How Do We Tell the Workers?

DATE DUE

BRODART, CO.   Cat. No. 23-221-003

How Do We Tell the Workers?

The Socioeconomic
Foundations of Work and
Vocational Education

Joe L. Kincheloe

Pennsylvania State University

Westview Press
A Member of the Perseus Books Group

To Cindy, Ronny, Brandon, Bob, and Mongo:
professionals all

Copyright © 1999 by Westview Press, A Member of the Perseus Books Group

Published in 1999 in the United States of America by Westview Press, 5500 Central Avenue, Boulder, Colorado 80301-2877, and in the United Kingdom by Westview Press, 12 Hid's Copse Road, Cumnor Hill, Oxford OX2 9JJ

Library of Congress Cataloging-in-Publication Data
Kincheloe, Joe L.
    How do we tell the workers? : the socioeconomic foundations of
work and vocational education / Joe L. Kincheloe.
        p.   cm.
    Includes bibliographical references (p.) and index.
    ISBN 0-8133-8736-1 (hc.) — ISBN 0-8133-8737-X (pbk.)
        1. Vocational education—Social aspects—United States.
2. Vocational education—Economic aspects—United States.   3. Work—
Social aspects—United States.   4. Critical pedagogy—United
States.   I. Title.
LC1045.K545   1999
370.11'3—dc21   98-11325
                                                                                                CIP

The paper used in this publication meets the requirements of the American National Standard for Permanence of Paper for Printed Library Materials Z39.48-1984.

10   9   8   7   6   5   4   3   2   1

Contents

Part 3   Coping with and Directing Change

Part 4   Race, Class, and Gender

Foreword

Fred Schied
Pennsylvania State University

Over thirty years ago, when I was taking my first high school shop class, vocational education seemed to be a much simpler undertaking than it is today. Everyone, or so those of us enrolled in shop classes assumed, understood the rules of the education game. The smart kids were placed in academic English, math, and history classes. The dumb kids were enrolled in a mind-numbing series of courses euphemistically called "practical" math and "practical" English. These courses were allied to an array of shop classes including wood, electric, machine, automotive, print, forge, foundry, and even aviation shop. My high school was inordinately proud of its shops. The number and types of shop classes were trumpeted as examples of a rich and varied vocational education program.

The view from the shop class floor was somewhat different. The main task of our shop teachers—tough, hard-nosed, World War II veterans who had escaped working in Chicago's mills and factories by earning their teaching certificates through the GI Bill—was to police a restless student body almost exclusively made up of male ethnic working-class whites and a sprinkling of African Americans and Latinos. What I understood, at least at some level, was that the shop classes were microcosms of the factories we were being prepared to work in. The skills we were supposedly being taught were mostly useless, the shops' equipment being badly out-of-date. But we were taught the rules of factory work, and went to class with the types of people we would be working with in the mills and factories. All this was accomplished under the watchful eye of a teacher, acting out the role of the factory foreman.

Yet despite the boredom, the harsh discipline, and the inadequate equipment, some amazing creativity and intelligence managed to seep through. There were shop students who at age fifteen could tune a car by simply listening to the sound of the engine, others who could machine tool a piece of metal down to specifications as small as one-twentieth of an inch by eyesight alone, and even one student who in a magnificent creative outburst, produced an exquisitely carved figure of a fist, middle-finger extended, as his final wood shop project. These students were, as Joe Kincheloe so accurately notes, the Rodney Dangerfields of education. Given little respect, the products of a system designed in the early years of the twentieth century to prepare working-class students to be fodder for industrial workplaces, vocational education students were consigned to the bottom rung of the educational ladder.

That this type of vocational education and the old Fordist forms of production that shaped it are obsolete is clear to even those who argue that vocational schools did at least serve the useful purpose of mitigating conflict by attempting to shape a more docile workforce. However, recent calls for radical reform of vocational education rest on the spurious notion that the previous decade's economic decline was solely based on a failing educational system, thus neatly avoiding corporate culpability in the U.S. economic decline.

The great value of this book is that Kincheloe explodes such myths by locating the debates over vocational education within the context of a changing economic and political arena marked by a corporate-shaped discourse on educational reform. Moreover, he turns the debate to the much more important and more useful issue of how to create a democratic vision for vocational education. In doing so, Kincheloe addresses the issue of worker empowerment, not in the language of management but in the language of workplace democracy. He has understood that creating more-democratic workplaces is not just a hope, but a necessity, if we are to continue as a democratic nation.

PART ONE

The Nature of Work

1   *A Sense of Purpose*

H*ow Do We Tell the Workers?* is an appropriate title for this book because education, with its central vocational function, whether consciously or not, has always been grounded on this question. The dilemma we now face involves how to tell workers about the workplace they will enter in the twenty-first century—a workplace with its downsizing, its profits being generated at the expense of workers' financial well-being, and its demand that workers compete with low-paid laborers around the world. How do vocational educators, progressives, and labor leaders tell workers about the stressful and difficult conditions they will inevitably face? With these issues at the forefront, this book is designed to help vocational educators and labor educators from various domains make sense of the social, economic, cultural, political, and educational world that shapes work, work education, and worker consciousness at the end of the twentieth century. This effort is contextualized within a vision of "what could be"—the special role that vocational education can play in the larger effort to make work a source of joy, satisfaction, respect, and financial reward.

In this context, *How Do We Tell the Workers? The Socioeconomic Foundations of Work and Vocational Education* becomes in a sense a worker civics—a citizenship book for workers, union members, cultural workers, and educators. A rigorous understanding of work and its context is essential knowledge for such individuals in an era where noncorporate-filtered information has become harder and harder for citizens to obtain. It is certainly not provided on television by the major networks or CNN or by mainstream newspapers and magazines. In response to the August 1997 teamsters' strike against United Parcel Service (UPS), "America's newspaper," *USA Today*, wrote of its inability to understand the strikers' motives. Arguing that increasing the number of part-time workers only made practical business sense, the editors of the newspaper dismissed the concerns of employees working two or three jobs without benefits. To provide such workers with full-time jobs would make the company less efficient and should therefore be rejected as a solution, they concluded (Jackson, 1997). Such reporting is typical of the mainstream press's coverage of labor issues. The message they choose to give the workers is clear: Labor's needs and concerns do not count.

In this information environment, worker civics becomes more important than ever before. The insights that emerge in this exploration of the "pedagogy of work"—the knowledge and values that are produced and transmitted in both schools and the society at large about work—are central to workers' ability to make sense of and actively respond to the obstacles they face. Such insights are essential to vocational and work educators' ability to understand and deal with the numerous vocational reform proposals of the last decade. The understandings that emerge from these considerations lead observers, I believe, to the vocational reform that makes the most sense: the end of vocational tracking of students and the integration of academic and vocational education. In this plan, all students would take an integrated form of vocational and academic education that would help students to understand concrete and practical applications of academic knowledge and the academic groundings of particular vocational tasks. For example, physics might be taught in an automobile repair lab, as physics and automobile mechanics teachers would work carefully together to build a curriculum that illustrated the connections between the workings of a car and the disciplinary knowledge of physics. If carefully planned, such an integration could produce new levels of motivation and understanding for students from a wide variety of backgrounds.

Although academic and vocational integration is an important dimension of how we choose to tell workers about the world that confronts them, it will not be emphasized in this book. I have written a previous book devoted to the topic; see *Toil and Trouble: Good Work, Smart Workers, and the Integration of Academic and Vocational Education* (1995). I also deemphasize much cognitive-related material in this work, since I have discussed worker thinking in detail in *Toil and Trouble*. This book concerns the nature and purpose of work and work education in a democratic society in an era marked by dramatic economic, political, and cultural change. Too often, the study of vocational education has focused on the practice and technique of teaching while ignoring the larger purposes of vocational programs. The nature of work, the workings of the economy, the social impact of technology, the power of cultural representations, and the ethics of business are not central concerns of the vocational field. *How Do We Tell the Workers?* makes no pretense of neutrality as it engages these topics: It begins with the assumption that present economic organization is unhealthy on many fronts. Indeed, corporations have gained inordinate power, in the process creating an atmosphere of unfairness that especially affects students who are pushed into vocational educational paths. Because of this reality, vocational teachers, students, union leaders, and workers more than anyone else must gain the ability to expose such injustice. To protect their own self-interest and the spirit of democracy, they must understand the way power works to undermine our way of life, our values, and our sense of right and wrong.

The Threat and the Vision

The vocational education envisioned here produces students who are aware of these threats to democracy, who understand the culture of work, and who can articulate a vision of what work should be (Giroux, 1993). For example, workers with a vision do not passively accept hazardous workplaces that produce toxic products that not only affect the health of the employees who produce them but harm the environment as well. Vocational educators and workers who share such a vision can no longer confine their activity to schools alone; they must take part in a larger project that involves the workplace, government, unions, and reform-oriented organizations. Vocational teachers and students have to realize that although vocational programs may help develop particular work skills of their students, such education cannot alter the reality of job scarcity (Jonathan, 1990). The availability of jobs depends on both economic circumstance and political choice—and political choice can be affected by the political participation of vocational educators who are motivated by a vision of economic justice.

The American debate over the politics of work over the last fifteen years has been reduced to a simplistic exercise in victim bashing. The reason individuals are unemployed or underemployed has little to do with economic conditions, the argument goes; their circumstances are a manifestation of their failure as individuals. Why develop vocational education programs or innovative antipoverty programs, many political leaders ask, when the cause of unemployment or underemployment involves the individual's moral inferiority or is the result of unsuccessful parenting. Family values are promoted as the "only way out" of the poor neighborhood or the degrading job. The problem with such arguments is that in many cases family values have little effect on economic success, especially when one *lives* in an economic circumstance (an inner-city neighborhood) where job opportunities are rare and informal networks through which openings are discovered are nonexistent (Coontz, 1992). Typically, if you live around people who are unemployed, you are the last to know when job opportunities are available. This is a bitter irony for those who seek a better life and economic mobility.

Pointing the finger of blame has become an art form in the last couple of decades. Not only are the victims of economic injustice deemed culpable but the schools have also been found guilty of undermining our economy. In 1983, Ronald Reagan's National Commission on Excellence in Education (NCEE) set the parameters of the national conversation on schooling (Copa and Tebbenhoff, 1990). The commission convinced millions of Americans that schools were largely responsible for America's economic decline. In no way am I attempting to protect the schools from criticism; this book will criticize both academic and vocational education at many points and on many levels. On the issue of economic decline, however, other factors must be examined and blame must be shared by a variety of institutions.

As corporate profits stagnated in Western economies in the early 1970s, corporations scrambled to cut costs. Managers realized that the quickest way to accomplish such a task involved lowering wages and taxes. Not only were workers pitted against each other in the struggle for jobs but local, state, and even national governments were forced into competition in the attempt to attract business and industry. The city of Greenville, South Carolina, for example, competed with Huntsville, Alabama, over which city would offer companies the lowest tax rates and the best infrastructures (roads, sewers, lax environmental regulations) in the race to attract companies and create jobs. The big winner in such competition, of course, was industrial management, as operating costs were cut, unions were undermined, labor was tamed, and executive salaries were raised. "What a great deal!" corporate leaders exclaimed. As executive salaries increased, the trade deficit and the budget deficit grew, and managers focused more and more on short-term profits rather than long-term stability (Pollin and Cockburn, 1991; Shelton, 1984).

The shrinkage of America's manufacturing base that began in the early 1970s has continued into the late 1990s; contrary to the pronouncements of the NCEE, this waning of manufacturing is not the fault of education in general or vocational education in particular (Chesneaux, 1992). One of the most important factors in the decline of American industry and economic institutions in general has been the reluctance of business and industrial leaders to reorganize the workplace in a way that eliminates low-skill positions and takes advantage of worker creativity and understanding of the specifics of the work process. This theme of workplace reorganization and worker empowerment will be central in our exploration of vocational education at the end of the twentieth century. Make no mistake about it, vocational education should assume that the workers it produces should have significant input into the workplace decisions that are of concern to them.

As our democratic vision has become clouded and the power of large private interests has set the national economic and political agenda, important decisions have been made without regard to their effect on working people. A major factor in this nation's decline to a second-rate industrial power has involved the massive military buildup of the Cold War and, unfortunately, the post–Cold War era. The complex network that President Eisenhower labeled the military-industrial complex employs 6,500,000 people in more than 135,000 factories, laboratories, and bases. Since 1974, the United States has spent more on the military than the entire civilian economy combined. In tens of thousands of factories, defense contracts have allowed managers to become the wards of the Defense Department, freeing them to act in arrogant disregard of the realities of the marketplace. In their secure cocoon, they have pursued inefficient and costly production strategies, undermining both their desire and capacity to compete with more productive foreign competitors.

As the Pentagon diverted more and more money into such inefficient enterprises, the nation found less and less money to invest in infrastructure and industrial education. The results of such economic policies were broadcast in the decline in productivity (the dollar value of output per hour of work), civilian technological development, and the enormous increase in the national debt. In the name of free enterprise, economic leaders competed for juicy defense contracts that guaranteed short-term profits. By the 1980s, economic management too often mutated into a high-stakes game of corporate buying and selling. A new breed of businesspeople, known as corporate raiders, burst on the scene. Depicted realistically in the movie *Wall Street*, such raiders made unprecedented and immediate profits. Unfortunately for the working people of America, no new jobs were generated in this legal pillaging of business and industry. No national wealth was generated in these winner-take-all, macho, boy's games that exposed the underside of the American dream of economic opportunity. The inequitable distribution of the spoils of such "victories" served to further undermine worker morale and the hope of the underemployed and the unemployed. Vocational education can expose this pathology, as it prepares skilled workers with a sense of what democracy means in the economic sphere (Melman and Dumas, 1990; Falk and Lyson, 1988; Rehm, 1989).

Contemporary social and economic conditions demand a vision—a vision that will bring meaning to the lives of Americans dispossessed by the chaos that marks the end of the millennium. The two dominant economic visions of the twentieth century are not working as proponents have hoped. Marxist-Leninist socialism has been a tragic failure; but (and this makes Americans very uncomfortable) multinational corporate capitalism has also manifested some fundamental flaws. In significantly different ways, the power elites that direct these systems escape the control of citizens. Indeed, the poisonous effect of these structures on the natural world and the social world undermines their viability as economic and social systems for the new millennium (Wirth, 1983).

The get-it-while-you-can ethic of laissez-faire capitalism is too insensitive for the needs of a fragile democracy, the mental health of individuals, and an overcrowded planet. Such an economic system transmits its values to all aspects of the society, undermining our ability to make meaning, to make sense of our lives, and to construct a humane vision for our future. This book explores a "third way," an alternative to doctrinaire state socialism and unbridled free enterprise. We will explore not only this individual-oriented, humane way of reconceiving economic policy but also the meaning and role of vocational education in the economic and philosophical context created by this third way.

Vocational education and the everyday world of work do not contribute to the development of a coherent picture of the world. In fact, such experiences tend to fragment our understandings of who we are and how our work fits into the larger society. We are isolated, shielded from many pieces of the social jigsaw puzzle, separated from a cognizance of the purpose of an operation. As a result, we become apathetic and withdrawn, released from responsibility for what ultimately happens in the schools, workplaces, and other organizations to which we belong. A humane vision of a democratic society demands that vocational education confront this fragmentation of reality and its resulting debilitation of the human spirit. A democratic vocational education struggles to empower future workers by helping them see themselves as living systems within larger living systems. In other words, an education of this sort induces students to ask, "How does my work fit into the larger economy, the ecosystem, the historical tradition of professionals or crafts people in this field?" Students and workers come to appreciate the fact that they are not Clint Eastwood–like "High Plains drifters," unconnected to anybody else, living and working in isolation. Workers are profoundly dependent on one another for the food they eat, the clothes they wear, and the homes they inhabit (Ferguson, 1984; Wirth, 1983; Bellah et al., 1991).

On the foundation of this interdependence, democratic vocational educators build an ethic of solidarity. While retaining their individual integrity, vocational students in democratic programs come to understand their connections to other people. Vocational teachers with a democratic ethic attempt to address the manipulative, inhumane tendencies that undermine the quest for authentic interpersonal relationships. In no way should this quest for human connectedness be interpreted as a demand to conform to a common set of precepts. Indeed, the best way to build community may be around a concept of difference. A heterogeneous community with differing principles may better contribute to the cultivation of critical thinking, moral reasoning, and good work. A community based on consensus is often unable to criticize the injustice and exclusionary practices that produce social pathology. We always profit in some way from a confrontation with another system of defining that which is important. Consciousness itself is spurred by the concept of differences, something we begin to understand when we gain our first awareness of who we are, that is, that we exist independently of another person or another's way of seeing.

The appreciation of difference between men and women, black and white, rich and poor must always be grounded on our notion of solidarity. Solidarity has two main aspects: (1) it grants social groups enough respect for others to listen to their ideas and to use them to consider existing social values, and (2) it permits us to realize that the lives of individuals in different social groups are interconnected to the point that everyone is accountable to everyone else. No assumption of uniformity exists here—just a commitment to work together to bring about mutually beneficial social change (Welch, 1991). In the vocational classroom, this valuing of difference creates a dialogue that helps students to understand their personal points of view as one socially constructed way of perceiving. As the classroom develops, vocational students are exposed to more and more diverse voices, to more and more ways of perceiving work. Through such exposure to differing points of view, their ways of seeing are expanded, their social imagination of what could be is broadened. Work no longer has to be a degrading and grueling trial by which we make our living. New vocational possibilities are open to discussion.

As we continue to develop a democratic vision for vocational education, the concept of freedom must be examined and reconsidered. In contemporary America, freedom has too often come to mean the right to be left alone. In the contemporary world, with its bombardment of information and unimagined forms of surveillance, freedom can no longer mean just getting away from other people. Institutions must take democracy and freedom seriously, in the process redefining freedom to involve the right to participate in the economic and political decisions that shape our existence and the future of the planet (Bellah et al., 1991). Of course, in the context of vocational education and work, this means that individuals play an important role in shaping both the nature of their education and the quality of their work. The word *empowerment* is promiscuously tossed around in the 1990s and has lost its impact as a result. But a true democratic empowerment of vocational students and American workers forms the basis for our vision. This book will attempt to reinvest meaning in the concept of empowerment, as it pertains to vocational students and American workers.

In order to act on this vision, vocational educators must delineate what active popular participation means in the everyday life of economic and educational institutions. As we redefine our notion of individualism, with its blindness to the ways the social context affects individual consciousness and performance, we must place individuals and their well-being at the beginning and the end of any social and educational reform (Bluestone and Harrison, 1982). The enhancement of the individual's ability to participate in social and educational movements is a centerpiece in our philosophy of education.

The difference between the democratic vision of empowered, self-directed vocational students and workers that is presented here and the many other "visions" discussed daily involves one key concept: The vision demands that we identify the social forces that impede its realization. No one in this society rejects outright the call for democratic institutions or smart empowered workers. Every expert guest on *Rivera Live* or *Sally* proclaims that men and women should be self-directed, be their "own person." You may ask, "So what's the argument, don't we all agree?" Sure, we agree that democratic self-direction is a good thing until we get down to specifics. As we begin to identify the way power elites undermine self-direction, the way business managers with their scientific modes of administering subvert the empowerment of their workers, we start to see what happens when the rubber meets the road. The key to uncovering the difference between our vision of self-direction and the pop psychologist on *The Vicki Lawrence Show* is that we name names, we identify the race, class, and gender oppression that undermines democracy. We finger from the witness stand the scientific conventions and the cult of experts who use their authority to prove the "deficiencies" of students and workers. We expose the mental models created by our interactions with school, media, and everyday life that insulate us from the consternation that learning entails.

To overcome the threats to empowerment, students and workers must act on their understanding of the forces that undermine their self-direction, their ability to participate in democratic communities. A democratic vocational education, unlike many technical programs of the present, helps students make sense of the way the world works, how the economy operates, and what the role of the everyday worker is in these processes. Vocational educators with a democratic vision endeavor to graduate students as "meaning-makers"—young people who can get behind the surface, understand the social construction of their identities, and detect the fingerprints of power at various "crime scenes." As vocational detectives, these students display a socially grounded consciousness that allows them to reinterpret old evidence, reopening cases in order to expose the way the world actually works.

Why, for example, are workers treated with such disrespect at the local meat processing plant? The managers of the plant are not bad people; indeed, on a one-to-one basis they are quite friendly and compassionate. As empowered, analytical workers examine the crime scene (the social dynamics of the workplace), they uncover some startling evidence. The procedures for management used by the supervisors and the top managers are derived from the tradition of scientific management. Such procedures assume that workers are incapable of running a plant themselves and that they must be controlled and supervised at all times to guarantee productivity. Their job descriptions must be narrowly and precisely delineated so that they will know what to do at any particular moment. The company managers act as the science of their field dictates they act. They do not understand that the very principles on which their managerial training was based creates an inhumane and degrading work life for their employees. As vocational students and workers begin to understand these realities, they refuse to accept degrading work as simply a necessary evil in our daily lives. They reject political officials' explanations that poverty is a permanent part of the human condition. Such visionary workers do not accept the notion that the violence and social pathology that accompany poverty is an inevitable reality (Senge, 1990; Coontz, 1992).

As demystifiers of the language of management and the public conversation about work, visionary students and workers challenge the legitimacy of the condescending cult of the expert (Giroux, 1993). This challenge confronts the very meaning of work in contemporary America. The democratic vision renders work less like a technical and utilitarian act and more like a calling. Interesting work that contributes to the good of others becomes its own reward. Our democratic vision moves students and workers to rethink the dogma that insuring private profit is the only criterion for an industrial policy (Bellah et al., 1991). Instead, a reconceptualized industrial policy insists that a rising standard of living for working people becomes a primary goal. A policy of this sort requires that there be an adequate supply of useful goods and services, whether or not they can be produced for a profit. The model for democratic work becomes an ethos of art and craftsmanship that engages the spirit of the worker. Working men and women are regarded as sacred individuals whose thoughts, feelings, and insights are valuable resources to be protected at all costs (Wirth, 1983). From this perspective, the democratic society demands that work become more hospitable, more engaging, less authoritarian, and safer. Our dedication to our sacred workers allows nothing less.

"We Don't Get No Respect": Workers and Vocational Education

Workers, vocational education, and vocational students are the Rodney Dangerfields of the late twentieth century. Often treated on TV as emotional dummies, workers understand all too well where they stand in the pecking order. As Americans, we have no choice; our democratic principles demand that we respect workers. Such respect is especially important in the nation's attempt to increase economic productivity. Since American society fails to value the knowledge workers need to accrue for job preparation, vocational students are often viewed as failures. By contrast, success in the academic curriculum has become a symbol not only of prestigious work but of virtue itself. Being academically schooled has become confused with the concept of being well-educated. It really does not matter what you know or what you can do; as long as you have academic diplomas and high standardized test scores, you are deemed "intelligent." The dirtying of one's hands is not an activity in which an "educated" man or woman engages. For employees who are not in management, thinking is considered an unnecessary activity (Copa and Tebbenhoff, 1990; Rehm, 1989; Goodlad, 1992; Kolberg and Smith, 1992).

To provide insight into the effects of this lack of respect for workers and vocational education, consider the fact that this nation financially subsidizes students who attend college seven times more than those who plan to enter the workforce as full-time workers (Hudelson, 1992). It is no wonder that such vocational students are often referred to as "the forgotten majority." In a democratic society with fundamental values demanding respect for workers and their work education, such disrespect and unfair funding could not take place. The renewal of this democratic respect is a necessity. But until certain attitudes change, such renewal will remain a dream. One of the most important themes of this book involves the notion that it is the role of vocational educators to help in the larger effort to renew such democratic values. Here at the end of the twentieth century, many American leaders have come to believe that the restoration of our moral and economic strength depends on it (Wirth, 1983).

Powerful agencies such as the media and corporate management have portrayed workers as incompetent. If workers can be portrayed as lazy and inadequate, then managers can justify the disparity between their own salaries and workers' wages. This portrayal allows managers greater freedom to design jobs that allow workers little input into how the workplace is administered or how particular tasks should be performed (Ferguson, 1984). It also releases corporate leaders from any responsibility for American economic decline: "You must understand," they tell the American people, "that workers these days have little commitment to their jobs" (Zunker, 1986). And their poor work habits are deplorable. Many analysts make the argument that workers are treated like children in industrial and clerical factories. Despite all the rhetoric of workplace reforms that "empower" workers, still in the late 1990s only a small percentage of workplaces have joined such a movement. Working is still very similar to going to high school, workers report. The principal turns into your general foreman, and teachers mutate into your superintendents; constant surveillance based on distrust joins the workplace and schooling in an antidemocratic alliance. Such unproductive arrangements are perpetuated by the Great Deception—the argument that American workers are unable to take responsibility for the direction of their own lives.

These excluded workers find it difficult to engage in their work with their hearts and their brains. How can you commit yourself when jobs require only minimal thinking? Workers execute plans they do not develop and that mean little to them. Rarely do workers know how their everyday tasks fit into the larger goals of the business or into the general economy. When they do understand these concepts, they typically figure things out on their own—not with the help of their superiors. Too often, workers in America are seen as economic instruments, men and women estranged from not only their fellow workers but from meaning itself. The great educational philosopher John Dewey argued years ago that workers often become no more than "industrial fodder" in a society controlled by money interests. Denied access to information and accumulated wisdom, workers are disempowered and removed from the realm of decisionmaking. This reality holds dramatic implications for the health of a democratic society (Brosio, n.d.).

When the society views workers as clerical and industrial fodder, it loses respect for workers' bodies. America has allowed its workers to breathe asbestos, to endanger their eyes and ears, to develop cancers from exposure to carcinogens, and so on. The job insecurity that workers increasingly experience, with its dramatic psychological and physiological effects, is viewed by neoclassical economists as a positive trend. Too much security undermines work effort and productivity, they argue. In this way worker security subverts the capital accumulation process, the conservatives conclude. How has such "logic" become the "common sense" of American economics? This book attempts to answer this question (Copa and Tebbenhoff, 1990).

Although Chapter 5 deals with this question more fully, the answer to it begins with the development of industrialization in the nineteenth century. The early industrialists saw work as a system based not on the creativity and autonomy of the individual producer but on the rational division of labor and the standardization of products. As a result, craftspeople such as shoemakers were turned into machines, or at least into extensions of machines (Brosio, 1985). For those who performed only one small function in a shoe factory (gluing a heel to the sole of a shoe), the sense of craft was lost. Thought was removed from the execution of everyday tasks. Many critics have argued that this deskilling of workers affected not only blue-collar factory workers but white-collar office workers as well. The legacy of this early deskilling can be found in the workplaces of the late twentieth century. Recent studies have found that many employers are more interested in the "attitudes" of workers than in their skills. Employers frequently want dependable, passive, and cheerful workers who will fit into a simplistic work organization that demands little analysis or creativity. As the Commission on the Skills of the American Workforce puts it: "U.S. businesses have adopted a low skills, low wages outlook" (Kolberg and Smith, 1992).

This deskilled orientation toward workers and the workplace spills over into other social venues—schools, in particular. The disrespect shown workers is similar to the disrespect shown teachers, especially vocational education teachers. In the view of many business leaders and popular politicians, the blame for American economic problems in the 1970s, 1980s, and 1990s rests squarely on the shoulders of our educators. The job shortages of the last couple of decades have been reinterpreted for the public as skill shortages. In media discussions of this issue, viewers almost see the message "Blame the Schools" trailing like a tornado warning across the bottom of the TV screen (Jonathan, 1990). All of this disrespect transfers to vocational teachers and students who reside, unfortunately, at the lowest rung of the educational status ladder. Students from vocational programs are often seen as undesirables, as people who could not make it in the academic track. Such perceptions must be challenged and clarified. This is not to argue that American education (vocational education, in particular) should not be improved; it should be (Oakes, 1985). But it is important to set the record straight and provide fair criticism of the responsible institutions. In other words, business and industrial leaders must be held accountable for their dehumanized and failed economic policies.

Vocation, Identity, and a Sense of Ethics

In studies of work and vocational education, the meaning of the word *vocation* is rarely addressed. In its best sense, vocation is a calling involving meaningful activity (Rehm, 1989). As the American economy developed, fewer and fewer jobs carried with them this notion of vocation. For example, the sense of vocation understood by workers in the retail trades was undermined decades ago by the advent of corporations like McDonald's and their standardized selling strategies. In such a social and economic context, we have lost our ability to distinguish labor from work. The distinction, as obvious as the difference between an Arrested Development and an Osmond Family concert, involves simply making a living (labor) and engaging the self in the production of products that enrich life (work) (Wirth, 1983). Dewey expanded this definition of work, arguing that work in the vocational sense connects an individual's ability with the benefits of social service. Indeed, work in the Deweyan sense provides meaning to one's life as it transforms the world and human interaction (Litz and Bloomquist, 1980).

Vocation in a truly democratic society should never become a blind technical process; in fact, it is a form of self-creation. Once vocational education understands that work helps shape who we are, the field will have to change. Vocational educators will appreciate the fact that they are preparing not just workers but also democratic citizens. Identity formation is constantly taking place in schools and workplaces. For example, when vocational students are placed as office workers and are told they need very few skills, expected to behave passively, not informed of their rights as workers, and sheltered from discussions about an ethical and democratic workplace, their identities and self-perceptions are negatively affected (Rehm, 1989; Simon, Dippo, and Schenke, 1991; Valli, 1988).

The hidden message of this vocational educational activity is that office workers are low-status laborers. Clerical workers are unconsciously taught to tell their bosses, in the words of Wayne and Garth, "We're not worthy." As vocational teachers locate work in a moral context, such students and workers must be taught that they are indeed worthy. They must come to expect that in a progressive democratic society, all jobs—office work included—should encourage creative input and the exercise of judgment. When individuals argue that low-skill jobs constitute the reality young workers face, progressive vocational educators tell them that workers may face such a reality but they do not have to accept it as inevitable. Workers can be empowered to imagine democratic forms of work and join in the struggle to make such visions a reality. Students in progressive vocational education programs learn that the way they see themselves as workers often reflects the way power elites want them to see their roles. When vocational education fails to challenge such domination, it plays into the hands of the dominant culture. It plays the social role of simply adapting vocational students to jobs that are unfair and undesirable (Giroux, 1993; Richmond, 1986).

As a construction worker during my years in high school and college, I came to understand on a variety of levels the brutality of the workplace. I learned that any attempt to question the sadomasochistic male culture of the construction site could be construed as not simply misdirected but as dangerous. Because of my refusal to accept the violence of the interpersonal relations among bosses, craftspeople, and laborers, I was subjected to forms of physical violence by my bosses. Generally, in fact, the language of the workplace is often violent, as it expresses itself in metaphors of war: We "attack" a task, "raid" the stock of a company, prepare "action commandos," engage in "cutthroat competition," wage economic "warfare," develop marketing "strategies," participate in corporate "espionage," and so on. The study of economics, of course, often reflects the same metaphors, as it erases human concerns and questions of work and identity from its curriculum. The dismal science, as economics has been called, needs to rethink its goals vis-à-vis the moral imperatives of the democratic tradition (Chesneaux, 1992).

Work and Democracy: Producing Meaning in Authoritarian Workplaces

Progressive vocational educators take democracy seriously. This means that they expect democratic values will shape the purposes and everyday activities of our social institutions. No democratic society can maintain its liberty if major discontinuities separate its professed values from its schools and workplaces. But in *America 2000: An Education Strategy*, the blueprint for the future of American schooling released during the Bush administration with great input from then governor Clinton, the guiding concept of democracy is dismissed. Indeed, social criticism or concern with the reality of democracy at the end of the twentieth century is viewed as impractical analysis, as a type of thinking that is too dangerous to pursue (Giroux, 1992). This perspective illustrates the crisis in contemporary American democracy. The crisis is also revealed by the pervading belief that democracy has little to do with the economic sphere of life (Brosio, 1985). Educators and economic analysts who speak of the inseparability of democratic precepts and the arrangement of workplaces often meet with silent stares from a public socialized to see no relationship between the two.

This book is grounded on the belief that the collision between democracy and the workplace should produce something called "economic democracy." This economic democracy would mandate that all people who work get a stake in the enterprise in which they work, while at the same time cushioning the harshness of the unrestricted labor market (Bellah et al., 1991). When workers gain a stake in their workplaces, they become participants in decisionmaking. When workers become decisionmakers, private corporations become more responsive to the needs of the public and more protective of the creative energy of their workers. In an environment like this, workers no longer look at themselves as fellow cell mates on death row and view their supervisors as wardens.

Supporters of democracy in general and economic democracy in particular know that democracy is incompatible with meaningless, deskilled jobs. In the early twentieth century, John Dewey argued that one of the most important functions of school involved providing students with information concerning the relationship between work and society and the role of industry in democratic society. I would argue that one of the most important goals of vocational education is to address the political, social, and economic realities that shape work. Vocational education students must understand the underlying assumptions and values that shape their vocational education. In the spirit of John Dewey and other advocates of democracy, they must be able to discern the difference between a truly democratic education and one that merely claims to be democratic (Rehm, 1989; Lakes, 1985; Giroux, 1992).

Shaping the Nature of Vocational Education: The Social and Political Role of Work

How we see work is central to the way we see education (Lyons, 1988). The issue of workplace democracy raises questions about the quality of life outside the workplace: For example, how do we allocate power and resources? Who makes decisions about what types of economic policies we should pursue? If some of the contemporary moves to construct a more flexible, high-skill workplace actually take place, vocational education could be profoundly affected. In this more flexible economy (some call it "post-Fordism"), workers might be used for more demanding, diagnostic, troubleshooting tasks. Vocational education would have to adjust accordingly. No one is sure, however, how economic and technological changes are going to affect work; the jury is still out. What we do understand is the direct impact that our vision of work life will make on vocational education. Do we choose technocratic efficiency or a more democratic orientation toward our work life?

The technocratic vision reduces vocational and educational questions to mere technical issues. This means that questions of purpose are subservient to questions of technique. When workplace managers separate purpose from work-related concerns, work is broken into little pieces. Each piece is removed from the context that gives it meaning and is considered in isolation. For example, bread making is an art that requires great skill and much knowledge. When it is technicalized, however, and broken down into a matrix of subskills, work at a bread factory is trivialized. For instance, a bread worker may work eight hours a day and do nothing but stuff loaves of bread into a plastic bag. In situations like this, the fragmentation of the work has trivialized the bread-making process and undermined the dignity of the worker. Unfortunately, the technocratic vision has held sway in the United States throughout the twentieth century and is still setting the socioeconomic agenda. Current projections indicate that the majority of jobs that will be created in the early years of the twenty-first century will require only low-skill workers (Feinberg and Horowitz, 1990).

Because of the indignity of the twentieth-century workplace, Americans still hold to the notion that blue-collar work is a badge of social failure. Indeed, this technocratic vision is accompanied by an ethic of decontextualization that removes individuals from their surroundings. Such an ethic makes the individual solely responsible for personal deficiencies, often blaming victims of injustice for the existence of the injustice. In this situation, the moral breakdown of poor families is promoted as a cause of poverty. Thus, the argument is made that if the poor only possessed traditional family values, they would not be poor. Undoubtedly, many of the social and economic problems Americans face in the 1990s manifest themselves in the guise of family dysfunction; and there is little doubt that many poor families engage in pathological behaviors that exacerbate their misery. But the tendency to blame poverty on family breakdown decontextualizes the issue and induces the public to scapegoat the poor and dispossessed. Such blaming of the victims does not modify the economic and social context of contemporary family life. Accordingly, it does little to remedy the problems that induce people to manifest personal behavior that subverts their family values (Coontz, 1992).

Vocational education cannot be separated from these issues, as much as some advocates might want it to be. For vocational educators, to ignore the technocratic travesties committed in the name of efficiency and the social pathologies generated by the cruel contemporary social context is to lose sight of our humanity. However, this is exactly what happens much too often in late twentieth-century vocational education. The social, political, and economic context of work is ignored, as vocational programs devolve into training programs to inculcate work survival skills. In such vocational programs, students are molded to fit the existing jobs—no matter how deskilled and degrading such work might be. Democratic vocational educators maintain that there has to be a better way, a more humane way.

Democratic vocational educators ground their programs on the concept of freedom—intellectual freedom, freedom of inquiry and expression, freedom of association at work, and freedom from manipulation, whether overt or covert. To protect workers from the abuse of these freedoms, progressive vocational education understands that workers are more than simply a supply of labor; they are citizens. And citizens need to learn to think, analyze, and make informed choices. Workers must understand what they can expect from their employers in a democratic society. In the United States, workers should expect that their jobs will not damage their physical or mental health, will not exacerbate inequality, and will allow them to produce socially beneficial products. Of course, vocational education should promote such expectations as it prepares workers for such jobs.

Under the old paradigm, the technocratic way of understanding democracy in the workplace was deemed ineffective and inefficient. The low-skill training and attitude-adjustment vocational education programs that come out of such a paradigm are based on several unstated assumptions: (1) only a small number of people are capable of making managerial decisions; (2) workers will never exert the effort demanded by the managerial process; (3) workers operate simply on self-interest and have little concern for the larger good; and (4) productivity and profitability depend on a division of labor that rationalizes a hierarchical system of authority and workplace organization.

Our vision of vocational education that prepares highly productive worker-citizens for work and life assumes that (1) when workers are granted access to information, (2) are given the opportunity to deliberate on workplace matters of importance, and (3) are accepted as full participants in the decisionmaking process, they will make a significant contribution to economic progress (Kolberg and Smith, 1992; Wirth, 1983). It is not as though the regressive models of authoritarian and hierarchical systems of work are highly efficient; they are not efficient at all. Industrial and business leaders in positions of authority are fearful of workplace reform. Empowered workers carrying the flag of justice are dangerous when they invade the sanctuaries of power. In male-dominated, authoritarian workplaces, such rethinking of work smacks of a loss of power and status for those in managerial positions.

Challenging Taken-for-granted Assumptions

One of the most important purposes of a democratic vocational education involves its ability to challenge the taken-for-granted assumptions about work, schooling, and the role of the economic sphere in public life that shape what workers are told. Concerning vocational education (and academic education) textbooks, for example, few teachers ask who produced them, who authorized their use, or what particular meanings they legitimate. The dominant conversation in vocational education rarely depicts schools as more than places where students are trained for work. Few observers see vocational programs as political agencies that operate in ways that privilege one group over another (e.g., management over labor) and engage in specific types of political regulation. In a recent vocational education textbook, for example, labor unions are mentioned on only one page out of 350—and that reference is very negative. Business and industrial leadership is referenced throughout the book in a consistently positive way. The authors of the book in question would certainly bristle at the suggestion that they promoted particular power interests over others; they see themselves as objective and fair observers of the vocational field. One of the goals of a democratic vocational education is to point out the footprints of power, especially when observers are unaware of its presence (Lather, 1991).

The vocational education of the old paradigm was not grounded on a democratic vision of good work. Without such a vision, vocational educators were unaware of what to look for in their schools and workplaces. Often, these educators failed to notice the ramifications of ability tracking that involved socioeconomic class segregation of middle and upper-middle class students into academic programs and working class and lower class students into vocational programs. Such educators frequently failed to notice that when students were trained in vocational education for specific jobs, rarely did they enter jobs in the area in which they studied (Kolberg and Smith, 1992). Without a democratic sense of purpose, vocational educators had no point of view, no criteria for making educational and vocational assessments. Vocational educators must analyze the social, philosophical, and historical foundations of their field. In this examination, questions of purpose naturally arise: (1) what personal skills do we want vocational graduates to possess? (2) what types of attitudes and behaviors? (3) what understandings should vocational students acquire that will help them become better workers? (4) better citizens? (5) what have the historical purposes of vocational education been? (6) what should the purposes of vocational education be? (7) how do factors of race, socioeconomic class, or gender affect various aspects of vocational education? (8) what is the role of unions in vocational education? and (9) what governmental actions are needed to help empower vocational students and future workers? The purpose of this book is to develop a democratic system of meaning and then ask these questions in light of it. In accomplishing this task, assumptions about vocational education that have long been taken for granted will naturally be exposed. Also, a starting place for conversation between vocational education practitioners, workers, and managers will be provided. Regardless of our perspectives, we must begin to consciously address these important issues that shape our working lives and our society (Copa and Tebbenhoff, 1990).

In this "foundational conversation" about the central questions of vocational education, democratic educators challenge the political innocence of power elites. They expose the taken-for-granted "neutrality" of TV news programs, for example, that provide hours of business news and no labor news. They challenge the authoritarianism that accepts a rigidly hierarchical workplace and the complicity of schools in the production and acceptance of social and economic inequality and oppression (Giroux, 1992). In the name of democratic justice, they confront the legitimacy of private businesses and corporations that are dedicated to private gain while denying their public responsibilities. And management, while denying its public responsibility and claiming the *absolute* right to control the production system of businesses and industries, is uneasy with our conception of the public responsibilities of private interests—but that is OK. In a democratic society, we can disagree about such issues. Vocational students can make up their own minds about the role of industry, work, and schooling in a democratic society. We owe them, however, the right to confront what is typically taken for granted in America in the last years of the twentieth century.

One of the most annoying of these generally accepted assumptions is that vocational education students are not capable of understanding the economic and work system into which they are being taught to fit. They are learning "how" not "why"; indeed, "why questions" are often deemed downright insubordinate. Such educational assumptions, like most educational assumptions, are derived from larger social understandings. In this case, many Americans hold a view of economics that assumes that it does not matter whether workers understand the socioeconomic "big picture," nor should their educators be much concerned with providing them with it. This so-called neoclassical view of economics requires that if workers simply do what they are told, the big picture will take care of itself. This means that if workers will merely "do their jobs," this automatic mechanism we call the economy will, through the self-interested actions of millions of unrelated men and women, produce prosperity. Such a simplistic and dehumanizing view of the social and economic realms of American life cannot simply be taken for granted in a society that sees itself as democratic (Copa and Tebbenhoff, 1990). Workers need to be told about these dynamics.

I can almost see Rod Serling stepping out of a bathroom at Frederick W. Taylor Vocational High School and speaking to the camera:

Witness if you will a vocational student, a frustrated young woman being told that she is unable to understand the ambiguities and complexities of the workplace. We will call her "Martha the clerical worker," her mind controlled by a larger society intent on filling her both with democratic platitudes and a barrage of low expectations packaged as a vocational education curriculum. In the backdrop of this dilapidated typing classroom, Martha learns to type on her ancient typewriter. But, more important, she learns her place in the hierarchy, learns to take orders from the man who is her boss and to consider herself merely a clerical worker unequipped to direct the day-to-day operations of an enterprise. Consider the flagrant contradiction, if you will, between these attitudes and the democratic notion that in America anyone can make it. (Serling takes a puff off his Winston, then concludes while exhaling.) A contradiction is a dangerous entity, a time bomb ticking in the mind of an innocent ready to explode in the most unexpected of places. Now witness, if you will, what happens when the phosphorus of low expectations is thrown into the water of democracy. Join us, as we follow Martha's vocational journey into the Twilight Zone.

Our democratic form of vocational education is capable of rescuing Martha from the Twilight Zone. As she begins to see the assumptions about the role and status of a clerical worker, she begins to understand the role of gender in the construction of one's self-concept. She begins to think about how many times she has visited an office in pursuit of help or information, only to find that the secretary knew much more about the operation of the office than the *man* allegedly in charge. She remembers how much she laughed at the truth contained in the movie *Nine to Five*. The office it depicted reminded her of the one in which her mother works. She giggles when she recalls how her mother would fantasize abut what she would like to do to pay back her boss—the monster with coffee breath, she called him. Coming from a proud but poor home supported by her mother's low secretarial salary, Martha begins to see that her family's economic status is not a result of a lack of hard work or a lack of family values, as many people believe. It has more to do with the vocational expectations laid on her mother and the ones now being dumped on her. She is empowered by such understandings, as she comes to believe that she cannot only type and file but can administer as well. Martha's liberation is the result of her having challenged the taken-for-granted.

In its concern with an analysis of work, vocational education occupies the catbird seat, the central location in any curriculum design. Beginning with the study of work, one can concretize the examination of society and culture. Through work, one can depict power and status differences, social stratification, the subtle ways that racism and sexism operate, the ways that a philosophy manifests itself in everyday lived experiences, and how the taken-for-granted shapes the lives of men and women. As vocational students study work both in the classroom and at the work site, they begin to see how particular human values were abandoned in the quest for profit maximization. In the context of such observations and realizations, students begin to raise questions about the nature and importance of meaningful work. As they raise such questions, they become ready to analyze the contradictions that characterize the relationship between the nation's humanity and its material vitality (Wirth, 1983; Rehm, 1989).

The democratic vocational education that might be created has as its purpose the production of thoughtful worker-citizens. Such students understand the contradictions in their education and their work experiences, are aware of unspoken (tacit) assumptions in definitions and standardized procedures, and understand how power shapes the way they see themselves and the world—in other words, such students have the ability to deconstruct work (Harvey, 1989). Deconstruction is a word that has been used in recent years to refer to the ability to uncover meanings in situations that were unintended and unseen even by those who created the situations. Deconstructionists use the word *text* in lieu of the term *situation* in order to make the point that the world can be viewed as a text to be read—often between the lines. Thus, vocational students come to read between the lines of textbooks; but they also read classrooms, workplaces, the language of management, TV, and so forth. They expose the power relations and the assumptions of that which is taken for granted about work, thereby uncovering the ways the world operates.

Thus, in the name of democracy, a new type of vocational education that is grounded in the best traditions of America's sense of justice is proposed. Under this system, democratic vocational education students learn how to evaluate current issues of work and recognize flaws in the conditions of work as they learn how to perform cognitive and technical tasks common to workplaces. This education demands a sophisticated understanding of what work is and what is happening to it in this new, post-Fordist era. As industries seek to become leaner and meaner, more flexible, and far quicker in their response to consumer demands, the possibility exists that the role of the worker may change. Some economic prophets foresee a world where workers must diagnose, recognize, and solve problems and deploy higher-order thinking skills on a daily basis. Indeed, some workplaces already demand such abilities; but as of this writing, low-skill, low-wage jobs still predominate. In fact, many economists project that such deskilled jobs will persist well into the twenty-first century. To allow the reader to understand why such realities afflict the American way of work, Chapter 2 examines the evolution of America's economic and organizational mind-set. The chapter is developed around two questions: How did the American workplace lose touch with the humane and democratic values so central to our national self-definition? How do we tell the workers about this human tragedy?

2 Modernism and the Evolution of the Technocratic Mind

It is not simply by accident that Western societies have come to build workplaces and conceptualize work as they have. Very specific historical forces have helped shape our economic institutions. In a book of this type, there is not the space to do justice to the complex of forces that have shaped work; however, it would be remiss not to attempt to contextualize the Western way of seeing the world that has uniquely influenced the American economic cosmos. Chapter 2 will thus explore the development of the modernist mind-set and its socioeconomic influence. Do not confuse the use of the term *modernism* with the term *contemporary*. Modernism is a particular Western way of seeing that developed under particular historical conditions. In order to understand the nature and future of work, vocational educators must appreciate the mind-set that has constructed not only our view of work but our consciousness as workers. Modernism has shaped the philosophical context that has spawned many of our contemporary problems.

The Birth of Modernism

Modernism was born with the realization that the Western medieval way of seeing was no longer adequate. The Black Death, for example, had swept across Europe in the fourteenth century, killing at least one-fourth of the population and changing the social order of the West forever. Every technique derived from the medieval ways of understanding the world was used in the attempt to control the plagues. Prayer, mysticism, scapegoating, and magic had no effect on the disease. When a society is unable to understand or solve a major problem that challenges its existence, its organization of reality will collapse or a new one will develop. Under the pressure of the Black Death, Western society began to develop a new way of seeing. This new impulse, which would lay the foundation of Western modernism, enabled the society to understand and control the outside environment, the world of matter and energy (Bohm and Peat, 1987; Leshan and Margeneu, 1982).

The foundation of the modernist science emerging in the 1600s and 1700s rested on the separation of the knower and the known, a cardinal tenet of the Cartesian-Newtonian (René Descartes and Sir Isaac Newton) way of organizing the world. Descartes's analytical method of reasoning, often termed reductionism, asserted that complex phenomena can best be appreciated by reducing them to their constituent parts and then piecing these elements together according to causal laws (Mahoney and Lyddon, 1988). All of this took place within Descartes's separation of the mind and matter. Known as Cartesian dualism, human experience was divided into two distinct realms: (1) an internal world of sensation, and (2) an objective world composed of natural phenomena. Drawing on the dualism, scientists asserted that the laws of physical and social systems could be uncovered objectively; the systems operated apart from human perception, with no connection to the act of perceiving. Descartes theorized that the internal world and the natural world were forever separate and that one could never be shown to be a form of the other (Lavine, 1984; Lowe, 1982; Kincheloe, 1991). We understand now but could not have understood then that despite all of the benefits modernist scientific methods would bring, this separation of mind and matter had profound and unfortunate consequences. Our ability to confront problems like the plague undoubtedly improved as our power to control the "outside" world advanced. At the same time, however, we accomplished little in the attempt to comprehend our own consciousness, our "inner experience" (Leshan and Margeneu, 1982): If we could not experience something directly through our senses, then we could not deal with it.

Thus, the Cartesian compass pointed the way to modernism, with its centralization, concentration, accumulation, efficiency, and speed. Bigger became better as the dualistic way of seeing reinforced a male-controlled, expansionist sociopolitical order grounded on a desire for power and conquest. Such a worldview often served to dehumanize, to focus attention on concerns other than the sanctity of humanity. A foundation was laid that allowed science and technology to transform the world. Commerce increased, nationalism grew, and European civilization could conquer at a rate previously unimagined. Rationality became a new deity, and around this god, the credo of modernity was developed: The world is "rational," and there is only one meaning of the term. All phenomena can be described within the boundaries of this encompassing rationality, whether we are studying atoms or the solar system, dreams or engines, learning or gunpowder, electricity or forms of government. Rationality applied to politics and government, for example, unleashed the most progressive aspects of modernism—its ideals of freedom, justice, and equality. In the attempt to develop ways of transcending the regressive features of modernism, this progressive dimension must not be forgotten (Leshan and Margeneu, 1982; Hannam, 1990).

This emphasis on reason, this attempt of philosophers in the 1700s to produce forms of objective scientific inquiry and to establish a rational organization of everyday life, is central to our understanding of modernism. Indeed, modernism is the story of the struggle of reason against manifestations of barbarism or the absence of civilization—the emotions, the animal instincts, or Freud's id. It is the story of science against religion, magic, and superstition. Such depictions of reason over irrationality allowed Western culture to constitute itself as different, superior, and as the benchmark of civilization itself. As the paragon of civilization, Western modernist culture could lust for absolutes and speak without qualification about certainty. Michel Foucault spoke of modernism as a way of relating to reality, a way of thinking and feeling that grants a sense of cultural belonging. Modernism is the force that has helped Europeans and Americans understand their relationship to the cosmos (Smart, 1992; Lather, 1991).

The Epistemology of Positivism

Epistemology is often viewed by students as a frightening word with few practical applications; but it is neither frightening nor impractical. Simply defined, epistemology is the branch of philosophy that studies knowledge. What constitutes knowledge? How do we know if something is true? What is the difference between a fact and an opinion? All of these are epistemological questions. The epistemology that has grounded modernism has been referred to as positivism. If we understand the nature of positivism, we are well equipped to understand exactly how modernism has affected our view of work and vocational education. Few philosophical orientations have exerted so much influence on everyday life as has positivism. At the same time, few philosophical orientations have been so little understood.

The label *positivism* was popularized by Auguste Comte, the nineteenth-century French philosopher who argued that human thought had evolved through three stages: the theological stage (where truth was based on God's revelation), the metaphysical stage (where truth was based on abstract reasoning and argument), and the positivistic stage (where truth was based on scientifically produced knowledge). Comte sought to discredit the legitimacy of nonscientific thinking that did not take sense (knowledge obtained through the senses, or empirical) knowledge into account (Kneller, 1984; Smith, 1983). He saw no difference between the ways knowledge should be produced in the physical sciences and the human sciences. From Comte's perspective, sociology should be studied just like biology. Society, he argued, is nothing more than a body of neutral facts governed by immutable laws. Like nature, society is governed by natural laws. Therefore, social actions would proceed with lawlike predictability (Held, 1980). Likewise, education is governed by unchanging laws; the role of the educator is to uncover them and then act in accordance with them. For example, educational laws would include pronouncements on how students learn and how students should be taught. To the positivist educator, there is only one *correct* way to teach.

Positivism shapes the way we look at the world without our being aware of it. It is useful to begin our analysis of modernism and the ways it has shaped our view of work and education by delineating the characteristics of positivism.

1. *All knowledge is scientific knowledge.* Positivism insists that only scientifically produced information should be regarded as an authentic form of human knowledge. Scientific knowledge is knowledge that can be proven. It is knowledge about which we are positive, which is the reason it is called positivism. When Newton formulated the theory of gravity, he told us that the apple *always* falls to the ground. What goes up must come down—there are no exceptions to these scientific generalizations. Scientific knowledge is not merely one form of knowledge, the positivists maintain, but knowledge can only be produced by science. Nonscience is held in disdain, with ways of knowing such as religion, metaphysics, and intuition dismissed as unverifiable nonsense. This way of seeing the world dramatically affects workers. If expert-produced scientific knowledge constitutes the only valuable information about work, then there is no problem with simply telling workers how to perform their jobs. In this situation, experts do the thinking and workers provide manual, deskilled labor. The knowledge that workers have accumulated over the years is useless because it has not been produced by strict scientific procedures. Workers, thus, should not seek input into the work process; they should not criticize the separation of mental (the job of management) from manual (the job of workers) labor in American factories. Workers should leave the thinking to their supervisors and simply do what they are told. Concepts of democracy and democratic work arrangements are not compatible with such epistemological assumptions.

2. *All scientific knowledge is empirically verifiable.* Positivism assumes that when we use the phrase *scientific knowledge,* we are referring to knowledge that can be verified empirically, that is, through the senses. What the eye sees, what the ear hears, what can be counted, what can be expressed mathematically—this is what constitutes empirical knowledge. There are many aspects of work and vocational education that cannot be validated empirically. These invisible factors may include ways of seeing or sets of assumptions. Indeed, the existence of positivism itself as a force that shapes what we "see" cannot be empirically verified. In other words, positivism cannot study its own assumptions because they are not empirically verifiable. Thus positivism tends to study only the *consequences* of certain actions, not the

causes of these actions. What we understand about the world is, therefore, very limited.

3. *The same methods that are used to study the physical world should be used to study the social and educational world.* When physical science methods are applied to the study of education and work, serious problems result. A key aspect of positivistic research in the physical sciences involves the attempt to predict and control natural phenomena. When these physical science methods are applied in education and work, social knowledge is produced as a tool to control not nature but human beings themselves. As a result, students and workers come to be viewed, understood, used, and controlled just like any other *thing*. Positivism loses sight of the idea that the objects of social research—humans—possess a special complexity that sets them apart from other objects of study. Positivist social and educational scientists fail to understand that the physical scientists they emulate impose their observations on the objects being observed. Physical scientists do not have to consider the *consciousness* of their objects of study or their history and sociocultural context. This makes research on humans different from the study of, say, rocks. If we do not understand this difference, we will miss the very things that make us human, that shape us, that restrict our freedom. Here rests one of the key points in our discussion of modernism in general and positivism in particular: Modernism and its positivist epistemology lead to a devaluation of human beings, a depersonalization of our institutions.

4. *If knowledge exists, it exists in some quantity; it is measurable.* If something exists, positivists argue, we can measure how much of it exists. In fact, the generalizations, principles, and theories derived from positivist data can be expressed in mathematical language (Beed, 1991; Garrison, 1989). Positivists define systematic observation that produces valid knowledge in terms of mathematical experiments. The researcher therefore looks for mathematical relations between variables. If such mathematical relations are found, they may be generalized to produce a universal law. Many of us who call for democratic vocational education and democratic research methods find ourselves very uncomfortable with the positivist assumptions that "to be is to be measurable" and that human endeavor can be expressed in mathematical terms. Much of what vocational education researchers want to study does not lend itself to easy measurability or, for that matter, to direct observation. In order to address this problem, positivists developed what they call "reduction sentences," that is, characteristics that reduce statements in a way that makes them more observable and measurable. A hard-to-measure concept such as hunger is defined as "80 percent of original weight" for a mature man or woman. Since weight is a measurable concept, hunger is expressed in terms of it. Behavioral psychologists who operate within a positivist context label such reduction sentences "operational definitions." Thus, we develop operational definitions for concepts such as intelligence

(what one scores on an IQ test) or productivity (output by workers per hour). Positivists even argue that concepts such as love or worker creativity can be operationally defined and measured.

Such operational definitions may or may not help us understand the phenomena under investigation. This kind of orientation often focuses our attention merely on the symptoms of larger problems—on the consequences, not the causes. Thus, the belief in the measurability of everything actually distorts our understanding of reality, as it hides the assumptions often made in the production of knowledge. What mental characteristics are addressed by questions on an IQ test? Short-term memory? The ability to store and call up a wide range of factual data? Certainly, the ability to see connections between ostensibly unrelated concepts or the skill to apply such understandings to the identification and solution of problems is not measured by such tests. Such difficult-to-measure but important abilities are deemphasized, whereas easy-to-measure but trivial abilities gain center stage. Academic and vocational education alike are undermined by this hidden process of knowledge production.

5. *Nature is uniform; that which is studied is consistent in its existence and behavior.* Positivists assume that the objects they study will remain constant. There is an underlying natural order in the ways both the physical world and the social world behave. Positivists argue that these regularities, or social laws, are best expressed through quantitative analysis and the language of mathematics. The goal for vocational educational research within this tradition, therefore, is to develop theories that give expression to the *regularities* in human expression. Human beings are not as regular and predictable as the positivists portray them. As humans exhibit their irregularities and unpredictabilities, nonpositivists begin to make the case that men and women defy positivistic attempts to reduce their behavior to measurable quantities. Teachers, students, and workers, for example, are not uniform in their makeup, contrary to the pronouncements of the positivists; humans are not machines whose behavior can be easily broken down into separate parts. As researchers coordinate their study of these separate human parts, they work to provide a full and final explanation of how humans work.

6. *The factors that cause things to happen are limited and knowable; in empirical studies, these factors can be controlled.* This perspective allows us to know for certain what causes what; it refuses to acknowledge the complexity of the world, especially the world of human beings. The world, positivists believe, is neat and tidy. The noise and confusion foisted upon the world by the "humanness of human beings" makes positivists edgy. Research would be so much easier, they dream, if researchers and the researched did not have to work in an untidy world and communicate through the imprecise medium of verbal language. Positivists fantasize about a spick-and-span social science where researchers are all identical, unbiased, infallible measuring

instruments. Modernist positivism accepts a cause-effect linearity that works like a machine. For example, when the human body breaks down, doctors may identify a certain factor, but the cause of the illness is always multiple. These multiple causes do not work in a simple, easily traced manner. Life processes, like social processes, are never neat and tidy; they must be viewed in the context that shapes them, if we are to make sense of the way they operate.

Consider the positivist assumption that the factors that cause things to happen are limited and knowable, and then imagine the way we study classroom management or, as some call it, discipline. Hundreds of studies have been conducted on classroom discipline in the last thirty years. In addition to problems of sample size, of the relationship between what is defined as good discipline and desirable educational achievements, and of cause and effect, the control of variables in discipline research presents special difficulties. Literally thousands of unmentioned factors have a significant influence on what happens in any classroom (Fiske and Shweder, 1986; Barrow, 1984). One student may respond to a specific teacher's disciplinary action in a particular manner, not because of the disciplinary action itself but because that student is accustomed to a certain type of disciplinary action at home. A Native American student, for example, raised in a permissive home may interpret a subtle, mildly coercive, noncorporal disciplinary act very differently from an African American student raised in a strict home where the rod is not spared. To the Native American student, the disciplinary action is understandable and consistent with prior experience; to the African American student, it is a sign of the teacher's weakness.

Another student will react differently to the subtle, mildly coercive disciplinary act because of the nature of her relationship with the teacher. This student, whose parents are longtime acquaintances of the teacher, knows the teacher as a trusted friend. When confronted with corrective action of any kind, she may feel very embarrassed because she is unaccustomed to conflict in her relationship with the teacher. What appears to the observer as mild admonishment elicits a great deal of embarrassment from this student. Another student may be affected by the presence of an outside observer and may react in a way that is inconsistent with prior behavior. There is no way that the observer can account for all of the possible variables that may affect what is being observed (Barrow, 1984). And this is the point: The various facets of a student's or a teacher's nature, of every individual's background, of every context, and of all the interrelationships and combinations of factors may be the key elements that help to explain what is going on in a vocational education classroom. These are the elements that are not addressed by positivist researchers.

7. *Certainty is possible.* The goal of positivist research involves the quest for certain answers to human questions. Because we cannot control all vari-

ables, because the factors that cause things to happen are *not* limited and knowable, the quest for certainty is quixotic. If we can learn anything from science, it is that our ideas about the world change and that they will continue to change in the coming years. The chance of arriving at some juncture in human history where research will become unnecessary because we will understand the nature of reality is slim. We must abandon the quest for absolutes that consistently focuses our attention on the trivial—on that which can be easily measured. One of the reasons that history tests often emphasize dates, people, places, and battles is that teachers find it easier to measure whether students have "learned" such information than it is to evaluate an essay test with all of its ambiguity and complexity. The result of the quest for certain evaluations is that the lowest form of thinking is emphasized (rote memorization) while higher-level thinking (analysis, interpretation, contextualization, and application) is dismissed. For these and many other reasons, antipositivists ridicule the certainty with which positivism makes "valid" arguments. Humans cannot achieve a God's-eye view and must, therefore, accept a more humble and limited perspective.

8. *Facts and values are separate; objectivity is possible and desirable.* Value judgments, convictions, beliefs, and opinions, positivists maintain, should not be factors in knowledge production (Beed, 1991). Empirical inquiry is always value-free and objective, for values are subjective and therefore tainted. As such proclamations are issued from the positivist pulpit, the illusion of political and moral neutrality is created. The magician must be exposed; the epistemological rules that dictate exactly what we can and cannot count as a fact must be uncovered (Garrison, 1989). The implicit rules that guide our generation of facts about work and vocational education are formed by specific worldviews, values, political perspectives, and definitions of intelligence. Research can never, therefore, be nonpartisan, for we have to choose the rules that guide us as researchers. Particular rules for research will focus our attention on certain aspects of vocational education and away from others. In the case of positivism, our attention is focused on vocational education as a technical act. When we measure certain aspects of education to determine how well school systems, or particular schools, or particular teachers are doing, we cannot separate this question from the political issue of what schools should be doing. Therefore, if positivist research can establish the criteria by way of their research instruments that measure how well we are doing in schooling, they have also established what we should be doing. Positivism thus becomes a political instrument of social control while its adherents are proclaiming their neutrality, their disinterestedness, their disdain for mixing politics and education (Bowers, 1982).

If vocational researchers describe a student's readiness for work as the ability to follow orders, respect authority, and work as a team player, then in order for vocational schools to get good evaluations, they must teach these skills. The "objective" process of defining work readiness holds some hidden but very specific values. There are, of course, a variety of ways to define work readiness; the researchers in this case chose the definition that best suited their political and economic beliefs. A value choice has been made; and the researchers are no longer political innocents. The same is true with a teacher who gives an *objective*, multiple-choice test. The test is presented as an objective, value-free instrument of evaluation, but a closer examination reveals a set of hidden value assumptions. In making the test, the teacher had already chosen the textbook from which the test material was taken—a value choice that privileged one book over several others; the teacher chose particular material from the book because it seemed more important—a value choice of some facts over others. A multiple-choice format was chosen over other test formats—a value choice that privileged certain forms of learning (fact memorization) over others (the analysis, interpretation, and application of an essay test). Such value choices are necessary to living and teaching in the world. The point is not that we avoid such choices, just that we understand that we are making them. Such consciousness is a key goal of a democratic form of vocational education. It is a cardinal aspect of a higher order of thinking.

9. *There is one true reality, and the purpose of education is to pass that reality along to students.* Ultimately, positivists argue, there is one best way to accomplish a task. For example, there is one best way (best method) to teach. The purpose of positivist teacher education is to pass that method along to students. Educational science that is grounded on positivist research assumes that the laws of society and the knowledge of human existence have been verified and are ready to be inserted into the minds of children. Operating on these assumptions, educational "engineers" devise curricula and organizational strategies for schools as if there were no ambiguities or uncertainties in the social and educational world. In this context, scientific knowledge achieves the status of the sacred, the holy word. Contemporary culture teaches us to revere science and the scientific method unscientifically, that is, by faith. The authoritarian voice of positivist science silences our natural language—the way we talk about schools and our professional lives as teachers. The worth of such language is undermined by a positivist science that regards it as soft, effeminate, impressionistic, and nonscientific. Cowed by the authority of positivistic science, we accede to its demands and humbly allow it to define our role as *mere* practitioners (Aronowitz, 1983; Koller, 1981; Eisner, 1984).

In his studies of the street-corner culture in Toronto's Jane-Finch Corridor, Peter McLaren found that lower socioeconomic class students questioned the school's view of them as passive recipients of sacred and official facts. Teachers, unfortunately, have less frequently questioned their own passive position in relation to the expert producers of knowledge (McLaren,

1994). When positivists control knowledge and student-teacher evaluation in schools, the range of behaviors that can be considered good teaching is considerably narrowed. Supervisors admit that creative lessons that fail to follow the "one best method" must be evaluated as unsatisfactory. Thus, rewards for vocational teachers are not based on reasonable notions of competence and creativity but on adherence to prescribed format. Like workers in a top-down authoritarian factory, teachers in positivistic school systems find themselves playing the role of rule followers who have little input into how the rules are made. Teachers, thus, become executors of plans. Among the best and brightest teachers, the passion for creativity and engagement with students and ideas is slowly lost. This reality is one of the great tragedies of our era.

Now that the modernist epistemology—positivism—has been introduced, we can turn our attention to the analysis of modernism in general and the ways it affects vocational schooling and work. Indeed, the quality of our everyday lives and our goals as human beings are directly affected by modernism.

Modernism and the Technical Fix

We live and work in a technocratic culture. The word *technocratic* is not used here to label a culture simply because it has developed a battery of technical activities. The Hopi Indians have developed techniques (skills, procedures, and routines), but we do not think of them as having a technocratic culture. We consider twentieth-century American culture technocratic and Hopi culture not technocratic because American culture embraces a rationalism that excludes other ways of knowing. This rationalism sees everyday life as a series of problems to be solved by experts applying scientific knowledge. The natural world is viewed as something to be conquered and used for the benefit of men and women, and time is seen in a linear manner that moves the individual to control the future. An important characteristic of this technocratic culture involves the tendency to see the technological method of solving a problem to be reproducible in a number of different contexts. This tendency to embrace technological solutions, or *technical fixes*, is illustrated in so-called teacher-proof reading programs with point-by-point instructions that leave nothing to the instructor's ingenuity and in work management systems that are designed for all workplaces, regardless of their differences. Such management systems seek to control all aspects of a production process, again leaving individuals (in this case workers) with little input into any aspect of designing the work process. In order to understand how teachers and workers are stripped of their skills (deskilled), one has to appreciate the power of technocratic thinking (Bowers, 1982).

Those of us who are interested in studying and teaching vocational education must understand this technocratic consciousness and the way it shapes the nature of the institutions with which we deal on a daily basis. All of our institutions—whether workplaces, schools, courts of law, or hospitals—have been shaped by the technical fix mentality, which assumes that systems problems, be they mechanical or human, can be solved by technical solutions designed by outside experts (Wirth, 1983). For example, if a group of vocational education students are failing English courses, the technical fix would involve adjusting classroom teaching methods. Students would sit in a circle rather than rows, workbooks and worksheets would be adapted to increase students' time on tasks, and assertive discipline programs would be implemented to maintain order in the classroom. Such a technical fix mentality would never think to examine the purpose of instruction, the assumptions one holds about the students' abilities, or the forms of knowledge and the skills students bring with them to class. Such issues are irrelevant in the mind-set produced by the technical fix.

This all-the-king's-horses-and-men way of addressing problems allows us to look at the possibility of changing everything in the world but ourselves. The problems of work and education cannot be solved by technical fixes. Democratic and progressive solutions to such problems demand structural changes in the economic and political system as well as alterations in the values and consciousness of individuals. Such changes lead us to understand that to treat a sociotechnical system at a workplace as if it were simply a technical system is a pathological act. In the spirit of the modernist tendency to ignore the connection between the various aspects of a situation, the human dimension is removed from the technical (Wirth, 1983).

When workers describe a problem that needs resolving, they select and name the aspects of the situation that they feel are important. When civil engineers, for example, direct the building of a road, they may attend to drainage, soil stability, or ease of maintenance; they may ignore the economic effects of the road on the villages that lie along its path. Problem setting involves a form of world making, as the problem solver selects the factors that should be attended to and organizes them in a way that provides coherence so that action can commence. Depending on our frame of reference, we see problems in very different ways. An economist, for example, may notice the very aspects of the road project that the engineer ignored. Thus, depending on our personal contexts, our disciplinary backgrounds, our interests, our values, and our political and economic perspectives, we examine problems in different manners (Schon, 1987). As a result of our differences, some of us will fail to see problems that others find central to the health of the community or the society.

Therefore, simply possessing problem-solving techniques or technical fixes provides little help to a worker. A mechanical engineer, for example, has learned a variety of technical methods for solving problems that are routinely encountered. What happens when a problem arises that cannot be solved with the learned repertoire of technical methods? Unique cases—

which beset the world—fall outside the range of technical fixes. To solve problems, workers have to be able to think on their feet, improvise, create strategies of their own devising. With this point, the type of thinking that vocational education should provide its students has been identified. The uncertainty and uniqueness of most work problems will escape workers supplied only with technical fixes.

Modernist Fragmentation and the Embrace of Short-term Goals

Modernist science teaches us to break apart problems into smaller pieces that can be more easily understood. Modernist schools do the same thing, breaking skills into subskills and knowledge into bits of data that can quickly be learned and inserted into the mind. Such activity is supposed to make complex tasks and school subjects more manageable, but in practice it tends to fragment our world. Unable to perceive the consequences of our actions or the relation of the parts to the whole, we lose sight of the big picture. How many times have students lost (or probably never gained) sight of the purpose of high-school algebra, as they sit day after day practicing algebraic subskills? Rarely do students have a sense of where such skills might be usable outside of school. This fragmentation of the world produces a short-term mentality, a way of seeing that cannot look beyond the task at hand to see how it fits into a larger vision, a larger sense of purpose (Senge, 1990). And this fragmented mentality can be detected at all levels of the society. Our political life, for example, is as shortsighted as our educational life. In his 1980 campaign against President Carter, Ronald Reagan captured this short-term perspective in the phrase: "Are you better off now than you were four years ago?" When decisions are made on the basis of such a question, it is hardly surprising that long-range planning is not a common activity in the halls of government. Former President Bush was so uncomfortable with the idea of long-range planning that he struggled to find a precise phrase to express it. Sounding more like Dana Carvey than himself, Bush frequently talked about "the vision thing." Vision and the connection it requires between the everyday and the long term was lost on George Bush.

   The vision thing has never been compatible with Cartesian-Newtonian modernist science. Positivism has tended to separate rational activity from moral values and religious experience. Efficiency in our factories and workplaces has typically been thought of only in quantifiable terms; questions of ethics and morality have been rendered irrelevant in such situations. Production decisions are based on short-term concerns for profit, not on the need for ethical workplaces or good work. If work takes on a more humane face, the inducement comes more from greed than from a sense of ethics. Modernist ways of thinking have rarely allowed us to synthesize our democratic ideals with an economic agenda (Lyons, 1988). A progressive vocational education demands just such a synthesis.

Educational philosopher John Dewey zealously opposed the fragmenting effects of Cartesian-Newtonian science. He argued that learning has been victimized by science of this sort, as it has been separated into neat and ordered compartments: vocational versus academic education; the mental versus the manual; and science versus the humanities. Such fragmentation has served to produce narrow specialists who are unable to perceive the world and its problems from a variety of vantage points. As a result, higher orders of thinking have been undermined, and our moral, ethical, economic, and political progress as a people has been thwarted. The same process has affected work and vocational education in particular. Both industrial training programs and vocational education have often opted to simply adapt workers to perform compartmentalized, functional, immediate tasks (Chesneaux, 1992). In such fragmented programs, educators are not interested in engaging *trainees* in intellectual pursuits. After all, the mental and manual are separate activities. Educational leaders maintain that their mission is to provide specific men and women with limited technical skills.

As with workers, managers have become victimized by modernist fragmentation. The dominant management style in America is grounded on the achievement of short-range goals. Contemporary management incentive programs are often based on quarterly earnings, not long-range goals of increased productivity (DeYoung, 1989). Such strategies not only indicate ethical failure but economic failure as well. Although they have attempted to lay the blame for America's economic decline on the shoulders of educators and incompetent workers, managers and their short-term ways of thinking have undermined America's economy. Unlike managers of a previous generation, today's corporate leaders rarely stay with a company more than ten years. Moving from position to position, these managers have little direct interest in the products their company produces. In many situations, this has led to a precipitous decline in firms' concern for quality, allowing foreign producers the opportunity to capture what were exclusively American markets. Slowly, consumer confidence in the made-in-U.S.A. label began to evaporate. Soon, corporate leaders were having to beg consumers to "Buy American," while concurrently asking Congress for bailout moneys and for tariffs and quotas against foreign products.

In an economy where short-term profit drives all activity, nothing is surprising. Activities on Wall Street in the 1980s resembled an Old West gunfight, with young investment-banker gunslingers seeking profits no matter who they hurt or destroyed. U.S. Steel typified the company seeking short-term profits, as it diversified by purchasing nonsteel corporations. Such acquisitions had nothing to do with increasing U.S. Steel's competitiveness in the steel industry; they had much to do with short-term profit making. The effect of such policy allowed U.S. Steel to ignore the necessities of owning steel plants with obsolete technologies. This strategy eventually led to the collapse of the American steel industry and the loss of thousands of American jobs. In the "paper economy" of late twentieth-century America, long-term investment in our industrial strength has given way to short-term acquisitions and mergers. Our industrial base is weakened when firms pursue all opportunities for profit and believe that the stability of workers' lives and communities' financial security are irrelevant. This analysis is not meant to suggest that profit seeking be abandoned by industries and business. The point is that profit must be sought within boundaries shaped by considerations other than profit. An economically just society can be achieved only through long-range planning and a way of seeing the world that does not separate economic efficiency from larger democratic values (Falk and Lyson, 1988).

Centralization, Bureaucratization, and Modernist Experts on the Loose

This modernist way of seeing the world has numerous effects—all of which are hidden from public view. It is this unseen feature that makes them so powerful, so influential in everyday life. The modernist tendency for centralized, top-down, bureaucratic management has dramatically affected the nature of American work. People are divided into roles, segmented, and specialized. Men and women are subordinated within the bureaucratic structure for the singular purpose of increasing the output of goods. Worker development, happiness, and even dignity are irrelevant—greater efficiency in the use of resources is all that really matters. Complex webs of human management have been developed over the twentieth century to deal with workers. The technocratic ideology that emerges in this context reduces humans to organisms whose behaviors are to be molded by well-intentioned behavioral engineers. The technical fix employed here removes the notion of individual free choice or the possibility of human development, substituting instead a scientifically produced strategy for manipulating human behavior. The democratic notion of a free society with individuals empowered to transform themselves by way of critical reflection and analysis is irrelevant in the centralized, bureaucratized, and expert-directed society (Wirth, 1983).

It is important to note that workplaces are not simply work sites, they are ambiguous agencies involved in the dynamics of controlling individuals. We are just entering into an era when individuals are beginning to react to these forms of control. An important aspect of this enlightenment involves the recognition that such forms of human management are incompatible with the principles of democracy. Indeed, democracy cannot survive the centralized organizational patterns of the expert-controlled society. When problems emerge and turbulence sweeps through an organization, the only way the culture of the expert can respond is by intensifying the control and supervision of the parts. As this occurs, bureaucratic structures become increasingly unwieldy, complex, and *more* dysfunctional. However, alternatives to these modernist patterns do exist. Democratic administration, for example, involves smaller units, the facilitation of self-management, and worker empowerment. Concrete examples of such organizational strategies can be found. The Norwegian navy provides a fascinating case study for a decentralized, democratic reorganization of a hierarchical institution. Not only did efficiency actually improve as the result of the reforms, but individuals from all ranks reported more congenial and interpersonally rewarding working conditions (Wirth, 1983).

Modernist Breakdown of Community and Public Space

One of the main points being made here involves the ways the modernist mind-set undermines democracy and good work. This analysis of modernism, therefore, is not merely an examination of work but an analysis of the survival of American democracy, for the two issues cannot be separated in our worker civics. Democracy cannot survive without the existence of community and its strong social ties. This does not mean that we have to go back to some idealized notion of community past, some mythical Mayberry with Andy, Barney, and Aunt Bea. Those days are past, or better, never were. Our charge is to build a new community within the boundaries of present reality. Vocational education plays a central role in this process, as it produces workers imbued with both technical abilities and social, political, and economic understandings. These workers will understand that community is destroyed when a large percentage of workers is condemned to labor in an economic and social reality not of their own design, one that denigrates their abilities and rejects their input.

Modernism has undermined our identity with the group (e.g., the trade, the village, the community), as it has emphasized a detached individualism. The modernist individual can be described as *Homo economicus*—a person who counts in terms of profitability. "We must learn to sell ourselves," the success evangelists preach. The gospel of economic success anoints us with the oil of market maximization after it baptizes us in the river of quarterly profit margins. This econo-theology sabotages our ability to maintain our interpersonal relationships, as it induces us to see one another as competitors in the savage marketplace. The omnipresent irony underlying all of this is that materialistic conceptions of human life undermine the economy itself. If communitarian values made us economically poorer, there would still be countless reasons to advocate them; the truth is that such values facilitate economic growth.

American schooling, as traditionally conceived, has often contributed one more brick in the wall that separates individuals from one another. Academic and vocational education has trained generations of students to think and behave in terms of an individual competitive success ethic. The logic of the common good has not played a major role in school or in the public sphere in general. John Dewey understood this reality early in the twentieth century and attempted to identify the impediments to a community-based democracy in which worker-citizens could live and work. Corporate power and its misuse rested at the top of Dewey's list, followed by an inequitable distribution of wealth, and an irrational system of production that focused not on human needs but on profit making. He also delineated misinformation disseminated by power groups, technology not adjusted to human need, art's captivity in museums while men and women worked and lived in ugly factories and cities, the bureaucratization of American life, and the undemocratic use of technology.

The politics of self-interest has undermined the quality of all of our lives. In particular, it has caused us to lose faith in our public institutions. Faith in government has vanished in the wake of lies, deceit, and permanent scandal. Faith in the corporate world evaporated in the wild 1980s, as arbitrage, corporate raiding, and materialism ran amok. Even the church, with the revelations about greedy and hypocritical televangelists and the sexual abuse of Catholic altar boys, has lost its halo. One of the most important symbols of the breakdown of community and the erosion of the public space involves the elevation of "family values" to the center of the moral dialogue about public life. The ethic of individualism found its highest expression in the substitution of political convictions with personality traits and the supplanting of political analysis with scandalmongering. As the family-values language of the private sphere appropriated the lexicon of political conversation, discussions of public life became more abstract and removed from lived experience (Coontz, 1992).

This phenomenon was exacerbated by the rise of the New Right and Reaganism in the late 1970s and 1980s. As the Falwells, Bakkers, Swaggarts joined forces with the right wing of the Republican Party, public morality came to be expressed in personal and individualistic language. By the end of the 1980s, young Americans described a "good citizen" not in terms of voting or political involvement but as an individual who was personally generous and caring. Evoking family metaphors as prototypes for public involvement yields an unrealistic, if not dangerous, definition of community. Chained to such private imagery, citizens lose their capacity to think in terms of public and impersonal issues. All social facts in the grand public arena must be translated into private, personal, and familial terms in order to gain meaning. That process leaves the American public vulnerable to crass manipulation by public figures who have the ability to appear sincere and intimate on television. "Bill Clinton looked presidential at the meeting with Yeltsin," Sam Donaldson tells us. Questions of economic justice and social morality give way to questions of personality and vague patriotic pretense. It is not surprising that as such tendencies have intensified, fewer and fewer Americans care to vote. Questions of workers' rights or safety in the workplace give way to descriptions of Marla Maples's attire first at the Trump wedding and then at the divorce. The analysis of childhood poverty gives way to *Hardcopy* reports on Rob Lowe's videotape of his latest ménage à trois. The specifics of union demands fade into the latest picture of O. J. Simpson playing golf.

Irrational Production and Ecological Destruction

Over the last two centuries, social analysts have repeatedly noticed a persistent irrationality embedded in modernist thinking that tends to devalue human beings and their needs. Nowhere is this impulse easier to identify than in the ways production decisions are made. Because modernist economists fail to account for natural and social realities, industrial policy often undermines the local and concrete concerns of workers and citizens. Raising the gross national product (GNP) becomes, in the spirit of raising standardized test scores, the purpose of economic activity. The GNP fails to distinguish among different kinds of production. The construction of more Burger Kings and Pizza Huts or shopping centers is just as important as steel or oil production. In this type of economy, the value of economic activity and products is determined by considerations that have nothing to do with social needs. The short-term visions that dominate the economic sphere destroy concerns such as worker creativity; in fact, workers are reduced to mere pawns if profit parameters are modified (Chesneaux, 1992; Falk and Lyson, 1988; Aronowitz, 1992).

The same neglect of social needs and irrational perspectives toward production have produced an industrial machine that laughs derisively at those who raise questions about ecological concerns. George Bush in the last days of the 1992 presidential campaign called Al Gore "Ozone Man" because of his book on the environment. Rush Limbaugh elicits a very positive response from listeners and viewers when he attacks the environmentalists as kooks and screwballs. Examining the health hazards of modernist workplaces in the past and present makes clear the irresponsibility of American corporate leadership. Organized labor has finally begun to address the dangers posed to workers by the various chemicals and substances produced or used in production. The near epidemics of cancer and other industry-related diseases are forcing industrial leaders to reassess their policies of shameful neglect. One out of every four citizens in the United States now gets cancer, and one out of every five Americans dies of it (Kellner, 1989). Although corporate America has begun to earmark more money for public relations concerning environmental issues, the cleanup of industry has only just begun.

A revolution of thinking must occur before environmental protection becomes a common theme of management training. Accounting methods, for
example, must begin to view the environment as something inseparable
from issues of economic production (Block, 1990). Under the new thinking, improvements in the environment of the workplace and increases in the
quality of air and water must be treated as material contributions to the
larger economic good. Growth for its own sake would no longer serve as an
axiom of economic life. Suggestions that growth be considered in light of
social needs or environmental concerns would no longer elicit cries of
heresy in the corridors of the corporations (Aronowitz, 1992). The disor-
derly growth of California's high-tech mecca, Silicon Valley, would become
a symbol for modernist failure, with its ecological and human damage.
Toxic waste overruns the area; chemical leaks and accidents are hidden from
public view; housing costs are ridiculous; traffic is horrendous; desperate executives take amphetamines to get going and tranquilizers to calm down.
The technological consciousness that produced Silicon Valley would be re-
assessed vis-à-vis the demands of democracy—and it would not become the
prototype of the American future.

Thus, contrary to the prevailing wisdom, technological development does
not necessarily improve the quality of work and the quality of life. The irrationality of modernist economic production with its emphasis on short-term
profits has created an atmosphere where technological development has
been viewed as a way to reduce labor costs. Technological development has
allowed machines to take the place of skilled labor. Those involved in the
production process, therefore, could be reduced to a few highly paid managers and R and D (research and development) experts and a division of
low-wage unskilled or semiskilled workers attending to machines. Although
there is evidence of need for higher-skilled workers in some high-tech industries, most advanced technological operations can be operated by low-skill,
low-paid workers. The computer, for example, shows no sign of eliminating
or even reducing the monotony and stress of service and information workers. Indeed, some studies indicate that word processing typists experience
twice as much fatigue and lack of challenge as traditional clerical workers.
The irrationality of the workplace continues; little effort is made to address
the human consequences of work (DeYoung, 1989; Pollin and Cockburn,
1991; Harris, 1981).

Efficiency, Rationalization, and Decontextualization

Modernism has promoted itself in the language of efficiency. One of the
highest values of a modernist institution involves its ability to raise the level
of output in relation to input, for example, raising the quantity of production in relation to hours of work or raising test scores vis-à-vis expenditures

for education. Measuring efficiency may not be as objective or value free as it first appears. Subjective decisions must be made concerning what to include or exclude in its calculation (Wirth, 1983). Should, for example, environmental effects or worker alienation be a part of the formula? Or are these merely extraneous factors that cloud the issue? As advocates of economic justice and democratic workplaces explore such dynamics, they come to realize that, given the influence of this bottom-line-oriented, *vulgar* efficiency, issues of social effect are swept under the carpet. Workers who are content to merely repeat one low-skill machine process day after day, year after year are more valuable to the quest for efficiency than creative, thoughtful, and industrious workers (Wilms, 1979). At this point, the irrationality of modernism again raises its ugly head: In this case, the development of individual growth is betrayed by the kiss of efficiency.

In the name of efficiency, the scientific managers have rationalized work—the consummate act of modernist scientism. The rationalization of work involves a three-step process: (1) a particular activity is subjected to a task analysis; (2) on the basis of this analysis, the experts divide the task into component subtasks; and (3) workers are then assigned to one of the subtasks. This classic description of the process of worker deskilling degrades workers, as it transfers the knowledge of production to managers (Simon, Dippo, and Schenke, 1991). Without such understanding, labor power is undermined, as workers are reduced to machine caretakers with little hope for advancement and social mobility. In a society driven by an ethic of individualism that places the responsibility for success exclusively on the shoulders of individuals, such an economic arrangement can extract tragic human costs (Aronowitz, 1992). Hard work allegedly pays off for everyone; when it does not, individuals can only conclude that they themselves are failures. The system is not to blame—culpability slides off the modernist experts like eggs off Teflon.

Practically every school in America reinforces this belief in the individual's responsibility for personal success. America is the land of opportunity, a place where impediments to success are personal, not social. Economic inequality results from differences in ability and motivation, not from differences in social circumstance. What about the poor and dispossessed who inconveniently keep popping up in public places? What about those children who grow up in conditions of dire poverty? Does their economic status simply reflect a lack of ability and motivation? Americans too often attempt to hide such individuals. We are made uncomfortable by their living testimony to the failure of both the ethic of individual responsibility and the absurdity of our claim to be a society unaffected by the dangers of class division. Because of continuing attachment to the ethic of individualism, Americans have been able to disabuse themselves of concern for those who have *failed* to take advantage of economic opportunity.

The ethic of individualism and the education that is grounded on it have obscured the truth about work. Contrary to the prevailing wisdom, we are not isolated and independent individuals laying bricks or buying and selling companies. Corporate policies and beliefs about economic theories profoundly affect the quality of our working lives. Economic institutions educate and shape us, just like schools and churches do. Definitions of efficiency make some experiences available to us as workers, while precluding the possibility of our involvement in others. The Social Darwinist, survival-of-the-fittest theme song is the Muzak of the modernist workplace; it is always there, always subliminally shaping worker consciousness. In the name of efficiency, it cultivates a short-term focus on naked self-interest. The time has come to change these ways of thinking—our conception of efficiency, our glorification of rationalization, our obsession with an individualism that removes women and men from the social contexts that help shape them. Efficiency and productivity do not countermand social and human values. Students who will become workers in a democratic society must understand these contradictions, as they uncover the influence of power in their lives as citizens and workers. This is the subject of Chapter 3.

3 Power and the Development of the Modernist Economy

Most Americans are unaware of the enormous power that business and industrial interests exercise over American society and culture. In the realm of vocational education, this political dynamic is practically invisible in the literature of the field. In order to understand how student conceptions of work and education are formed, vocational educators must understand how power works. How is it that we so often hear the opinions of business and industrial leaders on TV but not the voice of workers? Why is it that CNN devotes several hours a day to business news but no time to labor news? Why is there a business section in every newspaper in the country but no labor section? These are questions related to power and how it works. As a society, we have grown so accustomed to inequitable and dangerous power relations that a newspaper section on labor would seem strange to us. Newspapers and TV networks that are dedicated to the service of business needs seem almost natural, a part of God's larger plan.

The Organization of Work in Relation to Power

The concept that follows is simple and central to this book: One cannot understand workplaces or vocational education without understanding how power shapes such institutions. To grasp this concept, we must understand how the goals of management differ from those of the workforce: (1) business and industrial managers want to increase output (productivity) without raising wages; (2) they want to reduce worker turnover; (3) they desire a decrease in the conflict between labor and management; (4) they want workers who are loyal to the company; (5) they want workers who respect their authority; and (6) they prefer workers who value the work ethic. Whatever manipulations it takes to achieve these goals will be used by managers; all aspects of the work site will be shaped by these objectives (Simon, Dippo, and Schenke, 1991; Lamphere, 1985).

Social relations in the workplace often seem to have nothing to do with the power of management and its attempt to implement its agenda. This is not unusual; critical sociologists often describe how power hides in the shadows of everyday life. Worker rewards often hinge on how well an individual conforms to the goals of management. A subservient worker who is more loyal than thoughtful is often more valued than a more assertive colleague, even though the assertive colleague has the potential for significant accomplishment. Both workers may find that their self-esteem and positive sense of self are undermined by the ways they are rewarded and punished by management. How workers relate to each other and to managers cannot be viewed outside the context of power. Conflicts between workers or between workers and supervisors are typically framed as individual disputes, as personality conflicts (Simon, Dippo, and Schenke, 1991). The ways that power shapes these relationships is often missed. Mary finds herself drawn into a conflicting relationship with Rhonda at a hair salon. Neither recognizes that management has pitted them against each other in an attempt to encourage competition and higher profit margins. Workers who understand power will appreciate the ways in which the goals of management have subtly created a situation where Mary and Rhonda see one another as competitors, not as sisters with common interests.

When workers understand such dynamics, they come to see that such interpersonal problems are not simply private matters but social issues reflecting larger concepts of workplace organization. Power so regulates the conversation about economic policy and the organization of the workplace that open communication is undermined. To question the absolute legitimacy of the goals of management is to be positioned as antibusiness, as anti-America. The goal of higher productivity cannot be questioned even if it means placing greater stress on workers and undermining the quality of their lives (Webster, 1985/1986). The goal of reducing conflict between workers cannot be questioned even if it means placing the needs of workers on the back burner. The goal of workers' respecting the work ethic cannot be questioned even if it means that workers do not have the right to ask who benefits as a result of their respect for hard work. Once workers and vocational education teachers begin to understand these dimensions of power, social relations, and worker identity, then the possibility for alternative conceptions of work greatly increases.

The Power of Corporations: Subverting the Ethic of Democracy

Authority and power in late twentieth-century America reside not only in government but in what is commonly referred to as the market—corporations, businesses, and industries. The coercive power of the market is far more insidious, hidden, and elusive than that of the government. The elusiveness of private power undermines progressive elements to confront it, for most citizens are not aware of its existence and its modus operandi (MO). The market will not stay in its place, as corporate power spills over into the realms of culture, politics, and education (Brosio, 1994). This spillover has exerted detrimental effects on the efforts of democrats to protect the fragile democracy of the late twentieth century. Although individuals hold the freedom to vote, they have to submit to coercion in their economic lives. Many progressives argue that without a public understanding of the way economic wealth amasses political power, democracy cannot survive. Again, advocates of democracy are thwarted by the invisibility of the political impact of power. Indeed, the greatest challenge democracy faces at the end of the millennium is to expose the forces that undermine it (Wirth, 1983; Brosio, 1985; Giroux, 1993).

Controlling vast resources, American corporations have, in essence, become a fourth branch of government. They are more a superior branch than a coequal branch, for corporations can avoid the checks and balances that restrict legislative, executive, and judicial institutions (Wirth, 1983). The push for privatization that became the mark of the national politics of the 1980s has worked to put more and more power in the hands of corporations. As corporate taxes were reduced in the name of trickle-down economics, more power was transferred to business and industry in the name of corporate freedom and the rule of the market. With corporate leaders making more and more decisions about economics and political affairs, progressives have tried to point out that those who exercised the most power over the daily lives of Americans were not elected by anyone and had no obligation to act in the public interest (Giroux, 1993). These realizations are by no means new: Alexis de Tocqueville, a French visitor to America in the 1830s, wrote extensively about the impact of the industrialization of America. Understanding the tendency of power to follow wealth, Tocqueville warned that industrial development might lead to the creation of a new aristocracy. This so-called economic royalty, he concluded, could not coexist with the belief in democratic equality. By necessity, democracy would suffer (Bellah et al., 1991).

Since the beginnings of industrialization in the first half of the 1800s, corporations have consistently increased their power in American life. Not content to control the workforce and the process and distribution of production, early twentieth-century corporate leaders sought new techniques to help them control consumer demand. The second decade of the 1900s witnessed the birth of marketing, as cars, clothes, cigarettes, and processed food were presented as objects of desire. The invention of credit buying, annual model updates, and the psychology of packaging coincided with the development of advertising and marketing research to produce forms of social regulation unimagined in the nineteenth century. With the development of radio and television, the possibility for even newer forms of social control expanded exponentially. With innovations in market research, such as Nielsen ratings for TV viewership patterns, citizen surveillance and strategies of manipulation would place even greater power in the hands of corporate leaders (Webster, 1985/1986).

This scientific management of political life has reshaped the way Americans live their lives. Particular social sentiments (e.g., the belief that wealthy people have worked harder than poor people and thus deserve their fortunes) promoted by corporate leaders mesh with dominant ideologies (ways of making sense and meaning of the world) cultivated by the media, religious institutions, and schools, to profound effect. This notion of ideology is an important concept in our attempt to make sense of how power shapes the nature of work and the self-concept of workers (Harvey, 1989; Aronowitz, 1992). Social and educational theorist Peter McLaren (1994) has maintained that the public often thinks of ideology as simply the "isms" of communism, socialism, anarchism, or existentialism. But in his opinion, it is much more and is far more influential than these formal systems of belief. Ideology is a way of viewing the world that men and women "tend to accept as natural and as common sense" (pp. 184–185). Such ways of seeing are the result of the pervasive influence of power in everyday life. The customs, beliefs, and values that power helps formulate produce perverted understandings of people's place in the social and economic world. As a result, individuals come to accept their lowly position in the hierarchy as just. The inequitable relations of power and privilege that put them in their unenviable situations are hidden by the ideology.

I have often seen such ideology work with students in vocational education classes. Randy is a brilliant junior-high student from East Texas. He has been raised in a home where his father has a garage fix-it shop, where he repairs everything from lawn mowers to automobiles. Randy has watched his father work for as long as he can remember. By the time Randy was six, his father recognized that his son possessed great mechanical talent, as Randy took apart washing machine motors and other gadgets and put them back together perfectly. Randy's father finished only the fifth grade, and when Randy was a baby, his mother died. Randy is not sure whether his father can read; there are no books, magazines, or even newspapers in their home.

Although he has terrific talents, Randy has never been good at school. Because he came from a home devoid of reading materials and the awareness of the importance of words, Randy was always behind other students, especially those students whose parents were college graduates. As he performed poorly on language-based standardized tests, Randy was tracked into a low-ability group and was told that he was not college material. Although Randy always wanted to become a mechanical engineer, the ideology that presents standardized intelligence tests as infallible measurements of ability told him such a dream was ridiculous. Finding its roots in modernist scientism, positivism, and the cult of the expert, this dominant school ideology in collaboration with power convinced Randy that it was only common sense to forget mechanical engineering. Upper-middle-class students in Randy's junior high rarely have to overcome similar impediments, as they typically grow up in homes with written materials and linguistic consciousness. These upper-middle-class students, contrary to the ideology of the tests, are not by nature more intelligent than Randy. Indeed, very few of them will ever equal him in their ability to work with machines and motors.

The levels at which such ideological influence operates are numerous. Social theorists tell us that knowledge is power and whoever controls knowledge exercises great power. Often, corporations are able to hide information or issue misinformation, in the process shaping the consciousness of those who contribute to the making of social and economic policy. For example, consumers who eat Perdue chickens usually do not know that their prices reflect unfair labor practices. Most Perdue workers receive only minimum wages, no benefits, and many suffer from repetitive-motion illnesses due to labor speedups. Because they can manipulate public access to information with their advertising and sophisticated public relations strategies, many corporations are able to hide unfair and dangerous practices. Every day many firms dump toxic waste into the ecosystem, but because of their control of information, the public perceives them as concerned environmentalists. To the degree that business leaders can suppress their sins against workers and the environment, they can manipulate not only consumer behavior but also voter activity (Pollin and Cockburn, 1991).

Corporate control of information also affects the everyday life of workers, as managers hide data on job costing or company profit margins from the rank and file. Such knowledge control keeps workers off guard, unable to enter negotiations on an equal plain (Roditi, 1992). Media domination by interlocking corporate boards subtly shapes the perspective from which news stories are covered. Michael Apple (1992) recently examined a series of network news stories on unemployment. Few stories attempted to explain the rise in unemployment. Most of the reports, like TV news in general, focused on consequences, not causes, of everyday events. This is because any direct attempt to explain the conscious attempts by management to control workers would be quickly countered by charges of media bias. In lieu of analysis of causes, network reports spoke of tough times, stressful times for individuals. Economic ups and downs, newspeople implied, are part of a "natural" progression of events that operate outside the control of human beings.

Corporate power operates on a multitude of levels. In addition to information control, corporations have steadily increased their demands on local governments to create "good business climates." Such climates typically involve deals between business and government to lower corporate taxes, provide infrastructural improvements, and relocate people living on land needed for the work site. Barry Bluestone (1988) has written about the deals between Detroit and General Motors (GM) that preceded the construction of the "Poletown" Cadillac assembly plant. After having lost two GM production facilities, Detroit—not unlike other cities with high unemployment—was anxious to replace lost jobs. GM leaders hinted that they would be willing to build a new Cadillac plant in Detroit if the city was amenable to some concessions. GM asked the City of Detroit to (1) grant the company two-thirds of a heavily populated square mile of land in the middle of the downtown, (2) relocate the 3,000 people who lived in the area, (3) raze 160 small businesses in the neighborhood, (4) demolish a 170-bed hospital and 3 nursing homes, (5) redirect 2 major highway on-off ramps and move a railroad right-of-way, (6) transfer a Jewish cemetery to another location, (7) clear the area to a depth of ten feet so GM would not have to worry about water, sewer, telephone, and gas lines, and (8) grant a 50 percent tax reduction for twelve years.

The cost of the concessions totaled almost one-half billion dollars, and the City Council voted for it unanimously. Ironically, after the plant was built, it was not used for Cadillac production. Even if it goes into full operation, only 6,200 jobs would be available for Detroit workers. In a similar situation, International Harvester informed Fort Wayne, Indiana, and Springfield, Ohio, that it was going to shut down a plant in one of these two cities. Exercising its power, the company told city leaders that the community that offered the most concessions would get to keep its plant. After much analysis and debate, Fort Wayne offered International Harvester $30 million in tax breaks, loan guarantees, and a series of subsidies. Springfield countered with an offer of $31 million. Soon thereafter, the Fort Wayne plant was closed. Never in the twentieth century have corporations possessed so much power.

Of course, school programs—both vocational and academic—do not escape the influence of corporate power. School-business partnerships have become increasingly popular in the 1980s and 1990s. Although many companies have proclaimed such setups a success, the mainstream media have awarded such arrangements little analysis. Studying the research that has been conducted reveals that schools possess little power in their relationship with firms. As a result, businesses exercise veto power on any findings that portray companies in anything resembling a negative light. Individuals who have worked with the development of national student performance standards report that although many of their colleagues might want to encourage questions on unionism and democratic issues in the workplace, businesses would immediately withdraw their support the moment such topics were broached.

In recent years, an interest conflict has developed as businesses demand "ideological purity" (i.e., the unquestioning support of the ideology of laissez-faire economics) in vocational education programs. At the same time, progressive vocational educators turn to the Perkins Act and its demand that students be schooled in "all aspects" of their trade. Illustrating the power of business and industry once again, most states ignore the spirit of the Perkins Act's intent. In recently passed state and federal youth apprenticeship legislation, little attention has been granted to democratic workplace issues. Uninterested in critical reflection on issues of economic justice, many programs instruct students to simply identify skills and adopt attitudes that meet business needs. Hannah Roditi concluded her research on apprentice programs with the observation that the goals of most apprenticeships involve the production of *docile* workers. The education of worker-citizens well versed in democratic principles and capable of independent thought, Roditi added, is too dangerous (Bluestone, 1988; Roditi, 1992).

Cultivating Inequality: The Widening Chasm Between Workers and Management

Nothing illustrates the power of corporate management better than the grounding of the U.S. economy on a segmented workforce. One does not have to look far to find that some jobs are defined as information-based management positions, whereas others are described as low-skill, low-status, and low-income assignments. Even more disturbing is the realization that a disproportionate percentage of recently created jobs are of the low-wage variety (DeYoung, 1989; Block, 1990). As the middle class has shrunk, more and more workers have suffered from underemployment and unemployment. A new economic category has emerged to describe the experience of thousands of workers: contingent employment, jobs that offer few benefits and no assurance of job security. By the end of the 1980s, the percentage of full-time workers making low wages was growing. Workers without college degrees, the constituency of vocational education, found that their earnings declined by 18 percent in the 1980s. By the early 1990s, the real earnings of male high-school graduates had fallen below those of comparable workers in 1963. A large percentage of the jobs created in the 1980s were part-time and low wage, often performed by women (Coontz, 1992; Block, 1990).

The conservative tenor of the 1980s produced policies aimed specifically at cutting government spending on poor people. Welfare spending was slashed by an average of 30 percent per recipient, and in only a few years, the social safety net for economically disadvantaged people unraveled (Ellwood, 1988). By 1990, 12 million Americans received incomes that constituted less than half the amount specified by the federal government as poverty level. This growing economic inequality has placed great stress on the American social fabric. Inequality has always existed in America, but in the 1950s and 1960s, when incomes and wealth were growing, a more equal distribution of wealth was not an urgent concern. Hope was alive in the 1950s and 1960s as people assumed that people in every generation would live better than their parents had. As the economic health of America faltered in the early 1970s, hope began to fade, and inequality slowly came to be a serious issue again. By the 1990s, economists were able to make the observation that the distribution of private wealth had surpassed the degree of inequality that Marx documented in the middle of the nineteenth century (Coontz, 1992; Lather, 1991).

From the perspective of America in the late-1990s, we can observe the movement of high-technology-based capitalism ("techno-capitalism," as Doug Kellner has labeled it). This economic reality presents conflicting possibilities: the necessity of constructing a new and more democratic social organization versus a more and more repressive class-stratified society that exacerbates the inequality of wealth. The initial stages of techno-capitalism give us little to pin our progressive hopes on. While the rich got richer (that is, in the 1980s and 1990s), the public sector deteriorated, homelessness exploded, permanent unemployment increased, health care systems broke down, infrastructures (bridges, roads, public works) disintegrated, farm bankruptcies became the agricultural status quo, bank failures multiplied, the public debt mushroomed, and savings and loan and banking scandals proliferated.

Nothing better illustrates the social inequality of workers than workplace health issues. The media have devoted thousands of hours covering stress-related health concerns of managers and professionals. The stress-related problems of blue-collar workers, which are much greater than white-collar health concerns, are rarely discussed. Imagine a foundry worker in a large automobile assembly plant who faces daily an intensely hot workplace with an oil mist constantly in the air. After working in this situation for a few months, workers begin to notice a substantial degeneration in their health. Reflecting on their situation, workers conclude that they are being paid for five years that will be taken off their lives. This sort of situation is not the everyday fare of newspapers or TV newscasts. Not only is it representative of many factory jobs in the 1990s but it illustrates a *growing* inequality between management and labor. Unfortunately, the dominant trends of recent social development indicate a shrinking but more wealthy upper class, an expanding lower class, and a struggling middle class unsuccessfully attempting to maintain its economic equilibrium (Kellner, 1989; Ferguson, 1984).

Prophets of the new age of technocracy forecast the coming of a "techtopia," a great society built upon the shoulders of technology. On one level, these prophets are correct: Technological development always holds social consequences (Wirth, 1983). Progressive social analysts and vocational educators must study the social and political implications of new technologies and how they affect not only production but the everyday lives of workers. On another level, however, the prophets of techtopia miss the boat. Economists have found that although technological development has been used to increase productivity, it has also been employed by managers to maximize control over workers. The modernist science on which technology is based accepts predictability, repeatability, and quantifiability as its central goals. As such science devises new technology, it also lays out the procedures for its *proper* use. In such situations, the need for human judgment can often be eliminated (Pollin and Cockburn, 1991). As uncertainty and ambiguity are removed, workers simply follow preset rules and leave the thinking to their superiors. Although technology can produce countertrends that upgrade the skills demanded of individuals, this deskilling impulse still degrades far too many high-tech workers.

A debate over this question of high-tech industry and its relation to worker skills rages in economic circles in the late 1990s. No doubt exists that throughout the late nineteenth and early twentieth centuries, large factories fragmented and deskilled the labor process in order to increase efficiency, control workers, and reduce labor costs (Valli, 1988). Managers did not care whether such policies separated the planning, execution, and evaluation of work. Planning and conceptualizing are the domain of managers who design the production process; execution is the domain of deskilled workers who simply follow the plan devised by the experts; and evaluation is the domain of management-controlled supervisors who check to see if workers are actually following directions. Not only does this process undermine the dignity of workers, but it also deprives managers of the valuable input workers might provide to the planning and evaluation phases of production. No one in management can see this process from the perspective of workers. In the view of corporate leaders, however, worker insight is insignificant in light of the goal of worker control. Deskilled workers are easier to control because they are dependent on those who conceptualize and plan production (DeYoung, 1989; Pincus, 1980).

Indeed, deskilled workers in the twentieth century have often come to accept the mindlessness of their work lives. Some workers come to see their jobs as a paid incarceration much like prison, the army, or school. Deskilling has usually been used as a characterization of blue-collar, assembly-line work, but the fragmentation and rationalization of work has permeated all aspects of the workplace (Ferguson, 1984). White-collar positions have increasingly been affected in a way that deskills such workers. White-collar jobs can be rationalized and fragmented just like assembly-line positions. Decisionmaking is replaced with procedure following and demands for strict conformity with the rules of the organization. Such conformity is illustrated in the book and movie *The Firm*. The young lawyer played by Tom Cruise quickly recognizes the unstated rules he must follow and the conformist norms he must adopt if he is to succeed in his position.

This penetration of deskilling in new venues does not end with the rationalization of white-collar labor; workers can gain technological skills and still be deskilled in relation to their access to the logic of workplace management and organization. Vocational schools, operating in a culture of deskilling, can unconsciously mimic such an orientation toward human beings as they attempt to adapt students to the realities of the workplace. As they attempt to adjust students to the status quo, vocational educational leaders may argue in response to progressive critics: "We're teaching them survival skills; our purpose is to get them ready for the workplace." Progressive vocational educators understand the need for students to survive in the workplace but do not accept the notion that survival means the inability to make meaning of and critique the sociopolitical assumptions on which work is grounded. We do not need more of the Homer Simpsons who supervised operations at the Three Mile Island Nuclear Plant. Unaware of the overall planning and conceptualization of the facility, workers like this were lost when unanticipated breakdowns occurred. Nothing in the operations manual outlined procedures for surprises.

In light of these disturbing differences in public perspectives toward manager and worker health and deskilling's undermining of worker access to knowledge and the resulting degradation of worker dignity, differences in pay only add insult to injury. Since worker pay has actually declined since 1973, wage-earning Americans find it extremely difficult to fathom the salaries of corporate leaders (Coontz, 1992). Imagine hardworking men and women reacting to the following: In the year that Texaco, Inc. endured bankruptcy proceedings and a record $4.4 billion loss, Chief Executive James W. Kinnear was awarded a 14 percent pay raise, making his yearly salary $723,000; in the late 1980s, the median yearly earnings for chief executives passed 1 million dollars; the chair of Lotus Development Corporation currently makes $26.3 million a year; in the same two years that Chrysler profits fell 7 percent, former chair Lee Iacocca made $38.4 million; Japanese businesses are amazed by the size of American executive salaries that pay managers more than fifty times the salary of the lowest-paid line worker (Japanese executives earn only ten times as much as such workers).

Despite the protestations of corporate defenders that such disparate pay is simply the result of the free market in action, the dictates of the law of supply and demand, and compensation for the higher levels of stress that managers have to endure, progressive critics offer a different assessment. Pointing to the fact that executive raises have little correlation to their performance—failure is rarely penalized—critics emphasize the ethical absurdity of such disparity. This arrangement undermines the basic tenets of American democracy and forces us in the name of economic justice to provide greater educational and economic opportunity for our dispossessed vocational students. Contrary to the propaganda of corporate puppets who insist this disparity is the result of fixed economic laws, federal, state, and local governmental policies in cooperation with both academic and vocational educational reforms can play an important role in reversing these trends. The contemporary talk about the principle dubbed Total Quality Management (TQM) falls on cynical ears when workers believe that managers are benefiting unjustly from the fruits of their labor. Progressive vocational educators understand the necessity of a just workplace, where there is a more equitable sharing of gains and losses (DeYoung, 1989; MacLeod, 1987; Block, 1990).

Mystifying Power: Control in the Name of Democracy

In democratic societies, power attains its goals by *appearing* to promote equality while producing the stratified workforce demanded by corporations and employers (Livingstone, 1987). Many scholars label this process "hegemony." Peter McLaren (1994) has defined hegemony as the maintenance of control *not* by the employment of force but by way of social practices in churches, government, the mass media, the family, and the school that win the consent of individuals. These individuals, McLaren noted, are not aware that they are giving their consent to those in power and, as a result, participating in their own oppression. When schools, for example, teach the individualist ethic (i.e., the myth of individual achievement), the dominant culture ensures that economically or racially marginalized students who fail at school will blame themselves for their failure. In other words, such students are hegemonized to accept quietly their subordination. When these students find themselves unemployed or in low-paying jobs with little possibility for promotion, they have no one to blame but themselves. This attitude serves the needs of corporate power brokers, as it blinds such workers to the injustice of a system that requires people to be prepared to accept low-skill, low-wage, dead-end jobs.

Because of their power to control information and manipulate public opinion, corporate leaders can convince people that an economic system built upon such a stratification of jobs is in their personal interest. Over the last couple of decades, such leaders have convinced the public of a plethora of hard-to-swallow, bizarre ideas. For example, corporate-backed politicians convinced a majority of Americans that tax decreases for the richest citizens would "trickle down" in a manner that would improve the economic lives of the poor. These same politicians convinced many Americans that no regulations were needed to stop American companies from moving their factories to Third World countries leaving hardworking Americans unemployed— and they even convinced many of us that these companies should be rewarded with tax breaks for such migrations.

Many Americans were persuaded that weak schooling was the cause of American economic problems in the 1970s, 1980s, and 1990s. The fact that corporate leaders failed to update their workplaces or to create jobs where high skills were necessary was conveniently omitted from the story. If large percentages of employees were working in jobs that required minimal skills, what did it matter whether they were well educated or not? Production quality did not seem to be undermined when American factories were transferred to Third World countries where many of the workers were totally unschooled and illiterate. Something about these arguments did not add up, but few voices who opposed them were heard in our social institutions. Hegemony is complete when everyday people speak out and vote against their own self-interests. I suppose we have to give the corporate and political leaders credit for such successful public relations strategies.

Even allegedly "democratic" discourses of the late twentieth century, such as TQM and Quality of Work Life (QWL), can be used for hegemonic purposes. Instead of striving for worker empowerment, plans like these have often degenerated into deceptive slogans designed to manipulate workers to support the status quo. Unions have often come to realize that management support of industrial democracy programs may be used to subvert employee-run organizations. As a result, many unions caution workers about such programs, urging them to distinguish between genuine power-sharing plans and attempts at union busting. In an era where public relations and administration science have become such well-developed arts, workers have to understand that yes means no, black means white, and peace means war. Wrapping themselves in the flag of democracy, industrial leaders often covertly seek totalitarian ends (Wirth, 1983).

In this context, school leaders often wrap themselves in that same democratic flag while designing school programs that train students for corporate needs. Too often, vocational programs have been long on adjusting students to the workplace and short on helping students understand economic realities that undermine their participation in determining the nature of the workplace (Simon, Dippo, and Schenke, 1991). Topics such as democracy, public morality, or inequality have rarely played an important role in American schools and their preparation of students for work. Historians of education are explicit in their analysis of the historical purpose of vocational schooling in America. John Hillison and William Camp, for example, have argued that from the very beginning, federally funded vocational education in this country "was designed primarily to serve the needs of industry and secondarily to consider the needs of the individual" (Hillison and Camp, 1985, p. 48).

Sociologists of education have been quick to point out that operating in the name of democratic opportunity, academic and vocational schooling have both worked to reproduce the division between technically qualified professionals and managers, on the one hand, and low-skill, manual labor, on the other (Livingstone, 1987). School leaders and their business associates have little interest in opening the economy to more democratic participation by lower-level workers from disenfranchised groups. Often their primary objective is to produce obedient workers who have accepted the goal of increasing productivity within the boundaries of undemocratic workplaces and subservient worker roles. This is why the noncognitive skills of punctuality and rule following become so disproportionately important in school settings. Docile workers are rarely militant workers who advocate strikes or policies of labor resistance. Corporate ideology permeates the halls and classrooms of American schools, but few individuals comment on it or even notice it (Pincus, 1980; Giroux, 1993).

When vocational educators lead students through a study of democracy in the workplace and the various programs designed to implement it, they must help students develop ways of distinguishing the genuine from the bogus. Students must understand that all genuine democratic workplace reforms meet four principles: (1) workers are participants during all phases of the planning and change process; (2) any alterations in workplace organization must lead to increased worker autonomy; (3) workers, like managers, must share in economic benefits; and (4) workers must retain the right to pull out of the reform program if they find that it is not serving their interests (Wirth, 1983). The time for school silence concerning questions of genuine democracy in the workplace has passed. Schools must begin to live up to the sacred democratic principles that many claim serve as a political guide and an ethical anchor for this country. To better understand the mystification of democracy and its cooptation by antidemocratic forces, we must understand the development of scientific management.

Sophisticating Power: The Development of Scientific Management

The publication of Frederick W. Taylor's *The Principles of Scientific Management* in 1911 changed forever the way managers wielded power over workers. Since then, not only has business operated on these principles, but much of American society in general has been divided into hierarchical strata, with the work broken into parts and individuals assigned to these parts based on a scientific measurement of their ability (Kolberg and Smith, 1992). Frederick W. Taylor is undoubtedly one of the most important individuals not only in American economic history but also in American social and educational history. Born in 1856 in Philadelphia to wealthy philanthropist parents, Taylor was educated as a mechanical engineer. As the consummate modernist, Taylor worshipped at the altar of science and reason (Nelson and Watras, 1981). He believed that scientifically grounded social engineering and rational planning could help create a wonderful new world.

Unfortunately, Taylor's vision turned from utopia to dystopia as scientific management degenerated into social engineering and rationalistic regulation of men and women (Lather, 1991). Scientific management begins with the assumption that workers and other humans are *objects* to be manipulated in a manner that fits the needs of an organization. Managers often engage workers in activities that may not be conducive to their physical or mental well-being. The history of clerical work grants insight into the impact of scientific management on the nature of work and workers. In the nineteenth century, over 99 percent of clerical workers were men, and more than one out of every five American jobs was described as clerical. In 1850, clerical workers found themselves making more money than 90 percent of all other workers. As women began to enter the clerical market in the late nineteenth century, the high status of the occupation began to shift. No longer was clerical employment viewed as a high-skill and demanding task.

In 1917, William Henry Leffingwell published *Scientific Office Management*, introducing efficiency and time management into the clerical office. Typewriters were outfitted with devices to count strokes for the purpose of calculating payment for typists; they would be paid for the number of strokes they typed per day. It did not take typists long, of course, to outwit the managers, as they devised strategies to increase their daily strokes; for instance, they used the space bar and not the tab keys to increase their strokes *and* their pay. Naturally, such actions worked against efficiency, as they slowed down production.

Complex systems were designed to monitor the output of the workers and to devise time-saving improvements to increase productivity. Scientific managers became obsessed with the layout of the office, tinkering with the placement of water fountains and conveyor belts. Eventually, everything was designed so that the workers would never have to leave their desks. The goal was to eliminate misspent worker energy. Managers were uninterested in the mental and physical well-being of workers and the value of walks to the bathroom and water fountain. They consistently failed to understand that the most efficient way to arrange a clerical office is not always the most humane or even the most *productive* way (Simon, Dippo, and Schenke, 1991). Of course, clerical work is merely one of many forms of labor where scientific management changed the nature of everyday activity. In factories as well, the dehumanizing impact of rationalistic management reveals itself in the history of American labor. Because scientifically managed factories left employees with so little room for task variation, workers rarely had the opportunity to exhibit creativity or intelligence on the job. It soon became apparent that in a scientifically managed workplace, individuals could be reliable or unreliable from the perspective of their supervisors, but they could never be outstanding or excellent (Ferguson, 1984).

By the second decade of the twentieth century, the American public had become fascinated with scientific management and had begun to see it as a panacea for all social ills. Advocates of women's rights attempted to apply the principles of scientific management to the home in order to free women from the grind of housework. Clerics spoke of applying rational management to church projects to make redemption a more efficient enterprise. Indeed, on a variety of levels, scientific management inspired a religious sense of wonder, a reverence for its possibilities. To become efficient in the eyes of scientific managers was to achieve salvation. While it continued to describe a high ratio of return on an investment, efficiency began to take on new meanings.

By 1915, efficiency was connected with social relations, social harmony, and the suppression of class tensions. Sin was described as personal inefficiency, and personal success was seen as a question of efficient programming. Even perennial labor-management problems could be solved by efficiency. Make the self-interest of employers and employees the same, Taylor argued, by using scientific standards to figure production rates. If the necessary movements of a work task could be broken down into basic units of action and measured by scientific time-and-motion analysis, then an absolute equitable rate of production could be designated. Workers would understand that their pay was grounded upon *scientific* measurement, not the whim of greedy managers. By the grace of science, scientific managers theorized that there would no longer be any need for workplace disagreement. Modernism had reached its zenith: Scientific rationality was going to save the world (Nelson and Watras, 1981).

Of course, schools were part of the world, and it did not take long for the prophets of efficiency to aim their guns at education. Just as industrial efficiency experts fit the right worker to the right job, educational efficiency experts would fit the right curriculum to the right student. To Americans in the first decades of the twentieth century, the efficiency notion of training the individual in relation to personal capabilities had a commonsensical tone. Few scholars understood that such an ostensibly innocent premise would demand that assumptions be made about the intrinsic abilities of children to perform academically. Educational sociologists would later confirm the intuitions of educators such as John Dewey that marginalized children would be placed in ability tracks that would condemn them to "live down" to the low expectations of their teachers. Why should the children of the poor or the nonwhite study algebra, trigonometry, physics, international relations, and advanced composition? How would such courses help them in their future low-skill, low-wage jobs? In essence, such scientific policies sealed the fate of multitudes of marginalized students: School would not serve as an escape from poverty; it would serve to condemn them to it.

School, as the result of scientific management, increasingly came to resemble the factory. Reflecting the modernist tendency for fragmentation discussed in Chapter 2, scientific managers applied their task reduction to teaching. Dividing each educational activity into its most basic elements,

Taylor's apostles W. W. Charters and Franklin Bobbit set out to rationalize the schools. Analyzing, for example, the role of secretary, Charters identified twelve basic secretarial duties and divided them into 871 specific steps. Each step was then taught to each young woman in secretarial education programs. Soon thereafter, Stephens College for Women asked Charters to create a curriculum for the *job* of being a woman. Identifying 7,300 categories, he devised a scientific training program for women. It is easy to see that such a program left no room for evolution in the role of women; the elements that constituted an effective and efficient woman were determined by how the society defined femininity. Charters invoked the same logic for the teaching and learning of spelling and math, as he identified the words individuals would need to spell or the math abilities they would need in particular jobs or life situations. Once these functions were identified, the components of the curriculum would be segmented into smaller units to make sure learning proceeded efficiently.

Emerging from this same modernist mind-set was behavioristic psychology, a science of the mind that would profoundly affect teaching for the rest of the twentieth century. Drawing upon the intellectual foundations of modernist science and efficiency, John B. Watson fragmented human behavior into its most basic expression—stimulus and response. Like Charters's atomization of the curriculum, Watson reduced behavior to the point that it could be studied through scientific experimentation. Both curriculum efficiency and behaviorism tended to erase concern with both larger purpose and ethical consequence while exaggerating attention to the empirically quantifiable—that is, those human actions that lent themselves to measurability. The behaviorists failed to take into account that the trivial may often be the easiest to quantify, whereas the profound may be the most difficult (Nelson and Watras, 1981; Garrison, 1989).

Scientific management never lived up to its grand promise, but it has continued to influence work and vocational and academic education. Even though managers understood the unnecessary bureaucratization the system required with its army of supervisors, planners, and inspectors, they could not let go of the control over workers that it provided. Grounded as it was on an unsettling disrespect for workers, scientific management insured tension and hostility between workers and managers. Workers were aware of Taylor and his disciples' reference to them as "drays and donkeys." One of Taylor's most famous derogatory statements concerned his opinion of the men most qualified to shovel pig iron—men like oxen, he maintained, so dumb that they are unable to do anything else. Such well-known comments were not conducive to good labor-management relations. Despite numerous denials, the human relations schools of workplace management that have developed in years since early twentieth-century Taylorism still assume that workers are objects to be manipulated. In many ways, human relations management is Taylorism with plastic surgery. Aimed at men and women with a more middle-class educational and cultural background, human relations management depends more on the development of consent than on naked coercion. In this way it fits our definition of a hegemonic practice, as it wraps itself in the banner of humane and democratic values. As a consequence, it is far more effective and thus more dangerous to workers in particular and to American democracy in general (Wirth, 1983; Ferguson, 1984; Nelson and Watras, 1981).

The Consummation of the Modernist Economy: The Rise of Fordism

In conjunction with Taylor's scientific management, the business ideas promoted by Henry Ford produced the modernist economy. To appreciate the development of vocational education, it is important first to turn our attention to the evolution of Fordism. For many nineteenth-century economists, the iron law of wages dictated that the affluence of business and industrial managers depended on the poverty of workers. For profit to be made, raw materials would have to be procured cheaply, wages kept to the lowest rate possible. Many observers understood that such realities produced an inevitable conflict between management and labor. Cheap raw materials demanded economic imperialism with struggles between weak nations and strong nations, whereas the attempt to keep wages low necessitated sweatshops, packed tenements in the cities, and dangerous working conditions. Marx argued that the situation would eventuate in a worker revolution and the opening of a new era (Nelson and Watras, 1981). Henry Ford offered an alternative. His factories would produce more at reduced costs—and this would boost sales. As sales increased, so would profits, Ford contended, leading to more prosperity for everyone. Some of the huge profits would be used to pay higher wages, which, in turn, would create a larger group of consumers. Marxism would therefore be defeated, as workers with free time and money in their pockets were unlikely revolutionaries. Thus, a Faustian deal was made between workers and owners—a deal that would define Fordism. Workers would tolerate the meaningless and boring work of the factory in return for consumer rewards. Workers would buy into the system (with a little help from advertising and time payments), working hard with one hand and spending freely with the other (Aronowitz, 1992; Wirth, 1983).

The Fordist era began in 1914, when Henry Ford introduced his five-dollar, eight-hour day at his car assembly line at Dearborn, Michigan (Harvey, 1989). The mass production system employed would not only shape the workplace but would mold social institutions, vocational education in particular. Drawing upon the rationalism of modernism, Fordist production procedures became the highest expression of modernism and the lowest expression of worker dignity. Ford's four production principles included (1) the standardization of products, (2) the development of special-purpose machinery to be used in the construction of each separate model, (3) the fragmentation of tasks into their component parts, with task assignments developed around the scientific management time-motion principles developed by Frederick W. Taylor, (4) the replacement of static model assembly with flow lines, in that instead of workers working around the static product, the product (the car) flowed past the workers on a flow line. Ford, of course, was not the originator of mass production and assembly lines. There are examples of such methods being used as early as the eighteenth century, but Ford was the first to bring the forms of modern industrial organization together in concert with higher wages for workers. Once brought together, the new technology marched across the American landscape like a plague of cultural locusts devouring the traditions of the society. Fordist production strategies and their socioeconomic consequences in only a few years changed America forever (Murray, 1992).

The one nineteenth-century critique of industrialization that Ford could not address was the tendency of industrial work to separate itself from the creative spirit of the worker. A form of existential death accompanied a job where a worker tightened bolts to wheels over and over again, day in and day out. Like other forms of modernist fragmentation, Ford's assembly line made every task a standard self-contained unit. Each worker who became an integral portion of the line was rendered just as interchangeable as any other part. When scientific management and industrial psychology were added to the recipe, workers were progressively deskilled. Ford brought Taylorism and the gospel of efficiency to the automobile plants, supplanting traditional notions of fairness with the magic of efficiency (Nelson and Watras, 1981; Kellner, 1989; Harvey, 1989).

Other industries separated managerial planning and control of work from worker execution, but Ford's project was unique in the totality of its scheme. Ford wanted to create a new type of worker and a "new man"—not just the productive worker but also the worker as a consumer. Such Fordist laborers would live, work, and consume in a new society, a modern, rationalized world. Writing from one of Mussolini's prisons in Fascist Italy, Antonio Gramsci recognized Fordism as a new "mode of living and thinking and feeling life" (Harvey, 1989, p. 126). Indeed, so total was Ford's system that in 1916, concerned that workers would not learn how to consume properly, Ford sent a division of social workers into the homes of his workers to teach them morality, proper family life, and the characteristics of rational shopping. Fordism became synonymous with scientific forms of regulation associated with modernism (Grossberg, 1992).

The phrases "regime of accumulation" and "mode of social and political regulation" refer to the consistent, long-term ways that products are produced and consumed and the way the population is regulated to support such production and consumption (accumulation) processes. Working as Ford envisioned it, Fordism is the perfect example of a regime of accumulation and a mode of sociopolitical regulation. Between 1914 and 1945, Fordism faced numerous problems that disrupted its attempt to function smoothly in these roles. Two of the most serious issues involved labor's resistance to the devaluation of craft skills in the routinized, deskilled jobs created in Fordist factories and the reluctance of the state to employ activist fiscal and monetary policies to accommodate capitalism's inability to control discontent resulting from its unequal distribution of wealth. Only after World War II were their problems dealt with in a way that allowed for the ascendancy of Fordism as a fully operating regime of accumulation and mode of sociopolitical regulation. In this capacity, Fordism set the stage for the economic boom that lasted until 1973. Fueled by strong growth in cars, shipbuilding, transport equipment, steel, petrochemicals, rubber, electrical goods, and construction, the American economy devoured massive supplies of raw materials from the noncommunist world and came to dominate world markets with its products (Harvey, 1989).

Labor, with its tendency to resist the degradation of work, still presented a problem for Fordism. With the defeat of radical labor movements in the immediate postwar period, Fordism began to devise strategies of labor control. Vicious attacks were launched against unions for Communist infiltration, while the Taft-Hartley Act of 1952 undercut union organizing power in the workplace. Although unions retained some say in collective bargaining, social security benefits, and the minimum wage, they maintained this influence in return for their acceptance of Fordist production strategies and corporate schemes to boost productivity and worker discipline. A grand compromise was arranged that charged corporations with assuring stable growth in investments, guaranteeing growth in productivity, and raising living standards. This would be accomplished through the corporations' commitment to technological upgrading, mass capital investment, greater expertise in production and marketing, and the use of economies of scale by way of even greater standardization of products. Corporations would extend and sophisticate their use of Taylor's scientific management in order to better control production, personnel relations, on-the-job training, product design, and even planned obsolescence in their struggle for bigger profits.

The grand compromise was grounded on the faith that if wage increases were linked to increased productivity, profits were sure to increase. Business and labor were partners in a common economic struggle. Government would serve as a bow-tied referee, protecting in theory each institution from the excessive power and the low blows of the other. For example, the traditional exclusion of African Americans from the mainstream labor force was beginning to cause everyone problems. The state forced the inclusion of the excluded into the world of labor and business, even sending troops when necessary to overturn the forces of discrimination. Giving the appearance that it was operating in everyone's best interests, government presented itself as the neutral guardian of the egalitarian impulse. In reality, however, the leaders of this consensus (political liberalism), while avoiding the control of corporate power, found themselves subordinated to it. Although there were differences between the major political parties, in the long run they were insignificant. Both Republicans and Democrats agreed to the goals and strategies of Fordism, and a politics of general consensus blessed by the ghost of Henry Ford dominated the political and economic landscape of postwar America (Harvey, 1989; Grossberg, 1992).

The Breaking Point: The Decline of Fordism

As the Fordist compromise began to break down, observers saw not simply an economic decline but a decline of a way of life as well. Fordism as the economic expression of modernism carried the torch of Western civilization, as it reflected the modernist faith in progress, technological development, and rationality. These very elements and the arrangements of the Fordist economy based upon them undermined the supremacy of the American economy (Borgmann, 1992). For vocational education schools, and for other institutions grounded on this technocratic rationality, the news was not good. Technique became an end in itself, while human concerns and the goal of deeper forms of understanding were devalued. The decline of Fordism signaled a decline in the modernist faith in rationality as a panacea. As American products became shoddier and shoddier, as profits from planned obsolescence rose, as students emerged from schools seeming to understand less and less about the world, the evidence of decline mounted (Bellah et al., 1991).

As the recession of 1973 destroyed the stable environment for corporate profits established by Fordism, the transition to a new regime of production and mode of social regulation began. Many economists locate the beginning of the end of Fordism in the mid-1960s with the rise of the Western European and Japanese economies, the displacement of American workers as a result of the success of Fordist rationalization and automation strategies, the decline in corporate productivity and profitability, and the beginning of an inflationary trend (Harvey, 1989). The ability of Fordism to contain the contradictions of capitalism began to be seriously weakened during this period, as the inflexibility of American economic arrangements became more apparent. In long-term, large-scale fixed capital investments in systems of mass production, inflexibility undermined attempts to adjust to new designs necessary in changing consumer markets. In labor markets and contracts, inflexibility subverted attempts to reform workplaces with new forms of worker deployment. As social security, pension rights, and other entitlements expanded, government revenue collection was thwarted by a stagnant economy. The only avenue of flexibility led to a change in monetary policy that involved printing money at an accelerated rate to keep the economy stable. Thus began the inflationary spiral that ended the postwar boom. All of these specific rigidities were fastened to a configuration of political power that united big labor, big capital, and big government in the embrace of a set of narrow vested interests that undermined the productive capacity of the national economy.

Of course, many Americans were excluded from the benefits of Fordism, and as time passed, their discontents became more and more apparent. Only certain sectors of the Fordist economy benefited from the compromise; those spheres where demand was volatile or where there was insufficient investment in mass production machinery never prospered. Therefore, conditions for workers in so-called monopoly sectors did not improve. These excluded men and women were beset by social tensions that lay the foundation for civil unrest and social movements based on race, class, and gender. The civil rights movement unleashed resentments that expressed themselves in a revolutionary anger that particularly affected the inner cities. As women found themselves confined to low-paying jobs, the stage was set for an angry women's movement. As expectations increased and mobility declined, discontent with the Fordist arrangements festered (Murray, 1992).

This conservative response to the decline set the tone for policymaking on a variety of fronts—political, military, educational, and economic. Committed to economic policy with faith in the "wisdom of the market," the conservatives attacked the liberal Fordist compromise with its embrace of the welfare state. As they attempted to dismantle the welfare state's safety net for the disadvantaged, conservatives in the 1970s, 1980s, and 1990s redefined freedom in economic terms. Freedom, they argued, implies the right to compete and fail, which is more an entrepreneurial liberty than a civil liberty. With the conservatives in power, the state abandoned its Fordist role as the "Great Mediator" of the competing interest groups and unabashedly embraced corporate interests and their need for profits. While conservatives were winning their political victories, many businesses were desperately seeking to escape the confines of Fordist inflexibility in the workplace (Grossberg, 1992; Murray, 1992; Borgmann, 1992). These activities would lay the foundation for post-Fordism, a concept to be analyzed in Part 3. It is extremely important for vocational education teachers and students to understand these macroeconomic issues and their impact on work and education. If a humane and productive workforce is our goal, these understandings are essential. Workers must recognize their role in the larger economic, social, and even moral order. Chapter 4 continues this attempt to contextualize work for vocational educators, focusing attention on the ethical debate over work in late twentieth-century America.

4   *Good Work, Bad Work, and the Debate over Ethical Labor*

Any attempt to contextualize and analyze the nature of work cannot ignore its ethical dimensions. In a democratic society, for example, what constitutes good work? Socially beneficial work? Just work? Fulfilling work? Democratic work? These are the questions that underlie the foundations of vocational education, that involve the social, political, philosophical, and economic analyses of the field. Unfortunately, these questions are too often ignored in schools. These are the questions that this book in general and Chapter 4 in particular asks and analyzes. In the process of studying them, we begin to develop a democratic image of a just future grounded on a vision of good work. America must develop an ethical basis on which social, educational, and, contrary to prevailing sentiments, economic institutions are constructed (Simon, Dippo, and Schenke, 1991; Dewey, 1908).

Workplace Democracy

The concept of work is separated from the notion of a job on the basis of our ethical understandings. A job is simply a way of making a living; work involves a sense of completion and fulfillment. In a job, items are produced for consumption, whereas work produces items that are put to use in people's lives. An individual's purposes and meanings are engaged in work, but they are repressed in a job. As work becomes democratic, workers begin to ask how human possibility is being denied (Giroux, 1992, p. 139), and questions concerning workplace democracy begin to arise. In the negotiations over workplace democracy, observers can quickly discern how seriously the ethic of democracy is being taken. The democratic workplace will ensure workers that they will be more engaged in the day-to-day activities of a work site. The barometer for such engagement will involve the workers' ability to discern the results of their own actions. The critical democratic workplace demands more than management homage to Total Quality Management or quality circles. For the workplace to be genuinely democratized, it must demand an arrangement that guarantees that workers' voices will be heard and that workers will be shielded from the capricious exercise of management prerogative. If this is not the case, employees will not possess the freedom to speak their minds for fear of reprisal.

Workplace democracy also requires that workers appropriate significant power in the operation of a plant or corporation—power that would help protect them from the special dangers posed in the unstable contemporary corporate landscape. For example, in recent years the notion of shareholder democracy, with its diffusion of ownership, has proven ineffective in the attempt to subdue the power of corporate management. Managerial abuses have multiplied as corporate leaders have granted themselves golden parachutes and extravagant executive compensation packages. In this greedy context, corporate raiders ride into town wearing white hats and promising to clean up executive abuses. In the name of reform, the raiders take over the company. But the language of reform is soon forsaken, as evidence indicates that corporate raids do not improve the economic life of the corporation. Most important for workers, these takeovers disrupt employee lives and can be used as a threat by management to undermine their democratic demands. Employee stakeholding in the power of the corporation could lessen the possibility of a greedy set of managers overcompensating themselves, at the same time giving the workers input into the corporation's response to a corporate takeover bid. Such conditions become more and more essential in the effort to establish workplace democracies in the last years of the twentieth century (Block, 1990).

Good Work and the Struggle for Worker Dignity

If schools and workplaces are to contribute to the reinvention of democracy and challenge the antidemocratic tendencies of the contemporary era, good work must be carefully defined and pursued. Those characteristics of good work might include:

1. *The principle of self-direction: good work as a labor of risk.* This principle is grounded on the notion that workers are ultimately their own bosses. Workers operating under this principle would not be subjected to the humiliation of supervision that holds them under suspicion and surveillance. Utilizing a traditional concept of craft, work that is self-directed becomes a labor of risk in that workers are responsible for the success or failure of their work. Good work utilizes the judgment and skill of the individual worker, not some mass production technique characterized by automatically controlled production methods. Self-directed workers think analytically to identify and solve problems by making use of skills, knowledge, and aesthetic and pragmatic intuition to create products of worth (Richmond, 1986).

2. *The principle of the job as place of learning: work as a research laboratory.* Good work creates work conditions that treat workers as human beings

rather than hired hands. When this happens, workers cease being passive instruments and become active learners. Workers as active learners utilize and develop their intelligence, ingenuity, and capacities in such a way that they are empowered to direct their own fate. Such workers begin to understand the degrading way they have been treated in the restricted factory. These realizations sensitize them to the fact that large numbers of people are employed in firms that take no interest in their capacity to learn. They are outraged when they find that the number of these positions is expanding. Advocates of good work understand that there are material limits to growth but there are no boundaries to worker learning. Workers who are self-directed view the workplace as a learning and research laboratory. Good work privileges workers as equal partners in research and development, for their "shop-level" experiences provide unique insights into the production process. In sites that value good work, workers become researchers who produce knowledge about those things that affect work in general and their work in particular (Simon, Dippo, and Schenke, 1991; Wirth, 1983; Block, 1990).

3. *The principle of work variety: freedom from repetitive boredom.* Workers in both industrial and postindustrial contexts are plagued by repetitive, boring tasks. In the democratic workplace, workers struggle to provide opportunities for variations of routine that preclude boredom. Workers who are self-directed learners and thus are involved with the analytical mind-set of research and reflection are rarely bored. A good workplace allows employees to perform periodically in varied roles, not only to relieve monotony but to provide experiences where workers can better understand the interrelationship between the different aspects of the work site.

4. *The principle of workmate cooperation: overcoming the fractured social relations of the workplace.* The industrial ethos unfortunately produced conditions where it is not in one worker's interest to help another; indeed, in the workplace ruled by the competitive impulse, one person's gain is often another person's loss. In a good workplace, workers learn a form of self-discipline that attunes them to the needs of others. Understanding that the nature of good work is collaborative, good work induces workers to overcome their egocentric tendencies and join others in a common task. Good work transcends the fractured social relations of the scientifically managed workplace, as workers as collaborators sit down together, exchange information, and discuss the nature and purpose of their work (Rehm, 1989; Wirth, 1983).

5. *The principle of individual work as a contribution to social welfare.* When workers employ this principle, they reconceptualize their work so that it serves the public good. If work is not socially beneficial, then it must be made so. Good work encourages questions such as: Do the goods being produced serve human needs? Do they meet the criteria of permanence,

healthiness, and artistic and creative integrity? Are the products ecologically harmful? Good work makes sure that exploitative relations between work and the environment are changed to synergistic and symbiotic interactions. Workers who are self-directed learners are more likely to recognize the socially deleterious effects of production strategies and goals than alienated "hired hands" (Emery and Thorsrud, 1976; Lyons, 1988).

6. *The principle of work as expression of self: workers as more than a sum of their behaviors.* Since the introduction of scientific management, workers have often been reduced to organisms whose behaviors should be molded by expert social engineers, also known as scientific managers. As a vision of expertly controlled workers has been substituted for self-directed workers, people have come to be seen as a sum of their behaviors. Good work rejects these views of men and women, as it insists that workers explore their powers as creative human beings. Such powers include the ability to make sense of that which is present (or not present) in a work environment, to conceive and communicate ideas, to risk confrontation, to utilize dangerous memories in the process of democratic social change (Wirth, 1983). Thus, good work becomes an individual expression of self that redefines both the role of creativity in the everyday life of the workplace and the very meaning of output. Critically reconceptualized output cannot be separated from worker creativity and well-being (Block, 1990). In fact, a critical definition of output would not be complete until it included concerns with the intrinsic satisfaction of work, the economic security of workers, and the role of work in the workers' pursuit of happiness.

7. *The principle of work as a democratic expression: freedom from the tyranny of authoritarian power.* Good work is a democratic act operating in a free and autonomous workplace. It is self-creating and dedicated to critical forms of change. Good work transforms self and world as it strives to preserve democratic ideals. Work as a democratic expression is obligated to resist those often-hidden manifestations of power that subvert good work (Brosio, 1985). When managers squash intellectual and moral freedom, freedom of inquiry, freedom of association in or out of the workplace, or freedom of religion, democratic workers do not sit still. Because such antidemocratic actions take place at a covert level unrecognized by the public, democratic workers must carefully refine their resistance strategies in order to effectively expose the insidious nature of power. For example, the antidemocratic workings of power often take place in the ostensibly neutral medium of personnel administration (Ferguson, 1984). Democratic workers must have the insight to expose alternative meanings of management's attempt to increase "human efficiency," to develop "proper work habits," to "improve morale," and to "reduce conflict." All of these goals sound sensible and benign, but all implicitly carry particular views of the arrangement of the workplace and the role of workers. To resist this form of manipula-

tion, democratic workers must gain the power to deconstruct texts in such a way that hidden meanings become part of the public conversation about work. As a democratic expression, good work alerts the public to the way words are deployed to mystify and confuse, in order to maintain unequal power relations.

8. *The principle of workers as participants in the operation of an enterprise: Until workers are participants, talk of workplace cooperation rings hollow.* Workplaces at the end of the twentieth century are arranged in a way that excludes worker participation in their operation. Workers still execute directives they did not formulate and frequently do not understand. Attempts to create cooperative workplaces characterized by dynamic flexibility are undermined by the exclusion of workers from participation in the making of important decisions (Block, 1990). In the name not only of good work but of effective and profitable workplaces, workers should become stakeholders in firms. Indeed, democratic notions not only have humane benefits but pragmatic advantages as well. When workers are participants in the decision-making process, empirical evidence indicates that they are motivated to improve the quality of their own work and the profitability of an enterprise. When workers are well informed, convinced that their proposals will be seriously considered and allowed to criticize an operation without fear of reprisal, they become an invaluable force for innovative change (Bluestone and Brown, 1983). Workers as participants devise novel ways to train new employees, propose new management strategies, develop new production techniques, create new workplace arrangements, and revise criteria for hiring workers. As participants, workers refuse to sanction disparate economic benefits for management over labor and insist on a more equitable sharing of both gains and burdens in an enterprise. Worker participation in the fundamental functions of a business or industry is necessary to good work.

9. *The principle that play is a virtue that must be incorporated into work: play principles as path to freedom and fairness.* The rationality of the workplace supported by scientific personnel management has created a context less than hospitable to play. The workplace as we have come to know it has become the binary opposite of play. To argue that good work encompasses a spirit of play is, from the perspective of workplace management, to make a dangerous argument that can be framed as fatuous and juvenile. Herbert Marcuse (1955) maintained that play is basic to human civilization. Once we overcome our adult-centered bias against play as one of the highest expressions of human endeavors, its principles can be incorporated into our work and lives. Play principles that can extend our notion of good work include the following: (a) Rules of play are not constructed to repress freedom but to constrain authoritarianism and thus to promote fairness, (b) the structure of play is dynamic in its relation to the interaction of the players—and by necessity this interaction is grounded on the equality of the players,

(c) the activity is always viewed as an autonomous expression of self, as care is taken not to subordinate imagination to predetermined outcomes. Thus, in play, exhaustion is not deadening, since the activity refreshes the senses and celebrates the person. Good work can be viewed as a form of play when participating workers labor together for shared purposes (Aronowitz, 1973).

10. *The principle of better pay for workers in relation to the growing disparity between managers and workers.* Obviously, good work cannot tolerate the obscene differences between management and worker pay. The policy that has fueled the growth of corporate profits in the 1990s has been managerial slashing of labor costs. This cannot be allowed to continue.

The failure of democracy in the industrial and postindustrial workplace has shaped the failure of American education. If we want to change the schools, we must analyze the nature of work in America (Lyons, 1988). One of the reasons for the failure of so many school reform proposals involves the neglect of this relationship between school life and work life. Critically minded, reflective students often are perceived as troublemaking misfits in the workplace, and school leaders are pressured in a variety of subtle and not so subtle ways to turn out more compliant, less thoughtful graduates.

Henry Levin has argued that moves toward greater worker participation in a more democratic workplace could hold dramatic implications for school reform—for the reform of vocational education in particular. He maintains that if new production requirements demand more collaborative human interactions and more thoughtful workers, then vocational education will have to meet social orders for students with such skills (Wirth, 1983, p. 167). Levin's principle underlies a central theme of this book. A reality like this could create a new era of work-school interaction. If we are serious about good work with its notion of workers as participants, then such employees will demand a more stimulating education. The path to school reform is inseparable from work reform.

In an environment created by democratic work reform, employers and corporate leaders will have to reassess the firm's status as a "democratic citizen" (Bellah et al., 1991). Profit making as the sole purpose of the corporation produces a "Jaws Meets Wall Street" horror movie. A perspective of this sort positions corporations as sharks that live off the community, not human agencies that help construct and transform our politics and values. The idea of the corporate embrace of democratic as well as profit goals is not as far-fetched as one might initially think. Successful corporations have begun to embrace such goals: Anita Roddick's Body Shop, Ben and Jerry's Ice Cream, and Patagonia have all proven that profits can be made without ignoring democratic principles. The president of Volvo has argued that businesses in democratic societies must help maintain the public good, protect natural resources, and create economic growth as well as make profits; corporations must not simply provide jobs, but they must also provide meaningful employment where workers operate in dignified workplaces with opportunities for individual development. Vocational education students must be aware of the possibility of good work and its connection to the foundations of American society (Wirth, 1983).

Identifying and Subverting Bad Work

By now, we understand the concept that although modernism has brought us tremendous material progress, it has created a world that threatens our well-being, if not our very lives. Regressive modernism has left its fingerprints on bad work. Modernist bad work is grounded on a specific set of ideological assumptions:

1. *Social Darwinism: Workers must operate under the law of the jungle. Those who succeed at work are the fittest.* The strongest and the most resourceful will gain the rewards and privileges; the weakest will fall by the wayside into demeaning situations. This position is inherently naive, as it fails to question the forces that privilege certain groups and impede others. Thus, success is founded not simply on one's resourcefulness but on one's initial acquaintance (often attained through socioeconomic background) with the forms of knowledge, the attitudes, and the skills required for success, often called "cultural capital." This cultural capital is a very important concept, because both schools and workplaces reward individuals who possess the cultural capital of the dominant culture. Few employers or teachers recognize that individuals' cultural capital is shaped by where they grow up and what socioeconomic class they fall into (McLaren, 1994). When cultural capital intersects with Social Darwinism, tracking in schools and undemocratic hierarchical work arrangements are the result. The most damaging aspect of this unholy fusion is that it causes us to view these human hierarchies not as inhumane and unjust but as natural and just.

2. *Nature as enemy: One of the most basic of human struggles involves man versus nature.* Ever-increasing material growth requires that nature be viewed as a collection of objects to be acted upon, conquered, exploited, and controlled—to the victor goes the spoils. Nature is not intrinsically valuable: To hold significance, it must serve the ends of human beings. Scientific research is the human creation that allows for this, that is, the laws of nature can be known and thus manipulated and controlled. Human beings as products of nature can be known in a similar way and, as a result, can be manipulated and controlled. Like the ancients with their myths designed to control nature, scientific man attempts a similar goal. The control of men and women in the workplace is simply a natural extension of the "control impulse" (Held, 1980).

3. *Science as fact provider: Positivism covertly shapes the nature of the workplace.* Scientific data provide managers with indisputable knowledge. Values,

as the positivists have long contended, are subjective opinions and have little role in the world of schooling and work. Operating from this assumption, scientific managers have objectified the workplace, focusing on measurable factors related to the bottom lines of productivity and profit. The examination of human values as represented by Dewey's assertion that good work must be pursued as an ethical imperative does not fit into a view of work based on such a notion of science.

4. *Efficiency as maximum productivity: worshipping the bottom line.* The productivity of humans and their machines can be measured in only one way—quantitatively. This assumption can exist only in a social context where human beings and nature are not valued for their intrinsic spiritual worth. The notion of efficiency becomes deified in bad work. Worshipping this false god, workplace supervisors reward workers only on the basis of efficiency; the nonquantifiable goals of good work be damned. In schools, an outlook of this sort leads to the encouragement of modes of teaching that answer to the goal of efficiency rather than to human nurturing. Methods of evaluation in both school and the workplace are developed around efficiency and bottom-line concerns rather than as an attempt to understand students or workers, the forces that move them, and the possible strategies that might be taken to help individuals reach their potential. The subtle cultural forces that move students or workers to pursue excellence are crushed by this sordid love affair with efficiency.

5. *The supremacy of systems-efficiency and cost-benefit analysis models, or the effectiveness of standardized inputs in the quest for agreed-upon outputs.* Such models assume that work goals are already agreed upon by all parties involved. "Isn't the omnipresent goal of the workplace to increase profits?" the systems analysts ask. "Isn't the ultimate goal of schooling to increase test scores?" educational systems analysts ask. The systems researchers view the goal of scientific inquiry as the identification of so-called production functions. These entities refer to the effectiveness of certain inputs in the attempt to reach prespecified objectives. Effectiveness involves the cost-benefit ratio of the production function, as it is examined in terms of its economic efficiency. Thus, the effectiveness of educational methods could be compared in terms of test score results. When researchers combine this measure of effectiveness with an analysis of cost-benefit factors, decisions could then be made on which task procedures to require of workers and which educational methods teachers should use. All teachers or workers, regardless of context, would be expected to teach or work in the same standardized and efficient way. Questions about nonmeasurable outcomes such as dignity of the worker at the job site or student happiness in the school are irrelevant in systems analysis. Questions concerning the knowledge that teachers and workers pick up through their everyday experience in the school or the workplace are suppressed by systems-efficiency and cost-benefit analysis ways of seeing the world. Concerns with worker or teacher happiness and

the control of the planning and conceptualization of their work are deemed trivial and unscientific (House, 1978; Wirth, 1983). Understanding the big picture, that is, how one's work fits into the larger scheme, is irrelevant. Workers and even teachers are enslaved by supervisor and managerial control of their purposes as employees. To escape bad work, workers must get the whole story (Kolberg and Smith, 1992).

6. *People-proof jobs: designing work so that no matter how dumb a worker might be, the job can still be done.* Managers shape tasks into minute trainable steps, and psychologists ensure a close fit between workers and work tasks in the engineering of people-proof bad work. This orientation to job design demands that workers be closely supervised by managers utilizing sophisticated, high-tech surveillance and information systems. As managers create the institutional structures that keep workers from assuming responsibility for the quality of their labor, workers develop an antipathy toward management that undermines communication. Faced with the indignity of worker-proof jobs, many workers invent ingenious ways to stave off boredom. Some workers devise schemes with friends: One night, one worker will do the job of a buddy while the buddy sleeps or plays; the next night, the buddy will work while the friend rests. Faced with people-proof jobs at General Motors, Ben Hamper described the daily rituals of his fellow workers as a "ballet for the dead." Look at any factory that promotes deskilled labor: Somewhere close to the plant, there will be a bar where workers can dull the indignity of their malignant, people-proof drudgery. For the alcoholics, management will often provide free counseling—a badge reflecting their progressive employee relations programs (Zunker, 1986; Ferguson, 1984; Hamper, 1992).

7. *Short-term goals: the absence of ethical vision.* Bad work holds no vision of work as an activity that concerns itself with the long-term welfare of other human beings or of subsequent generations. Little effort is made in the workplace to cultivate the notion of the community of human beings past, present, and future. That concept would negate tendencies such as dynamic obsolescence, which serves as a symbol of bad work's alienation from human need. Management often labels concerns with long-term human and environmental questions as frivolous and unscientific; such concerns have no place in a company's quarterly plans. Labor and teaching as well are ethically fragmented; workers and teachers see little connection between their work lives and the needs and concerns of the human community. Work is further separated from life.

8. *The contingency of human happiness and human motivation on the acquisition of better consumer items: The First Commandment of modernism is Thou Shalt Consume.* Industrial progress is viewed as the result of more centralized, more mechanized work. In a well-administered world, better consumer items will result from efficiently managed industries and institutions.

Education becomes an arm of the ideology that promotes this view of work. Schools are designed to turn out individuals who fit comfortably into the bad workplace. Students are taught (by a variety of teachers who are found far beyond the classroom, e.g., television advertising) to embrace the First Commandment. In a sense, consumption becomes a ritual of salvation for modernist workers as they attempt to regain psychic peace after a forty-hour week of mechanized bad work. It is not unusual that "Born to Shop" bumper stickers have achieved so much popularity in recent times, as shopping becomes a raison d'être. Social and educational researchers concern themselves with studies of how better consumer goods can be produced, how humans can be convinced that their happiness and self-worth depend on the acquisition of these goods, and how schools can contribute to the production of the labor pool needed to produce these items and even these attitudes. The only thing that can motivate us to do better work (in the workplace or in school) is the possibility of buying more and better consumer goods.

No one has to remind us of the psychic, social, economic, and educational effects of bad work since we are confronted with them every day. Bad work produces waste, shoddy products, apathy, hostility, alcohol and drug abuse, nihilism, reliance on "experts," and depression. Opinion polls conducted periodically indicate that Americans are alarmed by the poor quality of goods produced in the American workplace. A study published in the *Harvard Business Review* indicates that 20 percent of all consumer purchases lead to some form of purchaser dissatisfaction—and this does not include dissatisfaction based on price. Automobile recalls are legendary. Obviously, technological advance by itself does not ensure quality of workmanship. Indeed, we honor the label "handmade" as an indication of high quality. It implies a sociological relationship missing in modern industries that operate on the principles of bad work. Products that have been handmade historically emerged from cultures where producers and consumers were the same individuals or close kin. Men made their own spears; women wove their own baskets. Even when technology advanced, material culture grew more complex, and specialization developed, the relationship between consumer and producer remained intact.

Bad work, like an ex-lover, will not simply go away. In the coming years, most new jobs will be found in low-level service and clerical fields; the economy is projected to need more janitors, sales clerks, and cashiers. As a result, work dissatisfaction may continue to increase with more unscheduled absences, more sabotage, more alienated workers (Zunker, 1986; Rumberger, 1984). Ben Hamper, a self-described "rivethead" from General Motors, described the look on those alienated workers' faces as they left their eight-hour shift. In his own most alienated moments, Hamper would get drunk and watch workers pile out at quitting time, commenting that he was struck by their "monster gaze." How can we study the ethics of work and not think of such a gaze? How can students of work study the social foundations of vocational education and not confront the contradiction that in one of America's premier industries, General Motors, the barbed wire fence surrounding the truck and bus plant in Flint, Michigan, faces *in*? As one of Hamper's barfly friends put it: "They don't wanna keep others out, they wanna *keep us in*" (Hamper, 1992, pp. 141–142).

Debating Work Ethics and Economic Policy: The Rise of the New Right

The conservative New Right political movement that arose in the 1970s can be best understood as a response to the breakdown in the Fordist compromise and the concurrent decline in the American economy. The movement was unequivocally tied to unregulated free-enterprise capitalism, with freedom defined in economic terms: We all have the right to compete and fail. As the conservatives devised their response to a changing world, leaders of U.S.-based multinational corporations struggled to address changing relations among the American economy, the world economy, and changing labor constituencies. For example, the rise of service workers, the decline of workers involved in manufacturing, and the changing ethnic and gender composition of the workforce, coupled with the deterioration of profit margins, presented serious adjustment problems for corporations. These changes demanded a comprehensive reconceptualization of the role of the corporation in American politics and cultural life. In order to prosper in this new environment, American business leaders determined that they needed more political power—power that would allow them the latitude to operate more freely with fewer governmental restrictions and lower taxes. The corporate power play of the late 1970s and early 1980s involved strategies such as funding political action committees (PACS), conservative think tanks, and national advertising campaigns.

As these corporate actions took place, an alliance between New Right conservatives (often organized around charismatic fundamentalist Protestant church leaders, e.g., Jerry Falwell) and corporate wielders of power began to coalesce. New Right fundamentalists painted a Sunday-school morality play, depicting "liberals" in the 1960s as the demons whose ungodly permissiveness initiated the moral, spiritual, educational, and ultimately economic decline of America. Confident, divinely sanctioned ministers made the Puritan dream fashionable again, as they parroted John Winthrop's famous metaphor of America as a "city on the hill, a shining beacon" of Christian morality to a corrupt Old World. Although Brooks Brothers–clad corporate leaders found the evangelical crowd a little gauche and a bit embarrassing in their zeal, they nevertheless welcomed them into a political alliance that would change the social, political, and economic face of America. The fact that the evangelicals were political allies, business leaders reasoned, did not require their admittance to exclusive country clubs; we can be close, they thought, but not all *that* close (Grossberg, 1992).

The economic changes that were occurring in the 1970s and 1980s were devastating for some groups but exerted virtually no impact on others. For example, the per capita income of families under age thirty dropped 27 percent between 1973 and 1986—the same decline experienced by the same demographic group between 1929 and 1932 in the Great Depression. During the 1973–1986 period, older, more affluent families actually experienced an increase in income. Because the drop occurred gradually over a thirteen-year period and affected individuals with less power and media access, it was hidden from the public consciousness.

After 1973, the worldwide economic changes, coupled with the growing power of the conservatives, began to undermine government spending on the needs of the public sector. As revenues fell, taxes were lowered, producing a unique situation in contemporary industrialized societies—private affluence and public squalor. America's urban communities suffered a decrease in funding that produced environmental negligence, untidy and unsafe parks, dangerous playgrounds, deteriorated public housing, underfunded public transportation, and inadequate social services. Europeans were shocked by the absence of publicly funded planning strategies to shape urban growth and revitalize inner cities. Poor individuals (especially the young poor) grew poorer and their numbers swelled because of this economic decline, with its accompanying inflation and the right-wing undermining of tax revenues from the corporations and the wealthy. In human terms, this meant job disruption, marital stress, and family disintegration, resulting in the growth of single-parent families.

After 1973, America changed dramatically. The most disturbing aspect of that change involved the radical redistribution of wealth in American society. By the middle of the 1980s, the chasm between the rich and the poor expanded to a point unseen for almost fifty years. Income for the poorest 20 percent of the nation dropped 5.2 percent; at the same time, the wealthiest 20 percent recorded take-home pay increases of 32.5 percent. The income of the richest 1 percent of Americans increased *87 percent*. In 1950, U.S. corporations paid 26 percent of all local, state, and federal taxes. By 1990, they were paying only 8 percent. If the corporate tax rate had remained steady over those forty years between 1950 and 1990, then the local, state, and federal governments would have received more than an extra *$13 trillion*. What is shocking about these figures and the disparity they represent is not that the conservatives accomplished their mission so quickly; the jolting reality is that a majority of middle-class and low-income Americans accepted it without dissent. The acceptance of this reshuffling of the economic deck, this cardshark New Deal, may constitute one of the greatest hegemonic acts ever perpetrated (Coontz, 1992; Bellah et al., 1991; Grossberg, 1992).

Because of the "selective attention" of the economic decline, middle-class Americans did not perceive the existence of an economic crisis until the 1992 elections—and even then they were confused about its consequences and its causes. Facilitated by an increasing conservative influence on the production of public knowledge, many Americans (especially voting Americans) came to conceptualize the economic problems as a loss of American military, political, and economic leadership in the world (Grossberg, 1992). Caused by the decline of traditional values, this economic regression was seen more as a problem of national "manhood" and international domination than as a problem of economic justice and even economic survival.

Fanned by the embarrassment of the oil embargo in 1973 and the Iranian hostage crisis in 1979–1981, many Americans latched on to Ronald Reagan's nostalgic portrait of the way America used to be and *should* be once again. The politics of nostalgia, with its return to *Little House on the Prairie* and *Happy Days* images, evoked emotional responses from Americans who believed the nation was unjustly under siege. What the hell did we do to deserve the Iranian hostage crisis? they asked, unaware and uninformed by the mainstream media of U.S. complicity in the overthrow of democratic government in Iran (see my 1989 book, *Getting Beyond the Facts: Teaching Social Studies in the Late Twentieth Century,* for further explanation of this issue). The key themes—going back to the basics and an assertive militaristic foreign policy—pushed by Reagan, George Bush, and Dan Quayle were supported by many Americans and "blessed" by a lapdog, uncritical media.

The new conservatives were extremely successful in breaking up the old New Deal coalition, with its alliance of farmers, union members, and urban ethnic voters. After the Fordist prosperity of the 1950s and 1960s, the members of the coalition no longer identified with being the allies of the dispossessed. By the 1970s, they were persuaded to align their interests with the affluent. By the 1980s and 1990s, the children of the old coalition members, spurred by right-wing glorifications of greed and individualism, had become unwilling to empathize with the sorry predicament of the poor. As the rich grew richer and the children's finances continued to deteriorate, their parents' picture of the truly needy faded into images of welfare loafers and lowlife cheats. The right-wing amoebas had absorbed another group that should have been concerned with the growing disparity of wealth. By the mid-1980s, however, the existence of economic and political inequality raised few eyebrows. The language of "traditional values" was being used to condemn those who fell outside the mainstream (e.g., the nonwhite poor, advocates of women's rights, gays and lesbians, and so on). The New Right was firmly in power, and social and economic policy was conceived under a new set of rules.

Those rules typically involved neoclassical economic theory and its allegiance to the freedom of the market. This means that anything under free market conditions that turns a profit is permissible and that state regulation is the bugaboo of economic progress. Specifically, the right-wing rules involved the following: (1) the privatization of governmental service agencies, (2) the reallocation of wealth from the poor to the rich, and (3) the establishment of a free market philosophy that promotes individualism, self-help, human resource management, and consumerism, in lieu of ethical values in the public sphere. The game Monopoly emerged as a prototype for public life as market maximizers became paragons of success. Economics assumed the status of a total science that explains all human questions, all mysteries of life. One interesting exception to the belief in the unfettered market has involved the realm of the "defense" economy or "Pentagon socialism." Despite protestations of the virtues of privatization and free markets, right-wing government leaders have advocated and voted for battleships and weapons systems that even military leaders do not want—all for the purpose of maintaining jobs and economic health in local economies.

Market politics, despite contradictions, and the politics of nostalgia have produced a virtual revolution in American ways of seeing the world. Although Bill Clinton's victory in 1992 exposed some of the frayed edges of the conservative movement, Clinton's campaign and presidency illustrate a tendency not to counter right-wing ideologies but to appropriate them. The conservative deployment of "the decline of family values" as a smokescreen to block public view of the poverty caused by neoclassical economics has yet to be challenged by liberal politicians and educators. Right-wing deployment of the politics of nostalgia has successfully shaped American's picture of its family-oriented past. Today, describing the traditional family throughout American history evokes images of grandparents, parents, and children all working together, nurturing mothers protecting children from early exposure to sex and adult concerns, virginal couples consummating their marriage on their wedding night, and faithful spouses removing themselves from the community so that all their time can be devoted to marital and familial responsibilities.

Such pervasive images simply are not accurate. Children who worked in family enterprises with parents and grandparents had little time for activities designed for entertainment. Mothers who worked in such enterprises (e.g., the family farm) had little time to nurture young Wally and Beaver. Often they relegated child care to older children, rarely stopping to celebrate baby's first step or worry about school report cards. Conservatives, failing to check with family historians about the accuracy of their romanticized vision, argue that if these traditional families existed in the 1990s, America would not have to endure existing social dilemmas. As Bob Dole, Dan Quayle, and their conservative followers maintain, the "single-bullet theory" of America's problems is the epidemic of family breakdown. School leaders buy into such rhetoric, proclaiming that the cause of the American education decline is a "parenting deficiency"; divorce and unwed motherhood lead directly to poverty and inequality. In his 1992 State of the Union speech, President Bush claimed that the crisis of the city has resulted from "the dissolution of the family." In his 1994 State of the Union address, President Clinton echoed similar charges. Across the conservative and liberal spectrum, American politicians have accepted the family values argument—and by the late 1990s, it was beyond debate in the public arena.

Analysis of poverty and its relation to family status in the 1990s reveals a reality quite different from the "commonsense" mainstream portrayals. If the traditional family were to be magically revived, researchers have asked, how many of the social problems America faces would be solved? And the generally agreed-upon answer? Very few. Throughout American history, crises in family structures have typically followed substantial economic and political upheavals. The family problems of the 1990s are no different; our crisis follows the economic problems that emerged in the late 1960s, with their international market alterations and destruction of once highly paid union jobs. Such changes caused pain and suffering in families, and some families responded to the disruptions in ways that often made matters worse. But one thing is clear: The economic and social upheavals could not have been avoided if families had simply tried harder to reassert their familial commitments. The Census Bureau reported in 1991 that the average family that falls below the poverty line after the father leaves was already in severe economic distress before his departure. In most cases, the distress was caused by the father's loss of his job (Coontz, 1992).

Adam Smith, the Sequel: The Emergence of Neoclassical Economics

The belief in an unrestricted economy in which all decisions are left to the undisturbed functioning of the market, known as neoclassical economics, gained great favor in the late 1970s and 1980s. Gradually subverting the contributions of religion, tradition, and literature to a common moral language, neoclassical economics provides a moral code for modernists—self-interest. In this cult of the free market, economists maintain that economic analysis can be deployed not only to determine a strategy such as whether to increase overhead costs for the 1996 fiscal year but also in all types of decisionmaking situations. Thus, the message is proclaimed that marriage is less about love than about a matter of supply and demand within the market for spouses. Suicide occurs when people find their "total lifetime utility" falling to zero. In other words, from this perspective all human behavior can be perceived from an economic vantage point, no matter how related it may be to altruism, emotion, love, or compassion (Bellah et al., 1991). Many political and educational leaders who find their philosophical roots in this neoclassical tradition have attempted to analyze schooling as merely a function of the laws of the marketplace. Attempting to privatize schools in line with their market philosophy, such leaders undermine the human dimension of the educational act while diminishing the importance of democracy in the public space (Giroux, 1993).

Assuming that individuals always act rationally to maximize their self-interest, the neoclassicists present a model of a self-regulating market that harmonizes the demands of production, labor, and capital. Supply and demand will regulate prices such that all human and material resources are used in an efficient manner. The market is all-knowing, neoclassical economists claim, and, as a result, possesses the ability to adjust to dramatic changes. For example, technological innovation automates a process of production to the point that 80 percent of the workers are laid off. Always working to restore equilibrium, the market will provide a solution, according to the theorists. As the cost (potential wages) of the displaced labor declines and the profits of the automated industry increase, a situation is created where an enterprising entrepreneur will rehire the unemployed workers in a firm producing a different product. But what is wrong with this picture? Unfortunately, this simple neoclassical model works best when the skill levels of workers are low. If workplaces possessed high-skill jobs, it would be difficult for laborers to quickly adjust to disruptions. When an industry declines and loses positions, neoclassicists assume that displaced workers will be able to find work quickly because there are so few job-specific skills that would keep, say, sales clerks from adapting to computer jobs (Block, 1990).

Like other modernist expressions, neoclassical economics possesses a tendency for decontextualization. When analyzing economic issues, neoclassicists argue that such topics can be separated from the spheres of politics and culture. Just as an educational psychologist who is measuring IQ ignores the context in which a student was raised, neoclassical economists deal only with variables that are internal to the economy. As economics is stripped from its social and political context, it is also extracted from a moral context (Nooteboom, 1991). The prevailing rhetoric of economic battle—the appeal to win the economic war with the other nations of the planet—reveals the emptiness of the neoclassical conversation. Such advocates seem unable to grasp the concept that economic thinking might want to address the provision of joint prosperity for human beings and that the production of winners and losers seems to miss the point (Chesneaux, 1992). When a local government in an isolated rural area chooses to keep the only grocery store in the district open despite its persistent unprofitability, it has, according to the high priests of neoclassicism, broken the Intergalactic Federation's Prime Directive: "Thou Shalt Not Interfere with the Free Function of the

Market." Let the fact that local residents would either have to starve or move be damned. Hunger or cultural disruption are not *economic* issues, after all.

Some advocates of neoclassical economics take their case even further, contending that an unhindered market in babies would resolve troubles concerning unwanted pregnancies, teenage mothers, and surrogate mothers. If women could sell their babies on the open market and baby prices were publicized in the same manner that winter wheat futures were quoted, the free market would quickly solve the problem. Americans always seem shocked when the French and other foreigners refer to our economic system as *le capitalisme sauvage*, or "savage capitalism" (Bellah et al., 1991, p. 91). Unfortunately, in vocational and other forms of education, teachers and students cannot speak these words; they are taboo. Such silent censorship cannot continue in a democratic society that supposedly values freedom of speech and discussion of issues. We must demand the right to examine the problems that plague our economic system and our work lives.

Vocational educators must demand the right to discuss and debate who benefits from these neoclassical forms of unregulated capitalism. Critics of the free market argue that instead of offering opportunity for all, they provide an ideological curtain that hides the free market's tendency to bestow its greatest benefits to those already in possession of wealth and power (Richmond, 1986). Free market capitalism creates a climate that justifies the privileged few's view of reality. Market forces and competition are presented in this construction of the world as cherubs and angels who joyously but silently work to create a harmony between supply and demand, wages and prices, and goods and services. The free market never worked this way, even in the nineteenth century. It certainly does not work this way in the last years of the twentieth century, with multinational corporations powerful enough to sway governments and control markets, government obsession with military spending and the maintenance of the "defense sector" of the economy, and the formation of economic communities and oil cartels. No local economy is free from larger influences that undermine free trade and equal competition. The neoclassical market model does not account for these intervening factors. Despite all appearances to the contrary, neoclassicists operate in a simple universe—a fantasyland that exists only at Disney World (or is it Wally World?).

The social foundations of vocational education revolve around these issues, these questions of social, political, moral, and, of course, economic context. The field of economic sociology is especially important for our purposes as vocational educators. Economic sociology refuses to allow proponents of neoclassicism to get by with their socially decontextualized portrait of economics. Arguing that economic activity is continuously shaped by cultural factors, these scholars provide example after example of the influence of noneconomic "background factors" in economic affairs. The type of work deemed appropriate for different social groups, for instance, is not simply an *economic* issue. Because of particular social assumptions, black men in the early twentieth century worked as train porters. The *free* market did not dictate such a reality. Women were assigned to low-status clerical jobs near the end of the nineteenth century, replacing men whose status as clerks had been quite high. Again, the market did not dictate this development. How do individuals weigh the value of more money versus more leisure? What factors determine the decision of a graduate student to pursue or not pursue a doctorate instead of stopping with a master's degree? Obviously, economic factors are not the only "variables" at work in these situations (Block, 1990).

The folly of reductionist economic explanations of daily affairs is obvious. A man wants to buy a book on the relationship between education and the economy at a corporate-owned chain bookstore. He picks up a copy of Richard Brosio's *The Radical Democratic Critique of Capitalist Education* for $39.95. A salesman notices his choice and says, "Why Brosio for forty dollars? We have a special on books on economics and education." The buyer responds, "But I wanted a book that questions everyday assumptions about economics and schooling." The salesman picks up a new edition of neoclassicist Milton Freidman's *Free to Choose*. "But, sir, this one is our Red, White, and Blue Light special. It's a hot value at only $9.99. You'll save thirty dollars. Come, look at our other economics and education volumes. They're conveniently arranged by cost." Another customer interrupts the salesman: "I'd like a book on postmodern architecture in the eleven-dollar range." Economic considerations do not dictate all decisions concerning consumption.

This facetious example illustrates the larger point: We cannot ignore the social and moral context of economic affairs. This larger point becomes especially serious when we find that neoclassicists view labor markets just like any other commodity market. The fact that the labor market is occupied by living beings with feelings and emotional concerns is irrelevant. Such human factors are quickly dismissed in the neoclassicist mind-set—because it is not people themselves who are an "input" in the process of production but one of their qualities. What matters about human beings in the free market is not their sacred spirit but their capacity to do work. The most basic concern of vocational educators—and that is our students—is stripped of its humanity and reduced to merely another factor in the production process (Block, 1990).

Automation and the Future of Good Work

Bringing together this analysis of good and bad work with our understanding of the dehumanization and decontextualization of neoclassical economics prepares us to examine work in the future. The debate about the impact of high technology and automation is multifaceted and ambiguous. When it is examined in light of ethical and democratic concerns, considerable insight is generated for vocational educators. A central question emerges in the study of high-tech and automated jobs and the future of work: Will the emerging economy contribute to the authoritarian control of workers, or will it serve to empower workers to participate and use their creativity and intelligence in their daily work lives? Too often, we hear high technology and automation being sold to industrial and corporate leaders as a way of reducing labor costs and lessening their need for skilled workers. At the same time, new technologies and the use of automation are touted as ways to guarantee high-quality production and improve industrial flexibility (flexibility involves the capacity to change one product line to another with more speed or to produce a diverse array of products without interruption) (Copa and Tebbenhoff, 1990; Block, 1990).

Refusing to invest in workplace innovations in the 1960s and 1970s when an oversupply of baby boomers began to hit the labor market, American firms fell behind other industrialized nations in quantity and quality of production. By the 1980s, report after report demanded immediate workplace reforms, with the development of high technologies and high-skill workers. The authors of these reports realized that empowered high-skill workers are invaluable in a firm's attempt to improve its productivity and the quality of its products. As an organization undergoes the workplace reorganization required by technological changes, no one is sure how the labor process should be reconceptualized. In this situation, empowered workers can play a central role in redefining the organization of work and production. No manager possesses the everyday, practical knowledge that comes from dealing with the microproblems that plague the work process (DeYoung, 1989; Roditi, 1992; Block, 1990).

Analysts understand that technological development and its accompanying automation have slowed the growth of jobs in both the manufacturing and service/information sectors (Harris, 1981). After this joint pronouncement, economists, labor researchers, and businesspeople agree on little else. One of the most basic disagreements concerns the general nature of the economic future we are entering. As was discussed in Chapter 3, the twentieth-century economy has been described as the Fordist era with its famous compromise: Workers will tolerate meaningless and boring factory jobs in return for consumer rewards. With its mass production, inflexible technologies (the assembly line), standardized work routines, economies of scale (larger factories that produce larger numbers of products can produce each particular product for less money than smaller firms producing only a few products), and necessary cultivation of a market for standardized products, Fordism produced great national wealth for the United States. As Fordism began to decline in the 1970s with the oil crisis and the rise of foreign manufacturing, scholars began to argue over whether a new economic era had dawned. Is there such a thing as post-Fordism? The question is difficult to answer because evidence of both Fordist and post-Fordist production patterns coexist in contemporary society. Before we address this question any further, a quick delineation of the characteristics of post-Fordism is needed (a more detailed analysis of post-Fordism will follow in Part 3):

1. Post-Fordism witnesses a decline in consumer interest in mass-produced products, which is replaced by growing interest in specialized items. Consumers become progressively more interested in quality and more willing to pay for it.
2. Because of the demand for specialized products, shorter production runs are required. Thus, smaller plants with flexibility replace large factories producing uniform products in a post-Fordist economy.
3. New technologies make possible and profitable new forms of flexible production. Post-Fordist factories employ computerized ma chinery programmed to produce a variety of items.
4. Post-Fordist workers possess more skills than their Fordist predecessors. In order to deal with the sophisticated technologies, workers must operate not only with greater ability but with greater autonomy as well. Thus, a new, more progressive workplace is created.
5. Great diversity in the post-Fordist workplace is mirrored in the society as a whole. Post-Fordist workers demand more differentiated products, lifestyles, and social activities (Ritzer, 1993).

Where are we, then? The economic world in the late twentieth century is an amalgam of Fordist and post-Fordist dynamics. The impact of technological innovation and automation has been paradoxical. Some employers use the same technology in very different ways; some ways empower workers, others deskill them. Because of these and other factors, it is difficult to generalize about the *nature* of the era. Employers who want to automate their factories can reduce labor costs by eliminating repetitive work tasks, but often there is a conflict between reducing a plant's reliance on skilled workers and simultaneously working toward goals of improving quality and flexibility. Without diverse skills, workers will find their ability to cope with unusual machine problems to be very limited; indeed, such inability will undermine quality improvement. Thus, the pursuit of quality and flexibility should pressure corporate leaders to seek workers with higher skills. For example, the growing complexity of mechanical and repair operations creates a need for more highly skilled workers. Although some deskilling might be possible in auto mechanics, maintenance mechanics, and office-machine servicers with the development of self-diagnosing machinery, someone must be knowledgeable enough to fix the machinery when self-diagnosis fails (Block, 1990, pp. 94–98, 108).

At the same time, however, elements of Fordism live on unaffected by these post-Fordist trends. George Ritzer (1993) in *The McDonaldization of*

Society has traced these persistent Fordist trends, delineated in his Mc-Donaldization thesis. McDonaldization is "the process by which the principles of the fast-food restaurant are coming to dominate more and more sectors of American society as well as the rest of the world" (p. 155). The process is quite compatible with Fordism, with its homogeneous products, rigid technologies, standardized work routines, deskilling, and homogenization of workers and customers. While post-Fordist production processes have expanded in America, McDonaldization has moved from the restaurant business to education, the workplace, travel, vacationing, dieting, politics, TV evangelism, and the family. No one said understanding the social and economic context of the foundations of vocational education would be easy: In the contemporary American economy we have two expanding forces, McDonaldization and post-Fordism, moving concurrently in opposite directions (Ritzer, 1993, p. 155).

Although many progressive impulses exist within post-Fordist workplaces, with their emphasis on highly skilled and flexible workers, such jobs will account for no more than 30 percent of the workforce by the early twenty-first century. The U.S. Labor Department reports that the growth in high-skill jobs will stagnate by the late 1990s; at the same time, there will be steady job growth in fast-food restaurants, small retail stores, and service establishments. Other studies at the Bureau of Labor Statistics have found that many college graduates are not getting high-skill jobs. As the creation of high-skill jobs has stagnated, 568,000 college graduates have taken work as sales clerks, 475,000 as secretaries and typists, and 125,000 as bartenders, waiters, and waitresses (Weisman, 1991).

Another continuation, if not expansion, of the Fordist trend involves the rationalization and deskilling of professional jobs—Stanley Aronowitz (1992) has called this the "proletarianization" of professionalism. The term *proletariat* refers to the lowest class of citizens in a community. Thus, proletarianization indicates the debasement of what once were high-skill positions in a way that strips skills from professional practitioners. The medical profession would seem to be one of the last professions to experience rationalization and deskilling, but the past decade has witnessed just such a trend. Physicians find themselves under increasing external controls by managers and bureaucrats who are not medical doctors. These controls bring with them a predictability that removes mystery and passion from the everyday lives of doctors. In these situations, doctors no longer rely on personal medical judgment to determine procedure in a case; rules, regulations, or the demands of technology make decisions for them. Of course, such rationalization works to proletarianize and deprofessionalize the work of physicians. In other words, medical doctors are losing the power to control their own profession to the rationalizing structures of modernism. Even high-status professions are not immune from the deskilling pressures of developing technologies (Aronowitz, 1992, p. 229; Ritzer, 1993, p. 140).

The belief that service and information jobs are inherently more highly skilled than industrial jobs has been undermined by the developments of the last twenty-five years. When service and information workers watch their work being divided into deskilled separate tasks, they understand that their work has been debased. Good service work has devolved into industrial services. An uninteresting, simple, repetitive task performed in an office is the same bad work as an uninteresting, simple, repetitive task performed in a factory. The consequences of bad work in the services can be dramatic, as alienated nurses and hospital workers, for example, scar, maim, and even kill. The low pay of service and information jobs reflects this bad work—and a majority of such jobs fall within the low-level wage segment of the labor market. Indeed, white-collar work is *not* better paid, more prestigious, or brainier than blue-collar work (Harris, 1981).

As the old stereotypes about white- and blue-collar work fade, the matter is further complicated by the upskilling taking place in the blue-collar labor market. Many labor analysts have pointed out that the automation of the 1990s is very different from the automation of the 1950s. In the 1950s, machines introduced into industry involved major investment and were highly rigid in their contribution to Fordist forms of mass production. The automation of the 1990s generally involves computer innovations that allow for flexible changes in the production process. Such flexibility makes automation cost-effective for small-batch production and for products that will be produced only for a short time. When industries become computer automated and are highly flexible, continuous-process production can be achieved. Continuous-process production allows the transformation of raw materials into finished products without humans ever touching the product. Workers in such a situation are involved in the supervision and maintenance of production equipment rather than in the physical transformation of raw materials. Thus, demand for labor is lessened, and the role of labor is changed.

Industrial workers in the new automated plants find themselves in new roles with new demands. For example, they find in the automated and computerized plant that their skill depth is reduced while their skill breadth is expanded. Skill depth refers to the time it takes to master a specific task; skill breadth refers to the diverse types of understandings and skills workers need to perform effectively in a particular job situation. New technologies that promote flexibility reduce skill depth because workers no longer work directly with production—the hands-on knowledge they accumulated over time is no longer useful. Skill breadth is expanded as jobs become interdependent and one job position is marked by a variety of assignments. Because of the nature of the machinery and the demands of continuous-process production, errors become more and more costly. In a workplace of this sort, one small employee error can ruin the entire run of a particular product, as automatic equipment turns out five thousand flawed products before anybody realizes it. The workers who attend these machines must understand the nature of the process in great specificity and detail; thus, such work situations demand worker upskilling.

When workers have to deal with numerically controlled machines—computer-driven machinery that is programmed to operate either individually or in groups—they may experience long and frustrating periods of inactivity before they do anything. Even though skill demands may be high, the work is typically boring and unsatisfying. Workers who work with numerically controlled equipment often request involvement with computer programming in an attempt to ease the boredom. In a few factories, machine operators are encouraged to do their own programming—an activity that significantly increases their skill breadth. At the present time, only about one in five machine operators has been taught to program. Until such learning is undertaken by the majority of numerically controlled machine operators, we can expect to see worker skill increases accompanied by boredom and alienation. In similar situations in Japanese industry, machine operators make continual programming alterations and are expected to write new computer programs for all aspects of the workplace. These workers are typically referred to as "highly skilled engineers with multifunctional responsibilities." In addition Japanese firms take 300 percent more time than American companies to upgrade employee skills.

The introduction of robotics into the workplace dramatically affects the nature of work. As robotics substantially decreases the need for workers, it concurrently increases the skill levels of remaining laborers. Just as with numerically controlled machines, workers have to learn to repair and maintain robots. Some studies indicate that most jobs created in robot-driven industry will be high skill and that a majority of the positions will require two or more years of higher education. Like workers with numerically controlled machines, robotic workers experience long periods of inactivity and boredom, despite the demands of higher skills. As employers, unions, and vocational educators strive for the creation of good work, they must remember that in the high-tech workplace, there is no guarantee that higher-skill work will be good work. High skills are often matched by higher stress and increased boredom (Block, 1990).

The challenges presented by automation and technological development for the future of work are numerous and dramatic. Vocational educators committed to the principles of good work and economic justice must understand the complexity and ambiguity of the emerging workplace. The presence of competing workplace trends as expressed by Fordism and post-Fordism make generalized pronouncements difficult to make. The competing trends within post-Fordism add to the ambiguity. The concept of good work serves as a guiding beacon, as we navigate the murky waters and the thick fog of the unknown sea of the future. Without such ethical guidance, we lose our way—in that we tend to forget that productivity growth and rising GNPs are achieved in a human context—often with little concern for the downsizing made possible by automation. Our students in vocational programs deserve an education that addresses these ethical questions, that grounds them in the historical, philosophical, and sociological foundations of vocational education.

The Buck Stops over There: Reshaping the Workplace

No matter what future economic projections indicate, the message from American business is perfectly clear: American productivity has fallen because American workers have low skills. Millions of Americans accept such pronouncements and build their political lives around the assumption of worker incompetence. Prevailing opinions, however, may not reflect the perspectives of those outside the circle of power. It is becoming more and more apparent that major business decisions of the last two decades have not served the best interests of the nation. In failing to recognize the need to reshape the workplace in a manner that would have empowered and compensated workers, managers perpetuated bad work with its low-skill expectations and top-down style of administration. Such managerial methods dramatically lower incentives, and when combined with a reluctance to embrace long-term, global views of markets, American business has had to rely on lower labor costs to fuel its growth in profits.

Businesses have evaded calls for workplace democracy, the formation of worker councils that would help analyze and implement plans for workplace reorganization, and the call for a commitment to high-skill, high-paid jobs. American firms have generally refused to admit that they could better utilize talents and skills workers already possess. *America's Choice: High Skills or Low Wages*, a report prepared by the Commission on the Skills of the American Workforce in 1990, found that only one out of twenty U.S. firms had attempted to reorganize work in a manner that demanded high worker skills. A study by Towers Perrin and the Hudson Institute, also in 1990, indicated that only 13 percent of U.S. firms ever utilized self-managed work groups. Most companies (86 percent) refuse to teach academic skills at work, and a majority of managers confide that what they really need is a low-skill workforce that is obedient and accepts a hierarchical organization (Perrin quoted in Roditi, 1992). Still, in the last years of the century, most business leaders consider frontline workers incapable of playing a role in making a firm more profitable. Despite the post-Fordist trend for high-tech worker skill upgrading, low-skill jobs will continue to proliferate in the twenty-first century. Democratic vocational educators cannot accept such a reality (Kolberg and Smith, 1992; DeYoung, 1989; Weisman, 1991; Block, 1990).

In this debate over the future of the workplace, the voice of the neoclassical economists can be easily heard. Neoclassicists contend that the skills of
workers determine the nature of the labor market, that is, the types of jobs
available and the way the workplace is arranged. These economists argue
that simply by increasing educational opportunities, better jobs would be
created. Barry Bluestone has rejected that stance (1988), arguing that low
wages and bad work result from entrapment in bad jobs. Provided the opportunity to work in high-wage jobs, most of these workers would have no
problems. In a large percentage of cases, Bluestone concluded, workers in
low-skill jobs could perform well even without years of extra education,
without massive infusions of job training, or without indoctrination into
some new "industrial discipline" program (DeYoung, 1989).

Despite pronouncements from economists like Bluestone, the neoclassicist position has dominated the debate about the school's relationship to the
economy. The folk wisdom of the 1990s posits that bad work results from
ill-trained employees whose incompetence undermines America's ability to
compete internationally. High-skill jobs will be created only when the
schools have produced high-skill labor. Ever since the National Commission
on Excellence in Education published *A Nation at Risk* in 1983, the neoclassicist argument that educational improvements are necessary for America
to maintain its slim competitive edge in world markets has been the accepted orthodoxy (Weisman, 1991). Critics have argued that a more realistic assessment positions schools as the target of corporate leaders who have
mismanaged the economy in much the same way they mismanaged it in the
1920s and 1930s. Revisionists argue further that just when educational
scholars were beginning to appreciate the ways educational and economic
opportunity for disadvantaged students was being undermined, corporate
leaders leveled their attack on the schools.

The corporate attack on the schools ignored the way cultural factors help
undermine the school performance of marginalized students. Focusing instead on a perceived lack of rigor and discipline, corporate critics argued
that if school standards are raised, the national economy will prosper. If SAT
scores go up, they concluded, we can expect higher productivity and a
stronger economy; but if they go down, then the reverse is true. The problem with such portrayals is that the National Commission on Excellence in
Education and other advocates of the orthodoxy offer no proof. Little, if
any, evidence exists that schools alone can solve the riddles presented by international trade and economic development. They offer significant proof of
the failure of public schools but no proof of the relationship between academic failure and economic decline. For example, can the schools be blamed
for the decision by Detroit automobile manufacturers to keep producing
cars with low gas mileage, a decision that resulted in their losing domination
of the car market? Did poor teaching delay automation in American indus-

try until European and Asian manufacturers had already stolen a large share of the world market? Maybe schools should not assume the sole blame for such economic problems (Goodlad, 1992; Spring, 1984; Weisman, 1991).

If a direct relationship between the failure of schooling and economic development does not exist, then the educational reform movement of the 1980s and 1990s has been misguided. By absolving corporate and industrial leaders of any responsibility, the advocates of orthodoxy have allowed schools to serve as scapegoats for private sector mismanagement. The time has come to reformulate the foundations of educational reform with input from business management as well as from academic and vocational educators, labor unions, and advocates of a progressive view of good work. The argument being presented here does not contend that schools do not need reform—of course they do. The important point is that business, labor, and education must all change if we are to seriously address American economic, educational, and social problems. At the same time, friends of good work cannot allow powerful groups to paint an unrealistic portrait of the respective roles of schools and business in the shaping of American economic life. Few issues better illustrate the way power works to shape the nature of public conversations and public policies than this corporate attempt to blame schools for a broad, multifaceted socioeconomic problem. Many politicians with their campaigns financed by corporate interests have given their constituents the illusion they were aggressive on the issue of economic decline by advocating educational reform while ignoring workplace reorganization. In this way, their cozy financial relationships with the powerful corporate lobby could be left undisturbed, thereby preserving the status quo—a status quo marked by too much bad work (Weisman, 1991).

Developing a Vocational Education That Challenges Bad Work

The purpose of this book is to introduce vocational educators to the sociological, economic, historical, and philosophical factors that undermine and support their attempts to create a democratic pedagogy for the present era. Understanding the modernist context that has produced scientific management and bad work begins the attempt to make sense of vocational education, its problems, its successes, and its role in schooling in general and within society. In the modernist, scientifically managed organization, the driving dogma was managing, organizing, and controlling. Human resources, that is, workers, were treated as mere components of a physical system (Senge, 1990). As such, dehumanization could take place to the degree that worker well-being could be ignored. Operating under this mind-set, corporate power brokers looked to the schools to perform a very specific function: to prepare a child for an unchanging world where passivity and unquestioning acceptance of the scientifically managed workplace was necessary (Nelson and Watras, 1981).

John Dewey and his Progressive colleague Boyd Bode were very specific in their rejection of the mind-set of scientific management and its perspective on the role of schooling. Bode, for example, wrote in 1927 that scientific management missed the point when its proponents contended that progress came from doing the same things more efficiently. Progress, Bode wrote, came from creating a new vision; almost seventy years later, we still see Bode's vision deferred by the personnel management descendants of Taylor and his efficiency corps. Dewey argued that scientific management undermines social imagination and even thinking itself. Workers would have understood what Dewey was saying, if they only had access to his writing. They experienced, as have their descendants, the removal of thinking and creativity from their daily work. The memory of the way American workers have been underutilized and marginalized can help vocational educators of the present in the struggle for good work, in the effort to shift responsibility for planning and executing work to the level where the work is actually performed (Wirth, 1983). By engaging in such a struggle, vocational educators, guided by their vision of good work, can uncover the hidden abilities and the creative potential possessed by vocational students (Alvesson and Willmott, 1992). At the same time, they can make visible the possibilities for alternatives that democratic workplaces create.

PART TWO

The Historical Dimensions of Vocational Education

5   *The Origins of*
Vocational Education

Many academics have described America as a culture of amnesia. The emphasis on the new, the up-to-date, the obsolescence of the old contribute to this neglect of the past. In a culture of amnesia, schools take "presentism" to new heights. Teacher education consistently neglects the study of the past—and vocational education is no exception. Without historical insight, vocational educational policymakers fail to gain insights into the relationship between schooling and work that the past may provide. As a result, vocational educational leaders may devote great energy to reinventing a pedagogy incapable of addressing the demands of democracy and the needs of an evolving economy (Edson, 1979). When institutions fail, there usually seems to be ample evidence in advance that trouble looms ahead. Historical consciousness can help vocational educators recognize the inherent problems in particular assumptions or particular ways of operating and facilitate the development of pragmatic alternatives. Let us begin our historical analysis with a look at the social and economic context into which vocational education was born.

The Forgotten Context: The Impact of Industrialization

When French aristocrat Alexis de Tocqueville traveled to America in 1831 he was impressed by what he called the equality that characterized American life. The America that Tocqueville observed was a land of small farmers, self-employed artisans (blacksmiths, shoemakers, carpenters, and so on), merchants, traders, and professionals. Although the tyranny of slavery existed and an industrial movement was brewing, the majority of Americans were free from anyone else's control. Effusive in his praise for the land of opportunity, Tocqueville issued an ominous observation: The growing manufacturers, he noted, were forming small aristocracies in the midst of the larger American democracy. Like all aristocracies, these industrial variants divide people into classes made up of a few individuals who are very wealthy and a multitude who are wretchedly poor and have little hope of escape (Brecher, 1972).

Tocqueville further argued that these new industries positioned workers on the same detailed task every day, thus allowing greater speed of production. That process, he wrote, holds dramatic implications for the worker and the employer. When workers produce only one thing, they lose their overview of the relationship between their labor and the process of production. As their minds are removed from their daily work, their lives are slowly degraded. Managers, however, are so elevated in status that they begin to look like administrators of expansive empires. So unnerved was Tocqueville by these developments that he predicted a new form of tyranny based upon this industrialization process. Unfortunately, his predictions proved to be all too true, as industrialization exploded over the next fifty years. Labor leader Terrence V. Powderly reflected on the human effects of industrialization in his memoirs, written in 1889:

> With the introduction of machinery, large manufacturing establishments were erected in the cities and towns. Articles that were formerly made by hand, were turned out in large quantities by machinery; prices were lowered, and those who worked by hand found themselves competing with something that could withstand hunger and cold and not suffer in the least. The village blacksmith shop was abandoned, the road-side shoe shop was deserted, the tailor left his bench, and all together these mechanics turned away from their country homes and wended their way to the cities wherein the large factories had been erected. The gates were unlocked in the morning to allow them to enter, and after their daily task was done the gates were closed after them in the evening.
>
> Silently and thoughtfully, these men went to their homes. They no longer carried the keys of the workshop, for workshop, tools and keys belonged not to them, but to their master. Thrown together in this way, in these large hives of industry, men became acquainted with each other, and frequently discussed the question of labor's rights and wrongs. (Powderly, 1889, pp. 26–27)

Chicago, New York, and other large cities attracted both the hopeful and the hopeless, as millions of immigrants from Europe and rural America poured into urban tenements. Cheap, unskilled workers were in high demand in deskilled factory jobs broken down to their simplest task components. While the factory workers lived in squalor, shrewd businessmen accumulated vast overnight fortunes by manipulating the stock market (Wilms, 1979). Corporate managers employed deceitful strategies to get rich quickly, in the process angering their impoverished employees (DeYoung, 1989). While the industrial leaders built their opulent mansions at Newport, Rhode Island, workers performed tedious tasks fourteen hours a day for incredibly low wages. No social programs or economic "safety net" for the poor existed; if an individual was injured on the job, no worker's compensation was there to help. Times were frightfully tough for the factory workers.

But as educational historian Clinton Allison (1995) has pointed out, one would hardly understand the plight of working people from reading the public-school textbook histories of the era. Consider the popular use of the term "gay" to describe the 1890s: In that era, "gay" meant happy, and the decade was characterized as carefree and fun-loving to those generations that followed. The popular understanding of the time did not include the view from below—the perspective of factory workers struggling to make ends meet. For them, urban life was often a catastrophic nightmare. Several families, often sleeping in shifts, shared a single room in a tenement; a single water spigot sometimes served an entire city block; the streets were filled with garbage and human excrement; opium dens were found throughout the city; cocaine and other narcotics were used in patent medicine for both adults and children; prepubescent girls often engaged in prostitution just to survive; and urban crime was rampant, with young boys snatching purses, shooting guns, and stealing horses.

Living in such conditions, workers found no relief when they entered the factory doors. Life was hard in the textile mills, the manufacturing plants, and the steel mills. The Homestead Steel Mill on the banks of the Monongahela River in Pennsylvania was typical of scores of other plants. Employees worked every day of the year except Christmas and the Fourth of July, with no lunch break, few bathrooms, and no shower rooms. The plant was hot as hell in the winter and worse in the summer. The noise of the machinery and the screech of cold saws ripping through steel took many of the workers' hearing. Their lungs were often weakened by breathing the minuscule, shiny grains of steel that covered their clothes and their hair. Workers were frequently killed by hot metal explosions or falls into the molten pits; far more were injured. No one was compensated for injury or death, as the idea was unheard of in the latter part of the nineteenth century (Heilbroner, 1977).

Although women did not work in steel mills like Homestead, increasing numbers of them were working in low-wage jobs in the late nineteenth and early twentieth centuries. Women worked in clothes-making, textile, and food-processing plants. An exploding demand for clerical labor instigated by the expanding industrial economy brought women into offices as file clerks and "typewriters." Although most women prepared themselves for roles as wives and mothers, industry increasingly needed low-paid women's work. In these industrial jobs, women were expected to draw upon their domestic role and perform tasks closely aligned with homemaking. Thus, as office workers, women were expected to do the routine and household chores. Clothes-making, textile, and food-processing work was viewed as a "natural" extension of the female predisposition and ability. With little exception, women industrial workers earned far less than men, even for the same work. Industrial managers used women's entrance into the factories as one of numerous strategies to lower the pay of male workers (Violas, 1978).

In the years between the end of the Civil War in 1865 and the beginning of the twentieth century, the economic and social transformation of America took place. Extravagance in America was redefined, as corporate leaders built gilded mansions on huge estates, threw parties that put Roman emperors to shame, purchased railroad carriages and private yachts, married European nobility, and literally came to run the country. The budding labor movement pointed to the injustice, screamed its indignation, but was eventually subdued. Labor unions objected to the organization of industry that allowed for such an unequal distribution of wealth and such degrading and dangerous work (McDermott, 1980).

Some historians refer to the period between the late 1870s and the 1890s as the Era of Labor Wars. The economic depression of the 1870s initiated pay cuts that sparked a series of railroad workers' strikes, leading to a national railway strike in July 1877. Angry workers around the nation blocked railroads and stopped factory production. When fired upon by state militias, workers turned violent, shattering the authority of the status quo. Unsure of how to use their newfound power, the strikers hesitated. President Rutherford B. Hayes mobilized federal troops, big employers organized loyal employees into armed companies, and slowly the workers were subdued. Although the workers were thoroughly defeated, the strike demonstrated the potential power of organized labor. Stimulating greater union membership, the strike initiated a series of labor-management conflicts (Brecher, 1972). In 1886 alone, labor organized strikes against 10,000 different employers that involved 500,000 workers. Most Americans felt that the "labor problem," defined as worker resistance to the organization of the workplace in industrial capitalism, was the most important issue of the era (Tozer, Violas, and Senese, 1993).

By 1892, the labor wars reached their most intense period. At the Homestead Steel plant, management employed an army of Pinkerton guards to quell a worker's strike. Consisting of 32,000 men, the Pinkerton force numbered more than the U.S. Army at the time. The governor of Pennsylvania mobilized the state militia and sent it to Homestead. As the strike spread to other plants, Andrew Carnegie, the owner of Homestead Steel, brought in strikebreakers to operate the factory and persuaded authorities to arrest the strike leaders for treason against the state. Such tactics undermined the workers' efforts and ended the strike. When Carnegie reopened Homestead Steel, only low-skill workers were hired—because they would work for less and were less resistant to control by managers than high-skill laborers.

Such practices spread around the nation, illustrating that management would use all means possible to control its workers. State governments expanded their militias and constructed armories in urban areas in order to better control workers. Because of its power, management was able to dictate the way the labor wars were covered by the press. Such favorable coverage allowed owners to gain the support of everyday Americans who came to see the labor organizations as controlled by foreigners and inherently anti-American. By the end of the nineteenth century, management power was consolidated by the merging of rival capitalists into great corporations, or "great trusts" as they were known at the time. This collective capitalism would ultimately defeat the labor movement, fracturing the working class and setting the stage for twentieth-century economic and labor events. Although labor could effectively fight Homestead Steel, it could not fight the new U.S. Steel Corporation, formed in 1901 when 138 different steel companies consolidated. As the new century dawned, the power of the giant industrialists was awesome in its omnipresence. It is in this context that we consider the history of vocational education (McDermott, 1980; Tozer, Violas, and Senese, 1993).

Education for Economic Development

Before the common-school movement in the 1840s in Massachusetts, education for economic development was not a common topic for discussion in America. Few Americans before the 1820s and 1830s, when the Industrial Revolution began in America, had seen any relationship between schooling and vocational success. A nation predominantly populated by rural dwellers needed practical knowledge to make a living on the farm. Learning to read and write was not unimportant, but it was commonly believed that such learning could be easily accomplished in the home after work. As Americans began to understand that industrialization was ushering in a new era, they still failed to perceive a connection between economics and schooling. With the crusade for public schooling led by Horace Mann in the 1840s, such perceptions slowly began to change (DeYoung, 1989).

The development of an industrial, factory-based economy began in the 1820s and 1830s in Massachusetts. Such economic changes would create the context for the first state-supported, compulsory, and universal school system in America. Industrialists experienced great difficulty in their attempt to adapt male workers to the demands of deskilled factory work. Frustrated by such men, owners hired women, children, and inmates of charitable institutions as laborers. When Irish Catholics began to emigrate to Massachusetts in large numbers, industrialists hired them to replace American-born workers. Trouble with native men focused the owners' attention on developing "proper" industrial attitudes among both the next generation of Americans and future immigrants, moving the industrial leaders to consider the role of schools in such "attitude adjustment." Thus, the industrialists' support of public education did not simply reflect their concern with an educated citizenry or the vocational success of individual men and women; it reflected their economic self-interest, their need for workers with attitudes conducive to the industrial organization of labor.

The understanding of this point is extremely important for professionals in education in general and vocational educators in particular. It allows us to appreciate the fact that schools do not simply pursue academic goals but that all educational decisions are also political decisions, as they concern questions of power and its distribution among different interest groups. Americans often experience great difficulty understanding the dynamics of political questions. Too often, by reducing the meaning of the term "political" to the sphere of life associated with political parties, their candidates, and elections, we miss the power-related aspects of politics. As a result, the significance of the political dimensions of Horace Mann's Common School Crusade and its relevance for contemporary educators is lost. Engagement with questions of power and the understanding that power elites possess inordinate influence in the shaping of school policy will help vocational educators better understand how schools work. They will better appreciate the nature of their personal role in this larger sociopolitical, albeit educational, process.

Mann worked hard to "sell" the public schools to his Massachusetts contemporaries. In his conversations with powerful industrialists and business leaders in the state, Mann addressed their fear of social disharmony. Anxious because of the growing dissatisfaction of workers with the tedium, danger, long hours, and low pay of industrial jobs, factory owners were seeking ways to ensure social stability and order. When Mann talked of schools producing a "common core of values," he insinuated to the industrialists that such values would support and promote industrial development. The common schools, he said, would turn out factory workers who were docile, easily administered, and not prone to participate in strikes and working-class violence. Schooling would reduce poor people's hostility toward the wealthy, Mann promised. Such words were music to the ears of industrial leaders, who were far more concerned with orderly and docile workers than with well-educated and inventive workers.

Working in a nineteenth-century textile factory, under what circumstances would a line worker need to exercise creativity or employ a highly refined ability to analyze and interpret? As far as the owners were concerned, such traits would only induce workers to cause trouble. The political dimension of the common-school movement, much like all educational reforms, involved its alliance with the money interests. Although Mann's vision of public schooling transcended merely providing power elites with malleable workers, the movement would never have succeeded if the commercial, banking, and manufacturing interests had not believed that schools would provide them long-term benefits. The key element in the political coalition that brought universal, compulsory, state-supported education to America was the power elite's faith that public schools would inculcate upon students a core of values that would prepare them to accept the indignity of industrial life.

Although the common-school crusade held dramatic vocational educational implications, the notion of vocational education as a distinct feature of schooling was not considered. A major move toward the modern notion of vocational education can be detected in the debate centered around the Morrill Act in 1862. Granting land tracts to states for the purpose of developing colleges that specialized in the agricultural and industrial arts, the legislation provided support for vocational education at the college level. Before 1860, most higher education involved training for the ministry, characterized by a classical curriculum consisting primarily of Greek, Latin, and theology. Industrial interests called for a more scientific curriculum that would promote technological development. Although the Morrill Act did not produce vocational education in its contemporary form, it did create a climate where discussion of a vocational form of education for public schools could take place (Tozer, Violas, and Senese, 1993; Pincus, 1980).

Vocational Education: Manual Training

The Morrill Act sowed a seed in the public conversation about education that conceptually countered the generally accepted idea that all students should learn the same academic subjects—the notion of the *common* school and its *common* education for everyone. The first introduction in the 1880s of a more contemporary version of vocational education into public schools, that is, manual training, retained the idea of a unitary curriculum. As the early advocates of manual training developed exercises in woodwork and metalwork, they were not as interested in providing specific employment skills as they were in training students to use tools and manipulate materials (Wilms, 1979). In pursuit of a well-rounded education, these liberal manual training advocates sought to train the mind by training the hand. As one of its primary spokespersons, Calvin Woodward, put it:

> *Hail to the skillful, cunning hand!*
> *Hail to the cultured mind!*
> *Contending for the world's command,*
> *Here let them be combined.* (quoted in Grubb et al., 1991, p. 5)

Any thought of separating academic from manual training was not acceptable to the leaders of the early manual training movement. As students learned to master the use of carpenters' tools and mechanical drawing, they were encouraged to connect such skills to academic aspects of the curriculum. By the early 1900s, more and more vocational education advocates urged separation of vocational and academic skills—and only in the last few years have vocational educators returned to the integration model of the early manual training proponents.

Like most reforms and innovations in American educational history, manual training was supported by diverse groups and individuals with conflicting conceptions of its function in the curriculum and its relationship to the political conversation of the era. To business and industrial leaders, manual training served a purely vocational function, grounding a larger strategy to move American education on a two-track European curriculum. That curriculum was envisioned as training working-class and poor children in technical skills in one school, while liberally educating the children of the middle and upper classes in another. As business and industrial leaders gained power in educational conversation, this training of the working class and poor to adjust to the deskilled workplace became a more and more important purpose of manual training. Although both groups—the liberal proponents and the business and industrial proponents—supported manual training, their educational and political goals for the curriculum differed (Feffer, 1993).

Manual training first gained publicity in 1879 when Russian educator Victor Della Vos's "instruction shops" used at the St. Petersburg Imperial Technical School were exhibited at the Philadelphia Centennial Exhibition. Della Vos's ideas later significantly influenced the nature of the manual training curriculum, as did a Swedish series of woodworking exercises known as the Slöyd. Liberal manual education advocates attributed almost mystical power to the Slöyd system and its transcendence of mere mechanical skills. The Slöyd, supporters proclaimed, develops the student physically, mentally, and morally, and the system's manual regimen connects to the central nervous system, enhancing kinesthetic coordination, nurturing neurological complexity, and developing talents and habits that accentuate a variety of physical and mental skills. In addition to this cultivation of personal skills, advocates concluded, manual training will make school more interesting to students and thus will keep them in school longer.

Once business and industrial leaders began to champion manual training, liberal arguments for its use became less and less important. By the end of the 1880s, manual training schools, with the support of national and business organizations, were established in major American cities. It was undoubtedly in the economic interest of business leaders to support forms of manual training that their national and local organizations had helped to establish. Specifically, corporate managers lent support to manual programs, understanding that business-controlled corporate training would undermine union-controlled apprenticeship programs. Workers, under business-supervised manual education, would receive better "attitude training" in the values of respecting authority, embracing the work ethic, and following directions. Even the liberals of the day focused on these "industrial values," as they emphasized social order over issues of equal opportunity and justice. In a sociopolitical context shaped by "labor wars," Jane Addams, social reformer and crusader for more humane treatment of immigrants, blamed labor-management conflict on the growth of unskilled workers. She argued that because these laborers are unable to maintain a balanced outlook on the world, or "a sense of proportion," they rebel against their managers. Such actions, most educators agreed, could not be allowed to continue.

Charles Keyes, the head of the National Education Association's (NEA) Department of Manual Training, maintained that "ignorant labor," when motivated by a demagogue, is the most dangerous force in the modern world. No despot, Keyes concluded, is more unreasonable than the "tyranny of illiterate labor." With such perspectives guiding the mainstream of the movement, manual training advocates worked to instill industrial values, concurrently attempting to fill the void left by industrialization's subversion of skilled work and craftsmanship. Maybe, they hoped, knowledge of the use of various tools would help alleviate the alienation of industrial deskilling. When labor ignorance and alienation were coupled with immigration from Southern and Eastern Europe, manual education advocates promoted their curriculum with a sense of urgency. Educational leader and psychologist G. Stanley Hall labeled these late nineteenth-century immigrants "the great army of incapables" and demanded in unison with other reformers that such inferiors needed manual training. Without such a curriculum and with the passage of child labor laws, many of these "lower caliber young immigrants," reformers feared, would end up on the street.

In the attempt to understand the motives of the manual training advocates, it is important to rank the fear of social conflict as a very important factor. Nonetheless, the concerns of the reformers were very complex, like most human matters. Many of the advocates, even those who proclaimed their ethnocentric view of the immigrants and called for manual education for social control of the "rabble," hoped to improve the lives of the workers. From their middle-class vantage point, proponents of manual training wanted to "culturally enrich" workers' lives and grant them greater control over their work lives. Indeed, many of the reformers associated with manual training were leaders in the anti-child-labor movement. They thus promoted manual labor as an alternative to the degradation of child labor. That curriculum would draw upon the student's nonacademic interests, pulling the child little by little into intellectual study. Despite all the promise, manual training did not endure. Like its future vocational educational progeny, it became associated in the public mind with education for social deviants. Advocates of efficiency in education opposed manual training because it did not go far enough. David Snedden, commissioner of education for Massachusetts and well-known advocate of educational efficiency, maintained that manual training was liberal education in disguise. In his opinion, such training rarely resulted in any identifiable form of "vocational efficiency." That pronouncement was the death knell for manual training (Wilms, 1979; Feffer, 1993; Kliebard, 1987).

With the support of the industrial and business leaders, efficiency proponents turned the calls for a balanced curriculum of manual and liberal academic education into nothing more than empty rhetoric. By the turn of the twentieth century, educators were ready for vocational education and its promotion of specific skill training. The nation needed a corps of skilled industrial workers with "good attitudes." Quickly, separate vocational schools were constructed for lower-class immigrant youth. It was the perceived practical economic payoff of specific skills training that fanned the flames of its support (Oakes, 1985, pp. 32–33). In only a few years, the claims put forward for manual training and the Slöyd seemed quaintly romantic and passé. The new era of scientific management in education had arrived with the new century.

Industrial Education for African Americans

Vocational education students cannot study the origins of their field without examining the history of African American education in the late nineteenth and early twentieth centuries. Three important understandings for vocational educators emerge from this analysis: (1) consciousness of the way traditional historical accounts and other research in the field unwittingly perpetuate ways of seeing that distort our understanding of the impact of vocational education, (2) insight into the forms of institutional racism that are concealed in the structures and goals of vocational education, and (3) awareness of the social, economic, and political forces that shape vocational education. Let us begin with an analysis of the first understanding.

Contemporary historical scholarship has attempted to reveal the distortions and half-truths that have evolved over the last fifty years into the standard history of African American education. The mainstream story goes something like this: Benevolent Northern philanthropists, typically corporate and industrial magnates, were morally outraged by the vile racism foisted on Southern blacks by Southern whites. In response, the philanthropists sought to help blacks by supporting black public education. Far more realistic and pragmatic than the Radical Republicans of the Reconstruction era, these philanthropists entered into an alliance with the Southern upper class to protect blacks from lower-class white racism. Finding themselves overwhelmed by the power of the Southern white supremacy movement, the benevolent corporate leaders were diverted from their original goals of challenging racism by good will, political skill, and hard work. Thus, they did what they had to do and entered into a compromise with the white supremacists to salvage what they could for the former slaves.

The only thing the philanthropists could save for black students was public schooling—the institution that would serve as the last hope for black social progress. The key feature of this "great compromise" was that black public education would be modeled on the Hampton-Tuskegee style of industrial education. By adopting Samuel C. Armstrong and Booker T. Washington's industrial education model, the corporate magnates saved black education from total destruction. By advocating industrial education, the philanthropists gained the support of white supremacists for universal public schooling for black students. The standard portrayal concludes with a partial but important victory: The African Americans won the right to a public schooling characterized by industrial education. Such an interpretation is highly simplistic and reductionistic, as it fails to account for power relations, economic motivation, and the key players' views of educational purpose. More specifically, what separated the different sides of the argument was their conflicting views of the relationship between schooling and the economy. Educational historians have often missed this point, because they have ignored the importance of how one sees this relationship.

Like the efficiency educators' view of the role of schooling as the inculcation of industrial values for immigrants and the poor, the philanthropists and their supporters saw industrial education for African Americans as an important aspect of the larger attempt to build an industrial economy. Corporate leaders pushing black schooling in the South were not unlike corporate leaders in many industrial cities of the era; they held a social vision grounded on order and efficiency that viewed schooling as a means of training the lower classes to be better citizens and better workers. Black education in this context becomes not the magnanimous effort to transform the social position of an oppressed people but simply a small part of a larger effort to create a profitable and more efficient society. Industrial education for African Americans was a new and sophisticated approach to the older goals of socialization and control of potentially dangerous social groups.

The fear of black violence against whites in the tradition of Nat Turner's rampage in Virginia in that fateful August of 1831 never was far from white Southern consciousness. As the supporters of the experiment in industrial education pleaded their case, they collided head on with wealthy Southern whites whose wealth and power was based on the perpetuation of a large class of illiterate and subjugated black agricultural workers. The white aristocracy was hostile to the Northern philanthropists' argument for the value of black industrial education as a means to ensure social order and economic development. The world of the wealthy Southern planters was a preindustrial (premodernist) cosmos where social control was achieved by simple coercion. From their position in the web of reality, the Southern aristocrats saw no need for the trouble and expense of industrial education. From their vantage point, such schooling would do little more than inflate the social, political, and economic aspirations of black workers. Indeed, it would subvert the traditional social relations they had enjoyed with their black servants and field hands.

A more specific analysis of the nature, assumptions, and goals of the Hampton-Tuskegee model of industrial education is in order. In 1867, Samuel C. Armstrong founded a manual training school for blacks and Native Americans at Hampton, Virginia. Armstrong's disciple, Booker T. Washington, opened a similar institution in 1881 at Tuskegee. Both schools touted manual labor as a key to disciplining the mind and the will of children of "ignorance, shiftlessness, and moral weakness." Armstrong, the superintendent of the post–Civil War Freedman's Bureau, built his industrial education curriculum for blacks upon his assumption of black racial inferiority. Armstrong argued that black children could acquire knowledge with about the same facility as white children; but, he contended, black students do not have the mental facility to assimilate and digest such knowledge. Black children mature more quickly than whites, Armstrong observed, but fail to keep up with white children's "mental strength." Thus, one of the main leaders of the industrial education movement saw the curriculum as special education for "inferior Blacks" (Kliebard, 1987; Bullock, 1967; Anderson, 1988).

Although Booker T. Washington did not hold Armstrong's racial views, he did agree with Armstrong's vision of industrial education for African Americans. Washington's educational philosophy was formed during his student experience at Armstrong's Hampton Institute, where he came to see the purpose of black education as adjustment of ex-slaves to a subordinate position in Southern society. When Washington employed the term "industrial education," he was referring to the inculcation of good work habits and industrial values. Rejecting the academic purposes of black education, Washington established Tuskegee Institute in Alabama in 1881. If students came from farm backgrounds, Washington wanted to make them better farmers. If students knew something about mechanics, Washington's curriculum was designed to make them better mechanics. Hard work would "civilize" the freed slaves and their children. No attempt to cultivate political understandings or lessons designed to encourage thinking were necessary for Washington's vision of black education. Hard work would instill the right moral habits—and that was enough.

It is not hard to understand how attractive Armstrong and Washington's brand of vocational education appeared to Northern corporate leaders. Steel king and philanthropist Andrew Carnegie bestowed the first major endowment on Tuskegee, proclaiming that the U.S. economy demanded black industrial education. Educational historian Joel Spring (1994) has concluded that industrialists welcomed the idea of racially segregated industrial education for its promise of cheap labor and antiunion sentiments. As railroad magnate and Tuskegee supporter William H. Baldwin Jr. maintained, if the South was to prosper economically and compete internationally, it would have to repudiate the high wages demanded by labor unions and rely on cheap black labor. So strong was the corporate support for the Hampton-Tuskegee model that philanthropists refused to support black education that veered even slightly away from Armstrong and Washington's prototype (Bullock, 1967).

For example, Richard R. Wright Sr., a well-respected black educator was the president of Savannah State, an institution that offered both industrial and academic education. A skilled politician, President Wright was able to convince the all-white Georgia Board of Commissioners to approve the industrial-academic curriculum. The corporate philanthropists, however, would have no part of such a course of study. The mere trace of academic learning caused the industrialists to close their wallets and withdraw support of any type. Liberal whites were generally happy to support black schooling as long as their investment increased the return on their capital investments or such education did not challenge the assumption of black second-class citizenship. Whites of the day often remarked that they wanted to help blacks become "better cooks, better servants, better washerwomen, better workmen in the field and farm and shop." As long as this was understood, many white people were willing to support black industrial education (Anderson, 1988; Margo, 1990). William H. Baldwin Jr. advised Africans in 1899 to lower their expectations and "face the music, avoid social questions; leave politics alone; continue to be patient; live moral lives; live simply, learn to work and work intelligently . . . learn that it is a mistake to be educated out of your environment" (Bullock, 1967, p. 102).

Within the black community, there was strong disagreement with the Washington-Armstrong model for black education. Many of us may be familiar with the best-known expression of the conflict—the confrontation between Booker T. Washington and W.E.B. DuBois (Jennings, 1991). Of course, Washington maintained it was better for black people to acquiesce in racial segregation in the short run, in the meantime learning manual arts and industrial skills to gradually improve their economic situation. DuBois rejected Washington's plan, arguing that industrial education would simply perpetuate black second-class status. Industrial education, DuBois argued, must not place too much emphasis on the "practical" character of work. The best education is more than practical, he wrote, as it attempts to address not merely the present but a possible world not yet realized. Education, DuBois concluded, must always be driven by larger ideals, never forgetting that it concerns souls, not dollars. Within the black community DuBois won the debate, for in the black schools of the era, the Hampton-Tuskegee model was not exceptionally popular. Most black educators understandably thought that it made little sense for black students to spend their time studying to become janitors, porters, chauffeurs, cooks, and laundry women. From the perspective of most black people, industrial education was something the white community devised to keep them in their "place." Thus, it is not hard to understand the institutional racism and the social, economic, and political forces concealed within the industrial curriculum for African Americans (Margo, 1990; Kliebard, 1987; Anderson, 1988).

Expanding Secondary Schooling and the Quest for Social Order and Americanization

Vocational education would become a permanent feature of American education as the push for high schools merged with the call for agricultural and industrial training in the late nineteenth century. The confluence of the movements produced a separate vocational track in American high schools for future industrial and agricultural workers (Raizen, 1989). Leaders of the budding vocational movement argued that the days of the self-sufficient communities of rural preindustrial America were over. In that agrarian period, an individual's life and vocational education were naturally integrated into the everyday life of the family. With the advent of industrialization and its factory system, the world changed—in that work and life became increasingly separate activities. The power of the family to grant children skill training and socialization was permanently undermined. Even in the 1990s, New Right family values advocates still attempt to restore the family to what they perceive to be its preindustrial status. Industrial leaders of the 1890s understood the social dynamics of what was happening and worked to ordain the school as the agent of socialization for new generations of workers (Jacobs and Phillips, 1979).

The role of schools changed so dramatically around the turn of the century that nearly one hundred years later most Americans—and indeed many educators—still do not appreciate the implications of the change. Students of vocational education cannot lose sight of the understanding that the birth of their field was one part of a larger historical project. During the Progressive Era of the late nineteenth and early twentieth centuries, a bold new attempt to impose disciplinary order on individuals and social life was initiated. A number of *administrative* fields emerged at this time; administrative law, policy "science," social work, public administration, and rational planning all centered attention on questions of technique and procedure in the larger effort to make the lives of individuals, especially the poor and non-Anglo, conform to an upper-middle-class Anglo-Saxon norm (Ferguson, 1984). Such development returns us to the concept of hegemony discussed in Part 1. With the development of vocational education and the other disciplines of administration and social regulation, America entered into a transitional period during which domination by direct coercion was giving way to domination by the winning of the consent of the subordinate class. Having just passed through the violent labor wars of the 1880s and 1890s, American leaders were beginning to understand the benefits to be derived from institutions like vocational education and their inculcation of values aligned with dominant interests. When vocational students learned industrial values such as respect for hard work, submission to authority, the ability to follow orders, and political passivity, the interests of the dominant class were well served (McLaren, 1994).

Attracted by the promise of vocational education to serve their interests, several business groups rushed to sponsor and direct the Industrial Education movement of the early 1900s. The work of the powerful National Association of Manufacturers (NAM) is a case study in the dynamics of hegemony. The NAM's crusade for vocational education, for example, attempted to produce a form of vocational study that would hurt most of the groups that supported it. The industrial needs that the leaders of the NAM wanted vocational educators to address were *not* the needs of students and workers; rather, they were the needs of industry. The increase in individual production efficiency without a corresponding increase in worker pay was not in the best interest of working Americans (DeYoung, 1989). Infusing "good attitudes" into the minds of workers without developing an understanding of economic justice was not in the best interest of working Americans. Promoting a philosophy of Social Darwinism, with its acceptance of the survival of the fittest, was not in the best interest of working Americans. Cultivating a dehumanizing view of workers as "human capital" was not in the best interest of working Americans (Wirth, 1983).

In the shadow of the labor wars of the preceding years, proponents of vocational education targeted "social unity" as a focus of the vocational curriculum. Unity became a euphemism in the public conversation about education for labor passivity, for worker submission to management demands. Without the assurance that vocational schooling would inculcate an acceptance of concepts such as unity, social and political leaders could never have cultivated the public support necessary for the dramatic expansion of public schooling in the decades surrounding the turn of the century. Between 1890 and 1920, schools opened at a rate of over one a day; student enrollment increased by 812 percent, whereas the national population increased by 68 percent; and the percentage of youth enrolled in high school shot from 4 percent in 1890 to 28 percent in 1920. During this era, school came to be seen for the first time as the place where students were prepared for adult work roles. If corporate leaders and the majority of Americans had not seen the influx of 23 million immigrants as a national emergency, such a dramatic increase in school support in general and vocational education in particular could never have taken place.

The Northern European ethnocentrism of America in the decades surrounding the turn of the twentieth century cannot be overemphasized in
the attempt to portray the origins of vocational education. The vast majority
of the 23 million newcomers in this era were Eastern and Southern Europeans—Italians, Jews, Poles, and Slavs. The prevailing opinion of the era
was that these immigrants lacked the moral and social qualities of Western
and Northern Europeans. Concentrating their settlement in the cities of the
industrial Northeast and Midwest, these new immigrants often outnum-
bered other ethnic groups. Corporate leaders, social reformers, and educators often failed to understand the differences between Jewish, Italian, Pol-
ish, or Slavic immigrants. Lumping them into the generic category of
"foreigners," leaders pushed for a single moral standard based on Anglo,
middle-class values and mores. Writing in 1909, Ellwood P. Cubberley, the
U.S. commissioner of education and an educational scholar, succinctly expressed the dominant culture's position on the role of education:

> These southern and eastern Europeans are of a very different type from the
> north Europeans who preceded them. Illiterate, docile, lacking in self-reliance
> and initiative, and not possessing the Anglo-Teutonic conceptions of law, or-
> der, and government, their coming has served to dilute tremendously our na-
> tional stock, and to corrupt our civic life ... Our task is to break up these
> groups or settlements, to assimilate and amalgamate these people as a part of
> our American race, and to implant in their children, so far as can be done, the
> Anglo-Saxon conception of righteousness, law and order, and popular govern-
> ment, and to awaken in them a reverence for our democratic institutions, and
> for those things in our national life which we as a people hold to be of abiding
> worth. (Edson, 1979, p. 140)

Reformers like Cubberley were first and foremost modernists. They could
only see schooling and work as components of a rational and scientific cosmos. From their modernist efficiency vantage point, the cultural differences
of the Southern and Eastern Europeans were annoying distractions in the
task of implementing vocational education, insuring workplace unity, and
promoting American economic progress. Children of the immigrants, therefore, were typically discouraged from pursuing high-status, high-paying vocations. Vocational bureaus and schools began to provide career counseling
for students. Drawing upon the new scientific aptitude tests of the era, vocational guidance counselors made the children of the poor and the immigrants believe they had been "scientifically" designated for low-status work.
When Christianity was combined with modernist science, new dimensions
of oppression were heaped on the immigrants and their children. Operating
from a Protestant view of the world, replete with its famous work ethic,
Christian Americanizers argued that the inculcation of industrial values was
a spiritual process that enlightened the immigrant to Anglo-Saxon ideals. If

immigrants and their children turned out to be "incorrigible," then they should be excluded from America. Incorrigibility was often defined as the "subversive" tendency to join labor unions—an activity sometimes described as both anti-Christian and anti-American (Violas, 1978; Edson, 1979).

As the "cult of Anglo-Saxonism" swept through the American landscape, social and educational reforms with an ethnocentric edge gained increasing support. One of the more important ideas to emerge in this respect involved the alleged incompatibility of the "racial traits" of Southern and Eastern European immigrants with the tenets of democracy. Stanford University president David Starr Jordan proclaimed that national survival itself depends on the preservation of Anglo-Saxon values. Ellwood P. Cubberley agreed, arguing that the immigrants threatened "democratic education" and that it was no longer possible to teach that all are equal and that all have an equal voice in the democratic community. An education based on these premises was not appropriate for the exploding numbers of foreign students pouring into the schools of the era. Such considerations added fuel to the argument for extending a separate track for vocational education. When the vocational curriculum and its concern for the inculcation of industrial values was connected with the emerging psychology of behaviorism, a new era of social regulation had dawned. Social psychologists proclaimed their ability to mold the attitudes and behaviors of their clients, grounding such claims on Edward L. Thorndike's success in using positive and negative reinforcement to determine future behavior. From Thorndike's behaviorism, school leaders learned that other techniques of shaping human behavior were more effective than the appeal to the intellect.

Children were taught "correct" responses to stimuli that educational and corporate leaders thought were common in the everyday world of work. In this way, educational reformers hoped to construct particular personality types that conformed to managerial goals and values of political passivity and acquiescence. Vocational classrooms thus copied the actual physical appearance of the factory workplace. Critics of vocational education who claimed that vocational courses failed to teach the "correct skills" because of outdated technology and equipment failed to understand the purposes of early vocational education: These programs were not necessarily designed to cultivate specific skills to be used in the factory. Such skills could be quickly learned by new employees when they first entered the workplace. The key dimension of the industrial curriculum was the inculcation of industrial values; Paul Violas has called it "industrial intelligence." Such "intelligence" attempted to produce a consciousness that induced workers to passively accept the degradations of the industrial workplace as the natural experience of labor. No worker resistance or labor union could change this reality, workers were told, for it was preordained (Violas, 1978).

Missing the Point: Traditional Interpretations and the Quest for Order

Traditional historical interpretations of the late-nineteenth and early-twentieth-century vocational education movement still help shape the consciousness of vocational educators. Since all political perspectives are based upon particular interpretations of the past, the way we perceive the origins and development of vocational education is very important. Traditional histories of vocational education paint a very different picture from the one presented here. The story is given as follows: The rapid growth of industry in the late nineteenth century was creating a class system in the United States. The jobs people obtained were increasingly determined by the skills they had developed. Workers from the least-advantaged backgrounds were the most unlikely to gain education and skill training. Early vocational educators sought to confront this social injustice by providing these needy people with job skills for industrial work. By providing a wide range of vocational programs, vocational educators could help bring about more equality of opportunity. Drawing upon the best science of the day, vocational educators would analyze the various trades by breaking them down into their smallest components. Vocational students would then systematically master each of these components. At this point, the traditional story concludes, vocational counselors would help guide students to the right position for them. In the process, these well-trained students would be led away from dead-end jobs (Wilms, 1979).

Obviously, the revisionist interpretation offered in this book agrees with the traditional story in its depiction of industrialization as the creator of a class system. But that is where the similarities end. The revisionist interpretation rejects the notion that jobs were determined by the skills workers possessed. No matter how talented particular immigrants, women, or African Americans might have been in the late nineteenth century, their chances of obtaining good jobs were slim. In addition, owners of factories with low-skill forms of work often felt that worker skill was virtually irrelevant—because owners were more interested in worker attitude. Although there is no doubt that many of the early advocates of vocational education were genuinely concerned about the exclusion of economically poor boys and girls from school and a chance for mobility, it is also the case that many of the most important supporters of vocational education championed it for their own personal advantage. A basic difference between the two historical interpretations involves the concept that education is not always a source of personal empowerment and edification; the revisionist view asserts that in many ways, early vocational education actually exacerbated class divisions and inequality of opportunity. Instead of enhancing an individual's personal empowerment, it often worked to resign the person to deskilled, low-paid, and dehumanizing work.

As for the traditional story's celebration of science and its tendency to break jobs down into their smallest components for the purpose of more efficient learning, the revisionist interpretation refers to this as the hyperrationalization of modernism. In line with the critique of modernism and positivism in Part 1, the revisionist view argues that such a process undermines our ability to grasp the meaning and purpose of a job, as it fragments it into meaningless bits and pieces. As it fragments, it also decontextualizes, again stripping purpose and meaning from the learning exercise. The same mentality that produces this scientistic fragmentation in teaching a skill perceives no problem with industrialization's tendency to deskill workers in the attempt to increase efficiency and productivity. Viewed as a panacea in the first decades of the twentieth century, vocational education continues in the traditional historical interpretation to be viewed as the innovation that meets everybody's needs (Raizen, 1989; Pincus, 1980; Grubb, 1978).

Vocational education was everything to everybody—a breath mint and a candy mint. For business leaders, vocational education promised to create the values and attitudes toward work that would serve their interests. Education leaders found in vocational education a way to establish the legitimacy of schooling that had been attacked for its disjuncture with changing social and economic conditions. Vocational education also provided educators with a way to address both the dropout problem and the sea of immigrants entering the schools. Some democratic progressives sincerely believed that industrial education would provide all students with equality of opportunity. Such education would also, they thought, help working people gain control over their work lives by enabling them to become economically self-sufficient. Some democratic progressives argued that a vocationally educated workforce would become so skilled that managers would have to depend on their workers. Such a shift in power relations, advocates concluded, would force employers to include employees in the important workplace decisions. At the same time that these proponents of vocational education argued for worker empowerment, efficiency experts and their educational colleagues argued that vocational education would lead to better employer control of workers (Wilms, 1979; Pincus, 1980).

It was hard for many vocational educational advocates to understand the ways their programs could be used to deny economic opportunity and to perpetuate inequality—and indeed, it is still hard for them to understand. Analysis of the early vocational education programs, however, reveals one consistent feature: No matter how dangerous, deskilled, and degrading industrial work might have been, vocational education attempted to adjust students to it without criticism or question. The goals of those groups that supported vocational education concerned the effort to "regulate" large numbers of poor people in order to guarantee their stable and predictable behavior (Ferguson, 1984). The effect of the labor conflict of the 1880s and 1890s cannot be overstated: Many middle- and upper-class Americans at the end of the nineteenth century did not feel that they could risk inaction. They therefore sought to quietly and unobtrusively provide industrial values to poor people, immigrants, and African Americans. They felt the covert nature of their operations was necessary because overt signs of control or manipulation would possibly trigger dangerous outbursts of rebellion. Understanding such actions becomes extremely difficult when we add the fact that many of the vocational educators operated under the genuine humanitarian desire to improve the horrendous working conditions of the era. The work of the reformers and vocational educators of the time was always marked by a high degree of ambiguity (Feffer, 1993).

Traditional analysts have consistently missed this ambiguity, this effort of the industrial leaders to try to discipline the workforce. Knowledge gained in one subject area was appropriated by the powerful to consolidate control in an administrative domain. For example, the study of psychology in the early twentieth century produced knowledge that helped control workers in the workplace (Ferguson, 1984). The birth of industrial psychology merged psychology with the science of management, pushing managerial authority to new levels. It is hardly surprising that prisons, factories, and schools resemble one another, as all of them work to "process" individuals, to fit them to the larger needs of the culture. In the process of fitting students to the demands of factory and business managers, throughout its history vocational education has often failed to teach students about the nature of the world in general and the economy in particular. Vocational education, in both its early and its later forms, too often threatens the forms of knowing that poor people need to change the workplace and its inegalitarian structure. For example, an appreciation of working-class solidarity is an extremely important aspect of the infrastructure necessary for progressive change in the workplace. Early supporters of vocational education purposely undermined such identification, consciously attempting to subvert the threat that organized labor posed to corporate and business management (McLaren et al., 1995).

It is unfortunate but necessary to conclude that the early manifestations of vocational education did not encourage independence and creativity in America's youth. Dissenting voices, however, could still be heard. Numerous democratic reformers called for a vocational education that provided students with solid work experience that engendered critical and independent thinking (Roditi, 1992). In 1916, John Dewey clearly delineated the problems with mainstream vocational education: It perpetuates the weakest aspects of the industrialized economy, thus becoming an instrument in the construction of "the feudal dogma of social predestination." Dewey felt we must get beyond such social pathology and contended that a democratic vocational education would recognize and teach "the full intellectual and social meaning of a vocation." Such an attempt would include instruction in the historic background of present conditions; training in science to give intelligence and initiative in dealing with material and agencies of production; and study of economics, civics, and politics, to bring the future worker into touch with the problems of the day and the various methods proposed for its improvement. Above all, it would train power of readaptation to changing conditions so that future workers would not become blindly subject to a fate imposed upon them. (Dewey, 1916, pp. 318–319)

Dewey's ideas for vocational education are as powerful and visionary at the end of the twentieth century as they were at its beginning. Dewey accurately predicted that there would be great opposition to such a visionary purpose for vocational education, which would come from two sources: (1) the "inertia" of the extant traditions of schooling, and (2) most important, from the corporate and business leaders who command the industrial machinery and understand that such a democratic vocational education would undermine their ability to manipulate others to their own ends.

6 The Progressive Debate, the Victory of Vocationalism, and the Institutionalization of Schooling for Work

Only in the past thirty years has American historical scholarship begun to question the social impact of various forms of education and schooling. For example, prior to the 1960s, Progressive Education, the most dramatic reform movement in American educational history, was seen as a liberal set of school reforms designed to change the way American children were taught. Most scholars described Progressivism as a response to the urbanization, industrialization, and immigration of the late nineteenth and early twentieth centuries. Based on a rejection of old psychological theories and the traditional, classical curriculum with its tendency for rote memorization, Progressive Education embraced forms of teaching that focused on student interests and their relationship to the larger culture. Educational historian Herbert Kliebard (1987) has written that the term "progressive education" was "not only vacuous, but mischievous" (p. xi). Nothing existed that deserved a single name; instead, several educational reform movements evolved in the early twentieth century, each with a different social vision and set of goals. To understand the Progressive Education movement, we must be aware of what particular form of progressive education we are observing. To understand vocational education, we must grasp its relationship to the various strands of the movement.

The Scientifically Managed Workplace Versus the Dignity of Labor

The importance of the ways industrialization changed work in America cannot be overemphasized in the effort to understand the history of vocational education. As scientific managers came to control the production process, workers found themselves saddled with repetitive, monotonous tasks. Bad work marked by the destruction of creativity, self-expression, and pride in the finished product became the order of the day. Industrial leaders understood the potential social effects of such realities as they watched union membership grow, labor strikes increase, and the appeal of Socialist political candidates expand. Old adages about the moral benefits of work began to lose their meaning, as industrial labor demeaned the concept of "vocation." Hard work and a desire to succeed counted for little in a deskilled factory where a man in his fifties was likely to earn the same low hourly wage he had made in his twenties (Edson, 1979).

Educators were baffled and confused by one of the greatest contradictions of human history: The assumption that work is one of the most noble expressions of human dignity collides head-on with the stark reality of the degraded and deskilled work emerging from the industrialized and scientifically managed workplace (Kliebard, 1990). Vocational education proponents found themselves ensnared in the net of this conflict, as they concerned themselves with the preparation of students for working-class jobs rather than professional and managerial jobs (Grubb, 1978). The existence of dehumanized work and the traditional conception of what work ought to be came into direct conflict on the social, political, and pedagogical landscape of vocational education. Indeed, this conflict was part of a larger American contradiction between the democratic notion of civic equality and the industrial reality of economic inequality (Brosio, 1994). The emergence of vocational education and the debates about the social and political role of education during the Progressive Era *cannot* be understood outside of these conflicts and contradictions.

Social and educational leaders understood that negative consequences could result from these unresolved conflicts and contradictions. Without some type of work education to address the mindless jobs created by industrialization, educational leaders feared that factory workers would embrace "destructive and chaotic ideas." Without some form of vocational education, reformers proclaimed, workers would become "insurrectionists," maybe even "perverts or criminals." Given such anxiety, numerous movements arose in the 1890s and early 1900s to restore dignity to work and to provide a tight lid to cover the cauldron of boiling labor anger (Feffer, 1993). The handicraft movement of the era sought to resurrect an old form of craft labor in the attempt to restore a sense of job satisfaction to workers. Other reformers, of course, sought to use the schools in the effort to confront the degradation of labor. Jane Addams and John Dewey sought to increase workers' understanding of the social context in which their work took place. Jane Addams provided an example of such an industrial education:

> If a child goes into a sewing factory with a knowledge of the work she is doing in relation to the finished product; if she is informed concerning the material

she is manipulating and processes to which she is subjected; if she understands the design she is elaborating in its historic relation to art and decoration, her daily life is lifted from drudgery to one of self-conscious activity, and her pleasure and intelligence is registered in her product. (Kliebard, 1990, p. 19)

As the movement for vocational education progressed, however, concerns about the dignity of labor became less significant in the public conversation on educational reform. The confusion caused by the conflict between American work values and the realities of the industrial workplace was submerged in the discourse of vocational education (Edson, 1979). Industrial leaders were able to redirect the discussion away from the question of school purpose: Should schools adapt workers to the industrial workplace, or should they help workers understand the social dynamics of their work in the hope of eventually reforming the workplace? Questions such as those concerning the status of workers in industrial jobs in relation to professional workers were suppressed by efficiency reformers and their corporate supporters. To attempt to understand progressive education and its relationship to vocational education outside the context of the contradictions of industrialization and the power of business and industry is to distort the past and sabotage the memory of the vocational education profession (Wilms, 1979). The next step in this analysis is thus to examine the revealing debate for the soul of progressive education—a debate that would help shape the entire history of vocational education.

The Emergence of Conflicting Factions of Progressive Educators

Those who were to coalesce at the turn of the century around the term "progressive education" agreed that traditional education was beset with problems: (1) the classical curriculum was not motivating students; (2) schools were plagued by high dropout rates; (3) juvenile delinquency and illiteracy were growing among urban young people; (4) waste and inefficiency undermined the management of schools; and (5) the needs of a modern industrialized society had rendered the traditional curriculum irrelevant (Tozer, Violas, and Senese, 1993). Progressives agreed that schools needed to be changed, but the direction of such change was a matter of disagreement. By 1905, many self-described Progressives were speaking of social control; others were talking about economic justice, human opportunities, and restructured democracy. Some Progressives argued that schools should pursue the values and techniques of scientific management and engineering, whereas others spoke of freed intelligence and social democracy as moral values on which the reform of schools and workplaces would be based. Schools serve society, some maintained, by increasing social and economic efficiency, but others saw social service as inseparable from the enhancement of the personal and social growth of individuals (Wirth, 1983; Simon, Dippo, and Schenke, 1991).

Although these competing themes were swirling in the cultural whirlpool of the turn of the century, progressive education could be distinguished from traditional educational forms. Steven E. Tozer, Paul C. Violas, and Guy Senese (1993) have delineated four distinguishing features of Progressive Education; their interpretation by the competing Progressive factions varied widely. Progressive Education assumed that (1) a dynamic curriculum grounded on interests and needs of students should replace the traditional curriculum; (2) school learning should be based on student activities rather than on rote memorization; (3) the purposes of schooling should take social conditions into account; and (4) the solution of social problems is a primary aim of schooling.

All Progressives claimed adherence to these assumptions, but the nature of the dynamic curriculum grounded on interests and needs of students, the forms of student activities, the specific social conditions to be taken into account, and the specific social problems to be solved were all hotly contested. Although there are many levels of division within progressive education, the two most fundamental to our analysis are the Business Efficiency faction and the Democratic Deweyan faction. As might be presumed, the Business Efficiency Progressives and the Democratic Deweyan Progressives held very different views of educational purpose in general and vocational educational purpose in particular. On the one hand, the Democratic Deweyan Progressives sanctified the effort to promote equality of opportunity for students from diverse social backgrounds; the Business Efficiency Progressives, on the other hand, viewed education as a sorting mechanism that prepared students for their particular niche in the labor market. The tension between these two factions was always emotional and often strident throughout the history of progressive education (Grubb, 1978). Even after the "death" of progressive education in the 1950s, these factional viewpoints could still be detected in the conversation about the purpose of vocational education.

The convenient division of Progressive educators into two discrete factions runs the risk of stereotyping and oversimplification. Rarely did Progressives fit neatly into one camp or another. Much of the educational practice that operated under the flag of progressivism found elements from both perspectives in its pedagogy. Even John Dewey, who lent his name to the Democratic Progressives, cannot be viewed as a "pure" proponent of that particular perspective. Often writing in terms that would be acceptable to liberal businesspeople, Dewey qualified his calls for economic justice and industrial democracy. Frequently shying away from a direct challenge to workplace hierarchy, Dewey walked a political and pedagogical tightrope. Thus, accepting some form of vocational sorting, Dewey sometimes straddled the fence separating the two factions (Feffer, 1993). It is appropriate in this regard to analyze the two wings of the Progressive Education movement and their connections to early-twentieth-century vocational education.

The Business Efficiency Progressive Educators

Business and industrial leaders, scientific managers, and educational efficiency advocates all saw schooling as a key component in the construction of an expert-controlled society. Efficient schools would teach students to suppress their own intuitions and submit to the authority of experts who produced validated knowledge. The personal authority of students and workers was undermined by the positivist experts and their unambiguous pronouncements on a variety of subjects. A set of social dynamics was put in motion that let families know that only scientific experts could determine their functionality. Parents began to lose authority to experts in state-supported institutions that dispensed validated knowledge about child rearing. Individuals were conditioned to depend upon organizations, citizens upon the state, workers upon managers, and the poor upon the "helping professions." The gears were set in motion for the development of a professional oligarchy of doctors, psychiatrists, welfare workers, civil servants, guidance and career counselors, and social science researchers, all of whom provided expert assistance for the efficient regulation of the population (Kincheloe, 1991; Lasch, 1979).

Any groups or individuals that resisted this regulation had to be disciplined and controlled. The threat posed by immigrant workers and their labor organizations demanded an immediate response from the experts. The Business and Efficiency Progressives proclaimed that strikes were anti-American and motivated by foreign influences. Efficiency advocates called upon teachers to help put down labor agitation and its attack on the American social order (DeYoung, 1989). Business and industrial leaders and their Efficiency Progressive supporters did not hide their efforts to use vocational education to undermine union apprentice programs. Efficiency Progressives maintained that industrial managers should control the teaching of job skills and work values, a stance that elicited cries of approval from high-ranking managers from the Carnegie Foundation, American Telephone and Telegraph (AT&T), and National City Bank. The National Association of Manufacturers agreed, issuing a statement in 1906 declaring that vocational training must be "protected from the withering blight of organized labor" (Pincus, 1980).

NAM, AT&T, and the other corporate interests not only wanted labor removed from work training but wanted school vocational instruction to reflect the efficiency message of Frederick W. Taylor. Efficiency Progressives David Snedden and Charles Prosser were the answer to the industrialists' prayers. Snedden used his position as commissioner of education in Massachusetts to promote vocational education as a part of a larger curriculum of social efficiency. While he was commissioner, Snedden appointed his former student Charles Prosser as deputy commissioner for vocational education. Beginning in this position, Prosser became the key player in the development of vocational education in the United States. Both men held fast to the Social Darwinism of Herbert Spencer and its belief that only the fittest survive; that is, only superior people gain wealth and power. It is easy to understand how such a position won Snedden and Prosser popularity points with American industrial leaders (Kliebard, 1987).

Accepting the adage that what was good for business was good for America, Snedden and Prosser saw their goal as the restructuring of American education to meet the needs of industry. In order to accomplish this task, they believed, education must be made more practical and efficient (Sherman, 1974). Using the gospels of Taylor and Spencer, Snedden and Prosser brought tracking, scientific management, teacher ratings, cost accounting, and teacher accountability to the schools. An efficient, scientifically managed education would provide a trained force of workers, programmed to function safely and effectively. Efficiency Progressives were captivated by plans detailing how schools would be run as businesses. Using the industrial job as a prototype, the business-modeled school would serve as a custodial agent by removing dangerous youth from the streets and adapting them to commercial interests. As efficiency improved, Snedden and Prosser maintained that the size of the economic pie would be increased. In this way, the Efficiency Progressives predicted that all citizens, rich and poor, would profit (Wirth, 1983; Beck, 1991).

Every aspect of school and society was to be subjected to reformulation by the efficiency proponents. Even training for gender roles could be improved upon, as was evidenced by many of the Progressive programs to turn out more efficient and effective young women. Reflecting prevailing views of the social role of women, homemaking education curricula sprang up across the country. Cooking, sewing, millinery, and crocheting classes for girls were common, as were carpentry, repairing, shoe-repairing, and tailoring classes for boys. Except for gender-integrated classes in cooking, all courses were strictly segregated. Girls must learn to do the "drudgery of housework more efficiently," educators argued, seeing women as homemakers first and foremost. Because of such attitudes, Business Efficiency Progressives saw little need in the quest for efficiency to grant girls access to traditional vocational programs. The primary function of an efficient curriculum for girls was to make them more "womanly" (Biklen, 1978; Tozer, Violas, and Senese, 1993).

Snedden and Prosser were not very tolerant of those who disagreed with their vision of progressive school reform. They were especially stung by

John Dewey's articulation of disagreement, charging him with betrayal of the progressive goal of reforming the sterile and bookish education that passed for traditional schooling. Snedden and Prosser thought Dewey was a romantic impracticalist who did not understand the need for vocational education to produce specific skills that enable the student to perform a valuable service (Simon, Dippo, and Schenke, 1991). Dewey was seen as a naive intellectual, blind to the efficiency proponents' call to build an orderly society through a disciplined workforce.

The Democratic Deweyan Progressive Educators

To understand the Democratic Deweyan Progressive educators one must appreciate the fact that John Dewey and many of his fellow political Progressives believed the American economy had failed to develop in the manner predicted by Adam Smith (Bellah et al., 1991). The socioeconomic class divisions produced by the industrialized economy in the last decades of the nineteenth century convinced Democratic Progressives that serious action was needed. The issues that separated Dewey from Prosser and Snedden were political in that they involved democratic questions of equality, community, and power sharing. For example, Dewey's lack of faith in the free economy forced him to reject a vocational education that simply adapted students to a particular niche in the organization. Dewey contended that what Snedden's program did in its separation of vocational and academic education was to maintain the inequalities of the status quo while making both forms of education narrow and less relevant to students' lives (Wirth, 1983; LaBrecque, 1974).

The type of vocational education Dewey promoted was dedicated to the reform of the industrial system. This form of vocational schooling would attempt to develop the types of intelligence and skills that would help workers control their own work lives. Along with other Democratic Progressives, Dewey argued that vocational education should help students and workers grasp the meaning of their work lives, broaden their worldview, and confront ideas (Lakes, 1985). Understanding the way Snedden and Prosser's vocationalism manipulated students to become functionaries in the existing industrial regime, Dewey called for an integrated vocational and academic education that cultivated an ability to lead others in the crusade to reestablish the dignity of work (Feffer, 1993). Dewey was especially concerned with developing this ability among the children of the working class who were vulnerable to the whims of employers, market forces, and technological change.

Dewey understood that not only was something fundamentally wrong with industrial work but its social consequences were problematic. Especially interested in the effect of industrialization on an individual's psychology, Dewey traced the rural family's move to the city for the purpose of procuring industrial work. In the new urban context, the family lost its cohesion as an organic productive unit that it had enjoyed on the farm. Children in this rural context, Dewey contended, were provided almost constant learning opportunities, learning self-reliance, independent judgment, and action. Thus, the home was transformed from a workshop to simply a dwelling place where the child lost contact with life processes and useful occupations. In the process, urban families experienced less contact, not only with one another but with the community at large. Dewey maintained that Snedden, Prosser, and the Business Efficiency Progressives failed simply because they were unable to understand these human and social dynamics. Furthermore, Dewey thought that without an appreciation of the social dynamics of both industrial work and the vocational education that adjusts students to it, the Efficiency Progressives had no way of assessing either what constitutes a decent human existence or what form of education moves us toward such a way of life (Edson, 1979; Feffer, 1993; Wirth, 1983).

Dewey refused to see vocational education outside of its social, political, and economic context (Sherman, 1974). That view remains extremely important in the development of a democratic vocational education even at the end of the twentieth century. Unlike the Business Efficiency Progressives, Dewey understood the human and social costs of the industrialization process. Based on such an understanding, his theory promoted a vocational education that induced American students to distinguish between democratic and undemocratic work. Dewey's vocational education pushed students to ask what type of society was desirable in the social context shaped by technological and industrial development; at all costs, the decontextualized vocational program that takes the interests of students and renders them secondary to the needs of employers must be avoided. Questions of justice, Dewey surmised, must always be considered in the formulation of industrial and vocational educational policy.

Such issues were central to Dewey's opposition to the separate tracking of vocational and academic students. Dewey was quick to point out that in addition to economic issues such as the duplication of buildings, equipment, teachers, and administrators, tracking would separate children of the well-to-do from the children of those who have to work in manual and commercial jobs. All that such tracking would accomplish, Dewey argued, would be to produce a corps of industrial workers that employers would find easy to exploit. Using manual training's integration of hand and mind as a model, Dewey and his colleagues insisted that tracking was one of a plethora of industrial forces that segregated intellectuals from workers, in the process destroying ethical consciousness (Simon, Dippo, and Schenke, 1991; Hillison and Camp, 1985). Integration of mind and hand, Dewey told a teacher convention in 1906, is part of a larger educational synthesis of "play and work, of the intellectual and the informational and the dynamic and motor factor; of instruction from books and teachers and from self-guided productive activities; such as concern in short the development of a type of education which shall make at once a man or a woman and a worker" (Dewey as quoted in Feffer, 1993, p. 132).

The Democratic Deweyan Progressives pursuing an education that united the intellectual and the manual argued that all institutions, schooling in particular, should develop the capacities of all individuals regardless of race, sex, class, or economic status. Educational tracking undermines this goal, as it deems the children of the poor unable to pursue an intellectual education. The alternative of such class-biased tracking, the Democratic Progressives maintained, was to turn the school into a community where young people from all backgrounds would develop the academic and manual abilities manifested by the creative accomplishments of scientists and artists. Dewey called this higher-order form of thinking "executive knowing." Students would develop this cognitive ability in integrated academic and vocational classes that emphasized learning by doing, followed by reflective activity. The Democratic Progressives' vision of the vocational and academic integrated curriculum would grant all students access to various forms of knowledge, as it provided contexts in which industrial skills would be studied in relation to the theoretical knowledge of industrial, social, and economic organization (Raizen, 1989; Feffer, 1993). But corporate leaders and the Business Efficiency Progressives refused to buy the argument. Most educators agreed with Snedden and Prosser and chose what they perceived to be practical needs over democratic theory. This choice has shaped the nature and purposes of vocational education even to the present day.

Justifying Vocational Education: Producing the Workers Industry Wants

From the very beginning of the manual training movement up to the present, vocational education has been most promoted in times of economic stress and transition. It has been consistently touted as a solution to problems of productivity and unemployment, alleviating the need to debate more fundamental structural problems in the economy, for example, the structural inability of corporate capitalism to supply enough jobs. A major source of support has come from individuals promoting vocational education as providing a chance for success to economically disadvantaged students. It is the duty of each citizen, such proponents have argued, to provide stewardship to the less fortunate. Although such sentiments may be noble, they belie a naïveté about the motives of many vocational education supporters and the outcomes of vocational programs. In fact, such promotion of vocational education exposes the presence of ways of seeing that fail to account for the power dimensions that have been addressed throughout this book (Grubb, 1978; Wilms, 1979).

Any historical analysis of vocational education that attempts to understand the forces pushing its development cannot ignore these power dimensions. Beginning in the last couple of decades of the nineteenth century, business and industrial leaders have pressured schools to become more competent in preparing industrial workers. Schools began to take on more directly the important social role of promoting the objectives of capitalism (Zachariah, 1987). As the Business Efficiency Progressives consolidated their victory over the Deweyan Democratic Progressives in the second decade of the twentieth century, they issued grand promises for the future of vocational education. We can produce a hardworking, stable, and regularized workforce, they proclaimed. Efficiently educated workers will be prompt and loyal; social unrest will become a distant memory. When one examines the vocational education promoted by the Efficiency Progressives and the workplace procedures devised by industrial managers, it becomes apparent that industrial policy was predicated on the distrust of the worker. It is difficult to find investors or engineers at any point in the twentieth century who contemplated creating machinery that would empower workers and ennoble work. While attempting to maximize output, industrial leaders have tried to minimize the role of the worker. Such an outlook has saddled workers with routine and mind-numbing tasks (Shelton, 1984; Webster, 1985/1986; Edson, 1979).

As discussed in Part 1, one of the main features of vocational education and workplace acculturation has been the attempt to induce workers to accept the workplace as it has existed since industrialization, to resign themselves to the necessity of performing routine and mind-numbing tasks (Grubb, 1978). Obedience, punctuality, compliance, and deference to authority became the most valued attributes of industrial and business leaders' description of the "team player." Managers daydreamed about that special worker with the good attitude and disposition to stay at one task all day, week after week, month after month. The perfect employee was not an entrepreneur or a craftsperson, rather, a regular person who understood the needs of the firm and was committed to them. The managers' demand: "Get rid of those antiquated union apprenticeship programs designed to produce craftspeople, we don't need their inefficiency. Give us committed workers" (Simon, Dippo, and Schenke, 1991; Wilms, 1979; DeYoung, 1989; Shelton, 1984).

Although Business Efficiency Progressives argued that specific work-skill training for typewriting, stenography, bookkeeping, bricklaying, electrical wiring, plumbing, tailoring, and some dimensions of machine operations was necessary, they viewed it as separate from any academic concerns. Snedden, for example, argued that teachers from the academic realm of schooling were totally unacceptable as vocational-skill teachers. Only teachers selected from industry or the trades should be employed in such positions, he concluded. The vocational education Snedden envisioned had nothing to do with academic learning—because it was a training system, *not* a learning system. The Deweyan notion of vocational students as problem solvers and future workers who learned how to learn was not important in the industrial scheme of things. Taylor's ghost haunted the Efficiency Progressives, as workers were not paid to think (Hillison and Camp, 1985; Copa and Tebbenhoff, 1990; Grubb et al., 1991).

Sometime in the first two decades of the twentieth century, a major shift occurred in the way Americans viewed education. Humanities, math, and science were important only to the extent that they helped a student procure a high-status job. Indeed, the purpose of education was not to simply elevate a person's human understandings and abilities, it was to get a person a job (Kliebard, 1990). The Deweyan vision of education for the purpose of developing the critical facility or encouraging the self-motivated pursuit of knowledge was the viewpoint that had been specifically rejected. Industrial leaders, along with their allies, the Business Efficiency Progressives, were suspicious of these "academic" goals of schooling (Grubb, 1978). Too often, they thought, such goals had done little more than create dissatisfied, unruly, "uppity" workers who held authority in little regard. The proper criterion for evaluating education should be its contributions to the economic health of the nation. So complete was this transformation in the American perception of school purpose that a contemporary observer finds it difficult to elicit a justification for schooling other than occupational preparation from a teacher, student, or a parent.

The Smith-Hughes Act: Consolidating the Victory of the Business Efficiency Progressives

In 1910 and 1911, the Business Efficiency Progressives pushed various state governments to adopt systems of vocational training, not yet having imagined the possibility of federal legislation for nationwide vocational education. Snedden and Prosser assumed the leadership for organizing support for a federal bill to fund vocational schooling, a bill that would set the tone for vocational education for the rest of the century (Kliebard, 1987). Prosser wrote the act, in the process bringing together a coalition of groups with compatible political, economic, and educational philosophies. Coalition members shared a conservative social philosophy, a belief in a pedagogy of specific training operations based on a behavioral psychology of stimulus and response and a curriculum theory that was shaped primarily by the needs of industry. Political necessities forced Prosser to make concessions to agricultural interests that wanted vocational schooling to help preserve the virtues of agrarian life. Through the industrial and agricultural alliance, the Smith-Hughes Act was passed in 1917 (Wirth, 1983; Hillison and Camp, 1985).

The bill offered a very narrow definition of vocational education that served to strengthen and legitimate the dual system of academic and vocational education. Clearly separating vocational from academic training, the legislation established the federal Board for Vocational Education, designed to advise local communities and states, administer money for vocational education, and publish research on the field. Smith-Hughes recognized three types of vocational education: (1) schools providing daylong vocational education, (2) part-time schools for beginning workers, and (3) night schools for adult workers. Distinguishing between students who were "abstract minded" and "concrete minded," the Smith-Hughes Act furthered the cause of a class-based education. The "concrete-minded" children of workers, Prosser and his cohorts assumed, could not handle academic learning. Based on such premises, a vocational guidance movement quickly developed that was designed to efficiently place students in their proper vocational niche. Such language ensured that class biases would be built into the guidance process (Spring, 1989).

Supporters of Smith-Hughes spoke at length of the morality of work, the dignity of manual labor, the equality of opportunity, and the patriotic duty to support vocational education. Some supporters even claimed that the bill would restore faith in American values. Upon further examination, one finds that the American values to which supporters were referring included the value of hard work undermined by the industrial economy, the respect of authority subverted by the labor movement, and the Anglo-Saxon value of economic mobility (bettering oneself materially) upset by Southern and Eastern European immigration. Vocational teachers and students of the present can thus begin to understand that the struggle for vocational education has never been simply an economic issue (Wilms, 1979). Indeed, from its beginnings it has always harbored difficult social and political questions; sometimes it has even erupted in cultural war.

The year after the passage of the Smith-Hughes Act, the National Education Association's Commission on the Reorganization of Secondary Education (CRSE) published its report, entitled *Cardinal Principles of Secondary Education*. As it included vocation as one of the seven most important objectives of American education, the CRSE institutionalized the work of the Smith-Hughes Act, forever establishing vocational preparation as a central concern of American education. Vocational education, the commissioners concluded, should prepare students to obtain secure employment, to serve the nation through their vocation, to establish good relations with fellow workers in particular and with the society as a whole, and to develop themselves through the pursuit of vocational excellence. The language and philosophy of the Business Efficiency Progressives permeated the commission's report (Edson, 1979). By 1920, the victory of the efficiency vocationalists was complete. Schools would never again be considered in this country outside the context of job preparation and the health of the national economy (Kliebard, 1990).

Savoring the Victory: The Post–Smith-Hughes Era

In relation to its public support and its universal integration into the curriculum of American schools, vocational education is the most successful educational innovation of the twentieth century. Although little evidence exists to support its value in promoting employment or higher salaries for its students, public support for vocational schooling has rarely wavered. Studies of schools in the 1920s found that vocational courses were thriving in American high schools. Students could choose from academic offerings, along with courses in shorthand, bookkeeping, applied electricity, mechanical drafting, printing, machine shop, manual arts, and home economics. Freshmen and sophomores were required to take English, but by their junior and senior years, students could choose from courses in commercial English. As such nonacademic classes proliferated, members of local business communities pointed to them as evidence of the schooling's quality and efficiency. Not all students should be taught as if they could become president, leaders concluded, arguing that they were taught now to simply get a job (Kliebard, 1987). This was a much more realistic strategy, they reasoned, given the different ability levels of students.

Schools of the 1920s and 1930s provided numerous vocational options for students. Typical schools of the era offered boys an eighth-grade shop class in which they spent a few hours a week sampling the course of the term offerings, in fields such as woodwork, metalwork, electricity, drafting, and textiles. The students were encouraged to discover in which, if any, of these vocations their interest and ability rested. Counselors pressured students to choose their high-school curriculum—liberal arts, sciences, or industrial vocations—by the end of the eighth grade. Often, boys met with the vocational director late in their eighth-grade year to discuss their choice. In the name of efficiency, of course, boys from working-class families were encouraged to choose the vocational track, whereas boys from the middle and upper-middle classes were encouraged to choose the liberal arts and science track. If a boy chose liberal arts or science, he had no more contact with vocational education.

When the vocational students returned to start their ninth-grade school year, they spent fifteen hours a week in shop work and the rest in academic studies. Vocational teachers attempted to make the shops as much like industrial workplaces as possible. Students were directed to produce the same products they would make in their future jobs. Of course, this was often impossible, for schools did not have the funds to purchase the same type of machines that were currently being used in the factories. In addition, vocational teachers attempted to impose the same type of discipline on shop students that would be encountered in the factory. The goal was to adjust students to the working conditions they would have to confront in the factories. In descriptions of vocational programs from the era, the status of recent graduates was frequently discussed. In addition to employment statistics, vocational directors announced how many students had or had not gone to jail, in an effort to demonstrate the value of vocational education in the control of delinquents. Such statistics reveal the perception of what types of students enter the vocational track; an educational historian is hard pressed to find such statistics for recent academic graduates.

Girls had a completely different experience in vocational education. One of the most important motivations for the development of a distinctive female curriculum in American high schools involved popular anxieties concerning the impact of industrialization on the family structure and the role of women in the home. The most important theme in women's vocational education in the first four decades of the twentieth century involved restraint, not opportunity. Vocational programs reflected the "natural" division of labor between the genders, as vocational educators refused to accept the possibility of women playing the same role in production as men. As a result, home economics was established as the female companion to industrial education for boys. When industrial education did exist for girls, it was limited to training for jobs in a restricted range of industries and for niches generally set aside for women.

Emerging at the end of the nineteenth century, the home economics movement was generally supported by the conservative wing of the women's movement of the era. The conservatives' goals involved emphasizing the nurturing abilities of wives and mothers rather than issues of equity in the social and political realms. This nurturing ability had gained new importance in a society marked by industrialization and its accompanying social problems; thus, home economics was not simply a matter of individual improvement but a larger attempt for social reform. Conservative reformers saw a threat to the role of woman as wife and mother in female teenage employment—which would not prepare women to assume their "true" occupation as homemakers. If women were not learning to become good mothers and wives, then vocational educators would take care of the matter in school.

Homemaker training became a primary concern of the efficiency experts. Efficient homemaking, they argued, could lead to more efficient use of social resources if practiced on a national scale. If wives could learn to prepare healthy meals cheaply and cut household expenses, family capital formation could be enhanced. Taylor protégé Frank Gilbreth applied his knowledge of scientific management to the home, inducing home economists to introduce girls to the use of time and motion studies in housework. A scientific management form of home economics soon developed, with leaders arguing that housekeeping was just like any other job and could be rationalized in the same way as factory work. Efficient homemaking would help women in their role as mothers; mothering, after all, was the process by which the nation's "human capital" was produced. Such an important social function could not be left to chance, for the nation's future social and economic development depended on it. Women were responsible for the social, economic, and even moral development of the nation's human resources; indeed, the family was the vocational sphere of women. The women who needed homemaker efficiency training the most, vocational educators argued, were the poor and the immigrants. As one educator put it during a conference on immigrant education in 1931:

> The immigrant woman is ignorant of the value of fresh air, and in our campaign of education we have to make the mother of a family realize that ventilation prevents sickness and that sickness means expense before she will attempt to ventilate her home. The educator has to create a horror of flies by drawing attention to the flies on the filth in the street, and then showing how they convey germs into the house. Such a thing as ventilating clothing or comforters or pillows is unknown, and the educator shows that unheard of things are possible by assisting at the first bed cleaning. (Rury, 1991, p. 145)

This quotation not only reflects the vocational educators' concerns with personal hygiene, cleanliness, and morality but also the decontextualized way they viewed the immigrants of the era. Examination of home economics literature rarely reveals any appreciation, much less concern, for a social structure that allowed slumlords to reap profits from overcrowded and run-down housing that leads directly to disease and malnourishment. Rarely did home economists realize that no other housing was available for immigrant families. The solution to such problems from the perspective of the home economists emphasized the moral turpitude of the mother and the sophistication of her understanding of the principles of home economics. If the immigrant mother could just be made to appreciate the necessity of good nourishment, sanitary living, and a rigid moral perspective, the nation could be saved from social decay. Vocational educators failed to understand that poor immigrant women lacked resources much more important to survival, health, and prosperity than the home economics education offered by the schools. That awareness has too often eluded vocational educators during the entire twentieth century.

The motto of many of the home economics programs of the 1920s and 1930s involved some variation of the following theme: teaching girls to live by living. Like boys, girls made a curricular decision by the end of the eighth grade, choosing a major in science, liberal arts, or home economics. Those who chose home economics often gained access to homemaking laboratories, one for food study, another for clothing study. Some schools designed dining rooms, adjacent to the food laboratory, where girls would often entertain their families, friends, and teachers. The clothing labs were typically equipped with long tables, irons, ironing boards, and kerosene stoves. Teachers frequently assigned home projects designed to induce the girls to view the home as a learning laboratory. Home economics students learned to make clothing, buy ready-to-wear items through field trips to clothing stores, and launder clothing correctly. Interior decorating classes taught girls how to select sofas and chairs to match attractive curtains and window dressings. Senior girls were instructed in child care, learning how to feed infants and encourage them to develop good habits. Personal charm classes helped girls to enhance their personal attractiveness and personality. Home economics curricula typically saw their goal as the production of "happy, healthy, wholesome, and well-poised women" adept at wifely duties and mothering chores (Rury, 1991).

Repressed Memory: The Lost History of Radical Vocational Education

The history of vocational education suffered for decades from interpretations that ignored issues of power and social control. Viewing vocational education as a logical scientific response to the needs of the American economy, questions of how such education undermined economic mobility for the poor, nonwhite, and women were simply not asked. The political implications of Edward Ross's comment in 1906, for example, about the social control role of education—collecting "little plastic lumps of human dough from private households and [shaping] them on the social kneading board" (Spring, 1994, p. 239)—were not of interest to most historians. Without such sensitivities, the *training* of vocational educators rarely involved social and political analysis of vocational education's effects on real-life students. This insensitivity allowed vocational teacher education programs to operate in a sociological vacuum that reinforced the power inequities in schools and society.

When revisionist historians of the 1960s began to focus on issues of power and social justice, they often viewed students and workers as merely pawns trapped by the power play of ruling elite businesspeople and academics. From this perspective, vocational students and workers were depicted as objects of choices made by grand conspirators—in that they had no consciousness and no effect on the flow of history. As revisionists called attention to the success of the social elite in its attempt to regulate and socialize workers, these historians gave little attention to the social conflicts that grew out of attempts to create and shape social institutions. Education, as Richard Brosio (1994) so eloquently pointed out in *The Radical Democratic Critique of Capitalist Education*, is a two-edged sword: On the one hand, it can be used as a means of social control; on the other hand, it can be used to promote consciousness of such control. Although education has been used consistently as a hegemonic force, a means to control the poor and dispossessed, it has not been imposed simply on a passive population. Different groups battled for control of school programs, each group holding a different vision of school purpose (Spring, 1994).

America in the late twentieth century is increasingly becoming a victim of social amnesia, a nation without memory. Dominant culture consistently erases the history of protest, taking with it our exposure to different points of view. This lost history of protest, or dangerous memory, is a valuable natural resource that is systematically rubbed out by schools and the media. As vocational educators, we can gain valuable insight into the future of our field from the conflicts, debates, and stories of those workers and educators who refused to capitulate to the dominant views of work and work education. When the past is forgotten, it shapes and directs without our awareness or resistance (Giroux, 1988). We come to believe everything that exists is natural; it could not have come to exist in any other form. An example of this appears in the notion that vocational education that adjusts workers to the savage realities of the industrial workplace is the only possible manifestation of education for work and in the idea that we had no other choice. Thus, our unconsciousness of history does not free us from the past but, to the contrary, traps us in the snare of an unconscious destiny (Jacoby, 1975; Lucas, 1985).

Vocational education has its own dangerous memory that has, for the most part, been erased from mainstream literature. Not everyone was content with a vocational education that was designed to accommodate the needs of the evolving corporate state. As a result, some union groups and radical democrats attempted in the first few decades of the twentieth century to establish alternative schools not under the control of business groups. One of the most important examples of such schools was the Modern School founded at Stelton, New Jersey. Founders of the school maintained that public schools were repressive in their attempts to control the minds of children. Believing that children were not taught to think but to obey the dominant social dogmas, the leaders and teachers at the Modern School stressed self-determination for their students. The role of the teacher was to help the child give meaning to the quest for self-determination.

The most important alternative schools of the period were labor schools established to combat the corporate domination of public schooling. One of the most representative labor schools of the period was Manumit, founded in Pawling, New York, in 1924. The school opened as a boarding school for children of workers on a 177-acre farm with cattle, hills, and a creek for swimming and fishing. The influence of Dewey was apparent, as organizers spoke of education acquired through life. The "community life of our school," the founders wrote, "is the socialized incarnation of our belief in industrial democracy." Students governed themselves by organizing their own work, play, and academic experiences. Manumit hoped to serve as a laboratory or demonstration school for the labor movement but never developed its program sufficiently. Thus, the labor schools never gained the level of influence their founders had hoped. By World War II, labor radicalism had been contained to such a degree that the founding of alternative schools was no longer a priority. Nevertheless, the legacy of criticism the alternative schools of the era left are important features in the social foundations of vocational education. Many students, teachers, and community members refused to sit on their hands and accept the corporate domination of work education (Spring, 1972).

Moving Toward Midcentury: The Russell Report, World War II, and Life Adjustment Education

Radical labor advocates were not the only analysts who were unhappy with vocational education. Dewey and the Social Reconstructionists were upset about the corporate influence and the class separation of vocational education. Emerging on the education scene in the early 1930s, the Social Reconstructionists viewed school as an institution that confronted social injustice and the underside of the industrial economy. Led by George Counts and Harold Rugg, the Social Reconstructionists charged that American education was serving the needs of only the selected few. The Great Depression brought about a social climate favorable to the reconstructionist message that students needed to learn the defects of the social system so they could do something about them. Many social leaders listened to Counts and Rugg's message about the way industrial culture, with the help of the public schools, was imposing a new conformity that undermined democracy. Vocational education, of course, was a key player in this corporate indoctrination (Kliebard, 1987).

Even mainstream educators were critical of vocational education, as evidenced in the Russell Report, issued in 1938 (Grubb et al., 1991, p. 6). As the first major review of vocational education, the Russell Report served as an evaluation of the impact of the Smith-Hughes Act. The Russell Committee, appointed by Franklin D. Roosevelt, claimed that the Smith-Hughes Act promoted an overly narrow conception of vocational education that trained students too specifically. So narrow was the training that students were inflexible in employment, unable to move smoothly from one job task to another. In addition, the report charged that such specific trade and industrial training produced few economic rewards, since school experience rarely reflected available jobs. Despite these indictments, the Russell Report reaffirmed the principles of vocational education. Unfortunately, however, it exerted little influence, appearing as it did immediately before American entry into World War II. Vocational education was too caught up in specific-skill training for the war effort to find it very useful (Grubb, 1978).

In fact, the war effort reenergized the vocational education movement. As a result of the meeting of the Conference on War Problems of Illinois Schools and Teacher Colleges on December 17, 1941, vocational educators were urged to reconceptualize their courses so that aeromechanics, aeronautics, auto mechanics, navigation, gunnery, and other features of warfare would be emphasized. Consumer and home economics were modified to deal with shortages and stresses precipitated by the war. With renewed zeal, the efficiency advocates emphasized afresh the value of good work habits and industrial values. Conventional academic subjects were subjected to a new round of criticism, as efficiency advocates argued that the central role of American schools should be to train students for their proper occupational role. This tone was reflected in a variety of wartime reports on education: *Education for All American Youth* in 1944 recommended that youth be provided with "salable skills" and a differentiated curriculum that would take into account the different needs and abilities of students. In 1945, a Harvard University faculty committee produced *General Education in a Free Society,* which, although more generous to academic subject matter than the 1944 report, still endorsed the development of occupational skills for students with "lower facility with ideas."

The most important wartime event for the future of vocational education involved the commissioning of a study by the U.S. Office of Education entitled *Vocational Education in the Years Ahead* (Kliebard, 1987; Spring, 1994). When the results of the study were presented in 1945 by Business Efficiency Progressive Charles Prosser, the first offensive in the call for Life Adjustment Education had been issued:

> It is the belief of this conference that, with the aid of this report in final form, the vocational school of a community will be able better to prepare 20 percent of its youth of secondary school age for entrance upon desired skilled occupations; and that the high school will continue to prepare 20 percent of its students for entrance into college. We do not believe that the remaining 60 percent of our youth of secondary school age will receive the *life adjustment training* they need and to which they are entitled as American citizens—unless and until the administrators of public education with the assistance of the vocational education leaders formulate a comparable program for this group. (Kliebard, 1987, p. 249)

A series of regional conferences was designed to implement Prosser's declarations on life adjustment. Invoking the old language, Prosser called for an *efficient* vocational education to address the "maladjustment of millions of America's citizens." As a movie, Life Adjustment Education could have operated under the title *Son of Business Efficiency Education,* as it repackaged the Snedden and Prosser arguments of 1917. Vocational educators were prodded to help schools offer courses in "Learning to Work," "School and Life Planning," "Growth Toward Maturity," "Boy-Girl Relationships," and "Preparation for Marriage." A feel for the nature of these courses can be obtained from many of the films developed by Life Adjustment educators of the post–World War II era. Simplistic, moralistic, and based on unexamined middle-class values, the films typically elicit laughter from the more worldly and self-conscious students of contemporary America. It is not surprising that such films have been shown for their unintended comic value on cable TV programs such as *Mystery Science Theater 3000* (MST3K).

Some measure of these feelings was not lost on academic critics of the postwar period. As Life Adjustment supporters promoted Basic Living courses as substitutes for the traditional academic curriculum, the attention of scholars was aroused. By the early 1950s, Life Adjustment Education was being portrayed as a caricature of anti-intellectualism in American life and schooling. Some of the criticism was undoubtedly associated with Senator Joseph McCarthy's attempt to flush out communists and radicals from all aspects of American life, but much of it came from respected academics speaking from behind their podiums on university campuses. The most sophisticated of the critics understood that Life Adjustment Education was not simply the latest incantation of Deweyan progressivism—although many of the conservative critics made that claim. Arthur Bestor, one of the most vocal critics, was quick to understand the difference between Dewey's philosophy and the Life Adjustment movement. He even used Dewey's ideas to criticize Life Adjustment's crass attempt to demonstrate the social value of education. Like a house of cards, Life Adjustment education could not withstand the winds of criticism. After the launch of Sputnik in 1957 and the accompanying call for improved academic education, Life Adjustment was dead (Kliebard, 1987; Grubb, 1978).

The 1960s and 1970s: Déjà Vu All Over Again

Emerging as a controversial issue a few years later in the 1960s as unemployment rates among unskilled workers grew along with the fear of technological unemployment, vocational education once again became an object of study. President John Kennedy appointed a national commission (the Panel of Consultants on Vocational Education) in 1963 to study the role of vocational education in light of the changing economy. The report of the committee was a déjà vu for longtime vocational educational professionals, as the committee criticized vocational education's narrowness, its limited economic benefit, and its failure to take into account labor market conditions.

Reflecting the Russell Report of 1938, the Panel of Consultants on Vocational Education laid the foundation for the Vocational Education Act of 1963. Although it never exerted much impact on American schools, the legislation attempted to redirect vocational education in a manner more flexible and less confined to specific job training. For the first time, legislators focused their attention on minorities, arguing that their particular socioeconomic position deserved special attention in work education.

In the maze of periodic reports that characterize the history of twentieth-century vocational education, the 1960s is an important decade. Five years after the consultants' report and the passage of the Vocational Education Act of 1963, yet another report was issued. In 1968, the Advisory Council on Vocational Education proclaimed that the 1963 legislation had been ignored; in particular, the council noted the bill's neglect of the vocational education of minorities. Once again, the report of a committee led to new legislation: the 1968 Vocational Education Amendments. Yet again, this new legislation was designed to make vocational teaching more flexible and more germane to the needs of marginalized students. Obviously, concerns with vocational education over the twentieth century have been remarkably consistent, as they focus on its tendency toward narrowness (Grubb et al., 1991; Grubb, 1978).

As previously noted in Chapter 3, it was in the 1970s that the Fordist compromise began to fall apart. The inflexibility of long-term, large-scale capital investments in systems of mass production began to undermine American productivity. As productivity declined, industry decreased its capital investments. There was no decrease in demand for workers in the 1970s, but unemployment rates rose rapidly, reflecting the entrance into the labor market of the postwar "baby boomers." The oversupply of labor caused wages to decline, especially for entry-level workers (Spring, 1984). We can therefore begin to understand government education policy in the 1970s and its concern with youth unemployment. While government vocational education policy continued to play the same tune, issuing yet another report on its narrowness, lack of effectiveness in preparing students for jobs, and neglect of marginalized students (the review by the comptroller general 1974), other voices were beginning to be heard—in particular those calling for career education. Business became more and more labor intensive, in the process reducing spending on new equipment or workplace reorganization. Instead of buying state-of-the-art equipment, many businesses added second and third shifts. American productivity stagnated between 1960 and 1977, while Japan's productivity over the same period increased by 255 percent. The world as Americans had grown accustomed to seeing it was gone forever.

Career Education can be understood as a response to the decline of Fordism and its myriad ensuing social effects. Obsessed with student and civil rights protests in the 1960s and the growth of a New Left countercul- ture, President Richard Nixon was intent on restoring law and order to America after his inauguration in January 1969. One of his strategies for ac- complishing this goal was to streamline the manpower-channeling orienta- tion of public schooling by linking the academic programs of the school to the labor market. As students were funneled into particular jobs, their atti- tudes could be concurrently adjusted. He hoped that in their concern for employment and job security, students would abandon their flirtation with social issues. Although no program of attitude adjustment ever works as it is originally conceived, Nixon and his supporters watched gleefully as Career Education, the end of the military draft, the scaling down of the Vietnam War, and a variety of other social circumstances undermined large-scale protest movements (Spring, 1989).

Appointing Sidney Marland as the U.S. commissioner of education, Nixon was confident that Marland could devise a Career Education pro- gram to accomplish these larger social and political objectives. By 1971 and 1972, Marland had begun to direct Education Office funding into the de- velopment of model Career Education programs. As money flowed from the Office of Education, educators began to write grants funding Career Education projects around the country. Marland was a true believer in the power of Career Education, contending that it was the answer to student re- bellion, delinquency, and unemployment. Much like the Life Adjustment educators of the 1940s and 1950s, Marland attacked academic education and its irrelevance for the majority of students. Laying the theoretical foun- dation for the Career Education movement, Marland's ideas were used to justify Career Education's inclusion in the 1974 Elementary and Secondary Education Act. The program continued to gain support over the next three years, culminating in 1977 in the passage of the Career Education Act. Even with all its high-level support, however, the program only received a small fraction of its authorized level of funding (Harp, 1992).

Career education never suffered from a dearth of grandiose claims as to what it could accomplish. Marland profoundly influenced Presidents Nixon and Ford, for both presidents claimed that career and vocational programs could solve the problem of rising unemployment. Nixon and Ford were re- flecting Marland's and a whole host of twentieth-century educational re- formers' naive belief that school reform alone, unconnected to larger social and economic reforms, could miraculously cure all that ailed the nation. Ca- reer Education advocates argued that their program could reduce the school turmoil that resulted from an inefficient method of vocational sorting. The curriculum as it was presently constituted, they maintained, was irrelevant to the career needs of students. In their view, vocational education, along with school in general, should emphasize the employment needs of all students, not simply provide training for specific occupational programs (Spring,

1984, 1989). The standard definition employed by career education proponents to describe the new program was this: "the sum total of those experiences of the individual associated with his [sic] choice of, preparation for,
entry into, and progress in occupations throughout his occupational life"
(Grubb, 1978, p. 76).

Echoing the language of the Business Efficiency Progressives of six
decades earlier, Career Educationists claimed that the new education would
restore the work ethic among young people. In the tradition of Life Adjustment Education of twenty-five years earlier, the reformers sought to turn
school away from the academic curriculum and its archaic goals. As it excluded traditional academic education, the movement tried to relegate vocational education to a subservient role under the larger Career Education
umbrella. As Career Education tackled every economic, educational, and social malady imaginable, it carried the torch previously held by the vocational
educators. The differences between career and vocational education involved Career Education's tendency to claim all aspects of education as its
turf. In the 1970s, after only a few years' time, it became increasingly difficult to discern what aspects of schooling did not fall under the larger category of Career Education (Luethemeyer, 1974; Grubb, 1978).

Below the surface, there are numerous hidden agendas in the Career Education movement. In addition to the desire to regulate youth and preclude
the return of the 1960s, the leadership of the movement was interested in
involving American business and industry more directly in the everyday life
of the school. One labor leader opposed the selection of Marland as commissioner of education because of his ties to an industrial-education complex "greedy for a share of the educational dollar." Soon after his appoint-
ment to the office, Marland spoke of the need for a new partnership
between schools and industry. Immediately thereafter, he appointed what he
described as a "businessman with a management background" as deputy
commissioner for management in the Office of Education (Sherman, 1974).

Marland and the proponents of Career Education assumed that social and
economic systems in America were fundamentally just. In a manner similar
to their Business Efficiency Progressive ancestors, Career Educationists saw
their role as simply matching potential workers to the existing jobs. That
such jobs were sometimes uninteresting, degrading, or unsafe was as unimportant to them as it had been to Snedden and Prosser. Richard Brosio
(1994) claimed that Career Education was designed to reduce expectations
and solidify commitments to the status quo, as it "conditioned" students to
a work culture that distributed rewards unequally. Stressing productivity as
it turned its back on questions concerning what is being produced and to
what purpose, the movement dismissed larger democratic concerns.

Like so many reformers before them, the advocates of Career Education
missed some important points, including the realization that business, in-

dustry, and technology are social and political forces that change our culture in a variety of ways. As such, the effects of these forces must be analyzed and evaluated in light of our basic democratic precepts. Such analysis was not a part of the Career Education vision; as a result, Career Education was less an *education* and more a *training* program. Concerns with citizenship, cultural matters, and academic learning were irrelevant. Like Life Adjustment Education, Career Education faded quickly from the scene. By the early 1980s, it was dead.

7 Failures and Reforms: The Recent History of Vocational Education

The history of vocational education has not been a peaceful journey through a gentle landscape. The fights and battles in America's vocational educational past have reflected the larger struggles that have shaped American history. Disputes between labor and management, the persistence of poverty in the land of opportunity, the uses of social control in the land of the free, racial and gender injustice, and the relationship between political justice and economic justice constitute only a few of the themes that can be teased out of the history of vocational education in America. In the shadows cast by these themes, many have proclaimed the failure of vocational education. Analysts have argued that vocational educators have failed to appreciate the relationship between these themes and the everyday functions of education for work (DeVore, 1983). Some critics push further, maintaining that the study of vocational education has not typically been marked by hard-nosed analysis, especially social and political analysis (NCRVE, 1992). This chapter will analyze contemporary vocational education, in the process connecting it to the historical themes delineated in Chapters 5 and 6 and the sociopolitical and philosophical concerns of Chapters 1, 2, 3, and 4. The first topic to be addressed is the charges made by critics of American vocational education.

American Vocational Education—a Failure?

According to many observers, vocational education has failed to accomplish the mission developed by the Smith-Hughes Act in 1917. Over the years, several criticisms have been levied against vocational education, including these: (1) it has segregated poor and minority youth into a curriculum that reduces their access to high-skill, high-status, high-pay careers. Such segregation creates the impression that vocational education is a dumping ground for "children other than mine"; and (2) it teaches skills that are obsolete in a rapidly changing economy. By the time vocational education students get to the job market, the specific work skills they have learned are out of date; (3) its instruction is narrow—so narrow that students who graduate are often unequipped for existing jobs. Vocational students do not have access to a curriculum that teaches them how to think and learn; (4) it has failed to offer students an alternative to dropping out of school. At the same time, it has not enhanced the employability of a large segment of the youth population, especially the poor and nonwhite; (5) its image revolves around a picture of students working with their hands but *not* their minds. The popular prejudice against manual jobs and the persistent reduction of such jobs to repetitive, deskilled labor has rubbed off on vocational education, making it a place where incompetent students can seek shelter; (6) it leads too often to nonprestigious jobs. Such positions in the twentieth-century American workplace have been described as bad work (see Chapter 4).

From its earliest inception, vocational education supporters have argued that given the unequal conditions of human beings, vocational teaching should be geared to the less able. In addition to David Snedden's proclamations of human inequality, the National Association of Manufacturers maintained in 1912 that different schools were needed for three types of children: the abstract-minded who learn from reading, that is, the future social leaders; the concrete-minded, who are unable to learn from books and written literature, that is, line workers; and the rest of the students who fall in between, that is, the low-level supervisors, the semiprofessionals. The identification and classification of children was a major goal in Business Efficiency Progressivism. You cannot squeeze blood out of a turnip, the reformers argued, meaning that you cannot train a "clumsy, slow-thinking boy" for a job that requires disciplined thinking. Of course, the concerns of the Efficiency Progressives were genuine, albeit problematic, as they called for an educational tracking system based on the probable vocational destinies of students. Another social factor, however, set the stage for widespread public acceptance of such expensive proposals (Parnell, 1990; Beck, 1991; Copa and Tebbenhoff, 1990).

In the decades surrounding the birth of vocational education, massive numbers of immigrants were crowding American schools. Many historians, of course, have argued that the infusion of poor, working-class, immigrants into the high schools elicited a fearful response from many Americans. They were frightened by the possibility that these "social undesirables" would undermine the prestige of high school (Oakes, 1985). Instead of modifying the nature of the secondary course of study to accommodate a multiethnic student population, the creation of separate vocational programs allowed the schools to offer different tracks for different students. Sorting students along socioeconomic class lines, the vocational advocates created an institution (the vocational school) that would inculcate the attitudes and skills (industrial values) industrial employers wanted. Vocational leaders often described this preparation for subservient roles in the workplace in mystifying language, saying, for example, that the "new education" would produce a society with the characteristics of a "winning team," where everyone would have a special function, some as leaders, others as followers. From the perspective of race, class, and gender, it was not hard to distinguish the leaders from the followers (Grubb et al., 1991; Beck, 1991; Wirth, 1983).

In one of the best examples of how power operates in an educational context, scientific intelligence testing was introduced into the school in order to offer an "objective" method of sorting academic from vocational students, the leaders from the followers. In the 1910s and 1920s, just as in the 1990s, there was a strong correlation between test scores and race, class, and gender background. Then as now, economically privileged, native-born, white students did better on the tests and were able to use the academic track in secondary schools as a bridge to college and "success." Economic and social inequality was exacerbated by testing and tracking, with vocational guidance counselors using intelligence testing as an indisputable scientific authority to justify injustice in the schoolhouse (Pincus, 1980). In a modernist context, who could dispute the power of the test: It "proved" what the Business Efficiency Progressives already believed in—the superiority of the white male. Intelligence test maker Louis Terman announced in 1923 that tests can determine whether a young child's ability better fits (1) the professional classes, (2) the semiprofessional classes, or (3) unskilled labor. Thus, young students could be efficiently and scientifically tracked (Edson, 1979).

The work of the vocational leaders in the first three decades of the twentieth century (as explained in Chapters 5 and 6) established a tracking system that purported to "train" some students and "educate" others. The division between vocational and academic education grew more and more distinct, despite the protestations of John Dewey, George Counts, Boyd Bode, and their intellectual progeny. Vocational schools were the places teachers sent their weakest pupils. Expectations for these students were lowered, and throughout the twentieth century, the vocational track ensured that students who entered it would experience little social or economic mobility. The best research indicates clearly that tracking lowers the achievement of those in the lower/vocational tracks without improving the performance of those in the higher/academic tracks. As far as questions of equity are concerned, vocational education has failed (NCRVE, 1992; Grubb et al., 1991; Shelton, 1984; Copa and Tebbenhoff, 1990).

Recent assessments of the value of vocational education have been characterized by harsh words. In 1985, the Committee for Economic Development concluded that many vocational education programs are virtually worthless. Educators, the report continued, perpetrate a cruel hoax on students seeking to gain marketable skills. As a strategy for teaching needed job skills and creating greater opportunity for its students, vocational education has been less than successful. Jeannie Oakes (1985) reported that most skilled workers did not obtain their training in vocational programs, more likely learning them informally on the job. Much less than one-half of the pool of vocational students gain jobs related to their vocational training. Indeed, programs often prepare young people for a world that no longer exists. Even when the effort to use vocational education as a means to raise student academic skills is considered, it has failed. Norton Grubb (1978) has concluded that all the talk about vocational education's unique role in integrating school and work is merely "rhetoric." On the national level, the use of vocational education as a means to raise the nation's productivity has been judged a bust. Successful completion of vocational programs has little to do with increasing worker productivity. The list of indictments goes on and on. In light of such findings, it comes as no surprise that recent critics of vocational education have questioned its need to exist (Kliebard, 1990; Raizen, 1989).

The Debate over Educational Reform in the 1980s

The decline of Fordism (beginning in the 1970s and 1980s), characterized by degenerating economic conditions and foreign competition, initiated a new wave of educational reform. Corporate officials and many political leaders criticized vocational education as the source of the failure of American schools to train a globally competitive army of workers and maintained that the only way to address such academic shortcomings was for government to align itself with corporate power. Together, these powerful agencies would produce school reforms that would restore America's competitive capabilities. Of course, the reforms that ensued were built on a faulty premise—that economic decline was simply the result of a declining education system. Rarely did the educational reform literature of the early 1980s mention changing international economic conditions and the response of American business and industry to such economic upheavals. As documented in Chapter 4, corporate-sponsored school reform exonerated business and industrial leaders of any responsibility for economic decline. To understand the political and economic currents that shaped vocational education in the 1980s and early 1990s, one must understand school reform as part of a larger corporate effort to reconstruct the social, political, and economic order (Tozer, Violas, and Senese, 1993; Apple, 1993).

Aided by right-wing political leaders, corporate managers worked to "rewrite" American values and political dispositions. The public value of the common good was shifted to the private domain—to private enterprise, private property, private schools, and privatization in general. Incensed by the attempts of labor and citizen groups in the 1960s and 1970s to question the absolute control of production by business managers via minimum wage laws, occupational health and safety regulations, equal employment opportunity, and improvements in worker compensation, corporate leaders directed investment away from firms located in the United States. Such disinvestment, deindustrialization, and capital mobility undermined regional economies; the *threat* of disinvestment held localities hostage, forcing them to provide firms with subsidies for research, lower corporate taxes, weakened antitrust legislation and environmental regulation, and new education designed to produce the type of workers employers wanted. If one does not understand the power of industry to manipulate political, economic, and educational policy, an analysis of corporate activity in the 1980s should provide significant insight into such processes (Margonis, 1989).

In addition to this policy of hostage taking, corporate America supported neoclassical economic policies that cut public sector budgets while supporting a massive military buildup. The refusal to invest in infrastructures such as roads, bridges, housing, and services undermined productivity. When considered along with business's steadfast refusal to consider workplace reorganization in line with high-skill work, an understanding of America's changing economy begins to emerge (Shor, 1986). The corporate-shaped national conversation about education, however, devoted little attention to such economic decline. Focusing instead on education, the national media began to notice that Japan was experiencing economic changes. Simplistically drawing a one-dimensional connection between Japanese student performance on standardized tests and rising economic productivity, corporate leaders and their conservative political allies called for emulation of the Japanese educational system.

The National Commission on Excellence in Education and its 1983 report *A Nation at Risk,* discussed in Chapter 4, took Japanese education as the model for excellence. Noting Japan's longer school day, mountains of homework, and family involvement in schools, corporate-supported school reformers envisioned American schools filled with students who imitated the work ethic and discipline of successful Japanese students. No need for vocational education existed in the minds of these reformers; all that was needed was a rigorous Japanese-like academic education for everyone (Holtz et al., 1989, p. 4). As a result of these views, enrollments in vocational courses declined by 11 percent in the decade that followed the NCEE report (Olson, January 19, 1994). Corporate leaders were not ashamed to pursue a policy that favored the advantaged students, the ones "who have the highest potential to contribute positively to society." Indeed, corporate leaders and conservative politicians maintained that the disadvantaged (racial minorities, the handicapped, women, and non-English-speaking minorities) had received educational attention at the expense of the best students (Shor, 1986).

This demonization of the marginalized became a central strategy of the right-wing advocates. David Duke explicitly articulated the concept in his political campaigns in Louisiana in the early 1990s: The real victims of discrimination are hardworking and decent white Americans. The poor and nonwhite are rewarded, Duke and his more subtle conservative colleagues maintained, for their laziness, immorality, and permissiveness (Apple, 1993). School reform was merely one aspect of a larger social strategy designed by corporate and educational elites to transfer resources to the privileged and the private realm while undermining union organization and strengthening managerial control. The architects of the NCEE's *A Nation at Risk* were not interested in teaching students to critically understand American economics and politics—and they certainly were not interested in providing them with the analytical tools to reshape the culture (Shor, 1986). While democratic educators concerned themselves with empowering students, conservative proponents of educational reform worked to grant schools more authority over students. Vocational educators need to understand the reform agenda of the 1980s in order to appreciate the purposes that have been assigned to education for work. The same issues that divided educators in the 1980s (and the entire twentieth century) are still at work here in the late 1990s.

The power of business heavily affected education at both the state and local levels. Adopt-a-School programs were developed, magnet school programs were created, and formal relationships were established at the insistence of business leaders (Spring, 1994). These programs were designed to represent business in a positive light, to promote business perspectives on American economic and political concerns, and to help shape school policy to respond to business's labor needs (Spring, 1984). The objective of business-directed reforms after the NCEE report, therefore, was not simply to help the schools but to benefit business. The same forces were at work in the report that followed *A Nation at Risk*—the report of the Task Force on Education for Economic Growth, *Action for Excellence*. This report, conceived by the task force of the nation's state governors and corporate leaders, reinforced the call for business-school cooperation. Education is the cure-all, the panacea, for America's problems, *Action for Excellence* proclaimed; our national defense, our social stability, our national prosperity, and our future success as a nation depend on the success of business-directed reforms (Tozer, Violas, and Senese, 1993; Spring, 1994).

Although *A Nation at Risk* and *Action for Excellence* represented the most publicized suggestions for educational reform in the 1980s, there were those who rejected the assumptions of these studies. The Carnegie Foundation for the Advancement of Teaching's 1986 report, *A Nation Prepared: Teachers for the Twenty-first Century,* produced under the leadership of Ernest Boyer, is the most compelling progressive response to the corporatist logic of the other two reports. Where *A Nation at Risk* calls for higher academic standards, more accountability for teachers, more standardized testing, and more emphasis on basic skills, Boyer's *A Nation Prepared* calls for corporations to "heal themselves." Corporations, Boyer argued, must restructure in a way that equips them to meet the new realities of the changing global economy. Such a restructuring would involve the creation of a high-skill, high-wage workforce.

All students, the Carnegie Foundation argued, need virtually the same type of education—learning experiences that emphasize higher orders of thinking, interpretive and analytical ability, and the capacity to work in teams. Boyer argued that an education of that sort benefits both economically disadvantaged students and boys and girls from privileged homes and should reject standardized, basic skills repetition and testing methodologies of instruction. The foundation was specifically critical of overenrollment in vocational programs that fail to teach either the ability to reason or to perform complex, nonroutine work assignments. But the conservative reformers, with their sympathetic colleagues in the White House, were not impressed by the Carnegie report. As a result, little interest could be generated to address the inability of vocational education to serve the needs of the majority of high school students who choose to enter the workforce immediately after graduating or dropping out of high school (Carlson, 1992).

As the 1980s ended, it was becoming apparent to most observers that the conservative reforms of the decade had ignored vocational education to such a degree that its reputation as a dumping ground for "undesirable students" was escalating. By 1992, studies indicated that the numbers of economically or educationally disadvantaged, disabled, or limited English proficiency students were growing dramatically in vocational education tracks. Disabled students, research revealed, signed up for more vocational courses than any other group. Also, students who were disadvantaged by physical or emotional handicaps or English deficiency were more likely to be concentrated in training for low-status occupations such as food service, auto-body repairs, and the metalworking trades. Analysts also found that these disadvantaged students were being tracked into vocational education for reasons contrary to their best educational interests. As conservative reforms ignored the viability of vocational programs and student populations in these programs declined, vocational program leaders found it necessary to recruit disadvantaged students for the purpose of keeping enrollments steady. As conditions worsened in vocational education, the William T. Grant Foundation released its 1988 report, *The Forgotten Half*. This report helped alert educators to the notion that vocational education should be reconceptualized and reformed. By the early 1990s, vocational schooling was beginning to elicit the concern of a new set of educational reformers (Olson, January 19, 1994; NCRVE, 1992).

The New Era: President Clinton and Goals 2000

Bringing together a multitude of reports and recommendations, President Clinton signed Goals 2000: Educate America Act in March 1994. Goals 2000, catalyzed by reports such as *The Forgotten Half* and agreed to by political, business, and educational leaders, was a compromise document designed to promote future economic growth. The compromise began during the Bush administration, when the nation's governors, led by then governor Bill Clinton and President Bush, prepared *America 2000: An Education Strategy*. This report delineated seven goals to be met by the year 2000: (1) all children will start school ready to learn; (2) all students will be competent in core academic subjects; (3) students in the United States will be first in the world in science and mathematics achievement; (4) the high-school graduation rate will be at least 90 percent; (5) every school will be safe, disciplined, and drug free; (6) the teaching force will be competent to further these achievement goals; and (7) every adult will be literate and possess the skills necessary to compete in a global economy (Pitsch, 1994).

Many democratic progressives have been disappointed by Clinton's refusal to move beyond the goals and language of the Bush administration's *America 2000*. Not only are the Clinton proposals silent on issues of citizenship, democracy, and poverty, but they couch reforms in terms of scientific management and efficiency (Giroux, 1993). In the terms developed in the preceding chapters, Goals 2000 and *America 2000* are examples of a modern form of Business Efficiency progressivism. Snedden and Prosser would be proud. At the same time that Goals 2000 held on to regressive silences, the Clinton administration supported the U.S. Secretary of Labor's Commission on Achieving Necessary Skills (SCANS) and the recommendations of the National Council on Educational Standards and Testing (NCEST).

The Revealing Debate over National Skills Standards

SCANS emerged in 1991 in the Bush administration's *America 2000* proposal, defining what work-readiness skills schools should teach. Upon successful completion of a work-readiness program, SCANS recommended that students receive a certificate of initial mastery indicating that they possessed skills necessary to start work (Hudelson, 1992). The work-readiness program was grounded on a set of "competencies and foundations" that the authors of the plan maintained were needed by all students, whether they were entering the workforce or higher education after high school. The purpose of SCANS was not to reform vocational education but to entirely rethink the way we prepare students for work. Instead of training specific students for particular trades or industrial jobs, SCANS contended that all students should be prepared for a dynamic and flexible future workplace.

Not surprisingly, business has played a central role in the development of the competencies and foundations (Pullin, 1994). For example, before the skills for workers in the retail industry were developed, analysts worked with retail executives who delineated what type of workers they wanted (Roditi, 1992). Generic competencies and foundational skills developed by SCANS include the following:

Competencies: Effective workers can productively use

- *Resources:* allocating time, money, materials, space, and staff.
- *Interpersonal skills:* working on teams, teaching others, serving customers, leading, negotiating, and working well with people from culturally diverse backgrounds.
- *Information:* acquiring and evaluating data, organizing and maintaining files, interpreting and communicating, and using computers to process information.
- *Systems:* understanding social, organizational, and technological systems, monitoring and correcting performance, and designing or improving systems.
- *Technology:* selecting equipment and tools, applying technology to specific tasks, and maintaining and troubleshooting technologies.

The Foundation: Competence requires

- *Basic skills:* reading, writing, arithmetic and mathematics, speaking, and listening.
- *Thinking skills:* thinking creatively, making decisions, solving problems, seeing things in the mind's eye, knowing how to learn, and reasoning.
- *Personal qualities:* individual responsibility, self-esteem, sociability, self-management, and integrity. (SCANS, as quoted in Pullin, 1994, p. 37)

In order to insure that competencies and foundational skills such as these would be considered throughout the nation, Congress established the National Council on Educational Standards and Testing in 1991. Since then, NCEST has proposed a national system of assessments, setting off a debate over national educational standards. Almost all states and many local school districts have begun to consider achievement standards and the curricular reforms that would accompany them. Several national standards projects have presented reports on the issue. Proponents contend that in any industry, there is a common set of skills that everyone needs. They argue that workers need to know the names of various equipment and processes and how to perform particular lab procedures. Some progressive supporters of national skills maintain that the training mandated by such standards would be so broad that narrow tracking of students into job categories would be avoided. The Clinton administration has supported that position, arguing that skills standards form the basis of its goal of upgrading the American workforce. Indeed, when Congress passed Goals 2000 in March of 1994, a national skills-standards board was an important part of the legislative package (Pullin, 1994; Hudelson, 1992; Olson, May 12, May 26, 1993, January 26, 1994).

Composed of twenty-eight members representing business, labor, education, community-based groups, and state governmental officials, the skills-standards board identifies broad occupational clusters and facilitates the development of voluntary systems of standards, assessments, and certificates. The process of establishing the board was filled with acrimonious congressional debate, illustrating the power dimensions that help shape vocational education. Points of contention revolved around the proper role of government in the development of skills standards, whether business and industry were properly represented on the board, the process by which the standards would be developed and how they would be used, and whether standards would inhibit the hiring of women and members of minority groups. The issue of racial equity was especially important in the legislative battles over the creation of the board. Civil rights groups lobbied diligently to make sure that the issuing of certificates complied with all federal civil rights regulations.

Another revealing controversy in the congressional debate involved the issue of business representation on the skills standards board. Both the National Association of Manufacturers and the National Alliance of Business argued that business representatives should dominate the board. Consequently, they induced former Kansas Republican senator Nancy Kassebaum to offer an amendment to replace the twenty-eight member board with an industry-dominated majority, under which arrangement six members would represent large businesses or industries and another six would represent small businesses. The three governmental officials, under the business-supported Kassebaum plan, would have no vote on the committee and workers would be granted only one voting member. "Without greater business and industry representation on the board," Kassebaum argued, "this legislation could become an exercise in futility." This debate illustrates how corporate power often works to privatize public programs in a manner that serves not the public interest (in this case job-seeking students) but their own private interest. The debate also illustrates that democratic interests can combat such naked power, for in this case the business proposal was rejected (Olson, May 12, June 2, 1993; Pullin, 1994).

Slowly, different industries began to present voluntary skills standards for their employees, the first being the American Electronics Association (AEA)

in March 1994. The AEA focused first on clusters of jobs that do not usually demand a four-year college degree, jobs that make up the majority of
the industry's frontline workforce. The electronics industry claimed that
skills such as "identifying customer needs" or "integrating improvement
processes into each critical function" require workers to engage in complex
problem-solving, communications, and analytical activities that were rarely
demanded in the past. The AEA has promised that in the future, the industry will identify the basic knowledge demanded by the skill standards (Olson, March 2, 1994). That process will be very important to federal and
state educational leaders and vocational educators, for it will set a precedent
for how the development and assessment of skill standards will work. Many
educators have voiced concerns that skill standards are grounded upon a
standardized test base that will trivialize the curriculum and reduce the role
of the teacher in determining what is taught in the classroom (Goodlad,
1992). Driven by standardized tests, vocational curricula can become mechanical and technical, losing sight of the twin goals of nurturing workers as
democratic citizens and creating good work.

The Great Conflict: Changing Vocational Education to
Meet Contemporary Demands for Smart Workers

Of course, the impetus for all of this vocational *and* academic education talk
of reform is the alleged need for a globally competitive workforce. A major
conflict emerges when educational, political, and business leaders embrace
such rhetoric, because too much vocational and academic education is designed to instill compliance and facilitate social control rather than to encourage questioning and democratic empowerment of students. We cannot
have it both ways; we cannot demand reforms that will produce a globally
competitive workforce while requiring a curriculum that fosters an unquestioning acceptance of the status quo. Teaching students to think, interpret,
and produce knowledge is a dangerous notion to the patriarchs of normalcy.
Do we merely train workers, or do we educate them? From the grave, the
voice of David Snedden speaks the language of training: No matter how important the production of a competitive workforce might be, many corporate and educational leaders cannot shake off the need to regulate students
and workers in the attempt to adjust them to the humiliating social relations
of the workplace.

In listening to the public conversation about the global or postindustrial
or post-Fordist economy, one would assume that all new jobs were high-
skill and high-wage—but it just is not so. Still, at the end of the twentieth
century, only about one out of every ten jobs in the American workplace has
been reconceived in a more dynamic and flexible manner. The argument is
correctly made that as companies become decentralized and more oriented

toward service, workers at every level of the organization will have to use their judgment in daily work activities. Following this contention, vocational educational leaders have argued for a broader and less job-specific form of vocational education for workers destined to enter this "workplace of the future." Unless employers work quickly to reinvent their workplaces for empowered and thoughtful workers, all of the vocational educational reforms of the present will amount to little more than, as Vice President John Nance Gardner put it, a bucket of warm spit (Marshak, 1993; NCRVE, 1992; Marsick, 1989; Pullin, 1994; Lather, 1991).

This is not to argue against such educational reforms. A group of empowered, visionary, and dissatisfied young employees emerging from an analytical and democratic education might motivate employers to take the big step, to reinvent their workplaces. Such empowering vocational programs would encourage students to understand the theory underlying the work skills they perform. An education like this would integrate vocational and academic education (see Kincheloe, 1995) in a way that would allow students to see the practical application of abstract concepts. No more narrow vocationalism, democratic progressive reformers would proclaim, as they structured a vocational education that taught higher-order thinking skills by way of experiences that connected the world of work to science, math, literature, art, and the humanities. President Clinton has talked the talk of such proposals, arguing that workers should become lifelong learners (Olson, March 2, 1994). Still, much work remains to be undertaken to turn the talk into concrete action, especially given the fact that the social control agenda remains so powerful in education at the end of the twentieth century.

The tendency to employ education as a form of social control is not the only impediment to the attempt to establish a democratic and empowering vocational education. As we move into the twenty-first century, the labor pool will become increasingly black and Latino—and these groups have not been traditionally well served by vocational or academic programs. When this reality is combined with the understanding that too many teachers do not possess a deep and complex understanding of the relationship between academic and vocational education (not to mention a sophisticated understanding of subject matter itself), the prospect for serious reform dims. The conceptual dimension of vocational teacher education, therefore, must become more and more sophisticated if we are to have any hope for profound reform. One of the greatest sources of hope in this regard is the Perkins Act.

The Value of the Perkins Act

The Carl D. Perkins Vocational Education Act was passed in 1984 and reauthorized in 1990 (Kolberg and Smith, 1992). Although it is tied in to the attempt to produce the workers that business desires, there are many progressive elements in the 1984 and 1990 legislation. In the tradition of federal vocational education legislation since the 1930s, the Perkins Act has attempted to move vocational education away from job-specific training toward a broader education that focuses on the integration of a variety of learning experiences. The architects of the legislation have maintained that the inculcation of specific skills is not the most important function of vocational preparation. Vocational students, they argue, should gain a critical understanding of industrial organizations in a context where vocational and academic education are integrated (Grubb et al., 1991). This notion from the Perkins Act lays a foundation for this book, as it attempts to provide vocational educators with a larger perspective on the relationship between vocational education and the organization of industry in the past and present. It is only in this type of context that vocational educators can provide a democratic education that truly provides students with a chance for dignified employment.

The 1990 reauthorization of the Perkins Act also mandated that secondary vocational education create stronger ties to postsecondary institutions through "tech prep" programs (Olson, January 19, 1994). Such programs link the student's last two years of high school with the first two years of college, leading to an associate degree or a skills certificate. Tied to the 1990 Perkins reauthorization, the Tech Prep Education Act allocated $63 million to promote and develop these "2 + 2" (two years of high school, two years of community college) programs. The justification for Tech Prep programs revolved around the changing needs of the American workplace demanded by the new global economy. Although the essence of this book is grounded on a notion of good work characterized by high-skill, high-wage labor, the advocates of Tech Prep have often assumed that business and industry have already created these conditions. As noted previously, they have not; political institutions and the American public itself must demand the reinvention of the American workplace. If this reorganization does not take place, many Tech Prep graduates will be "all dressed up" with technical skills but have "no place to go." If constructed around a concept of good work, an understanding of the worker as citizen, an integration of academic and vocational education, and a reconstructed American workplace, Tech Prep could possibly play a role in the improvement of education for students who do not choose college (Dornsife, 1992).

The Effort to Improve the Transition from School to Work

In 1991, the report of the Council of Chief School Officers, an organization of the public officials who head departments of public education in the United States, called for a major overhaul of the ways students moved from school to the workplace. The report, entitled *Connecting School and Employment,* argued that preparation for employment must begin in the primary grades and secondary programs must make sure students have access to postsecondary education, training, and employment. The report also cited the need for employers to share more responsibility in promoting the quality of the workforce, while insisting that schools provide less abstract and more work-based learning. This work-based learning should be grounded, the officers urged, on an integrated academic and vocational curriculum. However, they noted that none of this is possible if employers, schools, and post-secondary-education institutions fail to coordinate their efforts. (I find the absence of labor unions in this alliance noteworthy.) As coordination among these institutions is achieved, schools find it easier to expand cooperative education, youth apprenticeships, and focus schools. In their conclusion, the school officers suggested that a national framework of standards for employability skills be developed that would assess the workforce readiness of students.

The report stimulated action in state and federal education agencies. Realizing that 75 percent of American high school students enter the labor force without college degrees and that far too many cannot find stable, career-tracked jobs for five to ten years after they graduate, legislators devised school-to-work legislation. Bills began to take shape that would connect education and employment by coordinating school-based and work-based learning, academic and vocational curriculums, and secondary and postsecondary education. In addition to Tech Prep, the school-to-work programs in the School-to-Work Opportunities Act include Youth Apprenticeship Cooperative Education, Career Academies, and School-Based Enterprises (Olson, May 5, June 23, 1993; Pullin, 1994). An examination of each of these approaches is in order.

Youth Apprenticeship.   These programs connect structured learning in school and in the workplace with what is labeled a "broad occupational cluster" (for example, health care, manufacturing, engineering technology, and office technology). Apprenticeship programs usually begin in the eleventh grade and include at least one year in postsecondary education. Because students learn better in a real-life problem-solving context, learning in apprenticeship programs becomes more meaningful. Although still in their infancy, these apprenticeship programs have been catalyzed by the School-to-Work Opportunities Act and numerous state and local initiatives (Olson, January 26, 1994; Hudelson, 1992).

Cooperative Education.   Operated by traditional vocational education programs, cooperative education helps students obtain part-time jobs that connect to their chosen field of study. The students enter into written training agreements that specify what the student will learn as well as the responsibilities of the employer. One of the major problems of cooperative education involves the lack of coordination between the students' school and work experiences. Employers are charged with few responsibilities concerning the actual learning needs of the co-op students. Without the need for time or financial commitment, employers have viewed co-op programs as little more than screening devices to help them pick out students with "good attitudes" (Olson, January 26, 1994).

Career Academies.   Breaking down the depersonalization and alienation of large high schools, career academies create a "school within a school." In these minischools, students and teachers form cohort groups that stay together for several years. Academic and vocational curriculums are integrated, as both focus on a broad career theme. Employers are encouraged to supply mentors, workplace-based learning, and summer and after-school work experiences. The first career academy opened in Philadelphia in 1969, and the concept has spread throughout the country since then. By 1994, over two hundred career academies had been established nationwide (Olson, February 23, 1994).

School-Based Enterprises.   Another school-to-work program involves students actually producing goods or services for sale or use by consumers. These school-based enterprises include restaurants, child-care centers, construction jobs, and auto repair shops. Such experiences grant students the opportunity both to apply academic knowledge in the world of work and to gain a hands-on understanding of business operations. By 1994, almost one in every four American high schools had adopted some form of school-based enterprise (Olson, January 26, 1994).

Although these school-to-work programs are beginning to appear in a variety of schools throughout the nation, the United States in the late 1990s still has the worst school-to-work transition in the industrialized world. In the not-too-distant past, most high-school graduates could find steady employment even if they did not attend college. In the 1990s, one-half of all high school graduates have not found steady employment even twelve years after graduation. These young adults spend their twenties moving in and out of low-skill, low-wage jobs, with little possibility for training or career advancement. It does not seem to matter how they performed, for four out of five employers do not even read their high school transcripts. Those students not bound for college have little reason to be high achievers in high school. And they understand this reality, as they drift from one haphazardly scheduled, dull, low-level class to another. "Why do we have to learn this stuff," they ask, rarely receiving an answer.

Nearly one-third of high school students in the United States take general-track classes that get them ready for neither work nor college. Too often, vocational programs still offer only obsolete skills to students pushed out of academic tracks. The Perkins Act may mandate academic and vocational integration, but in the late 1990s, such programs are rarely found. When they do exist, many of the modes of integration are trivial at best.

Fewer than two out of every five vocational students find work that matches their preparation after they graduate from high school. Especially when it comes to poor and minority youth, educators hold fast to beliefs that such students cannot learn complex ideas in math, English, and science. Even though the school-to-work legislation specifically demands that the needs of "disadvantaged" students be met, the attitude that these students simply cannot do sophisticated work still persists. These attitudes must change before we can get beyond the tracking, sorting, and classifying of students that condemns "disadvantaged" students to meaningless school experiences and low-skill jobs (Olson, June 23, 1993; Frantz, 1992).

Impediments to Contemporary Vocational Education Reform

Contemporary vocational education faces many obstacles in the effort to create a democratic education for good work. Presently, very few coordinating organizations exist that can bring employers, academic educators, community-based organizations, students, parents, unions, and vocational educators together to plan work education and the school-to-work transition. Americans will have to examine European models of coordinating agencies if there is to be an effective school-to-work transitional experience for American students and workers. Germany and Denmark, for example, have special organizations that unite employers, educators, and organized labor to oversee school-to-work issues. American employers will have to alter some of their prevailing attitudes about their role in the school-to-work transition if progressive change is to occur. Employers have too often resisted providing structured and educational work experiences for students; also, they have resisted paying students for their work. Paul Osterman, an expert in human resources and management at the Massachusetts Institute of Technology, has maintained that the most formidable impediment to the implementation of practical school-to-work programs involves industry's reluctance to contribute time and financial resources to the effort (Olson, January 26, 1994).

A final problem that haunts these attempts at vocational education reform involves the assumption on the part of many reformers that American industry is in the process of building a high-skill, high-wage, high-performance environment for vocational graduates. Although a few employers have moved in this direction, there still is a long way to go on this journey. A high-skill, high-wage workplace is managed by visionary leaders who are unafraid to invest in the development of worker skills, to provide a career ladder for workers, and to explore the unknown terrain of good work. Vocational education reforms will never work until more business and industrial leaders pursue such courageous policies. Part 3 will examine more closely issues surrounding this need for workplace reform.

PART THREE

*Coping with and
Directing Change*

8   *Post-Fordism and Technopower: The Changing Economic and Political Arena*

Obviously, the vocational educational reforms of the 1990s have been grounded on the understanding—albeit a vague one—that the world is changing, the workplace is changing, and the organization of society is changing. If Clint Eastwood was "the man with no name" in his Westerns in the 1970s, then the contemporary world is "the era with no name." Analysts debate monikers for our contemporary society, throwing around such labels as postindustrial, techtopia, dystopia, postmodernity, late modernity, the end of history, and so on. The influence of technology is obvious; less obvious is the specific nature of the influence. Techophiles (those who love technology) assure us that new technology will make for more interesting, challenging, and diverse forms of work. Although there is no doubt that computers, virtual reality, and microchip technologies will change the face of work, there is much doubt about whether such changes will make for good work. Indeed, many of the techtopian versions of work are constructed around deskilled "people-proof" jobs that degrade the dignity of workers. One important role of vocational educators in contemporary America involves monitoring the nature of the changing workplace in light of our notions of good and bad work and informing students as to the nature of the workplaces they will enter.

Any social foundations of work and vocational education must examine the human costs of technological change and the workplaces and jobs it produces. Technocrats continually promote the idea that high-tech jobs are inherently good work, but closer examination tends to refute that generalization (Borgmann, 1992). Much too often, young people understand that the job market is not the avenue to creative self-expression. In their first jobs, they typically encounter demanding technological devices, impersonal supervisors, and anonymous customers. Indeed, their bosses manage them as if their lives were insignificant; any attempt to provide them with security is interpreted by many economists as a disastrous policy that will undermine worker motivation and productivity (Goodlad, 1992). In such a dehumanized context, it becomes acceptable to adjust workers' hours to the needs of machinery, in the process disrupting periods of rest and sleep. In the name of profit, almost anything can be justified—the destruction of the urban environment, pollution, undermining human health, and so forth. Vocational educators who take democracy seriously must analyze the meaning of progress in the contemporary socioeconomic order. This chapter will explore the political economy of contemporary society, analyzing the impact of new forms of social organization on the future of work and vocational education.

Work and the Rise of Post-Fordism

There is no doubt that many of the jobs being created in a high-tech post-Fordist economy demand higher worker skills than Fordist jobs. As was discussed in Chapter 4, the effort to mark a clean break between Fordism and post-Fordism is impossible; both Fordist and post-Fordist impulses coexist in the contemporary era. Post-Fordist high-skill work can be found in the shadows of Fordist low-skill jobs. Some post-Fordist firms have created a small core of high-skill jobs at the same time they have hired a new low-skill workforce. Certainly, high technology changes work roles; economists and vocational educators just cannot predict the nature of such changes. Post-Fordist upskilling requires workers who can perform abstract activities and respond to randomly occurring workplace events. Such skills cannot be behaviorally programmed into workers; high-skill post-Fordist vocational education combines academic and vocational experiences to teach future workers to diagnose, adjust, and problem solve. Such abilities rest on the development of workers who understand and can manipulate abstract symbols. Whereas Fordist workers were confronted with manufacturing processes involving concrete objects, high-skill post-Fordist workers must deal with representations of that concrete reality.

High-skill post-Fordist workers take responsibility not simply for a job assignment but for the quality of the final product or service. Progressive vocational educators study the skills needed to assume such responsibility and adjust their curricula accordingly (Carnevale, 1992). They teach self-management skills, communication skills, creativity, and interpersonal skills. Contemporary demands for high-quality and specialized products require producers to become anthropologists of consumption, first studying and understanding cultural dynamics and then targeting products and services at different "demographic groups" (Murray, 1992). For example, a retailer founded in 1907 as a single store in Atlanta expanded into a mass-production and marketing chain after 1945. As profits began to decline after 1973, the chain closed several stores that it had established in small towns. Struggling to stay afloat in the late 1970s, the company, on the advice of its marketing anthropologists, rearranged itself in the early 1980s as a niche market retailer with a group of specialized stores. Divesting itself of all manufacturing, the firm then focused its efforts on research and specialty design. A cadre of designers researched lifestyles, linking consumption patterns via commodities from wine to outdoor equipment, from children's clothes to investment counseling. They may even have named the lifestyle in question (e.g., neotraditional cottage, postmodern innovative chic, or outdoor health granola) in order to better coordinate commodity development in clothing, furniture, domestic services, food, travel, and recreation. New products were tested in the specialty stores, with the successful ones being ordered for more extensive distribution. By the late 1990s, the company's profits had skyrocketed as a result of this policy of flexible specialization.

Obviously, such post-Fordist firms worry about how to make the work site a place of learning that can respond to the unpredictable needs of the environment. The crowded market of the contemporary era demands that these flexible firms educate at least a portion of their labor force to deal with the dynamics of specialized production. With the level of computerized information access, transportation, and communication that exists in the late twentieth century, a businessperson and a small cadre of workers can put together an organization that previously demanded months of time and a small army of experts to create. Such realities allow for giant corporations to decentralize their structures in such a way that lifestyle-based production can efficiently proceed. Original descriptions of the economic paradigm shift were typically based on the distinction between the goods-production orientation of the old economy and the service orientation of the new one. Flexible accumulation or specialization is a much better representation of the shift that has occurred, as it directs attention to the ways post-Fordist capitalism is using information and anthropological market data to expand its economic power and social presence (Borgmann, 1992). The most *efficient* way to deal with these post-Fordist economic changes may be to create a high-skill, decentralized, power-dispersed workplace. The more corporate managers understand this concept, the greater the chance for proliferation of democratic workplaces.

Reluctant managers may be forced to share at least some power in the post-Fordist workplace. Their motivation will not be, as in the past, to temporarily improve worker morale or to soothe industrial relations. They may find that the post-Fordist workplace, with its technological realities and its market pressures, may simply require a cadre of knowledgeable and autonomous employees. Given such realities, a major conflict emerges within the consciousness of management: How do managers reconcile their traditional need for worker control with the high-skill autonomy needed in the post-Fordist workplace? Over the last two decades, white-knuckled American managers have watched and listened to Japanese corporate leaders proclaim the death of Fordism and Taylorism (Murray, 1992). Japanese innovators have argued such systems gave central management limited access to the information needed for innovation in production. Further, they discarded the valuable knowledge gained by workers in their everyday activities—knowledge the Japanese managers referred to as "the gold in workers' heads."

As workers are granted the autonomy to deal with unpredictable variables, managers can move away from assembly line production toward a more dynamically flexible approach, one that is shaped to respond to rather than regulate markets. Innovative managers see their companies as a cadre of learners who monitor the market, research patterns of taste, and dissect the nature of style. Managers build economic SWAT teams rather than bulky police forces, as they think of economies of scope rather than economies of scale. Production is based on limited runs, reducing costly reliance on large inventories. This strategy requires high-tech, flexible machinery and workers as learners who change duties with each alteration in consumer demand (Grossberg, 1992). Business time is permanently altered, as the period between design, manufacture, and sales is contracted.

New information and supply systems allow businesses to order supplies to keep up with demand. For example, every evening a firm receives detailed computer printouts of the movement of thousands of products in its various outlets. Based on such data, warehouse deliveries are immediately set into motion. With computerized access to stocks in the individual outlets, transportation matrixes, and automatic loading and unloading, this flexible system has overcome Fordism's stock dilemma. In its shift from mass production/consumption to flexible accumulation/specialization, post-Fordism has accommodated a social change that Robin Murray (1992) has described as not "keeping up with the Joneses" but attempting to "be different from the Joneses" (pp. 270–271). Basing their organization on this consumer desire for uniqueness, Benetton, for example, developed an automatic dyeing plant that enables it to modify the color of its clothes based on unexpected changes in demand. In another example, Toyota reduced the time General Motors took to change the dyes on its presses from nine hours to two minutes, while also managing to cut the average lot size of body parts from 5,000 to 500. Obviously, such changes have altered the textbook on manufacturing: Rather than using specific machines to produce large quantities of standardized products, post-Fordist flexibility employs general-purpose equipment to make an assortment of products.

The question reappears: Can these high-tech, dynamically flexible, post-Fordist arrangements of the workplace function with workers who are alienated and detached? A democratic progressive view of the workplace and vocational education maintains that workers' commitment is directly related to the level of autonomy and control granted to them at work. There is little doubt that when managers allow for worker self-direction, job satisfaction and initiative increase. Managerial forms that allow for more self-direction and worker autonomy have exerted less influence in countries with the strongest Fordist traditions—the United States and the United Kingdom. In these countries, many firms have attempted to develop post-Fordist flexibility while retaining Fordist shop-floor relations.

Taylor in Disguise

The conversation about vocational education and the high-tech workplace in the 1990s requires a reality check. As much as many observers would like to find progressive tendencies in post-Fordist industry, there is no post-Fordist techtopia on the horizon where countless high-skill jobs keep being created by new technological innovation. Stanley Aronowitz and William DiFazio have been blunt enough to refer to "the jobless future" (1994). American businesses continue to "dumb down" their work tasks, in the process cutting wages and benefits. Projections continue to indicate that the highest level of job growth will be found in positions for custodians, cashiers, secretaries, general office clerks, and sales clerks. No general monolithic trend emerges; some businesses and industries will upskill, others will downskill (Levin, 1984). Despite the promise of post-Fordist progressive democratic work, the ghost of Frederick W. Taylor returns, disguised by high-tech surroundings. Turnkey operations and step-by-step manuals are developed on the assumption that workers are dumb—and such prejudices undermine any possibility for worker growth or development (Raizen, 1989).

Despite the rosy picture painted by proponents of technology, many high-tech workers are still trained, not educated. Millions of dollars have been spent to produce computer programmers. Because of the modernist assumptions about education, such training programs tend to fragment computer knowledge. In such contexts, computer programmers fail to develop the ability to apply their knowledge to new situations, lacking the creativity to innovate (Block, 1990). Their computer education has resulted in little more than trained incompetence. The Three Mile Island accident in Pennsylvania is an excellent example of this Tayloristic high-tech work education that fails to integrate theory, systems knowledge, analytical reasoning, problem identification and solving, and contextualized site-specific operations.

After an extensive investigation of the situation, the president's Commission on the Accident at Three Mile Island concluded that the roots of the debacle could be traced to an inadequate training program for workers. Virtually no attention had been given to the connection between the theoretical and the practical; questions relating to thermodynamics, saturation, enthalpy, decay heat production, or solid system operation were not asked. In other words, operator trainees were not granted a basic understanding of nuclear reactor plant design and operation that would have allowed them to identify potentially dangerous developments. Thus, a Homer Simpson syndrome was produced by a training program designed to *train* workers to follow dumbed-down manuals, not to understand the workings of the reactor at both a theoretical and a practical level. The deskilled curriculum trained operators to name specific pieces of equipment, to identify the workings of safety systems, and to follow preconceived, step-by-step procedures in emergency situations. When the minor failure occurred, plant operators had no idea what to do. With deskilled workers in high-tech jobs, the potential for disaster is frightening (Raizen, 1989). It is therefore important to analyze in more detail the social and political dynamics of the post-Fordist economy.

Technopower

The use of such terms as "post-Fordism" or "high-tech economy" sometimes inaccurately portrays economic and political power relations in contemporary society. The development of new technologies over the last few decades has not created a new era of power sharing. Indeed, corporate power in America has never been more entrenched than it is in the late 1990s. Workers, at the same time, have lost power, as production and distribution decisions are made by management with little input from labor. In this respect, perhaps the term "technopower" can be used to describe the expansion of corporate influence through the use of post-Fordist technological development. Using technopower, corporations have increased their ability to maximize capital accumulation. Via technopower, business and industries are better equipped to produce steady growth and thus higher profits, no matter what the social or ecological consequences. Technopower allows firms to be better equipped to control and exploit workers. In fact, corporate growth is grounded on the ability to widen the gap between labor benefits and labor production. This is not exactly a situation conducive to the prospect of power sharing in the workplace (Harvey, 1989).

Understanding this technopower, progressive democratic vocational educators need to expose vocational students to the dynamics of how it works. Liberal vocational educators, carried away by the promise of techtopia, sometimes fail to address the web of corporate power students will confront in the workplace—not to mention in the society at large. Some vocational educators have proclaimed that "the interests of business and education are beginning to converge," ignoring the fact that corporations still operate on the basis of their private interests even when they conflict with the public needs (Carnevale, 1992, p. 29). With corporate public relations people leading the crusade, Americans have retreated from their commitment to the maintenance of a "public space." The needs of low-salaried workers, the poor, the environment—the needs of the public space—have diminished in importance to Americans. Freedom has been redefined as the right of corporations to desecrate this public space in the effort to pursue private gain. Technological development has undoubtedly changed what vocational educators must know, but the dynamics of technopower are rarely considered a part of that knowledge.

Despite claims to the contrary by conservative politicians and fundamentalist ministers, American commitments to the "private space" of family remain very strong. What have diminished over the last quarter of the century are commitments to the "public space"—to community activities, political organizations, volunteer agencies, and so on. Most high-school seniors, for example, say they do not think that a company going out of business has any moral obligation to pay its outstanding debts. In the name of profit maximization, American companies have shut down thousands of factories, moved entire operations to Third World locations, and migrated from state to state in search of cheaper labor and lower taxes. In 1991 in Tarrytown, New York, General Motors embarked on a campaign to lower its taxes by $1 million a year. Announcing that it would close the Tarrytown plant unless workers made benefit and wage concessions and the city lowered its corporate taxes, GM held the city hostage. Because of the subsequent decline of tax revenues, the Tarrytown schools were forced to lay off personnel, eliminate new orders for books and school supplies, and delay needed repairs of school buildings (Coontz, 1992). Given technological advances enabling them to move operations from one state or country quickly, corporations have found themselves bestowed with new power. This is the nature of technopower.

Technopower, Knowledge Control, and Democracy

Technopower comes in many sizes and colors; it is the essence of dynamic flexibility. Since the early 1970s, technopower has steadily expanded, as technology has come to play a more and more important role in organizing and regulating both economic production and our everyday lives. With a few exceptions, technology has been deployed as a tool of corporate leadership in its attempt to maximize profits, to extend its power. Data banks, radio and TV transmissions, and transnational communications systems all contribute to a network that allows corporate leaders to regulate markets all over the world. As these communications systems filter into cities, villages, and rural areas globally, corporations present a view of the world that promotes their interests. The process takes place in a quiet and subtle way, as values such as competitive individualism, the superiority of an unregulated market economy (a tenet of neoclassical economics), and the necessity of consumption are implicitly promoted. People's identities—their sense of who they are—begin to be formed less and less in their communities and more and more by their radios and televisions. The popularity of video compilations of old 1950s and 1960s TV commercials and the emotions they trigger within those of us who grew up in that era is evidence of this media-based identity formation (Kellner, 1989; Smart, 1992; Giroux, 1992; Brosio, 1994; McLaren et al., 1995).

This corporate control of the media and the control of knowledge that accompanies it dramatically affects an individual's perception of the world in general and the nature of work in particular. As was argued in Part 1 of this book, the corporate ability to portray workers as lazy and unproductive dramatically affects the politics of labor-management relations. Managers can rally the public to support their denial of higher wages and more power on the shop floor to workers—because, after all, they do not deserve such rewards. These understandings of technopower are essential to the education of young workers who are citizens in a *democratic* society. Empowerment of these workers can only take place when they are able to see through the myth that technological developments in media have served to produce a better-informed community. Workers with a democratic vocational education thus begin to understand that private interests are building information monopolies, that the public nature of information is quickly mutating into information as a private commodity. As fewer and fewer large corporations control the flow of information (2 percent of publishers, for example, now control 75 percent of the books published in the United States), public accessibility to information contracts. In the process, technopower expands.

It is important for vocational educators to understand that this shaping of public opinion by way of media control is never simplistic. Often, efforts to manipulate opinion backfire, as men and women perceive what is happening to them and rebel. Furthermore, technologies such as computer links and information highways can be used to convey alternative messages that challenge corporate control. Still, most workers remain unable to comprehend the degree of influence corporate leaders attain as they control TV and other media that bypass reason and focus directly on the management of human feelings and emotions. Media presentations that are not obviously political play to our emotions on a level that shapes our political perspectives. Images of children, exuberant as they open gifts on Christmas morning, have no overt political message. At a deeper level, however, such images may be influential, as they tell us that such happiness in our children can be evoked only by the consumption of goods and services. If we truly love our children and want to see them happy, then we must support the interests of the corporations that produce these valuable products. The process of political opinion formation is not a linear, rational procedure but is grounded on our emotional hopes and fears. Thus, when Mattel Inc. calls for lower corporate taxes and a better business climate in which to produce its toys, we accede to its wishes. After all, this is the company that allows us to make our children happy. Vocational educators must figure out how to tell workers and future workers about these realities (Harvey, 1989; McLaren et al., 1995).

Thus, it is safe to conclude that the development of late-twentieth-century information technology has not simply served to promote communication in a democratic society. On the contrary, the primary use of these technological innovations has been to sell and to create consumer markets for particular goods and services. Technopower becomes a medieval alchemist that instead of turning base metals into gold transforms "truth" into "what sells." Valuable information in this context becomes not that which explains or empowers but that which creates a cooperative community, a culture of consumption. Communications media do not exist to help ordinary citizens improve their lives or understand the demands of democratic citizenship. The need to capture the attention and the emotions of consumers transcends all other uses. As it improves ratings, TV reduces everything to the same level—everything that happens must be reconstituted to capture viewer interest. In terms of traditional notions of importance, all events and messages are equally trivial—death, destruction, war, famine, unemployment, beer, feminine hygiene, weight loss programs, acne medications, and the rest. CNN presents the Gulf War, brought to you by Depends Undergarments.

The ethic of market values penetrates into our consciousness, into our everyday political observations. We do not ask about the views of Jack Kemp or William Bennett on information control in a democratic society; we ask who has best sold himself to the Republican Party constituency or who has best manipulated media coverage with his sound bites. Questions of power sharing and social justice give way to the market value of short-term profit making. The short term becomes the only future worth planning, as fashions, political opinions, personalities (your fifteen minutes of fame just ended), and even labor markets come and go in the life span of a mayfly. Academic institutions sacrifice their most cherished values as producers of knowledge and promoters of truth to these short-term market values. The promise of corporate capital quiets proponents of academic integrity, as universities produce data that extend the corporate power to open new markets. The famous Stanford–Silicon Valley or the MIT–Boston Route 128 corporate-academic alliances illustrate higher education's co-optation. Many of the industrial relations that determine the curriculum of vocational programs illustrate secondary education's accommodation (Chesneaux, 1992; Goodlad, 1992; Harvey, 1989).

As technology has extended corporate surveillance capacities, the need for coercion has decreased (Smart, 1992). Factory owners no longer bring in Pinkerton guards to control labor as they did in 1892 at Homestead Steel (see Chapter 5). In the 1990s, labor control methods attempt to induce workers to consent to control by management. Ben Hamper, a former rivet-head at GM's Flint, Michigan, auto plant, described one of the more unsophisticated efforts to win worker consent. After introducing a giant cat named Howie Makem to promote worker morale in the plant, GM personnel managers installed a giant electronic message board that flashed "motivational" dispatches to the line workers. Alongside Howie Makem's face, managers sent messages such as these: Quality Is the Backbone of Good Workmanship! A Winner Never Quits and a Quitter Never Wins! Safety Is Safe! Squeezing Rivets Is Fun! and Happiness Is Horses (Hamper, 1992, pp. 160–161)! Some expressions of technopower, I suppose, are more successful than others.

Throughout the era of TV, power wielders have become increasingly adept at the use of the media. In the 1980s, Ronald Reagan's handlers set new standards for governmental manipulation of the electorate via TV and other technologies. In order to win mass consent, these media experts had to constantly provide TV with a "positive spin" on daily events; that is, they had to present a version of reality that portrayed Reagan and his policies positively. Over and over, like TV commercials, the administration fed the media this reconstituted and pasteurized version of events. Because news is a commodity that seeks to increase ratings just like the entertainment sector of TV, networks never have enough information on the president. Knowing this, the handlers provided sound bites and visuals of Reagan that carefully presented the desired picture of reality. The corporate-driven worldview of the Reagan administration fit quite neatly with the corporate-run media.

Many students of power and media are amused by the common question: "Does big business control the media?" The only response to such an inquiry is that the media *is* big business. The corporate owners of the top three U.S. commercial networks—General Electric (GE), Westinghouse, and Disney—are media monopolies. Squashing or absorbing any competition that might appear, these corporate conglomerates are above public accountability. The prospect of any serious competition in the future is undermined by the prohibitively high cost of establishing a media enterprise. The Reagan administration was extremely cozy with corporate leaders—so cozy, in fact, that GE made $10 billion in profits during the first Reagan term (1981–1985) and paid not one cent in taxes. In these circumstances, the idea of democracy and the power of democratic institutions fade under the domination of corporate technopower. Accountable to no one, such power continues to shape the nature of post-Fordist production and consumption (Brosio, 1994; McLaren et al., 1995).

Rage and Apathy: The Subtle Workings of Technopower, the Politics of Corporatism

All educators, and vocational educators in particular, need to appreciate the economic and political impact of post-Fordist technopower. Because of its subtle and hard-to-identify workings, few Americans have understood the process. Thus, this becomes a central question for our times: How do we tell the workers about these dynamics? Post-Fordist technopower has produced a new political orientation in 1980s and 1990s America; it is a *politics of corporatism* that works to create a "good business climate" (see Chapter 3). This neoconservative politics of corporatism has induced broad segments of the population to accept the existing economic and political inequalities as well as discrimination against various racial and ethnic groups. The politics of corporatism redefines equality in terms of the right to form a business and compete in the marketplace, while it rejects discussion of economic and political alternatives to such beliefs. Corporatism thereby portrays worker empowerment as contrary to our "national values," characterizing it as an attack on the free enterprise system (Grossberg, 1992).

We can all understand why the politics of corporatism works to establish good business climates—which are marked by lower taxes, government-financed infrastructures, land grants, and so forth. The complex workings of technopower involve the attempt to win public support for this politics of corporatism—and this hegemonic process is never easy to understand. The discussion of hegemony in Chapter 3 used Peter McLaren's definition: the maintenance of control not by force but by way of social practices in schools and other institutions that win the consent of the disempowered to be governed by those with power. The workings of technopower cannot be understood outside of this hegemonic context. Add one more factor to this hegemonic process: The politics of corporatism has not been accepted by the American public through a rational public political debate. No public debate exists over questions such as these: How do we distribute income among classes? Should we regulate industry? Does the creation of good business climates serve the public good?

In an age dominated by the media, information explosions, computerization, and information superhighways, politics is boring and few people pay attention to it. At the same time, however, culture is fascinating and almost everyone attends to it. How many of us do not know something about Diana and Dodi, Frank and Kathie Lee, O. J. Simpson, Tonya and Nancy, Amy Fischer and Joey Buttafuco, the Menendez brothers, or the Cola Wars? But it is extremely difficult for Americans to understand that culture is the location where consent is won. Controlling the government may no longer even be necessary for corporate leaders to win political battles (Giroux, 1992). On many levels, such a statement may not make sense—and this is the point. Logical and rational argument may have less to do with winning public consent in this age of media than it did fifty years ago. This does not mean that the politics of corporatism does not want governmental power; but it does mean that the world of the late twentieth century has changed. The politics of corporatism, in other words, does not attain power by making the most persuasive political argument; it attains power by restructuring our private lives and our feelings and emotions at the level of our private experience (Grossberg, 1992).

Thus, here rests the secret of technopower. With its access to people's private, everyday lives, technopower is able to help shape our identities and, consequently, the ways we make sense of our experiences. Our consent is structured not only through political messages but through pleasure and feeling derived by way of popular forms of television, music, dance, movies, and so on. For example, when individuals experience self-expression through consumption and consumption-related practices, TV commercials may structure political meanings and dispositions through the pleasure these experiences provide. A consumer enjoys car ownership and the image such a purchase projects to the world, thus the effect of a Corvette commercial may be experienced on many levels. The ability of corporate advertisers to create imagery that connects and extends the consumer's pleasure produces a variety of effects. Consumers may identify the present economic arrangement as the one best designed to provide them with the pleasure the Corvette accords. They may have to adjust their life within the boundaries of particular social conventions to make the money required to purchase the Corvette and the pleasures it provides. Engaging in such practices privileges certain political orientations, in this case making for a conservative identification with the maintenance of the status quo. It is important to note at this point that similar circumstances may produce very different effects in different individuals.

Students of corporate power have traditionally failed to understand that people make sense of reality both with the mind and the heart/body. Corporate leaders, however, understood this notion long ago, designing their commercial advertisements not around a logical appeal to the buyer's rationality but around the regulation and reshaping of the consumer's desire and emotions. In their attempt to uncover the workings of technopower and the politics of corporatism, democratic vocational educators must understand what people know, how they come to know it, and how such knowledge and the process of obtaining it shape their consent to the powerful. In such an analytical process, educators begin to understand the hegemony of technopower, the ways popular culture undermines human potential, and the ways it helps construct human possibility for self-direction and empowerment.

This potential for self-direction and empowerment, however, is undermined by the collapse of politics in America. Until we look at the political conversation taking place among workers and other citizens in Poland, the Czech Republic, Slovakia, Hungary, and other former Communist countries, it is hard to realize the degree of the American disinterest in the political. This disinterest in politics does not mean that Americans are not outraged by workplace realities and inequity in schools and other institutions; they are. Every term, my students express their moral indignation and outrage over modernist forms of "stupidification"; like *Network*'s Howard Beale, they are "mad as hell and not gonna take it any more." But despite all of this anger and outrage, Americans remain for the most part politically inactive. American citizens have one of the lowest levels of voter participation of any industrialized democratic society. Participatory democracy is steadily weakening in the United States as fewer and fewer people are involved in formulating agendas. We have lost our faith in the possibility of changing things. The American conservatism that has developed since the 1970s reflects not a satisfaction with the status quo but a pessimism grounded on the belief that reform is impossible. The conservative resurgence of the 1970s, 1980s, and 1990s is grounded on a politics of pessimism (Grossberg, 1992; Brosio, 1994).

Under such circumstances, politicians can avoid dealing with political issues, questioning instead each other's character, family values, Americanism, military records, and so on (Coontz, 1992). These nonpolitical politicians manipulate voters with sappy stories about mama and images of their role as family men (picture slow-motion campaign videos of the candidate playing in the backyard with dogs and grandchildren or children). The complex aspect of this story of the workings of power and American depoliticization is that the same audience that understands many of David Letterman's subtle parodies of TV forms and formats also understands the less-than-subtle manipulative intent of the political commercials. In other words, growing numbers of Americans are becoming sophisticated observers of the media and are thus able to identify the manipulative practices of politicians. In a bizarre sense, the ability to manipulate effectively becomes an art form, as some politicos are judged more adept in the art form than others. The press often perpetuates such perspectives, with reports analyzing elections not on the basis of issues or substance but according to how well candidates exploit the media. Whose images were more successful? Who "came across" most sincerely? Whose political commercials were better produced? Such coverage exacerbates pessimism and cynicism.

As political activism is undermined, this neoconservatism is expressed by inactivity on a number of fronts. After the stock market crash of 1929 and the resulting economic depression, thousands of unemployed Americans marched on Washington. The return of massive unemployment to America in the 1980s elicited no such response, not even on a limited scale (Chesneaux, 1992). The hopelessness of the politics of pessimism had undermined any form of political action. The success of neoconservatism in the 1980s and 1990s cannot be attributed to its economic success, as an unbalanced distribution of assets and a high growth of indebtedness have persisted. Many analysts have argued that neoconservatism and its politics of corporatism have been nurtured by a shift from the collective values of the Fordist working class to a new embrace of competitive individualism. The celebration of the entrepreneur is a key feature of this competitive individualism; and this orientation has encouraged thousands of Americans to take the risk of going into business for themselves (Harvey, 1989). Although there are many success stories, there are far more failures. This rise of competitive individualism with its neoconservative politics and its entrepreneurial culture has helped induce a substantial redistribution of wealth to those who were already wealthy.

The return of competitive individualism has provided the camouflage for the politics of corporatism—corporate self-determination. Competitive individualism harks back to a nineteenth-century conception of Social Darwinism, as it reignites the flame of classical economics. In many vocational education programs, the impact of these political and economic positions on working men and women is not discussed. As technopower broadcasts the corporate message throughout the society, vocational students find that they have never been presented with political or economic viewpoints that challenge competitive individualism and the politics of corporatism. Understanding that technopower grants corporate leaders control of a photocentric, aural, and television-directed culture in which electronic images produce knowledge, political perspectives, and identity, progressive democratic vocational educators devise a curriculum for workers that confronts technopower.

That curriculum is based on three principles: (1) it examines the historical context of particular assumptions technopower makes about the role of workers and the nature of the workplace (the discussions of Taylorism and scientific management and their views of the role of workers and the nature of the workplace in Chapter 3 provide an example of this first principle); (2) it devises new ways of analyzing the pronouncements of technopower, as it refuses to passively accept corporate portrayals of the world (the discussion of workers as researchers in Chapter 10 is an example of this second principle); and (3) it grounds its examinations of the world views presented by technopower by asking whose interests are being served by the portrayals in question. All aspects of this book have been developed around this important issue. Here rests the foundation of the effort to tell the workers that the world has changed and that new understandings and actions are required of them.

The Growing Gulf Between Core and Peripheral Workers in Post-Fordism

A vocational curriculum that confronts technopower cannot ignore the dynamics of post-Fordism's tendency to create a two-tier workforce, composed of (1) core workers, that is, a small group of full-time, permanent status workers, and (2) peripheral workers, meaning part-time or short-term workers with low pay and low benefits. The United Parcel Service strike of August 1997 was based on this tragic development. The post-Fordist core workers are a steadily shrinking group that enjoys job security, a good chance for promotion, good educational opportunities, pensions, insurance, and other benefits (Gans, 1993). Managers expect these workers to be educated, adaptable, flexible, and, if needed, geographically mobile. When advocates of techtopia speak of the high-skill, high-wage jobs of the future, they are referring to these core workers. As previously argued, there are progressive dimensions to the creation of this post-Fordist core worker; a few of these workers enjoy work situations that approach our concept of good work. They are responsible in part for product improvement and the rearrangement of work processes. Democratic progressive educators should validate these developments and work to extend these benefits to more and more workers.

A vocational curriculum that confronts technopower, however, cannot ignore the more common underside of these post-Fordist changes. Even these prized core workers are barred from the status and power of corporate managers. More important, studies indicate that in the 1990s, one of every two or three jobs created is a peripheral position. In the language of management, these peripheral positions are filled by "disposable" workers. As the decade of the 1990s has become the era of the layoff, newspapers are daily filled with headlines such as these: "Sears Lays Off 50,000"; "Big Blue [IBM] Reduces Workforce by 40,000"; or "28,000 Get Pink Slips at Boeing." Many of these jobs are not being replaced; the hiring that is occurring, of course, is dominated by part-time peripheral labor. Peripheral workers make only 60 percent of the wages earned by full-time workers and about one in five is covered by employer-sponsored health insurance. The growing corporate use of temporary agencies in the 1990s indicates this corporate emphasis on downsizing core workers (Coontz, 1992; Block, 1990).

Even before the 1990s, the decade during which part-time employment has grown most dramatically, part-time work was increasing. From 1970 to 1990, the Bureau of Labor Statistics reported a 121 percent growth in part-time hirings. Corporate subcontracting of labor involves two somewhat different subgroups: (1) the part-time workers and fixed-term contract staff that have just been discussed, and (2) full-time workers with skills that are easy to find in the labor market, that is, clerical, secretarial, routine, and low-skill manual labor. It is for these jobs that managers use temporary agencies, thus making it easier for workforce expansion when times are good and cost-efficient workforce reduction when times are bad. A new, lower working class is being established by these post-Fordist labor policies. Such a development is unacceptable to democratic progressive vocational educators who are dedicated to the principles of good work. Vocational students must gain an awareness of this antidemocratic feature of the contemporary economy and formulate strategies to confront its effects on their lives.

9 *Democratic Post-Fordist Workplaces and Debating the Changing Purposes of Vocational Education*

As the context shaped by technopower and the politics of corporatism becomes clearer, workers need an alternative vision of both democratic post-Fordist workplaces and a progressive vocational education. Only by constructing an ever-evolving notion of vocationalism can Americans begin to take back power in the effort to rebuild a humane public domain. Chapter 9 will review some of the reform proposals for contemporary vocational education in light of this objective. The criteria for judgment are clearly stated: the democratic notion of good work and a critical educational form of teaching underlie this perspective. As always, democracy is taken seriously.

The Language of Possibility:
The Democratic Post-Fordist Workplace

The neoclassical view of the "workplace of the future" is of a happy and cooperative place with no need for unions or worker organization. Such a Disneyesque view not only holds out false hope but places workers (especially peripheral workers) in great jeopardy. Any workplace arrangement or vocational education that ignores technopower and the politics of corporatism in a post-Fordist or a Fordist economy is not in the best interests of workers. Thus, even if democratic vocational educators turn out thoughtful, creative, and high-skill workers, there will not necessarily be good jobs for them until workers understand the dynamics of workplace power. As discussed in Chapter 1, any democratic economic movement must provide working people with a more equitable share of corporate and business profits. Work sites must become safer, less authoritarian, and more hospitable spaces where workers play major roles in their everyday administration. In such places, jobs can be evaluated not only for their material rewards but also for the opportunities they provide for people to develop their knowledge and skills (Carnevale, 1992; Bluestone and Harrison, 1982; Simon, Dippo, and Schenke, 1991).

In order to set the stage for such thinking, democratic vocational educators must rethink the workplace and its dynamics within a power-sharing context. Such thinking induces us to reconceptualize notions such as the definition of a work skill. In everyday language, a skill refers to a person's ability to produce or accomplish something. Roger Simon, Don Dippo, and Arlene Schenke (1991) question the power relations hidden in such a definition, contending that a skill is not simply a worker's personal property. The everyday definition is decontextualized, they argue, as it releases industrial and business managers from their role in the production of a skill. The act of contextualization allows us to understand that a skill is contingent on the interaction between a human ability and the opportunities to develop and employ it in the work environment provided. As with students, therefore, it is unwise to evaluate a worker's ability on the basis of what that worker is demonstrably able to do in a particular context. For this and many other reasons, it is important to discard the Taylorist concept of employees having fixed jobs; good work is always characterized by flexible work assignments that enable individuals to acquire a variety of skills.

In the democratic vision of a post-Fordist workplace, skilled workers are rewarded for acquiring knowledge and skills related to the functioning of the larger operation. The degree to which an industry is democratic depends on what percentage of its workers are included in these high-skill, high-compensation dynamics (Grossberg, 1992). When skills, performance, and initiative are viewed as *social events*, a new type of thinking has begun to transform the workplace and our understanding of cognition. In *Toil and Trouble: Good Work, Smart Workers, and the Integration of Academic and Vocational Education* (1995), I analyze this new form of worker cognition, labeling it "postformal thinking" (Kincheloe and Steinberg, 1993). Thinking of this sort involves the ability to understand the origins and context of systems, while identifying patterns that characterize them via the development of new forms of analytical processes. Democratic post-Fordist businesses and industries become postformal learning organizations that are marked by a generative form of learning—learning that catalyzes our ability to create (Senge, 1990).

The democratic post-Fordist learning organization cultivates employees' abilities to identify and solve problems. Acting on the information and insight workers provide, post-Fordist learning organizations come to regard worker skills and knowledge as the most important dynamic of economic production. Taylorist notions of one person at the top of the organizational hierarchy discerning what to do and then making sure that everyone else does it are obsolete. When learning takes place at all levels, it becomes possible for a firm to develop a shared vision of its purpose. Such an enterprise requires that management listen to workers' insights into design and production matters. When managers take worker knowledge seriously, they find that greater worker autonomy is a necessity. Deskilling evolves into "multi-skilling," as leaders designate underutilization of worker insight as a primary organizational mistake. A sacred view of work develops that perceives material affluence as merely one of many goals of an organization. Individual learning and development and other "intrinsic" benefits become more and more important in our vision of the democratic post-Fordist workplace (Block, 1990; Senge, 1990; Kolberg and Smith, 1992; Rumberger, 1984).

The Never-ending Debate:
Vocational *Training* Versus Vocational *Education*

Part 2 reviewed the one-hundred-year debate over perceiving work preparation as vocational training or as vocational education. Unfortunately, this debate is still alive, as the United States moves into an era of changing economic arrangements. The training argument, led by the progeny of David Snedden, has changed in light of the need for more flexible post-Fordist workers; but, while the means of production has technologically advanced, the purpose of vocational training has remained faithful to the effort to regulate workers so that they can be fitted to the needs of the workplace (Copa and Tebbenhoff, 1990). Still dedicated to the attempt to train students for entry-level employment, training proponents are rarely interested in the goals of higher-order thinking or creativity. Trapped in the modernist mindset that fragments skills into a neat series of subskills, vocational trainers ignore the production of meaning (Brosio, 1994; Block, 1995).

There is no need for vocational teachers to study the social foundations of vocational education, if we believe that "a creative mind is a flawed mind." Indeed, through the history of vocational teaching, we have focused more on teaching obedience and compliance than on nurturing craft orientations and analytical abilities. Whereas vocational training values imitation, a democratic vocational education values inventiveness; vocational training has sought technical proficiency, but democratic vocational education has sought intelligence. As John Dewey argued at the beginning of the twentieth century, work education simply teaches skills—and such an education involves inquiring into what values are worthwhile and should be pursued. Only in this context can a vocational education be developed that supports the nurturance of each student and the development of the student's potential. As vocational students are educated to understand the nature and conditions of work, they gain the ability to shape their own personal agendas. In the process, they learn to protect themselves from the corporate public relations specialists who too often induce workers to act against their own best interests (DeVore, 1983; Marshak, 1993; Lakes, 1985; Nelson and Watras, 1981; Rehm, 1989; Giroux, 1993).

Rethinking the Five Traditional Emphases of Vocational Education

In this analysis of the social, economic, and historical foundations of American vocational education, five traditional emphases begin to emerge. The standing of each of these purposes varies in relation to the nature and perception of changing economic and social circumstances (Simon, Dippo, and Schenke, 1991).

1. *Facilitating student decisions about careers.* An important aspect of Taylorist efficiency involved fitting the right person to the right job. Correspondingly, advocates of the scientific efficiency curriculum and their educational descendants have attempted to fit the right students to the right curriculum. Fitting students to an education and a job that matches their ability (or lack thereof) seems to hold a pragmatic and innocent tenor until one understands that in practice it meant making stereotyped judgments about the genetic ability of students from particular race, ethnic, class, and gender backgrounds. A progressive democratic vocational education has no problem with the attempt to help students make career choices—it should. The point is that these choices should be made with the knowledge that stereotypes often play a greater role in career counseling than does the student's actual interest and ability. Students should be aware of these tendencies as they enter into the process of choosing career paths (Nelson and Watras, 1981; Babich, 1981).

2. *Helping students develop the skills needed to obtain and keep a job.* Few would argue that a central focus of any vocational education must involve preparing students for potential employment. The questions in this vocational education emphasis concern what skills are needed and how such skills are taught. A basic assumption of right-wing approaches to vocational education maintains that the potential worker must be changed to fit the needs of the larger economy and the workplace. Democratic perspectives reject that notion, grounding their concerns on the need to change the workplace to meet the needs of workers. Although the changing demands of a post-Fordist workplace require worker adaptability, such flexibility will be pursued within humane boundaries. Democratic vocational educators can support the work skills delineated by the secretary of labor's Commission on Achieving Necessary Skills, but such vocational teachers recommend that they be based on the principles of good work. SCANS competencies include

A. The ability to allocate resources, such as time, money, and materials.
B. Good interpersonal skills that allow workers to work on teams, to teach others, to serve customers.
C. The ability to acquire and evaluate information and data, including the ability to use computers.

D. The ability to monitor and to evaluate systems and performance so they can be improved.
E. The ability to use technology and tools. (Kolberg and Smith, 1992)

3. *Providing students an alternative educational environment that will benefit underachieving students and discipline problems.* Here, advocates from a variety of ideological positions contend that vocational education should help students develop the ability to direct their own actions and to assume responsibility for themselves. Deeper analysis is required in order to understand the dynamics of this vocational educational purpose. More conservative analyses assert that the alternative environment provided by vocational education should produce workers who value tradition and respect the authority of the industrial hierarchy. If it does little else, conservative critics argue, vocational education should produce compliant and deferential workers. Some groups of students are harder to motivate—to turn into docile workers—than others, conservatives contend. They argue that poor nonwhite immigrants and African Americans have lesser capacities than white middle-class students and as a result, have been more likely to follow more humble career paths (Herrnstein and Murray, 1994). Thus, vocational education has served as a successful "holding tank" for groups sorted by class, race, and ethnicity; minority and lower-class youth are kept away from the academic, college-bound curriculum where the best chance for socioeconomic mobility resides. Tracked into vocational programs, those students most likely to exhibit the social pathologies of crime, violence, pregnancy, and other forms of delinquency become the constituency of vocational education. What self-respecting student wants to enter such a program? As a high-school principal told one of my students, the daughter of a physician, after she had signed up for vocational auto mechanics: "I took you out of that class. You don't want to be around those kind of students" (Copa and Tebbenhoff, 1990; Grubb, 1978; Babich, 1981).

Democratic vocational educators understand that such perspectives make vocational education a dumping ground for underachievers and discipline problems. They discern, however, a progressive dimension in the alternative educational environment created by vocational education. Understanding the separation of schooling from life and the boredom and alienation that attends it, democratic vocationalists recognize the possibilities for motivation presented by education for work. Conservatives often fail to understand that motivation does not precede involvement with action; indeed, it occurs as a part of the action (Freire and Macedo, 1987). Unable to grasp this concept, traditionalists use tests, discipline, baseball bats à la Joe "Stand by Me" Clark, and the promise of future jobs. Auto mechanics provides a motivational context to understand the physical forces that allow a car to operate—

in other words, the principles of physics. Vocational classes, the progressives realize, can be used to validate the knowledge of those traditionally rejected by the culture of the school. For instance, a young man who has experienced little success in school may find auto mechanics a self-affirming course, as the knowledge he has gained from his father is finally recognized by the school as valuable. That experience may lead him into new studies, maybe physics. A dramatic use of vocational education as motivational strategy has taken place in such a circumstance. It is an experience that refuses to further exclude students but serves to include more and more individuals in the community of learners. For the first time, students may feel as if they count—and this is always a dramatic motivational experience. Great vocational teachers have always accomplished these goals.

4. *Teaching students technical work skills* (Simon, Dippo, and Schenke, 1991). For decades, of course, vocational educators have debated exactly what constitutes a technical work skill: Are they specific to a particular workplace? Are they sufficiently general to apply to a variety of workplaces? Regressive modernist vocational education was constructed on a Taylorist foundation, as it told workers what to do and how to do it. Vocational skill training followed the modernist script, dissecting skills into their smallest parts. If each portion of the skill is learned, they reasoned, then the whole skill will be understood (Raizen and Colvin, 1991). Progressive democratic educators realize such methods are ineffective; in fact, they argue that specific work skills cannot be effectively taught in a school setting because work experience cannot be adequately modeled there. Thus, they appreciate the importance of context in any learning situation. As post-Fordist technologies continue to develop in more and more sophisticated forms, the difficulty of modeling work in schools becomes less feasible. Progressive vocational educators, understanding these dynamics, call for less specific work-skill training in classrooms and for more emphasis on general skills, symbolic understandings, and cultural knowledge (Raizen, 1989).

5. *Solving larger society's economic problems.* From the early twentieth century to the present, vocational education leaders have claimed that vocationalism can increase economic production as it matches workers to jobs (Grubb, 1978). From David Snedden to Anthony Carnevale of the American Society of Training and Development, vocational promoters have promised to increase the wealth-producing capacity of society. Ignoring the inegalitarian effects of class and racial structures, many advocates have guaranteed that vocational education would make everyone equal competitors in the market place (Jonathan, 1990). Viewing vocational education as a human resource supply system, these advocates have underplayed or dismissed the civic and cognitive role of vocational education (Block, 1990). Questions that center on such issues as what constitutes good work, or what makes a smart worker, or what kind of society we want have played a minor

role in the American conversation about vocational education. Although democratic progressives are vitally concerned with such questions, they do not deny the important economic role of vocational education. They realize, however, that their effort to produce talented, creative, and thoughtful workers will serve little purpose if business and industrial leaders do not rearrange their workplaces to accommodate such workers, if labor leaders do not build unions that will extend the educational work of a progressive democratic vocational schooling, and if governmental leaders do not push legislation to reward firms that rearrange their workplaces so as to utilize creative labor and to punish firms that perpetuate bad work.

Rehm on the Three Dominant Views Concerning Vocational Education

Vocational educator Marsha Rehm (1989) helps us make sense of the three dominant perspectives promoted in the contemporary conversation about vocational education. The debate centers around this question: What knowledge should schools transmit? In the following passage, I analyze Rehm's three positions in order to contextualize the latest expression of a democratic progressive form of vocational education—a critical pedagogy of vocationalism.

1. *The conservative humanist perspective: Vocational education should be eliminated because it is trivial and obsolete.* No student should pursue vocational studies; rather, all students should study history, literature, science, and math. On some levels, conservatives are on target with their criticisms of vocational education in the late twentieth century. Vocational education has not reduced unemployment, helped students find *good* jobs, or facilitated their quest for financial mobility. Conservative humanists believe that school is where knowledge is gained and learning takes place. Conservative humanists maintain that no one is *properly* educated outside of school; the academic dimension of school holds the exclusive franchise for educational experience. Any information that exists outside the walls of academia is inferior and has little to do with the rigorous demands of intellectual preparation (Freire and Macedo, 1987, pp. 77–78). This attitude, often promoted by those who prosper in academics, is transferred to people who work in trades and crafts, eliciting from them feelings of self-disdain and intellectual inadequacy. As conservative humanists strip academic learning from its lived-world context, students fail to understand not only its relevance to their lives but also the dynamics of how the knowledge was produced and how it came to be validated as essential information for them to learn (Macedo, 1994, pp. 50–55).

E. D. Hirsch, author of *Cultural Literacy* (1987), is a key spokesperson for the conservative humanists. Arguing that students need to absorb a common core of academic knowledge if they hope to possess an equal opportunity to compete in the American marketplace, Hirsch has asserted that vocational understandings have little relevance to this quest. Indeed, he has contended that vocational education is directed to the needs of a particular time and place and thus becomes quickly obsolete in a world of changing technology. Hirsch's political ally, Diane Ravitch, made a similar argument, maintaining that job training will become less and less important in the twenty-first century because of the accelerating pace of technological change. All we have to do, Hirsch and Ravitch have written, is make sure that students become culturally literate and intellectually steeped in the traditional academic curriculum. This is the best "vocational education" we can grant them. Vocational education as now formulated, conservatives maintain, has no role in the quest for cultural literacy. Much of the knowledge associated with specific vocations has no value. Democratic vocational educators reject such claims, arguing that such an argument is an excellent example of power at work, privileging the knowledge of the core elite while devaluing the understandings of the cultural outsiders (Rehm, 1989; Thompson, 1989).

Although the conservative position is correct in some of its criticisms of the vocational education status quo and offers hope with its antitechnocratic humanist curriculum in a regressive modernist school system, Marsha Rehm has argued that our democratic hopes are quickly dashed by the elitism and instrumentalism of the conservative humanists. Just as they argue that vocational educators are narrow and vulgarly utilitarian, the conservatives fall prey to the same impulses when they simplistically contend that a traditional education will make the U.S. more economically competitive. Never examining the fragmentation, decontextualization, and rote memorization of information that takes place in the name of traditional education, conservative humanists fail to delineate exactly how such academic experiences turn students into competitive workers.

The conservatives see no problem in designating the specific academic knowledge they include in their curriculum as the information everyone should possess. Henry Giroux (1993) and Donaldo Macedo (1994) contend that the conservative humanists see culture as an artifact frozen in the image of a warehouse or a storehouse. The value of this icy knowledge is determined by those who have the power to designate its worth. And the power brokers leave no doubt: The craft and trade knowledge of the vocations are not high-grade expressions of intelligence. The contradiction inherent in such pronouncements becomes obvious when we understand that the conservative humanists value efficient production but reject the notion that schooling might study the complex attempt to achieve it, with all its pitfalls and inhumane traps.

Many of us involved with the critical study of culture (cultural studies) understand that one learns as much about a school of thought from what it excludes as from what it includes. Conservative humanists rarely study the history and sociology of work, the dynamics of democracy in the economic sphere, or the struggle for justice in the workplace. Under the banner of sustaining a "common American culture," conservative humanists reject the study of African-American, Hispanic/Latino, and women's cultural experience. The struggle of these groups in the workplace is simply not a conservative concern. The study of the political and economic effects of vocational education is also neglected, as conservative humanists turn away from questions of inequity in the education of the poor and culturally different. Hirsch and Ravitch and their ideological brothers and sisters are perplexed by the anger of African-American and Hispanic/Latino students toward traditional education. They fail to understand because they refuse to acknowledge the elitist nature of their classical approach to teaching and learning. Questions concerning how teachers might deal with less-privileged learners do not bother conservatives. So opposed are they to vocational education that the idea of using a student's vocational interest to build a bridge to academic understanding is deemed absurd. If students do not bring an intrinsic motivation to academic classes, then there is nothing the conservative humanists can do for them; they are lost (Thompson, 1989; Rehm, 1989).

2. *The vocational specialist perspective: Job-specific vocational education should be provided to all students who are not going to college.* Vocational specialists are strongly opposed to the conservative humanist call for an end to vocational education. Advocating that a vocational curriculum should run parallel to an academic track throughout high school, vocational specialists reject the findings of Jeannie Oakes (1985) and others that tracking results in hurtful discrimination. Just the opposite occurs, they argue, citing statistical evidence that vocational students who graduate from programs with state-of-the-art facilities are hired by industry. Vocational specialists have debated conservatives and advocates of teaching general vocational skills throughout the twentieth century. Where conservative humanists look to the traditional knowledge of Western civilization as the basis of their educational proposals, vocational specialists turn to the needs of industry. Like David Snedden and Charles Prosser in the early twentieth century, the specialists worship at the altar of economic efficiency. Moved by appeals to market demands and financial rewards, vocational specialists see the purpose of vocational education as revolving around the transformation of the undisciplined student into the productive worker.

Traditionally, business groups have been the strongest allies of the vocational specialists. They understand that special-skill training benefits employers, as public school funds, not their own private monies, are used to train their workers. Specific skills involve the specialized tasks that one employee performs at one factory; for example, a worker who checks the quality of hops at the Miller Brewing Company possesses a specific vocational skill. Because of the time needed to develop a vocational program to train students for a specific job skill needed by industry, there is a good possibility that the program and the equipment it requires will be obsolete before implementation. An example of this tendency involved the spate of low-level computer programming projects created in the early 1980s just as new technologies wiped out jobs in the area. Indeed, most efforts to deliver specific skills to vocational students have failed (Babich, 1981). Specific-skill training should take place in on-the-job programs, apprenticeships, and special-purpose schools intimately connected to workplaces. The plethora of contemporary reforms analyzed in Chapter 7, emanating from the Perkins Act and including Tech Prep, Youth Apprenticeships, Career Academies, and School-Based Enterprises, indicate dissatisfaction with job-specific training. At least in the minds of their developers, these programs emphasize the relationship between broad concepts and technical principles supporting a variety of related occupations. Thus, teachers in these programs are encouraged to confront general vocational understandings, as they back away from emphasis on specific job skills (Rehm, 1989; Raizen, 1989; Grubb et al., 1991).

3. *The vocational generalist perspective: Vocational education should be provided to all students because it teaches valuable work concepts, values, and skills.* Simple job training is not the only purpose of vocational education; well-planned vocational programs give students the options of individualized instruction, leadership opportunities, cooperative learning, motivation, understanding the why and how of skills, career guidance, and leisure skills. Vocational generalists are interested in students' understanding the role of work in society. They see vocational classrooms as places where abstract concepts can be illustrated through their concrete applications. Through student experience in field placements, vocational generalists assert that students can learn about work in particular and the socioeconomic world in general. For example, students could learn general vocational and academic skills via a school-initiated building construction project. During their daily encounters in such a learning environment, students would come to understand the connections among drafting, marketing, home economics, and horticulture—not to mention concrete situations where they could employ and improve their math, language, and science skills.

Vocational generalists want to use vocational education to prepare lifelong learners who understand the principles of science and the dynamics of technology. Such learners possess analytical abilities that enable them to communicate effectively, recognize and solve problems, and produce knowledge. Most employers, generalists contend, find such abilities valuable, especially the general literacy skills and the productive work habits (critical democratic vocational educators question this assumption). Traditionally, labor has sided with proponents of general skills, whereas business leaders have promoted specific skills. Although vocational education reform after reform pushed general skills in order to provide workers with skills that can be transferred among different jobs in an ever-changing economy, the constant perception of need for such reform reveals that in practice, vocational education tends to be specific. After much analysis, Rehm maintained that all three positions are flawed: None of the perspectives examines the socially constructed nature of work and the roles that the politics of corporatism and other manifestations of technopower play in such constructions. New forms of vocational education must be developed, she has concluded, to produce workers with civic knowledge and courage who can challenge these antihumane, antidemocratic, and antiegalitarian dynamics of the present era (Rehm, 1989).

The Fourth Perspective:
Vocational Education for Jobs and Justice

The hidden political practices that support the processing, labeling, and stratification of students are left untouched by the conservative humanists, the vocational specialists, and the vocational generalists. There has to be another position, another perspective on the purpose of vocational education that confronts questions of justice and oppression. Thus, the fourth perspective that Rehm has developed contains the understanding that the purpose of vocational education is not restricted to an effort to enhance occupational mobility for vocational students or to simply ensure the student's economic survival after high school. A vocational education that is concerned with survival and mobility works merely to pit individuals against each other (Simon and Dippo, 1987). Thus, the fourth perspective on vocational education is not simply instrumental, as it provides students with knowledge, skills, and abilities needed to both understand and participate in the political dynamics of the changing workplace. As vocational education helps students make sense of the economic, social, and cultural relations that influence their workplace performance and sense of possibility for their future, it moves into a new, uncharted dimension. At first, students themselves may have trouble understanding this new dimension of their vocational education, trained as they are to see education as directly instrumental. Asking questions of worth (what is the worth of your knowledge?), progressive democratic teachers can begin to expand students' social imagination, their sense of possibility (Letiche, 1992).

This social imagination and sense of possibility always involve the belief that democracy is achievable, that hope for a better future exists. Understanding this context leads to transformation—and is a remembrance of Dewey's response to Snedden's efforts to use vocationalism to adapt workers to the needs of business and industry. An appreciation of the political and social aspects of work induces students to ask, "Of what use is this education if all I will do on the job is turn screws and fasten bolts to a product as it comes down an assembly line?" Such insightful questions lead to an appreciation of why a fourth perspective is needed, an awareness that there has to be more than this. Without a set of experiences that enable them to see beyond the cult of individualism, with its vocational education for individual mobility and economic survival, students will see no reason to cooperate with their fellows in the struggle for justice, equal opportunity, and good work.

A cultural focus of the fourth perspective, a vocational education for jobs and justice, involves rigorous analysis of how individual mobility is undermined—the central focus of Part 4 in this book. As vocational students understand the processes and patterns that thwart mobility, they take a giant step down the road to self-direction and toward the ability to control their own fate. Such students are critical in that they are not passively accepting, as they gain the ability to understand the hidden meanings of the workplace. Listening to the communiqués of their superiors in the educational and industrial hierarchies, for example, they begin to read between the lines of administrative speech. In the process, they uncover minefields of political meanings and assumptions that they expose for all to see. It is in these situations that vocational students begin to gain awareness of themselves as thinking agents. The realization begins to dawn on students that high school is not a place where analysis occurs or where students are permitted to choose their own thoughts. Imagination is forbidden; imitation and memorization form the safe path to success (Simon, Dippo, and Schenke, 1991; Rehm, 1989; Letiche, 1992; Grubb, 1978; LaBrecque, 1974).

It is useful at this point to return to the discussion of hegemony and its concept of winning the consent of the governed. This process of winning consent is a teaching-learning process that can only be understood when students understand how their own backgrounds help shape the way they make sense of the world in general and hegemonic authority in particular (Giroux, 1992). For example, a vocational education student raised in a small town in South Carolina in a fundamentalist religious family might understand the hegemonic process very differently than other students. Having been raised to defer to authority and do what he has been told, this student might grant consent to powerful figures with little hesitation. The effort of a critical democratic vocational education program to analyze the nature and effects of particular political and economic arrangements may strike this student as contrary to all of his innate impulses. Students of vocational education need to appreciate the social dynamics at work in this and many other situations—their own situations in particular. Because of these individual differences, students and teachers make sense of the world around them in many different ways. Thus, critical democratic vocational educators teach students to analyze the ways individuals legitimate and delegitimate certain forms of authority in their lives. In other words, students in progressive vocational programs investigate the way personal consciousness is constructed.

Here, we bring in the study of oppression and the impact of race, class, and gender forces. One factor that allows racial oppression to continue involves the "consciousness construction" of white people via TV and visual media. When white people are interviewed about their understandings of racism, they speak of their perceptions of black entry into the mainstream of American life, as evidenced by black sports figures with lucrative financial contracts, the growth of black TV news anchors, and sitcoms where African Americans are portrayed as professional, upwardly mobile people. Thus, many white TV watchers often conclude that racial discrimination is a thing of the past; the 1990s, they argue, is a time of unjustified privilege for African Americans. Anyone can make it in America now; because of affirmative action and racial quotas, black Americans have an easier time getting jobs than white people. Unfortunately, these attitudes have become popular at the same time that African American prosperity is declining. Black income in relation to white income is falling; since 1980, there has been a significant increase in black poverty, fewer black families own homes, and more than one out of three live below the poverty line (Jhally and Lewis, 1992). White perceptions of African American privilege and white victimization hold profound political implications. A fourth perspective on vocational education must examine the complex ways in which power constructs consciousness, while forming social and political perspectives that facilitate the perpetuation of existing power relations.

Engaging in a progressive democratic analysis of work in America involves not only an in-depth examination of the way the media represent the economic sphere but also a sensitivity to the contradictions between what we say we do and what we actually do (Trend, 1994; Grubb et al., 1991; Murray and Ozanne, 1991). For example, Americans often believe in following the ethical path as long as it does not interfere with the imperative of profit making. I recently watched a local news reporter interview a spokesperson for a fundamentalist Christian political coalition in Louisiana that had supported legislation to force businesses to close on Sundays. "We must respect God and his day of rest by keeping the Sabbath holy," he argued, "and force anti-Christian owners to close their stores on Sundays." "We must get back to God and follow His commandments to the letter," he continued. When asked if there could be any exceptions to the ban, the spokesperson quickly retreated: "Well, of course, the ban wouldn't include any firms that needed Sunday business in order to turn a profit." As Donaldo Macedo has asserted, Americans are concerned with ethical and democratic behavior as long as it does not conflict with our capitalistic interests. If corporate profit making is threatened, we can sacrifice democratic values, as happened with President Clinton's retreat from campaign promises to connect democratic progress with China's status as a most-favored-nation trade partner. When it

was understood that enforcement of such a policy would clearly have undermined corporate trading profits, Clinton quickly capitulated to the demands
of business and industry (Macedo, 1994).

Students in a vocational program grounded on a belief in democracy and
social justice come to see school as more than a consciousness-raising exercise. Such students are empowered to act, to take part in a larger attempt to
reshape economic institutions. Understanding that corporations in a democratic society are obligated to act in the public interest as well as in their private interest, students inform themselves and their communities of the indi-
rect consequences of irresponsible corporate activity. As vocational teachers
and students define freedom and justice in the context of work and their occupational goals, the level of educational concern transcends considerations
simply revolving around fitting in, coping with, or adjusting to the workplace. At this point, feelings of solidarity begin to develop with other students, teachers, and workers, and collaboration and cooperation replace
competition. All participants gain from their intimacy with the experience of
others, as they start to identify the forces that push natural allies apart—
forces like racism, sexism, cynicism, a mystified understanding of democracy,
a pathological desire to succeed, and so forth (Bellah et al., 1991, pp.
107–108; Murray and Ozanne, 1991; Rehm, 1989; Coontz, 1992).

As empowered vocational students grasp the words and language necessary to question tyranny, private displacements of public concerns, and social injustice, their sense of solidarity moves them to form participatory democratic collectives that enhance their political power. They can use this
power to gain a voice in the public conversation about work. Such organizations hold great potential; if organized intelligently, they can form the infrastructure for new forms of decentralized, worker-directed economic organizations. Examples of such organizations can be found around the world.
Such models should be studied by progressive democratic vocational teachers and students and workers who are interested in such alternatives. In a society that hires only a small percentage of its workforce for jobs that provide
an opportunity for high skills and sophisticated thinking, grassroots democratic organizations of this type can create workplace models that will influence vocational teaching around the country (Rehm, 1989; Kellner, 1989;
Brosio, 1994). A democratic synergism can be formed as the consciousness-
raising activities of democratic vocational education and the alternate workplace models constructed by grassroots democratic collectives mutually reinforce each other's work.

Economic Citizenship

The time has come for workers to demand a social compact that grants
them economic citizenship, a bill of labor rights that promises maximum

participation for every worker in the affairs of the public corporation. The call for economic citizenship is not simply a moral appeal; it is also a coldly pragmatic necessity that will pressure American business to upgrade skills and wages in the journey to higher productivity. The reference here is not to cosmetic forms of worker participation where "shop rats" get to choose the location of the water cooler. Economic citizenship demands a vocational education that emphasizes the acquisition of both technical and academic skills. Students in such programs learn to teach themselves and conduct research when necessities demand it. Most vocational education operates on the assumption that students placed in the vocational track are incapable of learning such skills. Vocational education from the fourth perspective expects not only that students learn self-education and research skills but that schools provide students with a broad variety of educational experiences. Much too often, students tracked into vocational education are not the ones who get to participate in the field trips and community-based experiences. Democratic vocational educators will not allow such exclusion to persist.

An education for economic citizenship explores the causes of poverty and the forces that oppress and disempower. At the same time, it provides insight into the ways workers can act both individually and collectively to change work conditions from bad work to good work. Economic citizens in a democratic society understand the demise of a public sphere and the way the politics of corporatism has successfully redefined public concerns as private matters. The effect of such redefining is very important to the consolidation of power, as it removes from public discussion issues that affect all members of society. To argue that corporate pollution is a private matter that the corporation has a right to deal with on its own terms free from public interference is an antidemocratic proposition. To maintain that TV and print media are private interests opens a yellow brick road to domination by political and economic elites. In such contexts, the notion of public opinion carries less and less weight. Perverting the concept of freedom to mean "freedom from public interference" is a distortion of the American democratic imperative (Lather, 1991; Fraser, 1994).

Economic citizens in a democracy understand the purposes of schooling, the ways that it can be used for both democratic and hegemonic purposes. Citizenship education in this respect develops the intellect, ingenuity, and initiative to understand the connections among power, school experience, and an individual's future. The role of technology is an important feature in the analysis of these relations. A vocational education for democratic citizenship promotes both an understanding of contemporary technologies and the ability to use them; it simultaneously encourages an appreciation of the social and political side effects of technology, as it focuses attention on issues such as toxic wastes and technological disemployment of workers. Vocational education is often arranged at the end of the twentieth century so that students leave school with little meaning-making experience; indeed, the idea of economic citizenship sounds alien and unrelated to the purposes of education (Sherman, 1974; DeVore, 1983; Parnell, 1990). Everyday vocational experience does not allow for such questions as these: How do economic citizens help the society provide all workers with a meaningful role in the economy? How does vocational education prepare us for those meaningful roles?

Meaning-making is central to a vocational education for economic citizenship. Economic citizens realize that much of the political talk of elections in the United States has little to do with the larger concerns of economic citizenship and sociopolitical meaning-making. Economic citizens understand that the American political conversation should be concerned with the right of workers to use their minds in the workplace. Political debates should revolve around which strategies are best equipped to bring about such a democratic goal. In light of the post-Fordist changes occurring in the contemporary American economy, public debate should be concerned with the growing numbers of peripheral workers and with strategies designed to undermine such growth. A vocational education for economic citizenship analyzes this problem and the diverse international responses to it, for example, Sweden's attempt to widen access to the core through a policy of full employment as opposed to Japan's exclusive preoccupation with core workers and their well-being (Murray, 1992).

One of the key objectives of a vocational education that promotes economic citizenship involves the understanding that *meaning is produced*; it is not something that simply exists. All meaning is inseparable from meaning-makers. Democratic vocational educators therefore understand that people who control technology, hold the power to provide monies for investment, and manage the communication and transportation infrastructures of the society exert more power to make meaning (to make *our* meaning) than does the average man or woman. In fact, Henry Giroux (1993) has pointed out that the production of meaning has become as important to the acquisition of political power as the production of consumer commodities. Understanding this disconcerting aspect of contemporary society, economic citizens begin to design strategies to resist this technopower. They make use of computers, for example, to disseminate information and to exchange ideas about worker empowerment and alternative forms of industrial ownership (Murray and Ozanne, 1991; Giroux, 1993; Kellner, 1989). Vocational educators and their students study these forms of political and economic organization in the hope of interrupting the control of technopower.

Understanding Craft, Making Meaning

Democratic vocational educators operating from the fourth perspective develop a conversation about meaning in vocational schooling. As educators

transform everyday activities into a set of abstractions unrelated to work experience, they sabotage the act of meaning-making (Slattery, 1995). For example, instead of having students learn electrical wiring terminology as part
of learning to wire a house, modernist educators separate the activities, removing students to a classroom for such memorization. Such fragmentation
of the learning process removes the immediacy, the motivation for such
knowledge. A progressive democratic vocational education attempts to understand work in the context that gives it meaning, even though it would be
less complex and ambiguous to remove it from the reality in which it is
found in everyday life. A student studying electrical wiring, as taught from a
textbook, would not encounter the "bugs" that confound a professional
electrician. Real-life electricians encounter real-life problems that must be
solved before a wiring system runs smoothly. The factors that separate a
good electrician from a bad one involve the technician's ability to deal with
these unexpected, unique wiring problems. Standardized in-school vocational education removes the very complexity that a professional must successfully confront.

Students often leave school understanding little about the matters that
will most concern their lives. How does my job fit into the general scheme
of things? workers ask. A democratic progressive vocational education asks
this question, as it challenges students to think at higher levels, uncovering
connections between job, society, and self—and these are connections that
form the infrastructure of a lifetime of self-knowledge, professional expertise, and social insight. In much of the research undertaken in vocational education, scholars find that questions concerning what work means in a
worker's life are rare sights in the contemporary vocational classroom. A
progressive democratic vocational education is more concerned with lived
experience than with the vocational curriculum as a set of facts and skills to
be mastered; students are more than empty vessels to be filled with information. Progressive vocational educators combine this notion of lived experience with Paulo Freire's concern with the language of students. When the
language and lived experience of students is taken seriously by teachers, vocational education becomes a process where one's work life can be appreciated in the context of one's anxieties, fears, and dreams. The politics of corporatism and its influence can be viewed in terms of our personal lives
(Block, 1995; McLaren et al., 1995; Feinberg and Horowitz, 1990).

Vocational education therefore examines not only what students experience and know but also how they came to experience and know it. Students
begin to examine why they chose to enter vocational education, how they
came to construct their vocational aspirations, and how they developed their
perceptions of school and academic experience. With such understandings
in mind, vocational educators realize the complexity of the teaching act, rejecting simple notions of what methods "work" and replacing them with
questions involving what it means to know something. For example, what

does it mean for vocational students to understand the concept of bad work? Does it require a reconceptualization of one's self-image as a worker? Does it require a form of meaning-making never previously needed? Does it require a need to keep up with current events and the production of what is referred to as "news"? Does it necessitate a form of action/activism never before imagined?

When vocational education touches lived experience, a new dimension of motivation is exposed. Students begin to study themselves in relation to these larger issues of good and bad work, economic citizenship, workplace democracy, technopower, and the politics of corporatism. No longer can vocational education be co-opted as a "Romper Room Wonderful World of Work Curriculum," an approach that ignores any talk of bad work. It pulls the plug on Ben Hamper's microphone, as he described line work at GM as "being paid to flunk high school the rest of your life"; whenever the foreman disappeared, Hamper and his buddies played Rivet Hockey and Dumpster Ball, got high or drunk, and generally raised hell (Hamper, 1992, p. 185). Such testimonies fall outside the homogenized curriculum, with its fragmented factoids and skills. There is little atmosphere in situations of that sort to develop a sense of craft; indeed, Hamper and his friends on the line find discussions of craft humorous, given their working conditions.

What does it mean for vocational students to develop a sense of craft? The original meaning of craft involved strength, force, power, and virtue. Slowly, craft began to be used in reference to a skilled occupation in which useful or decorative objects are made. The craft tradition coming out of preindustrial society stands in stark contrast to the standardized efficiency of Fordist industry. Unlike line workers riveting an automobile chassis, craft workers are personally responsible for the success or failure of their work, as they control the making of a product from beginning to end. A craft worker's judgment and skill are on the line for everyone to judge, thus the development of the concept of craft as work of risk. The modernist workplace had no space for craft work, no place for a worker to exercise subjective understanding and interpretation. Too many forms of contemporary work training fail to engage workers with the meaning of craft and the analytical thinking, problem solving, and aesthetic sensibilities it demands (Richmond, 1986). The progressive tradition of vocational education going back to John Dewey has promoted vocational education as craft development. Such a process, Dewey argued, could not be separated from greater socioeconomic understandings and the development of citizenship.

The Ramifications of Knowing

There is no limit to worker learning. We are sense-making organisms; we are capable of understanding the irrationality of economic rationality. Given the dangers of technopower, we have reached the end of an era where knowing and learning can be denied to large segments of the population without negative side effects. There is no contradiction between teaching someone how to perform a job and teaching that person to conceptualize it, to think about it in a number of different contexts. Teacher education is beset by this belief that performing and conceptualizing the teaching act are opposite poles that must be separated. It is for this reason that vocational teachers are often *trained* in particular teaching methodologies—techniques that are separated from thinking and contextualizing experiences. When we fail to teach vocational teachers to contextualize their teaching, we insult their intelligence. The same is true for workers. The purpose of this book rests on this notion of contextualization of work and the teaching of workers (Hinchey, 1993; Wirth, 1983; Simon, Dippo, and Schenke, 1991).

Surely any education for work designed to explore the social and intellectual meaning of a vocation would include analysis of the historical background of present conditions, the scientific principles on which production methods were grounded, and the economic and political knowledge required to acquaint workers with contemporary problems and their proposed solutions. Any examination of this type must take power relations into account. Economic histories, of course, often accept the politics of corporatism without question and offer a representation of the past that has been fashioned by dominant groups. Progressive democratic vocational educators must be careful of such work and its neglect of the history of working people, women, nonwhites, and the poor. Teachers and workers must produce new histories and new forms of analysis that examine the social and technical aspects of work in light of larger concerns with democracy (Block, 1995; Vattimo, 1991; DeVore, 1983).

When the political ramifications of the technical aspects of work are analyzed, we focus on tools, machines, technologies, and work flow employed in the production process and their impact on the everyday lives of workers. When the political ramifications of the social aspects of work are examined, we study the personal relations between workers and management and among workers themselves. Students and teachers ask how and why these social and technical processes have changed over the years. How has production changed, and how has this change affected the nature of the economy and the everyday lives of workers? Have such changes influenced American political life, our ethical orientations, or our psychological well-being? Through such questions, vocational students come to realize that although these social and technical forces help shape both their work lives and the way they see their reality, individuals can still affect their own futures. This does not mean that workers are autonomous humans who simply pull themselves up by their own bootstraps regardless of their social circumstances; they are not. Schools and workplaces are "contested terrains," meaning that a variety of groups struggle to assert their own interests and to privilege their own way of making sense of the world (Murray and Ozanne, 1991; Brosio, 1994). Because of the constraints of these conflicting power arrangements, people are not simply free to do what they want. When workers decide, for example, that they want more input in the production decisions of a firm, they are constrained by the power of corporate managers to retain their decisionmaking prerogative. Thus, to achieve their goal, workers must understand the constraints, the power dynamics with which they are faced.

All jobs hold economic, political, technical, and social ramifications that must be exposed by students of vocational education. These dynamics form an ecology, an interactive dynamic of forces that continuously shape and reshape one another to construct a larger ever-changing whole. A major industry has developed in recent years around issues of group dynamics, conflict resolution, and communication skills in the workplace. Much too often, these concerns are viewed outside the context of our economic, political, technical, and social ecology of work (Block, 1995; Copa and Tebbenhoff, 1990). When group dynamics in the workplace are isolated from the ecology of work, interesting patterns begin to develop. Instead of viewing the interactions between workers and managers in light of unequal power relations, the unequal playing field on which they compete, the politics of corporatism, and the politics of representing reality, experts in group dynamics focus on human relations as if these contextual factors never existed. Close examination reveals that the assumption underlying the group dynamic process involves an acceptance of workplace organization as it is. The goal of the counselor is to *adjust* workers to the status quo in a way that reduces stress and conflict. Such a process may be undermined by our concerns with technopower and good work; counselors may argue that these issues inject "unnecessary" conflict into the workplace. Although presenting themselves as neutral, nonpolitical experts, some workplace counselors promote a hidden politics of corporatism.

Students and Workers as Learners

At their best, democratic vocational classes can provide a unique context in which concrete manifestations of abstract ideas and concepts can be viewed. This is the beauty of the integration of academic and vocational education (see Kincheloe, 1995): Students can explore the ways knowledge is discovered and applied. A home renovation course, for example, will allow students a concrete experience with geometry that is impossible in a traditional classroom setting. Such integrated experiences engage students in the understanding that democratic workers are first and foremost learners and that good workplaces zealously protect this worker role. The fact that the role of workers as learners must be justified to educational leaders and corporate executives is evidence of the social and psychological scars of modernism and scientific management. Maybe the argument that workers should be learners is too threatening to the protectors of the economic status quo. A worker who is a learner, as John Dewey put it, begins to reconstruct personal experience. By "reconstruct," Dewey meant that a worker rethinks what has happened in such a way that new meanings are made and new insights are garnered. Such meanings and insights, when related to power, may move workers to reject their marginalized positions—and that smells like trouble to managers. Thus, a major contradiction of the American economic system is exposed: Smart workers may not fit the needs of business and industry; democracy may at times be at odds with free enterprise economics.

A democratic progressive vocational education based on the premise that workers should be learners sabotages the illusion that the world is made of separate and unrelated forces. Dewey (1916) argued that a reflective individual injects personal knowledge into the context of a broader and longer course of events, thus connecting ostensibly unrelated experiences. The connective process is necessary, he concluded, if a learner is to transform "mere happening" into meaningful experience. Contrary to popular opinion, the lessons of experience can be woefully misleading if individuals do not understand this ecological notion of context. Experience does not speak for itself; it must be reconstructed and interpreted. The tendency within a modernist, media-saturated society and its standardized test-driven schools is to misread experience by focusing upon isolated events. Focusing on isolated events was of primary importance in an earlier evolutionary moment in human history. When survival meant reacting quickly to the charge of a woolly mammoth entering your cave, focusing on isolated events was mandatory. In our contemporary lives, however, such an approach is not as important, because the primary threats to our well-being come from long-term, gradual processes, for example, ecological damage or the dehumanizing effects of modernist ways of understanding the world.

Workers as learners understand the gradual impact of an individualist ethic that undermines an appreciation of the social construction of our consciousness while it tears apart our solidarity with one another, our interdependence. In this context, workers as learners constantly recreate themselves, as they gain the ability to do things they were previously unable to do (Senge, 1990). Such workers learn to reconceptualize the world and their relation to it. They expand their ability to create with both their hands and their minds. Worker learners reconstruct the relationship between their jobs and the society, at the same time analyzing the ways that their jobs detract from or contribute to their own personal development. Workers as learners develop a more sophisticated ability to systematically examine the culture of which they are a part, gaining a more complex understanding of where they stand in the society and the economy; that is, they become able to determine their location in the web of reality (Feinberg and Horowitz, 1990). Workers with such appreciation gain the ability, in the words of Henry Giroux, "to intervene in the formation of their subjectivities" (Giroux, 1993, p. 102). Thus, workers as learners engage in an introspective process of analyzing the way they have come to be who they are.

On the job, Ben Hamper wrote, "Thinking tears you apart" (Hamper, 1992, p. 233). In order to overcome the deformities of the workplace culture and the technopower that perpetuates it, worker learners gain the ability to decode the hidden messages of the politics of corporatism. Civic participation is a waste of time, the encoded message reads. Neoclassical economics subliminally tells us that attempts to show compassion to the needy always backfire; attempts to modify the operation of the labor market will consistently produce disastrous outcomes. Such economic "folk wisdom" must be challenged by workers as learners who have gained the ability to produce historical, counterhegemonic knowledge. Pointing out the dramatic failure of classical economics in the Great Depression of the 1930s, progressive workers and vocational teachers defy technopower and the politics of corporatism (Block, 1990). Cultivating this ability to produce knowledge is one of the most important features of a democratic vocational education. Student and teacher knowledge production involves acquiring the ability to do research. As vocational students learn how to use a library, analyze everyday experience, and interpret the symbols and codes of the workplace, they begin to produce an unofficial form of knowledge. As researchers who study themselves, curriculum guides, course texts, and their own language about the world, progressive vocational teachers and students create a new curriculum, a grassroots literature that connects work, school, economy, political system, and personal experience (Shor and Freire, 1987; Block, 1995).

When vocational teachers become research-based "problem posers," they relinquish the mantle of expert and unite with their students as fellow learners. Teachers both with and without students study workplaces, analyzing the social, political, and technical problems that confront them. In the course of this research, the distinctions between practical and theoretical knowledge are blurred, as students are introduced into the workplace as both researchers and technical workers. Work-site placements, research trips, and apprenticeships become common activities that are taken back to the traditional classroom setting for reflection, analysis, and interpretation. No longer is the teacher presented as the all-knowing authority dropping morsels of knowledge into the mouths of hungry students. Good students are no longer passive receptors of data who never actively inquire about the nature of the world: Knowledge is not received; it is produced. Henry

Giroux has argued that this complex, ambiguous process requires a sophisticated teaching methodology that understands the relationship between classroom knowledge and student experience. It does not matter if the knowledge is expert-produced, authoritarian data or teacher-and-student-produced, grassroots information; vocational students can only understand it in the context of their own experience. This means that vocational teachers must also understand the backgrounds of their students and the ways these environments shape students' sense-making capacity (Murray and Ozanne, 1991; Wirth, 1983; Raizen, 1989).

As they transcend forms of vocational teacher education obsessed with validated techniques and methodologies, democratic vocational educators begin to think in terms of "why do we" rather than "what do we" (Hinchey, 1993, p. 22). Such teachers take seriously the call to teach higher-order thinking and to refocus attention on the forgotten 50 percent of American students who will enter the workforce immediately after high school (see Kincheloe, 1995; Kincheloe and Steinberg, 1993, on postformal thinking). All of our talk about the production of a new generation of workers—a generation that possesses civic courage, higher-order thinking skills, an ecological understanding of work, politics, economics, everyday life, and research skills—is for naught if business and industrial leaders do not have the courage to reshape the American workplace. Chapter 10 will expand our understanding of the education of this new generation of American workers.

10 *Confronting and Rethinking Educational Theory: Critical Vocational Pedagogy and Workers as Researchers*

Over the decades, both academic and vocational teachers have come to resent education professors in their ivory-tower offices making pronouncements on what teachers should do in classrooms. "That sounds good in theory, but . . ." has been repeated in thousands of schools by thousands of teachers. In my opinion, teachers have every right to feel this way: Their resentment of the outside expert dictating what they should do is justified. Emerging from the modernist tradition, educational theory used rigorous scientific investigation to produce a body of data about "regularities" in educational practice. This set of laws formed the foundation for the validated ways teachers should function in their classrooms. Theory in this modernist sense represented the unimportance of teachers in the educational workplace. Teacher experience is irrelevant; the generalizations produced by experts are what really matter.

Democratic progressive vocational educators reject this technical view of educational theory. In its place, they substitute a different way of seeing the world, a different view of what constitutes educational knowledge. Theory from this new perspective is not a set of official laws; on the contrary, it is a filter through which men and women view information and the world around them. Henry Giroux (1988) has argued that theory allows teachers "to see what they are seeing" (p. 47). In this reconceptualized sense, theory (or theorizing) helps us formulate questions about the world, providing in the process conceptual tools that allow us to think about the way knowledge is legitimized. Throughout this book, theory has helped me shape the issues I wanted to address, the format each chapter has taken. As theory provides us with the conceptual lenses to make meaning, it helps us understand what possible actions are needed to bring about social and educational justice at a particular time and place. It is important to note that our reconceptualized notion of theory does not dictate practice. It does not provide a set of universal principles or a blueprint for educational activity. Sometimes this characteristic frustrates practitioners who are accustomed to officials handing them a list of strategies and goals they can apply on Monday morning. Our reconceptualized notion of theory respects teachers' abilities to organize and teach their classes in the manner they deem appropriate.

If vocational teachers fail to develop their theoretical insights, their ability to distinguish and help their students distinguish between "truth" and "social construction" will be undermined. Such differentiation involves the ability to think about thinking. In this process, all "facts" must be questioned; such questioning means that students and teachers must explore the origin of what is known. How do issues of power figure in its production? Whose interests benefit from the dispersion of such information? Chapter 10 engages these questions as it attempts to introduce vocational education to the world of social and educational theory, thereby connecting the theoretical with the everyday work life of millions of Americans.

Grounding Critical Theory

The theoretical tradition that grounds our view of vocational education comes from the critical theory emerging from the Frankfurt School of Social Research in Germany in the 1920s. Seeing the world from the vantage point of post–World War I Germany, with its economic depression, inflation, and unemployment, the critical theorists (Max Horkheimer, Theodor Adorno, Walter Benjamin, Leo Lowenthal, and Herbert Marcuse) focused on power and domination within an industrialized, modernist age. Critical theory is especially concerned with how domination takes place, the way human relations are shaped in the workplace, the schools, and everyday life. Critical theorists want to promote an individual's consciousness of self as a social being. An individual who has gained such consciousness understands how and why a person's political opinions, worker role, religious beliefs, gender role, and racial self-image are shaped by dominant perspectives.

Thus, critical theory promotes self-reflection that results in changes of perspective. Men and women come to know themselves by bringing to consciousness the process by which their viewpoints were formed. Strategies that can be taken to confront individual and social pathologies can be negotiated once self-reflection takes place. Critical theory is quick to point out that such strategies do not take the form of rules and precise regulations. Instead, a framework of principles is developed around which possible actions can be discussed and analyzed. Vocational teachers who are conversant with critical theory are never *certain* of the exact path of action they will take as a result of their analysis. This can be quite frustrating to those raised in the modernist tradition who are accustomed to a specific set of procedures designed to direct their actions. Critical pedagogy is the term used to describe what emerges when critical theory encounters education. Like critical theory in general, critical pedagogy refuses to delineate a specific set of teaching procedures. Critical pedagogues, Peter McLaren (1994) has maintained, confront the modernist/positivist ways of seeing that dominate traditional liberal and conservative critiques of schooling. Moving beyond these analytical forms, critical pedagogy helps students and teachers understand how schools work by exposing student sorting processes and power involvement with curriculum.

Advocates of a critical pedagogy of vocational education make no pretense of neutrality. Unlike proponents of many other educational approaches, critical theorists expose their values and openly work to achieve them. Critical pedagogy is dedicated to the notion of egalitarianism and the elimination of human suffering. What is the relationship between social inequality and the suffering that accompanies it and the schooling process? The search for an answer to this question shapes the activities of the critical teacher. Working in solidarity with subordinate and marginalized groups, critical teachers attempt to expose the subtle and often hidden educational processes that privilege the already affluent and undermine the efforts of the poor. When American vocational schooling is viewed from this perspective, the naive belief that such education provides consistent socioeconomic mobility for working-class students disintegrates. Indeed, the notion that vocational education simply provides a politically neutral set of skills and an objective body of knowledge also collapses.

A Critical Pedagogy of Vocational Education and the Politics of Skepticism

A critical vocational pedagogy builds upon Deweyan progressivism, challenging comfortable assumptions about work and work training. A critical vocational curriculum begins to emerge that focuses on labor economics, the political and economic consequences of schools, the dynamics of unemployment and underemployment, the nature of racial and gender discrimination in the workplace, and larger patterns of wage inequality. Given such a body of understanding, critical teachers develop students' ability to analyze alternatives and make ethical career choices. Faced with decisions about production and consumption policies, critical vocational students balance health concerns resulting from pollution with the need for safer and more equitably remunerated work (Simon, Dippo, and Schenke, 1991; Grubb, 1978; Kellner, 1989).

Critical vocational teachers understand that all knowledge about vocational education is partial and is often shaped by social and economic interests. This power relationship produces inequalities in the ability of vocational students to delineate and ultimately realize their needs. An understanding of how power shapes identity helps individuals in their attempt to examine the ways that their "positionality" (where they stand in the web of reality in relation to race, class, and gender) shapes their view of the world (Mingers, 1992; Macedo, 1994; Giroux, 1992). It is at this point that the critical theorist's use of the term "pedagogy" emerges. As opposed to the concept of teaching, pedagogy expands our understanding of the classroom, viewing it as a "site of production." This means that school is a place where identity, desire, direction for change, and the taken-for-granted can be analyzed, challenged, affirmed, or reconceptualized. When critical pedagogues view school as a site for cultural production, they reject traditional notions of education as the transmission of a specific set of skills, a body of knowledge, or a core of values.

Pat Slattery (1995) has argued that critical teachers understand that all thought is connected to power relations. Skeptical to the end, critical teachers know that consciousness construction is never simple. If a student's view of the world is always influenced by power, then it falls to the critical pedagogue to attempt to illustrate the nature of this influence to the student. Pierre Bourdieu used the term "habitus" to describe the situation in which a student (or anyone) is culturally located. Habitus is embodied culture that shapes styles of knowing, learning, and relating to the world. It is personally felt and experienced, but it is the product of history, socioeconomic structures, and enculturation. Habitus is internalized culture that helps an individual make sense of the world. It works within a larger structure of power to maintain patterns of socialization; for example, working-class children are predisposed by their socialization to enter manual vocations. Such children learn through their body ("stand up straight"; "don't hold your knife in your left hand") an entire way of life, a mode of being (Mostern, 1994; Robbins, 1991; Gibson, 1986).

Habitus, Popular Culture, and Identity

Critical pedagogy is obsessed with this habitus, the way of seeing that students bring to a teaching situation (McLaren et al., 1995). Critical teachers therefore argue that one of the best ways to expose student consciousness in the late twentieth century involves the analysis of popular culture and its impact on student habitus. The emergence of cultural studies in the past few decades has increased interest in popular culture. Cultural studies is an interdisciplinary mode of academic study that focuses on discursive practices in a contemporary context. A discursive practice is a set of rules that regulate what can and cannot be said, who can speak with the blessing of authority and who must listen, and whose socioeducational constructions are scientific and valid and whose are unlearned and unimportant. The emphasis on discursive practices that is made in cultural studies is derived from its concern with the way power works in various cultural contexts (Kincheloe, 1991; Grossberg, 1992). Thus, in the everyday world of vocational education, legitimized discourses insidiously tell teachers what labor practices are legitimate, what work skills are indispensable, what instructional methods may be utilized, and what views of success may be taught. In response to such analyses, cultural studies consistently privileges the position of the outside and the marginal. Therefore, cultural studies, like critical theory, is always political, always partisan, as it seeks to develop strategies of resistance to dominant expressions of power.

Thus, with the help of cultural studies, critical pedagogy embraces the study of popular culture in the attempt to understand the investments students bring to the classroom. When vocational teachers fail to affirm popular culture as an important basis of knowledge, they dismiss the understandings students bring to class. Such teachers thereby undermine the possibility of formulating a pedagogy that connects academic and vocational understandings to the dynamics that constitute the lived world of students. Critical teachers who take popular culture seriously gain insight into student identity formation and the role that work plays in it. Teachers and students analyze the way work is portrayed in popular cinema, paying special attention to how they interpret and connect such portrayals to their own subjectivities, their own attempt to make meaning. One of the first lessons learned in such analyses involves the fact that learning and identity formation often take place outside the limits of rationality. The realm of feeling, pleasure, and desire is much more important to the formation of our identity, to our view of work and its role in our lives, than we may ever have realized (Giroux and Simon, 1989).

In the middle of such popular culture–based learning experiences, vocational students may come to realize that their career choices have had more to do with internalized notions of gender role than with a set of rational choices. Young men in training for the construction trades may have identified with a masculinist imagery of physically challenging labor that affirms manhood and that provides a ticket to acceptance within a male peer group. The point of the critical vocational curriculum is not to undermine this masculine investment but to understand it in a way that exposes both the ways it limits and expands human possibility. The important point here is that the use of popular culture in critical vocational education does not involve using the pleasure it produces to better individualize and administer student adjustment to the work force. From a critical perspective, popular cultural forms are used to provide a meeting ground for students and teachers—a terrain on which students can be engaged in a personal and empowering educational conversation.

In fact, critical teachers realize that identity formation is a site of struggle and conflict. Unlike some forms of teaching that have simply endorsed student experiences with popular culture, critical education demands that such experience be explored and interpreted. Such a pedagogy encourages students to speak in terms of their lived experience, while at the same time inducing them to uncover and disentangle the maze of popular cultural codes that shape experience in ways that silence and disempower. Since work is so central to self-esteem and is a primary form of social engagement, the relationship that unites work, popular culture, and student identity becomes central to a critical vocational pedagogy. As long as vocational education is viewed as a core of skills to be mastered (and maybe even tested by state and federal standards boards), the attempt to gain self-knowledge and the empowerment that accompanies it is doomed to fail. Whenever an educational program is organized around the skill-based principles of scientific management, people—the teacher included—are not asked to understand themselves, to trace connections between identity and social structure, or to use their education as a basis for social action. In this situation, teaching is reduced to a procedural technique, for example, to exploring what method should be used to teach carpentry skills (Giroux and Simon, 1989; McLaren et al., 1995; Rehm, 1989; Block, 1995).

Critical Pedagogy and Worker Empowerment

A few months after taking an education course with me that emphasized the limitations of modernist forms of teacher training due to their inculcation of technical methods of skill delivery, a group of my teacher-education students ran into my office to describe a final exam given in a technical audiovisual education class they had just completed. They were eager to tell me about the way the exam served as an example of, in their words, "the ultimate technocratic form of evaluation." Fragmenting all aspects of the teaching act, the test required students to list the five steps involved in making a bulletin board. All five had to be in correct order or they would all be marked incorrect. One of my students had missed all five of the steps because he forgot the first step, which was "get an idea." The absurdity of the exam struck us all as very funny, reminding us of a George Carlin comedy sketch. We imagined a future teacher, proclaiming in frustration after making a bulletin board, "Damn, I forgot to get an idea."

Donaldo Macedo (1994) has picked up on the pedagogical implications of this story, arguing that a critical pedagogy is always an antimethod pedagogy. It is antimethod in the sense that critical teacher education provides no specific road to the way a critical educator must teach or a student must learn; there are no five correct ways to construct a bulletin board. Drawing upon the poetry of Antonio Machado, Macedo illustrated that critical teachers will make their road as they walk. Vocational educators caught in a technocratic modernist program are required by supervisors to make mastery of particular tools or the production of certain items the primary goal of a course. In such situations, students are denied intellectual responsibility for both selecting the materials and instruments that best fit a task and developing their own model and plan of work. Students in a critical vocational program learn to analyze the degree to which a job allows worker discretion. In this way, student dignity is protected and an ethic of democratic good work is constructed. Work is viewed in a larger social and technical context, preventing the deskilling of the modernist fragmentation of work (Lakes, 1985; Valli, 1988).

Empowerment occurs when students gain the power of self-direction. A critical pedagogy of empowerment cultivates cognitive, intrapersonal, and motivational changes that enable students to gain greater control as concerns the quality of their present and future lives. Such vocational education grants students a sense of possibility, a sense that positive change can take place. Empowered vocational students look for the footprints of power and domination not only in the construction of their own consciousness but also in the literature and curricula of vocational education. They question inequity, asking why some jobs confer more status than others. Acting on their empowerment, they weigh existing social institutions against their own claims of integrity and democracy. Do social institutions pursue policies that insure the realization of different abilities, or do they inhibit their accomplishment? Simply put, do social institutions, the workplace in particular, work to expand what it means to be human? As a critical vocational education expands the possibilities of "humanness," it joins with other critical social agencies (unions, worker councils, churches, women's organizations, racial organizations, and so forth) to coordinate and supplement its work. Critical vocational teachers build a context in which the meaning of work can be examined in a critical rather than a simply technical perspective (Rehm, 1989; Copa and Tebbenhoff, 1990; Simon and Dippo, 1987).

A critical pedagogy of vocational education engages students in projects—for example, home restoration in poor neighborhoods, large-scale cooking for the homeless, an ethnography of the unemployed in the local community—that are grounded on democratic values, good work, worker participation as learners and researchers, workmate cooperation, and a larger vision of social change. Taking a cue from William Heard Kilpatrick's democratic progressive "project method" devised in the second decade of the twentieth century, critical vocational teachers construct research-based experiences for students. Instead of teaching random skills and facts, Kilpatrick argued that classrooms should be organized around the purposeful activity of a project. Although the project method is undermined by several flaws, it holds great potential when reconceptualized within the framework of a critical vocational education. The central feature around which this critical project method is constructed involves the notion of student as researcher and interpreter of reality. The ability to make sense, to uncover meaning, to interpret, and to produce knowledge about the worth of work becomes the guiding goal of the critical project method (Spring, 1994; Kliebard, 1987).

Too often, however, the "common sense" of vocational education maintains that just getting students experience of any kind in the workplace is the best form of work education. Many vocational educators operating from this perspective might support the basic aim of the project method: getting students out of the classroom and out into the world. They contend that experience is the best teacher, and since the project idea provides students with experience, then they would support it. Critical vocational educators reject this simplistic celebration of experience, arguing that such a position disconnects the workplace from the classroom. Although any critical pedagogy of vocational education is grounded on student experience, it never simply celebrates that experience uncritically. As Roger Simon and Don Dippo have put it: "We must avoid the conservatism inherent in confirming that which people already know" (Simon and Dippo, 1987, pp. 103–104).

Critical vocational educators transcend the traditional view of experience, experience being information and techniques people develop through their involvement in new or unique situations. It is here that one learns what to do and how to do it—and generally, this practical form of learning is what vocational teachers expect their students to acquire in their projects and work placements. Critical teachers understand that simply reaffirming students' experiences and work stories is insufficient. An important aspect of a critical pedagogy of work involves the generation of a language for critically studying the experiences that shape a student's view of both work and the world (Shor and Freire, 1987). A critical pedagogy always starts with a student's comprehension of personal lived experiences. Whether through work placement or experience with a project, critical vocational teachers give students the opportunity to reflect upon and examine what they have done. Such reflections demand confrontations with meanings and feelings. Stories are exchanged, then compared, contrasted, and discussed. Experiences are worked on, viewed as social and historical constructions, and challenged. Contradictions are exposed, and forms of response to unjust circumstances are developed. In the process, new forms of analysis and student empowerment emerge.

Critical Pedagogy and the Community of Workers

A critical pedagogy of vocational education is always concerned with community building in a democratic context, with rethinking the nature of the community of workers. In the struggle to bring about good work and build community, critical vocational educators realize that worker inability to deal with cultural, racial, or gender difference has undermined the struggle for justice in the workplace. Although this issue will be examined in more detail in Part 4, an analysis of difference and worker community building is in order. A critical pedagogy of work makes use of voices and perspectives that have been traditionally excluded. Such viewpoints help educators and workers clarify the central cultural and economic values, an exercise that precludes power elites from freezing corporate and other dominant perspectives into modes of control. With these perspectives, a critical pedagogy of vocational education utilizes the marginalized voices of ignored workers throughout history, African American perspectives on work, the cultural/economic perspectives of indigenous peoples, and women's viewpoints on labor from their location in the economic order to create a counterdiscourse.

Traditional modernist scholars have long contended that the foundation of political and ethical thinking has rested on a close-knit community with a common set of precepts. Sharon Welch (1991) has challenged that perception, arguing from a critical perspective that heterogeneous communities with differing principles may better contribute to the cultivation of critical thinking and moral reasoning. A homogeneous community is often unable to criticize the injustice and exclusionary practices that afflict a socioeconomic system. Criticism and reform of cultural pathology often come from the recognition of difference—from interaction with communities that do not suffer from the same injustices or that have dealt with them in different ways. We always profit in some way from a confrontation with another system of defining that which is important. Consciousness itself is spurred by difference, in that our first awareness of who we are occurs only when we become aware that we exist independently of another or another's ways.

Welch has maintained that the concept of solidarity is more inclusive and transformative than the concept of consensus. Even if we perceive consensus as involving a common recognition of cultural pathology and the belief that we must work together to find a cure, we first have to accept the value of solidarity. For Welch, solidarity has two main aspects: (1) the ethic of solidarity grants social groups enough respect to listen to their ideas and to use them to consider existing social values; and (2) the ethic of solidarity realizes that the lives of individuals in differing groups are interconnected to the point that everyone is accountable to everyone else. No assumption of uniformity exists here—just the commitment to work together to bring about mutually beneficial social change. In the classroom, this valuing of difference and its political and cognitive benefits exhibits itself in a dialogical sharing of perspective. Students therefore slowly come to see their own points of view as one particular sociohistorically constructed way of perceiving. As the classroom develops, students are exposed to more and more diverse voices in various texts and discussions, a process that engages them in other ways of seeing and knowing. Thus, their circle of understanding is widened, as difference expands their social imagination, their vision of what could be.

Vocational students begin to realize that because they can imagine good work, it is possible.

Drawing upon the value of the worker community of difference, a critical pedagogy of vocational education engages students in the development of not only their technical imagination but their social and political imagination as well. Students who have developed such imaginations are dangerous—because they no longer see themselves as interchangeable human parts designed as replacements for the workforce. They have become members of a valued community, united as participants in the democratic political arena and the democratic economy. As knowledge producers who design counternarratives, these workers challenge entrenched networks of power and privilege. Around the country, vocational educators are witnessing the establishment of several critically grounded vocational education programs. One important example is a home economics course established by the Wisconsin Department of Public Instruction. Emphasizing the family's construction of meanings, values, and ways of seeing the world, the course examines the impact of technological changes on the everyday life of the family. Students taking this course learn to analyze and critique the influence of technology on family life as well as the impact of family life on their own consciousness (Rehm, 1989; McLaren et al., 1995).

Buoyed by these critical orientations, students and teachers begin to redefine learning in the critical community. In modernist schools, learning has typically involved the acquisition of specific task-related behaviors that lend themselves to quantitative measurement. Success in this context is individually oriented and is evaluated on the basis of short-term results (Marsick, 1989). The attempt to redefine workplace learning is concurrently an attempt to redefine workplace community. No longer do workers labor in isolation, simply following directions. The critical work community is rich with interaction between workers who are developing and employing their judgment on a variety of matters. Problems are viewed as human-generated, not preexistent, and as such can be changed by human effort. Once the origin of problems is revealed, human beings working together in a critical community can begin to expose "avenues of change" in the status quo (Wirth, 1983; Senge, 1990; Murray and Ozanne, 1992).

The student/worker community established by a critical pedagogy of vocational education is baptized in dialogue and dedicated to "thinking together." Learners analyze patterns of interaction that sabotage learning and keep them from working together toward common goals. Students and workers in the critical community value the process of working cooperatively toward their objectives; although they are guided by democratic principles of solidarity and equality of all community members, students and workers refuse to work toward a *final* goal, some predetermined state of liberation. A critical perspective is not a commodity that is peddled like snake oil. Students do not leave class saying "I have finally achieved universal consciousness; I am everywhere and nowhere; I now *understand*." A critical vocational pedagogy and the community of learners it produces is a precarious enterprise, an endless process. Students, workers, and teachers in a critical project struggle endlessly to counter traditions, prejudices, scientific management, and other dominant forces that undermine democratic action. One of the most important ways to insure the success of this counterhegemonic struggle involves vocational teachers, vocational students, and workers in learning to become researchers. Knowing that knowledge is always tied to power, critical teachers set out to produce their own (Alvesson and Willmott, 1992; Murray and Ozanne, 1991).

Workers as Critical Researchers

Empowered workers in a learning-centered workplace can become researchers who uncover the ways power operates to construct their understanding of their role in a company and to undermine their autonomy as professionals. As they explore the market-driven objectives that shape the way their jobs are defined, workers can begin to see themselves in relation to the world around them and to perceive the workplace as a site within larger economics of power and privilege. Such explorations can serve as invitations to workers to understand both the way the workplace is "governed" by a top-down series of directives and the way power is utilized on a day-to-day basis. They come to see the language of the marketplace as a tradition that defines whose knowledge is most legitimate and whose voices count the most. In the workplace of the late industrial era, workers as critical researchers are encouraged to challenge their position as objects of administration, defined by prevailing discourses of what counts as "work" and "being a worker." As critical workers uncover the assumptions that construct the meaning of work within the context of a post-Fordist global economy and workplace and the organizational hierarchy that supports them, they can begin to realize that the systems of discourse that help shape them as workers operate within a society driven by the logic of capital. Further, questions of production and profit take precedence over questions of justice and humanity. Workers as researchers discover that concerns with the intellectual or moral development of the workforce often cannot be granted serious consideration in the "no-nonsense" ambience of "business values." The democratic vision of critical workers who are capable of evaluating a job in terms of its social significance or its moral effects becomes, from the perspective of management, the talk of an impractical and quixotic group of workers too removed from the demands of economic survival in a global marketplace (Ferguson, 1984; Feinberg and Horowitz, 1990).

Confronted by the antidemocratic features of the post-Fordist condition, workers as critical researchers become translators of democracy in a power-dominated landscape. In their struggle to translate and interpret the conditions that define their own labor, critical workers recognize capital's growing control over information flow. They come to understand that fewer and fewer corporations control more and more of the production of information. They discover that the post-Fordist corporation frequently regards the advertising of products as secondary to the promotion of a positive corporate image. Controlling information in this way enhances the corporation's power, as it engages the public in relating positively to the goals and the "mission" of the corporation. In this way, corporations can better shape government policy, control public images of labor-management relations, and portray workers in a way that enhances the self-interest of management. As a result, corporate taxes are minimized, wages are lowered, mergers are deregulated, corporate leaders are lionized, and managerial motives are unquestioned (Harvey, 1989).

So powerful is this corporate control over information flow that other social institutions often defer to its authority. Because it is part of the corporate empire, television news often covers only the consequences, and not the causes, of news events. In its coverage of unemployment, for example, TV news has typically avoided analysis of miscalculated corporate policies or managerial attempts to discipline employees. Operating in this corporate context, broadcasters frame explanations of unemployment within a "times-are-tough" motif. The current situation victimizes workers, but reporters assure us that bad times will pass. Unemployment is thus causeless, the capricious result of a natural sequence of events. There is nothing we can do about it. This is the point of intervention for worker researchers; critical workers attempt to uncover the causes of unemployment that are unaddressed by the media. As they demand access to the airwaves, the public comes to understand that unemployment is not as natural a process as it has been portrayed. A democratic debate about national economic policy is initiated (Apple, 1992).

Bringing an understanding of power in the workplace to the negotiating table, critical worker researchers question the productivist biases of post-Fordist industrial capitalism. In place of a model of unlimited growth and ever-increasing productivity, critical worker researchers propose an ecological model grounded in attempts to shape economic growth in a manner that improves the quality of life. Thus, workers as critical researchers begin to push on the walls of regressive modernity with their concerns for autonomy and self-reflection in opposition to the instrumental rationality of scientific management (Kellner, 1989).

This notion of self-reflection is central to the understanding of the nature of critically grounded research. As critical researchers attempt to restructure social relations of domination, they search for insights into an ever-evolving notion of social theory and the understanding it brings to their struggle for self-location in the net of larger and overlapping social, cultural, and economic contexts. In analyzing their location in the hierarchy of the workplace, worker researchers uncover ways in which they are controlled by the diagnostic and prescriptive discourse of managerial experts in their quest for the perfectly controlled workplace. Workers as critical researchers draw upon critical social theory to help them employ their understanding of their location in the corporate hierarchy in an effort to restructure the workplace. Social theory in this case becomes a vehicle for resistance, a means of social transformation through collective participation. In line with the project of critical research, worker researchers attempt not simply to describe the reality of work but to change it (Brosio, 1985; Ferguson, 1984).

Not only do workers as critical researchers attempt to change the demeaning reality of work, but they also endeavor to change themselves. Critical worker researchers view their own roles as historical agents as a significant focus of their research. Analyzing the various discourses that shape their subjective formation, critical workers attend to the effects of the disjunctures in the social fabric. These disjunctures reveal themselves in routine actions, unconscious knowledge, and cultural memories. Workers trace the genealogy of their subjectivities and the origins of their personal concerns. At this point in their self-analysis, critical workers acquaint themselves with the politics of corporatism and its powerful mobilization of affect. Workers study technocapitalism's production of desire, its culture of manipulation, and its electronic surveillances by large organizations. Fighting against the social amnesia of a media-driven reality, critical worker researchers assess the damage inflicted on them as well as the possibilities presented by the post-Fordist economy.

Indeed, the post-Fordist workplace co-opts the language of democracy, as workers are positioned within by Total Quality Management programs and other "inclusive," "worker-friendly," and "power-sharing" plans. Workers as critical researchers are forced to develop new forms of demystification that expose the power relations of the "democratic" plans. Upon critical interrogation, workers find that often "the elimination of we/they perceptions" means—as it did in the Staley corn processing plant in Decatur, Illinois—increased worker firings as disciplinary action, required "state-of-the-plant" meetings marked by managerial lectures to workers about the needs of the plant, the development of new contracts outlining "management rights," the introduction of twelve-hour shifts without overtime, and the formation of work teams that destroy seniority. Although the managerial appeal to efficiency was a guise in the modernist workplace to hide worker-control strategies, worker researchers find that in the post-Fordist workplace "cooperation" becomes the word du jour. Add to this illusion of cooperation the appearance of upward mobility of a few workers into the ranks of management, and attention is deflected from insidious forms of managerial supervision and hoarding of knowledge about the work process (Giroux, 1993; Ferguson, 1984; Cockburn, 1993).

The only way to address this degradation of worker dignity is to make sure that worker researchers are empowered to explore alternative workplace arrangements to share in decisionmaking concerning production and distribution of products. Workers distribute their research findings so that the general public understands how the present organization of work has served to concentrate wealth and power in the hands of industrial leaders. Worker researchers explore alternatives to present forms of bureaucratic control. One of the best sources for such alternatives involves recent feminist research (Cook and Fonow, 1990). Feminist research illustrates how traditional interpretations of reality that rely on class analysis of the workplace are insufficient. Modernist radical literature frequently used class as a unitary conceptual frame and as a consequence, the male-centered structures of the worker worldview were left unquestioned. Critical forms of analysis drawing upon feminist reconceptualizations of research alert critical researchers to the multiple subject positions that they hold in relation to the class, race, and gender dimensions of their lives. Critical worker researchers, for example, come to understand that the speaker in the discourse of the workplace is most often male, whereas the silent and passive object is female. Only recently has the analysis of workplace oppression highlighted the special forms of oppression constructed around gender and race. Issues of promotion and equal pay for women and nonwhites and sexual harassment are relatively new issues in the public conversation about work (Fraser and Nicholson, 1990).

The focus of critical worker research can vary widely—from the fragmentation of worker lives to industrial processes that pollute and deplete the environment. Worker researchers turn their attention to the effects of workplace bureaucracy, especially its tendency to isolate portions of the self from the whole. For example, the worker as laborer has little to do with the worker as spiritual entity. In a classic Cartesian manner, the body is separated from mind and spirit in the workplace, as worker researchers uncover the way power and knowledge inscribe and position the body. Workers come to realize that the physical maladies that accompany work not only in manufacturing but in the service sector are reflections of inegalitarian power relations; they are not simply manifestations of "the way work is." As worker researchers examine the origin and nature of industrial conflict, they come to find that in the TV and media-dominated contemporary era, such conflict becomes a war of representation. Swedish worker researchers studied media portrayals of a wage dispute that resulted in a lockout by management. Workers produced a seventy-page analysis of the conflict that was widely distributed. The critical theoretical principle of research leading to action was illustrated when Swedish workers filed a complaint against Radio Sweden, drawing upon their own research as proof of prejudiced media coverage (Ferguson, 1984; McLaren, 1992).

One of the most traumatic experiences workers have to face involves the closing of a plant. Taking advantage of contemporary technology, factory managers have engaged in "outsourcing" and have moved plants to "more attractive" locales with lower business taxes and open shops (often in Third World countries, where it is easier to exploit workers). Since more attractive locales exist only for management, workers have few options and typically have to scramble for new lower-paying jobs in the old venue. Worker researchers caught in such a situation have analyzed alternatives to closings or relocations. Worker researchers in plants marked for closing from Detroit to the British Midlands have researched the causes of shutdowns as well as the feasibility of the production of alternate product lines, employee ownership, or government intervention to save their jobs. In relation to the causes of shutdowns, worker researchers employ what feminist researchers call "situation-at-hand" inquiry. Such research takes an already given situation as a focus for critical sociological inquiry. Researchers who find themselves in an already given situation possess little or no ability to control events, because they either have already happened or have happened for reasons that have nothing to do with the research study. Plant managers would probably be far more guarded about offhand comments made about plant closings if they were taking part in a traditional interview or completing a questionnaire. Finding themselves in sensitive and controversial situations in which millions of dollars may be involved, critical worker researchers can make good use of situation-at-hand inquiry as a creative way of uncovering data (Eiger, 1982; Cook and Fonow, 1990).

When critical workers turn situation-at-hand inquiry upon themselves, they analyze their own experiences in the workplace. Workers in a variety of industries and occupations have examined the skills of their craft and their group and personal relationships in light of the ebb and flow of workplace politics. Such documentation can serve as valuable information for workers in similar settings and for craftspeople in the future. Workers with such research goals can make valuable use of photography and videotaping to collect or elicit information. For example, worker researchers concerned with workplace safety could document through videotapes problematic features of their everyday lives. Such tapes could then be used to pressure management to abandon public relations stonewalling and actually address workplace hazards. Such techniques, when combined with theoretical consciousness, can initiate great changes in the workplace (Cook and Fonow, 1990).

Critical research can be exceedingly practical and can contribute to progressive change on a variety of levels. The following is a summary of some of the progressive and empowering outcomes offered by critical theory-based worker research.

1. *Produces more useful and relevant research on work.* Worker research provides an account of the world from the marginal perspective of the workers, taking into consideration perspectives from both business and labor (Hartsock, 1989). Research from the margins is more relevant to those who have been marginalized by the hierarchical discourse of mainstream science

with its cult of the expert. Worker researchers ask questions about labor conditions that are relevant to other workers (Garrison, 1989).

2. *Legitimizes worker knowledge.* The discourse of traditional modernist science regulates what can be said under the flag of scientific authority and who can say it. Needless to say, workers and the practical knowledge they have accumulated about their work are excluded from this discourse (Collins, 1989). Worker research grounded in critical theory helps legitimate worker knowledge by pointing out the positionality and the limitations of "expert research." James Garrison (1989) has contended that practitioner research tends to distort reality less often than expert research because the practitioner is closer to the purposes, cares, everyday concerns, and interests of work. With the growth of worker research in Scandinavia, analysts report that the gap between scientists and workers is being diminished. Such reports point to the progressive impact of worker research and the value of such inquiry in the movement toward a more egalitarian community (Eiger, 1982).

3. *Empowers workers.* Critical worker research operates under the assumption that the validation of worker knowledge can lead to worker empowerment. But worker researchers must not be satisfied simply with producing a catalogue of incidents of worker exploitation. Worker researchers must produce a provisional vision of empowerment as part of a larger critical project. This provisional vision must decide which concepts from the present study are essential for worker empowerment (Cook and Fonow, 1990) and which can be extended and elaborated for larger consideration, such as the development of a critical democracy.

4. *Forces the reorganization of the workplace.* Western science has produced a set of fixed hierarchical binarisms, including the knower and the known, the researcher and the research, the scientific expert and the practitioner. Critical worker research subverts the existing hierarchical arrangement of the workplace as it challenges the assumptions upon which the cult of the expert and scientific management are based. Without Cartesian epistemological structures to justify them, the hierarchical binarisms of modernist science are significantly weakened (McLaren, 1992; Garrison, 1989).

5. *Inspires the democratization of science.* As John Dewey maintained decades ago, narrowly conceiving of science as a technique puts the power of inquiry in the hands of those at the top of the hierarchy, who, by way of their education or status, are pronounced the most qualified. These elites engage in research, turning over the data (the product), not the methods (the process), of their inquiries to the low-status practitioners who follow their directions. When workers take part in research and legitimate their own knowledge, then scientific research will be better able to serve progressive democratic goals.

6. *Undermines technical rationality.* Technical rationality is an epistemology of worker practice derived from modernist Cartesian science. Technical

rationality maintains that workers are rationalistic problem solvers who apply scientifically tested procedures to workplace situations. Well-trained workers solve well-formed problems by applying techniques derived from expert-produced knowledge. Worker researchers have learned, however, that the problems encountered in the workplace are not reducible to simple propositions or assertions. For instance, workers in a garbage recycling plant must decide how to balance environmental concerns with business survival demands. They must not only know what waste materials cause environmental damage but what materials bring high market prices. When extraction costs are calculated into this problem, it becomes apparent that no simple technical procedure exists that can lead workers to the solution of problems that confront such a workplace. The relationship between worker competence and expert knowledge needs to be flip-flopped. In the modernist workplace hierarchy, managers start with research provided by "experts" and train workers in accordance with such findings. A democratic workplace would start instead with research by the workers themselves on the conditions of their labor. For instance, worker researchers could document the forms of intelligence competent workers exhibit. An important aspect of the worker's job would be to help create nonexploitative conditions that promote such competence (Schon, 1987; Raizen, 1989; Feinberg and Horowitz, 1990).

7. *Promotes an awareness of worker cognition.* Critical worker research encourages a relationship to worker production that is expressed in love of craft, awareness of the relationship between craft and world, and solidarity with other craftspeople. In addition, this critical productive orientation highlights an awareness of reality by way of both logic and emotion. Critical research holds many cognitive benefits that transcend Piagetian forms of formal analytical reasoning. As workers as researchers transcend procedural logic, they move to a critical realm of knowledge production. In this realm, researchers organize and interpret information, no longer caught in the hierarchy as passive receivers of "expert" knowledge. As critical researchers, workers learn to teach themselves. In this context, learning in the workplace becomes a way of life, a part of the job. Workers as researchers come to see events in a deconstructive manner, in ways that uncover privileged perspectives within the dynamics of the workplace not necessarily apparent before critical reflection (Kincheloe, 1993, 1995; Feinberg and Horowitz, 1990).

Rethinking Vocational Pedagogy in Light of Critical Worker Research

When rethinking the foundations of vocational education, one of the most basic conceptual understandings on which we build contends that learning via practical experience is superior to learning via the memorization of factual material (Raizen, 1989). This is why worker research is such a central practice in a critical pedagogy of vocational education. Although Alan Block was writing about learning to read, his point is relevant here: "Language is not learned to be used; rather language is learned in the exercise of its use" (Block, 1995, p. 30). Vocational students learn to conceptualize and analyze in the context of observing the workplace and through the process of working itself. They do not learn to think so that *someday soon* such an ability can be put to use. Traditional forms of modernist teaching distance us from the world. Students too often lose touch with concreteness; they learn to separate concepts about reality from reality, to quarantine the present from the future (Shor and Freire, 1987).

John Dewey, as usual, understood these educational concepts decades ago, arguing that the classroom and the town or city surrounding it should be inseparable in the educational process. As students travel back and forth between the world and school, they learn methods of inquiry. Such immersion in inquiry (or research) would help students learn how to learn; students would discover information as they attended to issues of context and sequences of events. As interpreters of the world, vocational students and workers analyze texts, refusing to accept any text on face value. Thus, critical vocational education draws upon what philosophers call hermeneutics, the form of research that involves the interpretation of texts. Unlike modernist empiricists and positivists, who seek certainty and final truth, hermeneutical researchers understand the context-specific, ambiguous nature of knowledge about human beings. Focusing on the process by which we come to understand the meaning of texts, hermeneuts expose layers of meaning in various situations. Once again, a democratic education revolves around the act of interpretation. Although it may sound odd to contemporary ears, workers and vocational students as hermeneutical inquirers form the central core of a critical pedagogy of vocational education (Lakes, 1985; Block, 1995; Slattery, 1995).

I do not want to be misunderstood on the following point: Workers who can do research and interpret the world around them can also learn to execute the technical and manual skills required by their jobs. Critical teachers, students, and workers understand work itself to be a form of discovery and creation. Indeed, every aspect of work can be transformed into a research act. To cultivate this perspective, Ira Shor (1988) asked his students to write reports on their best and worst job experiences. In this exercise, after a series of students were asked to read aloud their worst job experiences to the class, Shor asked his students to become interpreters (hermeneutic researchers), posing the question, What do these worst jobs have in common? After students had performed this independent content analysis, they might be ready to read the description of bad work given herein and compare it to their own interpretations. The same process can be repeated for good work, with subsequent reading of the notion of the concept and the comparisons it evokes. Shor and other critical educators realize that research designed simply to describe is insufficient for the critical democratic task. Critical theory demands that inquiry lay the foundation for "transcendent thought"—that is, thinking that allows us to go beyond common sense, to unveil power, to disclose democratic alternatives. That cognitive process sets the stage for a theoretically grounded program of democratic action (Rehm, 1989; Murray and Ozanne, 1991).

The possibilities for vocational teaching that arise out of the concept of student or worker as researcher are infinite. A group of workers in Scotland involved in an adult-learning research project, for example, found that a large percentage of workers were alienated and culturally isolated. On the basis of their research, several programs were initiated. One of the most important of the worker-initiated programs was called the Skills Exchange. Because high unemployment in Scotland had left many men and women with unused skills and hours of deadening inactivity, workers developed a mutual skills exchange called Tit for Tat. Workers shared a wide variety of services, negating the need for money. Those involved with the project registered their skills, and a volunteer core group kept records of the jobs done. Vocational students have much to learn from such a project. Like the Scottish workers, they could set up skill exchanges or skill teaching exchanges where individuals with two different skills could teach each other new job skills.

Students in vocational programs could visit work sites with cameras and VCRs to record the images of good work and bad work. Not only would students be learning about the different types of workplaces and how to make a film or photo essay, but they could integrate language arts skills into the research with written reports and presentations. Teachers need to schedule class time for discussion and analysis after outside inquiry has taken place to allow students to reflect on and analyze the research the class has produced. Student business projects (for example, students producing pizzas in a simulated factory) can initiate sophisticated research activities. During the course of the project, some students could serve as researchers, exploring the type of work required by the student managers, the skills required of workers, and the social effects of such labor dynamics (Shor, 1986; Rehm, 1989; Marsick, 1989). In these situations, vocational students can begin to trace power relations that play out so importantly in the lived world of the workplace. Part 4 will extend the analysis of these power relations, examining vocational education and work in light of race, class, and gender issues.

PART FOUR

Race, Class, and Gender

11 *Plausible Deniability: The Skeleton in Vocational Education's Closet*

In my first year of college teaching, after a discussion of student marginalization and vocational education, a student told me a story from her high-school experience, a story I mentioned previously but will expand upon here. My student had grown up in a small town in Tennessee, the daughter of a physician. In the spring term of her senior year in high school, needing only a couple of classes to finish her degree requirements, she decided to take a vocational class in automobile repair—a skill she had never had an opportunity to learn. On the morning classes were to begin, the principal, a longtime patient of her father, called her to his office during her homeroom period. "I was just looking over your schedule," the principal told her, "and noticed that you had signed up for auto repair." My student told the principal why she wanted to take the course and that she was excited about it. "I've removed you from the class and placed you in a sociology course," the principal announced confidently. "I know you don't want to associate with the type of people who take vocational education." My student's brief foray into vocational education ended before it started.

You Study Vocational Education, You Study the Marginalized

No matter how you cut it, vocational education has always involved students marginalized around the intersecting axes of race, class, and gender—the "type" of people with whom my student's principal did not want her to associate. Indeed, it was ironic that he wanted her to take sociology, for the sociological lessons he was teaching her were more profound than those any sociology textbook could provide. If the sociological issues of race, class, and gender have always been important to vocational education, they have become even more important in the 1980s and 1990s. The growing presence of African Americans and Latinos in American cities, the feminization of poverty, the expansion of an underclass and a homeless population, and

increasing racial and ethnic conflict have all upped the social and educational ante in America (McLaren, 1994). African-American and Latino students are frequently enrolled in classes for low-wage, low-status occupations—in building maintenance, commercial serving, and institutional care
(Banfield, 1991). As vocational education enrollments have declined, students who are economically or educationally disadvantaged, disabled, or
English-deficient have increasingly been concentrated in vocational education programs (Olson, January 19, 1994). This concentration, simply
stated, is not in the best interests of the students involved; a better word for
the process is "dumping."

"Shhh...We Don't Talk About Race and Class in Our Vocational Program": Tracking as Resegregation

This dumping is rarely discussed in American schools. I have walked down
the halls of many an American high school with a school or district official,
inspecting all-white advanced placement classes and all-black/Latino vocational classes, with no reference being made to the racial dichotomies confronting us. Traditional forms of racism have involved the ascription of unfair
generalizations about racial groups to individuals in a manner that leads to
prejudicial treatment of them. In previous decades, the public expression of
such generalizations was relatively (depending on circumstance, e.g., geographic locality, type of vocation/profession, political predisposition) open.
Since the 1960s, however, such pronouncements are heard less frequently—
especially in public spaces. In order to avoid the topic, many individuals, especially teachers, have found it safer to act as if they did not see skin color.
White teachers especially have tried to suppress what they perceive about
nonwhites, choosing a stance that erases color as a human feature (Sleeter,
1993). Thus, my tour guides sought shelter in racial silence, in the process
assuring that nothing would be done to explain the existence of such classroom demographics or to subvert the processes that led to their existence.

This new silence about race is a form of "politeness" that equates talk of
race not only with social impropriety but also with "*race-ism*" itself (see
Clinton Allison, 1995, for a historical discussion of racial silence in education). In the context of education in general and vocational education in
particular, this racial silence can be extended to include a "power silence" as
well. Indeed, the structures of domination that lead to the racial demographics in college prep and vocational classrooms are also erased in late-
twentieth-century American culture. If teachers work to see a "colorless"
school where "it doesn't matter if we're red, green, or purple," then individual students are different *only* to the degree that they study hard and
work or they do not study hard and work (Frankenberg, 1993). In our
color-blind and power-erased microcosm, teachers have no way of appreci-

ating the complex issues that lead African Americans, Latinos, Native Americans, or poor people from all backgrounds to score lower on IQ tests or achievement tests and to be placed in remedial and vocational curricula. In the culture of racial silence, white-dominated educational institutions have nothing to do with the low station of the poor and nonwhite. Individuals are entirely responsible for their own fate, as the social context in which one grows is deemed "inadmissible evidence" in the everyday world of educational evaluation. In this world, the consideration of individuals in terms of the social aggregate of which they are a part is forbidden by the grammar of race silence.

Decontextualized individuals, an ever-increasing percentage of them nonwhite and handicapped, inhabit the high schools lowest track, vocational education. Simply stated, tracking isolates and segregates (resegregates) African Americans and Latinos within a school, denying them the opportunity to gain academic skills that would increase their possibility for social mobility. From the early twentieth century to the present, vocational education has been based on the concept of tracking (see Chapter 6)—separating the college bound from the work bound. That separation contributes to high dropout levels among the work bound. Such dropouts, from a purely economic perspective, cost the nation literally tens of billions of dollars in social services and crime fighting—and from a human perspective, such statistics indicate men and women caught in a trap of hopelessness. Not only is tracking inhumane, but it is un-American in its denying low-track students the equal opportunity for an education (Banfield, 1991; McLaren, 1994; Giroux, 1988; Oakes and Lipton, 1990). All students can benefit from a diversity of learning experiences, an integration of academic and vocational education that synergizes the best aspects of both (see my *Toil and Trouble: Good Work, Smart Workers, and the Integration of Academic and Vocational Education* for a detailed analysis of the synergy between academic and vocational education).

Tracking undermines the notion of school as a neutral environment in which students compete against one another equitably. In fact, tracking and the organization of schooling themselves may both undermine marginalized students' ability to learn. Such students are "taught" that they are stupid by being placed in low tracks and referred to as "sweathogs" or "dummies." The whole process is a humiliating experience for them. Tracking creates the illusion of individualized attention for the needs of each student, as it pushes them into their "proper" slot. Placement in the lower track transforms school into a grueling waste of time that degrades students and undermines their sense of worth (Oakes, 1988). Much of the low-track curriculum involves the socialization of students to accept their own inequality as well as the unequal nature of the larger society. Studies of the differences in the treatment of high-track and low-track students consistently indicate that high-track students find their identities as intelligent human beings affirmed with fewer classroom rules and restrictions, more intimate and egalitarian relationships with teachers, and more joking and good-natured kidding characterizing student-teacher interactions (Giroux, 1988, 1997).

Ben Hamper's socioeconomically grounded description of the impact of tracking on his group's self-concept is revealing. "We were," he said, "the who-gives-a-shit-hey-have-you-heard-the-new-Cream-album-yet-yup-my-daddy's-a-stinkin-shoprat-too track" (Hamper, 1992, p. 11). Such characterizations remind us of the often denied class-based nature of American society. Conservatives refer to questions of class and social justice as "tired issues of the left that refer to conditions that no longer exist." On the contrary, there is abundant evidence that we are devolving into a more rigidly divided two-class nation, rich and poor, black and white (Gaines, 1990). Thus, the struggle against tracking and its segregation of rich and poor students is part of a larger social struggle against class bias, racism, and sexism in the larger American society. Racism and sexism are often expressed in terms of socioeconomic class, as race and gender dynamics undermine the quest for economic mobility. Critical vocational educators must study the specific nature of this process and the way it presents itself on the vocational terrain. In this respect, critical vocational educators must become students of power and the way it relates to their students—their poor, African-American, Latino, and women students in particular.

The conservative assertion that class divisions belong to a different era of American history is one of the great distortions of the contemporary public discourse. Before we leave the issue of tracking, it is important to examine Jeanne Oakes's (1985) study of class and race hierarchies in vocational courses themselves. The dynamics of the workings of power are specified in her research. Oakes asserted that vocational courses are divided between higher-status courses such as home economics, business, and technology studies and lower-status courses such as institutional cooking and building maintenance—and it is not surprising that white students dominate the enrollments of high-status courses and nonwhite and poor students the low-status courses. For example, even in the business courses, Oakes found hierarchies of status involving race and class dynamics. Courses in business management and finance are located primarily in white schools with predominantly white enrollments. Only students in primarily white schools take business courses in banking, taxation, the stock market, business machines, and business law.

Courses offered in specific trades and employable manual skills differ between predominantly white and minority high schools. Although both types of schools offer courses such as drafting, machine shop, auto repair, and hospital and health occupations, only students at white-dominated schools took marine technology, aviation, and power mechanics. Students at nonwhite-dominated schools take cosmetology, building construction, institutional cooking and sewing, vocational child care, mill and cabinet shop, needle trades, upholstery, printing, commercial art, commercial photography, and housekeeping and food services. Such courses are not offered at predominantly white schools. Oakes also found differences in the format of courses most likely to be populated with white as opposed to African-American and Latino students. Courses and programs at white schools tend to be offered on campus and are easily fit into the regular school schedule. White students taking these courses see them as "typical" school classes and see themselves as "regular" students in school. Low-status courses taken by nonwhites, however, are less closely tied to the regular activities of school and more likely to be offered at off-campus venues.

Oakes concluded from these data that white students tend to feel more of a sense of belonging to school than nonwhites. Not only do nonwhites feel less connected to the school, but they encounter far less access to high-status vocational courses. African Americans, Latinos, and poor students are directed in school toward lower-class social and economic roles. The programmatic divergence in the vocational education of whites and nonwhites in American schools clearly indicates a race and class-based stratification of students. Minority and poor students are advised as early as junior high to adjust their curriculum for low-level occupations. They are removed from their high-school classes for work-site training (most often low-level skill, "gofer" types of experience, not analytical research into the nature of the job, its connection to good work, and so on) and, perceiving that they possess marketable skills, leave school early. The pattern is all too consistent: These students find themselves in the workplace unable to translate their vocational education into vocational advantage (Oakes, 1985). Many of those who argue that the U.S. socioeconomic structure of the late 1990s is "open" to everyone have not carefully studied the forces at work in contemporary vocational education (Rehm, 1989; Olson, January 19, 1994).

Becoming a Successful Worker—and Justice for All

Critical vocational educators are haunted by and obsessed with questions of how social, political, and economic power works to undermine the educational progress and economic mobility of nonwhite and poor students. Educators, economists, social workers, and cultural workers of all types need to understand such dynamics in order to counter the charges of inferiority against African Americans, Latinos, women, and the poor made by talk radio commentators and corporate leaders in the 1990s. We have learned much about this insidious process, but little of it finds expression at the public level. Differences in academic achievement are not the result of primary effects such as deficiencies in intelligence but relate more to secondary effects, such as the deficit of poor and minority students' cultural capital and the social practices resulting from particular cultural experiences. Cultural capital involves ways of dressing, acting, thinking, or representing oneself. For example, the knowledge that one would need to deport oneself gracefully in an expensive restaurant is a form of dominant cultural capital. Thus, style, manners, courtesy, language practices, moving, and socializing are all forms of cultural capital. Teachers and managers often identify the possession of dominant cultural capital as an innate quality that emanates from a student or a worker's "inner essence." However, such traits are culturally determined and are inseparable from the cultural and socioeconomic class backgrounds of the individuals who exhibit them.

Thus, students and workers who do not possess the cultural capital of the dominant culture are in big trouble. They are viewed as rude and uncouth, not the type of people a "cultured" person would want to have around. The type of students middle-class educators want to represent their school are not those without cultural capital; and they are not the type of workers who will get promoted. Students from dominant cultural backgrounds manifest different cultural capital than students from poor or minority homes. Schools will always privilege those students who exhibit the dominant cultural capital—they are the school leaders, the leaders of tomorrow. Thus, modernist teaching and evaluation strategies that do not examine contextual factors focus only on test scores and IQs. They thereby dismiss factors such as cultural capital and its effect on academic and workplace performance. Critical analysts examining educational and workplace dynamics that cannot be quantified come to understand that student and worker performance often does not reflect an individual's innate ability but represents the school and management science's validation or rejection of a particular form of cultural capital. That argument does not rest well with the Limbaughs and Gingriches of the late twentieth century and their decontextualized logic. It is obvious, they argue, why minorities and the poor often perform poorly in school and fail to get promoted on the job: They are lazy, unmotivated, and mentally deficient (McLaren, 1994; Aronowitz and Giroux, 1991).

Thus, culture is connected to power: Our culture plays a major role in determining our access to social, political, and economic rewards. Schools and workplaces legitimate specific forms of language, reasoning, and style, while delegitimating other forms. Many of us who have taught in American public schools have listened at faculty meetings to colleagues warn us not to expect too much from a particular group of students, maybe those Laotian immigrants or the kids from Highland Park. Those kids are inferior to "our" kids, the monologue continues, they are not motivated to work. In all of these ways (and more), schools perpetuate race, class, and gender inequality, all the while draping the pathology in the language of democracy. One of the most devastating ways poor and minority students are disempowered involves the false promise of our vocational education. Being a student in the vocational track is often taken as a message to employers that an individual does *not* possess forms of dominant cultural capital; thus, the vocational education label precludes students from gaining access to jobs with economic power (Giroux, 1988; Atkins, 1986).

A basic question to be asked in relation to minority and poor vocational education students involves the relationship between their investment in vocational training and the reward they receive in obtaining a job with economic power. A key feature of the analysis of vocational education discloses that the reward is greater for whites than for African Americans and Latinos, for men than for women, and for middle-class students than for poor students (Falk and Lyson, 1988). The unfortunate reality is that poor and minority students are often left outside the job market. The key point that too many mainstream educational analysts want to ignore is that a student's race, class, and gender exert a central role in the acquisition of both job skills and good work. My position in this book is that such a reality is unacceptable and that vocational educators must learn how to disrupt this antidemocratic pattern. If we do not develop the capacity to subvert it, the present unjust organization of the workplace will remain intact: Jobs populated primarily by women or minorities, or both, are characterized by low pay, low skills, little autonomy, constant supervision, and few opportunities for promotion; jobs populated primarily by white males are characterized by high pay, better intrinsic rewards, more autonomy, and better opportunities for promotion (DeYoung, 1989; Tomaskovic-Devey, 1993).

When vocational education, workplace culture, and labor patterns are studied in relation to issues of race, class, and gender, analysts are bombarded with insights into the ways power operates. In the context of such examination, the claims of the "angry white men"—Rush Limbaugh, Newt Gingrich, Bob Dole, and Pat Buchanan, and the rest—that white men are the victims of a feminist and minority-driven society are exposed as bunk. For example, to argue that women have an upper hand in getting good jobs over men in contemporary America is simply not true. An ever-increasing percentage of American low-skill jobs are filled by women. At the same time, attempts to rationalize such jobs—managerial control both of job content and how it is performed—has never been greater. Indeed, labor historians argue that a strong relationship exists between the feminization of an occupation and its transformation into a deskilled job. As pay is decreased, it is argued that more supervisory control is needed. Thus, women's work is deemed less important or of lesser status because *it is women who perform the work*. Although much effort has been expended by the women's movement to dispel such attitudes and many people have transformed their predispositions about such matters, these female labor dynamics remain firmly intact. The white male domination of the workplace is in no immediate danger (Apple, 1985).

The most effective way to get ahead in a workplace hierarchy involves mirroring the looks, style, and ideology of one's supervisors. Given the depersonalization of the workplace, superficial signs of reliability such as social and ethnic similarity take the place of direct personal understanding. The greater the similarity that exists in recognizable, surface-level characteristics, the greater the possibility a worker will be designated as a "quality person." Only quality people are given access to positions of decisionmaking and economic power. The greater one's difference along the lines of color, gender, ethnicity, language, and style, the more one needs to prove one's support of group values. Black males in predominantly white workplaces, for example, report that they feel great pressure to prove their acceptance of group values. When authors of "rules of success" preach the gospel of "getting ahead" at work, all agree that the primary virtue of a good worker involves the willingness to *conform*. Such conformity is not always easy; workers who speak with a dialect or display characteristics that reflect their ethnic backgrounds cannot simply turn these traits on and off. Even if they have developed that ability, the emotions engendered by this necessity of denying self may fan flames of anger that cannot be understood by workmates and workplace supervisors (Ferguson, 1984; Ellwood, 1988). Thus, in the eyes of those who surround them, this "different" worker may be perceived as having a "bad attitude" or as not being a "quality person."

These are problems that poor, minority, and some female workers encounter after they secure a job. The act of securing a job when one does not possess the dominant cultural capital, is unsure how to conform, or is undeniably culturally or racially different can be a complex task. Contrary to pronouncements that anyone who works can make it, marginalized workers experience great difficulty finding jobs with any possibility of promotion. Jobs that require more than low skills or hold the promise of becoming a "career" are typically filled through informal (good-ol'-boy, grapevine) networks, wherein employers hire workers they know or who have been recommended by members of the network. Women experience great difficulty with their difference from men, falling outside job networks and the male culture of the workplace. "That girl just won't fit in here," male managers remark daily, making informal reference to the conflict between women job applicants and the male culture of the workplace.

Male-dominated workplaces develop forms of communications that employ metaphors from and references to sports, the military, and pornography. The knowledge assumed in this discourse excludes women, whose life experiences fall outside these domains. When the language of a male-centered workplace or a male-dominated managerial staff is researched, analysts typically uncover what outsiders perceive as secret codes, double meanings, and esoteric slang. When students understand that the factor most important to success at work involves not so much competence on the job as access to these informal networks and comfort in these workplace cultures, empathy for the difficulties experienced by women and minorities will expand. Right-wing molders of opinion have been so successful in the 1980s and 1990s that empathy of this type is lacking. One of the main tasks of critical work educators involves the effort to promote empathetic understandings of race, class, and gender dynamics in the workplace. Such awareness can help lay the foundation for the support of policies promoting good work.

As long as these dynamics of exclusion characterize American workplaces, they will remain racially and sexually segregated, with most white men working with white men, most minorities working with minorities, and most women working with women. White women, black women, and black men will continue to earn much less than white men and have far fewer opportunities for jobs with career ladders and economic power. Many of the economically disadvantaged students we will see in our vocational education classes will have spent their whole life poor, surrounded by unemployed and underemployed adults financially unable to move out of their urban neighborhood or the rural area; these students are buoyed by little hope that they will someday share in the material rewards of mainstream, middle-class America. Why has it been so hard for education professionals to appreciate the hopelessness of these students and the frustration that comes with it? Research indicates that African-American high-school students see the value in obtaining an education, but they harbor serious doubts about the practical value of education in the lives of black people like themselves. Why bother? they ask, when the cards are stacked against them (Tomaskovic-Devey, 1993; Ellwood, 1988; Zweigenhaft and Domhoff, 1991).

Critical vocational educators understand that they must learn how to intervene. First, they must be aware of the demographics of the workplace in the present and projections for the future. They cannot hide the stark realities of the racial, class-based, and gender-based injustice of work in late-twentieth-century America. They must confront head-on the fact that poor and minority students are tracked into the secondary labor market (e.g., as laborers, janitors, food service workers, and so on). They must deal with the realization that high-tech workplaces perpetuate low-skill, low-paying jobs and that such jobs, as in the past, are being filled by poor, female, and minority workers. They cannot avoid addressing the thesis that the absence of a national industrial policy targeting the race, class, and gender-based injustice of the workplace as a pathology in need of a cure allows such realities to embed themselves more securely into the national fabric (Falk and Lyson, 1988; DeYoung, 1989). These realities cannot be swept under the rug; but, just as important, they cannot be allowed to snuff out the flame of hope. Strategies for the empowerment of poor and minority students to survive in the face of such adversity are at the heart of a multicultural, critical vocational education. Students must learn to participate in a democratic society in order to resist those forces that work to maintain the pathologies of the status quo.

Desperately Seeking Mobility

By 2010, two out of five Americans will be nonwhite. Since racial and ethnic minorities are more than twice as likely to live below the poverty line, dramatic consequences accompany such demographics. By 2050, one out of every two Americans will be nonwhite. In the twenty-first century, four out of five new workers will be women, nonwhites, or new immigrants. Virtually nothing is being done to prepare for these eventualities. In late-twentieth-century America, the marginalized have few friends and are divided among themselves. White men are told that they are privileged—and relative to other demographic groups, they are. But to working-class or poor white men, the label of "privileged" seems like a dirty joke, as they hang precariously over the edge of poverty. In such circumstances, many of them feel threatened when minorities or women gain access to formerly all-white-male terrain. Failing to understand questions of mobility in macrosociological context, white men blame the victims of an inegalitarian system. The possibility of working-class solidarity or a unified challenge to the greedy is thus subverted (Banfield, 1991; Wolfe, 1991; Rubin, 1994).

It has been hard for Americans, for working-class Americans in particular, to grasp the nature and meaning of the disintegration of Fordism after 1973. For young people from poor families, it means that the American ideal of universal upward mobility is a cruel irony (West, 1993). As Peter McLaren (1986) and Jay MacLeod (1987) have so clearly pointed out, the American social ladder is not as easy to climb as we thought. Young people from the lower half of the class structure feel so ensnared in the net of poverty that upward aspirations seem an indulgence. Working-class Americans have traditionally harbored the hope of "moving up"—if not themselves, then for their children. Maybe the hope was always greater than the possibility, but it persisted nonetheless. Poor and immigrant parents dedicated to the possibility of a better life for their children did the "dirty work" so sons and daughters could do the "clean work." The promise of upward mobility was a tangible reality—and it shaped American lives. Indeed, the belief shaped America itself (Rubin, 1994).

The post-Fordist era, the last quarter of the twentieth century, has not been kind to America's young people. Their economic hardship is especially bitter and discouraging, coming as it does after a dream of financial security and *upward mobility*. They entered vocational programs on the assumption that they were being prepared for economic prosperity in their adulthood. In their late twenties, many of these men and women still have the jobs they obtained in high school. With such prospects, it is not surprising that many males and some females from poor families have found gang and gang-related activity attractive. Nothing speaks more directly to the breakdown of the hope of social mobility than the rise of gangs over the last fifteen years in large and small urban areas. America's poor and minority youth face tremendous obstacles to social mobility but few barriers to gang involvement and the financial rewards such organizations offer. Having studied and emulated organized crime networks of the past, contemporary gangs have effectively colonized illegal markets. In doing so, they have turned impressive profits, offering the possibility of economic mobility to young people excluded from the prosperity of the legal economy (Gaines, 1990; DuBois, 1973a; Rodriguez, 1994; Jankowski, 1991).

The Double Disadvantage of Black Women

The dynamics of socioeconomic mobility among marginalized groups at the end of the twentieth century is well illustrated by the particular problems encountered by African-American women. Black women, not surprisingly, are disproportionally placed in vocational programs. They are concentrated in low-paying jobs and underrepresented in supervisory, managerial, and executive positions. Writing about her childhood, bell hooks (1993) commented that she was taught as a black woman of the hardships of her social position. It was a given that black women would work hard in domestic jobs, in the fields stripping tobacco, or wherever necessary. The history of black women and work in this society is a chronicle of brutal, backbreaking labor. Given the stereotypes of black female laziness traditionally held by white Americans and the reality of black women's working lives, the realization emerges that many white people have no idea who black women are (Banfield, 1991; Malveaux, 1992a). Ralph Ellison's invisible man has had a sex change—and is now transmuted into the invisible woman.

"Doubly disadvantaged" is the functional term for black women workers. Having both membership in a minority group and a gender at the bottom of the power hierarchy does not sufficiently relay the extent of the disadvantage endured by black women. In fact, the pay and status difference between black and white female workers is greater than the difference between black and white male workers. On the job, African-American women face an added prejudicial dynamic from supervisors who often feel they are "too uppity"; that is, they do not display the "proper" submissive attitude of a "subordinate." Such factors push black women into dead-end jobs as maids, domestics, institutional cooks, janitors, nurse's aides, welfare service aides, and low-skill machine operators. Seven out of ten black women in service jobs are employed in positions where women's full-time, full-year pay was less than $7,500—a salary below the poverty line. Black women make 56 cents to every dollar earned by white males, and only seven out of one thousand collect a salary of $50,000 a year.

Media depictions do little to dispel the myths or contextualize the struggles most black women face. Consider director John Singleton's portrayal of black women in *Boyz 'n the Hood:* The mothers of Tre and Doughboy are one-dimensional characters who are probably responsible for their babies' troubles, their dangerous lives in the streets. These representations are not sympathetic. The daily stress endured by black women who work in often degrading jobs by day, who come home to more work and financial pressures, and who are often called on to provide care and comfort to friends and relatives in need is a story not often told in contemporary America. Whereas work-related stress of corporate managers is a common topic of discussion in the media and in medical research, the statistics concerning black women's stress-driven heart disease, depression, ulcers, hypertension, and addiction are buried issues in the public conversation (Falk and Lyson, 1988; hooks, 1993; Malveaux, 1992a, 1992b; Johnson, 1991). A critical pedagogy of vocational education examines these dynamics on a variety of levels, seeking at the same time to improve the chances for the socioeconomic mobility of black women students.

The Wages of Hopelessness

From the perspective of many poor and minority vocational education students, the world they have been told to trust no longer works. As they realize that their childhood is over, such students begin to appreciate the speed with which they assumed responsibilities and grew up. It is at this point that they face the fact that theirs was a childhood denied (see Steinberg and Kincheloe, *Kinderculture: The Corporate Construction of Childhood*, 1997, for an expansion of this theme). Poor American children have seen their dreams stolen from them, replaced by a hopelessness that narrows their choices and undermines their sense that their actions can make a difference. Youth suicide was not even a statistical category before 1960; by the 1980s, it was second to "accidents" as the leading cause of death among young people. By 1990, suicide among kids was described as an epidemic. What kind of hopelessness must a young person feel to commit suicide? By the time many kids enter a high-school vocational education program, they are world-weary, drained of any sense of possibility for their future. They have heard it all, the charlatans with their manipulative pseudo-hope grounded on everything from televangelism to drugs to schooling. They have watched the false prophets of education-for-success corral them into the low-track classes and have figured out the consequences of that process (Ferguson, 1984; Gaines, 1990; West, 1993).

Vocational education students want and deserve the truth. Too infrequently, vocational education teachers level with their students. We must explain to them that the training they often get in vocational classes is hardly enough to prepare them for social mobility. Students must understand that good work and a democratic workplace will not automatically appear. Vocational educators must take the lead in organizing students, workers, and other citizens to reshape our conception of work in relation to our lives as democratic participants. Hope for our young people, especially our poor and minority youth, can only be restored in such a movement. The attempt to tell the truth will not be easy. Vocational educators will not be rewarded for such an effort by school and community hierarchies. Donna Gaines (1990) has searched for humor in the delivery of the cold facts: "So what if it's the end of the world as you know it. You'll find a new place, eventually. Meantime, have you thought about the service sector? I hear they have lovely jobs! Why not put in an application *today*. Meanwhile, even though the world around you is falling to bits gloriously, please say no to drugs and don't forget to use condoms" (p. 167).

The victories of right-wing political philosophies in the 1990s heralds a refusal to examine the social context into which poor and minority students are born. The right-wing movement has pushed questions of social justice and the conditions of socioeconomic mobility aside, couching inequality as the necessary price we pay for freedom. In a world like this, economically disadvantaged students have four choices:

1. Despite the bad odds, play the game and try to get ahead. Of course, if you are poor you typically do not have the dominant cultural capital (the ways of talking and acting that represent the inscription of the middle and upper-middle class) necessary to social mobility. Middle-class individuals are sought to fill middle-level positions in the workplace, thus eliminating from consideration those who begin at the bottom rung of the social ladder.
2. Accept the fate of your parents: Work hard at a dead-end job and seek consolation in God and family or sex, drugs, booze, and rock 'n' roll. Work in such jobs is painful psychologically and physically—and the pain must be addressed in one manner or another.
3. Join the military. Some young people do learn a skill in the military, but far too many return to the same conditions they left. Veterans often report that they wanted an adventure where they could learn electronics, radar, or airplane mechanics but often say, "I ended up stacking trays" in the mess hall.
4. Take the big risk, leave school, run scams, break the law, work for the big payoff. Chances for mobility for poor and minority students who stay in school are bad enough, but they are worse for dropouts. Poor and minority dropouts experience poorer health and have higher chances of going to jail. There is an important distinction between the effects of dropping out of school if you are white and male as opposed to, say, African-American and female: Only three out of twenty white male dropouts will live in poverty, as opposed

to almost two out of three black females (McLaren, 1994). Students who choose to live outside the law are often motivated by one simple fact: Given the choices, crime seems to them to offer the best opportunity to escape the pain of poverty and the hopelessness that accompanies it.

With this in mind, consider the growth of youth gangs in America over the last two decades. The conventional wisdom about youth joining gangs involves the assertion that the young person is beset with identity problems and the gang provides them with a new one. Although there may be kernels of truth in this explanation in individual cases, most kids join simply because they want better living conditions (Jankowski, 1991). Bombarded with images of failure—street derelicts, individuals dependent on government assistance, parents who have worked in degrading jobs leading nowhere—young people join gangs in an act of resistance, a refusal to allow themselves to succumb to their environment. And a hostile environment it is, with its unrelenting fear and nagging possibility of violent death. Often, middle-class observers ask why youth put themselves in such physical jeopardy by joining a gang. They do not realize that urban poor and minority youth often feel that very sense of danger as non-gang members and join the gang as a means of finding some protection against it. Thus, like individuals who have organized themselves throughout human history, they join together on the basis of their anxiety, fear, and suspicion.

These kids take the advice of corporate America, as voiced by its hired guns, its advertisers: "Go for the gusto"; "You can have it all"; "Just do it." They know they may speed to the top or crash to the bottom—but, they tell us, there is nothing to lose if you are going to end up a loser anyway. Such kids tell the same story over and over again: Their greatest fear is having to take the "shit jobs" that ruined their parents' lives. And besides, if nothing else, being in a gang provides a temporary deliverance from the life such jobs entail. And maybe, just maybe, as one gang member from Boston put it: "I could hit it big at something we're doing and get the hell out of this place" (Jankowski, 1991, p. 46). As a twenty-year-old gang member from Los Angeles told the story: "I just joined the T-Men to kick back [relax, be carefree] for a while. My parents work real hard and they got little for it. I don't really want that kind of job, but that's what it looked like I would have to take. So I said, hey, I'll just kick back for a while and let that job wait for me. Hey, I just might make some money from our dealings and really be able to forget these jobs" (p. 46).

Many gang members reveal painful memories of their parents' vulnerability to the whims of their employers, the bad work they faced day after day, the defeat they lived with. An eighteen-year-old expressed these feelings:

A few years ago I would be pissed at my old man 'cause he didn't do things like save his money and move from the projects. He just seemed to be unwilling to have a desire to improve himself so that my mother and us kids were better, you know? . . . Later I could see that he didn't have much of a chance, given that he was just a worker. I resented that, not him, but the situation. But you know, after I talked to him, I was more pissed at the way he felt than anything else. He felt like he had no control over the situation; and I said to myself, I'll do everything I can not to let the fuckers make me feel like that. And I hustle all the time trying to develop projects to get money. (p. 108)

Who among us cannot relate to the pain, the "social death" of dead-end bad work. Social death entails dealing with the loss of dignity and self-worth that accompany bad work and the loss of hope for any way out of it. Even for kids who join gangs, those who live through the experience often end up taking the no-future jobs after their will to resist wanes. For those who are yet to figure it out: America has a *big problem* that is just beginning to come to a head. A nation cannot teach and broadcast without consequence the mythology of social mobility, advertise the notion that one's self-worth revolves around the acquisition of expensive consumer items, and refuse to acknowledge the social and cultural dynamics that keep poor and minority youth as mere sideline observers of this process. When the public reaches the political decision that nothing can be done to include the observers in the action, the ingredients for a violent recipe come together. The words of the prophets of America's future are inscribed in urban rap.

Confusing Refusal with Inability: The Costs of Resistance

Much too often, the poor and minority students who are tracked into vocational education are individuals resting near the bottom of the schools' status hierarchy. Peers reject them, and teachers give up on them. Often, the closer these marginalized kids find themselves to the mainstream school culture, the worse they feel about their identity. In order to separate themselves, they improvise clothing styles that differ significantly from the dress conventions of their teachers and more affluent peers. In this and scores of other acts of resistance, such students begin to form a distinctive cultural style—a subculture of opposition. Much to the detriment of these marginalized students, the professional culture of education has never quite understood the dynamics of youth resistance, often mistaking the need for students to protect their identities with the personal rejection of the teacher. Indeed, the professional education culture does little to help teachers distinguish a student's refusal to participate in an educational activity for the purpose of identity protection with incompetence, the inability of the student to successfully execute participation. The ability to make this distinction is necessary to the development of a critical pedagogy of vocational education for marginalized students.

If critical vocational educators can illustrate the fact that the conscious refusal of African-American, Latino, Native American, and many white students to participate in many mainstream school rituals, then new understandings of student school performance can become possible. Schooling emerges in a new light that reveals the insight that school failure is not based simply on the limitations of particular students. Teachers thus begin to understand what marginalized students have known all along: Schools are set up to reward the values of the already successful, those whose culture most accurately reflects the mainstream. Even though they have understood this sociological reality all along, marginalized students have not known what to do with it. They have too infrequently applied the understanding to the preservation of their own self-worth; educational science's ascription of "slow," "dull normal," or "failure" to them still leaves profound scars. A critical vocational education is dedicated to helping marginalized students figure out where they can take their resistance, their sociological intuition, their unfocused anger.

An important lesson for all marginalized students involves the appreciation of the costs of many forms of resistance. Rejection of middle-class propriety often expresses itself as an abrasive classroom behavior antithetical to mutual respect and focused analysis. Clinton Allison (1995) has reminded resistant students that their silence, disruption, nonperformance, lateness, and absence may "cost them the possibility of using school for their own liberation" (p. 36). Also, Paul Willis (1977) taught us in the late 1970s in his study of the "working-class lads" in Birmingham, England, that their resistance to class inequities helped to reinforce the class structure by locking them into their working-class status. Marginalized student resistance to mainstream norms often expresses itself in terms of a cultivated ignorance of information deemed important by the so-called cultured. It is, if course, the dominant culture, not the students, who benefit from this cultivated unawareness, as young people lose the ability to critique, to make sense of the world around them. Such resistance leaves them no escape, no way out. In the last years of the twentieth century, they are often unable to enjoy a sense of solidarity with their fellow resisters because of race, ethnic, or gender antagonism. Their disempowerment and isolation in this context is complete (McLaren, 1994; West, 1993).

All that is left for such students is the enjoyment of maintaining an oppositional social identity. Blacks develop oppositional identities in opposition to whites; poor white students develop oppositional identities in opposition to popular "socials" or upper-middle-class student culture. In addition, marginalized students develop an oppositional cultural frame of reference or an alternative way of making sense of the world (Zweigenhaft and Domhoff, 1991). Critical educators have always granted great respect to such a way of seeing, because within the frames of such perspectives, there are insights on which resistance to injustice can be constructed and which pedagogical alternatives can be theorized. Ironically, this oppositional culture and its view of the world created as a response to and protection from racism and class bias is employed as an important justification by guardians of the status quo for rejecting the marginalized. "*They* are weird," mainstream apologists contend, "have you listened to the way they talk? I hate the way those black athletes carry on after a touchdown. I'm glad the school outlawed it."

This oppositional identity, simply stated, is a shield against the hurt often imposed on marginalized students by individuals and groups who see the marginalized as their social inferiors. One of the most important features of the oppositional identity involves the projection of a "tough gaze," a suspicious, confrontational attitude toward authority. Many African-American, Native American, and Latino students develop the tough gaze, with its low affect and dismissive attitude toward schooling as a white institution. An integral aspect of the stance involves its predisposition to reject "whiteness" as a universal marker of appropriate behavior and affect. Such a rejection is often read by teachers and white students as the manifestation of a "bad attitude." This oppositional identity, this "nigger with an attitude" (NWA) has become a symbol of racial pride in many portions of the African-American community. Vocational educators must understand this oppositional identity, its origins, its codes and unstated messages, its social consequences, and its effect on educational performance. These understandings are important for many reasons, not the least of which involves a teacher's (often a white teacher's) ability to interpret the resistant behavior not as a personal attack but as an understandable reaction to a constellation of social, economic, and cultural dynamics.

Understanding the Oppositional Identity:
The Marginalized Student as Defiant Individual

To facilitate the understanding of the resistance of poor and minority students in vocational education, a tentative description of the oppositional student is in order. Wishing in no way to essentialize or universalize a "personality type," I offer the description as a heuristic device (a method of developing insight and understanding), as an attempt to discern patterns in resistant behavior. Recognizing such patterns, vocational teachers can avoid some of the personal and impassioned reactions that undermine communication and trust in vocational programs. An oppositional identity is marked by a sense of mistrust or suspicion. Many marginalized young people spend their entire lives in communities where they must compete for scarce resources. In such situations, trust cannot be taken for granted but must be studied and carefully, if not strategically, calculated. Given this adoption of mistrust as a survival skill within a student's community, it is not likely that such wariness will be reduced outside the home community. When the new context is one dominated by individuals from mainstream upper-middle-class Anglo culture, suspicion will only increase.

This mistrust is typically accompanied by a strong sense of self-reliance. Because there are so few resources in the families and communities of marginalized students, they learn early in their lives to depend on their own resources to procure those things they need. That characteristic points to a view of poor people that is quite different from the one painted by conservative advocates of massive cutbacks in welfare and social programs. Many individuals who grow up in families that have had several generations of welfare recipients are *not* passive, unmotivated young people. Although they may be unmotivated by academic learning possibilities, this does not mean that they are not moved by the effort to improve their economic well-being, even if it takes superhuman and danger-filled efforts. Their absence of academic motivation does not have as much to do with laziness as with education's inability to convince them of its intrinsic worth, its relation to their lives, and its capacity to lift them out of their uncomfortable lives.

This sense of self-reliance produces another trait of the oppositional personality—social isolation. Because self-reliance is so important and trust is granted so tentatively, marginalized individuals forge fewer ties with others. Emotional connections with others can subvert one's self-reliance, constrict freedom and options, and set one up for emotional hurt. Such understandings are made as part of a larger survival instinct that marginalized students feel pressured to cultivate. If one has to deal daily with drug dealers, drug addicts, pimps, and robbers who see the young as prey, then a mark of intelligence involves the ability to negotiate, elude, and, indeed, survive these interactions. Survival of this sort is accomplished in a variety of ways that draw upon sophisticated forms of intelligence and creativity. The cool pose referred to earlier reemerges in this context, manifesting itself not simply as cool and detached but as mysterious and intimidating—a defiant air. "Don't mess with him, you never know what he's going to do," one's peers may report. To survive, resolve must be firm and steady.

Outsiders are often amazed when they learn about the innovative business sense and work ethic displayed by urban gang members. Grounding their self-concept on a Social Darwinist survival-of-the-fittest ideology, marginalized youth, males in particular, assume the role of ghetto entrepreneurs. Again, what a wide gulf there is between portrayals of these young people as dim-witted, lazy, dependent children of welfare and as hustling, savvy financial operators conjuring yet another money-making strategy. Mainstream Americans and middle-class educators fail to recognize such traits, generally because when the diverse groups interact, the marginalized kid assumes a reticent pose, a cool-driven, low affect that hides individual talent (Jankowski, 1991). Attempts to compare the abilities of these self-educated ghetto entrepreneurs to the financiers who occupy the highest offices of our corporations typically elicit a derisive laugh from the halls of academia and the professional elite. Understanding the cultural and political dynamics of defiance, critical vocational educators make use of the broad range of talents these students possess in order to provide them with new forms of hope. Proving to the community the unquestionable intelligence of these students, critical teachers work to restructure schooling in a way that provides both respect and opportunity to these victims of institutional racism and class bias.

The Adult World's Dismissal: Marginalized Kids as Aliens

Education in America has never quite understood its students—especially those who are "different" from the mainstream norm in some way. In the 1990s, it is not hard to find educators who even hold young people in contempt. Students are quite sensitive to such feelings and, much to the surprise of teachers, are hurt when they uncover them. One of the characteristics of young people that seems so threatening to many adults involves the libidinal energy, the sense of desire, enthusiasm, passion, and even rage that youth in a variety of places and times have experienced. Such emotion—expressed as a desire for experience and adventure, a longing to escape the boredom of contemporary school life—threatens modernist rationality and the order of the scientifically managed school. Understanding how out of place they are in such institutions, many young people, marginalized youth in particular, have sensed that the tacit social contract between adults and youth no longer exists (Gaines, 1990).

Youth culture emerges from this context as an important villain. Not understanding the social field from which youth culture emerges and the complex dynamics surrounding how it is received by kids, adults often see youth culture one-dimensionally—as a harmful and destructive presence in the lives of young people. Working-class survival strategies such as shop-floor pranks, loyalty invested in friends not institutions, and break-time fraternizing have always vexed school authorities. To many middle-class guardians of educational order, these behaviors are manifestations of moral depravity. Often modernist-oriented psychologists have interpreted them as evidence of emotional disturbance, sociopathic behavior, or brain damage. Those of us who have never been diagnosed in such a way often have trouble empathizing with those who have. Being labeled as mentally ill, retarded, or maladjusted is not fun and cannot help but elicit anger and, at one's lowest moments, feelings of worthlessness.

Although not all kids have to face such specific labeling, all young people, especially the poor and nonwhite, have suffered from the media's portrayal of them in recent years. Serving as symbols for social decay, they have been viewed more and more as not just social victims but as the *victimizers* of adults. Many kids see TV shows about "youth in crisis" as conversations between adults about youth—not as dialogues between kids and adults about growing up at the end of the twentieth century. Many of the experts on youth who are interviewed in such programs elicit gales of laughter from kids with their pomposity, condescension, and academic language. The advice such experts give parents about opening lines of communication with their children are doomed by their naïveté to failure. When kids are interviewed, many young people argue, they are asked such stupid questions that they themselves come off looking dumb. When a song mentions suicide, for example, reporters sometimes assume that a simplistic relationship exists between the song and the actions of young people; that is, kid listens to song about suicide, kid then commits suicide. Reporters then ask, "Why do you listen to music that advocates suicide?" The question is so outside the context of the world kids inhabit that they stumble through an answer. The song is not necessarily a literal statement but rather speaks to their anger and despair, their frustration over parental misreadings and misunderstandings. In many ways, the music is a "legal stimulant" to assuage boredom, to address their suppressed desire. Adults too infrequently understand these dynamics.

Thus, even that which is often important to young people, that which touches their desire and rage, is dismissed by adults. It is not surprising therefore that students often feel that school success demands they surrender themselves, cut their connections to youth culture. Such realities affect poor and minority students most directly, but even the children of the middle class are not immune (Gaines, 1990; McLaren, 1994). All young people are coming of age in an unfair economy where bad work is proliferating and high-skill post-Fordist core jobs are contracting. Given such realities, TV news reporters should not be surprised by youth anger directed at them and the stories they produce about kids in America. It is as if the adult population has been blinded to the desire and passion of youth. A critical pedagogy of vocational education refuses this blindness, focusing its efforts not on some facile romanticization of young people but on a concerted attempt to understand the issues involved with being young in the 1990s. When alienation and dismal vocational prospects are added to this mix, special understanding by vocational teachers is needed.

12   *A Touch of Class*

Chapters 12, 13, and 14 will examine the foundations of vocational education in light of issues of class, race, and gender, respectively. Before beginning such analysis, however, it is important to understand that this separation of class, race, and gender into different chapters does not imply their conceptual isolation from one another. The chapter separation is made in the attempt to bring analytical clarity to the book. In each chapter, one of the dynamics will be analyzed, often in relation to the other two. The study of class, race, and gender must be carefully integrated in order to gain new insights into the nature of oppression. Vocational educators need to understand the complexity of these integrated dynamics in their attempt to build a democratic and critical pedagogy of vocational education. As they study class, race, and gender and their relationship to work and school, the realization emerges that sometimes, for example, race and class dynamics work together to engineer a "double whammy" of reinforcing oppression; at other times, one's racial experience can mitigate the effects of one's oppression in relation to class and gender issues, for example, in the case of a woman who is in a lower socioeconomic class but is *still white*. The point is simple: The interactive dynamics of class, race, and gender confound attempts to study them as isolated phenomena.

Class Blindness in America

Since vocational education deals so frequently with job training for poor students, one would think that a central feature of the study of vocational education would involve questions of socioeconomic class and mobility. One of the most important questions students of vocational education ask might be: What is the effect of vocational education in the attempt to help students obtain employment and socioeconomic mobility? When it fails to ask such a question, the study of vocational education also turns its back on questions of wealth distribution and the nature of equal opportunity to succeed in a democratic society (MacLeod, 1987; Jonathan, 1990). If such topics are ignored, tacit approval is provided for the view that individuals are equal combatants in the struggle for economic success. Without a consciousness of such questions, vocational classrooms become places where skill and status hierarchies are taken for granted and questions concerning worker wages and pay are off-limits. Worker pay is a private matter, vocational teachers assume, and accordingly, it should not be addressed in a public venue (Gaskell, 1987; Simon, Dippo, and Schenke, 1991). Thus, vocational students leave their vocational courses unaware of the political and moral issues that surround wages in specific workplaces and the larger economy. Such unawareness is severely disempowering.

As they adopt a silence about socioeconomic class, vocational teacher education and secondary vocational education itself fail to confront reality. As they ignore issues of class, the leaders of vocational education miss the connection between the consequences of schooling and the socioeconomic background of students. In the everyday world of human beings, this scholarly blindness expresses itself very concretely. Students who are intelligent and creative are convinced of their intellectual inferiority, as experts fail to understand the socioeconomic context in which they have matured. Without certain exposures to, say, an ethic that values the importance of education or the linguistic conventions that are implicitly used in schools, these students are incorrectly and unjustly deemed intellectually inferior. The same mind-set shapes the formulation of educational reforms such as Goals 2000; concern with socioeconomic class and its effects on American schooling is missing in such proposals. Some reformers are so worried that someone will charge them with using the concept of "class" in their reform proposals that they invent euphemisms such as "economically marginal," "disenfranchised students," "disadvantaged students," and "at-risk students" to express the idea (McLaren, 1994; Macedo, 1994). When the term "class" is used, conservatives often proclaim that since America is so egalitarian, class analysis has no use in the U.S. context. They then accuse analysts of "playing the race card," that is, using the idea of race and class to agitate the people. Such demagoguery must be stopped, the right-wingers conclude.

This battle over the use of class analysis to understand education is nothing new in American history. As documented in Part 2 of this book, vocational education for the poor and marginalized was always a class issue. As part of a larger effort to *discipline* an industrial workforce laboring in low-skill and boring jobs, vocational education was surrounded by the trappings of socioeconomic class issues. Indeed, had it not been for such issues, vocational education would not have existed in the first place. Corporate and business leaders would have been reluctant to support any work education that did not result in commercial profit for themselves and other dominant power groups. The elite control of local school boards guaranteed that school policy would rarely run counter to the interests of dominant groups. The use of class analysis as a tool to help make sense of American society has never been more important than in the 1990s, with the massive redistribution of wealth from the poor to the well-to-do. In 1980, for example, the average business or corporate chief executive officer (CEO) earned thirty-eight times the salary of the average school teacher and forty-two times as much as the average factory worker. By the end of the decade and its redistributive policies, the average CEO earned seventy-two times as much as a teacher and ninety-three times as much as a factory worker (DuBois, 1973b; Giroux, 1988; West, 1993; Coontz, 1992).

When such unequal realities exist and continue to grow, the use of class analysis is certainly appropriate. When the specific dynamics of the polarization of wealth in America are analyzed in further detail, new insights into American mobility are uncovered. Americans have always placed great value on hard work. People who work hard should be rewarded for their effort; and in fact, Americans believe that hard work is the backbone of the society. Most Americans would be surprised to find out, therefore, that the redistribution of wealth over the last fifteen years has been accomplished in inverse relation to hard work. Much of the new wealth created in the 1980s and 1990s did not come from inventing a better mousetrap or long hours of study or working overtime. Most new wealth befell those with enormous assets who were able to reap "instant wealth" from rapidly fluctuating return rates on their speculative investments. Dividends, tax shelters, interest, and capital gains were at the center of the action—not hard work (Coontz, 1992). The connection between class position and one's willingness to work hard may be less direct than many Americans have assumed. The attempt to dismiss class as an American issue must be exposed for what it is—an instrumental fiction designed to facilitate the perpetuation of the status quo by pointing to the laziness and incompetence of the poor as the cause of their poverty.

Four "class myths" perpetuated by power elites lay the ideological foundation for dismissal of class in the economic, political, and educational life of America: (1) the *myth of equal opportunity* contends that schools play the role of democratizer in America. Economic success awaits anyone possessing ability and willpower; (2) the *myth of meritocracy* maintains that those who succeed in schools and society deserve the spoils of victory. This myth is often expressed by the cliché "cream rises to the top." Richard J. Herrnstein and Charles Murray, authors of *The Bell Curve* (1994), support the myth of meritocracy when they argue that poor people in America tend to be the least intelligent members of the culture. In this context, conservatives can easily make the argument that biological factors form the infrastructure for class divisions—that poor and nonwhite students will never successfully compete with white middle-class students because of the qualitative differences in their gene pools; (3) the *myth of equality as conformity* asserts that when democratic progressives advocate social and educational policies grounded on the goal of equal access to upward mobility, they envision a Communist Chinese–like society characterized by zombielike conformity. This argument is absurd, as advocates of good work and a critical vocational education value individual differences and the right of individuals to fight demands of conformity; (4) the *myth of power neutrality* maintains that informal (nonelected) constellations of power will always work to maintain their own interests. Such activity is not neutral, as it strives to maintain the status quo, that is, extant power relations. Elite groups tend to interact with one another more than with nonelite groups. Clinton Allison (1995) has pointed out that the various elites are the members of the same golf and civic clubs; their wives (if the elite are men) are members of the Junior League; and they attend the same parties. If they do not sit on the local school board, then they know somebody who does. The important point here is that they have connections, informal access to policymakers. Poor and marginalized men and women do not have such connections (McLaren, 1994).

When the four class myths are widely accepted and the socioeconomic context is ignored, racism and class bias come out of the shadows. Why waste the school's money on students who are inferior? Why attempt to make access to jobs more equitable when particular class and racial groups will never perform as well as others? Such questions are being asked daily at the highest levels of power in 1990s America. The mind-set behind them perceives nothing wrong with tracking policies that place over 95 percent of white students in college prep and advanced placement tracks while relegating over 95 percent of African-American and Latino students to the lowest track. This modernist decontextualized way of seeing has allowed almost $300 million of the $981 million appropriated by the Perkins Act in 1991 for disadvantaged students to be returned to the federal government unspent (NCRVE, 1992). It is a way of seeing that views unskilled and semi-skilled workers as expendable fragments of production—as a contingent workforce to be hired and fired at the command of the market. The short-term corporate profits gained in this regard pale in comparison to the long-term effects on the nation and the workers in question. When a middle-aged worker cannot depend on a permanent job, the social compact between the worker and the nation is damaged. Given such realities, it should come as no shock to Americans that the United States, the land of opportunity, has greater disparity between the rich and the poor than Japan, Sweden, Australia, the Netherlands, Germany, the United Kingdom, Norway, Canada, and France (Rubin, 1994).

Relating Class Polarity to the Vision of Vocational Education

Why are socioeconomic classes so polarized in the United States? Why is the polarization increasing? How does vocational education fit into these class dynamics? The definitive answers to such questions, of course, are enormously complex and beyond the scope of this book. Nevertheless, it is essential here in Part 4 to consider the dynamics surrounding these questions in light of issues of socioeconomic class. Much of the work on class polarity and the causes of poverty tends to fall into one of two categories: (1) individualistic blame, and (2) contextual blame. This dichotomy denotes a simplistic view of the way power works in its subjugation of individual human beings. Of course, power is exerted through social structures, but the way such structural or contextual power operates appears in the everyday experience of specific women and men. To argue that class polarity is caused by one or the other is to fall into a conceptual trap. The distinction between individualistic blame and contextual blame sets up a false dichotomy. Thus, critical vocational educators examine the complex dynamics of power at work at both the individual and structural contextual levels in their attempt to understand the polarization of socioeconomic class in America. These concepts demand more attention.

Conservatives believe that anyone who has the ability and exerts the effort can "make it" in America. Those who do not, they argue, are held back by their lack of morals, their lack of family values (Ellwood, 1988). Such talk ignores thousands of poor people who embrace the work ethic, labor year upon year with hardly a break, and still remain at the bottom rung of the economic ladder. Those who make this "character" argument often refuse to address the social context, with its political and economic structures that work to privilege the privileged and punish the poor. Concurrently, they refuse to discuss the nature of white racism, sexism, and class bias; such talk, they confide, induces the poor to see themselves as victims, not agents. The purpose of empowerment involves the ability to move beyond victimization and to take charge of one's own destiny, but the way to do it does not involve the denial of history (West, 1992; Jennings, 1992). Social, political, and historical analysis grounds our understanding of the forces that overtly and covertly undermine socioeconomic mobility. Such knowledge is essential in a critical vocational pedagogy that is dedicated to the empowerment of the poor.

The Conservative Position: Individualistic Blame

Poverty results from individual pathology, conservatives argue. The conservative position is validated by Herrnstein and Murray (1994) in *The Bell Curve*, as they maintain that there is no mysterious dimension to the polarization of wealth in the United States: The poor are poor because of their low intelligence and pathological behavior. A major cause *and* effect of this pathological behavior, the argument goes, involves the absence of strong family values—middle-class family norms in particular. The model middle-class family existed at one point in our golden past, but in their rejection of

American values, progressives and liberals undermined the institution through welfare and giveaway programs. Such actions, the conservatives continue, by providing something for nothing, so reduced self-initiative that the poor have subsequently refused to work. In this "golden past," mothers were totally available to their children and intensely intimate with their husbands, a construction that placed so much pressure on women in the 1950s that thousands of them were driven to therapy and using tranquilizers and alcohol. Ignoring these midcentury problems, conservatives of the 1990s ascribe a large part of the blame for deteriorating family values on women's embrace of feminism. The feminist ethic, they argue, undermined women's dedication to the family and began the process of family breakdown (Coontz, 1992; Stafford, 1992). Decontextualizing the rise of feminism, conservatives speak of that time when women were peaceful, happy, traditional, and dedicated to their families. The femi-Nazis, as Rush Limbaugh puts it, destroyed that wonderful world.

The argument that poverty is caused by the lack of family values is not new to America. Over the last quarter of the nineteenth century, white essayists used the family values argument in reference to newly freed African Americans. The problems of blacks, they wrote, are not the result of racism and poverty but of their family values and personal behavior. Black parents were commonly believed by whites to raise their children without discipline or morality. Such inferior rearing produced boys born to roam and sexually promiscuous girls who frequently gave birth to illegitimate babies. Some commentators were more vitriolic, declaring that African Americans knew no more about fidelity in a marriage than a bull or heifer. Throughout the first half of the twentieth century, black families were described using such adjectives as "vicious" and "depraved." One disturbing aspect of the family values argument in the late twentieth century is that both conservatives *and* a sizable number of liberals have ascribed poverty to family breakdown. A middle- and upper-middle-class consensus has developed that attempts to repress understandings of context and structure and their role in shaping poverty.

This new consensus speaks of its anger toward the poor and nonwhite and their incessant whining about their victimization. Liberal politicians scramble to realign themselves with the anger, arguing that in the 1960s the cause of poverty was the lack of opportunity caused by class bias and racism; in the 1990s, they contend, the problem involves not class bias and racism but pathological patterns of behavior on the part of the poor themselves. Thus, all we can do is cut social services, education, job training, college aid, and welfare support for the poor; Herrnstein and Murray (1994) argue that since the poor are less intelligent, such programs are not likely to help them anyway. In a time where such arguments occupy a central position in public policy, critical vocational educators have an important role to play. Because they are concerned with social justice and economic opportunity, they must claim a voice in the conversation (Coontz, 1992). They must be able to speak to the problems in the individualistic blame position and articulate a vision of economic democracy and good work.

Responding to the New Consensus: Truth Versus Myth

Middle- and upper-middle-class Americans know very little about poor and nonwhite people. Indeed, much of the prevailing wisdom about the underclass is simply not true. For example, the folk wisdom of the 1990s asserts that the poor—black women in particular—have been producing "exploding" numbers of babies out of wedlock. The truth is that birth rates among single black women have fallen by 13 percent in the last twenty-five years. During the same period, birth rates for unmarried white women increased 27 percent. Such information might induce some right-wing politicians to temper their descriptions of poor black mothers as "brood mares" and "welfare queens." As the rate of monetary polarization increased in the 1970s and 1980s, new problems emerged in poor communities (especially poor urban black communities) that cause concern for all of us. Levels of violence have worried all Americans, though the poor suffer the effects disproportionately. The attempt, however, to ascribe the cause of such problems simply to the pathology of the poor is both logically simplistic and emotionally unempathetic. The causes of the urban crisis have been reduced to a few basic factors: broken families, high divorce rates, unwed pregnancies, family violence, and drug and alcohol abuse. The same problems confront families whose members serve as police officers or in the military, yet most Americans refrain from blaming them for their dysfunctionality. Typically, we have little trouble understanding that the context in which police officers and soldiers operate is in part responsible for such pathologies. Work stress from danger and conflict can produce devastating results. With this in mind, it is not difficult to imagine the stress that accompanies living for just one week in an inner-city war zone. Now imagine living there with no hope of getting out.

The argument can therefore be made that the strong family values that the socially and economically marginalized possess actually serve to impede economic mobility in some cases. Imagine that an elderly poor couple living in rural West Virginia inherited $5,000 from a deceased uncle. For years, they had tried to save enough money to buy a new house with indoor plumbing, with a heating system that worked consistently, in a location closer to the grocery store and the doctor's office. The money was just enough for a down payment on a modest two-bedroom home on the outskirts of town. Right at the time they were closing the deal on the new house, a cousin who had lost his job in the coal mines told them he was being evicted from his house; he owed $1,200 in delinquent rent. Another relative, the wife's sister, who was recently widowed, needed money to pay a long-distance phone bill she accumulated talking to her husband's four brothers living in various parts of the country about her husband's medical condition, his death, and the funeral arrangements. Another relative had a car repair bill of $1,000 she was unable to pay. If she were to keep her job, she had to get her car fixed, but she did not have the money. In the end, the house deal fell through—and within a month, the inheritance was gone. It had not been spent on a Cadillac, drugs, booze, or fancy clothes; it was not lost because of the poor couple's inability to defer gratification or plan for the future, a charge frequently leveled at poor people. Because of the couple's commitment to their extended family, their socioeconomic mobility was subverted. Strong family values alone cannot solve the polarity of wealth in America.

Many analysts contend that if all poor people who do not now possess traditional family values were to miraculously develop them by next week, very little would change in relation to the widening disparity of wealth in America. Even if poor families are tightly knit, few of them will advance economically if jobs are not available. No matter how hard conservatives might try to prove that individual pathology *causes* poverty, they will not succeed. Indeed, it may even be possible to establish a link between deviant social behavior and *high* income. Obviously, many make the observation that a large number of the most well-to-do young people in inner-city neighborhoods have made money through violent and pathological crimes—the reward of pathological behavior.

Social analysts make the point that one feature that separates the poor from the middle class is the pathological inability of the poor to delay gratification. When corporate behavior in America is examined over the past twenty-five years, one is struck by the emphasis placed on short-term quarterly profits at the expense of long-term development. The credit card debt compiled by middle- and upper-middle-class consumers in the 1980s and 1990s points to the possibility that the pathology of the poor is not all that different from other Americans. This ascription of pathology and individualistic blame to the poor is not based on some objective body of facts pointing to their complicity. Rather, it is an example of power at work: The maintenance of the existing polarization of wealth is a condition that is imposed on the poor by the powerful guardians of the status quo (Coontz, 1992; Ellwood and Wise, 1983; Jennings, 1992). This does not mean that there is some secret conspiracy operating behind the social curtain. However, it does mean that conditions are perpetuated that benefit those who hold power at the expense of those who do not. When Senator Jesse Helms, for example, airs TV campaign ads that pit the black and white poor against one another in the scramble for the working-class jobs that still exist, the status quo is defended. By dividing the poor people into competing racial groups, the possibility of their uniting to fight for good work and economic democracy is negated.

Separating Difference from Deficiency:
The Poor, Not the Stupid

A strange alchemy occurs when the cultural baggage carried by poor students encounters the middle-class dynamics of the school. The middle-class mind-set views poverty as a badge of failure. One African-American child learned this lesson in her first experiences in school, as evidenced by her response to the question "What is poverty?" "Poverty," she said, "is when you aren't living right." Such a lesson takes its psychic toll, moving students from poor backgrounds to reject the academic world and the culture that surrounds it as a matter of self-protection. School leaders still have trouble understanding that the poor are not stupid. Often, children from working-class and lower-socioeconomic-class homes do not ascribe importance to academic work in the same way as middle- and upper-middle-class students do. Working-class and poor students often see academic work as unreal, as a series of short-term tasks rather than as something that has long-term importance for their lives. Real work, they believe, is something you get paid for after its completion. Without such compensation or long-term justification, these students often display little interest in school. This lack of motivation is often interpreted by teachers, of course, as inability or lack of intelligence. Poor performance on standardized achievement tests scientifically confirms the "inferiority" of the poor students (Oakes, 1988; Nightingale, 1993; DeYoung, 1989; Woods, 1983).

It happens every day. Educators mistake lower-socioeconomic-class manners, attitudes, and speech for lack of academic ability. Some teachers report that they place some students in low-ability groups or recommend their placement in vocational education because of their *class* background. Their rationale involves the poor student's social discomfort around students from a higher class background; lower-socioeconomic-class students should be with their own kind. The standard practices of American schooling are too often based on a constricted view of the human capacity for development and an exclusive modernist understanding of human diversity. Intelligence in this view is defined operationally as one's performance on an IQ test, not as the unique and creative accomplishments one is capable of in a variety of venues and contexts. The social context and power relations of the culture at large and the school culture in particular are central in the attempt to understand the class dynamics of student performance.

Research on the education of low-status groups in other countries provides some important insight into the performance of marginalized students in American schools. In Sweden, Finnish people are viewed as inferior—and the failure rate for Finnish children in Swedish schools is very high. When Finnish children immigrate to Australia, however, they do well—as well as Swedish immigrants. Koreans do poorly in Japanese schools, where they are viewed as culturally inferior; however, in American schools, Korean immigrants are very successful (Zweigenhaft and Domhoff, 1991). The examples are numerous, but the results generally follow the same pattern: Racial, ethnic, and class groups that are viewed negatively or as inferiors in a nation's dominant culture tend to perform poorly in that nation's schools. Critical vocational educators must attend to the lessons of these findings in their attempt to undermine the class bias that consumes their students. Such research helps dispose of the arguments that school failure results from the cultural inferiority of the poor or the marginalized. It teaches us that power relations among groups (class, race, ethnic, gender, and so forth) must be considered when the performance of various students is studied. Without the benefits derived from such understandings, brilliant and creative young people from marginalized backgrounds will continue to be relegated to the vast army of the inferior and untalented. Such an injustice is *intolerable* in America.

Obviously, something is wrong here—something that rewards the privileged for their privilege and something that punishes the marginalized for their marginalization. Not only do we find worldwide evidence that those groups viewed as inferior perform poorly in school, but even after those deemed "inferior" leave school, we cannot find any connection between school-measured intelligence and occupational attainment or economic productivity (Zweigenhaft and Domhoff, 1991; DeYoung, 1989). This means that for those students who come from similar backgrounds, differences in school-measured ability do not seem to matter in the workplace. There are a couple of reasons for this ostensibly surprising condition: (1) as discussed in Chapter 4, it often does not matter how intelligent a worker might be in a workplace that does not require creativity or skills to perform daily tasks; and (2) the way intelligence is measured has little to do with the types of thinking required outside the world of school. Thus, critical vocational educators work to protect their vocational students—the group most damaged by the discourse of intelligence—from the lived ramifications of class bias.

Rethinking Intelligence

The struggle begins with the attempt to rethink intelligence in light of the tacit class, race, and gender assumptions that ground it. Although this project is not within the purview of this book, Shirley Steinberg and I have detailed this reconceptualization in other work (see Kincheloe and Steinberg, 1993; Kincheloe, 1995). A brief description is in order. Jean Piaget theorized

formal thinking as the highest order of human thought. Such thinking implies an acceptance of a Cartesian-Newtonian mechanistic worldview that is
caught in a cause-effect, hypothetical-deductive system of reasoning. Unconcerned with questions of power relations and the way they structure our consciousness, formal operational thinkers accept an objectified, unpoliticized
way of knowing that breaks an economic or educational system down into its
basic parts in order to understand how it works. Emphasizing certainty and
prediction, formal thinking organizes verified facts into a theory. The facts
that do not fit into the theory are eliminated, and the theory developed is the
one best suited to limit contradictions in knowledge. Thus, formal thought
operates on the assumption that resolution must be found for all contradictions. Schools and standardized test makers, assuming that formal operational thought represents the highest level of human cognition, focus their
efforts on its cultivation and measurement. Students, teachers, and workers
who move beyond formality are often unrewarded and sometimes even punished in educational and work-related contexts.

In this book, an attempt is made to define the type of thinking that might
occur when individuals, workers in particular, move beyond the boundaries
of Piagetian formality. Many theorists (Lave, 1988; Walkerdine, 1984,
1988) over the last two decades have sought to formulate a post-Piagetian
cognitive theory. Too often, however, they have not used the critical theoretical understanding employed throughout this book (especially in Chapter
10) to understand the way our consciousness is shaped by the world around
us. On the foundation of such understandings, we can construct a new vision of cognitive theory, a new conception of what "being smart" entails.
We can move beyond Piaget's notion of formal thinking, with all of its narrow assumptions about the ways intelligence is expressed. We refer to the
new vision of higher-order thinking as *postformal* thinking. As they move to
postformal thinking, critical vocational educators politicize cognition; they
attempt to desocialize their students and themselves from the conventions
of school-based pronouncements of who is intelligent and who is not. Postformal thinking is concerned with questions of meaning, self-awareness, and
the nature and function of the social context. Such concerns move postformal thinkers beyond formalist concerns with the proper scientific procedure
and the *certainty* it must produce. Postformalism grapples with purpose, de-
voting attention to issues of human dignity, freedom, power, authority,
domination, and social responsibility.

One of the main features of postformal thinking is that it expands the
boundaries of what can be labeled "sophisticated thinking." When we begin
to expand these boundaries, we find that those who were excluded from the
community of the intelligent seem to cluster around exclusions based on
race (the nonwhite), class (the poor), and gender (the female). The modernist conception of intelligence is an exclusionary system based on the

premise that some people are intelligent and others are not (Case, 1985; Klahr and Wallace, 1976). Intelligence and creativity are thought of as fixed and innate, as mysterious qualities found only in the privileged few. The modernist definition of intelligence has stressed biological fixities that can be altered only by surgical means. Such an essentialism is a psychology of hopelessness that locks people into rigid categories that stay with them throughout life (Bozik, 1987; Lawler, 1975; Maher and Rathbone, 1986).

Piaget's developmental description of thinking falls captive to the modernist tendency to separate the object of study from its environment; in this case, a person's intelligence is separated from the social context (one's class, race, gender, ethnicity) that produced the person. However, the theory is its own captive because it views intelligence as a process that culminates in an individual's mastery of formal *logical* categories. The development of thinking seems to come from thinking itself, separate from the external environment. This reflects the innate fixity of earlier Cartesian-Newtonian views of intelligence as a specter emerging from innate inner structures. The young Piaget, in particular, maintained that the desired pedagogical course was to move students' development away from the emotions so that rationality could dominate the progress of the mind. Stages were thus constructed around this logocentrism—stages that would become key supports in the commonsense, unquestioned knowledge about intelligence (Piaget, 1970, 1977; Piaget and Inhelder, 1968).

Since one of the most important features of postformal thinking involves the production of one's own knowledge, it becomes important to note in any discussion of the characteristics of postformality that few boundaries exist to limit what may be considered postformal thinking. Postformal thinking and postformal teaching become whatever an individual, a student, or a teacher can produce in the realm of new understandings and knowledge within the confines of a democratic pedagogy and good work. Much of what cognitive science, and in turn the schools, has measured as intelligence consists of an external body of information. The frontier where the information of the disciplines intersects with the understandings and experience that individuals carry with them to school is the point where knowledge is created (constructed). The postformal teacher facilitates this interaction, helping students to reinterpret their own lives and uncover new talents as a result of their encounter with school knowledge.

Viewing cognition as a process of knowledge production presages profound changes in education. Teachers who frame cognition in this way see their role as creators of situations where student experiences could intersect with information gleaned from the academic and vocational disciplines. In contrast, if knowledge is viewed as simply an external body of information independent of human beings, then the role of the teacher is to take this knowledge and insert it into the minds of students. Evaluation procedures that emphasize retention of isolated bits and pieces of data are intimately tied to this view of knowledge. Conceptual thinking is discouraged, as schooling trivializes learning. Students are evaluated on the lowest level of human thinking—the ability to memorize, the ability to follow directions. Thus, unless students are moved to incorporate school information into their own lives, schooling will remain merely an unengaging rite of passage into adulthood.

The point is clear; the way we define thinking exerts a profound impact on the nature of our schools, the characteristics of vocational education, and the shape that work will ultimately take. Notice in the brief delineation of the characteristics of postformal thinking that follows that each feature contains profound implications for the future of work and work education. Indeed, the postformal thinking described in the following passage can change both the tenor of work and the future of vocational education. Self-reflection would become a priority with students and workers, as postformal educators attend to the impact of school and work on the shaping of the self. In that context, working and learning would be considered acts of meaning-making that subvert the technicist view that thinking involves the mastering of a set of techniques. Vocational education could no longer separate technique from purpose, reducing teaching and learning to deskilled acts of rule following and concern with methodological format. Schools and workplaces guided by empowered postformal thinkers would no longer privilege white male experience as the standard by which all other experiences are measured. Such realizations would point out a guiding concern with social justice and the way unequal power relations at school and work destroy the promise of democratic life. Postformal teachers would no longer passively accept the pronouncements of standardized-test and curriculum makers without examining the social contexts in which their students live and the ways those contexts help shape student performance. Lessons would be reconceptualized in light of a critical notion of student understanding. Postformal work educators would ask if their classroom experiences promote, as Howard Gardner has put it, the highest level of understanding that is possible (Gardner, 1991).

A Brief Description of Postformal Thinking

Critical vocational educators expand "what counts" as intelligence by using these four basic features of postformal thinking:

1. Etymology (the origin of validated knowledge): the exploration of the forces that produce what the culture validates as knowledge. An individual who thinks etymologically pays close attention to the source of personal intuitions and "gut feelings." Rarely do we come

up with such feelings independently, for most thoughts and feelings are collective in origin (Bohm and Edwards, 1991; Senge, 1990). Consider, for example, language: It is entirely collective. We may think that our assumptions are self-generated, but typically we get them from the kitty of culturally approved assumptions. The concept of "thinking for oneself" must be reconsidered in light of these concerns; indeed, without an awareness and understanding of etymology, people are incapable of understanding why they hold particular opinions or specific values. Without such appreciations, the ability for reflection and analysis is seriously undermined. It is not an exaggeration to maintain that the capacity for critical thought is grounded upon the postformal concern with etymology.

2. Pattern: the understanding of the connecting patterns and relationships that undergird the lived world. Having spent a harrowing night in a small bathroom with three of my children, my wife, and three dogs seeking shelter from Hurricane Andrew, I am aware of the power of the cyclonic weather pattern known as a hurricane. Picking up energy from the warm ocean waters, hurricanes develop a rotation pattern that creates unfathomable power. High and low pressure centers developing in differing locations become part of the hurricane system as they interact with prevailing wind patterns to direct the path of the storm. Each component of the pattern influences the others in a way that is typically hidden from view. One can only comprehend the system of a hurricane by thinking of it as a totality, not as independent, discrete parts. Work, education, and economic systems are also constructed by invisible patterns characterized by interlocking activities. From our vantage point in the middle of these patterns, they are extremely difficult to identify. Modernist science and education have typically focused on separate pieces of the patterns, often missing the system itself. As a result, serious problems go unsolved as mainstream "experts" focus on specific events. "American worker productivity falls again," Tom Brokaw tells his nightly news audience, fragmenting our understanding of long-term deskilling patterns in the workplace and causing us to fight the wrong battles in the effort to increase productivity. Indeed, no matter how educated individuals become, if they cannot escape the confinements of formal thinking they will be held hostage by unseen patterns (Senge, 1990).

3. Process: the cultivation of new ways of reading the world that attempt to make sense of both ourselves and contemporary society. The way modernist civilization has developed with its Cartesian-Newtonian logic and scientific reductionism has taken its toll on human creativity. All human beings naturally hold the potential for

creative thinking processes, but through their acculturation and especially their education, many people have lost that capacity. Many analysts argue that prehistoric peoples lived a more creative existence than we do now—which comes as a shock to our "modernocentric" systems. They devised not only tools and useful objects but creative ornamental and spiritual articles as well. Unlike many workers and students today, they did not follow a mechanical routine. For prehistoric humans, every day was different, new, and possibly quite interesting and exciting. The postformal notion of process attempts to recapture that excitement and interest, by devising new ways to perceive the world. The postformal process attempts to break the mold, to rethink thinking in a way that repositions people as active producers, not passive receivers of knowledge (Bohm and Edwards, 1991).

4. Contextualization: the appreciation that knowledge can never stand alone or be complete in and of itself. When people abstract, they take something away from its context. Of course, this is necessary in everyday life because there is too much information out there to be understood in detail by the mind. If an object of thinking cannot be abstracted, it will be lost in a larger pattern. The postformal thinker is certainly capable of abstraction, but at the same time, such a thinker refuses to lose sight of the conceptual field, the context that provides separate entities with meaning (Raizen and Colvin, 1991). For example, modernist schooling has typically concentrated on teaching students the "what" of school subjects. Life and job experience has traditionally taught us "how" and "why." Data (the "what") are best learned in the context of the "how" and "why." Thus, academic knowledge may best be learned in a vocational context, maybe in an apprenticeship or a work-study situation. If deeper levels of understanding are desired, tasks must be learned in the context in which they fit. In light of such a pronouncement, we can begin to see that a novice is one who possesses no specific knowledge of a particular work setting, despite perhaps bringing to the situation everyday knowledge and academic information. Such greenhorns become seasoned veterans only after they gain familiarity with specific social, symbolic, encoded, technical, and other types of workplace resources, that is, the context of the workplace (Raizen, 1989).

A definition of intelligence that takes these notions into account begins to recognize the abilities and resourcefulness of students tracked into vocational education. I frequently visit with or am told about students deemed unintelligent by the school who make up creative games that can be played in the confines of an urban neighborhood, who build vehicles out of abandoned car and bicycle parts, who write their own music and choreograph their own dances, who have collected junk from the neighborhood, fixed it up, and sold it at their garage sale, who have used paint found in the bottom of discarded paint cans to produce sophisticated portraits of themselves and their communities. Gang members, who are portrayed by the media as universally dim-witted and violent, are often in actuality precocious entrepreneurs who devise complex business deals and commercial relations (Jankowski, 1991). Postformal thinking recognizes the genius of such young people early in their school experience. Assuring them of their abilities and engaging them in activities designed to sophisticate such talents, postformal teachers create situations for these kids that replace their need to employ their talents in illegal, dangerous, and socially damaging activities.

Vocational educators learn from their introduction to postformal thinking that students tracked into their classes can learn academic skills in the context of vocational education. Changes in the perception about who can learn and who can achieve set in motion an avalanche of changes in the organization of schooling. The purpose of vocational education can no longer involve merely the attempt to adjust students to the culture of the workplace. Students emerging from a critical postformal vocational program are able to examine workplaces in larger contexts, understanding the relationship between power and authority, skills and wages, the rhetoric and the reality of democracy, and so on. Students with this background are able to assess how difficult it is for vocational graduates to break into a particular workplace. Having done so, they can figure out how realistic the possibility of establishing good work is in a specific work setting. In other words, vocational students emerge from such programs empowered to ask the questions that open doors for them.

The Irrelevance of Individualistic Blame: The Extreme Difficulty of Escaping the Class Barrier

Many economic analysts "just don't get it." They often fail to examine the attempt to escape poverty in the trenches, in the everyday lives of poor people. The collapse of Fordism in the early 1970s dealt Americans working in the manufacturing sector a fatal blow. The number of employed steelworkers was cut in half in less than a decade. The ranks of rubber workers were decimated. Competition with the Germans and Japanese rearranged America's manufacturing heartland, while the emergence of the economic strength of Taiwan, Hong Kong, Singapore, and South Korea with their thousands of low-wage workers cemented the fate of American blue-collar laborers (West, 1993). In 1970, 26 percent of American workers had jobs in the manufacturing sector; by the early 1990s, that percentage had fallen to

18 and by the year 2000, it will fall to 12.5 percent. Not only has the federal government failed to provide support to the victims of this decline, but it has encouraged the American corporate Diaspora to the Third World (Rubin, 1994).

For example, the U.S. Agency for International Development (AID) gave financial grants to trade organizations in El Salvador to help them recruit Decaturville Sportsware, a company previously based in Tennessee, to Central America. In addition, AID provided $5 million for the construction of a new plant, $1 million for corporate insurance, and thousands of dollars in low-interest loans to cover other moving expenses. Hundreds of American firms have been seduced to abandon American communities for foreign locations by AID and other governmental agencies. In their new foreign venue, they pay lower wages (about 45 cents an hour), provide fewer benefits to workers, pay no corporate taxes to either the United States or the host country, and pay no shipping duties. Meanwhile, the community back in Tennessee struggles to cope with the loss of the company's tax base and the lost income from the migration of high-wage jobs. Former employees and their families struggle to put their lives back together—and most will never recover. All of this and thousands of situations like it have been made possible by officials who campaign on the platform of family values.

In the Fordist era, working-class white men had access to low-skill jobs that, although often dangerous and demeaning, paid relatively good union wages. With such employment, those workers and their families were able to participate in middle-class consumption patterns and save money for a college education for their children. Even though work in low-skill manufacturing jobs was often an assault on one's dignity and sense of self, hardworking men could take solace in the knowledge that they were sacrificing daily to provide socioeconomic mobility for their children (Rubin, 1994; Weis, 1988). As the rivethead, Ben Hamper, put it: "Working the line for GM was something fathers did so that their offspring wouldn't have to" (Hamper, 1992, p. 13). After the 1970s and 1980s, a large percentage of these jobs were gone; today, the best available path for the mobility of poor and recent immigrants accommodates only a decreasing trickle of workers.

The industrial manufacturing path to socioeconomic mobility was often closed to African Americans, but as a result of union reforms and the civil rights movement, such jobs did open up a little after World War II. The post-Fordist decline in American manufacturing has been devastating to the black community, as one of the few avenues for black mobility has been closed. Although many have argued that the loss has reduced the number of employed role models for young African-American men, a more important effect has been the dissolution of job connections and employment networks for young black men and women. When youth do not live near successfully employed people, then the grapevine through which one worker tells another about a job opening and makes a recommendation to the employer is destroyed (Coontz, 1992; Ellwood, 1988).

Much to the horror of African-American young people, the loss of these connections and these manufacturing jobs has helped turn inner-city neighborhoods into hopeless wastelands. To white workers and their children, such changes have undermined the possibility that they will ever possess secure jobs. The forty-hour-a-week position that pays a livable wage and provides health and retirement benefits is becoming a dinosaur, a relic of a previous age. As noted earlier in the book, one of the fastest-growing types of employment in the post-Fordist era is so-called contingent work, that is, part-time, low-benefit, low-pay work. There are nearly 34 million of these "disposable" workers in the American workforce of the 1990s, already constituting about one-third of all U.S. workers. Because of such economic trends, the average take-home pay of employed black men in the 1990s is so low that it would take the salary of *four* of them to enter the middle-class mainstream. With the decline of full-time unionized jobs and the growth of the contingent workforce, vocational students (especially women and African Americans) find themselves unable to translate school attainments into reasonable employment. Critical vocational educators must join the struggle to challenge the corporate and governmental policies that contribute to these deteriorating economic conditions—conditions that further polarize social classes and undermine the American dream of socioeconomic mobility (Rubin, 1994; Coontz, 1992; Oakes, 1988; Johnson, 1991).

Critical vocational educators address the misinformation about the marginalized that is propagated by the proponents of individualistic blame. From the pens of mainstream scholars to speeches in the halls of Congress, the poor are vilified daily, the common charge being that the poor are poor because they are lazy and shiftless. Such charges are not only *untrue* but constitute an attack on the unprivileged by the privileged. If poor people are *uninterested* in work, then the number of unemployed poor people should have little to do with the ebb and flow of economic conditions. But such is not the case. When the unemployment rate increases 3 percent (moving from 6 to 9.5 percent, for example), the numbers of the unemployed *poor* almost triple. At 6 percent, for example, 341,000 husbands who are *poor* with children are unemployed; at 9.5 percent, 1,017,000 such husbands are unemployed. The fact that poverty rates are contingent on the number of jobs available indicates that poor people do not generally choose unemployment (Ellwood, 1988).

A democratic vocational education promotes awareness of these issues; in a time when the marginalized possess few advocates, critical vocational educators expose the war on the poor. A critical vocational education is honest with its students about the fantasy world often portrayed by educators that promises that all those who apply themselves and work hard will have a successful life. The point here is not to discourage student dreams but to prepare young people for the difficulties they will face and to help them develop strategies to overcome the obstacles in their paths. Critical vocational educators support the notion in the name of good work, economic democracy, and *family values* that any American two-parent family with children should be able to avoid poverty via the full-time work outside the home of one parent. Of course, at the end of the second millennium, we are far away from such a goal, but the future of American democracy rests on its accomplishment. Around this one objective, critical vocational educators can establish a program of outreach to the community, an outreach that forges larger networks and advocacy groups for the support of marginalized students attending our schools. And in the 1990s, such students desperately need help.

Examples of the despair of poor kids abound. Because of the deindustrialization precipitated by post-Fordist globalization and corporate America's flight to Timbuktu, factories around the nation have closed their doors. In the communities surrounding the factories, the science of economics wears a human face—and in the case of economically disadvantaged kids, it is a face of desperation. Studies of young people in these communities reveal consistent patterns of youth response. There is an increase in juvenile crime. Youth counselors in the local communities attribute such an increase to the malaise of economic hopelessness that devours young people after the factory jobs disappear. The aimlessness and nihilism is real and manifests itself in all-too-real ways: most disconcertingly in the increase of "untimely deaths." Gunshot murders, fatal drunk-driving accidents, and drug complications all lead to previously unimagined horror in the daily lives of the young.

The point being made here is that the economic conditions of the late twentieth century, marked by an increasing polarization of America's wealth, have created a situation where our society's economic machine no longer needs young, inexperienced people. Adolescence as a preparatory stage for adulthood is obsolete. In the 1990s, it has become a corral for unneeded young people drifting in a socioeconomic purgatory. Demographers report that elderly men have the highest suicide rate in this society. Perceived by society and themselves as socially superfluous, America's old men are removed from the workforce, stripped of a future, and left to wait for death. Over the past quarter century, the group with the fastest-growing suicide rate was males aged fifteen to nineteen (Gaines, 1990). Devoid of hope for socioeconomic mobility and burdened with the masculine expectation for self-sufficiency, these young men reflect America's dilemma in the 1990s. Critical vocational education must provide a voice of hope, an avenue of participation for students victimized by contemporary economic strategies and youth policies.

Controlling the Poor: Inferiority as Self-Image

As discussed in Part 2 of this book, powerful groups in America have always promoted conservative goals for schools. Maintaining social order and social control have typically been viewed as educational purposes superior in importance to the promotion of social mobility. Learning to obey the rules and defer to authority is often more important than academic learning. Social control usually refers to the control of the poor. Researchers have discovered that classroom management strategies differ significantly between classrooms composed primarily of poor students and those composed primarily of middle- and upper-middle-class students. But control of the poor is never achieved easily—if it is achieved at all. The dynamics of social control always involve contestation and conflict; students who perfect an oppositional identity, as discussed in Chapter 11, do not lend themselves to being controlled by the school or anyone else. The identities that students wear are directly affected by the dynamics of this struggle for control—and critical vocational educators study these everyday power struggles very carefully.

How does it affect a young man or woman from a poor family to discover that most of the resources of the school are devoted to the more "promising" (read middle-class) students? What happens to poor students when they learn that they can expect little from the school? How long does it take them to understand the often subtle and sometimes not so subtle procedures to persuade them to enter the low-ability classes? Many of the young people I have talked to have been livid when they finally appreciated (often years later) the ways their opportunities were undermined by their high-school experience. Once they have gained some wisdom in the workaday world and some insight via self-education or maybe a return to school, these students explode with anger when they recall the ways standardized intelligence tests rationalized their relegation to the low-ability groups. They are flooded with emotion as they recognize that the knowledge they acquired in vocational education had little exchange value in the open marketplace (Giroux, 1988).

In such circumstances, how could marginalized students be motivated to learn or be excited about school? Educational sociologists have for decades reported the cold, impersonal ways teachers often treat their lower-socio-economic-class students. Rarely do teachers show empathy for poor students and the painful existential choices they must make between acceptance by their peers and school success (Banfield, 1991). School is sometimes like a jealous lover who demands that marginalized students must choose between their peers or school; if school is chosen, then such students must give up their culture and adopt the identity of a school achiever. So hard are these choices for marginalized kids that students from poor backgrounds who remain in school and are at least moderately successful in their classes are, when compared to school dropouts, more depressed, less politically conscious, more passive in the life of the classroom, and more prone to conform. The price of success in the modernist school for marginalized students may be a form of coerced cultural hara-kiri.

Under such circumstances, it is not surprising when schools that should exist to empower lower socioeconomic class students actually serve to demoralize them and strip them of a desire for self-determination. Indeed, studies indicate that the school does a good job of convincing the poor of their inferiority. Since they often fail in school, individuals from the lower socioeconomic classes often feel that they have no right to help make political and economic policy, that is, to help govern. There is little that could be done that would better maintain existing power relations, to keep the poor in poverty. Poor people in this failure mode should not even attempt to voice their concerns and fight the injustice that chains them to their dead-end jobs—after all, they are incompetent, resting as they do at the base of Herrnstein and Murray's bell curve. This psychology of inadequacy supplements more obvious forms of domination such as factory ownership, control of information and expertise, placement in governmental positions, and lobbyist access to political officials. All of these dynamics work synergistically to maintain the polarization of power and wealth (Zweigenhaft and Domhoff, 1991).

Marginalized students often believe the equal opportunity fable propagated repeatedly in their classrooms. Caught in the psychology of inadequacy, they internalize the psychobabble and the labels it ascribes to them: "We're problem children, emotionally disturbed, and learning impaired," they tell us. On one level, they understand the absurdities of some of the labels and laugh uproariously at the irony of their usage; but on another level, a very personal one, they accept the classifications as transcendental truths about themselves (MacLeod, 1987). A critical pedagogy of vocational education intervenes in this context, assuring mislabeled students of their intrinsic worth and helping them understand the social dynamics that contextualize their bizarre position in the culture of American schooling. Clint Allison (1995) has written in *Present and Past* that American schools have traditionally feared the poor and the nonwhite; school leaders argued in the middle of the nineteenth century that something had to be done about them: Their "inferior cultures and dangerous ideas" must be addressed by the schools; students from these groups must be taught order and self-control (p. 187). What better way to accomplish this holy mission than by convincing marginalized students that they are failures and that they have no one to blame but themselves?

Critical vocational educators help inform their students of these dangerous educational memories that allow marginalized students to see beyond the horizon of their poverty. The contextual understandings achieved by students at this point, contrary to prevailing assumptions, do not merely provide excuses for their educational failure. My experience and the experience of many of my colleagues who have taken part in such critical interventions is often quite exciting. Students often gain an unprecedented sense of excitement about school and the power of ideas. Many of them gain a new sense of efficacy, an empowerment that induces them to join the fray—both for personal development and social justice. They are awestruck by truth telling, motivated by the desire to get the whole story, and moved by the vision of what education *can be*. In such a context, teachers come to understand their own unconscious complicity in the subversion of marginalized student success. This understanding begins with the recognition that school failure is, in the words of Peter McLaren, "structurally located and culturally mediated" (McLaren, 1994, p. 216). When teachers are educated as technicians, unexposed to the socioeducational forces that concretize prevailing race, class, and gender relations, they inadvertently transmit a debilitating message to marginalized students: Your low status in the school is a manifestation of your personal inadequacy. Thus, students are initiated into the sixth circle of educational hell—the realm of the low achiever.

Understanding the unfairness of the race and the terror of their descent into educational hell, many marginalized students simply drop out. Most efforts at resistance are unproductive acts of anger directed at everyone in general and no one in particular. A crude form of class consciousness sometimes emerges outside of the appreciation of democratic values, community building, and politics of difference grounded on solidarity. A young African American from New York City delineates this consciousness:

> Take the white society in this city, they just keep you poor by giving you bad schooling, you know, giving you no skills, paying you low wages, and then not letting you live in certain areas. You see they get the good things in life because they get profits from paying you low. And then when you do get some money, they don't let you live in any area but the one they say you can live in, which is not where the better houses are—you know, the bigger and cleaner houses. So most of the big things in life they keep for themselves and then the scraps they let us niggers and spics fight with the spaghetti and potato heads [Italians and Irish] for. So all the brothers know if you don't belong to an organization at least some of the time, you just a sittin' duck for their organizations. (Jankowski, 1991, p. 85)

When the poor white kids, especially poor white males, grasp their position in the mobility hierarchy and the disappearance of the industrial working-class jobs held by their fathers and grandfathers, they react angrily. Unable to draw upon the discourse of racism, there is little to comfort them.

It is at this point that the anger of white lower-socioeconomic-class men turn on nonwhites. Blacks, with their affirmative action, have received preferential treatment, white men argue, and have taken jobs from better-qualified whites. Since racism is no longer a problem, the argument continues, affirmative action serves to promote the interests of those with inferior ability. Blacks are not the victims any more, whites conclude—we are (Jones, 1992). The anger and racial antagonism that emerge from these social dynamics have led to two serious consequences: (1) they have undermined any vestige of solidarity among the victims of the polarizing policies of political elites. Marginalized groups are too embroiled in internecine conflict to address larger political realities; (2) they have insured the political victory of power holders in U.S. society. Lower-socioeconomic-class whites (men especially) have sided with corporate interests to end any attempt to address the injustices of race, class, and gender. Thus, racial antagonism, as it has since the beginnings of industrialization, has undermined the solidarity of the marginalized.

When this racial subversion of class solidarity is combined with the decline of working-class identity in general, the plight of democratic progressives at the end of the twentieth century comes into focus. Stanley Aronowitz (1989) has argued that since the loss of assembly line, construction, and other heavy industrial work of the last two decades, working-class identification has quickly evaporated. The old urban working-class culture that once existed will never return, Aronowitz pointed out, and as a result, political organization strategies must change. Kids who a generation ago would have identified with their father's shop-floor, barroom culture find their identities shaped more by the mass media with their TV, radio, Walkmen, stereos, personal computers, computer networks, movies, and so forth. If media depictions of the working class are analyzed in this context, one discovers that this culture is no longer represented in any direct way. Media depictions of the working class after the 1970s have been centered around beer commercials and police shows. Here, male working-class characters jostle with one another in bars (Miller Lite Beer) and the police station house (*Hill Street Blues*, *NYPD*, *Homicide*, and so on). Male bonding within a working-class culture survives in these dramas, but the solidarity between production workers with mutual political interests is a relic of a lost past (Aronowitz, 1989). Most lower socioeconomic class students do not understand these cultural dynamics and the ways they influence their lives. A critical vocational education helps students contextualize their feelings, their sense of cultural estrangement, their loss of hope. By providing theoretical constructs, critical vocational educators empower students not simply to understand their situations but to act to change them.

Developing the Economic Empowerment Curriculum

The decline of working-class consciousness has affected no group more profoundly than economically disadvantaged young people in their late teens (West, 1992). Without traditional manufacturing jobs, such individuals feel superfluous and lose hope. In the 1990s, government help in the creation of jobs and other employment opportunities has ended—because the public has decided not to support funding for such projects. It will take a monumental effort on the part of the poor and the friends of the poor to rekindle support for such policies. It is absurd that at the same time that $150 to $200 billion (a conservative estimate) was being spent to bail out savings and loans in America, aid to the employment of the poor was being slashed. To combat such misguided policies, new forms of political organization are needed. Vocational education must play a central role in such organizational efforts (Gaines, 1990; Nightingale, 1993; Cotton, 1992; West, 1993).

The first step in this larger process involves the development of an economic empowerment curriculum for vocational education students. That curriculum centers around the existence of poverty and the knowledge and skills one needs to escape it. As a multidimensional holistic course of study, the economic empowerment curriculum views men and women in more than simply egoistic, self-centered, and rationalist terms. Individuals, especially poor ones, need help making meaning in their lives, developing a sense of purpose, constructing a positive identity, and cultivating self-worth. Unlike previous forms of vocational education, the economic empowerment curriculum would address these issues, using the categories covered in this book as the program's theoretical basis. Understanding poverty in the larger context of historical power relations, students would understand that poverty is not simply a reflection of bad character or incompetence. Students would thereby appreciate the organizational dynamics necessary in the effort to "pull oneself up by one's bootstraps"—an undertaking often referenced but infrequently explained. Vocational teachers and their students would help poor individuals develop strategies to take control of schools, social agencies, health organizations, and economic organizations. Understanding how these organizations work to undermine the interests of the poor with their narrow and often scientifically produced definitions of normality, intelligence, family stability, and the rest, the curriculum helps students devise strategies to resist the imposition of policies grounded on such definitions (West, 1992; Ellwood, 1988; Jennings, 1992).

Providing the poor with a context for making sense of the way power works and poverty develops, the economic empowerment curriculum equips students with the knowledge to initiate public conversations about the relationship between poverty and wealth (Jones, 1992). The American people have yet to actually discuss the social, political, and economic aspects of privilege vis-à-vis deprivation. A national debate on the problem of the existence of an underclass in America might be a first step in the larger attempt to reinvigorate the public sphere of American life. Any effort to empower poor people that ignores the political development of the economically marginalized will fail. The poor must gain the political clout to castigate those who attempt to undermine their solidarity by appealing to their racial, gender, ethnic, or religious prejudices. The cultivation of this political power is the key to attacking poverty in America—but such a development will not come easily (Cotton, 1992). Critical vocational educators understand these realities and thus lend their efforts to providing their marginalized students with the knowledge needed to begin the process of change.

Such educators understand that job training alone will not solve the polarization of wealth in America. The traditional route to socioeconomic mobility has involved *first* achieving income stability and *second* investing in education (Coontz, 1992). In light of this understanding, the basis of governmental policy should revolve around job creation/full employment policies that provide child care for workers and reward and punish businesses on the basis of their contributions to the creation of good jobs and democratic workplaces in poor areas. The curriculum of economic empowerment calls for an increase in wages and a commitment to end welfare by providing jobs to welfare recipients. In two-parent families where one or two of the parents is a full-time worker or in single-parent families where the parent works either full-time or part-time, work should be rewarded. Health care for such workers should be guaranteed and tax burdens should be reduced (Nightingale, 1993; West, 1992; Ellwood, 1988). Students of the economic empowerment curriculum are motivated by their vision of good work and economic justice and, as participants in a democratic community, fight to make the vision a reality.

13   *Accounting for Gender*

$\mathbf{M}$y teacher education students almost universally possess an acute sense of fairness, a desire to do the right thing. As our discussions turn, as they inevitably do, to issues of race, class, gender, mobility, and school performance, this sense of fairness expresses itself in ways consistent with the public conversation, the conventional wisdom. "Why should we talk about issues of race, class, and gender?" they ask. The only fair way to deal with questions of difference, they posit, is to erase them from our consciousness. As teachers, they propose to ignore questions of difference and treat everyone the same because they are not prejudiced.

Such viewpoints are heartfelt and are expressed with great passion and commitment. The question for me and thousands of other teachers is where to engage this passion and commitment so that a more textured understanding of race, class, and gender dynamics and their relationship to schooling can be attained. Chapter 13 focuses on gender and its relationship to work and vocational education. Before beginning this analytical task, I want to explore in some detail the dynamic relationship among gender, class, and race. Serious strides have been made over the last fifteen years to understand the way such dynamics operate to shape our lives, our education, and our work. This chapter will begin with a brief exploration of the development of social theoretical explanations of the relationship and then move to specific analyses of gender dynamics at work in a vocational context. Do not be intimidated by the term "social theory." We have been involved in social theorizing throughout this book. Just for clarification, all social theory refers to is the attempt to explain on a rather general level why things happen as they do. In vocational education, social theory helps us understand why a man hired for a particular position advances more quickly than the woman who helped show him the ropes. Or it may help us understand why one does not see as many women over fifty in managerial positions as men (Hacker, 1989). How do these patterns develop? Who benefits from these arrangements? Who loses? Questions like these that relate especially to gender provide the infrastructure for this chapter.

Connecting Gender with Race and Class:
Mainstream Perspectives

The connections among race, class, and gender have been little understood by educators. Mainstream liberal and conservative educators have not only failed to understand the interactions among race, class, and gender but have also been relatively uninterested in probing the connections that unite the spheres of politics, culture, and the economy with education. The mainstream disinterest in such issues accounts for the absence of foundations courses in many vocational teacher education programs around the country. Without such study, educators and educational leaders view their task as merely to address prejudicial attitudes toward women and minorities. American life, from these modernist perspectives, is seen in fragmented segments—with education here being isolated from politics, economics, and culture. Like my students, conservative and liberal analysts see "unattached individuals" unaffected by their membership in racial, gendered, or class collectives or groupings. Critical researchers maintain that such fragmentation distorts our view of how schools and workplaces operate.

When conservative and liberal scholars fail to account for power dynamics in schools, workplaces, and the socioeconomic context that shapes them, specific processes of domination and subordination of students and workers cannot be exposed. In the place of such specific exposé, the individual behavior of irrationally prejudiced men and women is embraced as the cause of unfair treatment. Although such isolated irrational acts of prejudice certainly occur, they are not responsible for most of the oppression of racially, sexually, and economic "outsiders." To get to the point where we can explain the particular processes of subordination, critical vocational educators must understand not only the dynamics of race, class, and gender but also the ways their intersections in the lived world produce tensions, contradictions, and discontinuities in everyday lives (McCarthy and Apple, 1988; Arnott and Matthaei, 1991).

In this regard, Carol Gilligan (1981) was on the right track in her study of taxonomies of moral reasoning and the ways they privilege male over female approaches. Subsequent analysis, however, has indicated that gender is just one of the plethora of social categories that shape the ways individuals engage in moral reasoning. When race and class (as well as geographic place, national origin, religion, and other categories) are added to the social caldron, we discover that women from different social locations reason differently. In this circumstance, gender analysis is insufficient; we must examine the way gender interacts with other social categories to get a deeper and richer picture of moral reasoning (Stack, 1994). Such understandings are important in our effort to understand why different individuals engage with schooling and the workplace in divergent ways. Such awareness can help us distinguish between being different or being deficient—a distinction that when left unmade can perpetuate forms of institutional sexism, racism, and class bias.

Understanding Gender in Relation to Class and Race

My argument is simple: Racial, sexual, and class forms of oppression can be understood only in structural context. This means that gender bias plays itself out on the terrain of economic and patriarchal macrostructures. An economic macrostructure might involve white male domination of the highest salary brackets in American economic life. A patriarchal macrostructure might involve the small percentage of upper level corporate managers who are women or, in a domestic context, the high rate of spousal abuse perpetrated by American males. Differences in women's lives in general and economic opportunities in particular revolve around inequalities of power. For example, African-American women, Latinas, Asian-American women, and Native American women experience gender as one aspect of a grander pattern of unequal social relations. Indeed, the way one experiences gender is contingent on its intersection with other hierarchies of inequality—other hierarchies in which the privileges of some individuals grow out of the oppression of others. There is no shared experience of gender subordination among women (Zinn and Dill, 1994; Zinn, 1994; Arnott and Matthaei, 1991).

An important aspect of the role of a critical vocational educator involves pointing out to students where gender bisects the axes of race and class. Some intersections create privilege. For example, if a woman marries a man from the upper class, gender and class intersect to create privileged opportunities for her. However, if a woman is Haitian-American, forms of racial prejudice will exacerbate the ways in which she experiences gender bias. Thus, whether it be through subordination or privilege, race, class, and gender dynamics affect everyone—not just those at the bottom of the status hierarchy. The problem is that those at the top of the race, class, and gender hierarchies often do not understand the ways the intersections of the various axes affect them. The economic divisions of class serve to structure the ways race and gender manifest themselves. Although we understand that connections among race, class, and gender exist, we never know how to predict the effects of the interactions. Racial and gender hostilities, of course, can subvert class solidarity. Class solidarity can undermine gender-grounded networks. Working-class women, for example, have rarely felt a close affinity to the middle- and upper-middle-class feminist movement (Zinn, 1994; Arnot, 1992).

As these race, class, and gender forces interact, sometimes in complementary and sometimes in contradictory ways, school experience cannot be viewed simply as an uncomplicated reflection of social power. The school experience is exceedingly complex, and although there are general patterns of subjugation that occur, such patterns play out in unpredictable ways with particular individuals. Cameron McCarthy and Michael Apple (1988) have maintained that school mediates rather than imposes its power upon students. This means that students from lower-socioeconomic-class backgrounds are not simply classified and relegated to low-status classes and ultimately to low-status jobs; instead, forces of race, class, and gender create a multilevel playing field on which students gain a sense of their options and negotiate their vocational possibilities. Race, class, and gender dynamics combine to create a larger playing field with more options for some and a smaller, more limited field for others. In these contexts, students struggle to make sense of and deal with triple or more divisions of the social gridiron—here they wrestle with fractious social classes, genders, and racial and ethnic groups. Star Trekkies understand the three-tier gridiron in terms of Mr. Spock's three-dimensional chessboard—all three dimensions are in play at the same time.

On their 3-D social chessboard, young women must deal with gender destinies and representations of women. Due to the social assumption that women are *destined* for eventual marriage and motherhood, female employment or *un*employment is not viewed as an important problem, as it is with males. Vocational teachers need to examine the ways families and vocational programs construct relationships between future work and a young women's everyday life (Arnot, 1992). In the process, they can begin to formulate interventionist strategies to subvert the disempowered destinies that await many of their female students. Social organization based on—in the case of young women in vocational education—*biological* determinism must be exposed as part of the *social* context; the placement of women into low-status, low-paid vocational roles is not a piece of a larger *natural* order. Liberal vocational educators who fall into Marsha Rehm's category of vocational generalists (see Chapter 9) often argue (persuasively) that gender diversity is important and that we should emphasize women's vocational needs in our programs and curricula. Critical vocational educators agree such action is necessary but insufficient. We must go beyond the recognition and inclusion of difference, using women's experience both socially and vocationally to reshape the most basic concepts and articulations of vocational education (Mullings, 1994; Zinn and Dill, 1994). We will return to this issue later in this chapter.

Educators and policymakers have not often put together the perception that America has a high level of unemployment among specific population groups and that among those groups there are an inordinately high number of female-headed families. Avoiding the connections between these realities, such professionals fail to discern that the causes of poverty among women are often different than those among men. Thus, the same remedies, the same educational experiences, for women and men will not address these gender-related differences. Gender expectations define different locations in both the cultural terrain and the vocational arena. Women's lives are intimately involved with caring for others. Most people understand that women devote much time to child care, but the effort they devote to taking care of men, aged parents, grandchildren, friends, and distant relatives is less frequently acknowledged. As weavers of the fabric that connects us, women have less time and energy to devote to making a living. When their domestic work in housekeeping and child rearing is added to the mix, time for paid work decreases even further. Gender expectations once again intersect with class to produce a socioeconomic context hostile to contemporary women (Sidel, 1992).

When these dynamics are traced in the post-Fordist economic terrain, with its hopeful promise of good work, interesting revelations appear. Silicon Valley, located in California's Santa Clara County, is widely recognized for its high-tech microelectronics industry and the economic revolution it catalyzed. As the home of the nation's most celebrated computer jocks and financial whiz kids, Silicon Valley hides a labor force that is more heavily stratified by race, class, gender, and nationality than any other economic segment in the United States. It does not take a rocket scientist to figure out that the celebrated, multimillionaire Silicon Valley executives are almost all white males, whereas the vast majority of low-paid manufacturing workers are minority women. The tendency of Silicon Valley managers to hire minority women—primarily Third World Asian and Latina women—is not limited to Santa Clara County but is typical of high-tech glamour industries around the world. Thus, race, class, and gender hierarchies structure the most high-tech industries of the late twentieth century, and the news is not good for those who are small, poor, foreign, and female. Employers argue that women can work for less, even though they possess little if any specific knowledge about their female employee's family circumstances. Post-Fordist microelectronics company managers generally assume that their female workers are married to men who are earning a "livable" salary. In actuality, over four out of five women employees in the industry are the main moneymakers in their families.

Karen Hossfeld (1994) has contended that when employers assume women, nonwhites, or immigrants accept low-paying work because they are content with it or because they are unprepared for or undeserving of better work, they are in complicity with forces that keep the marginalized in their place. She labeled these managerial assumptions racial, immigrant, and gender "logics." In the high-tech microelectronics industry, there is no conflict between these logics and "capital logic"—business strategies that contribute to profit maximization while increasing class stratification and the control of labor. Obviously, white employers' use of racism and sexism to construct an exploitative division of workers is nothing new and is not limited to the microelectronics industry. We can find the same social dynamics in the international textile industry, with its racial and gendered labor hierarchy. In many industries, managers justify their use of Third World women in assembly line repetitive tasks because of such workers' alleged superior hand-eye coordination and patience. White male managers frequently report that the tiny size of many Asian and Mexican women allows them to sit still for hours at a time performing detailed work that would push larger white people beyond the limits of sanity. When workers are asked to respond to this manager's comments about them, they agree that he preferred to employ small female workers so that he could feel superior and appear more intimidating around the plant (Hossfeld, 1994). Here, the intersection of race, class, and gender can easily be seen on a variety of levels, including the masculinist anxieties of industrial supervisors.

The Feminization of Poverty

Since 1970, the daily lives of millions of women have been transformed. In a relatively short period of time, women have entered the workforce in massive numbers: In 1950, about one in three women worked outside the home; by 1990, seven out of ten did. Since the early 1970s, more women have entered professions such as law, medicine, business, banking, film directing, and publishing. In the same time period, they have broken blue-collar taboos and have found partial acceptance in the male provinces of police work, firefighting, and, in limited roles, the military. As their lives were transformed, socioeconomic changes created a climate of vulnerability that women had not previously experienced. After the conservative victories in the 1980 elections, social and economic policy changed in such a way that poverty rates among women and children began to grow. Cuts in human services such as Medicaid, maternal and child-health programs, community health centers, family planning, and child nutrition programs placed poorer and minority women especially in precarious economic situations. All training and employment programs under the Comprehensive Employment and Training Act (CETA) were eliminated in the 1980s, 80 percent of Youth Employment Demonstration Projects' funds were cut, and Employment Demonstration Projects' funds were significantly reduced. The desire to cut and eliminate such programs has intensified throughout the 1990s. Over fifteen years' worth of such cuts have affected all poor people—but no group has been more adversely affected than female-headed families. Reductions in socioeconomic government programs have more than doubled the percentage of working mothers living below the poverty line—and their numbers are still growing (Malveaux, 1992a; Sidel, 1992).

In the 1990s, women have higher unemployment rates than men, women college graduates earn less than men with an eighth-grade education, minority women make less money than any other demographic grouping of workers, pregnancy is the leading cause of dropping out of high school, and 60 percent of women living in poverty dropped out of high school. Two-thirds of women who work outside the home are the sole or primary source of support for themselves and their families (McLaren, 1994; Sidel, 1992). Obviously, not all women are in imminent danger of falling into poverty. Gender intersects with class in such a way that excuses most upper- and upper-middle-class women from such anxieties. Such women typically have the financial resources, the cultural capital, the education, and the skills to control their own lives even if they are left without a man. Still, the socioeconomic and political changes of the last third of the twentieth century have left *all* women more financially fragile than their male counterparts. At the end of the twentieth century, the new poor includes far too many women—women who were not born into poverty but have been pushed into it by the social, economic, and personal dynamics that shape their lives. When the globalization of the economy, with its corresponding depletion of good jobs, is combined with governmental budget cuts in education and social programs for the poor, women are placed in a precarious position. All it takes for them to fall through the cracks of economic stability is a job loss, a divorce, a sickness, or a childbirth.

This new vulnerability for women sets into motion a vicious circle of poor women's oppression that is grounded on a loss of hope for good work. Low-income teenage women, for example, who find few economic options even after intensive self-sufficiency and employability training, fall into the trap of single-mother welfare-recipient status time and time again. Without social services, adequate child care, and hope of meaningful employment, American teenagers exhibit the highest rates of pregnancy, abortion, and childbearing in the industrialized world. U.S. teenagers under fifteen are five times more likely to become pregnant than youth the same age in other industrialized countries. Wealth polarization correlates significantly with high teenage birth rates. The poverty rate among these children born to teenage mothers is extremely high. The lack of options experienced by poor women holds devastating consequences for both their children and for the society at large. With poverty just a divorce away for millions of women, vocational educators must understand the dire importance of career counseling and economics education for young women in high school (Fine, 1993). Americans in general must appreciate the need for a humane environment in which women can work and raise their children. Critical vocational educators understand the political action that must be taken to insure the interests of women in America.

Women need a form of political action that takes account of the connection between their role as caretakers of children and the feminization of poverty. Whereas men may impregnate and run, women are faced with a twenty-year commitment. Young women must understand that they cannot count on a man's taking care of them, and, as a result, they must make preparations for economic self-sufficiency. This belief in men as caretakers is a cultural dinosaur from a previous era. The culture of feminine dependency, however, is still cultivated by social, political, and educational institutions, thus rendering transcendence of traditional gender roles very difficult. When such cultural realities are viewed in relation to the intolerable neglect of prenatal and well-baby care, accessible day care, after-school care, and the lack of an adequate child welfare system, the harsh reality of patriarchal negligence is exposed. That reality undermines the dignity of women and the sacredness of children. When child care for working mothers, for example, is closely examined, the human results of the logic of capital once again display themselves in cagelike cribs, dog leashes used to restrain children, and minimum numbers of caretakers for maximum profits (Aronowitz and DiFazio, 1994; Sidel, 1992). A coherent, democratic, mother-friendly, child-oriented American family policy is the victim of fatuous moralizing about family values and patriarchal irresponsibility. Until political action is taken, poor working women will continue to be victimized.

Keeping Women in Their Place: The Nature of Patriarchy

Patriarchy is the gender arrangement in which men form the dominant social group. In a patriarchal society, the male role is granted higher status than the female role. Although the original use of the term "patriarchy" meant control by the father, this book employs the term in a more expansive sense to involve the power men gain by birthright to define reality and enjoy the rewards of privilege by way of their domination of subordinates (Balsamo, 1985; Ferguson, 1984). Patriarchal power, as with most power, constantly interacts with the axes of race and class, either finding itself undermined or enhanced by the interaction. Patriarchal power's capacity to define reality, for example, is more pervasive when it is combined with the power of socioeconomic class privilege and the racial privilege of white people. The male definition of reality in this privileged context is inseparable from the tenets of Cartesian-Newtonian modernism discussed in Chapter 2. This view sees the world constructed of physically, socially, and biologically disembodied "things," ruled by predictable laws that can be rationally perceived and deployed by "men of science." Thus, the world can be viewed objectively and disinterestedly in this patriarchal cosmos. From this perspective, scientific work is deemed a high-status enterprise that seeks to predict and control those of lower status. Such activity has been called "bad science" by some individuals—bad in the sense that it places research "purity" and rigor above the needs of people and the problems of the community. These critics urge us to rebel against the rules of patriarchal ways of seeing and reestablish our connections with one another and the natural world (Ferguson, 1984; Williams, 1992).

Many men, especially Anglo men from well-to-do backgrounds, form their male self-identity through the denial of their connections with other people. Late-twentieth-century American patriarchal culture defines manhood in terms of separation and self-sufficiency—a character like Clint Eastwood in *High Plains Drifter* comes to mind. Here was a man who was such a loner he needed no name. Some critics claimed that Eastwood's acting style consisted of "squinting and not-squinting," a humorous reference to his low-affect style of acting. Male self-identity in patriarchal societies is grounded on the repression of affect, the disruption of connection (Ferguson, 1984). Eastwood in the man-with-no-name Westerns and later in the Dirty Harry movies set the standard for male disconnection, for man as self-sufficient loner. He repressed his hurt feelings and learned to hide and disguise them from the world. Indeed, in a traditional patriarchal culture the only approved techniques of dealing with one's emotion involve evasiveness, bravado, boasting, bluster, lying, and various forms of aggression. In the attempt to master such techniques, young boys in our culture begin to cultivate a "cool male pose" around the time they enter the fifth or sixth grade. Such a pose negates public emotional display; obviously, crying is forbidden, and even smiling and displays of enthusiasm are restricted (Nightingale, 1993).

The emotional repression and lack of interpersonal connection that patriarchy breeds creates severe social dysfunctionality, especially in the areas of family, child care, and women's issues. Men who are unable to deal with emotional conflict and the interpersonal dynamics of marriage and familial relationships have left their wives and families in ever-increasing numbers over the last third of the century. Such fathers are unable to deal with the "breadwinner-loser" male character who forfeits his patriarchal power (his "male energy") in his domestication and subsequent acceptance of fidelity in marriage, dedication to job, and devotion to children. This "domesticated loser" has been the subject of male ridicule in post–World War II America: To the beatniks, he was square; to *Playboy* devotees, he was sexually timid; to hippies, he was tediously straight. The search for a hip male identity in a patriarchal culture of disconnection has devastated the stability and nurturance of the family. In fact, to connect with one's family and to develop a faithful and communicative relationship with one's wife is to lose status among one's fellow men in a patriarchal culture.

Thus, the male's escape from commitment has become the order of the era, with its panoply of negative consequences for women. The majority of men who flee the family refuse to offer any assistance to the wife and children left behind. Child support has become an important women's issue in the last decades of the twentieth century because of the dramatic increase in female-headed families. When men's failure of commitment is combined with women's inability to earn high wages, female-headed families, as described earlier, too often fall below the poverty line. When the courts mandate child support, more than one out of four women never receive a penny of the money awarded—less than one-half ever receive the full amount. A more telling statistic reveals the average *annual* child-support payment for white, Hispanic, and black women: white women, $2,180; Hispanic women, $2,070; and black women, $1,640 (Sidel, 1992).

In patriarchal societies, men's claim to knowledge, its production and validation, carries more weight than women's. Although different classes and racial groups of women hold different perspectives on this social dynamic—white working-class women seem to defer to it more than other groups of women, for example—men's knowledge about work and other activities garners the most status in this society. This power dimension is illustrated daily on the individual level, with men in board meetings, union meetings, shop-floor meetings, or teachers' meetings interrupting and speaking over women or appropriating authority over what women have said, as in the example, "What Cindy meant was that . . ." The same pattern is discernible on TV when an advertisement promotes a household product for a woman (dishwashing detergent). While the video depicts a woman using and enjoying the product ("my hands are softer after washing the dishes"), a male voice-over provides technical information ("three out of four dermatologists conclude that new, improved Bongo Liquid . . . ") and the trappings of authority. The woman alone with her "inferior" form of knowledge is an inadequate authority in a patriarchal society. Bring in the man with the deep voice (Luttrell, 1993; Meissner, 1988).

This power differential between men and women in the patriarchal society is also seen in other forms of media. In many movies, women are marginalized as parents, as, for example, in *Boyz 'n the Hood,* where director John Singleton drives home the point that boys without fathers fail—and mothers are irrelevant. Both *Boyz 'n the Hood* and *Jungle Fever,* two brilliantly written, powerful, and appealing movies, designate female sexuality as a threat to male (in these movies, black male) heterosexual identity. Indeed, Singleton and Spike Lee are so seductive as moviemakers that women can actually enjoy their own symbolic denigration. Similarly, network news accounts of economic issues such as unemployment also reflect patriarchal structures in their verbal and visual focus on unemployment in the male-dominated industrial sector. Stories on the dramatic increase in layoffs and permanent unemployment in service-sector, predominantly female positions such as secretaries, information processors, and government workers constitute only *1 percent* of TV news stories on such matters (Wallace, 1993; Apple, 1992). It is no secret that TV producers, scholars, and researchers in vocational education devote less attention to women than to men (McLaren,

1994). Critical vocational education teachers and researchers are aware of this situation and are working to change it.

This patriarchal context induces some women, especially working-class women, to devalue their own knowledge and abilities. Instead of understanding what they know as valuable forms of knowledge about the world, working-class women have been conditioned to view it as "*just* common sense." When women view their knowledge as affective and not cognitive, as feelings and not thoughts, their subservient role is perpetuated and their power is diminished. Women scholars have argued that such working-class female forms of understanding make it impossible to distinguish emotional from objective/rational thinking. Such a cognitive form, they conclude, is important for women to study and analyze because that can challenge the false dichotomy patriarchy constructs between feminine emotionalism and masculine rationality. In the economic sphere, this false dichotomy produces lower-status emotional and intuitive feminine care-giving work and higher-status masculine "skilled" labor. The false dichotomy perpetuates an unjust system that exempts men from nurturing, service types of work while holding women responsible for such unpaid forms of domestic toil. It is essential for vocational educators to understand these patriarchal dynamics, for it is these forces that work to hide a young woman's abilities from her teachers, her potential employers, and, most important, herself (Luttrell, 1993).

Critical vocational educators are keenly aware of patriarchy and its effects on both their female *and* male students. Such teachers know that two-thirds of all poor people over the age of sixty-five are women; that four out of five single-parent families are headed by women and a substantial majority of them are poor; that one in six wives is beaten by her husband; and, that one in six women is sexually assaulted. In almost all of these situations—from poverty to abuse to assault—women tend to hold themselves responsible:

> If your life does not fit the middle-class, or even better, the upper-middle-class, image that appears on TV, something is wrong with you. For, if you are poor in America, you are an outsider and it's your own fault. If you are blind, disabled, or old, there is some excuse; you are one of the worthy poor. But if you are a welfare mother, you must be doing something drastically wrong. (Sidel, 1992, p. 8)

Patriarchy's Women: The Ideology of Domesticity and the Culture of Romance

Resting at the basis of the patriarchal system is the marginalization of women's work—a form of oppression that highlights the intersection of the forces of class and gender. The ideology of domesticity and the culture of romance refer to women's responsibility for unpaid work at home and their acquisition of status by way of their male relationships. Home and family in this context become central concerns for working-class female students, whereas their interest in wage labor is secondary. That perspective sets them up for failure in a patriarchal society—and in a sense, they become patriarchy's women. Because of their identification with the domestic sphere, they become especially vulnerable to the whims and moods of their male partners. If a man leaves a domestically identified woman as the sole supporter and caretaker of the family, she has little experience to draw upon in her attempt to find wage labor outside the home. This is not an isolated scenario in the late-twentieth-century feminization of poverty, as women face the patriarchal reality that devalues their talents and abilities. Indeed, the "domestic code" dictates that women's work in the economic marketplace is not worth as much as men's work and does not provide single mothers with sufficient resources to support their families by themselves (Valli, 1988; Weis, 1988).

Lois Weis has contended that women are caught in a double bind: They define themselves around themes of home and family but are forced by economic realities to work outside the home. When the post-Fordist economy forced married women into the workforce, little change took place in the social dynamics and work responsibilities within the home. Women found themselves bound by a double workday—full shifts in both the home and the workplace. Recent studies indicate that employed, married women perform three hours of housework for every one performed by their husbands. In addition to their jobs outside the home, married employed women work in the home an average of five hours a day. If a married woman's domestic work were monetarily compensated, her family's income would be increased by more than 60 percent. Critical vocational educators understand the negative impact of the domestic ideology and romance culture on women, on working-class women in particular. In so doing, they appreciate the reality that has been created by American society's refusal to provide special support for women in these circumstances. Therefore, critical vocational educators prepare their female students to deal with the social dynamics surrounding these gender issues, while engaging them in a larger struggle to help increase public awareness of the need to redistribute some of women's caring functions. Such redistribution can relieve women of their mind- and body-numbing double workday. One hopes that the critical consciousness that surrounds such an appreciation of these complex gender issues can be used to help the American public employ these caring qualities of women to humanize society, schools, and workplaces (Sidel, 1992; Wolff, 1977).

This feminine ethic of caring holds great potential when applied to the reconceptualization of vocational education and other social institutions. At the same time, it can undermine women's best interests when it is employed without cognizance of power relations between women and men. When working-class women operating out of an ethic of caring place their own concerns and own needs last, they inadvertently reinforce patriarchal power relations between themselves and their husbands. In fact, many working-class women can justify their educational pursuits only in terms of their commitment to husbands and families: "I'm doing this for them," they often tell their teachers. That nurturance ideology, that way of making sense of woman's role in the world, reached the level of social obsession in the years immediately following World War II. The ideology of domesticity and the culture of romance were expressed in TV's June and Ward Cleaver, Alice and Ralph Kramden, and Lucy and Ricky Ricardo—with visions of mother in the kitchen and father at work. The roots of late-twentieth-century feminism can be traced to the emotional toll this view of womanhood exacted on the "loving housewife" of the 1950s and early 1960s. Housewife depression, increasing divorce rates, and a general discomfort with family life characterized this era of hyperdomesticity (Luttrell, 1993; Rubin, 1994).

Women caught in the patriarchal trap who fail to understand the underside of the ideology of domesticity and the culture of romance are less able to protect themselves from the social forces that have feminized poverty. Self-sacrifice and passivity, common features of traditional notions of femininity, should come with the surgeon general's health warning in the 1990s. Young women who embrace such traditionalism, Michele Fine (1993) has reported, are far more likely to find themselves with unwanted pregnancies and child care than more assertive teenagers. In a study of girls in a public high school in New York City, Fine noticed that a large number of the students who got pregnant were quiet and passive—not those girls whose dress and manner signified sexuality and experience. Such an observation should not be interpreted to mean that teenage mothers are always a certain type of female; obviously, the issue is far more complex than this. What it does mean is that the traditional practices of femininity often subvert the economic, social, and educational development of young women.

Some of my students often assume that this ideology of domesticity and culture of romance are now behind us, a relic of an era past. Such is not the case, I tell them, focusing their attention on the second curriculum, the "girl curriculum" that operates covertly in American schools. Researchers have found that schools offer more career choices to boys, white upper-middle-class boys in particular, and fewer for girls, lower-economic-class nonwhite girls in particular. Career education booklets often list four career options for boys for every one listed for girls. Thus, vocational career counseling often directs female students to career choices that dramatically undermine their wage-earning possibilities and lead them toward a life of poverty (Johnson, 1991). Even in the newest vocational programs, I explain to my students, these gender dynamics are still at work. Analysis of the fifteen federal school-to-work demonstration programs developed in the 1990s indicates that three of the programs enrolled no girls and four enrolled three girls or fewer. The types of programs attended by students conformed to traditional gender stereotypes: Girls were guided into office, allied health, and clerical programs; boys enrolled in electronics, metal-working, and automation programs (Pullin, 1994).

Patriarchy on the Job:
Institutional Gender Bias in the Workplace

Women's paid work is constructed around two types of divisions: (1) a *vertical* division of labor where women as an economic grouping receive less wages than men, and (2) a *horizontal* division of labor in which women are concentrated in specific types of work. Women workers are more vertically and horizontally divided in the United States than in any other country in the advanced capitalist world. Many Americans are surprised to learn, for instance, that women with three years of college earn less than a man who finishes only the eighth grade. In the early decades of industrialization in the nineteenth century, women worked alongside men in vocations as widely diverse as mining, manufacturing, and printing. In the first decades of the twentieth century, however, a new form of patriarchy began to arise that associated "heavy" labor in the industrial sector with manliness and male strength. The "gender wisdom" that developed in tandem motivated legislators to pass laws "protecting" women from industrial work and crafts. Such perspectives have helped shape the domestic ideology and romance culture that have limited women's job opportunities throughout the twentieth century. World War II, of course, interrupted such viewpoints, but the system struggled to reassert itself when the men came home from the war. The cultural debate about women's "proper" place has raged ever since (Apple, 1985; Coontz, 1992; Johnson, 1991; Aronowitz and DiFazio, 1994).

An important thread in this debate has involved the equation of paid work with masculinity. Skill is a male discourse. If women pushed their way into the workplace where a particular skill was performed, then the skill was devalued. Thus, the male attempt to exclude women from the workplace was not simply a matter of men thinking that women were not capable of performing a job skillfully; rather, it was more an attempt to protect their craft's integrity from the devaluation caused by women's involvement with the work skills in question (Aronowitz and DiFazio, 1994). "I think a lot of the men were threatened," women steelworkers reported after encountering extensive male resistance to their presence in the mills, because "here was a woman coming along who said she could do it just as well as they could" (Livingstone and Luxton, 1988, p. 31). In addition, male steelworkers were embarrassed to disclose their shop-floor behavior to women. As one female steelworker put it:

> For them it's like having two personalities. Like Jekyll and Hyde sort of thing. . . . At work they swear, they throw their garbage on the floor. I'm sure they don't do that at home. . . . They're like kids at work . . . and I could just see them

go home and be, you know, straight and narrow, very serious with their wives, and as soon as they get to work it's crazy. . . . Some of them just cannot handle women being in their line of work. (Livingstone and Luxton, 1988, p. 32)

Thus, gender bias in the workplace never operates in some simple manner. It can be understood only as a constellation of social, cultural, economic, political, and psychological forces that intersect at various points in the web of reality. In order to intervene in a democratic manner, critical vocational educators must grasp the complexity of the forces at work.

This workplace gender bias expresses itself in a variety of ways and on a number of levels. For example, the double workday problem that working women face with their "day shift" at work and their "graveyard shift" at home is rarely addressed by individuals in leadership positions. If men were plagued by such a problem, corporate, government, and educational organizations would scramble to solve it. As long as the double shift is a women's problem, little action will be taken—because women are expected to take care of domestic tasks *no matter what their circumstance*. In the political climate of the 1990s, many elected officials have ridiculed the idea that society should provide assistance for women who are both mothers and workers. The most obvious form of assistance, public child care, would provide a wider range of choices to working-class mothers seeking employment. Despite women's increasing participation in the American workplace, public policy has continued to be based on the assumption that outside-the-family child care should be reserved for children with inadequate parental care.

American day care is woefully inadequate for the needs of contemporary working mothers. Indeed, day care funding has declined by almost 25 percent since the early 1980s, and further cuts are threatened. The dire state of day care reveals important insights into gender dynamics in America at the end of the twentieth century: (1) despite the women's movement and the national conversation about family values, women and children remain quite powerless; (2) despite the rhetoric of equal opportunity for women and men, political leaders do not want women workers taking employment opportunities away from men; and (3) despite repeated denials as to the existence of a patriarchal power structure, men in positions of power do not want to give up their place in the patriarchal family. Public provision of day care, they fear, would empower women to the degree that the hierarchical relationships of the patriarchal family would be disrupted (Ferguson, 1984; Palmer and Spalter-Roth, 1991; Pascall, 1994; Sidel, 1992).

Patriarchy on Parade: Men's Workplace Culture

"It's a Man's World," James Brown sang in the 1960s in reference to the patriarchal control of the workplace. The workplace's continued existence as a male domain has taken a heavy toll on the career aspirations of the millions of women who have had to enter it in the economically troubled post-Fordist era. As with all of our critical analyses of the workplace and the school, an understanding of the patriarchal control of the workplace demands an appreciation of the power dynamics between women and men. In the conversation about work, the *male* workplace has been designated as the *normal* state of a workplace. Women's entry into the workplace in the context of this dominant conversation comes to be viewed as deviant, as *abnormal* (Jacques, 1992). Thus, we can observe the ability of the dominant power to classify and name; in this case, the orientation to connectedness and the cooperation of many women come directly into conflict with many men's notions of self-sufficiency and isolation. Critical vocational educators argue that these larger social issues involving unequal power relations are not esoteric theoretical notions; rather, they shape the material realities of the workplaces we enter daily.

It does not take a long time to uncover the effects of unequal power relations in the gender dynamics of the workplace. The subordinate status of male factory workers, for example, has produced generations of men who have been forced to forfeit their dignity, sometimes on a daily basis. The impact of this reality on male self-esteem and sense of worth is dramatic—indeed, it is one of the most tragic effects of both the industrialization process and market-driven capitalism. One of the few domains of male workers' lives over which they can exert power and exercise control involves their relationships with women. It is this social dynamic that creates the context where working-class women find exaggerated assertions of patriarchal power by their husbands. Scarred by the indignity of the workplace, many such husbands seek to reestablish their dignity through the domination of their wives in the domestic sphere. In the workplace, these male workers may hang pictures of sexually available women in submissive erotic positions. Such pictures grant men a symbolic position of power over women that substitutes for the lack of power they possess in the daily affairs of the firm (Livingstone and Luxton, 1988; Weis, 1987).

In the context of their powerlessness, working-class men search for hidden passages to dignity. The dangers and brutality of many industrial workplaces are not typically viewed as employer-imposed hazards by male workers, but as tests of masculinity. Male dissatisfaction with unsafe or uncomfortable work is not formulated as a form of political resistance to insensitive bosses but is expressed in terms of sexual aggression through language and sadomasochistic play among workers. Difficult work is characterized as something feminine to be conquered: "We'll beat this bitch." Exploitation by managers is described by terms for rape: "We're getting screwed by the boss." Women bosses or coworkers are separated from the male group and placed into a separate category by name-calling: "bitches," "whores," or "sluts." Such categorization of women serves to justify different treatment of them, to relegate them to a less powerful position in the workplace. These male power plays are central to many men's self-definition in their reassurance that they (the male workers) are the only ones "man enough" to accomplish dangerous and dirty work (Livingstone and Luxton, 1988; Rubin, 1994).

In addition to these direct attempts of males to dominate women in the workplace, a set of inadvertent gender practices also serves to marginalize women workers. Men's conversational practices, which are aggressive and characterized by shared experiences and by military and sports metaphors, tend to silence women and make them invisible in an organization or a workplace. The conversation community established by male communication is exclusive and tends not to be open to women workers. Studies indicate that many women workers experience feelings of loneliness and isolation in the workplace. Social isolation at work strips women of the informal connections needed by individuals who want to rise in the workplace hierarchy; thus, men continue to occupy positions of power at work. These institutional impediments to women's success in the workplace illustrate cultural conflicts between particular forms of masculine and feminine identity patterns. When women view their work more as a process than as a specific outcome, they introduce an alien culture into the masculinist job site (Meisner, 1988; Bhatnagar, 1988; Ferguson, 1984). Critical vocational educators understand these dynamics and strive to prepare vocational students to recognize and address them as part of their work education. Young female workers who are able to map the male culture and communication patterns at a job site are much more likely to develop practical forms of resistance to the exclusionary practices that accompany them. Young male workers who recognize the dynamics are empowered to model more just ways of operating in a gender-integrated venue.

Patriarchal Dynamics: The Sexual Identity of Women

The most publicly discussed aspect of gender bias in the workplace involves sexual harassment. Sexual harassment is a form of domination that reproduces patriarchal domination in general. The form sexual harassment may take depends on the context that surrounds it. Vice presidents of corporations corner file clerks between filing cabinets and massage their backs while telling them how good they look. At the same time, however, a group of maintenance workers may make catcalls and other sexual sounds each time a female coworker walks by them. Although those who engage in harassment may come from diverse points in the status hierarchy of the workplace, they all share a view of women that emphasizes their sexuality rather than their skill and work abilities. When women attempt to extend kindness and care to these traditional male colleagues, the men often interpret such acts as manifestations of the women's sexual desire for them or as evidence of their subordination as servants or quasi-servants (Meisner, 1988).

Vocational programs for women often fail to examine the power relations and patriarchal context in which sexual harassment thrives. Indeed, some programs actually contribute to the maintenance of the context, as they promote an ideology of the "glamorous young woman." Such an orientation induces women vocational students to prepare for job interviews not by presenting their work knowledge but by highlighting their bodily image (Valli, 1988). In a vocational education context of that sort, women are reduced to frills, to window dressing in the workplace. Ray Kroc, the founder of McDonald's, illustrated this view of women as frills when he wrote in his autobiography about June Martino, one of the most brilliant of the early core of McDonald's businesspeople who made the fast-food restaurant one of the most successful corporations in history.

> I thought it was good to have a lucky person around, maybe some of it would rub off on me. Maybe it did. After we got McDonald's going and built a larger staff, they all called her "Mother Martino." She kept track of everyone's family fortunes, whose wife was having a baby, who was having marital difficulties, or whose birthday it was. She helped make the office a happy place. (Kroc, 1977, pp. 66–67)

From this description the reader would not have known whether June Martino knew anything about business.

June Martino's business acumen was not recognized by Kroc because she was a woman. Had she been a man, Kroc would not have written of her ability to keep up with everyone's birthday—a man would have been insulted by such a trivialization of his *serious* work. As with June Martino, secretarial work has been devalued simply because it is performed by women. The complexity of the work secretaries are assigned has to be constantly denied in offices where male managers make ten times the wages of their female secretaries. It is no secret that secretaries daily perform the same functions as managers—the only difference is that they receive fewer rewards, less compensation, and only token recognition. Women clerical workers remain the lowest-status group in a firm not because of the lack of complexity of their job skills but because of the low status of their gender role. Definitions of the complexity of particular job skills are not innocent descriptions of the nature of the work but are socially constructed labels that justify the socioeconomic advantage of some jobs and the disadvantage of others. Typically, such skill definitions are used to maintain existing power relationships in the workplace by privileging those abilities usually associated with masculinity (Block, 1990; Gaskell, 1987).

The patriarchal dimensions of work have not, of course, been viewed as central concepts in mainstream vocational education. Indeed, vocational education for women has often focused on simply adjusting students to the mentality of clerical work as unskilled, low-pay, low-status labor. Clerical training in late-twentieth-century vocational education is a separate island in the world of management training or computer education; the status differential is so great that a student is not allowed to enroll in one program and take a set of courses from another (Gaskell, 1987). Many how-to-get-ahead-in-the-workplace books for women reflect mainstream vocational education's goal of adjusting women to the reality of the patriarchal workplace. Use your feminine attributes, the books exhort their women readers. The same manipulative skills women learn in dealing with men in romantic and domestic relations, the success authors argue, can be utilized to get ahead at work. These manipulative skills are described by the authors as "an unlimited repertoire of manipulative, two-faced, guileful tricks" (Ferguson, 1984). Such reprehensible advice is derived from the same patriarchal mindset that encourages sexual harassment and violence against women. You can almost hear such language ("manipulative, two-faced, guileful") used to justify misogyny and workplace abuse of women. Ben Hamper provides a realistic but sobering picture of the mind-set:

> It wasn't easy for a woman on the Rivet Line. They were under constant siege by legions of moronic suitors. Almost every guy down there perceived himself as some kind of rodent Romeo. A woman working in the midst of so many men was looked upon as willing prey. Personality, looks, marital status hardly mattered. If it had tits and ass and jiggled along, it was fair game. Being that she was young and attractive, Jan was swarmed nightly. She deflected them nicely, defusing their advances with talk about her husband and snapshots of her little boy. Sooner or later, the vultures would hang it up and drag their libidos toward the next shapely bottom. (Hamper, 1992, p. 146)

Drawing upon Women's Subjugated Knowledge to Fight Patriarchy

People who fall outside of modernism's white-male nexus often discover that their ways of making sense of reality are not valued by the mainstream. These efforts to make meaning have been labeled subjugated knowledges by Michel Foucault and numerous women scholars. Critical scholars uncover them when they attend to the specific histories of oppressed peoples—a practice neglected in American historical scholarship until only recently. When scholars of African history analyze traditional African gender roles, for example, an alternative model of gender relations is presented that in its blurring of gender boundaries restructures relations between men and women, a subjugated knowledge of gender (Ferguson, 1984; McCarthy and Apple, 1988; Mullings, 1994). Because subjugated knowledge is produced often within a culture in subjugation, it reflects a "double knowledge," an understanding of both the subjugated culture and the ways of the oppressor culture. W.E.B. DuBois called this double knowledge the gift of second sight. This second sight constitutes the type of subjugated knowledge that can revolutionize vocational education. Too often, mainstream analysts have conceptualized diversity as "spice," as the mere inclusion of differences in the tossed salad of American life. A critical understanding of vocational education uses gender or racial diversity as DuBois conceptualized it: as a means of rethinking the basic assumptions, concepts, and theories of a discipline. In the context of this chapter, women's subjugated knowledge forms the conceptual base on which vocational education and work itself is transformed (West, 1993; Zinn and Dill, 1994).

Writing about the rural Kentucky of her youth, bell hooks discusses the African-American woman's perspective toward work. "Work makes life sweet," her elders told her; pride can be taken in a job done well. Subjugated notions of work permeate her memories:

> My Aunt Margaret took in ironing. Folks brought her clothes from miles around because she was such an expert. That was in the days when using starch was common and she knew how to do an excellent job. Watching her iron with skill and grace was like watching a ballerina dance. Like all the other black girls raised in the fifties that I knew, it was clear to me that I would be a working woman. Even though our mother stayed home, raising her seven children, we saw her constantly at work, washing, ironing, cleaning, and cooking (she is an incredible cook). And she never allowed her six girls to imagine we would not be working women. No, she let us know that we would work and be proud to work. (hooks, 1993, p. 41)

A work philosophy that stressed commitment to any job was an important coping device for African Americans stuck in a racist society. That viewpoint is similar to Buddhist perspectives that teach that any work becomes sacred when undertaken with dignity and care. When such an ethic was connected to what black women often referred to as "motherwit," work became not only something sacred but something that allowed one to display her intelligence (hooks, 1993; Luttrell, 1993). Such intelligence was essential when working for white people, with their predisposition to believe the worst about black people—their lying, cheating, stealing, and so on. These forms of women's knowledge become not only valuable vocational lessons for students, but they can form the value base on which resistance to bad work can be constructed.

Women's subordinate position in the workplace, like African Americans' subordinate location in the social hierarchy, has necessitated the development of these subjugated knowledges as survival skills. In an era where poverty has been feminized, women must draw upon such knowledge to help them understand the race, class, and gender power dynamics that lead to exploitation and control in the workplace. This insight into the workings of patriarchy allows women to fight male domination on a variety of levels. A critical vocational education joins this fight, as it exposes these power relations. In this context, it helps young women devise skills and analytical abilities that help them in their struggle to participate equally in the workplace. In an era of misogyny where women's attempts to achieve justice at work earn them the labels of "aggressive bitches" and "femi-Nazis," women's economic self-sufficiency becomes a serious issue. Statistics show that a large percentage of women will be forced to lead independent lives, despite their individual preferences.

In addition to the exposé of patriarchal power relations in the workplace, women's subjugated knowledges provide an alternative to patriarchy's hierarchical and bureaucratic conception of the organization of work. Women's subjugated knowledges often cultivate the understanding that the struggle for social justice is as much a matter of emotion as factual data, related as much to human empathy and connectedness as analysis. Often, those who struggled for justice in the past were men who did not appreciate the power of such *feelings*, and who, as a result, failed to link their social analyses to the domain of the visceral. Women's subjugated knowledges operating at this affective level provide an antihierarchical orientation that sutures the fissure between private and public life. Connection with others is a primary feature of most women's lives, as their self-assessments often revolve around questions of responsibility and care of others. In this arena of caring and feeling, women humanize the workplace with their production of informal activities such as birthday celebrations, baby and wedding showers, covered-dish luncheons, and retirement gatherings, as well as with their networks of people with common identities such as mothers and wives that bridge cultural and economic divisions in the workplace. This notion of women's networking presents valuable possibilities for vocational education, with hundreds of examples of women's labor networks around the world. Microsyster is a network of women computer technicians, workplace technicians, and clerical workers based in London. The Women's International Information and Communication Services is a source for names and addresses of scores of groups that are involved with the various aspects concerning women and their relation to work and technology. Vocational education teachers and their students need to link up with these organizations in their struggle for good work and gender justice in the workplace (West, 1993; Lamphere, 1985; Hacker, 1989).

Struggling Against Patriarchy:
What Women Want in Their Vocational Life

Why all this fuss about gender identities? Why all this talk about patriarchy? What is it that women want? Such questions, which are not uncommon in my teacher education courses, are asked by students who do not understand the dynamics of patriarchy or the effects of gender bias. Teacher education students are not the only individuals who do not understand these concepts. Almost daily, I speak with men and women who express opinions based on such confusion. The most basic answer to this question is that this is little more than a simple quest for self-determination—for a woman to gain the ability to control her own life. Many ask why this quest is so important. Again, the answer is simple: Many women are not allowed to do so. Traditional modes of feminine socialization at home and at school undermine women's ability to exercise self-direction, as they assume passive and deferential behavior—a form of conduct often described as sweet and agreeable. The point, of course, is not that women concerned with self-sufficiency should refuse to be pleasant and engaging human beings; the point involves making sure that sweetness is not synonymous with subordination.

The public has often failed to understand not only this issue of self-sufficiency but also its relation to women's economic and political agendas. Americans ask why women want to perform jobs traditionally held by men. Again, the answer is quite simple, actually: Many women want an opportunity to obtain "men's work" because such jobs pay so much more than jobs traditionally performed by women. For example, whereas a secretary's income averages around $15,000 a year, a plumber makes about $30,000; an electrician earns $470 a week, a female sales clerk, $200. For twenty-five years, women have attempted to break down the patriarchal barriers to equal access to higher wage jobs—sometimes successfully, other times unsuccessfully. Critical vocational educators understand that social action is needed to secure such job access for women. They therefore work to ensure that the federal government enforces the antidiscrimination statutes presently on the books (Ferguson, 1984; Johnson, 1991).

It is in this regard that women's groups have fought rigid gender role differentiation—a perspective that ultimately harms both men *and* women. The traditional masculine role as sole breadwinner puts too much power in a husband's hands and too much stress on his heart. More flexible sex roles encourage both cognitive and emotional growth in both men and women, while expanding justice and opportunity in the society. Vocational programs that are grounded on such notions of gender-role flexibility make great strides in the attempt to cultivate the self-sufficiency of marginalized female students. As such students begin to gain skills, knowledge, and understanding of gender role flexibility, they begin to take control of their lives. Buoyed by such appreciations, they are empowered to avert pitfalls of early pregnancy and welfare motherhood—a role that is often connected to disempowered notions of feminine subordination and acceptance of rigid definitions of women's role. Subjugated histories provide thousands of examples of women who have transcended such role restrictions. African American women in the early industrial period, for example, smelted iron, laid railroad tracks, and made bricks. Asian-American women, Chicanas, and Puertoriqueñas, despite stereotypes of passivity, courageously worked and organized for better wages in the sweatshops, factories, and the farms to which they were relegated (Fine, 1993; Banfield, 1991).

Thus, women want the power to reject traditional role designations that undermine their dignity and their life options. A critical pedagogy of vocational education as it pursues diverse forms of knowledge confronts the patriarchy-induced imbalance of gender power. It builds networks of working women and sympathetic men to share announcements of job openings, workplace knowledge, craft topics, economic news, updates on litigation, and other matters. Such connections help bring political coalitions together, as they inform members about instances of injustice that demand political resistance. Both men and women in low-status, low-pay secondary sector jobs can, when they are working together with committed vocational educators, demand the restructuring of such positions. Women in child care and institutional kitchen work can demand reasonable wages and more control over the conditions of their work. Recent actions by service sector workers such as the Justice for Janitors campaign in Atlanta have obtained a higher wage for office cleaners. At the same time, organizations of office workers have won better pay and more dignified treatment on the job (Luttrell, 1993; Arnott and Matthaei, 1991). Such campaigns represent the interests of all workers, regardless of whether their oppression results from race, class, or gender. Thus, such campaigns illustrate one of the central theses of Part 4 of this book: The struggle against patriarchy cannot be separated from movements against racism and class oppression (Mullings, 1994).

It thus becomes important for women workers to organize in some way. In the 1990s, only about one out of ten women workers belongs to a union. That figure is not surprising in light of trade unions' historical lack of sympathy toward women. Even when numerous women joined unions, however, the union leadership was drawn almost exclusively from men—a situation that still exists all too often at the end of the twentieth century. In addition to these factors, women's union organization is thwarted by the types of jobs typically reserved for women: positions in small shops where they work in isolation from other women; clerical, secretarial, child care, and health care jobs that mimic the patriarchal role designations of the family; jobs that are temporary or seasonal. The patriarchal socialization of women to be "good girls" or "ladylike" has produced a passivity that is at odds with the assertiveness necessary in the struggle for good work. As uncritical vocational education and the realities of bad work condition women to low expectations, too many women ease into a state of disempowerment that accepts little reward or recognition for a job well done (Sidel, 1992; Weis, 1987). Such women are not top candidates for the role of leading the organization of women in the workplace. Despite all of these impediments, however, women workers in the 1990s are building new forms of labor coalitions. Nine to Five is a successful women's work organization, and a variety of new organizations have attracted women clerical workers. These beginnings, it is hoped, will lead to a new era of women's labor organization in the twenty-first century.

Developing a National Economic Program for Economic Justice for Women

When women are subjected to the double whammy of the work-home double shift, this society's sense of justice is undermined. Those who promote family values rarely connect such a call to the economic realities that families, and women especially, face on a daily basis. Critical vocational educators must help convince employers that women as workers are placed in a special circumstance by their family responsibilities and reproductive role. It is in everyone's interest to support women with these responsibilities, to pay them fairly, to promote them equitably, to encourage their self-sufficiency, and to respect their various commitments. *All* women, married or unmarried, with or without children, deserve such treatment—and few have traditionally received it. Poor working mothers do, however, constitute a special group—a category of workers who, in America at the end of the second millennium, cannot make it alone. Economic support must come from somewhere if these women are ever to possess a hopeful future. Critical vocational educators dedicated to a progressive democracy and economic justice understand that Americans must reconceptualize their social responsibility to working women, to mothers and their children. To this end, a national program for economic justice for women must be developed, with the following features:

1. *Flexible hours, part-time work as parental option.* Tremendous stress accompanies the attempt to raise young children while working full-time. Viewing one's work life holistically allows women (or men) to work part-time during both their children's early years and their own older years. If parents with children under six were allowed, for example, to work three-quarter time for reduced pay, there would be more work to go around, family values in the *authentic* sense would be promoted, and stress on day care centers would be reduced.

2. *Salary bonuses and specialized education for women workers.* To aid working mothers with the financial burdens of raising children, governmental salary bonuses or tax breaks could be offered to women in this precarious position. Hard work would thus be rewarded and the quality of children's lives would be improved. Specialized vocational training for women needing

to update job skills would be made available, as well as internships and mentorships to help women concerned with vocational advancement.

3. *Fringe benefits for working parents.* In addition to health care benefits for themselves and their children, working parents would be provided with child care and opportunities for sick leave for themselves and family members.

4. *Child care for working parents.* All working parents must deal with child care in one way or another. The United States must therefore establish a system of day care and after-school care that addresses the needs of working parents and their children. Without a network of day care centers, women in particular are eliminated from the workplace or placed at the mercy of the slipshod day care that does exist. High-quality child care must be a central feature of any program designed to cultivate economic justice for women and good work in particular.

5. *Women's support services networks.* A few vocational education programs for women have begun to construct a support service component to accompany the educational process. Such service networks either provide services such as transportation, job placement, and child care or refer students to such resources in the community. The establishment of these services would allow women to grant full commitment to job training, while reducing absenteeism and drop-out rates.

6. *Parental insurance.* Financed by taxes and employers' contributions, such insurance would allow either parent to remain at home for up to nine months after childbirth, while receiving around 90 percent of his or her salary. The nine months would be divided between the parents in a way that is most convenient, but the leave could not be taken by both parents concurrently.

7. *Payment of delinquent child support.* Law enforcement agencies must become far more committed to the prosecution of fathers who do not honor their legal responsibility to support their children. The U.S. government should assume the responsibility of guaranteeing child support when fathers do not pay. This policy would make the federal government the agency directly concerned with recouping delinquent payments, thus creating a bulwark of support for children's right to financial support.

8. *Alternatives to welfare.* Programs must be implemented that provide welfare recipients with career planning, job training, education, and aid in locating and securing a job. Pilot programs at work in some locations have already developed creative strategies of facilitating the transition from welfare to employment for many women (Rendon and Nora, 1991; Sidel, 1992; Johnson, 1991).

9. *Women-sensitive vocational education programs.* Critical vocational educators will not have addressed their mandate to produce socially just programs and to educate for good work until they demonstrate an awareness of

the special problems women face in school and at work. An understanding of the gender dynamics that shape our work lives is a central component of any democratic vocational program.

Patriarchy Fights Back

There is no doubt that women have won victories in the economic sphere over the last twenty-five years. There are more opportunities for some women in some workplaces in the 1990s than there were in the 1960s. The impact of such gains must not be overstated in light of the feminization of poverty and the other problems that continue to plague women at the end of the twentieth century. Indeed, even the limited gains made by women have elicited a frightening backlash that threatens to erase any progress achieved. The supporters of patriarchy have declared a war against women, accusing them of destroying the family unit, abandoning children, and subverting intimate relationships with men. According to the neopatriarchal doctrine, our downfall began when women embraced feminist values that encouraged them to abandon their nurturing of husbands and children in the pursuit of self-gratification (Coontz, 1992). The forms of misogyny that have emerged in the last decade are disturbing, with their radical defense of traditional forms of gender relations that position women as sexual objects to be "overpowered" in a man's effort to assert his masculinity. Critical vocational educators must fight such patriarchal power dynamics in their struggle for good work. Like other democratic battles, the movement for socioeconomic justice for women will require the efforts of thousands of dedicated teachers, students, and workers.

14 Howlin' Wolf at the Door: Race, Racism, and Vocational Education

Working with rural teachers a few years ago on the subject of race, class, and gender, I observed a fascinating phenomenon. White teachers for the most part were very reluctant to speak frankly about racial matters when African Americans were present. In a class of thirty, for example, only a handful of white teachers would address interpersonal dynamics relating to race in their private or professional lives. After class, however, when all the black teachers had left, these white teachers wanted to talk about their perceptions of race in their everyday lives. During this "private time," they told me stories of "reverse racism," of incompetent black teachers and preferential hiring of nonwhites.

As Aaron Gresson put it, these teachers constructed a bridge between us on the ideological basis of our whiteness. It was as if my antiracist in-class pedagogy was irrelevant, a public facade that either the school or the discipline required. Once *we*, as white people, were alone, honest talk was possible. During these conversations, the teachers spoke in hushed tones, constantly looking around to make sure *we* were alone, that is, racially segregated. When they spoke the word *black*, they spoke even more quietly—sometimes only mouthing, not even whispering, the word. It quickly became apparent to me that there were two conversations about race in the culture of these white teachers: (1) a public discourse of feigned civility, and (2) a private discourse of racial solidarity, grounded on the perception of whites as victims. Only in the private conversation did the teachers' authentic feelings emerge. It is therefore important to examine the nature of racism and its relation to vocational education, work, and economic policy. For the sake of clarity, I will examine different forms of racism. In reality, these forms are difficult to separate and distinguish.

Essentialist Racism

Racism must be understood as a historically specific, constantly mutating phenomenon. The most common historical expression of white racism in America is known as essentialist racism—the belief that there are *essential* qualitative, biological differences between different races. From the beginnings of European exploration, white people viewed the "savages" they encountered in new lands as primitive and inferior. African "natives," it was assumed, could never achieve the heights of civilization attained by Europeans. Today, when racism is discussed in the public culture, most Americans see essentialist racism as the *only* form of racism; that is, to be racist is to exhibit an essentialist racism. Many Americans who identify with right-wing politics ascribe to an essentialist form of racism, though they often express it only in the company of like-minded white people. Manifestations of essentialist racism reveal themselves in schools when black or Latino students are placed in vocational programs because of their "cognitive deficits" or "cultural deprivations." Nonwhite youth are assumed in these contexts to lack qualities necessary for educational success—*academic* educational success in particular. Essentialist racism reveals itself in social policy when white voters assume that African Americans and Latinos are unequipped to "do their jobs right" and therefore take advantage of employment policies that favor them over whites. This is *our* country, essentialist white racists proclaim, not theirs (Frankenberg, 1993; Hacker, 1992; Banfield, 1991; Rubin, 1994).

Essentialist racism works to shape the way its adherents see the world and their role in it. At the same time, it shapes views of the purposes of academic and vocational education. A few examples of essentialist racism in education are in order. Teaching materials thought by many to be wholesome and totally innocent have been some of the most flagrant perpetrators of essentialist racism. One of the most popular and long-lasting children's book series, the *Bobbsey Twins*, entertained hundreds of thousands of students with Dinah, the family cook. As the ultimate stereotype of an African American happy servant/slave, Dinah told the children outlandish stories reflecting her laughable superstitions, ate watermelon whenever she could get it, and was not above stealing from the family. Hugh Lofting's "innocent" Dr. Doolittle taught generations of children about ignorant Africans. With his superior knowledge, Doolittle fulfilled the "white man's burden" by ministering to the needs of these "grotesque and uncivilized" peoples. Laura Ingalls Wilder's *Little House on the Prairie* and Walter D. Edmonds's popular *The Matchlock Gun* portrayed Native Americans as hated and feared "savages," and Claire Huchet Bishop garnered great praise for her *The Five Chinese Brothers*—a book that depicted Chinese as yellow, disturbingly similar in appearance, slant-eyed, and morally suspect.

Textbooks were frequently even more blatant in their essentialist racism than trade books. Well into the last quarter of the twentieth century, some American educational textbooks have continued to represent Native Americans as a bellicose, warlike people, African Americans as incompetent and violent, Asian Americans as passive and duplicitous, and Puerto Rican Americans as violence prone and dangerous when living together in urban areas. A few quotations illustrate these stereotypes from textbooks published in 1975: from Harcourt Brace Jovanovich's *America: Its People and Values* we read, "The Iroquois were a fierce and warlike people"; from Allyn and Bacon's *The Pageant of American History,* "Many slaves did not know how to live without their former masters"; from Addison-Wesley's *The American Experience,* "In San Francisco, the historically compliant Chinese aggressively resisted attempts to bus their children to schools outside of Chinatown" and "groups such as the Puerto Ricans in New York City . . . form additional suburban populations which keep the nation's cities seething with discontent and conflict" (Banfield, 1991, pp. 79–80). To many observers, given the nature of the pictures of nonwhites presented throughout our nation's history, it is not surprising that essentialist racism lurks within racism—in expressions that privilege white genes over those of nonwhites and white intellectual capacities over those of racial "others."

Employing the logic (or illogic or irrationality) of essentialism, nonwhite economic failure is not the fault of our unjust system, it is a problem of nonwhite inferiority. Indeed, in this mind-set, slavery was not a moral and political problem of whiteness but was the result of the "slavishness" of African Americans. Prejudice, discrimination, and institutionalized racism such as vocational tracking are concepts generically flawed, irrelevant in the American experience. The belief structures of white supremacy not only discount such sociological concepts but are poised to quickly deny the existence of white privilege in educational and economic institutions. The common belief that African Americans or Latinos are unemployed because they are lazy and incompetent merely reflects this way of making sense of the world.

Obviously, all white people do not buy into white supremacy; many white Americans have courageously fought such an ideology at great risk to their lives and financial well-being. Many white vocational education teachers have risked job security to expose essentialist racism, white supremacy, and other forms of racial injustice. Tragically, nevertheless, the 1980s and 1990s have witnessed a regrowth of racisms of all types, even a resurgence (albeit in new guises) of essentialist racism. Radio talk show hosts, right-wing politicians, superpatriots, and many traditional educators fan the fires of the essentialist racism resurgence, arguing that minority groups in America must "get with the program," change their attitudes and conduct, and get to work. Such views are often self-contradictory, as they argue that nonwhites should start applying themselves but at the same time question their talents to "make it" even if they exert the effort. In a society historically shaped by essentialist racism, minority groups have had nowhere to turn, no way out; this sort of ideology structures their failures no matter what avenues to mobility they choose.

It is unfortunate that at the end of the twentieth century the point has to be made; but, alas, it must: The essentialist racist charge that nonwhites (African Americans in particular) are unwilling to work hard for a living is a ludicrous assertion. When a new hotel publicizes openings for porters and chambermaids, lines of predominantly black men and women snake around the block. Military recruiters know their best prospects are often black youths unable to find a career-type job anywhere else (Hacker, 1992). Clint Allison (1995) has described the fervent desire of African American ex-slaves to attend school. In places where schools existed, young and old aspiring black students lined up at their doors; where there were no schools, black communities pooled their resources and built them. One of the most tragic stories in American educational history, of course, is that the African American faith in schooling fell far short of its promise. One of the most pernicious fables of essentialist racism is the welfare-mother stereotype, with its depiction of multiple-child-bearing, stupid, and lazy black women. Contrary to the stereotype, young nonwhite women on welfare want good work. Often, welfare mothers seeking socioeconomic mobility run into pathological hostility from welfare functionaries who remind them that welfare will not pay them a penny for their college degree. It is often emotionally easier for such women to sit home watching TV than to make the sacrifices demanded by the attempt to better themselves (hooks, 1993).

This damned-if-you-do, damned-if-you-don't position that African Americans, Latinos, Native Americans, and many Asians experience in situations structured by essentialist racism induces nonwhites to ask just what is it that white Americans want. If black students and black communities, for example, ask schools to teach more about black culture, they are shocked when whites demand in response that schools teach more about white culture to keep things equal. "What do white Americans think their sons and daughters have been learning about in school for the last few centuries?" black observers want to know. Schooling in America, they contend, has been the story of white people, their lives and accomplishments. To protect the "white story," many white Americans in the final two decades of the twentieth century staged what some scholars have labeled a "white counterrevolution." The post-Fordist economic reorganization has been accompanied by a white-dominated movement to decrease social spending for nonwhite citizens. The movement seeks to undermine or revoke affirmative action, subvert the enforcement of civil rights laws, slash grants and loans for minority higher education, and cut funding for minority-oriented vocational education programs. It is apparent that what many white people want is a return to a pre–civil rights movement, pre-1960s America—a time when this country was much too comfortable with economic injustice, unemployment, and bad work for nonwhite men and women (Hacker, 1992; Rubin, 1994; Zweigenhaft and Domhoff, 1991).

"Institutional Racism," or Alleged Nonpersonal, Structural Racism

As compared to essentialist racism, another form of racism—called institutional, or structural—tends to be far more subtle and difficult to identify. In separating institutional/structural racism as a distinct category from essentialist racism, there is no intent to imply that the two practices operate in isolation from one another. Essentialist assumptions held by individuals in institutions, for example, cannot be separated from the structural discrimination institutions exhibit toward nonwhites. The distinction is made in order to facilitate an understanding of the ways racism operates. Most white Americans do not identify what is defined here as institutional/structural racism as a form of racism at all. Most institutions develop informal cultural practices that are internalized by their members (and vice versa). Such institutional cultures are diverse in their expression and specific to particular organizations; but in the United States, they do tend to be white. Historically, most of the individuals who work in the upper and middle management of General Electric, who teach at the University of Virginia, or serve in the FBI have been white. That reality has created the public image of such institutions as well as their modus operandi, or MO. The organization "thinks" and carries on its business in a white manner. Via their cultural experiences, white people are perceived to be better suited for inclusion in these cultures, although class and gender issues obviously affect dimensions of "suitability" as well. As has already been discussed, the dynamics of cultural capital exert dramatic influences on social relations between job applicant or employee and organizational culture.

Policies that produce racially discriminatory effects do not have to be conscious or intentional—though in expressions of institutional/structural racism, consciousness and intentionality are difficult to determine. Setting aside questions of consciousness and intent for the moment, institutional/structural racism is judged on the terms of its effects: Do the institutional structures reinforce and extend racial exclusions and subordinations? When businesspeople make hiring decisions, the logic of profit induces them to ask how customers will respond to, for example, nonwhite salespeople, or nonwhite technicians' creating complex equipment. Upper-level managers often express concerns about the effect of promoting nonwhites to supervisory roles in the firm: Will white subordinates work for them without resentment or resistance? Obviously, expressions of racism are present in these issues, but everyone denies personal culpability. Managers squirm uncomfortably when asked about such dynamics and assert that racism is simply not involved. When outside observers leave, however, white-only coteries of supervisors and managers may express how hard they find it to work with Puerto Ricans or blacks, citing instances of nonwhite individuals having chips on their shoulders. All too infrequently do they question why interpersonal difficulties between races develop. Their response is generally to avoid the problem by hiring and promoting as few nonwhites as possible, finding "safe" token hiring enough to deflect outside criticism (Anthias and Yuval-Davis, 1992; Hacker, 1992).

Such situations do not typically evoke the self-reflection and institutional reflection needed to expose and remedy structurally embedded racism in the economic sphere. Thus, cultural practices develop that encode the racist practices into the formal structures of the organization. For example, the on-the-surface innocent use of the term "quality" can develop into one of these cultural practices of encoding. No one is against standards of quality. When questions of admission into a law school or hiring in a service industry arise, "quality-based" decisions can become the organizational code word for whites-only policies. Criteria for hiring and admission decisions are narrowed, and suggestions for alternate guidelines that might culturally widen the pool of applicants are often characterized as attacks on the integrity of the institution. Codes proliferate, taking on a national character: "the closing of the American mind"; "cultural literacy"; "transitional or good neighborhoods"; "at-risk students"; "dressed for success"; "welfare mother"; "inner city"; "safe schools"; "traditional American values," and so forth. The racial decoding process is an important dimension of the work of critical vocational educators and all people who value social justice. Contrary to the belief of some, individuals can confront institutional/structural racist practices, expose them, and change them. No matter what its form, racism can be overcome.

Institutional/Structural Racism at School and Work

Many of the reforms suggested and adopted for academic and vocational education in the 1980s and 1990s have reflected the institutional/structural racist dimensions discussed here. Because of high minority student percentages, vocational education has been particularly affected by such reforms. One of the key instruments of institutional/structural racism in education is standardized tests. Educational leaders who are aware of who wins and loses when such tests are employed frequently use such tests as the preferred method of judging student ability and educational success. IQ tests, for example, undermine the possibility for school success for vocational students from poor or nonwhite backgrounds. Because they are inseparable from the prior assumptions of test makers, IQ and other forms of achievement tests keep educational barriers in place for those traditionally excluded from avenues to high-paying jobs. These tests provide legitimacy for structures of exclusion, in the process providing upper-middle-class white people with a conscience-soothing, scientifically validated rationalization for the privileges they enjoy (McLaren, 1994; Kincheloe, 1991).

A large body of evidence points to the fact that standardized tests fail to predict the future achievement of nonwhite students (Kincheloe, Steinberg, and Gresson, 1996; Banfield, 1991; Beane, 1985; Rosser, 1989). Since the justification for using such tests is tied to the need to track a student's future educational programs, the revelation of such failure should work to call the use of such tests into question—but so far this has not happened. Vocational education students are not the only ones to be adversely affected by testing; the use of standardized testing for teachers (for example, the National Teachers Exam) works to keep nonwhite men and women out of vocational teaching. When nonwhite teachers are barred from vocational education, student access to diverse worldviews and different frames of reference is curtailed; the practice especially restricts student access to viewpoints that confront both obvert and covert racism (Sleeter, 1993). Many progressive educators and legal experts have worked to remove standardized test requirements from educational, workplace, and other public spheres. Such analysts understand that institutional/structural racism will never be weakened as long as such tests subvert opportunities for minorities.

A Nasty Intersection: Institutional/Structural Racism Meets Regressive Modernism

Standardized tests and the uses to which they are put in American education have come to represent the intersection of structuralist and essentialist racism with the regressive forms of modernism discussed in Chapter 2. Thinking, of course, is universal, something human beings in all cultures do; but the types of thinking that are privileged and respected differ from culture to culture. Thus, students from different cultures will "test differently" based on the types of thinking that have been valued in their homes and communities (McLaren, 1994). Modern developmental psychology has become so much a part of the conversation about intelligence that we overlook the contradictions embedded in the discourse. A critical pedagogy of vocational education wants to expose existing definitions of intelligence as specific social and historical constructions grounded on a particular set of assumptions about the mind (Riegel, 1973; Maher and Rathbone, 1986; Walkerdine, 1984). As modernist science decontextualizes and strips away layers of the social from its analysis, intelligence and cognitive development are essentialized; that is, their characteristics are written in stone. The social features (race, class, gender) that influence patterns of thinking and cognitive development are ignored, allowing what are actually social constructions to be seen as natural processes. Our understanding of the limits of modernism and the nature of various racisms helps us overcome this social decontextualization, as it denies the existence of men and women who are outside the sociohistorical process.

Intelligence, then, is not a static, innate dimension of human beings; it is always interactive with the environment, always in the process of being reshaped and reformed. We are not simply victims of genetically determined, cognitive predispositions, good with only our heads or only our hands (Lawler, 1975; Walkerdine, 1984). Because modernist schools have traditionally valued abstract forms of knowing, the mental has been privileged over the manual. The way of knowing in a Cartesian-Newtonian context ascribed to "rational *man*" defines logical abstraction as the highest level of thought—as in symbolic logic, mathematics, and so on, which are signifiers far removed from their organic function in the world (Wirth, 1983). Piaget's delineation of formal thinking (his highest level of cognition) failed to escape this removal of thought from its context (Bowers, 1982). This modernist formality sees a world that consists of discrete entities, each demanding a particular form of analysis. Modernist schooling and the thinking it promotes reflect this isolating tendency, as they explore "things in themselves" (Poster, 1989; Ferguson, 1984; Gergen, 1991; Reinharz, 1982; Fee, 1982; Mahoney and Lyddon, 1988). This intersection of racism and modernist ways of looking at the world works consistently to privilege middle- and upper-middle-class white (often male) students in American schools. The effects of the intersection extend even further, causing American educators to underestimate the potential of their vocational students. This tragic situation can be tolerated no longer by Americans who believe in race, class, and gender justice and the promise of democracy. In *Toil and Trouble: Good Work, Smart Workers, and the Integration of Academic and Vocational Education* (1995) I explore these issues in far greater detail, addressing specifically the question of what now constitutes and what should constitute the definition of a "smart worker."

These issues are not generally understood by American society in general or American education in particular. Most white people do not perceive their nation, its economic and educational institutions, or even its science as "white." The assertion, for example, that there are Eurocentric cultural dynamics involved in intelligence testing, school success, and the way knowledge is produced raises the hackles of many white people. African Americans, Latinos, Native Americans, and many Asians are always aware of their white surroundings at school, work, and play. Although O. J. Simpson, Oprah Winfrey, Colin Powell, and Michael Jordan are celebrities known to all Americans, the institutions and the culture that makes the rules are still predominantly white. Nonwhites understand that such a social reality de-mands they need to work harder and be smarter about it than whites if they want to succeed. Nonwhites know that when they walk on to the job the first day, all eyes are on them; they are the guinea pigs in the Noble Experiment (Allison, 1995; Hacker, 1992). Too few white people understand what pressures this generates and how bad such a position can make a man or a woman feel. It is at *this personal level* that all our talk about epistemology, critical pedagogy, and the social axes of race, class, and gender matter.

Undermining Dualisms: The Complex Nature of Different Forms of Racism

In multicultural education, a debate has developed between those who focus on essentialist racism and those who emphasize the institutional/structural form. Those who focus on the essentialist dimension tend to believe the purpose of multicultural education involves addressing problems of individual prejudice; those that emphasize the institutional/structural form tend to believe multicultural education's greatest contribution involves exposing social, economic, and political impediments to racial equality—structural dynamics that shape patterns of distribution of social goods and power. There is no doubt that simply addressing racism as a form of individual prejudice does little to undermine white racism. Appeals to the rationality of racist individuals through curricula that seek to expose the irrationality of racism are not very successful. At the same time, however, multicultural approaches that privilege institutional/structural dynamics often assume that institutions possess a generic nature that is separate from the perspectives and practices of individuals. Separate from the actions of living human beings, institutional racism seems beyond reproach. Taking that position leaves individuals powerless to change these generic structures, and the possibility of democratic reformulations of the educational and corporate domains is negated. Workers interested in social justice are left in the lurch, with no idea where to begin the struggle for good work, economic justice, and race, class, and gender equality.

The key concepts that help critical vocational educators get beyond this dualism involve the notions that (1) social institutions are and have always been constructed by individuals; and (2) individual racial prejudice and essentialist racism help shape racist structures and institutions. As will be discussed in more detail later, progressives must understand that racism is viruslike. Although we can identify particular prototypes of racism and come to understand the way they interact in the lived world, it is more difficult to appreciate that a viruslike racism is always mutating, taking on new forms and posing new dangers. New contexts such as the dawning of post-Fordism and the advent of technological innovations that have created an era of corporate technopower have helped shape new forms of racism. Although general features of racism persist (it is important, for example, that we should understand essentialist and institutional/structural prototypes), racism is context specific (Rizvi, 1993; Sleeter, 1993; McCarthy and Apple, 1993). In an era where innovation and technological change alter contexts so quickly, racist forms mutate in frightening sci-fi rapidity. The task, admittedly, is exceedingly difficult, but critical vocational educators must make the effort to comprehend the mutating nature of racism and the ways it distorts academic and vocational education, the economic sphere in general, and work in particular.

The Mutating Virus: Post-Fordist Racism

Drawing upon the discussion of the decline of Fordism in Chapter 3 and the widening gap between rich and poor and between core and peripheral workers in the emerging post-Fordist era in Chapter 8, we can begin to explore the effects of recent historical trends on American racial dynamics. The recessions and stagflation that accompanied the death throes of the Fordist compromise in the 1970s intensified a perception of scarcity among Americans. At exactly the same time, affirmative action and minority-preference hiring policies allowed a few nonwhites to make small but visible intrusions on what had been an all-white terrain—and the combination of the two social trends was electric. Throughout the 1970s, 1980s, and 1990s, the economy for vocational students kept faltering, local, state, and federal governments continued to cut services, the quality of life of the middle- and lower-classes continued to deteriorate, and the economic debate over what remained accelerated. Indeed, as power became concentrated in the hands of those occupying the predominately white and richest segment of society, social discord among everyone else intensified (Rubin, 1994).

This social dissonance has taken many forms. One of its most important and influential manifestations involves the claim made by many conservative whites that racism in America is a thing of the past—that we live in a "post-racist era." America is the land of opportunity, the white narrative reads, and since everyone is granted access to material well-being, those who do not achieve it have no one to blame but themselves. The reencoding of black and Latino inferiority is connected to a Social Darwinist survival-of-the-fittest social theory: "*Those people* who keep bitching and moaning about discrimination would be better served to shut up and get their lazy butts to work." The mobility experienced by a small portion of middle-class African Americans over the last thirty years and the high visibility this successful group receives has been misinterpreted by many struggling white working-class Americans as evidence of the economic success of African Americans as a group. A closer examination does not support this interpretation. In fact, such black middle-class success has intensified fiscal inequality in the African American community, as tens of thousands of black Americans have fallen into poverty and joined the underclass. Thus, the very groups that have been victimized by the inequitable distribution of wealth in America— African Americans and working-class whites—have found little solidarity in their similar plight. Instead, they are political enemies reduced to fighting for a slice of the economic pie (Stafford, 1992; Rubin, 1994; Jones, 1992; Cotton, 1992).

Gresson's Recovery of White Supremacy: Whites as Victims

Post-Fordist economics and the social dissonance that follows it can be, and is, nasty. Vocational educators operating in the 1990s do not have to be told of the racial tensions they witness in their everyday professional lives. Dealing with the poorest segments of high-school students, such educators are aware of the distrust and suspicion engendered by interracial competition for limited opportunities. This context places racial interaction in a pressure cooker, exacerbating the racism-mutation process. New forms of racism emerge that call for new understandings and approaches on the part of democratic progressive vocational educators. The corporate use (commodification) of nonwhites and the superficial celebration of diversity in media cannot be confused with genuine democratic movements to decentralize wealth and more equitably distribute political power in America (Fusco, 1992). Critical vocational educators must stand ready to point out that such movements have not taken place in this country. They must gain the language to tell their students that this corporate commodification of "ethnicity," expressed in terms of "Shaq attacks," "Be Like Mike," and "Oprah at 5:00," cannot be equated with a pervasive nonwhite access to economic mobility. When people consider the relationships among hard work, schooling, and financial success, misconceptions like these distort both the public conversation about it and individual perceptions of it.

The post-Fordist era has been hard on most Americans; only the upper-middle class and the wealthy have been spared. I empathize with the white working class and poor, as they have watched their financial security and opportunities for economic success be pulled out from under them during the last quarter of the twentieth century. I appreciate their frustrations and anger, as they work hard and struggle daily to make ends meet. It is difficult to write about these racial issues that surround vocational education in America—difficult because they evoke such passion and fury on the part of everyone. Critical vocational educators must appeal to the best instincts of their students, colleagues, and communities; that is, they must appeal to their compassion, sense of justice, and empathy. African Americans must empathize with working white people and their frustrations concerning their lack of mobility and crushed aspirations. At the same time, white Americans must empathize with nonwhite Americans and their continuing frustrations with their inability to gain access to the promise of the American dream. Until such empathy is engendered, the possibility of dialogue and unity among Americans victimized by viral forms of racism, sexism, and class bias cannot be realized. Such empathy will lead to dialogue and unity; and such unity will form the basis of an American prodemocracy movement, an interracial, interethnic struggle for political and economic justice.

These words may sound idealistic—and they are; but we must retain the ability to envision a better day, to dream social dreams. This book, of course, is itself a social dream that lays out a sense of possibility for vocational educators and their students. This chapter focuses attention on one of the most important impediments to hope—racism, and its context, effects, and mutating expression. Vocational teacher and student awareness of this phenomenon takes on more importance than simply the understanding of racism itself. The awareness of the ways our consciousness is socially constructed around issues of race (not to mention class and gender) grants us insight into the way the world works, into the way power relations in a society work ambiguously to induce us to adopt identities and perspectives that undermine our self-interests and our collective interests as a culture or a nation. In this regard, Aaron Gresson's description of "racial recovery" and its social divisiveness becomes very important.

Hegemony, as previously discussed, makes the world seem natural, as if it can be explained by a dominant cultural story. Certain stories become privileged at particular historical junctures because they fit so well with the maintenance of existing power relations. Gresson has called to our attention the emergence of a *new dominant story* over the last couple of decades—the narrative of the recovery of white supremacy. In many ways the new story is a white story that inverts a traditional black story. The new story rejects essentialist racist descriptions of nonwhite inferiority, substituting in its place a narrative of nonwhite *privilege*. Because the media have constructed the illusion of black and other minority group success, the story contends that nonwhites have greater power and opportunity than whites (Gresson, 1995). Thus, nonwhite privilege has been gained *at the expense of white Americans—especially white males*. The story is portrayed at a variety of levels and in a multitude of ways, but always with the same effect: the production of *white anger* directed at African Americans, Latinos, Asians, Native Americans, and sometimes women. Such anger works, of course, to divide poor and working-class people of all races and genders and to support the interests of privileged power wielders.

This story induces white Americans to see themselves as a people under threat. Sociologists have long maintained that individuals and groups under threat often react with an attempt to reassert their power and former social position—the social phenomenon of status anxiety. This reassertion, of course, takes many forms and comes in many degrees. Manifestations may include modest efforts to reassert one's self-worth by way of private expression of racial disdain ("I hate the way Deion Sanders struts around the end zone like a rooster every time he scores a touchdown") or racial superiority ("Many of the people who work in my office don't make a very good impression—with their loud 'street talk' and everything"). Another example of white reassertion may work more at the level of group recovery with the passing of "English only" legislation in heavily Latino areas in such states as Florida, California, and Arizona or in battles over "multicultural curricula," as evidenced throughout the nation (Frankenberg, 1993). More extreme expressions involve the dramatic growth of white supremacist organizations in the 1980s and 1990s and the terrorist activity associated with some of them, for example, the April 1995 bombing of the Oklahoma City federal building. The vast majority of Americans are dismayed by this level of angry white reassertion, yet the perceptions of whites as victims becomes more and more deeply embedded into white collective consciousness as the century comes to an end.

The Andromeda Strain:
The Contemporary Mutation, Crypto-Racism

In a so-called postracist era, when supposedly the only form of racism left is a discrimination directed at whites, all the rules of racial talk in America have changed. The critical analyst's attempt to track neoracism is analogous to the effort by the Center for Disease Control (CDC) to track the evolution of the ebola virus, with new outbreaks popping up in diverse venues. This "Andromeda strain of racism" can best be described as crypto-racism ("crypto" meaning concealed, secret, not visible to the naked eye), a racism that employs thinly veiled racist code words that often evoke images of white superiority (Nightingale, 1993). Steve Haymes (1995) has uncovered that virus and its damage to the public conversation about education, as concealed in discussions of issues of illiteracy and basic skills, with their cryptic identification of nonwhites with these problems. The subliminal message conveyed involves the depiction of illiteracy and lack of basic skills as a black and Latino problem so severe that educational resources needed for students who could make good use of them (read: white students) are dramatically reduced. Thus, shortfalls in educational funds for middle- and upper-middle-class white students are not the sins of communities and the political leaders who have cut educational funding in general—rather, such deficits are the direct fault of minority groups. According to the authors of the best-seller *The Bell Curve,* such funds are wasted because the nonwhite and the poor are not capable of profiting from the programs the funding subsidizes (see Herrnstein and Murray, 1994; and Kincheloe, Steinberg, and Gresson, 1996). The story of white victimization is extended: Fuel is added to the fire of white anger.

Crypto-racism produces a form of doublespeak that not only transforms whites into the victims of racism but also redefines the word itself. "Antiracism," in this new discourse, becomes racism. References to the existence of racism and the call for its eradication are redefined by crypto-racists as racist practices, that is, "playing the race card" or "evoking the tired cries of discrimination." So pervasive has this neoracism become that many workers are afraid to make reference to racism on the job. Workers know that merely bringing up issues of race in the workplace can undermine their chances for advancement (Macedo, 1994). Crypto-racism has developed a "proper syntax" of racial reference that involves an encoding maneuver that escapes identification as racism. It is a language of white supremacy that constantly denies its racist undercurrent. As it distances itself from any expression of biological inferiority (also known as essentialist racism), crypto-racism aligns itself with notions of (1) *common culture,* meaning that all Americans hold particular, sacred values and understandings. Implicit in the assertion is that many nonwhites do not share these values and understandings; (2) *urban troubles,* meaning that the cities present mammoth and unsolvable problems in the late twentieth century. Unstated here is the recognition that since urban demographics have changed so fundamentally over the last thirty years (nonwhites now constitute the majority of many urban populations), urban troubles can be directly blamed on nonwhite social pathology; (3) *family values,* meaning that America is in decline because of the breakdown of family values. The unsaid in this discourse involves reference to the pathology of the nonwhite, especially the African American, family; (4) *the epidemics of drugs and violence,* meaning that something must be done to end this attack on American communities formulated by unscrupulous drug dealers. The message encoded here involves the connection between drugs and the nonwhite. Drugs and the violence that surrounds them are products of the ghetto, of black and Latino gangs.

What is amazing about the crypto-racist coding of these four assertions is their distortion of the truth. The first assertion concerning common culture assumes that a national culture is grounded on the notion of consensus, that is, that all citizens ascribe to an unchanging homogeneous culture characterized by a universally known and accepted core of uniform values. National cultures, especially the American variety, have never been constructed on this level. The second assertion blaming nonwhites for urban troubles is consummately misleading. The flight of middle-class residents and corporate interests from the inner city has spawned an economic, political, and social crisis for the people left behind. The refusal of citizens and politicians to address their problems and needs resulting from the flight has contributed to their hopelessness. Who is at fault here? The third assertion concerning the decline of family values fails to account for the amazing strength of black family structures throughout American history. Regardless of historical context, African American families have often produced individuals who were equipped to cope with and sometimes transcend violence, poverty, and other manifestations of their powerlessness. The fourth assertion concerning drugs and violence ignores the sociological data that refute the myth that inner-city nonwhites are primarily responsible for drug use and violence. White women are statistically more likely to use and abuse drugs than nonwhite women—despite the reality that black female drug users are ten times more likely to be reported than white women users. Almost 80 percent of illegal drug use in America takes place outside of inner-city nonwhite communities. The prototypical crack addict is a white middle-class man between the ages of forty and fifty. At the same time, FBI statistics indicate that although the proportion of African Americans arrested for aggravated assault is three times greater than the proportion for whites, the National Crime Survey, which studies victims of assault, has found black and white aggravated assault statistics to be almost the same. Crypto-racist codes portray a misleading picture of the world (Rizvi, 1993; Haymes, 1995; Coontz, 1992).

In no way do I want to undermine our appreciation of the ambiguity and complexity of crypto-racism. Indeed, I will devote a great deal of space in this chapter to the delineation of the conflicting ways such racism undermines the position of nonwhites in the labor market and education. Before moving on to that issue, however, a demonstration of the value of an encoded racism for power wielders in American society is necessary. The recovery of white supremacy is in the interests of corporate and political leaders who overwhelmingly tend to be white. The economic and political advantages of white recovery were specifically outlined by political analyst Kevin Phillips in his *The Emerging Republican Majority,* published in 1970. Phillips understood the political power to be derived from exploiting the developing perception of white workers that minority groups were unjustifiably gaining too large a percentage of the economic pie. Struggling to retain Fordist profit margins of the 1950s and 1960s, many corporate leaders and their political allies employed the rhetoric of white recovery to gain the electoral cooperation of their natural adversary, the (in this case white) working class. So strong were the racial concerns of the white working class that it was induced to support economic and political policies contrary to its own interests. Employing the crypto-racist codes of the welfare slate, drugs, crime in the streets, family values, and the liberal assault on Western and Judeo-Christian values, right-wing and centrist political candidates began the process of creating favorable business climates, with lower corporate taxes, reduced governmental regulations, lower wages for workers, higher public expenditures for defense-related business contracts, and so on (West, 1993; Amott, 1993).

It is not difficult to trace this political and economic trajectory throughout the last three decades of the twentieth century. Richard Nixon deployed "busing" as a crypto-racist term as early as 1968. Quickly, the Republican Party became adept at using the language of white male recovery to woo white voters away from the labor-identified Democrats. By no means do I mean to absolve the Democratic Party from complicity in the recovery efforts (the Democratic Party role in this puzzle will be discussed in detail in Chapter 17). The Republicans, however, perfected the politics of white recovery by using race and gender codes to divert white worker attention from the politics of the workplace. Ronald Reagan, with the help of advisers Michael Deaver and Roger Ailes, was the master of crypto-racist recovery, as evidenced in his ability to elicit worker support of a no-tax business policy and government grants to corporations.

Lacking Reagan's charm, George Bush was forced to employ negative black visual imagery such as the picture of rapist Willie Horton in his 1988 campaign TV ads to link the recovery rhetoric to his (Bush's) persona. The racial imagery worked so well that by 1990, in his race against a black challenger, North Carolina Republican senator Jesse Helms was able to use TV ads that made references to minorities' taking white working-class jobs—all the while denying racist intent. Of course, such references had little to do with reality; job loss in North Carolina involved corporate flight to the Third World. And that flight was made possible by tax incentives passed by the business-friendly Senator Helms and his corporate-financed colleagues in government. The success of such strategies kept raising the racial ante, proving that racial scapegoating works. Candidates began to ask how far they could go. What are the most effective ways of conveying the codes? By the early 1990s, such questions prepared the American political landscape for more radical and daring crypto-racists. David Duke—former essentialist racist Ku Klux Klan and Nazi Party leader—pushed the racist envelope. The work of Nixon, Reagan, Bush, and Helms had plowed the ideological and cultural terrain, making it more acceptable to racist seeds; Duke, for example, in a gubernatorial race in Louisiana in 1991, received nearly two-thirds of the white working-class vote (Marable, 1992). By the middle of the decade, the rhetoric of white recovery was a common element in political campaigns in all regions of America.

Reasonable Paradoxes: The Complexity of Crypto-Racism

In order to better understand the complex workings of crypto-racism, it is important to examine it at the level of ideology. Ideology is a complex concept that can be expressed rather simply: It refers to the way our ideas, values, and beliefs are shaped and the manner in which we incorporate them into our everyday life, our way of being in the world (McLaren, 1994). We use our ideology to organize our lived experiences, to make sense of our predicaments. This organizational and sense-making process is never stable, as it changes from context to context. Thus, the process is contradictory and disjointed, with sometimes bizarre and paradoxical belief structures cohabiting in our consciousness. Power wielders in the society help shape our ideologies through a process known as hegemony, a process through which the powerful win the consent of the oppressed. When hegemonized, the oppressed are induced to buy into ideologies that are not in their best interests; for example, workers who grant their consent to corporate leaders around issues of race are induced to support business policies that ultimately cut employee wages and limit their input into the organization of their work lives—a process that results in bad work. The central form that hegemonic action has taken over the last decades has involved the corporate winning of working people's consent to the politics of racial and corporate recovery. Thus, their private, public, and work lives are structured in part by the hegemonic ideologies they internalize.

The way this structuring takes place cannot be separated from the workings of the existing hegemonic ideology. This way of seeing is successful in helping working people make sense of their lives to the degree that it renders power-driven depictions of the world natural. Crypto-racism naturalizes the relationships that structure racial relations in a way that erases the historical processes that have helped mold the present social order in general, and existing racial dynamics in particular. We therefore come to believe that the world could only exist in the way that it does today. Our sense of the possibility of a better social order, of racial harmony between working people, is undermined. Please do not infer from these descriptions some simple process by which hegemonic ideology is transmitted into the consciousness of white workers. Individuals acquire their racist orientations and their connection of these ways of seeing to corporate ideologies not through a simple duplication of the ideas to which they are exposed. The process is one of reception, construction, and reconstruction that helps them make sense of, *deal with*, and act in their lived worlds. Political depictions of crypto-racist blame of, for example, unqualified minority workers for taking white jobs helps white workers organize their realities and focus their anger.

Conflicting forms of consciousness in this process are not unusual. Studies indicate that students who sincerely ascribe to tenets of multiculturalism and racial justice are untroubled by patterns of isolation between racially different students, a rhetoric of "us" (whites) and "them" (nonwhites), linked with the perception that school values are and should be "our" (white people's) values. The crypto-racism that is encoded here has been described as "aversive racism," a liberal form of race consciousness that denies its tendency for discrimination at the same instance it asserts its low opinion of the racially different. These reasonable paradoxes are expressed in a common and recognizable rhetorical style: Rejection of racism is asserted in preliminary phrase ("I am not a racist but . . . ") followed by the delineation of an explicitly racist characterization ("these Cubans are so pushy and arrogant"). Of course, the ability to identify the various ways racism manifests itself is extremely important for vocational educators. At the same time, it is important for such professionals to understand that no matter what guise racism assumes, its structural consequences are similar. Victims of discrimination are marginalized, excluded, and denied equal access and treatment by institutions.

By way of the message systems of schools, students' ambiguous aversive racism is legitimated and reinforced. Students' perceptions of who they are and the nature of their social identities are inseparable from these educational message systems (Rizvi, 1993). In this context, we can understand the ways that vocational education fits into this complex social puzzle. The tracking and social stigmatizing so central to the logic of vocational schooling coincides with contradictory crypto-racism. Vocational education is a place for the academically and intellectually inferior. As white students watch the nonwhite and handicapped segregated into the vocational space, they are reminded of their "separateness" from this group. Vocational students are the abnormal, those distanced from the norms of middle- and upper-middle-class whiteness. The message is clear: Although the world is populated by different groups, cultures, and ethnicities who deserve our verbal respect, we live separate lives. It is *we*, as white students, who live within the boundaries of the norm; it is *our* culture that constitutes *the* culture; *our* friends and daily associations come from those within the boundaries of academic education; *we* may never use these words to express it, but we are the dominant group. These are a few of the ways that racist consciousness is *constructed* and inequality is perpetuated in the everyday life of the contemporary era.

Crypto-Racism and the Dynamics of Vocationalism: Hispanics/Latinos

Latinos are profoundly affected by the racist forces analyzed here. Any examination of the relationship among racism, Hispanics/Latinos, and vocational education must begin with a recognition of the diversity within the umbrella term "Hispanics/Latinos." Five principal groups are represented in the U.S. population: Mexican Americans, 63 percent; Puerto Ricans, 12 percent; Central and South Americans, 11 percent; other Hispanics/Latinos, 8 percent; and Cubans, 5 percent. Hispanics/Latinos constitute the fastest-growing demographic group in contemporary America. Over one-third of them are tracked into vocational education, most of the time without any counseling as to the social and educational consequences resulting from such a placement. In Los Angeles, for example, Mexicans, Salvadorans, and Guatemalans struggle in school and in the job market. When Latinas find jobs, on the average they make 53 cents for every dollar earned by white males. Hispanic/Latino students are victimized by crypto-racist educational practices that are represented as antiracist, multicultural, and equal-opportunity oriented. Although couched in the language of democracy, these practices exclude Hispanic/Latino students from honors and higher-level programs, making them more likely to drop out, be enrolled below grade level, and less likely to attend postsecondary programs than any other ethnic or racial group in America. Given the proliferation of these ostensibly helpful programs, Hispanic/Latino students have lost educational ground in respect to measurements such as rates of high-school graduation over the last three decades (Rendon and Nora, 1991; McLaren, 1994; Perez, 1993).

Rarely do educators set out to impede the academic and vocational progress of Hispanic/Latino students; crypto-racism simply does not work this way. Vocational counselors do not think, "Oh, here's a Salvadoran; I'm going to put him in metal work in the vocational department." The process is much more complex, but the dynamics of social regulation of the poor and nonwhite do come into play. Studies indicate that minority students and their parents often have little input into curricular track placement. Counselors and teachers take responsibility for these decisions, typically basing their judgments on the student's grades and test scores. Interpretation of test scores rarely takes into account that many Hispanic/Latino students employ English as a second language. For the large number of Hispanic/Latino students who are recent immigrants, testing takes place long before students have had an opportunity to integrate themselves into North American life. Decontextualized assessment procedures fail to account for these and other mitigating factors, guaranteeing unmediated placements of Hispanic/Latino students into low-ability tracks on the basis of their understandably low scores.

Thus, Hispanic/Latino students make the long march into vocational education, finding themselves before they consciously realize it being trained for low-pay, low-status, bad-work jobs traditionally held by Hispanics/Latinos or other minorities. The process is perpetuated year after year by counselors operating within the modernist paradigm of their profession, grounding their counseling activity with crypto-codes such as the "cultural deficiency" of Hispanic/Latino students. Given such a degraded situation, the only *realistic* form of vocational counseling must involve lowering illusory professional aspirations, in the process inducing such students into a curricular track that prepares them for low-status roles commensurate with their talents (or lack thereof) (Oakes, 1985; McLaren, 1994; Banfield, 1991). In his historical contextualization of such unjust practices, Clinton Allison (1995) has described the historical reactions of educators to poor, minority, and immigrant parents who refused to accept teachers' descriptions of their children's cognitive or academic limitations. Throughout the twentieth century, educators have looked contemptuously at parents who failed to recognize "scientifically validated" assessments of their children's limited aptitudes. Educators understood that one of the most important aspects of their professional role was to dispel poor and minority parents of their delusional hopes of upward mobility that would eventuate in professional careers for their children.

Critical educator Donaldo Macedo—who entered the Boston public schools with Portuguese as his first language—has described his encounter with a vocational guidance counselor. Although Macedo was in no way interested in such a job, his counselor advised him to become a TV repairman (Macedo, 1994). As one who was pushed by a high-school guidance counselor to become a piano tuner (a vocation in which I had absolutely no interest), I can empathize with Macedo and the tens of thousands of Hispanic/Latino students whose counselors relegate them to an exclusively vocational track, based on encoded perceptions of them as incapable students. Donna Gaines (1990) described an all-too-common encounter between a marginalized student and the vocational counselor:

> "So, Roy, what do you see yourself doing five years from now?" And Roy is thinking what did I do wrong, what does she want me to say, what is going to come down on me now? And then the guidance counselor will say something about Roy's lack of spectacular grades—"not on any teams or in any clubs, are you, Roy?" And Roy starts feeling stupid and maybe he fiddles with himself nervously, and says the first thing that comes to his head, like how much he enjoys working on his car. Like she shouldn't think he's a total loser. And that's that? He's never really given much thought before now, but today, the future is laid out before him and now Roy's going to vocational high school and he's going to learn about cars. (pp. 145–146)

Hispanics/Latinas, of course, face special forms of cryptic-encodement, as literature and media depict them as powerless and sometimes pathological. As subjugated, subservient, loyal daughters, wives, and mothers, they are blamed for their own victimization. They are portrayed as unresistant to their positioning as sex objects and as befrilled consorts with a proclivity to excessive praying. Obviously, vocational teachers and counselors need to understand these cryptic codes and reformulate their teaching and counseling to address them. Critical vocational professionals must help Hispanics/Latinas learn to confront such ethnic encoding by developing strategies of resistance. Hispanics/Latinas and their teachers and counselors must insist that

Latinas not be excluded from academic courses, be given access to programs that teach them about career and life options that are available and the curricula necessary for access to them, and understand the power and ethnic dynamics that force them into dead-end careers and life choices. Schools at various levels need to connect these racial, ethnic, and cultural appreciations into integrated academic and vocational curricula, building, when and where needed, centers designed to help all marginalized people (Hispanic/Latina students in particular) cope with the unnerving stress, role conflicts, vocational dynamics, and crypto-racism that they will inevitably face in contemporary society. Such centers might specifically provide such services as child care, apprenticeships with Hispanic/Latina workers, mathematics-anxiety reduction classes, social foundations of vocational and economics education seminars, financial aid, and financial planning study groups (Rendon and Nora, 1991).

The Lived Consequences of Racism: Disparity in Black and White

The interethnic fighting in the former Soviet Union and the former Yugoslavia is viewed by Americans as a social pathology both geographically and culturally distant from the lived experience of Americans. Contrary to such popular belief, America has its own strain of ethnic strife that exhibits no sign of imminent resolution. Indeed, America is still a segregated nation divided into ethnic enclaves, the most dominant division involving the separation of black and white. Obviously, spaces exist for different ethnicities to mingle, but the separation still exists both geographically (in terms of space) and politically (in terms of power). This segregation is imposed by white Americans who feel better when nonwhites are not around them and by blacks, Hispanics/Latinos, Asians, and Native Americans who are more comfortable without whites. Even after twenty years of fair-housing legislation, for example, blacks *no matter what their income level* still live with other blacks. Residential patterns that do not contribute to interracial ethnic groups are an active indicator of the degree of segregation and integration within a society. In America, interethnic marriage rates have risen for all groups except blacks. Black-white intermarriage rates are lower in America than any other nation in the Western world. In many respects, America is still two nations (Hacker, 1992; Zweigenhaft and Domhoff, 1991).

Of course, a major force perpetuating this separation between whites and nonwhites (African Americans in particular) involves the shocking disparity of wealth between different racial and ethnic groups. Race intersects with class in this context, manifesting outlandish inequities in terms of material well-being. White people who claim to be the victims of racial preferences in hiring and other forms of special privilege for African Americans and other nonwhites should consider these economic realities: The net worth of the average white family is $46,706, compared to the average black family's $4,054; a white female-headed family has an average wealth of $26,853, compared to a *black married couple* family's average holdings of $15,588. The great redistribution of power and wealth that conservatives insist took place over the last thirty years between whites and nonwhites simply never happened (Cotton, 1992).

Critical vocational educators must understand that a key element of a multicultural vocational education involves preparing minority students to understand the workings of power and power inequalities so that they can *gain* power in its political, economic, and educational guises. That is, they need to organize their communities and their allies in elections, lobbying, and other forms of political pressure; build economic institutions, cooperatives, capital-generating enterprises to raise individual and community living standards; and formulate both academic and vocational school programs that reflect the culture and needs of the community. Such efforts are connected to the previously mentioned political and economic goals, viewing empowerment as a central mission of minority schooling and exposing and eliminating hidden forms of racism embedded in school bureaucracies. Grounded on these types of understandings and activities, critical vocational programs will be able to expose and suggest positive responses to the ways racism is embedded in political, economic, and educational structures. Although it will be difficult, we will have to deal with the fact that the maintenance of such structures is in the interest of well-to-do white people. For example, white business owners profit by the maintenance of a cadre of low-paid and disempowered laborers; indeed, racial inequality is in the *short-term* interest of businesspeople (Hatcher, 1992; Sleeter, 1993).

Students in critical vocational educational programs grounded on a power-conscious multiculturalism would appreciate the fact that deindustrialization and corporate restructuring of the post-Fordist era has hurt nonwhites as a social group far more than whites. Deindustrialization, with its job migration to the Third World, hit the industrial Midwest with its heavy African American populations very hard. Automobile, steel, and tire plants moved to suburbs, rural areas, and, of course, to Mexico, Southeast Asia, and other foreign locales. In a five-year period in the early 1980s, 50 percent of black workers in durable good manufacturing in the Great Lakes region saw their jobs disappear. Outside of the Midwest, the numbers were still sobering; just for example, Philadelphia lost nearly 200,000 jobs in the 1970s and 1980s alone. Such losses were accompanied by a 32 percent decrease in employment that demanded less than a high-school degree. Black college graduates have made economic progress during the last quarter of the twentieth century; of course, those who fit this demographic category constitute only a small fraction of the African American population and the percentage *is dropping*. In this deindustrialized post-Fordist context, the number of black Americans who are dismally poor—defined as individuals with incomes constituting only one-half of that income demarcating the poverty line—has increased by 69 percent since 1978. Since 1973, the gains made in the 1960s by African American workers have been reversed, and contrary to the pronouncements of many angry whites, the average income of young black men has fallen by 50 percent since 1973. By the end of the 1980s, the average earnings of a black high-school dropout had fallen by 61 percent (Bluestone, 1988; Coontz, 1992; West, 1993; Nightingale, 1993).

Americans identify with winners, exerting little anxiety over the plight of those who lose in the great capitalist race. White Americans for the most part are not aware of the vicissitudes of black workers in the post-Fordist economy. Their plight is certainly not the daily fare of the exponentially expanding variety of cable TV channels. As displayed by the growth of crypto-racism and other forms of white racism, most white Americans not only do not understand these racial dynamics in the economy but fail to appreciate the benefits that accrue from their whiteness. If you are white, blue-collar, and struggling economically, such words hold little solace; but the fact remains that whites (even blue-collar whites) have fared better economically over the last thirty years than nonwhites. Low-skill jobs have migrated away from heavily populated black urban centers; the sight of African American workers commuting to such jobs is a more and more common sight. Such a vignette serves as a symbol for what has happened to the African American losers in the great economic race of the late twentieth century. After hopes of a brighter economic future were raised by political rhetoric and government actions in the 1960s, the corporate search for better business climates transformed such hopes into anger and despair. Economic deprivation in the early portion of the twentieth century, structured by overt forms of essentialist racism, was in some ways not as bad as the new hopelessness catalyzed by crypto-racism that is couched in the language of democracy and equal opportunity (Ellwood, 1988; Hacker, 1992; Nightingale, 1993).

Governmental Neglect: The Politics of Discrimination

After the death of Fordism and the economic turbulence of the early 1970s, the primary objective of the most powerful individuals in American politics—corporate and business leaders—was to deploy their political machine of lobbyists and elected representatives whose political careers they had financed to preserve their profits and power. Their strategy was four-pronged: (1) move their operation to cheaper regions of the United States and foreign countries, (2) undermine the power and wages of workers and cripple their unions, (3) downsize the workforce in a way where more peripheral labor, that is, part-time workers, would be utilized, and 4) make use of their political clout to ensure the passage of business-friendly laws, such as emasculating environmental regulations. By 1981, their power maneuvers had worked so well that the greatest redistribution of income from the poor and middle class to the rich, from the nonwhite to the white, in American history had begun. This was skillfully (cynically) accomplished in an orgy of banal clichés about patriotism, respect for the flag, and the love of God. Homelessness skyrocketed, jails filled, working wages fell 20 percent, taxes for the wealthy were slashed, social programs were decimated, take-back contracts were signed by unions faced with managerial threats of plant relocations, and many of the top 2 percent of income earners were able to buy new yachts. The press played its role dutifully, reporting periodic "good news tonight on the economy"; what reporters failed to divulge about these economic "rallies" involved the fact that financial improvements during the era concerned the interests of the upper and upper-middle classes and such rallies had little to do with the worsening predicament of the poor and the nonwhite (West, 1993; Amott, 1993; Macedo, 1994).

At the same time government leaders were gnashing their teeth over government spending on welfare and social programs for the poor and nonwhite, welfare programs for the wealthy remained outside the realm of public debate. One of many examples of such aid for the rich involved the McDonnell-Douglas Corporation. By late 1990, the corporation was facing such severe fiscal problems that the Pentagon devised a secret plan to provide the firm with two cash payments of $148 million and $72 million (Macedo, 1994). Julianne Malveaux (1992b) used the metaphor of a wolf with sharpened teeth to describe the governmental response to minority economic problems during the 1980s and early 1990s. So vicious was the wolf that at the same time hundreds of millions of dollars were being paid directly to corporations, governmental leaders were cutting social programs for pregnant women, the blind, aged, and disabled. Such cuts of services so important to their recipients saved taxpayers at the most $3.5 million (Macedo, 1994). Cuts in government services exerted double damage on nonwhites, because not only recipients but a high percentage of service providers were African Americans, Hispanics/Latinos, and other minorities. Partly because of such cuts, African American men with college degrees watched their income fall by an average of 11 percent in the 1980s (Hacker, 1992). Poor nonwhite people found it difficult to hide from the wolf.

The Wolf at the Door:
Structural Impediments to Minority Mobility

For the purpose of emphasis, following is a short list of factors impeding nonwhite, especially African American, mobility in the late 1990s. Critical vocational educators understand these impediments and make sure that all

their students, nonwhite and white alike, appreciate their impact. It is extremely important that nonwhite, especially African American, vocational
students grasp the meaning of the list so that they can develop individual
and collective strategies to counter each impediment.

1. Stores and service providers with predominantly nonwhite customers overcharge and underserve them. Compare prices, for example, in a suburban grocery store with prices in an inner-city store in
   a black community.
2. Consumer credit is denied more often to nonwhites and, when
   available, costs them more. Real estate redlining practices (the refusal of lending institutions to loan nonwhites, particularly African
   Americans, money for houses outside specific nonwhite areas) keep
   poor nonwhites confined to increasingly squalid ghettos, preventing
   them from following in the path of whites who escaped years before. Even middle-class African Americans face tremendous discrimination in their efforts to secure home loans.
3. White monopolies over high-skill, high-pay jobs and career ladders
   in many labor markets frequently undermine nonwhite efforts to
   obtain good work. When nonwhites do find good work, their efforts to move up the bureaucratic ladder are often thwarted.
4. Funds for schools in poor nonwhite communities have disappeared
   with shrinking ghetto tax bases. The white flight from such areas
   was followed by business and corporate moves to suburban and
   rural locales. As a result, inner-city infrastructures, especially relating
   to school maintenance, have deteriorated. To exemplify the state of
   inner-city schools, Jonathan Kozol described in *Savage Inequalities*
   the vocational classrooms in a high school in East St. Louis, Illinois:

In the wing of the school that holds vocational classes, a damp, unpleasant odor
fills the halls. The school has a machine shop, which cannot be used for lack of
staff, and woodworking shop. The only shop that's occupied this morning is
the auto-body class. A man with long blond hair and wearing a white sweat suit
swings a paddle to get children in their chairs. "What we need the most is new
equipment," he reports. "I have equipment for alignment, for example, but we
don't have money to install it. We also need a better form of egress. We bring
the cars in through two other classes." Computerized equipment used in most
repair shops, he reports, is far beyond the high school's budget. It looks like a
very old gas station in an isolated rural town.

Stopping in the doorway of a room with seven stoves and three refrigerators,
I am told by a white teacher that this is a class called "Introductory Home Ec."
The 15 children in the room, however, are not occupied with work. They are
scattered at some antiquated tables, chatting with each other. The teacher explains that students do no work on Friday, which, she says, is "clean-up day." I

ask her whether she regards this class as preparation for employment. "Not this class," she says. "The ones who move on to Advanced Home Ec are given job instruction." When I ask her what jobs they are trained for, she said: "Fast food places—Burger King, McDonald's." (Kozol, 1991, p. 27)

5. Blue-collar jobs in urban areas have often been filled by nonwhites (men in particular) in positions such as craftsmen, operators, fabricators, or manual laborers. These jobs have been the ones most likely to be exported or "technologized" out of existence. Any growth recorded in such job categories over the last couple of decades has been found in suburbs and nonmetropolitan areas far away from concentrations of nonwhites.

6. Because American electronic and print media devote so little time to the coverage of such issues, most white Americans have little understanding of these economic dynamics. As a result they blame the nonwhite victims of these racist policies and structures, arguing that their incompetence or laziness has brought on both their unemployment and the deterioration of their neighborhoods. Thus, proposals to help nonwhites solve these formidable problems are rejected as undeserved preferential treatment.

7. White employers have made no secret of their preference for immigrants (either legal or illegal) to native-born black workers. Apartment house and retail shop owners, for example, are more disposed to lure immigrants for their service staffs than African Americans. Such hiring practices not only cause economic hardships for African Americans but also result in tremendous resentment directed toward both employers and the immigrant workers they hire.

8. An alarming tendency among businesses and corporations in recent years has been identified involving the selection of sites for new U.S. facilities in geographic areas with minimal nonwhite populations. Such tactics are not limited to American corporations, as Japanese firms such as Honda and Toyota use the same criterion for choice of plant sites (Cotton, 1992; Nightingale, 1993; Zweigenhaft and Domhoff, 1991; Falk and Lyson, 1988; Ellwood, 1988; Hacker, 1992).

By no means is this list intended to be comprehensive. Scores of other forms of racial discrimination undermine minority efforts to "break out" of the traps that thwart them. In my conversations with white students in high school, college, and even graduate school (not to mention nonacademic white citizens), I am frustrated by their unfamiliarity with these impediments and their effects. Such obstructions to economic mobility can be central elements of any economics curriculum or any political campaign. A strange silence concerning such matters falls over curricular discussions and campaign forums—and that silence insidiously tears America apart as it allows the wolf to scratch and howl at the nonwhite door.

The Collapse of the Inner City: Hyper-ghettoization

The racist forces discussed here have worked to destroy the unity and viability of inner-city neighborhoods. As jobs and incomes in the cities were lost and middle-class residents moved to the suburbs, city governments built prisons, low-income housing, homeless shelters, methadone clinics, and drug treatment centers. Middle- and upper-class citizens marshaled their power to keep such "trouble makers" and "property devaluers" out of their own backyards, leaving the powerless to deal with the ill effects. Hyper-ghettoization was left in the wake of these factors, for all parties involved could claim no malice, no intent. All parties except the poor inner-city residents were acting simply in their own interests. It was only "common sense" (1) for industrial managers and service industry executives to follow their preferred, chiefly white workers to the vanilla suburbs, (2) for chain stores and conglomerate-owned retail establishments to evacuate the inner cities, (3) for bankers to finance white-owned suburban developments rather than those in the ghettos, and (4) for mayors and city councils to support tax plans, transportation systems, and job creation policies that reward the already privileged instead of the poor. The results are obvious: The affluent prosper while the underclass struggles to survive its hopelessness.

This struggle with despair is often missed by educators and the white public. Unable to empathize with inner-city dwellers' "sociological depression," mainstream Americans attribute their condition to personal pathologies. Urban black neighborhoods that lack networks of employed friends to pass along upcoming job opportunities and to provide counseling and support when conflicts occur often find it difficult to sustain a functional community, resist invasions of drugs, or offer a range of positive vocational and other educational options to their residents. Many commentators speak of the development of a new underclass in America beset by despair and nihilism. If the defining characteristic of the underclass is little hope for mobility, then there is little new to chronicle. Among African Americans, there has always been a significant population with minimal chances of escaping poverty. Vocational educators must unite with various cultural workers in social services, religion, counseling, and other professions to fight the human effects of hyper-ghettoization (Coontz, 1992; Jones, 1992; McLaren, 1994).

The Children's Defense Fund reports that the United States is one of the worst places to be born in the industrialized world; a black infant born in sight of the White House is less likely to live to the first birthday than an infant born in Trinidad. Comparing the health dimensions of black urban areas with Third World conditions has grown common in recent years, but another aspect of the analogy has been neglected. Poverty and economic underdevelopment in the Third World is the consequence of Western economic exploitation of Third World resources; the economic retardation of urban African American communities in the United States began with the white power bloc's adoption of slavery and continues today with the underevaluation, the underpayment, and, thus, the exploitation of black labor. This economic exploitation, this structural racism expressed by inner-city homelessness, joblessness, crime, disease, hunger, and substance abuse, constitutes the human face of the economic policies formulated and implemented by American corporate leaders and their governmental cronies (Cotton, 1992; Wallace, 1993). The political influence of conservative interests in business and government and their power to gain consent for their self-interested policies among white workers is significant at the end of the twentieth century. Critical vocational educators must work to break the connection that corporate and political leaders have forged with American workers, with white males in particular, a connection that exploits their racial and gender prejudices and anxieties in the effort to win their support for policies designed to benefit the privileged. The racial politics of corporatism must be confronted.

While these business-friendly, trickle-down forms of public economic policy reward corporate management, inner-city minorities remain trapped in inadequate and expensive housing, victimized by bureaucratically impaired social services, and haunted by chilling manifestations of street violence. In living conditions marked by physical decay, young people lose hope of upward mobility. How can school be a priority for young people who face hunger as a daily problem, who have no warm place to sleep in the winter, rat-infested apartments, and landlords who allow houses to fall apart and fail inspection so that they can reclaim the property and use it more profitably. Such conditions eat away at one's soul; they break down nurturing systems for children. Chronic poverty does not contribute to stable family relations (Wallace, 1993; Nightingale, 1993). As the rappers tell it, kids who live too close to the edge have to struggle to keep from going under—and many do "go under" with drugs or violence. Indeed, for many middle-class Americans, the reality of urban ghetto kids "going under" is an abstraction, something far away from the pulse of their everyday lives. To follow individual children and watch the process is to observe one of the great tragedies of contemporary life. In these circumstances, how can parents and concerned adults transmit meaning and purpose to children with wounded souls (West, 1993; Coontz, 1992)?

Inner-city schools are not spared from the effects of hyper-ghettoization. Nonwhite urban students often attend schools in various stages of disrepair and devoid of the educational equipment found in middle-class schools. Because of the white flight and other dynamics of hyper-ghettoization, more nonwhite students attend predominantly nonwhite schools in the 1990s than they did in the 1970s. The decay, both physical and psychosocial, is omnipresent in corridors and classrooms. "How can these conditions exist?" many black and Latino observers ask. Many people answer such questions with the observation that many white educational leaders obviously do not want nonwhite competition for power and resources. Especially in hard economic times when social status is threatened, they argue, white leaders become even more protective of their educational and material advantage. Critical vocational educators must work to increase funding from government agencies to repair inner-city schools and make them livable (Banfield, 1991; Zweigenhaft and Domhoff, 1991; Sleeter, 1993). Increased funding could be used to provide school sociologists who could serve as liaisons between teachers, students, and educational leaders and community service agencies. Such groups must work together to coordinate the improvement of living standards with educational reform. Until these aspects of life are viewed as inseparable, little progress will take place.

Whiteness as Racial Identity

We have learned that one's position in the web of reality (one's positionality) shapes the way one sees the world. Yet when it comes to being white, a knowledge of where whiteness places a person in the web of reality has not been discussed. How whiteness shapes our view of the world of work and education is not a part of the multicultural curriculum. But, in fact, whiteness is an ethnicity that exerts a profound impact on how white people see themselves, nonwhite people, and political issues. African American scholars have long maintained that oppressed people can see not only their own position in the web of reality but also that of the dominant group; this form of subjugated perception has been labeled the double consciousness of the oppressed. Whiteness, however, has been erased as a racial marker. In this context, whiteness becomes a racial and cultural norm that has no effect on white people. Naming whiteness upsets the applecart of racial erasure; it assigns everyone a place in the dynamics of racism. When whiteness is named and described, everyone becomes complicit in race relations, whether they think they are or not. Many individuals, white individuals in particular, become very uncomfortable as a result of the "naming ceremony."

It is extremely difficult to define whiteness because it is continually shifting and changing in historical time and cultural space. Suffice it to say in this regard that whiteness has something to do with economic and political structural advantage, racial privilege, the subjective position from which white people see themselves, nonwhites, and the world around them, and a group of cultural customs that exist unnamed in everyday life. A critical vocational education that studies race and economics, therefore, does not simply study ethnicities other than white but examines the socioeconomic aspects of whiteness itself. Study of this sort would not attempt to find some universal, unchanging whiteness that occupied a fixed economic position but would understand both the sociohistorical construction of whiteness and its inseparability from questions of gender and class. As has been discussed, one's racial identity cannot be separated from gender and class considerations. In no way will the analysis of whiteness be easy. For many white people, looking at race has meant either disclosing racial hierarchies (white supremacy) or taking the more liberal position of not saying anything about race at all—and this is especially true among older white people. To those individuals, naming whiteness will come as a racial shock.

Focusing on White Privilege

In the politics of white erasure, nonwhite individuals stand for "difference" and white individuals stand for "sameness." It is not uncommon to hear a manager say, "I have a highly ethnic workforce." In this statement, the manager is conveying the notion that many of his workers are nonwhite; whiteness is erased as nonethnic. An important aspect of this erasure involves the hiding of white privilege. All white Americans understand at some level of consciousness that black Americans have suffered because of white racism and the inequities it has imposed. The question is not whether whites know this—they do. The more important question involves how whites deal with this reality. No matter how loudly contemporary whites speak of their victimization, few would trade places with black and other nonwhite Americans. Again, at some level of consciousness, whites understand that their skin color provides an unearned wage, that is, privilege. Whiteness opens doors, protects one from harassment on the street, provides assurance that one will not be regarded as black (Frankenberg, 1993; Carby, 1992; McLaren et al., 1995; Hacker, 1992). Peggy McIntosh (1995) has argued that white privilege is similar to a weightless backpack that contains "special provisions, assurances, tools, maps, guides, codebooks, passports, visas, clothes, compass, emergency gear, and blank checks" (p. 77). When such privilege is unexamined, white people often ignore the voices of the nonwhite and silence them with the unacknowledged power to speak. When this privilege of speaking and silencing is challenged, whites often react with great anger (McLaren, 1994). W.E.B. DuBois described white privilege in the first half of the twentieth century as follows:

> They were given public deference . . . because they were white. They were admitted freely, with all classes of white people, to public functions [and] public parks . . . the police were drawn from their ranks and the courts, dependent on their votes, treated them with leniency . . . Their votes selected public officials

and while this had small effect upon the economic situation, it had great effect upon their personal treatment. . . . White schoolhouses were the best in the community, and conspicuously placed, and cost anywhere from twice to ten times colored schools. (DuBois as quoted in Roediger, 1991, p. 12)

In light of such white privilege, the question Americans have historically asked is not "Who is white?" but "Who may be thought of as white?" Admission to the "white country club" is strictly limited, and one can be blackballed for a variety of "impurities." No matter how much of a failure a white person may be, white privilege guarantees that the person will not hit bottom and will be able to maintain that "at least God made me white." For poor whites in degrading, deskilled jobs, whiteness has been there to relieve some of the sting of their class status; here, whiteness has served as an analgesic for low-status white workers. Yet privilege has its underside. White privilege damages whites in ways very different from the way it victimizes nonwhites. Although I am not attempting by any means to equate the damage, the erased privilege of whiteness distorts the white psyche by impeding insight into the formation of self, the construction of consciousness. The erasure of white privilege undermines white people's intra- and interpersonal intelligence in a way that blinds them to the workings of the world and their relation to it. Much more research is needed on the negative effects of white privilege on whites (Roediger, 1991; Hacker, 1992; McIntosh, 1995).

Why is it so hard for white Americans to perceive white privilege? Usually, all one has to do to see it is to drive through any town and notice that people with European heritage control most institutions and desirable resources, whereas nonwhites are concentrated into low-status positions. Often, from the perspective of many of the townspeople, the low status of nonwhites is just and deserved. Indeed, school has traditionally taught white students not to see this reality, not to see themselves as members of a privileged but damaged group. We can therefore clearly recognize the effects of an abstract and decontextualized individualism that sees moral questions only in terms of individual moral will. A white student is thus encouraged to be "nice" to nonwhite students on an individual basis but not to think about the power relations implicit in group membership and the implications of such relationships for moral behavior. Since the school portrays whiteness as the invisible ideal, white work for others (especially racially different disadvantaged others) has involved helping "them" become more like "us." "We worked hard and made it," whites chant, assuming the same payoff for nonwhites' effort to better themselves as for whites. Rarely understanding the lived reality of nonwhite lives, whites assume that everyone in America plays the vocational game under the same rules. "Our ancestors were immigrants and made it without any help from anybody," white Americans maintain. The hidden wages of whiteness and their moral implications elude them (Sleeter, 1993; McIntosh, 1995; Rubin, 1994).

White immigrants, of course, had an out—they could "win" their white-ness. The Irish, for example, once considered nonwhite, were able to prove their whiteness by mimicking the racial attitudes of whites and leading as-saults against African Americans in the late 1800s. Such arguments about the hidden wages of whiteness and white privilege do not fall softly on white working-class ears in the late 1990s. "We worked hard for what we have," working-class whites maintain, and they are right. But still, as hard as their lives have been, in the 1970s, 1980s, and 1990s their whiteness is still a ben-efit. Compare, for example, white working-class and nonwhite working-class efforts to find a job, a school, or a home mortgage; whiteness still mat-ters in these pursuits. For whites to accept the reality of white privilege, however, is psychologically difficult. Such acknowledgment subverts their belief in meritocracy—that cream rises to the top—and, in turn, diminishes the significance of their accomplishments. Thus, a wall of whiteness is erected that keeps at bay any suggestion that being white holds special ad-vantages. As many white Americans explain it in the late 1990s: "We're just better and harder workers. Many blacks really don't want to work."

Fighting Racism: The Role of Vocational Teachers and Students

Critical vocational teachers must develop a vision of an antiracist pedagogy that is grounded on a set of vocational, intellectual, and social tools. These tools will help guide the effort to uncover and decode the conditions of racial oppression and help students lead the struggle against such injustices. It is important for critical vocational educators to develop a sense of mis-sion, a vision to fight the various forms of discrimination that undermine nonwhite students' possibility for vocational success. In this respect, voca-tional educators become an integral part of the movement for justice and equality in American schools and American life in general. As part of this movement, vocational teachers work with students and community mem-bers to empower themselves and others by raising consciousness about the mutating nature of racism. Empowerment in this critical pedagogy of voca-tional education also means becoming self-critical, exposing our limitations and hypocrisies as we struggle to overcome them. Rebuilding a minority freedom movement for economic and social justice is no simple undertaking as we teach vocational and academic skills; and critical vocational educators also teach leadership skills that empower them to address the racism that plagues their students (King and Mitchell, 1996; hooks, 1993; Jennings, 1992; West, 1993; Marable, 1992). Although we took a step forward in the long walk toward racial justice in the 1960s and 1970s, we have taken two steps backward in the 1980s and 1990s. We must get back on track.

PART FIVE

The Role of Labor and Unions in Vocational Education

15 *Democratic Unionism in the Global Economy and Corporate-Directed Vocational Education*

In America, labor unions and education have traditionally been kept far away from one another. Many have feared that something dangerous would happen if the two institutions ever got together. In 1996, higher education and organized labor got together during a number of seminars held at various colleges around the country. Large audiences turned out to listen to labor leaders such as AFL-CIO (American Federation of Labor and Congress of Industrial Organizations) president John Sweeney and philosopher Cornel West talk about their common interests in the welfare of workers, the poor, the marginalized, and the country in general (*Nation*, October 28, 1996). The same type of convocation needs to take place between organized labor and public school educators, vocational educators in particular. The "something dangerous" referred to earlier needs to occur in a way that would involve the meshing of interests between a critical education and a democratic union movement. The disparity of influence on vocational education exerted by corporations and businesses as opposed to organized labor is hard to fathom. Part 5 of this book explores the existing relationship between vocational education and labor, while speculating on what this relationship could be in a democratic society, in a critical pedagogy of vocational education.

Listening to Labor

As noted in Chapter 7, the Perkins Act, which was passed in 1984 and reauthorized in 1990, sets the stage for a critical study of organized labor in the vocational education curriculum through its mandate to analyze all aspects of industry and work. If vocational educators are to honor this injunction, they must begin to take the perspectives of labor seriously. Without such attention, the curriculum of vocational education will continue to reflect the narrow interests of corporate leaders who want a compliant, "safe," and nonunion workforce. Indeed, organized labor should have just as much access to students to speak about the virtues of labor union membership as corporations do to speak about the benefits of working for their organizations. To be purposely repetitive, the present disparity of access to vocational education between labor and corporations is unsupportable in a democratic society.

If critical vocational educators are serious about empowering students to shape and determine their working lives, a thorough understanding of labor, its history and possibility, is in order. A progressive work education that prepares students to understand workplace social relations cannot rationalize the prevailing exclusion of labor and union issues from the vocational curriculum. In American vocational programs, teachers are often uncomfortable challenging the discomfort many people harbor concerning the legitimacy of workers to organize for their self-protection. Too often, the only opinion vocational students hear concerning unions is that organized labor is in some way anti-American, that it operates in opposition to the nation's best interests. Since worker empowerment is a central goal in a critical pedagogy of vocational education, the banishment of knowledge about unions and collective bargaining contradicts democratic educational objectives. Students without such understandings are ill equipped to address unfair labor market practices and are more likely to suffer their effects in their own working lives (Levine, 1994; Lakes, 1990; Moberg, April 1, 1996; Zieger, 1994).

When the voice of organized labor is muffled in vocational education, a romanticized view of the workplace fills the silence. Questions of worker alienation are left unaddressed and issues of race, class, and gender discrimination can be more easily avoided. In fact, when the voice of labor is silenced, the way schools relate to work—a question central to this book—is profoundly affected. The nature of the vocational student's civic life in the workplace as well as the political arena is shaped by that student's understanding of the history and social significance of organized labor. Without labor's presence, schools and vocational programs come to be seen as arms of corporations where students learn their "proper" place in the grand hierarchy. A critical vocational education in its commitment to social justice and worker empowerment views knowledge about collective bargaining as a central feature of the vocational curriculum. A democratic vocational education is not neutral about collective bargaining, supporting, as it does, any form of collective bargaining *that justly empowers workers to democratically control their working lives.*

Of course, this lack of neutrality is bound to be misinterpreted. Many will ask how a public school curriculum can overtly support labor over capital.

The critical pedagogy of vocational education proposed here does not simply promote labor over corporate capital. Indeed, such an educational philosophy seeks not to glorify organized labor in America but to criticize it by using the same criteria it applies to the corporate world. And by the way, there is much to criticize about labor in America, both past and present. As Dennis Herschbach (1994) has argued, organized labor in America has traditionally been inhibited by its own social philosophy. Its belief system has centered labor's attention solely on wages, hours, and working conditions, not on larger questions of economic democracy, social justice, and cultural change. Because it has ignored the megatrends that undermine its power and influence, organized labor has failed to protect even its designated interests. Thus, a critical vocational education does not support unions wedded to an inequitable status quo, tied to outdated strategies of protecting existing jobs, or unconcerned with race and gender discrimination within worker ranks.

A democratic progressive vocational education asks hard questions of unions and their collective bargaining practices. It induces vocational students to ask not only how unions will help them but how unions will help the society at large. Will unions challenge bad work? Will they contribute to an economic growth and productivity that will be justly shared? How will unions react to post-Fordist globalization and the downsizing and depressed wages that too often accompany it? Will unions challenge technopower and the politics of corporatism? The type of organized labor supported in a critical educational context works in some situations for more worker influence in corporate decisionmaking, in other sites for elected workers' councils with a legally protected voice in the affairs of the firm, and in some locations for employee ownership through enterprise alliances. A critical vocational education, therefore, supports forms of organized labor that are serious about workplace justice and that seek out new and exciting ways of edifying and empowering the American workforce. The possibilities offered by labor unions with a critical social vision are exciting.

A Critical Unionism?

Many argue that a new era of organized labor is dawning at the end of the twentieth century. New labor leaders and a changing workforce are calling for a more critical form of unionism that comprehends the power of corporations. Unions that understand this politics of corporatism are aware that corporate influence is gained by the ability to explain the world to the public in a manner conducive to business interests. With their access to media and hyperslick advertising, corporations win the battle of ideas with right-wing justifications of growing inequality. The success of such corporate manipulation is manifested in how few workers possess a sophisticated ideological perspective: Many union members do not possess a basic framework for making sense of their declining incomes and lost jobs. The point here is not that many workers are merely uninformed as to the political, economic, and cultural issues of the day; what is alarming is that they have never been exposed to a theory of the world that would help them arrange and interpret their vocational lives. A critical progressive labor movement would provide such assistance: It would fight back against the corporate salvos in the battle of ideas. Critical vocational educators would work with such a movement to make sure that vocational students received another side of the story, a challenge to the right-wing fables with which they are presently bombarded (Bluestone and Bluestone, 1992; Lakes, 1994b; Moberg, April 1, 1996).

Democratic vocational educators want to see critical unionism take part in, if not lead, a new progressive movement dedicated to worker empowerment, economic justice, race, class, and gender equity, and a new era of democratic participation. At the very least, an American prodemocracy movement would provide a countervailing force to refute the corporate claim that American workers' troubles are caused by big government, irresponsible poor people, and dangerous minorities. Of course, such a countermovement by critical unions and the educators who supported them would be positioned by corporate disinformation as a call for class warfare. Vocational educators, contrary to pious corporate spokespeople and their political apologists, have the right to criticize the anticivic actions of American business. In no way does their private status shield corporations from the critical eyes of work educators.

Much of what Americans believe today comes from corporate-sponsored media and conservative think tanks. These ideas seep into vocational classrooms via a variety of conduits, proving that ideas do matter—albeit in ways quite different than in a preelectronically mediated cosmos. The corporate shaping of the political consciousness of workers is so powerful that it takes a socioeconomic earthquake to awaken them from the trance. Add to this the complex nature of the structural changes in both American and world economics over the final fifteen years of the twentieth century and one finds a land of politically confused citizens. Surveys by the AFL-CIO seem to confirm this, indicating that many of the rank and file are "adrift politically." A critical unionism joins with a critical pedagogy of vocational education to address this situation. Unfortunately, the earthquake necessary to awaken the worker "Van Winkles" may be provided by the runaway downsizing of the lean, mean, and automated post-Fordist corporations. However, we can hope that the critical union movement and democratic vocational education will move workers to action before downsizing turns into a jobless future. Organized labor and vocational education must come together in a dynamic alliance that addresses the ever-evolving crisis of the workplace of the new millennium (Moberg, April 1, December 16, 1996; Lakes, 1994a; Cooper, April 8, 1996; Samper and Lakes, 1994).

Keeping Unions Out of Vocational Education

The lack of union participation in secondary school vocational education is conspicuous in its absence. Ironically, apprenticeship training where novices learn a trade under the watchful eye of an experienced worker is the oldest form of vocational education. Such education still takes place, of course, but mostly outside the influence of high schools. No one pays much attention to this omission in the vocational education establishment. Because people are often blind to the power differences between workers and corporate managers, it is not surprising that school leaders infrequently question labor's exclusion. When confronted with the vast difference between the respective roles of organized labor and corporations in vocational education, many school leaders fail to see a problem. "We're not here to teach students about unions," they tell me, "we're here to provide them with the work skills businesses need."

Historically, many unions opposed vocational education because it was so obviously controlled by big business. Labor leaders argued that corporate-dominated vocational education would produce workers willing to labor for little pay and with loyalties to companies, not unions. Because of power differences, labor's concerns were generally dismissed, and as delineated in Part 2, labor eventually acquiesced to the Smith-Hughes Vocational Educational Act of 1917. Soon, however, labor discomfort resurfaced around a number of issues, not least of which was the fact that vocational education consistently failed to explain the purposes and concerns of organized labor. This discomfort has intensified in recent years, as is evident from research showing that vocational (and academic) students are unclear about the history and purpose of trade unionism. When this is combined with mainstream media pronouncements about how union wage increases only spark inflation and how strikes serve only to inconvenience citizens, the image students hold of unions becomes very negative. Make no mistake, critical vocational educators' efforts to include material on unionism in the curriculum will be systematically opposed by many corporations and their political allies (Roberts and Wozniak, 1994; Lakes, 1994a; Grubb, 1978; Pincus, 1980; Copa and Tebbenhoff, 1990; Shor, 1986; Roditi, 1992).

Justifying Unionism in Vocational Education

Work problems in general and work problems specifically in the globalized post-Fordist economy at the end of the twentieth century require more than individual workers struggling alone. Such problems demand collective action—and for this reason unions and collective bargaining need to be included in the vocational curriculum. Without collective organizations, workers are often helpless against authoritarian corporate managers who can require them to attend antiunion meetings on work time, subject them to numerous indignities on a daily basis, and fire them precipitously. At the end of the twentieth century, economic and political power resides asymmetrically in the hands of corporate managers. Critical vocational educators seek to bring balance to an educational and public discourse that assumes that the needs of business be protected at all costs. That view is supported by right-wing neoclassical economic assumptions that position unions as an interruption to the free market's efficient distribution of resources. Despite economic research to the contrary, this viewpoint continues to hold sway in many circles (Simon, Dippo, and Schenke, 1991; Lakes, 1994b; Candaele and Dreirer, 1996; Aronowitz and DiFazio, 1994).

The prevalence of this neoconservative view of unionism reflects the politics of knowledge that operates in contemporary societies. That politics dictates that some bodies of knowledge are more worthy than others. In the case of knowledge production about unions, studies that contradict neoclassical assumptions are often ignored in public debate. This politics of knowledge also shapes research findings, as procorporate studies are generously supported by government and private monies whereas research sensitive to the needs of workers is not. The most obvious example of this political dynamic is the difference between the coverage of business and labor in newspapers and on TV. Although there is a business section of daily newspapers and business news programs on TV networks, there is no similar feature for labor. It is thus not surprising that unionism is underrepresented in both the school curriculum and the public conversation. The tragic result of this, of course, is that without a powerful union voice, millions of working Americans become invisible in the political life of the nation. Such invisibility allows their concerns to go unaddressed and the quality of their lives to deteriorate (Shor and Freire, 1987).

Given these political circumstances, it is not surprising that many have dismissed the role of unions as central players in the democratic process, not to mention in vocational education. Reared in this antiunion information environment, most vocational education students and even most young workers do not understand that management has not always wielded such power over employees. In the medieval period, the master craftsmen of the guilds enjoyed power over the conditions under which journeymen and apprentices labored. As industrialization developed, the need for such expert craftsmen lessened, and power shifted from employee to manager. As more technological skill-displacing machines were invented, employers became increasingly able to undermine worker power. It is at this point in labor history that employers gained the confidence to increase the workday to twelve or fourteen hours and the workweek to six days. At the same time, managers began to bring child laborers into the factory. Abuses steadily increased until labor began to fight back in the last decades of the nineteenth century. Contemporary vocational students need to understand that no divine or natural law dictates the weakness of labor. Labor disempowerment is a human-produced phenomenon; and just as humans shaped such a process, they can similarly reverse it.

Thus, vocational students should be keenly aware not only of the need for unions but also of the benefits unions provide workers. Critical vocational educators point out that union jobs, for example, have fixed hourly rates with regular increments, sick pay, extra compensation for overtime, paid vacations, retirement plans, and other benefits. A brief study of unionism reveals that union jobs pay about 15 to 20 percent higher wages than nonunion positions. It also shows that unionized companies have consistently received higher productivity from their workers than nonunion shops. Contrary to corporate propaganda, it is difficult to find examples of cases where unions have harmed firms or the public interest. There are logical reasons that unions benefit corporations and the economy. Union workers have a lower turnover rate, which saves companies money that can be allocated for training new workers; union workers need less supervision; and a union presence in the workplace induces managers to devise ways to improve productivity in light of union demands for wage increases.

In many ways, this should not be surprising to those who understand that any business runs best when all workers are involved in management. Unions can organize workers in a way that corporate leaders cannot: Managers have to make decisions in the interest of stockholders. Such interests may involve selling the company, moving it to Malaysia, or cutting quality in the interest of increasing quarterly profits. Vocational educators do not teach that stockholders are bad for business or for the country—though maybe sometimes they should. One of the most powerful arguments against the corporate assertion that unions are bad for the economy comes from Germany. At the same time that U.S. unions were shrinking, West German unions were growing—a growth accompanied by some of the highest productivity increases in the world. Despite the rocky road labor has traveled over the last one hundred years and the adversity it has encountered in the last quarter of the twentieth century, labor continues to play a role in the struggle for social justice. At the end of the twentieth century, unfortunately, it remains one of the few national institutions involved in such an activity.

Vocational students should understand that organized labor led the fight against child labor and for the eight-hour workday, safer workplaces, social security, the funding of public education, affordable housing, and improvements in health care. American unions were the leading funder of Dr. Martin Luther King's famous march on Washington in 1963 and played a major role in the passage of the Civil Rights Act and the Voting Rights Act in the same decade. Even in the 1990s—labor's weakest era in seventy years—unions still remain the largest social issues educator for working people. Of course, public schools should take advantage of this union function in both vocational and academic education. Labor union involvement in work, social issues, and education is in the nation's best interest. Organized labor can increase the civic knowledge and political participation of students in a society marked by a debilitating political apathy. It is not difficult to articulate the need for union participation in vocational education; what is difficult is overcoming the business and corporate opposition to it (Bluestone and Bluestone, 1992; Shor, 1986; Candaele and Dreirer, 1996; Spencer, 1995; Moberg, December 16, 1996).

A Brief Overview of Recent Union History

Vocational educators and their students need to understand that unions exist as the result of an ongoing historical struggle over the legitimacy of certain forms of collective action. After the bitter and sometimes bloody labor wars in American cities in the final two decades of the nineteenth century, three great waves of unionization can be identified in the twentieth century. The first wave occurred in the construction trades in the first decade of the century. Among the huge numbers of immigrants who came to America at that time were millions of bricklayers, carpenters, plumbers, electricians, and laborers. Such workers found employment in the urban building boom taking place around the nation. The sophisticated skills of these men (almost all were males) allowed them to obtain union status through the American Federation of Labor. The second wave of unionization was found in the Fordist mass-manufacturing industries in the 1930s. Great armies of workers operated in huge factories and through the provisions of the Wagner Act formed the Congress of Industrial Organizations. This legislation in 1935 legalized worker efforts to fight business's attempts to prohibit unions from existing in their firms. By the end of the 1930s, millions of factory laborers had joined the United Auto Workers (UAW), the United Steelworkers, and the International Union of Electrical Workers, as well as scores of other industrial unions. The face of organized labor in America was dramatically changed by this activity (Simon, Dippo, and Schenke, 1991; Bluestone and Bluestone, 1992).

With the advent of World War II and the industrial production it stimulated, large numbers of new workers hired in firms continued to join industrial unions. The war ended with the power of organized labor stronger than it had ever been before. Fearful of this power, employers began to resist further union demands. Labor leadership in this postwar period became increasingly authoritarian and began to suppress the democratic voice of the rank-and-file membership. Such policies undermined the ability of unions to resist corporate America's quest for workplace control. In the 1950s, American work began to shift away from mass production and toward a service-providing orientation; union numbers continued to decline and political power was further undermined. This decline was temporarily halted in the early to mid-1960s with the election of the pro-union Kennedy and Johnson administrations. When President Kennedy signed an executive order in 1961 affirming the rights of workers in government and the public sphere to organize, the third wave of unionization was initiated. Within months, such unions as the American Federation of Government Employees, the American Federation of State, County, and Municipal Employees, and teacher's unions were founded. The power organized labor gained from this new pool of organized workers was negated, however, by competition between public sector unions. The labor movement was fragmented just at the time in economic history—the collapse of Fordism—when labor solidarity was most needed.

Corporations suffered a sharp decline in profitability as Fordism unraveled in the late 1960s and early 1970s. In order to discipline labor and keep workers from demanding a larger share of corporate profits, corporate leaders and their governmental allies pushed for policies that would increase unemployment. They gambled that fearing layoffs, workers would be less prone to make demands on their employers. Thus, the wages of union workers declined, hours of labor increased, and the ability to purchase housing and medical insurance deteriorated. In turn, union membership declined, organizational efforts fell short, secure contracts with management were abrogated, and public support of union politics diminished. When international competition, capital mobility, and dramatic technological change were added to this mix, labor became more and more subservient to capital. Smelling labor blood, corporations in the mid-1970s launched an all-out attack against unions. Union-busting consulting firms were hired, and corporations spent hundreds of millions of dollars to destroy unions. The hard work paid off for corporations, as unions grew so weak that they could not even hold on to the contracts they had previously negotiated; corporate managers forced labor to give up the hard-earned concessions of the past fifty years. Where unions refused to give up their contracts, corporate managers often closed their plants and moved them to a nonunion locale (Herschbach, 1994; Bowles, Gordon, and Weisskopf, 1990; Zieger, 1994).

Corporate managers called this plant-closing scheme their "Southern strategy." When they had targeted a particular union they wanted to bust, management would demand contract renegotiation, typically in a plant in the Northeast or the industrial Midwest. If the union balked, the corporation would move the plant to a Southern state where unions were weak or, better yet, nonexistent. Scores of corporations employed the Southern strategy, including Pepsi, General Mills, Mead Paper, Weyerhauser, Mobil Oil, Goodyear, Firestone, and Piper Aircraft. At the same time they were bashing labor with the Southern strategy, corporations used their political clout to push for both lower corporate taxes and the defeat of labor-law reform that would facilitate union organizing. The law known as the Labor Law Reform of 1978 was a very moderate piece of legislation designed to help unions survive in flagrantly antiunion companies such as J. P. Stevens, the Southern textile producer. The corporate overreaction to the law revealed the intensity of the corporate campaign against the unions. It also revealed the growth of corporate power, as the law was defeated in the Congress.

During this period of corporate aggression, which began in the 1970s and early 1980s, the press virtually ignored the sea change in corporate policy. Once again, the politics of knowledge reflected and exacerbated corporate power. In the Reagan era, from 1981 to 1989, the Republican Party's efforts to undermine unions were carried out with little public knowledge about what was happening to organized labor; indeed, it was a topic rarely broached in vocational education. The most visible antiunion action was taken by President Reagan soon after he took office in 1981. That summer, Reagan moved to defeat a strike by the Professional Air Traffic Controllers Organization (PATCO) by destroying the union. But not satisfied with merely destroying the union, the president mandated a lifetime ban on federal rehiring of the members of the ex-union. These actions signaled to employers everywhere that it was open season on organized labor. The AFL-CIO concluded soon thereafter that Reagan and his allies were operating under the belief that unions were a harmful dinosaur that disrupted an orderly free market economy. Soon, corporate raiders such as Frank Lorenzo at Eastern Airlines were encouraged to squash their workers' unions without mercy.

Reagan's response to PATCO was portrayed in the media as the action of a no-nonsense, take-charge president facing down a bloated, arrogant union at high noon. The corporate raiders were often depicted as lone gunmen single-handedly making themselves a fortune in the best American entrepreneurial tradition. They were "men's men" who would stand up to any group that interfered with their star-spangled right to make money. Thus, many Americans cheered the frontal assault on labor. And that political climate created a new economic world. In this corporate "econotopia," auto manufacturers such as Ford, for example, could tell the United Auto Workers to go to hell. If the union refused to relinquish benefits and wage levels, Ford would simply close its U.S. plants. General Motors acted similarly, pitting one plant's workers against another's in a bidding war to see which group would give up the most to stay open. In one incident, workers in Arlington, Texas, won a "concession contest" against workers in Ypsilanti, Michigan, by agreeing to a three-shift, twenty-four-hour work schedule with no overtime pay. Auto manufacturers had laid down the gauntlet to the workers: Concede, or face the consequences (Reich, 1995; Bowles, Gordon, and Weisskopf, 1990; Zieger, 1994; Barnet and Cavanagh, 1994).

With the advent of this corporate antiunion extremism, labor was forced to rethink its traditional modus operandi. The conservative tradition of American labor was unable to provide workers with responses adequate to the harsh new reality. Unions historically had not challenged management's prerogative to determine questions of production, the geographic location of plants, finance, marketing, and pricing. Traditionally, American unions had not challenged the assumptions behind management science and its efforts to efficiently (not necessarily humanely) deploy workers in production. In the management discourse, of course, men and women are less human beings than objects to be managed, that is, they are simply human capital. Personnel management strives to adjust workers to unequal power relations while inducing them to identify with the corporation—not with the experiences they have in common. Many union members and leaders armed with a detailed knowledge of how corporate managers have thwarted them over the last quarter of the twentieth century are calling for a new unionism that breaks with the conservative labor tradition.

In its new articulation, this critical unionism would educate workers to the insidious manifestations of corporate domination. They would not only study management's control of the workplace and production but also learn about the techniques of managerial science that are used to manipulate workers in ways that run contrary to their well-being. When these critical understandings are combined with union organizational efforts aimed at professional workers caught in the deindustrialization policies of their corporate employers, the possibility of democratic action emerges. Authors, writers, journalists and other knowledge-producers, along with women, minorities, and recent immigrants working in low-skill, low-wage jobs, compose the core of what may become a progressive fourth wave of unionization. A democratic, egalitarian, debureaucratized union movement with a critical educational agenda can help lead America in the twenty-first century toward the realization of the democratic dream that has for so long been given only lip service (Wirth, 1983; Ferguson, 1984; Bluestone and Bluestone, 1992).

Self-Inflicted Wounds: The Failure of American Labor

As if an all-out attack by corporations and conservative government were not enough, labor leadership in post–World War II America tended to be myopic at best, criminal at worst. As the corporate assault reached unprecedented levels of viciousness, one would think that unions could have rallied their troops to action. However, for the most part, the rank and file accepted the destruction of their job security and future plans often without raising a hand. The "strong arm of labor" corporate leaders had once so feared had lost not only its strength but also its will to muster it. Just at the time working people most needed their collective organizations, they viewed them as part of the larger problem afflicting laboring people. In many new plants that opened in the 1980s and the early 1990s, workers defeated union organizing plans, often dancing and reveling to celebrate their victories against organizations they held in disdain. The reasons for such attitudes are complex and must be carefully examined, but in many cases, younger white workers grounded their opposition on generational and racial issues. As established unions attempted to protect their longtime members by enhancing their job security, younger members felt pushed out and neglected. Also, the extent to which organized labor had worked with African American advocates to include more black members evoked a backlash from young white workers who saw the entry of nonwhites into their unions as another obstacle to their economic opportunity.

Having swallowed the omnipresent right-wing version of the "real" world as presented by Reagan, Bush, Limbaugh, Ollie North, and Christian fundamentalists, such workers saw their unions as part of the antiwhite liberal establishment. Corporate leaders could not have wished for a more fortuitous turn of events. Organized labor could provide little political or moral leadership to these confused and angry young workers. Unions not only had few leaders who could offer a compelling response to the right-wing narrative, they had no social memory of labor resistance to injustice to pass along to young workers. Indeed, a working-class culture of solidarity had disappeared over the decades and, along with it, any ideology of labor rights or recognition of the forces that threatened such rights. Before a new critical unionism that works with and informs a democratic progressive vocational education is possible, an analysis of labor's contribution to this degraded position (labor's own failures) must be carefully analyzed (Barnet and Cavanagh, 1994; Zieger, 1994; Cooper, April 8, 1996).

Without a strong sense of what it takes to empower workers, to help them make sense of power relations in the larger society, and to protect themselves from corporate domination, unions had no light to guide them through the turbulent period after 1945. In the 1950s, for example, the unions were caught up in management's celebration of new technology in the workplace. Accepting without sufficient analysis management's claim that automation in the factories would create more high-tech jobs than would be lost, unions were unprepared to counter the developing technopower of corporations. The only response labor seemed willing to offer was a call for more retraining. In fact, one of the most important fruits of labor political action was the passage in 1962 of the Manpower Development Training Act. This legislation was designed to provide training for workers who lost their jobs to automation. The central mistake labor made in this era involved not negotiating for a share of the productivity gains derived from automation. Since workers were "paying" for productivity by losing their jobs, they could have demanded shorter workweeks and increased wages. Instead, as more jobs were lost, union membership decreased and the decline of organized labor was accelerated (Rifkin, 1995).

Organized labor's leadership had chosen to live a comfortable life in ideological subordination to corporations. Labor leadership began to emulate corporate management, as union bosses became autocratic barons of organizational bureaucracies designed to keep workers in line and to not make waves (Aronowitz and DiFazio, 1994; Greider, 1992). During this era, workers in America lost the help of a mediating institution to protect them from the expanding power of the corporate world. Ben Hamper, the rivethead, expressed the growing cynicism of workers about the unions that had once represented their interests. The United Auto Workers Union, he said, was

> nothing more than a powerless puppet show groveling in the muck . . . The workers from Pontiac seemed cold, indifferent, resigned to the fact that their union was nothing more than a charade and that management took full advantage of the fact. The only guy I ever spoke with was the worker right beside me, a Pontiac native named Jim. The guy was a total mess. He used to show up for work drunk—an astounding accomplishment when you stopped to consider it wasn't even daylight yet. It wasn't long before the two of us were tippin' together. (Hamper, 1992, pp. 225, 227–228)

Whereas individual unions did advocate for the workers and addressed the pressing issues of the day, organized labor as a larger institution was for the most part impotent. Although labor supported civil rights legislation on the national level, its record in dealing with racial discrimination at the workplace level is far less impressive. Indeed, union membership was often (and continues to be) an obstacle rather than a facilitator for nonwhite workers wanting entrance into a skilled craft. Workers from all demographic backgrounds were unhappy with their unions, and in this context, unions as a political force collapsed. By the 1980s, almost one-half of union workers were not voting in national elections—and even fewer voted in state and local elections. By 1988, less than one-fifth of blue-collar workers voted for the Democratic presidential candidate—a statistic unimaginable a generation earlier. Understanding such an abrupt change in worker sentiment involves a wide range of social awarenesses that concern growing corporate power and the politics of knowledge. But incompetence and highly visible corruption in some unions also played an important role. In the Teamsters

Union, for example, President Jackie Presser flaunted his indictment for fraud and extortion in outlandish displays of arrogance and extravagance. At the 1986 Teamsters' convention in Las Vegas, for example, Presser spent $647,960 of union funds for the opening-night party. At one point in the evening, the three-hundred-pound Presser was carried into the party by weight lifters in Roman centurion attire, as the crowd shouted "Hail, Caesar!" This was probably not the best public relations operation ever devised for dues-paying union members and the American people in general.

Corporate-driven media had a field day with such union stupidity. Representing union leaders as dishonest buffoons who hang on to outdated work rules that undermine the nation's economy, corporate leaders and their allies were able to use union blunders to elicit a deep resentment against them among Americans from various demographic categories. Such public disdain induced unions to turn inward, forgoing recruitment and promising merely to take care of the members they already had. The dinosaurs who took control of many of the union locals during this period were not interested in issues of social justice, race and gender equality, a union-influenced vocational education, or anything else a critical democratic labor movement would value. Such local leaders demoralize workers and subvert attempts to establish a new labor movement dedicated to a critical education and worker empowerment. With the power cards stacked against it, organized labor cannot afford self-inflicted wounds. The need for a politically informed, smart, democratic, civic-minded, and ethical labor movement is greater at the end of the century than ever before (Herschbach, 1994; Zieger, 1994; Bluestone and Bluestone, 1992; Cooper, March 24, 1997).

Crumbling Support for Labor:
The Need for Unions in the Post-Fordist Economy

As argued throughout this book, the techtopian pronouncements by business, government, and education leaders concerning the high-skill workplace of the twenty-first century are a misleading hoax. Unfortunately, the primary victims are workers, although everyone will eventually suffer an adverse impact. With improving technologies in the 1970s, corporations were able to expand in ways and into places previously unimagined. New horizontal corporate organizations were created—multinational conglomerates—that owned companies in a variety of sectors. One conglomerate, for example, might own firms in steel, electric power, banking, and entertainment. U.S. Steel changed its name to USX after steel production was reduced to merely one division within a huge international conglomerate. As newer and bigger conglomerates emerged, they began to take advantage of their global access to achieve higher profit margins through lower labor costs. Having refused to make technological improvements in the 1960s that would have made them competitive with Japanese and European industries, U.S. conglomerates could not sell their products as cheaply as the more cost-efficient foreign firms. They therefore came to see lower labor costs as their only salvation, thus the unprecedented attacks on workers and unions during the period.

Economic historians will judge corporate leaders of the 1960s, 1970s, and 1980s very harshly because, in essence, they allowed their advantage as the leading industrial producers in the world to slip away. Realizing their failure by the mid-1970s, they went looking for scapegoats. First, there were the competitors, specifically the Japanese and the Germans. Although we can find some unfair trade practices that disadvantaged American businesses, such problems were not the cause of declining corporate profit margins or stagnation in domestic living standards. The improvements in Asian and European economies did not have to harm American industry at all. Indeed, more savvy managers could have exploited the new markets for American goods created by the foreign prosperity. The second scapegoat, of course, was labor, with its outrageous demands and growing incompetence. In retrospect, it is amazing that corporate leaders were able to sell the public on the view that U.S. economic problems were the fault of workers and their unions. The seed was implanted in the minds of many that organized labor undermined American economic competitiveness with its selfish interests and un-American social philosophy. Thus, in the post-Fordist era of corporate globalization, workers need the protection of organized labor against corporate attacks on both their image and economic well-being (Aronowitz and DiFazio, 1994; Bluestone and Bluestone, 1992; Herschbach, 1994).

Organized labor must gain a voice to counter the deflection by corporate spokespersons and corporate-influenced media of honest discussions of America's economic troubles and their causes. In an era of falling wages for workers and a continuing contraction of full-time jobs, it is indicative of the power of corporations that such issues are infrequently referenced in the public conversation. Why, for example, are there no TV shows on any of the "157" cable channels concerning the power, influence, and effects of multinational conglomerates? Little is said about the fact that the corporate profit boom of the 1980s and 1990s was unevenly shared and that in both the United States and the world in general, the chasm between those who gain and those who are excluded from the benefits continues to expand. Little news is reported about the new labor policies of corporations such as Caterpillar Tractor, which, for example, when faced with a strike by the UAW in spring 1992 refused to negotiate and hired replacement workers. After having bargained with the UAW for forty years, Caterpillar's management recognized the weakness of organized labor and decided not to deal with unions any longer. Thus, labor was further weakened, and the disparity in wealth between managers and workers grew even greater.

Caterpillar's success induced other companies to force strikes, hire lower-paid substitutes, and make their firms union-free. Whenever union activists fought back, courts imposed severe penalties and heavy fines. The message was clear: Organized labor's right to strike was being undermined. Between 1978 and 1992, for example, the number of strikes involving more than 1,000 employees fell from 235 to 35. After years of corporate power plays, government had begun to ignore the unfair labor practices that were further eroding the weakened labor movement. Employees who worked to form unions were being fired, whereas employers who broke the law could fight the charges with legal war chests and battalions of lawyers. When corporations were convicted of illegal dealings with their employees, penalties were notoriously minimal. Hopes were raised that such a poisoned atmosphere could be reformed by the election of Democrat Bill Clinton in 1992. Unfortunately, Clinton soon proved to be almost as corporate-friendly as his Republican predecessors, Presidents Reagan and Bush. In November 1993, Clinton worked for the North American Free Trade Agreement (NAFTA), despite organized labor's opposition to it. The president valued the agreement for its encouraging U.S. corporations to profit from Mexico's low-wage workers and feeble environmental protection laws.

Labor was shocked by Clinton's dismissal of their concerns and in the wake of the agreement's passage realized that working people had no one to help them but the union movement. The realization hit them that the "new Democrats" were almost as uncomfortable with organized labor and working people as the Republicans. Clinton's administration has not challenged the corporate co-opting of agencies designed to help workers, such as the Occupational Safety and Health Act (OSHA), the Environmental Protection Agency (EPA), and the National Labor Relations Board (NLRB). Although these agencies have differing origins and operate for different purposes, none of them presently serves the interests of working people in the ways originally intended. The NLRB, for example, formed in 1935 to facilitate collective bargaining, has been used in the last fifteen years to enforce federal decisions designed to curb union influence. Corporate leaders and their political allies have bought into a philosophy of economic growth at any cost; and if one of the costs involves the degradation of workers, then so be it. Both Republicans and Democrats now operate in the name of "progrowth," meaning they will not adopt any policies that interfere with businesses generating wealth. Sustainable economic growth is still possible when workers' rights and well-being are protected, when the environment is preserved, and when the forces that bind communities together are respected.

Organized labor is direly needed in an era when corporate and governmental leaders fail to think in terms of the relation of economic policies to the needs of human beings. Businesses at the end of the twentieth century operate as if they had no understanding of what life is like for workers who lose their jobs and their economic security in the downsizing of the lean and mean post-Fordist company. When the Staley Company was planning to fire a large number of middle managers in 1992, corporate leaders asked the local clergy in Decatur, Illinois, to help the group deal with the job loss. That move symbolizes the politics of the era, as economic leaders feign concern for the victims of their policies. Any worker who was fired so that quarterly profit margins could be raised is not going to be impressed by his bosses' arrangement of clerical counseling. Crocodile tears for discarded workers may be good public relations for a media-driven society, but workers understand the moral emptiness behind it. I am always amazed at how well corporations can muster public relations; even after all the layoffs, downsizing, and lowering of wages, corporate leaders have been able to convince many Americans that individual economic difficulty is caused by the personal weaknesses of the individual (Reich, 1995; Greider, 1992; Barnet and Cavanagh, 1994; Zieger, 1994; Cooper, May 27, 1996; Herschbach, 1994).

Globalization's Threat to Unionism: Corporate Infidelity

A new critically grounded labor movement that participates in a democratic vocational education is extremely important in light of corporate mobility and civic irresponsibility. Corporations have massaged the political system in a way that allows them to do virtually anything they want in a globalized economy, moving factories and jobs to wherever short-term profits can be enhanced. The key feature of this corporate economic freedom that unions must reveal to the American public involves business leaders' disregard for how their uninhibited pursuit of profit hurts both individuals and the society at large. If profits are to be increased, who cares what happens to the workers and the communities that are left behind? Although corporations speak the public relations rhetoric of patriotism and loyalty to America, their actions reveal a very different set of priorities.

Post-Fordist international conglomerates are no better international citizens than they are American citizens. With globalization and its capital mobility, American companies have exported their social irresponsibility. Take one international location of corporate mobility—northern Mexico. Over the past twenty-five years, around 1,500 American plants have been constructed along the U.S.-Mexican border. Jobs with wages over $10 an hour in the American Midwest are performed by Mexican (often young women) workers for around $1 per hour. Everyone except the corporate leaders is hurt by this arrangement. American workers, of course, lose their jobs and are forced to take lower-paying positions; contrary to the disinformation distributed by the corporations, Mexican workers and the Mexican economy have not gained from this economic setup. Wages from American firms are sometimes lower than subsistence level; and Mexican children as young as fourteen are being taken out of schools to work in the border (or *maquiladora*) plants. The impact of globalization both domestically and internationally is easily discerned in this circumstance: lower pay for workers, less job security, and more power for corporations. In America, the globalized future portends fewer and fewer jobs for American workers.

The long-term effects of the deindustrialization process, or corporate downsizing, in the globalized economy have yet to be felt by American society as a whole. Old factory-type jobs are long gone, of course, but well-paid professional, technical, and production jobs are now on the hit list. As more and more workers in these areas lose their jobs, a new socioeconomic class of people will begin to experience the effects of the new economic order. No matter what one's class, the loss of jobs now and in the coming years will cause great psychological trauma. Indeed, many argue that the industrialized modernist world is facing the disappearance of labor. As the exaggerated promise of high-tech jobs fades into the discourse of a previous era, poverty rates soar in the silicon corridors from California to Massachusetts. Because of corporate America's response to globalization, many middle- and upper-middle-class whites will be experiencing some of the same job-loss issues that have been faced by minority and blue-collar workers over the last couple of decades (Cooper, May 27, 1996; Greider, 1992; Aronowitz and DiFazio, 1994; Rifkin, 1995).

A strong democratic union movement could help vocational students and the general public not only understand these macroeconomic dynamics but also alert them to the policies that exacerbate their traumatic impact. Western European and North American governments have been cutting social programs for unemployed workers just as the effects of downsizing and capital migration have begun to intensify. In Europe, the effects of automation and corporate restructuring, combined with social cuts, have evoked tremendous anger among a variety of groups. One manifestation of this alienation and anger has been protests; another has involved an increase in crime and random violence. Signs that a *Clockwork Orange*–type of future is possible, with roving bands of unemployed individuals wreaking havoc on a frightened population, are sobering in their horror. Empirical studies have indicated a correlation between a rise in unemployment and an increase in violent crime. In one study, a 1 percent rise in unemployment was accompanied by a 6.7 percent increase in the murder rate (Rifkin, 1995, p. 208). The same study displayed a disturbing correlation between economic disparity and criminal activity, in many ways not a surprising finding on further analysis. The corporate-governmental decision arrived at over the last couple of decades that the United States could no longer afford social justice may prove to be one of the great mistakes of American nationhood.

When conservative groups speak of social breakdown in American society—the decline of the family, welfare mothers, teen pregnancy—further study reveals unmentioned issues of unemployment, falling wages, and job insecurity somewhere in the social mix. In the everyday discourse of politics, right-wing spokespersons often dismiss these factors, as they fix blame to the individuals in crisis. The cruel policies and the personal recriminations cannot continue without a response. A democratic union movement and a critical vocational education want the response to be forceful but grounded on a set of humane, life-affirming, and egalitarian principles. Unfortunately, the response may not take this form. In Germany, Italy, Russia, and the United States, one can observe in varying degrees emerging neofascist and hate-filled right-wing agitation. "We can't do anything about these problems," corporate leaders proclaim. "The market shapes our economic conditions," the argument goes, "and there is little humans can do about it. Leave things alone—the invisible hand will eventually make it well."

A democratic union movement is especially important in light of these corporate attitudes and actions. One of the most important reasons for the American economic downturn over the last three decades has been corporate mismanagement. As argued elsewhere in this book, declines in productivity and increases in unemployment and underemployment are the direct result of decisions made by corporate leaders. Emphasis on "portfolio management"—a euphemism for the cutthroat practices of mergers and acquisitions—drains the energy of the business world's best minds and diverts the attention of companies away from improvements and innovations in product lines. Operating units that produce goods and services are viewed as expendable, temporary properties to be disposed of whenever portfolios become imbalanced in one way or another. Workers in such a financial arrangement become expendable pawns whose lives and families are irrelevant in these immediate profit-making monopoly games. A democratic union movement is needed to help workers understand the difference between what employers and schools say they do and *what they actually do*. A critical union will inform workers and students of the desire of many corporations to control prices for raw materials, the costs of the goods and services they produce, and the inputs into their production systems. The desire for such control demands that government and unions keep away from what corporate leaders see as their free market prerogatives.

Workers and students need to understand that over the years, corporate leaders and their business organizations (the National Association of Manufacturers, for example) have fought against humane reforms such as child labor prohibitions, public education, the eight-hour workday, workers' compensation, unemployment benefits, social security, truth in advertising, food and drug safety laws, antiracial and gender discrimination laws, workplace safety, and environmental protection legislation. They have also worked to thwart workers' efforts to organize, to procure fair wages, and to gain information about the production process and the economic conditions surrounding it. Given the vicious demands of quarterly profit margins, corporate leaders continue to fight against policies that are in the long-term interests of workers, the job market, the environment, the society, or even their own companies. A democratic union movement and a critical vocational education must address the "tyranny of the short term." Corporate infidelity to the most basic features of civic responsibility must be addressed if the future is to hold any promise (Gordon, 1996; Rifkin, 1995; Bluestone and Bluestone, 1992; Barnet and Cavanagh, 1994).

16 *The New Unionism and the Struggle for a Democratic Social Movement*

Without a progressive social and labor movement to keep them honest, corporations can use their electronic public relations machines to convince the public of their patriotism, generosity, and compassion. Such image building helps corporations politically, as it provides armor against hostile political attacks from egalitarian critics. Positive corporate images also help hide firms' antisocial behavior and shape the public conversation about the political economy in a way that enhances their quarterly profit margins. Corporate public relations has been amazingly successful in light of its twenty-year-old class war against working people. Despite the increase in productivity and record corporate profits, wages continue to decline and layoffs continue to rise. The ratio between the earnings of U.S. corporate executives and the average U.S. worker reached 187 to 1 in the late 1990s. And, in the public discourse on economic issues, corporate leaders and their political allies have turned the term "class warfare" into their critics' acts of making reference to these inequalities (*Nation*, April 8, 1996; Greider, 1992).

Vocational Education as Diversionary Tactic: Battle Plans of Class Warfare

Obviously, these are bad times for workers, for the students who have traditionally been tracked into vocational education. Unions' ability to organize workers, for example, always declines during difficult economic times. Additionally, in technologically sophisticated contemporary workplaces, workers who sit at computer terminals all day long may have little time to interact with their fellow workers. The opportunity to develop a workplace culture and a sense of worker solidarity is undermined by the technical organization of the office. When work design is dictated by technology, the culture of the workplace is permanently modified. A progressive union movement understands this dynamic and reshapes its strategies to organize workers under these new conditions. Also, these technological innovations have created a new class of skilled technical workers who never identified with the goals of unionism—but neither has unionism identified with them. Until the 1990s, this group of workers possessed both high incomes and job security. In the late 1990s, with their wages falling and their job security long gone, these skilled workers need union protection. In the present climate, the new pool of part-time workers has also fallen through the cracks of traditional unionism. Obviously, new economic times demand profound changes in union operations (Herschbach, 1994; Aronowitz and DiFazio, 1994; Greider, 1992).

As corporations continue their class warfare, their struggle to maintain their power advantage against unions and workers, they keep developing new mechanisms of control. Frederick W. Taylor would be proud of the new methods of worker surveillance that have developed in the last couple of decades to supervise workers, including computer tracking of practically every move an employee makes. Economists estimate that around 34 million people in the United States are hired to police workers—about one monitor for every 2.3 workers. Never have unions faced the reality of such a well-supervised and controlled workforce. As discussed in Chapter 7, new reforms in vocational education such as the secretary of labor's Commission on Achieving Necessary Skills promote "adapting students to the high-skill workplace." Almost never do the reforms mention that unproblematized adaptation of vocational students to the high-tech workplaces is politically dangerous. Adaptation ignores the conflict between management and worker interests, the new methods of surveillance and control being deployed in technologically innovative firms, and the antiunion maneuvers of corporate leaders. SCANS, like many other vocational educational reforms, tacitly presupposes that management needs take precedence over labor needs in shaping work and vocational education.

When vocational education merely adjusts workers to high-tech jobs, it not only supports the interests of management but it provides corporations with a diversionary tactic to take the public's mind off of corporations' antisocial behavior. American businesses have used vocational education and worker retraining as ways to remedy the job losses that result from their own downsizing and deindustrialization. The Business Roundtable, a representative organization of American companies, maintains that vocational training is the best way to interrupt the downward mobility of workers. This assertion adeptly shifts the blame for joblessness away from corporations and onto the backs of vocational students and workers. The corporate argument is that when facing a shortage of skilled workers, better training is necessary. The idea of a "skill shortage" is a corporate hoax, many labor economists argue. Indeed, many corporations that use the skill-shortage ploy have dramatically reduced their American-based facilities over the last two decades and have moved their corporations to undeveloped countries with low literacy rates and a large pool of unschooled workers. General Electric, for example, has mustered much vocal support for the need for education to address the skill shortage, but since 1981, it has closed more than fifty U.S. plants and fired more than 50,000 workers. The workers fired were not merely unskilled laborers or low-level functionaries but skilled workers such as machinists, electricians, engineers, and even white-collar managers (Schwartz, 1994; Levine, 1994; Greider, 1992). Where is this skill shortage? Vocational students need to understand these dynamics.

The Emergence of a New Labor Movement in the 1990s

In many labor rallies in the late 1990s, one can sense a new union movement emerging. In some meetings, Latino dishwashers, African American maids, nurses of all colors, and white men wearing hard hats stood together calling for the solidarity of working people. New-style union activists are talking about preparing a new cadre of workers who will instigate a new wave of social justice in America. John Sweeney's rise to the presidency of the AFL-CIO has raised hopes and invigorated labor activists who have been fighting against the odds for years. Polls are beginning to reflect the moderate success of the new unionism, as after an era of overt hostility, Americans are expressing more and more sympathy for organized labor. Late-twentieth-century union organizers are finding, much to their delight, that millions of workers want to join unions. They have not joined up until now because of disillusionment with union corruption and the plethora of laws and regulations that inhibit union organizing. Indeed, because of this unsafe labor climate, many workers are afraid that attempting to join a union will induce management to fire them. About one-half of the U.S. labor force identifies with the interests of organized labor, but only about 15 percent belong to unions. That statistic implies the power of corporate politics and antiunion legislation to weaken the position of organized labor.

New labor leaders are reaching out to groups long alienated from unions. The series of academic meetings between labor and university professors and students referred to in the opening paragraphs of Chapter 15 have brought together intellectuals and workers in a manner unheard of since before their disagreements about U.S. policy in Vietnam in the late 1960s. Union members and academics are working together in this new labor movement because they believe the good of the country depends on it. They do not want to see the continuation of the growth of disparity between the well-being of the have and the have-nots and the multitude of problems such inequality precipitates. In these and other meetings, the new labor leaders are winning people's trust with concrete evidence of their commitment to clean up corrupt unions and turn them into democratic organizations. The new leaders are listening to the rank and file and are grounding their reforms on bottom-up recommendations. The entire culture of unionism is changing, as members connect activities such as recruitment, elections, collective bargaining, coalition building, and goal formulation with a commitment to share power throughout the organization. Although most unions have been democratic and corruption free all along, the organizations that were corrupt spoiled the image of the institution as a whole. The work of the new labor leaders is designed to reform those last few unions whose leadership has so seriously damaged the interests of working people (Cooper, March 24, 1997; McClure, 1992; Moberg, April 1, December 16, 1996; Zieger, 1994; *Nation*, October 28, 1996).

Of course, the new unionism not only addresses the antidemocratic practices of unions but also speaks out against the antidemocratic practices and ploys of management. In particular, participants in the new movements have asked union members and the public to examine the results of union attempts to cooperate with corporations and their worker-involvement projects over the last twenty years. Quality of Work Life programs, ostensibly designed to empower workers, have often served merely to quicken the pace and raise the stress of workers without even any compensation through increased wages. Labor cooperation has often been elicited by managers for joint management-union education programs. Too often, corporate leaders have failed to deliver on promises to include workers in decisionmaking and the formulation of the educational curriculum. The new unionism therefore views corporations with suspicion and is not as willing to sign cooperative agreements as labor has been over recent decades.

Several unions have elected leaders dedicated to many of these democratic principles. In the United Auto Workers, a group of workers formed what they called a New Directions Movement that offers an alternative critical vision for the entire union movement. In the United Mine Workers, Richard Trumka, a lawyer from the West Virginia coal fields, led a movement in the late 1980s against undemocratic and inept union leadership. In New York, Dennis Rivera helped guide a movement of hospital workers in an embrace of grassroots activism and social diversity. After seventeen years of organizing by Teamsters for a Democratic Union, Ron Carey beat two status-quo supporting candidates in the Teamsters' election in 1991. Reelected in 1996, Carey and his supporters have fought many battles against old-guard Teamsters and employers. The Teamsters ought to become a much more democratic and clean union as a result of these activists' work, although problems within Carey's camp set back the cleanup efforts. Similar types of reforms have taken place in the International Longshoremen's and Warehousemen's Union and in the New York City local of the Transport Workers Union (Roberts and Wozniak, 1994; McClure, 1992; Early, 1997; Zieger, 1994).

One of the most important unions in the new labor movement is the Service Employers International Union (SEIU). Representing men and women who perform some of society's most unpleasant jobs, the SEIU has developed fascinating strategies to call attention to their plight as workers. In 1987, the union deployed its "Justice for Janitors" strategy in various locations around the country. Because of the way government agencies have come to regulate union organizing and protesting, the SEIU has chosen to garner attention with one-night walkouts. The Justice for Janitors movement has used this and other tactics such as publicly bringing shame on the owners and tenants of office buildings where the unionized janitors work. In this modus operandi, janitors crash owners' dinner parties and ply the owners' neighborhoods with leaflets explaining their participation in unjust practices. The unjust practices involve actions by groups such as the owners and managers of urban office buildings. These individuals often hire independent contractors to clean their buildings who have won in competitive bidding for the job. The contractors who charge the least then pay the janitors who work for them the lowest wages. When the SEIU organizes janitors in a particular company and bargains for a better contract on their behalf, the owners and managers of the buildings immediately fire the unionized contractor and hire a new nonunion cleaning company.

That practice keeps individual janitor salaries below $10,000 for full-time annual employment. But, amazingly, most janitors at urban office buildings do not get full-time hours, as employers typically keep their shifts below four hours a day. This ploy works to exclude the janitors from the benefits firms must make available to full-time workers: health insurance, pensions, paid vacations, and sick leaves. Very few Americans are aware of the obstacles these hardworking individuals face in their effort to make a living and often classify them within the great species of humans deemed lazy, violence prone, and deserving of their low-status lot. Even individuals who work in the office buildings in question do not know about the janitors, since they leave work before the janitors come on their night shifts. Newspapers, not surprisingly, have ignored the entire controversy; even the creative tactics employed by the janitors are not reported.

The janitors and the SEIU have learned about the various dimensions of the economic situation they confront. Understanding how little janitor salaries take from the overall costs of building management, the workers have become even more assertive in pressing their agendas. And amazingly, in this era of labor disempowerment, they won some concessions from the office owners and managers who did not want to be publicly embarrassed any more. The Justice for Janitors campaign, inspired by its success, began to attack inequity for janitors in other contexts. Moving the campaign and its creative tactics to California's Silicon Valley, the SEIU has made important inroads into the gross disparities between janitors and professionals in this high-tech context. The union is pressing for a comprehensive master contract that guarantees its workers a 20 percent pay hike, health coverage, an education fund supported by employers, and a guaranteed ceiling on employee workloads. The Justice for Janitors program teaches a lesson to all vocational students about critical citizenship and union organizing at the end of the twentieth century. Unfortunately, political and economic changes are rarely produced via electing individuals to office or supporting the passage of legislation; the corporate grip on both political parties in America is simply too tight at this juncture. Students and citizens learn from the janitors that political and economic strides can be made by being well informed and by confronting power wielders directly and persistently (Cooper, May 27, 1996; Greider, 1992).

The emergence of a new labor movement at the end of the millennium depends on organizing the presently unorganized. Along with the SEIU, a number of well-informed, committed unions have worked over the last decade to organize disenfranchised service workers. Traditionally, individuals who worked in hotels, amusement parks, hospitals, nursing homes, and colleges and universities have not been unionized. Union activists in the SEIU; the American Federation of State, County, and Municipal Employees; the Hospital Workers Union, and the Communications Workers Union understood that unlike manufacturers, owners of these service enterprises simply cannot pick up and move to northern Mexico. As a result, significant progress has been made in organizing these neglected, underpaid, and unrespected laborers. Not surprisingly, a large percentage of the unorganized workers in the service domain are women and minorities. Such workers quickly became leaders in organizational and recruitment efforts, devising creative campaigns among workers such as Los Angeles Latinos employed as janitors and the Harvard University clerical staff. By the mid-1990s, two out of three newly organized workers were women. This statistic illustrates not only the ability to organize the unorganized but also the changing nature of the new union movement.

By the late 1990s, American unions had become more integrated by race and gender than any other institutions in America except for the military and the Catholic Church. Indeed, a critical democratic labor movement can do more to help low-wage, low-status workers than almost any other social institution. It can do much to help women workers, who, unfortunately, still have to manage households as well as hold down a job. Already, the SEIU and the Communications Workers Union have negotiated shorter workweeks for women in such a position. Consciousness of such problems and issues of race, class, and gender have moved progressive AFL-CIO president John Sweeney to fill the organization's leadership and executive council with far more women and minorities than ever before. Sweeney wants union leadership to reflect demographically the workforce that American unions are attempting to organize. A democratic union movement dedicated to making sure that marginalized youth get an education and a job could provide some hope to students who now believe that there are no jobs for them. Believing they have no viable employment future and that there is no institution concerned with their specific problems, such young people sense far more possibility in joining gangs and engaging in criminal activity (Gowen, 1994; Zieger, 1994; Greider, 1992; Moberg, April 1, 1996; Rifkin, 1995).

Sweeney and the other leaders of the new labor movement have come to acknowledge the relationship between multicultural issues and the reality of class oppression in America. Appreciating the point emphasized in Part 4 of this book—that race, class, and gender issues cannot be separated—the new union movement understands that white male workers must work for justice for all workers regardless of race, ethnicity, and gender if the new labor movement is to succeed. American labor cannot allow itself to be fractured around questions of race and gender any longer. Corporate leaders and right-wing politicians have counted on such divisions to subvert the power that an organized workforce might wield. To make sure the divisions stay in place, such individuals have often fanned the flames of racial, ethnic, and gender conflict. Nothing undermines the effort to create social and economic justice more than these racial and gender fissures among workers.

Guided by these precepts, Sweeney and the new leadership have learned from their new nontraditional members. Before his election to the presidency of the AFL-CIO, Sweeney was president of the SEIU. In his new position, Sweeney has brought tactics from the Justice for Janitors movement to American labor as a whole, teaching workers to use their information to embarrass corporate leaders about their antidemocratic, antienvironmental, and anticivic activities. Sweeney and the janitors want Americans to understand that economic unfairness is destroying their country, who the winners and losers are in the information-based economy, and that there is a need to transcend the traditional narrow concerns of American unionism. Sweeney, the janitors, and the emerging multicultural leadership of the AFL-CIO want unions to be educational agencies that hold up for examination the ways of seeing that allow for the growth of social and economic injustice and the steady increase of corporate power. In an electronic media–saturated culture, such pedagogical goals must be addressed in a smart, attention-grabbing, and creative manner. With this imperative in mind, the AFL-CIO has in the late 1990s established a $20 million organizing fund for both recruiting and political work. Young workers and students are being attracted to Union Summer campaigns, where they learn a wealth of information about union restructuring, corporate activity, and ways of energizing the labor movement. Vocational teachers and students could profit from attending such a program.

The new unionism is learning from Swedish unions that educational activities are central to union growth and goal attainment. So important is this dynamic to Swedish workers that they have formed the Workers Education

Association to organize 150,000 educational circles involving 1,400,000 people. With large governmental grants and union contributions, the pedagogical work of Swedish unions presents quite a model for labor and educational organizations. When such educational commitments are combined with strategies such as the United Auto Workers' "work-to-rule" campaign, the potential for dramatic cultural work presents itself. The work-to-rule effort pressured management to respect workers and accept the positive role of the union in the wake of corporate efforts to destroy unionism once and for all. When work-to-rule strategies to reinvigorate the "already organized" with frequent and enthusiastic parking lot rallies, ministrikes, and shop-floor network rebuilding are combined with educational groups that study corporate and governmental practices and their effects on workers, good things begin to happen. Benefits from such activities include the construction of a worker and citizen consciousness that values social and economic justice (*Nation*, October 28, 1996; Cooper, May 27, 1996; Moberg, April 1, 1996; Eiger, 1982; Zieger, 1994).

New Labor Strategies

Helping Prepare Workers for an Uncertain Future

Not only must the new unionism prepare workers to construct a democratic culture of work (good work), but it must help organize workers to fight the job-destroying policies of the post-Fordist corporation. With jobs of all types being terminated every day, workers cannot face the uncertainty of the future alone. A savvy, power-conscious union movement will insist that employers—not just workers—share the social and economic costs of the problems that confront the financial realm. So far in the United States, workers have paid the costs of globalization with their jobs and their wages. Corporate leaders have absorbed none of the liabilities, as their salaries have risen in relation to the number of workers fired in their industries. Thus, the money saved in corporate downsizing has not been used mostly for production improvements but rather for corporate managers' salaries and horizontal expansion (buying other nonrelated industries).

In light of these unfair and inequitable corporate job policies, the new unions must push for shorter workweeks. Aronowitz and DiFazio (1994) have called for a thirty-hour workweek with no reduction in pay. The last time working hours were reduced was with the passage of the federal wage and hour law in 1938. In the last six decades, the United States has witnessed a gradual increase in working hours, with people holding two and three jobs and scrambling for overtime. As many working Americans labor their lives away, the quality of their lives has deteriorated. Indeed, many of the family, health, and larger social problems we face result from overwork and low-pay in bad jobs. Concurrently, this expansion of working hours has fanned the flames of unemployment and poverty among those individuals excluded from the labor system. As the workweek and the workday become shorter, workers would begin to share in the economic gains coming from the rise in productivity. In the globalized, downsized economy, workers' rewards would not come in the form of rising income but, at least in the beginning, in reduced work hours. Given the economic projections, workers in the first decade of the twenty-first century may find that 20 to 30 million jobs may be lost unless the workweek is shortened (Roberts and Wozniak, 1994; Herschbach, 1994; Aronowitz, 1992; Aronowitz and DiFazio, 1994; Rifkin, 1995).

It is with ideas like these and many others that labor will contribute to the struggle for social justice. Sweeney at the AFL-CIO is very concerned with ideas and ideological understandings. One area of particular interest is international labor organization in the globalized economy. In this sphere, the new leadership at the AFL-CIO is attempting to move its international concerns away from Cold War issues and toward questions of global solidarity with workers exploited by multinational corporations. The union wants to challenge the power of corporations both in the United States and internationally as part of a larger movement for social and economic democracy. In this context, the need for a progressive labor newspaper becomes very important for the new unionism. Almost 2 million people a day read the *Wall Street Journal*, a paper that plays a significant role in setting the public conversation, not to mention the agenda of TV and radio, concerning corporate affairs. Everyone knows that the paper represents the world from the perspective of corporate leaders and the private sector, but that does not seem to undermine its influence.

If businesspeople and the well-to-do can have a newspaper, why not plumbers, mechanics, janitors, service workers, and progressive vocational education teachers and their students? Such a paper could help worker researchers and vocational educators gather information about white-collar crime as well as crime in the streets, formulate responses to power wielders, and analyze proposals for democratic renewal. Coverage of labor has practically vanished from daily newspapers and their wire services, and the press has all but abrogated its traditional responsibility as a corporate watchdog. A labor daily could provide a voice for those who hold the least power within the society and fill the moral void in U.S. journalism. The idea is not new, according to Fred Schied (1993), who has written about workers' newspapers in Chicago in the nineteenth century in *Learning in a Social Context: Workers and Adult Education in Nineteenth-Century Chicago*. In the first decades of the twentieth century, a Kansas City–based workers' weekly—the *Appeal to Reason*—had a paid circulation of over 760,000. If such a paper could exist almost a century ago, a modern labor newspaper can be produced for the twenty-first century (Sherman, 1997; Moberg, April 1, 1996).

Issues such as the formation of a labor daily newspaper are part of a larger critical social vision that sees education as a central objective of progressive social movements. Union members and vocational educators must understand in detail the economic conditions of American business and the context in which firms operate. The new union leaders understand that all the strides they have made through collective bargaining and educational campaigns may be lost if corporate leaders fail to concern themselves with productivity, quality, and innovation. When quarterly profits dictate that decisionmaking and portfolio building in the buying and selling of companies become the primary corporate goal, managerial disinterest in questions of production is often the result. This realization has been learned the hard way by many U.S. workers who have watched such disinterest destroy their jobs and undermine their wages. An educational campaign that alerts workers to such possibilities, provides them with the expertise to expose such destructive corporate practices, and teaches them to build coalitions among the many parties affected by them is a central priority of the new unionism.

Like a critical pedagogy of vocational education, the new unionism forges alliances with a variety of institutions and groups around social issues. Canadian unions provide a model for ways of addressing social issues and connecting a number of diverse organizations. Joining with women's groups and racial alliances, Canadian unions have produced information and provided classes on employment equity, sexual and racial harassment, the destructiveness of world poverty, domestic violence, and problems of individuals with physical handicaps. One of the most important issues for Canadian unions has involved the environment. The 1990s have witnessed the development of a number of courses on workers and environment by Canadian unions, among them Union Environmental Action, Workers and the Environment, and Pollution Prevention. Although environmentalism has sometimes been a divisive issue among union members, this is not to say that union workers are antienvironment. Too often, environmentalists have pursued a narrow agenda that has been less than sensitive to job issues. Frequently operating as an upper-middle-class movement, environmentalism has not attempted to see the world from the perspective of working-class individuals. Canadian unions have worked to bridge the gap between the two groups and show both environmentalists and workers their intersecting interests.

Canadian unions understand that long-term employment is an important goal, and they thus reject the crass environmental damage caused by some corporations in resource extraction. Some corporate activity may serve the interests of quarterly profit margins but not the needs of workers who want long-term jobs. Also, it is often the families of the workers who have to grow up in the shadows of factories with dangerous discharges. Many unions have issued policy statements that insist that it is not contradictory for workers to choose both economic security and environmental health for themselves, their families, and their progeny. In this context, Canadian unions published a book entitled *Sustainable Development*, which argues that this double goal can be achieved by way of a critical view of economic development. That viewpoint demands that economic growth take place only when the natural resource base is not merely conserved but enhanced. Sustainable development is grounded on the appreciation of renewable resources. In this respect, Canadian unions stand ready to expose those corporations that fail to respect these environmental concerns (Aronowitz, 1992; Bluestone and Bluestone, 1992; Spencer, 1995).

Turning Up the Heat

In an era when the legal system allows temporary and permanent replacement workers for strikers and the threat of deindustrialization and corporate transnational migration is omnipresent, labor strikes just do not have the impact they used to have. Thus, unions have to turn up the heat on corporations in ever-evolving ways. An excellent example of such labor strategies comes from United Steelworkers Local 9121 in its struggle against Bayou Steel and RSR, one of the planet's biggest lead smelters. The steelworkers bypassed the old tactic of striking by gathering information on their employers. They investigated the corporate conglomerate's affiliated companies, checked their environmental records, put together consumer boycotts, and informed regulatory agencies of their findings. Located in La Place, Louisiana, Local 9121 was offered a contract in 1993 that conceded no pay increases for six years and gave Bayou Steel's management the right to contract out any job the steelworkers performed. To gain leverage after such a profound defeat on their contract, the steelworkers begin to study patterns of corporate violations at Bayou Steel and its affiliated company, RSR.

It was not difficult to find such violations, and a series of the corporation's environmental abuses came to light. Illegal storage of hazardous waste, illegal exportation of hazardous waste to Mexico, the construction of a fourteen-acre mountain of toxic lead (the runoff was contaminating the land of Mexican farmers and small communities), violations of lead-emission standards in New York, and lead poisoning of minority children in Dallas were just a few of the corporate abuses exposed by the union. With this data in hand, the steelworkers found out where the corporation was planning to open new plants and inundated the local media with documentation of the company's checkered past. In Aiken, South Carolina, where RSR was preparing to build a $65 million operation, ads were published in local papers, billboards proclaiming "Lead Kills" were put up, and environmental groups were supplied with information. Just as RSR hired a public relations man to market itself to Aiken's African American community, the steelworkers exposed new indictments of RSR in Indianapolis for knowingly violating the Clean Water Act. Subsequently, RSR personnel (including an upper-level manager who would have directed the South Carolina plant) pled guilty to lead pollution of a waterway, and submitting falsified reports and false documents to the Environmental Protection Agency. In light of this revelation, the Aiken officials rejected RSR's proposal to open its plant.

The union also challenged what it considered bogus tax breaks by Bayou Steel. The company had been awarded $49 million in corporate tax relief for what it spent on tax-deductible "capital improvements." One of these improvements was a $177,000 security system used to maintain surveillance on union picketers. The steelworkers publicized serious violations at the Bayou Steel plant, including safety abuses and the overexposure of employees to airborne lead and cadmium. So successful was the union's strategy that environmental groups now overtly support the steelworkers and refer to RSR as a leading polluter and environmental offender in North America. The success of these turning-up-the-heat strategies has motivated corporations to pull out their big guns, to deploy the power of their legal departments to render union information campaigns illegal. Joining forces, corporate leaders have met to pressure federal lawmakers to bar such tactics under the righteous mantle of making sure "that the American workplace is a constructive arena in which the employee and the employer can work together" (Press, 1996).

Thus, in the name of happy and cooperative workplaces, corporations want to revoke contemporary unions' latest method of fighting against sometimes overwhelming corporate power. After the steelworkers' victories, both RSR and Bayou Steel sued the union under the provisions of the Racketeer Influence and Corrupt Organizations Act (RICO). The suit accuses the union of undermining the corporations' business contracts and financial relations by propagating misrepresentations and negative statements to third parties around the world. Other corporations began to follow RSR and Bayou Steel's lead: the Food Lion Supermarket company sued the United Food and Commercial Workers and the Sun Healthcare Group sued the SEIU. The AFL-CIO is confident that the First Amendment's protection of free speech will protect these education campaigns. One would think this would be the case, but given the legal and political climate of the last few years, one can never be certain. Corporations with cadres of lawyers and armies of powerful lobbyists have attempted to change the rules when unions fight back. Still, corporations would not be working so hard to squelch labor if the educational campaigns were not burning them.

Turning up the heat on corporations does not mean acting in an irresponsible manner. When facing a crass class war, unions must act in ways to defend themselves and their interests. When employers act in the interests of the economy, their employees, and the society at large, then organized labor is willing to help corporations face the tough demands of globalization. In this regard, the new unionism will embrace what Irving and Barry Bluestone label the "Enterprise Compact."

1. The union and management agree to pursue mutually established productivity growth targets.
2. Wage and compensation goals are set that are consistent with productivity growth in order to maintain global competitiveness.
3. Price setting in the company is subject to joint action by union and management.
4. Quality is a "strikeable" issue, to assure that products and service meet or exceed international standards.
5. Employment security is guaranteed for the company's workforce.
6. Extra financial rewards are provided through profit and gain sharing throughout the enterprise.

Finally, at the very center of the Enterprise Compact and reinforcing all its other provisions:

7. The union and management agree to joint decisionmaking throughout the firm, including labor representation on the company's board of directors. With this, the last remnants of the traditional workplace contract's "management-rights" clause are abolished. (Bluestone and Bluestone, 1992, p. 26)

The Enterprise Compact does not represent some Disneyland "Workworld," where labor and management magically become bed partners and live happily ever after. Unlike corporate proclamations that the workplace should be "a constructive arena in which employee and employer can work together" (Press, 1996, p. 29), the Bluestones' compact demands that workers be treated with dignity before any talk of cooperation can begin. If corporations are willing to meet the tenets of the compact, then the new unionism will drop clumsy and bureaucratic work rules designed under their fear of persistent job insecurity and the threat of capricious managerial workplace action. Such rules—often used by management to argue against the continued existence of unions—are exemplified by the concept of featherbedding: keeping job positions that are no longer needed because of changes in the needs of production or technological changes. Such flagrant impediments to productivity will have no place in an industry where good work is the order of the day.

A compact of this sort will be increasingly difficult to maintain in an era of job compression. Although such contracts should be pursued wherever and whenever possible, the new unionism must be ready to take unprecedented measures in the difficult years of the new century. Organized labor in the post-Fordist globalized economy will have to move into the arena of worker-union cooperatives. There are many styles and variations of this idea, starting with profit sharing (allowing employees to share in company profits via cash bonuses or granting of company stock). Although profit sharing allows workers to profit in line with the success of the company, it changes nothing about the nature of the labor process in which workers engage. Conceivably, profit-sharing workers could participate in low-skill, bad work, with managers still making all decisions and worker talent remaining untapped. Of course, critical vocational educators promote a more unprecedented form of worker-union cooperative, in which workers totally own companies and, accordingly, sit on boards of directors, plan how their labor should be organized, and shape the financial policies of the organization. It is for this type of economic activity that critical democratic vocational educators want to prepare vocational education students.

Such a progressive vision can work only if the new unions and their workers understand the multitude of demands it places upon them and their allies in various social and educational institutions. One of the most important of these demands involves effectively organizing workers from around the world—especially those who have been affected by multinational corporations and their oppressive practices. Already, Sweeney's AFL-CIO has developed the Center for Strategic Campaigns to help domestic and foreign unions counter the omnipresent power of multinational conglomerates. Unionists, social activists, cultural workers, and progressive vocational educators must understand that in order to achieve social and economic justice and the good work it supports, labor needs and strategies must be coordinated internationally. National unions are dinosaurs in the globalized economy. In the auto industry, for example, moves are being made to synchronize bargaining and positions on social issues in response to transnational automobile manufacturers. The new UAW is working to renew its affiliation with the Canadian Auto Workers Union, which broke apart in the mid-1980s. The New Directions Movement won the UAW election on a platform the Canadian union had been advocating for years. Now that they are more philosophically aligned, the U.S. and Canadian auto unions are in touch not only with each other but with Mexican and other automobile unions around the world. If the Mexican unions were affiliated with U.S., Canadian, and other auto unions around the world, they would not be so easily shoved aside by manufacturers.

I do not mean to sensationalize these issues, but the type of future that awaits us could depend in part on the success of these international organizational efforts. A dystopia of growing unemployment, falling wages, and global economic depression awaits us without a countervailing international force to curb the socioeconomic pathologies of the multinationals and to help educate the world's peoples about the destructive qualities of a unregulated market economy. Indeed, the success of these union efforts will help determine how the wealth of the globalized economy is distributed. If unions fail and the wealth generated flows only to corporate coffers, stockholder earnings, and elite knowledge workers, then the escalating gap between rich and poor and the hopelessness of the marginalized will lead to social and political convulsions around the world. A fair distribution of the wealth and the pursuit of good work are not only moral issues; they are hard, pragmatic questions of survival (Schwartz, 1994; Bluestone and Bluestone, 1992; Roberts and Wozniak, 1994; Moberg, April 1, 1996; McClure, 1992, p. 22; Rifkin, 1995).

Critical Networking: Constructing the Labor Curriculum

The new unionism provides an unprecedented opportunity for a labor–vocational education collaboration. Focusing on issues of economic democracy and social justice, union members and educators can begin to conceptualize the technical and academic skills and understandings students will need to survive and thrive in the evolving globalized socioeconomic and political environment of the twenty-first century. As I argued in *Toil and Trouble: Good Work, Smart Workers, and the Integration of Academic and Vocational Education*, the skills vocational students will need involve the integration of academic and vocational understandings. There is no longer any justification for an exclusively vocational education. Academic and vocational integration can be grounded in part on the labor issues addressed in Part 5. In this context, vocational educators can develop a curriculum that engages issues of economics, history, sociology, political science, literature, science and technology, and mathematics. What a powerful and empowering educational experience such a curriculum could provide when organized by teachers with an understanding of the concepts and subject matter involved, the purpose of such a pedagogy, and the social vision around which it evolved.

To pull off such an academic coup, vocational educators would need to cultivate allies within a variety of progressive unions who could provide them with resources, practical experiences, and other forms of expertise. A synergistic interaction could take place when the progressive union members sought out vocational educators and critical educators sought out union members. Together, these progressive agents could structure alliances with other groups and individuals in the local area and, with the convenience of E-mail and other forms of communication, establish relationships of ideological solidarity with workers and teachers around the planet. The corporate domination of the vocational curriculum can only be overcome with the establishment of large and diverse coalitions that transcend numer-

ous boundaries—racial, gender, class, religious, ethnic, national, and professional. As the new unions begin to build international worker solidarity,
they can share their networks with vocational teachers, who can then team
up with individuals around the world for pedagogical collaboration. In this
situation, teachers, students, workers, and other people could develop ongoing dialogues about their mutual problems and common values. They
could figure out creative methods of helping and supporting one another in
their struggle for good work and critical forms of democracy.

Experiences like these could help Americans overcome their intellectual
isolation from the rest of the world. Taking a cue from the Coalition for Justice, formed by the AFL-CIO in alliance with more than sixty environmental, religious, and community organizations to address corporate abuses in
the *maquiladores* (the American plants in northern Mexico), progressive vocational teachers could form international partnerships with like-minded vocational educators around the world. Such vocational educators, for example, could make contact with the worker researchers in Sweden and learn
how to form international research teams to support their mutual endeavors
and pedagogical projects. As the new unionism moves American labor organizations away from their exclusive concern with workplace issues such as
contract wages, benefits, and conditions, an excellent opportunity is presented for vocational educators to make use of unions' new attention to social, macroeconomic, and educational questions. With the Perkins Act mandate that "all aspects" of work be taught to vocational students, the window
for critical action is opened even more widely (Roditi, 1992; Spencer,
1995).

The critical labor curriculum and the alliances that can help support it are
both centered around the notion that there is absolutely nothing about
work that demands the treatment of workers as noncitizens, as entities to be
used and degraded. When employees are denied—as they often are in the
late 1990s—freedom of speech, privacy, the option to determine their own
style of life, freedom from searches and undue surveillance, and protection
from capricious discipline and unjustified termination, the efficacy of American democracy is subverted. When employees must submit to drug testing
and top executives do not have to, class position takes precedence over the
rights of citizenship. Recent court decisions have strengthened employers'
power by affirming their right to silence employee speech. In *Waters v.
Churchill* (May 1994), the U.S. Supreme Court sided with hospital administrators against a nurse in a matter involving employees' free speech.
Churchill was a nurse who was overheard criticizing the hospital's policy of
moving nurses from one department to another when staff shortages developed. In a conversation with another nurse, Churchill argued that the reas-
signed nurses posed a potential hazard because of their lack of training in
the new area. After the comments were passed along to supervisors,

Churchill—an employee of the hospital for many years—was fired for comments that were "nonsupportive" of the administrative leadership.

The inclusion of workers' rights and court cases such as *Waters v. Churchill* in the vocational curriculum illustrate to students the need for organized protection in the management-friendly work climate of the late twentieth century. Students would therefore come to appreciate the International Workers of the World (IWW) model of unions as communities rather than insurance companies. In these early-twentieth-century labor communities, the IWW imagined the integration of the political, the economic, and the social. Taking a cue from such a holistic integration of these various domains of life, the communities that we envision emerging from the networks formed by the new unionists and critical vocational educators would add another sphere—the pedagogical. Such critical communities would educate young workers as well as help them shape their ideological identities. From these diverse social spheres, the foundation for a new labor bloc would emerge that would permanently transform both American education and American politics. Vocational educators could draw upon the networks for information, materials, and resource people; political activists could make use of them as a reliable base of support for campaigning and grassroots activism.

One key aspect of the critical labor curriculum would involve alerting students to the way corporations and other power wielders "regulate" populations. Although the techniques of Taylorism have long been abandoned for a more subtle form of regulation, the spirit of Taylor lives on in corporate managers' discussions of the control of the "human element." As discussed in Chapter 3, the legacy of Taylorism dictates that managers mold employee work ethics, channel their emotional energy, deny the existence of conflict, and fashion a smooth-running but unjust workplace. Vocational students analyzing these dynamics come to understand that the language of management works assiduously to avoid any reference to power or power relations. When workers, teachers, or public figures do broach the topic, corporate leaders and their allies often misrepresent such power references as hate-mongering, fear-producing demagoguery. In the critical curriculum, vocational students learn the plethora of management techniques deployed to erase power and the inequality of power distribution (Reich, 1995; Aronowitz, 1992; Moberg, December 16, 1996; Ferguson, 1984).

As vocational students study the concept of workplace democracy, they work together with teachers to design a variety of research projects. In this curricular format, students might focus on the status of workers' rights in the globalized economy, making use of insights obtained from critical networks consisting of union members, academics, and social justice organizations. In such inquiry projects, these vocational students might establish E-mail connections with workers and unions around the world that have won victories involving issues of economic planning, the organization of work, and personnel management. Vocational students can learn from the experiences of workers around the world who have had to deal firsthand with the power of megacorporations and international conglomerates. For example, students can study what happens when a mobile post-Fordist plant decides to relocate. Swedish workers who have experienced such trauma and devised alternatives to it could help vocational students and teachers prepare others for this all too common post-Fordist occurrence.

Faced with such a depressing situation, many Swedish workers formed study groups to research the reasons for and the effects of corporate decisions to close factories. On one occasion, when a steel manufacturer decided to close down a factory, workers invited two TV documentary filmmakers to record what they were doing to respond to the policy. Not only did the steelworkers broadcast the reasons and effects of the shutdown, but they put forth their proposals on how they could use both their skills and the abandoned plant facilities to manufacture alternative steel products. By taking ownership of the deserted plant and inducing lawmakers to pass some supportive legislation, the Swedish steelworkers could take charge of their own lives and in the bargain help their community maintain its tax base and its economic health. Vocational students can learn profound lessons from such research involving the post-Fordist globalized economic realities they will have to face, vocational problem solving, the links between their jobs and the well-being of the community, and the necessity of worker solidarity.

This concept of worker solidarity is extremely important in the critical vocational curriculum. Worker and trade union solidarity, when grounded on a philosophical platform of social and economic justice, can not only change the workplace but begin to lay the groundwork for changing the world. This notion of solidarity among workers and its extension to human beings in general underlies the critical curriculum's emphasis on social action. Vocational students must come to understand the connection between knowing and acting. As Ira Shor (1988) has asked, "How do humans act on the knowledge we discover in the classroom" (pp. 107–108)? This knowledge-action connection demonstrates to vocational students that the critical curriculum is not merely empty talk; it has connections to the making of history; it cannot be separated from the way we live our lives. In this action orientation, the critical vocational curriculum becomes an integral aspect of larger democratic social movements. Vocational students who have previously felt like outsiders and outcasts find new self-definitions as players in the major sociodrama of our time—the quest for justice.

As players in the struggle for good work, vocational students gain a new vantage point on contemporary labor news and labor history. They listen to elderly union members recollect stories of labor disputes and strikes with a new consciousness, a new way of making such stories meaningful. The same goes for their analyses of Hollywood movies and TV's depiction of workers and unions, with the sensationalizing of physical conflict and tragedy and the downplaying of social, political, and economic significance. In this dramatic context, mainstream Hollywood is long on seamstresses flinging themselves out of windows in factory fires and violent gangsters' enforcing union bosses' control of, say, the waterfront. Vocational students with a critical consciousness begin to pick out the negative patterns and stereotypes within these media formats and to assess the impact they exert on labor's sociopolitical position. As critical researchers, vocational students and their teachers begin to compile data and data bases in conjunction with the new unions. Whereas Swedish and other international unionists built libraries for students and workers, critical students, teachers, unionists, and other cultural workers make web pages on the Internet and use resources such as Labornet. New labor wants a larger voice in work education in both the private and public sectors. As more international unions, district councils, and locals provide educational funding for their brothers and sisters, the networks that connect vocational educators, academics, and cultural workers become ever more essential to success. Union-directed education like vocational education needs a detailed understanding of the pedagogical, economic, political, epistemological, and social dynamics delineated throughout this book (Herschbach, 1994; Eiger, 1982; Lakes, 1990; Shor, 1988; Levi, 1996; Roberts and Wozniak, 1994).

Integrating Vocational Education, the New Unionism, and the Global Economy's Declining Need for Workers

The massive job loss caused by corporate downsizing has predominantly been viewed by Americans as private troubles, the burden of particular unlucky individuals. Thus, such escalating job decline has yet to affect most Americans' ideological outlook or the mainstream discourse of vocational education. Although evidence of the effects of such social realities can be found among the membership of the new unionism and other groups and individuals, debate among vocational educators about job loss and the increase in bad work is still hard to find. Does it matter to vocational educators that the fastest-growing job categories at the end of the century are often characterized by assembly-line work in cramped, dirty, dangerous, and unhealthful conditions, for example, work in the poultry industry? The other domain where job growth is occurring is in clerical work. Such labor has been drastically speeded up, controlled by high-tech surveillance, limited to repetitive tasks that are hazardous to workers' health.

One would think that such profound rearrangements of work—an upheaval as grand and convulsive as the Industrial Revolution—would move education for work to rethink its priorities in the new context, to reconsider its purpose. So far, at least, this has not been the case. Vocational educators must face the simple but important truth: A good work education matters little if there are no jobs. Despite the proclamations of corporate leaders and their Democratic and Republican political allies, no one has provided convincing evidence of where skilled jobs in the twenty-first century are going to be found. Contrary to the corporate implication that a better-educated workforce will keep employers from exporting jobs, factories will continue to be built in Third World locales and jobs will continue to be lost. When these factors are combined with increasing job loss from automation, the skilled-job future grows even more dismal. Government officials and vocational educators do not want to deal with this problem. How do we tell the workers of the future that they are being misled?

The old human-capital development approach does not wash in the post-Fordist globalized economy. Mainstream liberal reformers of vocational education speak from the beds they share with corporate leaders about high-techtopias fueled by innovative school-to-work programs. They just cannot admit that "better human capital" does not necessarily lead to job-market success in the globalized marketplace. Thus, vocational students need more than mere functional skills to negotiate the slippery slopes of the globalized economy. A critical pedagogy of work education in a way becomes a civics for workers. It is a citizenship education that provides a critical lens through which students can examine the social role of work, demonstrates how students can develop and deploy their critical powers, grants opportunities to cultivate solidarity through collective activities, and encourages a mode of thinking about labor as a contribution to the good of the community. In this critical civics context, vocational students understand the possibility of work in relationship to the ways it can become a source of alienation and injustice.

The importance of unionism is highlighted by the exaggerated alienation and injustice workers experience in the post-Fordist globalized economy. These exaggerated inequities call for a new paradigm in vocational education that transcends merely acquainting workers with more sophisticated electronic technologies or new managerial practices that call for more participation in shop-floor decisionmaking. In this new critical paradigm, students learn that the track record of recent American corporate leadership has not been exemplary, as managers have not exercised the best judgment in running their companies. Vocational students study these blunders in the larger effort to learn about the ways strategic decisions are made in companies. They come to appreciate in this pedagogical context the factors that help shape whether a firm succeeds or fails, including the dynamics of pricing, accounting, design, engineering, advertising, marketing, investment, and subcontracting. In this way, they learn those things about corporations that will empower both their personal participation in democratic unions and the unions themselves.

Just as the steelworkers learned in their struggle with Bayou Steel and RSR, vocational students in critical classrooms appreciate the patterns of managerial blunders and corporate abuse. They learn, for example, that companies that punish workers also tend to be irresponsible citizens and environmental polluters and that the advertisements companies produce for TV often promote corporate images that are very different from reality. When these corporate patterns are combined with job downsizing, the need for well-informed, courageous, and creative vocational students and workers takes on a new urgency. Such savvy citizen workers devise ways in which organized labor can induce corporations to work for the public good. Informed about these civic matters, critical citizen-workers can insist that the irrationality of the educational status quo be challenged: Instead of thinking in terms of how citizen-workers can be better trained to serve the economic order, we should consider how the economic order should be reformulated to serve the citizen-workers. These, of course, are some of the foundational concepts for the democratic new union movement (Reich, 1995; Rifkin, 1995; Roberts and Wozniak, 1994; Lakes, 1994a; Levine, 1994; Bluestone and Bluestone, 1992; Press, 1996).

Vocational Education and Critical Unionism's Push for Industrial Democracy

Critical vocational educators have hoped that the shared governance rhetoric of the high-tech post-Fordist workplace was genuine but have feared all along that it was not. Eager to embrace corporate calls for the democratization of work, such educators have seen worker hopes betrayed too many times. Because of the weak worker empowerment record of American firms of the 1990s, critical educators need to forge alliances with progressive unions in order to teach vocational students about industrial democracy. Workers in an industrial democracy govern themselves and often own their own companies. Given the problems facing workers over the coming years, lessons on industrial democracy and concepts such as consumer cooperatives become very important for vocational students. In consumer co-ops, for example, consumers are the proprietors. Students can help themselves and community members set up co-ops in which shareholders divide profits or divert them back into the organization. Entire vocational classes could be constructed around the formation of co-ops, through which students can make money for themselves, the school, and the community, learn about the formation of community-friendly businesses, solicit the help of labor unions in the administration of such enterprises, and discover practical alternatives to the unfair and unhealthy practices that often taint the contemporary marketplace. Consumer co-ops are one of many ways worker civics is encouraged, a process where vocational students, workers, and the community are brought together for the collective good.

When vocational educators and unionists join forces for industrial democracy, a critical pedagogy of worker self-rule emerges. Vocational education in this empowered context profoundly disconnects with the status quo and its human resource development. Students begin to learn about "what could be" and its relationship to "what is." Critical vocational teachers stimulate students' social imagination via their engagement with alternative democratic modes of economic and political community development. The imaginative is thereby integrated with the pragmatic, as teachers induce students to study the particulars of worker-managed companies such as the I.G.P. Insurance Company in Washington state, several timber cooperatives in the Pacific Northwest, and Valley Care Cooperative (a Waterbury, Connecticut–based home health care enterprise). Workers at Valley Care Cooperative not only own their company and earn a living but are constantly learning and improving their literacy through Freirean educational strategies. The cooperative consists of thirty African American and Latina home care aides who administer the health needs of elderly people in the local area. The women workers study labor-management concerns and examine the workings of cooperative business ventures. The cooperative is so successful that many new worker-operated home care cooperatives are being founded around the country (Lakes, 1994b; Schwartz, 1994; Shor, 1988; Samper and Lakes, 1994).

Valley Care Cooperative provides a model for the type of vocational education called for in this book. All vocational educators can learn from the multidimensional work taking place in this enterprise. If unions were to lend their support and expertise to such efforts, a new social movement could be initiated that would profoundly change the American social and educational landscape. Worker-owned and worker-operated, union-assisted, socially responsible, and education-based enterprises can become prototypes for twenty-first century democracy. Vocational educators can play a central role in this movement through their special ability to connect a critical social vision and an education for work skills and worker citizenship to a set of public problems. The way such a process could be aided by government and other institutions is the focus of Chapters 17 and 18.

PART SIX

*A Vision of Government,
Vocational Education,
and the Future*

17 *Worker Civics: The Decline of the Nation-State and the Rise of Corporate Government*

When the world changes and power shifts as much as it has over the past few decades, critical analysts maintain that changes in governance are necessary. The way a society views the role of the state directly shapes its educational institutions. The manner in which American government has responded or failed to respond to particular socioeconomic changes at the end of the twentieth century has directly affected vocational education and the role of work in our society. Political liberty has been jeopardized by economic forces—the same forces that dictate that economically poor and racially marginalized students be siphoned into vocational educational tracks characterized by low expectations. Critical vocational educators understand that the notion of free competition in the name of liberty does not work either in the marketplace or the schoolhouse. The assumption that everyone starts from the same location and holds equal access to necessary resources is false. Critical vocational educators thus advise pedagogical interventions into the education of marginalized students and governmental and civic interventions into unfair economic practices. Without such action, hierarchies develop and inequality is exaggerated. In relation to their understanding of power, inequality, the role of work in society, and a democratic pedagogy of vocational education grounded on social and economic justice, such educators develop a vision of a just and practical government for the new century. Such appreciations constitute an integral part of what might be termed a "worker civics."

A Critical Vision of Government

A regressive modernist view of government, like Cartesian-Newtonian thought in general, fragments our perspective and forces us to see government simply as a discrete political dynamic. Government in a more critical perspective is viewed as part of a larger political, economic, social, techno-

logical, and ethical context. Perceiving this complex context allows observers to understand that a decontextualized government that sees itself
functioning only in a political sphere cannot address the forces that shape it
in contemporary society. The concentration of economic power by corporations over the last twenty years, for example, has dramatically changed the
way governments operate. Without the benefit of this economic context and
the reforms that a knowledge of it necessitate, government would soon become as superfluous as socks on a rooster. To avoid such a reality, critical
observers argue that a new social contract is needed that explicitly addresses
the ways concentrated economic power undermines political freedom. That
contract would specify limits to the economic inequality that a democratic
society can tolerate (Freeman and Gilbert, 1992; Reich, 1995).

American government at the end of the century has lost sight of the fact
that when the poor fail, everyone will eventually pay for it. Thus, social justice is not merely a moral question but a pragmatic strategy for survival.
Government's modernist predisposition for scientific rationalism removes
political leaders and bureaucratic functionaries from the suffering of the
poor and their feelings of marginalization. Governmental efficiency does
not address the sense of injustice felt by the marginalized. When the marginalized speak of their hurt and their emotions, they cannot understand
why no one in policymaking positions listens. Policy experts who speak
about economics with the authority of science do not perceive the relevance
of the emotional pronouncements of the dispossessed to the subject. When,
for example, members from the Justice for Janitors campaign testify about
their plight, government economists operating on a different epistemological set of assumptions see only uninformed individuals emotionally clouding
the relevant issues at hand. The economists are blind to the connection between their policies and the economic difficulties groups like the janitors
must face daily. Operating outside the rationalistic discourse of positivistic
economics, the janitors, their neighbors, and their families recognize the
economists' blindness—their "rational irrationality."

A central feature of the power bloc's ability to dominate those who fall
outside its boundaries involves its ability to use scientific rationality over human emotions. The understanding of this epistemological dynamic, this rational irrationality is, of course, a central feature of a critical vocational education curriculum. In the governmental context, that understanding
grounds a critical vision of government; it opens the possibility of developing new forms of thinking that help us transcend the limitations of rationalism. This new form of thinking would help vocational students and working
people see through corporate attempts to mystify them about the politics of
self-interest. Corporate leaders and their conservative political allies have
been able to convince many individuals that democratic political and economic change is not in their best interest. Whereas conservatives attempt to

mystify Americans—especially those from the working class—about democratic reform, liberals tend to focus their reforms on the techniques of government, in the process avoiding fundamental questions of power and its
equitable distribution. A prerequisite for the creation of a renewed public
sphere is an exposure and disruption of existing power relations.

That path is difficult, there is no doubt. But those committed to a critical
vision of government have no choice; they must take the path of maximum
resistance, the path that contributes to the nurturance and cultivation of
democracy. Such critical citizens must make sure that government collects a
fair share of taxes from corporations, enforces laws regulating corporate pollution, protects American jobs from exploitive use of foreign labor, provides
health care and health insurance for those who need it, and helps the unemployed find good work. Critical vocational educators and their allies in other
social spheres understand that a democratic government has numerous
means of helping establish a more equal social order. And contrary to the
well-publicized pronouncements of right-wing commentators, the use of
such mechanisms will not constitute an attempt to "legislate equality." What
such spokespersons fail to realize is that leveling access and weeding out impediments to worker mobility is merely an effort to address a flagrantly unfair system. Policies such as these do not constitute a move to provide "special advantage" but are designed merely to lessen many of the disadvantages
poor and other marginalized peoples face daily. A critically grounded government can adjust fiscal policy, taxation, support of research and development, and regulation of collective bargaining, to mention only a few strategies for democracy (Gee, Hull, and Lankshear, 1996; Kallick, 1996).

As discussed in previous chapters, the power of neoclassical economics
and scientific progress plays a prominent role in shaping public consciousness and government policy at the end of the century. A critical vision of
government—a critical worker civics—understands the necessity of addressing neoclassical and scientific myths both in public and academic spaces.

The following is a list of myths of the inseparable discourses of neoclassical economics and scientific process:

1. *Unrestrained economic growth is an unmitigated blessing.* Embedded
   within this myth is the Western idea of progress, which in its single-
   mindedness fails to appreciate the disastrous consequences it produces. Pollution, industrial waste, dangerous radiation, and a cancer
   epidemic constitute only a few of the problems created by unrestrained economic growth.
2. *The free market is the best model for organizing social life.* This myth
   contends that the operation of the free market involves a group of
   self-directed individuals selecting from a wide range of options
   those things they most want. It is this situation that represents the

modernist utopia of personal freedom. The point missed, of course, is that the freedom assumed in the model does not exist in reality. Individuals are constantly constrained by the oppression resulting from power asymmetries of various sorts.

3. *All of the important social values shaped by the free market are measurable and quantifiable.* Economic growth expressed in terms of GNP or leading market indicators becomes the ultimate measure of social well-being.

4. *Political and economic decisions are made only in rational and dispassionate ways.* In the context created by this myth, emotion becomes a manifestation of weakness and rationality a sign of strength. Using the critique of modernist positivism, we can understand that the definition of "rational" is inscribed with power and political self-interest, so that those who dominate can define their position as rational and that of those who oppose them as irrational. By following the "objective" dictates of the free market, for example, economists, corporate leaders, and political functionaries make rational, disinterested, scientific decisions about governance. The fact that a wide range of subjective assumptions about the economic, social, and political cosmos are implicit in such scientific rationality is never mentioned.

5. *Science and technology lay the foundation for the good life.* Examining government pronouncements as well as scholarship in vocational education in the contemporary United States, one would never know about the intense debates surrounding science and technology and their social impact. The continuing dominance of science and technology in the pursuit of a positivist utopia is simply not problematized in the dominant discourse of American politics. The critique of scientific modernism and the technocratic mind-set provided in Chapter 2 is not a part of the public conversation.

6. *Biology and psychology in particular provide a verifiable picture of human beings that can be used to provide order and promote the good society.* One of the great ironies of modernity is that the same science that promised human emancipation and freedom has been deployed for purposes of control and manipulation. Biology and psychology are used to justify forms of rationality that undermine human freedom in a variety of social organizations, including education (Aronowitz and DiFazio, 1994; Schwartz, 1994; Gee, Hull, and Lankshear, 1996).

A critical vision of government understands the underside of each of these discourses. Those who hold such a vision appreciate the fact that promises have turned to nightmares and that public institutions often regulate individuals more than liberate them. In order to address such dysfunction, critical vocational educators must understand the unexamined belief structures on which it rests. In this regard, we can begin to rethink government, both its organization and its function. In our critical vision, government works hard to establish and maintain an economic democracy with as little bureaucracy and personal regulation as possible. No one here is advocating some form of blind faith in or reliance on big government. We know too much about the pathology of bureaucracy to fall into that trap. In the public conversation about American politics, it is rarely noted that the growth of government in the twentieth century did not take place in a social and historical vacuum. Governmental growth was a response to the growth of corporate power in the industrial era and the unprecedented problems such expansion caused. Small-business owners and farmers were unable to compete with emerging megafirms; monopolies tortured consumers with price fixing; labor lost the power to bargain effectively with its corporate bosses; intoxicated by their growing power, megacompanies lost interest in consumer and worker health and safety.

Creative Responses: A New Politics for a New Era

The creation of a powerful government as a countervailing force to corporate power was a logical move in the 1930s. And in the power-balancing act created in the Fordist compromise that responded to that need, big government achieved some modest successes in mitigating the impact of disparate wealth. But, of course, big government became, like other hierarchies of administration, more and more bureaucratic in its organizational culture, which resulted in rational irrationalities. When the public became sufficiently fed up with the dysfunctionality of government bureaucracy in the 1970s, corporate leaders took advantage of the impulse and manipulated it to their own ends. Instead of calling for a reform of government bureaucracy and inefficiency in its role as countervailing force to corporate power, corporate leaders and their allies convinced many Americans that neither government nor its countervailing power function were needed. Thus, reference to the all-too-real problem of bureaucratic pathology became a front for a much larger corporate agenda—the end of government interference in its affairs, the termination of attempts to mitigate the growing disparity of wealth (Bowles, Gordon, and Weisskopf, 1990; Wirth, 1983; Ferguson, 1984).

For those of us who promote the critical vision of government, the question thus becomes this: How can we create the political power to counter the expanding domination of corporations without the bureaucratic side effects the organizational structure of such an entity tends to produce? In many ways, this may be the most important political question of our era.

The concern with bureaucratic government should induce us to strengthen the democratic nature of the state, not to destroy it. Maybe government has something to learn from the more progressive aspects of post-Fordism's organizational strategies. If government believed this, it would move away from mass-produced administration to a more flexible and decentralized state. Public services in this model would abandon centralized and standardized forms of delivery and focus attention on differentiated, contextually relevant goals. The counterbureaucratic critical governmental vision would embrace a true notion of localism, not the pseudolocalism of post-Fordist megacorporations that paint a "ma-and-pa" façade on their franchises. Indeed, the critical vision holds that government would be big enough to thwart the oppression of corporations but smart enough to perform its tasks humanely.

Many argue that the time has come for a progressive government to relegate many of its functions to other, nongovernmental organizations. However, that proposal is dangerous and must be addressed very carefully. Critical educators and cultural workers need to study this question carefully before dismissing or including the proposal in their critical vision of government. Liberalism has undoubtedly been too single-minded in its reliance on government and in the process has ignored the reformist possibilities of other social sectors. Leaders of the women's movement understood this dynamic when they urged women to politicize the personal; democratizing power in personal relationships was not the province of government. Addressing such personal issues was the concern of men and women and groups in what might be termed "civil society." Women therefore did not push for passage of laws legally forcing men to change diapers and wash dishes. Instead, they sought a variety of social influences, including small groups that aided those who wanted change and educational groups that called attention to problematic forms of masculinity and patriarchal structures. In this context, such civil society efforts would be supported by governmental actions requiring equal pay for equal work, preventing sexual harassment in the workplaces, and increasing educational opportunities for girls in school (Murray, 1992; Gee, Hull, and Lankshear, 1996; Kallick, 1996).

The lesson to be learned from this example is that a socially concerned government is needed but is not to be relied upon to carry out all aspects of social action. Thus, cultural workers and critical educators must carefully distinguish between rhetoric that advocates action in civil society for the purpose of shutting down government's role of countering excessive corporate power and discourse that envisions a creative and progressive synergy between government and civil groups. Obviously, the point made here is that civil organizations—such as unions—can play an important role in the quest for social and economic justice, good work, and a critical vocational education. The possibilities raised by government, education, unions, and other civil organizations working together for such goals are exciting. I have no problem with including an active civil society working with the help of state agencies in our critical vision of government. If carefully planned, the civil agencies could help rebuild civil life by aiding the poor, extending health care, constructing affordable housing, cleaning up the environment, and helping with education for work. Part of this careful planning would involve the engagement of government support for these *supplemental* social actions from the civil sector.

The role of civil organizations becomes especially vital given the social, economic, and political changes wrought internationally by the globalized economy and its multinational corporations. The same forces that undermine the well-being of American workers are insidiously operating throughout the world. Americans, either with or without the help of government, must connect their democratic and justice-related interests with people with similar concerns in other countries. Working together, unions, educational organizations, and other civil groups can demand specific standards of behavior from multinational corporations. As we know, the post-Fordist economy pays no allegiance to national boundaries, and as a result, transgovernmental organizations are needed to police the transgressors. Critical vocational educators can connect with and help construct these transgovernmental organizations, so they and their students can learn and benefit from the knowledge gained in the effort to monitor and limit the irresponsible behavior of the multinational megacorporations (Moberg, April 1, 1996; Kallick, 1996; Rifkin, 1995; Greider, 1992).

The Decline of Government and the Realm of the Political: The Breakdown of Democracy

Electoral politics at the end of the millennium is a sham, as it attempts to hide the way government actually works from citizens. Of course, this circumstance holds dramatic implications for vocational education's "worker-citizen" students and for the worker civics curriculum critical vocational educators teach. The sacred values that Americans have associated with democracy are crumbling, as power shifts from the many to the few. Government now responds less to popular will and more to narrow financial interests and influential elites. New alignments of power interests decimate the democratic expectations of a public that grows increasingly jaded and cynical. Interestingly, despite the dramatic breakdown in democracy over the last decades of the twentieth century, the form and veneer of democratic government has stayed the same. The only change in the format of American electoral politics over the late thirty years has been that more money is spent by and for candidates than ever before. In an educational context, the way American government and civics are taught in elementary and secondary education despite such dramatic changes in the function of democracy is indistinguishable from the government classes of the 1950s. "Now, class, the three branches of government are the executive, legislative, and judicial branches; a bill becomes law by . . ." Such simpleminded teaching conveys a misleading impression of how government works in contemporary America.

A critical vocational civics asks questions left unexplored in most government classes: Why do some groups shape the government's process of decisionmaking while others have little voice? Why, critical vocational educators ask, do monied interests consistently gain government support for their needs while the vast majority of working people are ignored? In building a construct of the world that helps vocational students place themselves socially, critical vocational educators describe an American democracy that is a struggle for power not between citizens but between organized economic interests. How can unorganized working people, weak unions, or small civil organizations compete with corporations or coalitions of corporations that employ teams of lawyers and lobbyists, fund political parties, political action committees, and even TV shows? (*The McLaughlin Group*, for example, is a corporate-friendly weekly news program funded by General Electric.) The impact of such investments places corporate concerns on the government's front burner, moving the individual needs of citizens off the stove. The public perception that monied interests control government through bribery misses the subtle way influence is typically peddled. Corporate money employs lawyers and lobbyists with "connections." Their job is often to "build relationships" between corporate leaders with particular needs and government functionaries. Indeed, many of the lawyers and lobbyists are former—many of them high-ranking—governmental officials. Their job is to put the corporate leaders in touch with the government operatives who can help them.

What do the corporate financiers get for their purchased influence? Generally speaking, the answer involves the passage of legislation tailored to maximize the financial well-being of corporate management—and this payoff is often referred to as corporate welfare, or welfare for the rich. In 1993, the federal government, for instance, provided $104 billion in direct payments and tax breaks to American multinational corporations. The Sunkist food company received almost $18 million for the promotion of its orange juice. Farming conglomerates collectively received over $29 billion that same year. McDonald's received $456,000 to tout its Chicken McNuggets. Mining, timber, pharmaceutical, and many other types of corporations are annual beneficiaries of such government handouts. Another bargain corporations get for their money is velvet-glove treatment for corporate or white-collar crime. Sixty-two percent of Fortune 500 corporations have been involved in one or more significant illegalities; forty-two percent have been found guilty of two or more corrupt activities; fifteen percent have been convicted in five or more cases (Greider, 1992). Corporate influence allows major offending companies to avoid the penalties most working Americans would suffer. Ordinary Americans who are criminals are prohibited from engaging in politics; corporate convicts continue to play dominating roles in the political process.

Corporate lawyers have slyly won legal rulings that consider corporations—as organizations—the same as people under the law. This means that corporations as a legal entity, not individual corporate leaders, are liable for corporate criminal activity. Since you cannot imprison a corporation and corporate leaders are shielded from prosecution, corporations literally get away with murder and continue to operate with little more than a slap on the wrist. The million-dollar salaries corporations pay their lawyers are lucrative financial investments, as their legal henchmen use their expertise to pervert legislation designed to protect labor unions and workers so as to serve corporate objectives. In fact, laws passed several decades ago to protect the interests of the weakest members of American society are now used daily to undermine the needs of the poor and protect corporations from legal penalties for their sociopathic actions. Such disparity of treatment insults the concept of equal protection under the law, since it pounds another nail into the coffin of democracy. Without a civic faith in the connections between the governed and the government, the country will descend into a civil chaos that produces more Tim McVeighs, white militias, and violent antigovernment movements of all stripes. The role of the critical vocational educator is to reveal these injustices and threats to democracy but to channel the outrage and cynicism of future worker-citizens into democratically affirming and socially responsible actions (Greider, 1992; Bowles, Gordon, and Weisskopf, 1990; Rifkin, 1995; Schwartz, 1994).

Bypassing Traditional Political Institutions

The decline of democracy and the decline of government in general is exacerbated by the globalization of the economy and the evolution of powerful national corporations into superpowerful multinational corporations. The multinationals are so powerful that they have subverted the capacity of governments to protect their citizens. Leaders of multinational corporations are now able to bypass established political institutions, among them tax laws, commercial regulations, employment policies, and environmental statutes. Nation-states no longer have the power to regulate their democratic economic spheres as they did even twenty years ago. Given the powerful role of megacorporations, national governments grow more and more reluctant to protect their domestic markets. So far, no governmental strategy has been developed to respond to the profound changes wrought by the power re-configurations of globalization. Asian, African, and Latin American governments are collapsing, as multinational corporations vie with indigenous people's movements and informal economies to fill the political and economic vacuums created.

The hand of government grows weaker as the invisible hand of the market strengthens in this era of globalization and privatization. Private corporations are better suited to the new electronic world, the privatization argument goes, than traditional governments. Not being connected to any specific geographical place, they can cope with the supersonic pace of global market forces. With their post-Fordist dynamic flexibility, they can move markets quickly from one continent to another, in the process shaping the commercial and political priorities of all countries they encounter. Thus, governments are adrift and on the retreat in the face of the march of privatization. A critical philosophy and pedagogy must attend to this expanding crisis of government and carefully delineate a new, globally conscious, justice-directed, democratic, and creative mission for the nation-state. Without a critical vision of government for the new globalized world, privatization is likely to create untenable conditions in the short run for the poor and working people and in the long run for everyone (Barnet and Cavanagh, 1994; Aronowitz and DiFazio, 1994; Rifkin, 1995).

We already see the results of the decline of democracy and privatization in the deterioration of the public space. Americans do not have to look far to see decaying cities, violence and the extra security measures it demands, air and water pollution, homelessness, unrepaired roads and bridges, under-funded parks, libraries, museums, and, of course, the decline of schools. Even though many argue that at the end of the century America is booming, corporate profits are rising, and new wealth is being created, still the public space continues to decline. Money is available for these desperate needs, but decisions have been made not to spend it on such problems. One of the few public domains where money is regulated is in the construction of new prisons. With prisons, the debate is not about allocation of funds but centers around where they are to be built—build them, proponents argue, but just not in my backyard. The wealthy can protect themselves to a large degree from the deterioration of the public space by withdrawing into their secure and self-sufficient fortresses. Working people and the poor, however, must suffer the brunt of such deterioration because they have no place to which they can retreat. Without an interruption in the march of privatization and the decline of government, more and more individuals will find themselves unemployed or underemployed, sinking ever deeper into an intractable underclass. They will engage in an informal economy to survive, bartering and trading for food. Many will turn to theft, crime, drug dealing, and prostitution to get by.

At one level, talk of privatization may be misleading, as it implies a boundary between the public sector and the private sector that has faded away in the last few years. Because of the overwhelming influence corporations exert on national, state, and local governments, it is hard to delineate exactly where the public ends and the private begins. This dynamic can be easily observed in vocational education, as business leaders direct the goals and curriculums of federal vocational programs from their presence on advisory boards and as supervisors of work practicums. This blurring of the private and public that comes under the umbrella of privatization is seen in the new business-operated schools with curricula, of course, that discourage questioning the path of the new privatized world and its sacred icons of deregulation, consumerism, competition, and individualization or, more accurately, customization. The highest expression of the communications revolution is the privatized battering of eyes and ears with inducements to consume. So pervasive and compelling are these advertisements that six-year-olds know more about beer than democracy. Using the neoclassical language of the free market and privatization, the power derived from controlling the global media empire, and their inordinate influence on governments domestic and foreign, megacorporations are becoming the emperors of the twenty-first century (Reich, 1995; Rifkin, 1995; Gee, Hull, and Lankshear, 1996; Barnet and Cavanagh, 1994).

Ford Motor Company's economy, for example, is already bigger than that of Saudi Arabia or Norway. The yearly sales of Phillip Morris are larger than New Zealand's annual gross domestic product. Such statistics are interesting but mean little if they are not accompanied by the understanding that the balance of power in global politics has moved from public territorial governments to nomadic private companies. The national state is being supplanted by the meta-state—a coalition of multinational corporations and their allies in national governments, international trade organizations, and higher education. These multinational corporation-led coalitions are the first secular organizations to plan and operate on a global level. Amazingly, little of the planning and organizational work of the corporate meta-state deals with the questions raised here concerning the deteriorating public space, the growing disparity of wealth, and the future of work. It seems of little importance to the new emperors that the profit needs of the multinationals are forcing governments to nullify protective labor codes. In this new context, employers in nations around the world are enabled to pay lower wages and to import cheap, undocumented workers. Thus, the disparity of wealth grows both *between* rich and poor countries and *within* rich and poor countries. In light of globalization's creation of the meta-state, there no longer exists a discrete entity called the U.S. workplace—we now have a *global workplace*. Such issues are central to the ability of vocational educators and their students to make sense of the forces that shape work in general and their working lives in particular. These understandings are central to the critical vocational curriculum (Smart, 1992; Aronowitz and DiFazio, 1994).

The Emergence of Corporate Government

To help workers, students, and other people around the world understand the emerging role of these multinational corporations, it may be appropriate to characterize such organizations as a new form of government—corporate government. That designation removes megacompanies from the shadowy realm in which they operate and exposes their function for precisely what it is. Along with their allies in public government and the media, corporations form a corporate governmental system. Such a system via its technopower regulates its worldwide empire more effectively than any previous form of governance. This ultimate privatization, or rule by private government, holds far more power over people's lives than "public government," as it dictates terms of employment and controls people's livelihood. As this corporate governmental system shapes workers' ability to make a living, it exacts a degree of subservience that public government could never equal. Corporate governments' ability to punish economically is a more powerful tool of domination than the laws deployed by public government. Dismissal from one's job can take place without warning and can be just as personally devastating as a prison term or even capital punishment. When the effects of dismissal from a job are studied, we find that getting fired often causes the untimely death of a worker—a form of death penalty by the economic government.

The social understanding we have of our governmental system has been skewed by the corporate government's ability to blame socioeconomic problems on the public government. Often, workers who themselves have been laid off by corporate downsizing or deindustrialization speak of getting "government off our backs," blaming the corporate action on public government. They often vote for candidates who promise to reduce the size of government and get government out of business affairs, not knowing that they are helping exacerbate the tyranny of an unregulated corporate government. Using this get-government-off-our-backs mantra, corporations since the late 1970s have steadily gained the power to govern and as a result make more money. Attempts to make life better for working people become more and more difficult as citizens and elected officials continue to turn power over to the corporate emperors. Despite the picture painted by business leaders and their political allies, public government has experienced a decline in power over the last decades of the twentieth century. Fewer and fewer decisions that shape our lives are made through the traditional political process as we enter the new millennium.

An important development that has served to strengthen this corporate government involves the defection of middle- and high-ranking government officials to corporate payrolls. From different presidential administrations, members of the Treasury Department, including legislative counsels and assistant secretaries, Energy Department lawyers, the chair of the Joint Chiefs of Staff, and even former attorney generals of the United States now work for big business. Their job is to influence the decisions their former departments make in a manner that benefits their corporate bosses—and there is no doubt that corporations get what they pay for in this respect. With these functionaries in place and buoyed by the heady freedom of action provided by deregulation, the corporate government is a post-Fordist version of the old urban "political machine." Differing in scale and power—there are hundreds of corporate "private" political machines in operation—the corporate government is less attentive to its constituency than the old party machine, as it teaches, leads, and dictates without the accountability sometimes forced on the machines by elections.

This politics of corporatism, armed with its technopower, claims like other governments to look out for various constituencies in need of protection. It is not public government, corporate government maintains, that speaks for workers but the humane corporation; in other words, your corporation, my McDonald's—they "do it all for you." In addition to workers, corporations speak for consumers, stockholders, the world of business in general, and Americans and their interests around the planet. Policies that are beneficial for us, corporate spokespeople maintain, are good for the masses. When particular groups oppose the needs of the corporate government, the myth tells us, they are hurting millions of Americans. Corporate welfare for the rich, for example, is justified on the basis that its real beneficiaries are the "little guys" that such funding allows the corporate government to help. Because of their unparalleled access to people via control of the various media, corporations provide appealing and simplistic explanations for complex socioeconomic problems. Do answers such as big government, a failure of personal responsibility, the waning of the work ethic, rock and rap music, schools not teaching our values, and welfare loafers sound familiar? What we need in addition to less public government, corporate government's philosophers conclude, is a positivist intelligentsia that issues indisputable edicts based on management science, neoclassical economics, evolutionary biology, and behavioral theory. By the way, from the perspective of corporate government's educational experts, such an intelligentsia can make use of these disciplines to build a damn good philosophy of vocational education. A critical worker civics appreciates the fatal limitations of such a pedagogy of regulation.

In light of the power and tyrannical behavior of corporate government, those Americans who have placed such great faith in the new day of freedom coming when the public government is rendered sufficiently insignificant are in for profound disappointment. Although their freedom to shop at Wal-Mart may well remain intact in the future, a wide variety of traditional political freedoms, such as having a voice in the making of political policies, will have vanished. The protections citizens enjoy from public government were guaranteed by the Constitution—but no similar document exists to limit corporate government. Indeed, there are no institutions to provide checks and balances on the privatization of government. Unless critical cultural workers act, nothing will impede the penetration of market values into all phases of human life—from romantic relationships to work. In this context, the term "free market" is used as a signifier designed to disguise the coercive process that devalues workers and their well-being, as corporate leaders pursue policies that save on labor costs (Reich, 1995; Greider, 1992; Schwartz, 1994).

Surrendering Public Government:
The Debasement of Republicans and Democrats

When push comes to shove in contemporary American politics, neither political party, Republican or Democratic, is willing to challenge corporate government. Both are far too invested in it, too ensnared in its tentacles to resist it. Most important, both parties are too addicted to corporate money to stray too far away. Thus, Americans find themselves in a peculiar situation: Their two political parties operate in the grasp of the corporate government. Corporate leaders and their political allies in the public government and the media perpetuate the myth that the views expressed by the Republicans and the Democrats represent the full spectrum of political opinion. Thus, it is easy to dismiss opinions such as the ones presented here; in the pseudo-universe of political perspectives, they simply do not exist.

The way to understand the difference between the Republicans and Democrats is to look at their corporate clients—or, as some analysts describe them, their investors. Ideological differences do not divide political parties at the end of the century; the needs of their clients do. At most, parties serve as mediating agencies between different corporations—not between individuals with differing political viewpoints. In fact, many of the most important issues of American politics involve conflicts between these investors and their Republican and Democratic gladiators. Such corporate control of the political agenda degrades the democratic process and the parties that claim to operate on particular civic principles. At the same time, it undermines the interests of workers and all those who fall outside the inner circle of corporate management. Republicans have been comfortable with corporate coziness for decades. Often involved with commerce, Republicans have found it easy to view voters as consumers. Their job as politicians, they came to believe, was to identify what voters think and feel and to then adjust their political advertising to those thoughts and feelings. Since Republicans represented the monied interests, no one was particularly surprised when Republicans provided increasing support to the corporate government.

The Democratic Party's sellout was a different matter. Known and identified at one time as the party of average working people, the Democrats have grown closer and closer to corporations and their money. By the close of the 1980s, the Democrats were in reality the party of corporate lawyers. Such political operatives rotate in and out of private and government jobs and have replaced the old networks of local party leaders, who decades ago formed the basis of the party. When political analysts argue that Democratic liberalism is dead, they are unwittingly referring to the fact that liberal operatives made a devil's pact with corporate money: They could not take corporate money and defy the rule of the free market. Liberals have few ideas because they, like the Republicans, have laid down their arms in deference to neoclassical economics and corporate rule. The Democrats have particularly courted high-tech corporate moneylenders, winning friends in Silicon Valley and other high-tech corridors. One of the starkest examples of the Democrats' corporate coitus involved their support of corporate raider Frank Lorenzo's attempt to crush the labor unions at Eastern Airlines. Hiring a host of Democratic party lawyers and influence peddlers to negate the influence of the machinists', pilots', and flight attendants' unions, Lorenzo fought these unions with the help of Democratic "friends of labor." Lorenzo was forced into mediation and eventually lost the airline, but the support generated in the Democratic Party for such a flagrant enemy of labor held profound implications (Cooper, May 27, 1996; Greider, 1992; Reich, 1995).

That forces in the Democratic Party could support Lorenzo illustrated the power of the corporate government in the most unlikely places. With the victory of Bill Clinton in the wake of these capitulations, it comes as no surprise that the New Democrats have consistently supported the freedom of multinational corporations to move, regardless of the consequences for workers in America and around the world. In his two administrations, Clinton has never promoted workers' interests to the point that his party's Wall Street supporters might balk. Indeed, it has never struck Clinton as a problem that average worker wages are 13 percent lower in the late 1990s than they were in 1973. The Democratic collaborators of the late 1990s are cavalier about the fact that one of three contemporary workers is unemployed, underemployed, or stuck in the peripheral workforce with no benefits or protections. No wonder so many Americans—working Americans in particular—are fed up with both political parties. So far has the Democratic Party strayed from its New Deal concern for worker well-being that only about one in ten Americans identifies it as the party of the average person. How do critical vocational educators tell future workers that in the existing political configuration, they have no one to represent their needs?

The corporate government fears the anger that permeates the electorate. Such discontent could lead to an abrupt seismic shift in the political landscape that could express itself in a frightening fascist extremism or, more positively, in a worker-friendly progressive politics that transcends senile liberalism and Social Darwinist conservatism. Many critical analysts have recently advocated formation of an American Labor Party—maybe one that at least in the short run would not run a slate of candidates but would campaign for public awareness of the political dynamics discussed here. Many union leaders have endorsed that idea, hoping to devise a way to respond to the corporate government's wildly successful efforts to divide workers around issues of gun control, race, and abortion. We keep giving the Democratic Party money, union leaders complain, and they kick our asses. A little time passes, they continue, and we reward them with more money. A labor party could learn from the ridiculous behavior of the existing political parties that spend hundreds of millions of dollars on vacuous TV advertisements but virtually nothing on grassroots organizing. If political money were spent on developing methods of responding to people rather than manipulating them, workers and other individuals would soon understand that the purpose of the party was not simply to win elections but to serve their needs. The present operations of the Republicans and the Democrats make it hard for Americans to imagine such a political reality (Bacon, April 1, July 8, 1996; Pollin, 1996; Kallick, 1996; Cooper, April 8, 1996).

The Need for Worker Civics

The political dysfunctions described here call for new forms of action, new types of worker education. So far, few Americans have objected to forms of education that overtly promote partisan corporate interests. Even traditional high-school economics has been pressured by business leaders to redesign itself as free enterprise economics—and such classes are often little more than crass celebrations of neoclassical economics and an unregulated market. And I have already alluded to business-operated vocational programs that teach workers little more than compliance to management demands and positive (passive) attitudes. To argue for a critical worker civics that provides a view of what is good for worker welfare, as previously maintained, is merely an effort to balance a curriculum dominated by the ideologies and economic interests of the corporate government. Since public government no longer works like the model taught in school, critical vocational educators teach a corrective civics that helps future worker-citizens understand the demands of citizenship in a new era. The corporate government has used its power to saturate the society with what many label as a hegemonic picture of the world. A hegemonic portrait attempts to win citizens' consent to a way of seeing their lives and reality that works to the advantage of those in positions of power. In other words, it provides individuals with a misleading map of reality (Reich, 1995).

The power of this misleading map of reality is hard to overestimate. A misleading map of reality is being promoted when individuals are induced to buy into a worldview that proposes that public government will not allow businesses and corporations the freedom to act in ways that would improve the lives of workers; when any growth of public government is seen as bad and any growth of corporations is good; when nonwhites and women are portrayed as having all the advantages and because of affirmative action are thriving while white men are suffering; when unions are described as outdated and as doing nothing but impeding the efficient operations of corporations; when education that teaches the necessity of an unregulated market and worker compliance to management is viewed as nonpolitical but a critical pedagogy of vocational education is seen as political. The success of such promotion has left us with a lack of social self-knowledge that undermines our ability to make sense of the macrostructures of which we are a part. Worker civics helps vocational students make sense of the larger social context and of their place in it, as it teaches them the hidden rules and assumptions that permeate the invisible social organism.

James Gee, Glynda Hull, and Colin Lankshear (1996) in *The New Work Order: Behind the Language of the New Capitalism* write of this corporate process, arguing that post-Fordist corporations more than ever before "need to socialize people into communities of practice that position people to be certain kinds of people" (p. 21). These post-Fordist companies—or as Gee, Hull, and Lankshear label them, "fast capitalists"—attempt to delineate a set of social values transcending profit that they want their workers to adopt. Johnson and Johnson (the pharmaceutical company) values decentralization, creativity, and productivity in the effort to alleviate pain and disease; Phillip Morris (cigarettes and other products) values the right to personal freedom of choice; and Disney values continuous progress through creativity and imagination. A critical worker civics reminds workers to be wary of such lofty language and to examine the ratio between management's and nonsupervisory workers' salaries before celebrating freedom, creativity, and corporate piety. Many analysts argue that the new corporate values are just an updated and highly polished form of mind control. A worker civics attempts to help workers construct a "corporate crap detector" that allows them to see through the manipulative personnel management strategies corporate leaders continuously devise (Bacon, April 1, 1996; Gee, Hull, and Lankshear, 1996; Reich, 1995).

Vocational Education and Critical Worker Civics

Present forms of vocational education, unfortunately, too often avoid the issues that worker civics addresses. When young women are educated for office work, for example, technical knowledge about office equipment and material processing takes precedence. Issues of social relations, the role of the work in the larger structure of the corporation, safety, worker rights, pay, unions, or the personal effects of new technology are not deemed a part of the vocational curriculum. A vocational program built around an awareness of worker civics promotes a metaconsciousness of the purposes of vocational education and school in general. With the rise of corporate government and its social and educational influence, an awareness of the objectives of a vocational program becomes more and more important. Students need to understand whose interests are being served by the curriculum, as well as the way the program views their own personal role in the enterprise. Questions concerning this massive corporate power and its ability to squash inquiry into the actual results of vocational programs are infrequently asked in the enterprise of vocational education.

If having power involves learning to act in one's own behalf, few vocational students study power. Corporate government attempts to train its workers to be passive in civics but active in the pursuit of corporate values. It is fascinating to observe this post-Fordist schizophrenia in operation, as workers are encouraged ad nauseum to use their minds, take chances, show initiative, ask questions, and break away from the chains of tradition—but not in relation to questions of worker rights and justice. Corporate leaders covertly induce workers, worker-trainees, and vocational students to do just the opposite in these domains. In the corporate mind-set, the idea of empowered worker-citizens who ask questions of democracy and insist on good work is not a pleasant thought. In order to keep such a civic empowerment process from occurring, corporations monitor vocational programs and spend millions of dollars on TV and other media to promote countermessages. Even without the conscious hegemonic messages promoted by corporations, TV as a communications medium seems to undermine the interest of younger viewers in the political sphere. Political participation has remained relatively stable among citizens who came of age before TV, but it has fallen precipitously among younger people. Research on younger workers indicates that political reporting seems remote and nonsensical to them—and as a result they quickly lose interest in it.

If TV has taught these viewers to be hip and cynical about the mediated world it presents, then such hip cynicism reaches its apex in young viewers' perspectives toward the political domain. Such perspectives position them as remote and impotent in relation to the political cosmos; citizenship thus becomes a concept that simply fails to connect with everyday life. No one profits from such civic alienation more than corporate government. This circumstance enables it to continue its transference of power from the public to the private with minimal interference. As corporations colonize the concept of empowerment, the term's connection with the political sphere is frayed. Empowerment in this corporate discourse becomes a privatized notion, revolving around the freedom to consume and to work within wider boundaries of creativity. Just as long as the empowered creative work contributes to an increase in productivity and short-term profit margins, workers can be as empowered as they want to be. In the lexicon of the post-Fordist corporate government: Enjoy the benefits of the Brave New Empowered World! A critical worker civics in this bizarre dimension becomes far more difficult to teach but far more necessary.

Worker civics is both a pedagogy and a political vision that struggles to provide vocational students and workers with an understanding of the social, economic, political, philosophical, and ethical context in which labor and schooling for it takes place. A critical worker civics attempts to counter the confusion created by corporate messages and the crazy-quilt media civics taught on TV. In an age marked by confusion and a loss of meaning, worker civics attempts to make sense of the socioeconomic and political world. In order to accomplish this difficult feat, the invisible must be made visible. For example, a central feature of any critical vocational teacher's worker civics curriculum would involve the recognition of the market's influence on vocational education. Indeed, this observation may form the basis of any worker civics program. This understanding can serve as a springboard to an analysis of the impact of twenty-first-century global economics on the work lives of vocational students. In this context, teachers induce students to question the ways public and corporate governmental decisions shape their work futures: Will students be able to gain steady, long-term jobs? Will they be able to achieve economic security? Will they have access to career advancement and financial mobility? Will the attainment of good work be possible? How as worker-citizens can they help shape political and economic policies to benefit themselves and their fellow workers around the world (Valli, 1988; Reich, 1995; Schwartz, 1994; Lakes, 1994a; Simon, Dippo, and Schenke, 1991)?

Seeing Through the Language of New Age Corporatism: A Critical Worker Civics

The corporate government—like all hegemonic agencies—changes with the times, incorporates popular culture and movements into its repertoire of regulatory strategies. The talk of worker empowerment and values beyond profit that emanate from corporate leaders at the dawn of the new century seems to find its origins in the most shallow corners of the New Age spiritualist movement. As a pop psychology for the workplace, management induces new generations of workers to become empowered by getting in touch with their "inner achiever." This pseudoempowerment diverts worker attention from the issues raised throughout this book. Truly empowered critical workers see through the language of New Age corporatism. They are researchers, knowledge producers, and analysts who realize that real empowerment involves understanding the social context in which work takes place and appreciating the motivations and reasons for both the programs management devises and the map of the world it distributes.

The term "critical thinking," as used by managers, often signifies an opposite meaning—uncritical passivity. Real critical thinking allows workers to understand that when corporate leaders use phrases such as "global competition," they are often actually participating in forms of global exploitation. Workers engaged in critical citizenship know that corporate phrases such as "decentralized control" and "diffused power" often cover up insidious forms of exploitation. Critical vocational educators collect stories about the specific effects of the multinational globalized economy from Malaysia to Flint, Michigan, in order to personalize the ravages of this abstract, hard-to-fathom entity. This is why it is so important for vocational teachers and international unions to establish close communications with one another; E-mail and Internet connections among workers are a necessity in the new economy. The personal economic stories told in this context are invaluable in the struggle for social and economic justice. Vocational students can identify particular corporations and the specific effects of their policies on individual workers. They can become an integral part of the call to end economic strategies that cause poverty, malnutrition, environmental cancer, and marginalization (Gee, Hull, and Lankshear, 1996).

Although it is necessary to delineate the social, political, economic, and philosophical foundations of work and vocational education and to develop visions of the way the world works, critical worker civics also demands that teachers, students, and workers engage in the messy world of everyday politics. As unpleasant and distasteful as the media has convinced us to consider this realm, work within it is noble, patriotic, and necessary. Critical civic work in this realm means reaching across racial, class, and gender boundaries and forming alliances with people who are in some way different from oneself in the pursuit of common goals. Such "good work" involves humbly engaging in dialogue about values and visions and their application in the complexity and ambiguity of everyday life. The work of critical citizenship requires a fidelity to the principles of social and economic justice and a commitment to marginalized individuals that is so strong it can overcome the divisive issues that separate us from one another. Middle- and upper-middle-class "experts" must refrain at all costs from "leading" such a movement and speaking for their lower-status allies. Such agents must develop the ability to work *with* exploited people in a way that is permeated with a genuine humility.

For all the cynicism that the political and economic events of the last several decades have generated in all of us, we can make a difference. Nothing shocks the unresponsive Congress as much as seeing several of their colleagues defeated in their reelection bids by a popular movement of organized people. Just because public government now takes a back seat to corporate government does not mean that the situation is irreversible. The "monied interests" have always feared the "strong arm of labor." Factory owners in the middle decades of the nineteenth century were obsessed with making sure that labor's strong arm was not raised against them in retribution for their work policies. Monied interests in the twenty-first century will be no different—and their fears are justified. A united labor movement around the world can interrupt the smooth operations of international corporate government. The basic tenet of worker civics for the New Age of corporatism is very simple and with concerted effort can be communicated to power wielders: Concerned citizens will not allow the new world economic order to turn productive individuals into "surplus human capital" unneeded in everyday commerce. Critical vocational educators cannot carry on as if this human disposal process does not exist. In Chapter 18, the book will conclude with more ideas about how this human tragedy of global proportions can be addressed by vocational educators and cultural workers.

18 *A Reconceptualized Government for the Twenty-First Century*

In our effort to explore and construct philosophical, historical, economic, political, and sociological foundations for work and vocational education, an understanding of the role of government is essential. This concluding chapter offers a vision for government as it relates to the promotion of good work, economic justice, and a critical vocational education. As Americans enter the twenty-first century, there is widespread confusion about the role of government—especially in light of corporate government's domination of the public conversation about the issue. This chapter is therefore grounded on four important questions: (1) what should the role of government be in society? (2) given the changes wrought by the dramatic expansion of corporate power in the latter part of the twentieth century, what new roles must government play in the twenty-first century? (3) how can critical educators and cultural workers promote sustainable economic growth and socioeconomic justice both through the construction of progressive government and innovative nongovernmental organizations (NGOs)? and (4) how do these social, political, and economic dynamics relate to vocational education and the student's transition from school to work?

Government as Critic: Addressing the Harmful Effects of Profit Seeking

A progressive government dedicated to socioeconomic justice guards the society from the negative effects of private profit-seeking activity. The market has historically, for example, never done well in setting a national economic development strategy, as it pushes and pulls the economy in conflicting directions—often in ways that undermine long-term goals; it has failed to provide even a minimal degree of financial security, adopting a cavalier attitude about its tendency to dismiss workers without warning and pay them wages as low as possible; it has never displayed an interest in mitigating the unequal distribution of income and economic and political power it promotes; it has consistently been unwilling to address undemocratic, authoritarian workplaces; and it has addressed its own environmental destruction only under legal pressure (Pollin and Cockburn, 1991). Without the help of a concerned public government, workers and citizens will be hard pressed to mitigate the social damage caused by the free market's historical neglect of these issues.

For these reasons, many progressive economists have argued that measurements of the GNP, indicating the nation's total economic production, should be supplemented by a figure called the gross national cost (GNC). Subtracting the GNC from the GNP would give Americans a far more revealing picture of the operation and status of the economy. The GNC would report on the depletion of natural resources, pollution, crime and violence, the welfare of children, the state of inequality, the psychological well-being of citizens, and the degree of waste of human talents. Health costs, the unmeasurable price of human suffering from cancer and other diseases, and cleanup monies could be calculated as part of the socioeconomic liability of environmental pollution. Such debits far exceed the costs of investments in preventive measures. The short-term, quarterly-profit-driven mind-set of free market economics has prevented the implementation of such ethical *and economically efficient* policies. Similar preventative long-term strategies could both save money and prevent human suffering in all of the categories delineated. Phenomenal savings in governmental, corporate/business, and individual expenditures could be realized by a society free to pursue such farsighted initiatives. Crime alone, *Business Week* has estimated, costs Americans $425 billion annually. The corporate lobby's successful thwarting of measures to prevent these costly problems is one of the greatest assaults on the public well-being in American history (Reich, 1995).

A critical vision of government demands that whether they want to or not, private firms must operate for the public good. That approach could be implemented not simply through government regulation but also by a cadre of knowledgeable, empowered employees who demand managerial fidelity to a core of responsible socioeconomic goals. Such critical workers would understand that the old ideological maxim "What's good for General Motors is good for America" is not, nor ever has been, true. They would appreciate the fact that this sort of concept is especially untrue at the end of the century because of corporate management's elevation of profit maximization over objectives such as productivity, efficiency, and quality of product or service. The pursuit of short-term profit even takes precedence over the development of the company or over longstanding commitments to employees and communities. Profit making in a world of predatory capital characterized by the buying and selling of companies is separated from all traditional business activities—even from production itself. A fictitious case study serves as a good example of such practices. Although the public relations department issues saccharine New Age proclamations stating that Acme Enterprises is all about personal freedom and the unfettered human spirit, the company is actually dedicated to the enhancement of short-term profits. Even the father of the owner of Acme Enterprises, who managed the firm when it called itself Acme Thimbles, maintained that his company's goal was to make good thimbles for a profit. We are referring to a difference of emphasis—but a very important difference of emphasis.

The difference between the old Acme Thimbles and the new Acme Enterprises shows up in shifts in management personnel: The former consisted of people primarily involved in production; the latter, of individuals primarily concerned with finance. In Acme Enterprises, finance people close down their 150-year-old plant in Factoryville, Massachusetts, and buy a chain of fast-food pork restaurants called The Speedy Pig. They have demonstrated on numerous occasions their lack of interest in thimble production and their willingness to sacrifice Acme's future for a high-profit quarterly report. Managerial salaries have increased 82 percent during a five-year period in which profits increased only 4 percent and worker wages dropped 3 percent. The few old-timers from Acme Thimble who are left in upper- and middle management are shocked by the fact that the company's expenditures on research and development is 30 percent less than it was in 1969. The harmful social side effects of profit seeking at Acme are not difficult to uncover.

Thousands of actual corporations now operate in America in a manner similar to the fictitious Acme. In such companies, loyalty to employees and communities is a lost virtue; in the lexicon of managers, it is a quality that inhibits the dynamic flexibility needed to maintain acceptable quarterly profit margins. The side effects of this value structure are disastrous for the nation's social fabric, not to mention for the lives of individual employees and particular communities. Corporate leaders and their political representatives have become adept at hiding their culpability from the public and even from those directly affected by such moral shallowness. Deftly using the organization as a form of camouflage, corporations operate on a daily basis to avoid responsibility for their antisocial behavior. The job description of corporate lawyers involves devising creative new strategies to avoid liability for a plethora of public transgressions. A critical democratically responsible government understands these realities and works to address them in a way that allows workers and communities to benefit (Block, 1990; Schwartz, 1994; Reich, 1995).

Government Strategies to Counteract the Antisocial Consequences of Corporate Behavior

Corporations, like other human inventions, are social constructions and therefore can be reconstructed by human action. The profit-generating antisocial corporation of the contemporary era is not the only possible model of a corporation. Critical social analysts understand that we can devise a new type of corporation that is employee operated, democratic, wealth generating, and socially responsible. Indeed, there is no inherent conflict between profitability and the pursuit of critical social goals. It is not economic heresy, though it may be represented as such, to argue that government should have as much say about corporate moves to another location as baseball owners have about the proposed move of the Montreal Expos to Washington, D.C. The owners ask whether the move is good for baseball. Likewise, government could ask whether the move is good for the country. In addition to the problems created in the lives of employees and in the stability of communities by migrating corporations, the efficiency of corporations is grounded on the stability of social relationships. Frequent migrations and corporate raidings undermine such relationships and the smooth operations they encourage.

To mitigate the damage caused by these post-Fordist capital migrations and by the orgy of buying and selling of corporations that has occurred over the last two decades of this century, a progressive government develops criteria of regulation. Policies emerging from such criteria are designed to discourage cities and counties from luring firms from other locations with low taxes, low wages, and cheap public services. When such migrations take place, no new jobs are created and opportunities for economic mobility are temporary at best. A worker can be sure that the jobs at the new plant will last only as long as it takes management to find a new location with even cheaper taxes, wages, and social services. Government policies must prevent migrating corporations from turning communities into revolving doors that waste valuable ecological and human resources in their attempt to induce firms to locate for a few short years. These socioeconomic dynamics are typically overlooked by state and local economic development officials, whose reports are almost always limited to merely the number of jobs created when a new industry moves into an area. The nature of the wage and skill level of the jobs and the infrastructure and tax costs to the community are not relevant questions. There are numerous examples of local communities in poor regions actually rejecting high-skill, high-pay jobs out of fear that their presence might force other employers in the area to raise wages. Such "rational irrationality" must be ended by requiring corporations to prove the positive impact of a move in terms of creating new jobs and promoting good work in the new community (Aronowitz and DiFazio, 1994; Block, 1990; Falk and Lyson, 1988).

The Need for a Post-Fordist Bill of Rights

Charles Reich (1995) has argued that in light of present economic realities, the time has come to take another look at President Franklin Roosevelt's new social contract, first broadcast in January 1944. Informed by Roosevelt's principles, critical vocational educators might want to offer a Post-Fordist bill of rights for the consideration of the American people. Such a delineation of rights would be primarily designed to protect American workers from the inordinate power that corporations have amassed via new technologies and media over the final decades of the twentieth century. As a set of amendments to the Constitution, the Post-Fordist Bill of Rights would be grounded on the assumption that political rights and individual liberty cannot exist without economic security and freedom from what I have called corporate government. Workers should possess:

Amendment 1. The right to good work in the nation's workplace.

Amendment 2. The right to monetary compensation for work sufficient to provide adequate food, clothing, and recreation.

Amendment 3. The right (for farmers and agricultural workers) to raise and sell their products at a return that will provide them and their families with a decent standard of living.

Amendment 4. The right of every family to an adequate home and medical care.

Amendment 5. The right to protection from the economic hardships of old age, sickness, accident, and unemployment.

Amendment 6. The right to educational opportunity.

Amendment 7. The right to live in a healthy natural environment.

Amendment 8. The right to protection from racial or ethnic discrimination.

Amendment 9. The right to live in freedom from monopolies, foreign or domestic, is guaranteed by:

A. The denial of corporations' right to claim status as individual "persons" under the Fourteenth Amendment.

B. The denial of corporations' right to control the political process or public communications.

C. The denial of corporations' right to move from one community to another, domestic or foreign, without adequate compensation for the abandoned workers and community and proof that the new community and workers will benefit from the relocation. In corporate moves to foreign countries, the same proof of benefit is required; workers must be paid a livable wage, environmental standards must be maintained, and communities must benefit.

Amendment 10. The right to enjoy the benefits of citizenship in the workplace, which includes freedom of speech; freedom to choose one's private style of life; freedom from search and intrusive surveillance; freedom from termination without fair treatment and the spirit of due process; freedom of religion, including the right to wear religious clothing on the job despite employer uniform requirements. (Reich, 1995)

Amendment 11. The right to special considerations because of gender-related social demands. The right of protection from sexual harassment. The right to corporate help with day care and reasonable family leave.

Amendment 12. The unabridged right to unionization.

Developing a National Industrial Policy

A study of the economic history of the twentieth century indicates to those concerned with good work and socioeconomic justice that neither the free market nor central governmental planning is adequate as a principle for organizing and regulating the economic sphere. A hybrid system focused on particular democratic social and economic goals seems to provide a more pragmatic answer to the economic problems that have plagued industrialized and postindustrial societies. The twenty-first century demands a national industrial policy that addresses those domains in which historical experience indicates the free market has performed poorly: the formulation of a national economic development strategy; the provision of a minimal level of economic security, the production of a fair distribution of wealth and economic-political power, and the protection of the environment. Without such planning, the free market unleashes economic forces that tend to swing between prosperity and poverty—boom today, bust tomorrow. Without a national industrial policy, we witness corporate migrations to Third World locales that leave many U.S. communities and workers economically devastated. Critical vocational educators understand the socioeconomic and political dynamics that necessitate a coordinated national economic policy.

What might such a policy do? A plan of this sort would encourage coordination of activities at the national, state, and local levels to gain a fair apportionment of job opportunities across urban and rural, prosperous and depressed regions. Programs would be developed to maintain existing industrial production, to facilitate the opening of new firms, and to attract growing industries that help upgrade the skills and wages of particular labor markets. In particular, an industrial policy would reject myopic state and local practices of providing increasingly expensive incentives to attract migratory companies to a particular locale. A basic tenet of such a policy would involve supporting activities that raise the standard of living for working people and increase their participation in the daily affairs of the workplace. Contrary to the convoluted theories of trickle-down economics, plans that reduce unequal income levels and social inequality actually do stimulate spending, increase demand, and result in job creation. Right-wing opponents of such a commonsense industrial policy argue that the United States could not afford a plan with such radical democratic objectives. New expenditures would be required by such a policy, but they could easily be financed by reducing existing governmentally funded corporate welfare provided to firms without requirements to produce socially beneficial outcomes. Closing corporate tax loopholes provided by political cronies would generate another source of funding, as would an increased sales tax on luxury products and services.

In light of the antiworker, antiunion, and anticommunity policies pursued by the corporate government over the last two decades of the century, the only industrial policy that will work must involve the effort to promote good work and higher wages around the world. Of course, such a task is daunting, as governments in the industrialized world would have to coordinate policies designed to promote higher standards of living for workers not only with one another but also with impoverished nations that fear being shut out of the possibility of prosperity. The struggle for justice is always difficult, but the struggle projected to a global dimension is even more overwhelming. The understanding we have gained of the globalization process leaves critical cultural workers and educators no choice: For the struggle for justice to win on the local level, it must be fought in the global, the national, and the local arena. No matter how hard one local area may push for such desirable goals as higher wages for workers to create an incentive for productivity growth and increased investment in high-productivity and high-skill jobs, the process is undermined when economically disadvantaged areas negotiate independently to "undercut" labor and other operating costs. Without (inter)national coordination around such issues, successful labor negotiations and progress toward good work can be wiped out in an instant (Pollin and Cockburn, 1991; Block, 1990; Falk and Lyson, 1988; Pollin, 1996; Bowles, Gordon, and Weisskopf, 1990; Greider, 1992).

With protection against capricious capital migrations of this type, worker-owned cooperatives can be established. Under the provisions of an industrial policy dedicated to good work and higher wages, such co-ops could borrow low-interest start-up funds now routinely denied them. With a friendly climate for worker co-ops, critical vocational educators could direct more and more of their curricula to the analysis of information necessary to such endeavors. For workers who hold jobs that are not self-directed and are labor intensive and physically difficult, a democratic national industrial policy would relegate special compensation for unpleasant but socially necessary jobs. That move would be one aspect of a larger effort to reduce the hierarchical division between intellectual and manual labor. One of the many reasons for integrating academic and vocational education comes from the belief that various tasks could be shared by people from a variety of backgrounds. Such integration is also grounded on the understanding that, contrary to the pronouncements of mainstream psychology, the difference in the abilities of people who perform intellectual versus manual labor is not very significant. This appreciation is central to a plethora of political, moral, and educational policies in our critical vision of government, labor, and schooling.

In addition, a national industrial policy advocated by critical vocational educators sees through the illusions of free trade policies so popular with Western neoliberal governments at the end of the century. According to the theory, freeing trade by lifting barriers to international commerce allows each nation to focus on products and services in which they hold a competitive advantage. In this way, all commodities are produced efficiently at the lowest cost, which benefits consumers around the world. When obstacles are presented to free trade, advocates maintain, customers must pay a surcharge that, in effect, subsidizes inefficiency. Like other celebrations of the free market, free trade is based on a view of a world that does not exist in globalized, corporatized reality. All nations employ numerous strategies to protect their industries: tariffs, quotas, and subsidies, to name but a few. Japan, for example, has used "dumping" policies—the protection of domestic enterprises by permitting them to sell their products to foreign consumers below prices prevailing in Japanese domestic markets—to establish a beachhead in the United States and other foreign markets. Soon, the beachhead evolved into total market domination. That industrial policy worked brilliantly, of course, to move Japan into an unprecedented economic position (Aronowitz and DiFazio, 1994; Bowles, Gordon, and Weisskopf, 1990; Bluestone and Bluestone, 1992).

Most nations in the world watched the United States gain world dominance in the production and selling of military hardware through its national policy of subsidizing its defense industries. Learning an important lesson, many nations focused a similar industrial policy on the subsidization of their commercial products. Various nations funded research and development costs for machine-tool industries, semiconductors, supercomputers, high-definition TV, and various industrial materials. By holding on to the fantasy world of free trade, the United States allows Japan, Germany, and other nations to gain an edge in commercial product innovation. Such neglect not only hurts the United States in an purely self-interested economic nationalist sense but allows the balance of wealth in the world to grow more disparate by discouraging international coordination of industrial policies. A democratic global industrial policy would not only provide grants and loans to innovative producers but also to firms that employ disadvantaged groups, both domestic and foreign. This policy would also reverse the decline in government-funded basic research. Our democratic industrial policy would focus increased funding of basic research on sustainable and equitable development, with issues of race, class, and gender equity constantly directing its moral compass.

Conservative opponents of a democratic national industrial policy would have us believe that such a governmental role in economic affairs is unprecedented and somehow anti-American. Governmental intervention of the type discussed here is as old as America itself. Although such policies have never been planned and coordinated around long-term socioeconomic visions, government in the nineteenth century promoted economic development via right-of-way grants to private railroad companies and protected struggling industries by way of high tariffs. Throughout the twentieth century, government has funded infrastructural needs such as highways and has subsidized research and development in industries such as synthetic rubber and integrated circuits. Curiously, throughout American economic history, zealous fidelity to the rule of the free market has been set aside in times of need. When Japanese computer chips began to undermine American domination of the market, for example, the sacred competition of unimpeded free enterprise was abandoned; IBM negotiated a cooperation agreement with its domestic competitors and successfully petitioned the federal government for research and development funds. Despite all of the rhetorical glorification of the unfettered free enterprise system by the leaders of Chrysler, the company survives at the end of the century only because of its bailout by the federal government—through ad hoc national industrial policy. Who among these free market evangelicals is complaining?

Of course, any industrial policy that facilitates the production of wealth in a context centered around the pursuit of socioeconomic justice must address the moral obligations of corporations in the globalized economy. The corporate oligarchy must be dethroned and called to social accountability. Such a process must be delicately handled, for the rights of free speech in a democratic society apply to potentates of concentrated technopower as well as to the disenfranchised. A critical socioeconomic vision does not imply the need for a "palace cleansing" with a denial of civic rights for selected groups. Simply put, this vision necessitates applying the obligations of citizenship to corporations in the same manner they are applied to individual men and women. As delineated in the Post-Fordist Bill of Rights, corporate abuses must be identified and addressed. A democratic national industrial policy, for example, would question granting corporate tax credits to companies undermining the quality of products and reducing the number of jobs. This policy would ask corporations to at least share the costs of remedying the social, economic, and environmental problems their policies precipitated. A democratic policy would carefully scrutinize the provision of state, local, and federal governmental subsidies and incentives to firms that failed to live up to their social obligations to their communities.

The free market orgy of deregulation that has dominated the last two decades of the century has failed—but as a society, we have yet to pay the full costs of such failure. Although corporate leaders have benefited from this politics of deregulation, the suffering it causes the poor and racially marginalized continues to escalate. In the shadow of the free market, thousands of small businesses have failed, many workers have lost both jobs and hope, and the quality of public services has disintegrated. The privatization process encouraged by deregulation has been unable to offer affordable housing, support services such as day care, and education. One of the most profound tragedies of this voodoo economic process has been the dismantling of the public sphere. Interestingly, as Aronowitz and DiFazio (1994) have astutely pointed out, the deregulation steamroller has been most consistently applied to corporate efforts *to undermine the position of workers*. Under the mantle of deregulation, corporate leaders have contracted jobs, closed long-operating and even profitable factories, broken unions, and undermined workers' health and pension plans. A society that allows such destructive operations to proceed unimpeded has fallen victim to a form of ideological fundamentalism in which fidelity to a free market orthodoxy takes precedence over good sense. A democratic national industrial policy can help restore our sense of values and humanity (Lakes, 1994b; Falk and Lyson, 1988; Greider, 1992).

A critical vocational education can be tied directly to this industrial policy by linking educational programs to our moral vision in general and to job creation and targeted employment opportunity in particular (Samper and Lakes, 1994). Students would not be mechanistically trained for jobs but would come to understand the socioeconomic context into which their jobs fit as part of a larger integrated vocational and academic education. Vocational teacher understanding of a vision of social justice, good work, democratic labor policies, and an (inter)national industrial policy are only a few of the pieces necessary to any effort to move vocational education beyond a low-level form of technical training. I am convinced by my decades of observations of students deemed academically incapable that many of them respond enthusiastically and competently to an education that connects them to the realities of the lived world. Once they appreciate both the personal and the social benefits of such integrated, visionary, and pragmatic learning, they will—like most people—avail themselves of it. Thus, the purpose of this book emerges yet again: The key dynamic to the success of such a process involves the ability of vocational educators to help students understand the vision, to make sense of the bombardment of unconnected information that confuses them. Without this ingredient, all of the brilliant reforms the most gifted among us can imagine will fail miserably.

Government Policy

Investing in People and Their Needs

As vocational educators sophisticate their democratic social vision, they come to understand that by denying government's role in the economy, the free market has cut off short-term governmental investments in people who pay long-term dividends. Thus, the logic of the quarterly balance sheet induces policymakers to cut social spending, as the costs resulting from socioeconomic inequality and the social conflict it produces consume *nearly one-half of the wealth produced in the United States.* The recognition of this phenomenal reality should ground every political and educational discussion that takes place. But like so many other social understandings at the end of the century, one is hard pressed to hear reference to it in the public political conversation. American politics, unfortunately, has operated for the last thirty years as if such real-life side effects of socioeconomic injustice did not exist—as if people could, year after year, generation after generation, operate outside the boundaries of hope and not be in some way damaged by the process. In the perverted logic of the free market, social investments in people, especially the most hopeless among us, were slashed while corporate welfare to the rich grew. Under the banner of getting government off our backs, corporate social obligations were lifted while new regulations on the poor were developed without hesitation: workfare, Ritalin for control of hard-to-teach poor children, new prisons for drug dealers and users, more severe penalties for cheap crack-cocaine convictions than for powder cocaine, war measures against illegal immigrants and denial of education and social services for their children, and armed guards in poor urban high schools, to name only a few.

Governmental investments in education, health, child welfare, transportation, and other social categories have now been neglected for a generation. Not only are such programs helpful to targeted individuals—especially if they are decentralized, locally administered, and personally operated—but the new jobs created by them are distributed in productive sectors of the economy. Many Americans presently hold down two or three jobs, working much of their time to maintain a home and raise their children. Investments in publicly financed privately owned homes and multiple-dwelling rental housing would dramatically improve the lives of millions of American workers. Currently, such workers are held captive by real-estate market fluctuations that have dramatically slashed their home equities and have much too often led to their eviction. There is simply no reason that the mercurial free market should be allowed to destroy the economic security of workers when a national housing plan could be easily formulated. In this regard, workers with children are also penalized by the absence of public child care services. No one should be surprised to learn that half the income of many struggling workers is absorbed by mortgage or rent payments and child care. The decline of the public sector is often viewed by Americans as not having human consequences—but nothing could be further from reality (Coontz, 1992; Pollin, 1996; Aronowitz, 1992).

Jobs

The socioeconomic changes fueled by the globalized economy and all of the forces it has unleashed have led to the firing of millions of workers around the world. Despite temporary fluctuations, the rising unemployment rate has fanned worker anger across continents, and projections for the first decade of the twenty-first century indicate the problem will only get worse. If such predictions are only partly correct, hundreds of millions of people will find themselves in a position where their talents and energies will be deemed unnecessary and irrelevant. If we do not make plans and develop (inter)national strategies to avoid such a future scenario, the world may find itself steadily plunging into an era of chaos and lawlessness. A key justification for any critical democratic industrial policy involves not only its moral imperative but a crassly pragmatic need to avoid the possibility of such a stark and frightening Mad Max future. Conservatives and liberals have consistently ignored the reality of the job market, not to mention the projections concerning the depressing effects of globalization and the automation that accompanies it. This reaction has served to downplay the impact of deindustrialization and the nearly 6 million jobs it has destroyed in the last fifteen years. The conservative and liberal dismissal of the consequences of such realities has been well illustrated by Newt Gingrich and Bill Clinton's shared belief that new high-tech jobs will fill the gaps in employment left by the globalization process.

The free market cannot generate enough jobs—high-skill, high-paid positions in particular—to make up for accelerating losses. Since the growth in high-skill jobs is over, a national job-creation policy tied closely to vocational education is badly needed. A government policy creating jobs that are grounded on the principles of good work, distributing them democratically by reducing the number of hours in the workweek to thirty-five, and redistributing overtime can help delay the social upheavals of mass unemployment and poverty. Since the 1960s, scores of federal job training programs have been developed and have been run haphazardly by groups of private businesspeople with little governmental supervision. Unconnected to a larger, coherent job policy or a coordinated overview of vocational education, such programs from CETA to Job Training Partnership Act (JTPA) and beyond have served as little more than a welfare program for business. Learning from the failures of the past, a government-directed job policy could be grounded on the needed repair of America's infrastructure: road, railroad, and bridge building and repair; the construction of waste disposal plants; cleanup of toxic and nuclear wastes; construction of the new housing mentioned earlier; and renovation of public libraries and schools. Such work would continue for decades, given the $5 to $6 trillion long-term costs of this undertaking (Weisman, 1991; Murray, 1992; Bovard, 1987; Melman and Dumas, 1990).

A corps of skilled, unionized workers organized around a larger international social vision could be employed for these and other socially valuable tasks. Contrary to conservative objections, such work would not be characterized as meaningless jobs designed merely to keep people busy. Unless job creation is tied directly to specific socially necessary tasks, we face the same question that has dogged President Clinton's job retraining proposals for high-tech work: Retraining for what high-tech jobs? Where are they? Department of Labor studies indicate that fewer than one in five retrained workers in the 1990s were finding new jobs at even 80 percent of their previous salary. Our democratic job policy is based on the assumption that everyone should benefit from productivity increases derived from technological innovations in information, communications, and industrial machinery. Various forms of compensation can be devised in this context for those who have lost their jobs as a result of these advances. The formulation of smart, creative, socially beneficent, individually rewarding compensation is a central concern of this chapter and the critical vision that guides us.

Corporate policies that dispose of good jobs and undermine communities, as I have consistently argued, must be carefully examined in light of the goals of a national economic plan and a democratic job policy. When corporations move, the plan would induce them to negotiate the provisions of such migration with unions, local communities, and governmental agencies at the local, state, and national levels. Joining with AFL-CIO proposals, the plan focuses much attention on the plight of workers displaced in these corporate migrations as well as on first-time workers and the problems they face as they enter the workforce. As far as these young workers are concerned, Republican free market advocates have fought for years for the enactment of a "training wage" below the minimum wage for inexperienced workers. Such a provision would create a profit bonanza for many corporate managers, who would hire such youth and fire them at the end of their so-called training period. Thus, labor costs could be saved, but at the expense of older workers, whose wages are used to support their families. A progressive jobs policy would support a flexible minimum wage that takes into account a variety of factors, including the portability of the job, the area of the country and the prevailing wage rates that exist, and the nature of the employee—Is that employee a middle-class teenage part-time worker or one of the millions of workers trying to raise a family on an inadequate income (Falk and Lyson, 1988; Rifkin, 1995; Roberts and Wozniak, 1994)?

Worker Safety

Since Congress passed the Occupational Safety and Health Care Act in 1970, almost 250,000 workers have been killed on the job, and 2 million have died from workplace-generated diseases. Other workers—1.5 million of them—have been permanently disabled as a result of workplace accidents. Yet the most amazing statistic regarding worker safety tells us that only a handful of companies have ever been prosecuted for on-the-job safety violations. Not only do workers continue to die en masse, but they are killed in the most horrible ways: suffocated by trench cave-ins, electrocuted while working on power lines, blown to bits by explosions in mines and refineries, minced into pieces in cutting machines, burned to death in iron and steel factory fires. In many ways, these types of deaths may be preferable to the long-term suffering caused by death from black lung, brown lung, cancer, or chemical and radiation poisoning. The point is clear: The lax enforcement of OSHA rules has failed to encourage corporate leaders to adopt policies that place the value of worker safety over short-term profits.

American society has demonstrated a lack of interest in issues of worker safety. An accident, for example, that kills several workers attracts little attention in the news and is quickly forgotten. When a construction worker is killed when scaffolding collapses on a high-rise project, people shake their heads and proclaim that the worker understood the risk that went along with the job. Even though OSHA demands a safe workplace, many observers ascribe accidents to the will of God, even when owners are negligent in addressing safety factors. When corporate executives are killed, the news media deliver long obituaries and a series of connected stories about the loss, the tragedy. The difference in news coverage and public concern is connected to a central concern of this book: class bias. This culture, simply put, cares more about the lives of the rich than about those of the poor. And the perspective is not new, as throughout American history the workplace has always been unsafe. The litany of U.S. workplace tragedies is overwhelming, with its descriptions of thousands killed in mine explosions, of seven hundred deaths in the construction of one tunnel, of hundreds dead in one factory fire after another.

Employers understand that it is cheaper to buy insurance and defer costs to workers and consumers than to actually make their workplaces safer. With the dawning of the age of fast, dynamically flexible post-Fordist capitalism, the quickened operating pace typically translates into reduced safety and health concerns for workers. "We'll give you your money back if the pizza is not at your door in thirty minutes," Breakneck Pizza executives announce, as their delivery drivers crash into unlucky pedestrians and immovable barricades. Attempts to increase and enforce employer penalties for workplace safety infractions have been successfully crushed by the corporate lobby. Emasculated during the Reagan-Bush era, OSHA only holds a small fraction of the resources necessary to inspect the nation's 7 million workplaces. OSHA, operating under the auspices of the corporate government, has adopted industry's own Milquetoast health and safety guidelines as its own. When technical help is needed, the office seeks the advice of the business-run National Safety Council. Of course, such meager regulation allows the massacre of U.S. workers to continue and corporate leaders to rest comfortably in their exemption from criminal responsibility for negligence. The only "good" aspect of such lax policies I can imagine is that with the further deterioration of workplace safety and health standards, U.S. corporations will have less incentive to move to Malaysia.

Taxes

The basis of a critically reconceptualized federal tax policy would be grounded on the effort to reward good citizenship and to promote social and economic justice. Fair taxes that redistributed just 1 percent of the income of America's most wealthy 5 percent could help lift 1 million people out of poverty. A 1 percent increase on only the upper 2 percent of America's wealthiest people would enable the nation to double federal spending on education and still have 20 billion dollars left over. But instead of moving in this type of just direction, tax policy over the last twenty years has worked to redistribute wealth from the poor and working class to the rich. The tax breaks and loopholes for corporations and their wealthy owners have been appropriated from the so-called socioeconomic safety net for the needy. Such corporate-designed breaks and loopholes work to subsidize the political campaigning of the most wealthy and powerful political voices in the world—firms and their political action coalitions receive tax write-offs for the production and dissemination of self-interested propaganda. Under this arrangement, General Motors can deduct the cost of flying its executives and lobbyists to Washington to lobby against workplace safety legislation, whereas workers have to finance their own trips to tell lawmakers about injuries or diseases caused by unsafe workplaces.

When a billion-dollar corporation—one of the few social organizations that can afford the costs of prime-time TV advertising—finds its political activities tax deductible at the same time an individual citizen's attempt to gain a voice in the public conversation is not, the spirit of participatory democratic has been snuffed out. An essential aspect of a democratic national industrial policy would expose the Never-Never Land fiction that corporate lobbying and "educational" activities are not political—not political because they are not tied directly to political elections. The cultural changes brought about by contemporary electronically mediated culture have moved much of the process of political consciousness construction outside of the realm of electoral politics. For this and other reasons, the study of the foundations of work and vocational education can no longer focus simply on the economic, political, and pedagogical realm and ignore the cultural domain—in this case, popular culture and the analysis of TV. In the past, it was assumed that economic and political processes were the domains to study in order to understand the "real world" of work and the financial system. To understand these spheres and their relation to vocational education, we have to grasp the processes by which cultural practices shape the way human beings understand issues such as government tax policy and the role various organizations play in creating cultural meanings about such practices. Such an appreciation ties the development of political and economic consciousness directly to the realm of pedagogy, where knowledge and values are produced and transmitted and where identity is formed (du Gay et al., 1997).

A national industrial policy would eliminate governmental subsidies for corporate political activity. The corporate government's transformation of tax laws into elaborate corporate giveaways would end. A democratic tax policy would not offer tax credits for the political activity of those most able to pay but for those least able—wage workers and ordinary citizens. Any individual who wanted to engage politically would be granted a tax credit of several hundred dollars. Political deductions for several hundred dollars' worth of contributions to election campaigns or political educational efforts would be a part of a democratic tax plan designed to stimulate national and state political organizations to refocus their energies toward neglected citizens and workers instead of megacorporations. Another aspect of the use of taxes to stimulate individual grassroots efforts to engage in political or civic activity involves the rebuilding of nongovernmental organizations dedicated to the improvement of communities. To fund such positive work, a wide variety of analysts have called for a so-called value-added tax (VAT), a tax that is levied on consumption rather than on income. If small businesses and the consumption of basic necessities such as food, clothing, medicine and medical care, and housing under a certain cost are exempted from such a tax, the VAT holds great possibility as a revenue generator for civic activities.

The tax could be specifically targeted to finance particular problems emerging from the inequities resulting from globalization. We might consider, for example, a VAT on all computers, information, and telecommunications services and products. Revenues collected from this would be used to pay for education and job creation needed in the transition of workers whose jobs were consumed by the technological revolution into new vocations—maybe even nongovernmental civic activity. To avoid regressive deployments of such a VAT, nonprofit organizations such as schools and humanitarian or philanthropic institutions would be exempted from it. Charles Reich (1995) has estimated that Americans spend more than $340 billion a year on entertainment and recreation—on videotapes, VCRs, cellular phones, home computers, boats, personal airplanes, amusement parks, toys, sporting equipment, movies, live entertainment, and gambling. If a VAT were levied on these expenditures and on corporate advertising, enough money could be raised to sophisticate vocational education through its integration with academic education and make sure the nation's poorer workers had better jobs and better pay.

Current tax policies—corporate tax breaks in particular—are resistant to such socially beneficial and democratic uses. Justifications are often mere smoke screens for crass corporate greed. Tax cuts for General Electric (among hundreds of other firms) allowed the company to reduce taxes on its $6.5 billion profits between 1981–1983 from $330 million a year to a minus figure of $90 million—the corporation received a net cash payment from the government of $283 million. The smoke screen justification for the tax cuts that in only a few years saved GE $1,300,000,000 (and even more in the long run) was that such revenues would allow the corporation to create thousands of new jobs. Of course, this was not to be the case. In an orgy of downsizing, GE during this period laid off 50,000 workers. Other companies followed this pattern, using their new job-creation monies to build cheaper factories, hire less expensive workers in foreign nations, and acquire new firms to add to their corporate assets. It was with the help of this tax cut that GE purchased the National Broadcasting Corporation (NBC) (Greider, 1992).

Government and the Politics of Knowledge

In the post-Fordist globalized economy, the production of knowledge and scientific and intellectual work in general has been steadily appropriated by corporations. In this process, knowledge has been captured and deployed in an effort to protect corporations against their critics and produce technological innovations that raise quarterly profit margins. This development, if not challenged, holds ominous implications for the future of democracy. Such a politics of knowledge silences citizens who do not have the fiscal resources to produce data at the same level as do corporations. How do individual citizens answer a corporation that produces a score of expert-generated empirical studies—heavily biased though they may be—that "prove" the corporate claim that the pollutants they dumped in the water supply did not cause miscarriages and deformed babies? Citizens do not typically speak this modernist language of the expert—nor should they. As an excellent example of the power of modernist science, expert empiricism silences the language of lived experience, of pain and suffering.

To make the often-heard argument that the American people are narcissistic and ill informed is to miss the epistemological dynamics at work in contemporary culture. The public is not ignorant because it does not understand the scientific rationalism of political and social elites—indeed, its suspicion of such a politics of knowledge illustrates the people's intuition about the irrationality of modernist rationalism. With the decline of political parties in the United States, no powerful group exists to help the people produce information that would lend credence to their intuitions. In some countries, such knowledge production is a primary function of political parties—but not in the United States. Even the knowledge production that takes place in the end-of-the-century American university has been curtailed by governmental budget cuts, making a higher and higher percentage of the information generated in higher education corporate-sponsored. It is highly ironic that just at the time when knowledge work has become more important to the commercial sphere, university budgets are being slashed—despite rising enrollments and overburdened faculty researchers.

There is nothing complex about the politics of knowledge in contemporary university systems. Scholars are often hired to turn out policy ideas for political debate that support the interests of their corporate benefactors. These scholarly data producers deliver their information to corporate lobbyists and lawyers, who use the ideas to influence public opinion and legislative decisions. The corporate seizure of information and its political effects have taught the American public a hard lesson: Scientifically produced knowledge is never objective. Such data emerge from particular questions motivated by particular interests and needs in specific circumstances. In other words, many scholars are "for sale"—and the only players wealthy enough to consistently participate in this knowledge game are the corporations. One of the most important ways corporations have operated in this context is by sponsoring ostensibly neutral think tanks (Wolman and Colamosca, 1997). The American Enterprise Institute (AEI), for example, once viewed as a reactionary little right-wing organization, began in the late 1970s to pick up wealthy sponsors who liked its probusiness message: AT&T, $125,000; Chase Manhattan Bank, $171, 000; Chevron, $95,000; Citicorp, $100,000; Exxon, $130,000; GE, $65,000; GM, $100,000, to name only a few. By the late 1990s, AEI has become a major force in American politics (Greider, 1992). Scores of other corporate-fed think tanks produce data that support specific business-related political projects: the Heritage Foundation, the Cato Institute, the Hudson Institute, the Hoover Institute, the Progress and Freedom Foundation, the Manhattan Institute, the Competitive Enterprise Institute, and so on.

As argued throughout this book, students and workers need to know that democracy has been taken captive by corporate knowledge producers, that government agencies designed to help curb corporate abuses are now operated by corporations themselves; for example, the Bureau of Mines is run by the coal industry. Such realities remove workers and other citizens from access to relevant information, from an understanding of how the political process actually works. In this context, political action by citizens—when it occurs—is often reduced to single-issue oppositional tactics. A polluting corporation with unfair labor practices may be confronted and even successfully deferred, but long-term political action that addresses larger systemic problems is more difficult to generate in this unfair knowledge context. Likewise, the needs of workers squeezed in the globalized economy are erased from the public conversation. It is amazing at the end of the century that the struggles and hardships of workers around the world do not make it onto the national news or the national political agenda. Such erasure allows a large percentage of Americans to believe that poverty is caused by poor people—not by corporate leaders, who, in alliance with one another, set wage structures.

No matter what they might do, corporations in such an information climate are released from blame. Thus, vocational education is injected into the debate as the social agency that can "repair" the poor by granting them job skills. If corporations can produce information that focuses on the limitations of workers and their need for a "practical" and pacifying vocational education, the battle for the soul of vocational education is almost over before it begins. This is why, as argued in Chapter 10, workers and vocational teachers and students must become researchers who can counter these self-serving corporate claims. This educational dynamic takes on dramatic importance in an era where few groups have the expertise or power to present alternatives to the corporate agenda. Critical vocational educators maintain that government grants could be provided to high-school vocational programs to carry out research on work-related issues. The research of students and teachers could in this way be supported, opening a new day for the potential of work education (Carlson, 1997; Aronowitz and DiFazio, 1994).

The Search for Painless Policies:
Youth Apprenticeships as Panacea

American political and corporate leaders have avoided the huge effort it will take to improve the lot of American workers. Constantly seeking painless remedies, they have searched the world for easy solutions. Rejecting many European governments' social spending on worker protection and well-being, they began to focus on vocational education and training as the answer to the problem of labor. Employing a simplistic and reductionistic form of thinking, they began to look at the educational programs of nations that have achieved recent economic success. Unfortunately, no nation has an exemplary program, and in addition, it is hard to display the relationship between vocational educational policy and national economic progress. Nevertheless, many Americans have sought to emulate various characteristics of foreign programs—especially Germany's youth apprenticeship program. In the minds of some, Germany's recent economic success is grounded on its apprenticeships.

In 1950, West Germany adopted the Federal Youth Plan, which addressed the academic and vocational needs of young people aged fourteen through twenty-one. Those students who move from school directly into the labor force are required in this plan to enter an apprenticeship program or have vocational training. Students begin to make decisions about their career track at age ten, when they take a national test designed to place them in an educational track. Two out of three German students are placed in the vocational track and learn very quickly where they stand in relation to academically tracked students. German vocational students know they operate in a very rigid system that does not allow them to escape their assigned track. Grounded on the belief that the workplace is the best vocational learning environment, the German system mandates that apprentices attend vocational classes only one day a week. During that day, they study German, social studies, and theoretical and practical information related to work placement. Students who want to be machinists take courses in algebra, geometry, and trigonometry. Teachers work to display the applicability of such mathematics to the making of machine parts. Apprentices in office work use their one day at school to study accounting.

The German apprenticeship system, no doubt, prepares German vocational students to work in more intellectually demanding jobs than American young people. At a time when American vocational students are working in McJobs in fast-food restaurants, mopping floors, and operating cash registers, German students are entering higher-skill, career-type jobs. At a very young age, such students are expected to perform adult jobs such as car repair, police work, bank telling, and TV repair. Even after graduating from secondary school at age eighteen, German apprentices continue taking vocational classes until they take a state-sanctioned examination that grants them the credentials to pursue their chosen vocation. Making use of its highly trained workforce, the German economy has concentrated on high-quality niche products in the manufacturing sector. That focus has paid tremendous dividends for Germany's economy, as it has accelerated the nation's standard of living. Understanding such benefits, many German corporations and unions have lent their support to government plans to maintain and extend the apprenticeship system. Unions, for example, encourage apprentices to participate in their activities, even developing sports and youth activity centers for them (Kolberg and Smith, 1992; Rifkin, 1995; Banducci, 1985; Roditi, 1992; Hamilton, 1992; Hamilton and Hamilton, 1992; Hamilton, 1986).

In light of the German program, vocational educators clearly see the lack of interest Americans have had in apprenticeships: Apprentices constitute less than 0.5 percent of the U.S. workforce. But the times they are a-changing, as presidents, state legislators, educational policymakers, and blue-ribbon commissions have embraced German-style apprenticeships in the 1990s. As is typical of one-shot panaceas, little analysis has been conducted to examine the contextual factors that have contributed to the success of the German program and to explore how a different context may affect the wholesale adoption of apprenticeships in the United States. Although many aspects of the German program are admirable—the integration of academic work into the vocational curriculum for working apprentices, for example— apprenticeships in the United States will not work outside of a social vision accompanied by progressive governmental action, strong democratic unions, and a vocational education closely integrated with academic understandings. Without policies that combat racial and gender discrimination and embrace good work, apprenticeships will join a long line of vocational education reforms in the panacea cemetery. Since job skill level is typically not the main criterion for employers when they hire young workers, apprenticeships will not necessarily improve the job outlook for American youth.

Apprenticeships without a sufficient number of full-time jobs or positions that require high skills are irrelevant. Much of the support for apprenticeships comes from corporate leaders and their apologists, who argue that workers' skills are currently so low that firms cannot afford to create jobs with high skill levels. Apprenticeships, the argument concludes, will allow firms to create high-skill, high-pay jobs. This absurd position would have us believe that business leaders are champing at their bits to pay their highly skilled workers high wages. If this is true, why are so many of them moving their factories to Third World locations where the formal educational level of the population is significantly lower than in the United States? The answer is simple: The jobs that are moved to poor countries are deskilled positions requiring little expertise or knowledge of any kind. Even if Albert Einstein and John Dewey filled such positions, the low-level work skills that characterize these jobs would not allow this talented duo to exhibit their respective genius. Indeed, apprenticeships without the governmental commitment to jobs and union support discussed in this book will simply perpetuate the injustice that plagues students who enter vocational educational programs—and such young men and women will still be viewed as the incapable ones unable to make it in the academic track (Hamilton, 1992; Kantor, 1994).

Apprenticeships take place in the everyday world of workplaces. What actually goes on in these situations? Although there is a wide variety of apprenticeship experiences, all too often the apprenticeship becomes more an unthinking adjustment to managerial interests than a rigorous and reflective educational practicum. A critical apprenticeship should provide vocational students with an opportunity to confront ill-defined problems and to develop a variety of ways to solve them. Such lived-world experiences should be supplemented with a time for reflection about the larger context in which problems are situated, with the aid of highly skilled workers and vocational and academic teachers. An example of a critically grounded apprenticeship might involve students in a house construction project. Not only would students learn carpentry and construction skills but they would also study the politics of housing, ways of examining contemporary housing problems, the manner in which housing is viewed in different cultures and historical eras, and various solutions to the problem of housing the homeless.

Unfortunately, this critical vision of apprenticeships is not the reality. With businesses firmly in control of the curriculum of apprentice experiences, many students in highly touted programs spend their time photocopying, pressing buttons that take pictures of checks, getting coffee for employees, or sweeping the hair from the beauty salon floor. In the few academic classes they take, teachers often bombard them with an uncritical delineation of the virtues of free enterprise capitalism. Arguing that the free market is the economic extension of democratic freedom and choice, many teachers present a corporate-friendly curriculum. In too many apprenticeship programs, students are not encouraged to imagine and evaluate new possibilities for accomplishing various work tasks in the society. As with other vocational programs, questions concerning fair pay, health and safety conditions at work, collective bargaining, the ethics of the post-Fordist practice of hiring mainly part-time workers, alternative ownership systems, labor history, and environmental issues are infrequently asked. As most apprenticeship programs are now organized, they merely prop up the inequalities of the end-of-the-century status quo (Lankshear, 1995; Gabbard, 1995; Shapiro, 1995; Raizen, 1989; Rehm, 1989; Roditi, 1992).

Government as Coordinating Agent: Addressing
Empty Innovations of Post-Fordist School-to-Work Programs

The new vocational programs of the 1990s, such as the School-to-Work Opportunities Act signed by President Clinton in 1994, fail to take into account the global economic dynamics discussed in this book. Because such legislation celebrates high-tech, high-performance workplaces, it lays out no plan to stimulate the generation of such jobs. One potentially important initiative proposed by the Clinton administration involves the development of a national work education and training strategy. The most important feature of this plan employs government as a coordinator of vocational training programs among industries, schools, unions, and other institutions. Such a coordination function represents the quintessential act of the type of critical democratic government visualized here. Without such coordination and the values of socioeconomic justice so central to the critical mission, programs like these inevitably gravitate toward the corporate power mass and its need to adjust workers' attitudes in a manner conducive to the short-term interests of profit. Outside of this critical coordination, new school-to-work programs become empty innovations in the name of educating world-class workers for the globalized, competitive marketplace.

Several post-Fordist companies have developed educational programs for workers that embrace democratic goals: making the workplace a learning place; building worker-led problem-solving teams; and giving workers the right to present their solutions to problems directly to their managers. Undoubtedly, from the perspective of good work, such goals constitute a step in the right direction. In their pedagogies of work, these post-Fordist companies use the latest innovations in cognitive theory to develop contextualized cooperative learning opportunities that stress interpersonal communication skills. In such employer-developed vocational education, terms such as "team player" are bandied about in management pronouncements about the importance of workers' cooperating in the effort to accomplish innovative production goals. Such corporate talk comes directly from the new paradigm in management theory that emphasizes cooperative workplaces and empowered workers. Those of us concerned with economic justice may become enamored with such postmodern managerial changes until hit with the realization that often the purpose of such humanistic innovations still involves the traditional managerial effort to adjust students to the inequalities of the economic sphere. At this level, post-Fordist worker empowerment becomes little more than a Taylorist (or post-Taylorist) disempowerment (Levine, 1994; Nichols, 1996; Carlson, 1997; Gee, Hull, and Lankshear, 1996).

Thus, the innovations in vocational education are much like the old vocationalism in their narrow view of work roles and worker knowledge. The paradox critical vocational educators face involves helping future workers discern the difference between a genuine worker empowerment and corporate lip service to empowerment. Such corporate pseudo-empowerment claims that workers are wanted who are critical and can think for themselves; upon further examination, however, we find that workers in many of these "empowered" workplaces are limited in the actions in which they can engage, the types of options they can choose, and the prerogatives they can exercise. The managerial message is confusing: "Be empowered, think for yourself; but don't let it get out of hand." Even in companies where managers truly want to grant workers a greater voice in the operation of the firm, the educational strategies utilized to accomplish such an objective often subvert it. One reason for this is ideological: Managers do not want to give away inside knowledge and the power that attends it. A second reason is pedagogical: Many corporate training and development personnel do not quite understand what a pedagogy of empowerment—a critical pedagogy of work—actually entails.

This lack of pedagogical understanding reveals itself in socioeconomic class–inscribed perceptions of front-line workers as mentally deficient children. In accordance with such a condescending sensibility, work curriculums developed by trainers remind critical observers of traditional top-down information delivery pedagogies of the traditional elementary classroom. Trainers deliver unproblematized information to passive worker-students who are required to pass the data back to the teacher on written tests in the same form it was presented to them—in other words, by rote memorization. Critical observers of this form of vocational training report that they are hard pressed to find classes where students are induced to respond critically to the material: to question its validity, to compare it to their own work experiences, to inquire as to its source, to uncover hidden assumptions buried within it, and so forth. Indeed, much of the time worker-students take their multiple-choice, fill-in-the-blank, and matching tests and go on to the next predigested topic.

Instead of operating to empower workers to take initiative and make decisions, the corporate training curriculum often implicitly teaches employees to accept managerial pronouncements without question, when in doubt to be passive, and to do what they are told. This implicit curriculum often co-exists with no ostensible conflict with corporate mission statements proclaiming the need for workers to think, to troubleshoot, and to diagnose and act accordingly without supervisory permission. The post-Fordist managerial rhetoric and the training and workplace reality seem to exist in two different and conflicting space-time dimensions. In one corporate training class called "Accepting Change," Gee, Hull, and Lankshear (1996) reported that workers were taught to accept it "appropriately." Corporate trainers told student-workers to find out what the change involved and how it affected their work, then to support it. Much to the observers' surprise, trainers never talked about the possibility of student-workers evaluating the change or relaying their perspectives about it to managers. After completing such courses, workers found themselves accepting foolish organizational changes as matters of standard operating procedure. Of course, workers saw through such empty rhetoric, became justifiably cynical about the "innovations," and made fun of the entire process.

Tech Prep programs, touted by a variety of political and educational agencies, often fall into the same regressive syndromes as these corporate empowerment classes. Tech Prep at its best promises workplace literacy and applied academics in the last two years of high school. Such experiences are tied to the vocational students' immersion in an occupational cluster curriculum. After high-school graduation, students enroll in two-year occupational training programs in a community college that prepare them for "middle-range occupations" such as law enforcement, nursing, computer processing, engineering technology, and office-machine maintenance. The problem with Tech Prep is that it too is shaped by corporate values and business needs. Labor and other social agencies concerned with issues of justice for workers and a critical form of empowerment are notoriously missing in the Tech Prep pedagogical recipe. A critical pedagogy of vocational education teaches vocational teachers, vocational students, and workers to identify the ways that ostensibly neutral programs like Tech Prep are inscribed with corporate values (Carlson, 1997; Gee, Hull, and Lankshear, 1996; Kolberg and Smith, 1992).

The vocational education for the twentieth-first century advocated here responds to these governmentally backed programs by offering an alternative set of values on which to ground future school-to-work programs. In the spirit of good work and worker dignity, vocational education ought to engage students in an analysis of how corporate power in the media and in schooling helps shape their identities, their views of the political, economic, and educational realms of society, and their role in these contexts. By expanding their vision, by helping them construct a critical consciousness of that which surrounds them, critical vocational educators help develop student and worker cognizance of the ways power operates in the globalized cosmos—an awareness that moves worker consciousness far beyond the stage corporations would find comfortable. Although worker immersion in the communities of practice of the workplace helps develop worker skills in the way delineated by avant-garde cognitive theory (situated cognition), the same type of involvement is needed in the context of worker analysis and critique of the values and assumptions that reside in corporate economic and educational operations.

A government focused on decentralizing many of its functions, dedicated to good work, and wedded to the democratic policies enumerated earlier in this chapter can positively contribute to both a critical work education that produces smart workers and to economic justice. It is ironic that at the same time the United States has dismissed the ability of government and the public sphere to contribute much to the improvement of the lives of its citizens, governments in many developing countries have adopted policies that have successfully spurred economic growth. For example, in the countries known as the four tigers of East Asia—South Korea, Taiwan, Singapore, and Hong Kong—government has developed national economic plans tied closely to research and educational policy to produce unprecedented economic success. The economic troubles of late 1997 and 1998 in this part of Asia have not been caused by governmental planning as much as by inept business practices by corporate leaders. Without such economic and educational coordination—a task only government is equipped to administer—Americans who make their living by muscular and intellectual work will find themselves in the twenty-first century laboring harder and longer but earning less. Such a future prospect necessitates a national governmental policy that demands high educational expectations for students of all backgrounds and the pedagogical attention necessary to achieve such a goal. Of course, such an educational goal is worthless unless the economy is restructured in a manner that helps create and reward industries and worker co-operatives that create high-skill, high-paid jobs (Wolman and Colamosca, 1997; Gee, Hull, and Lankshear, 1996; Carlson, 1997).

The need for coordination is well illustrated by the current arrangement of youth employment in the United States. America has the highest youth employment rate of any nation in the industrialized world—but the jobs young people occupy are almost always unrelated to school and learning. Indeed, these jobs frequently steal youth's time for school and scholarship. It is patently absurd that government is not coordinating youth employment with schools, unions, businesses, welfare departments, and a variety of nongovernmental organizations such as women's groups and social justice–oriented institutions such as the National Association for the Advancement of Colored People (NAACP). Here, in a decentralized, grassroots, and personal manner, government could help promote the community as a site of learning. If this were accomplished, not only would youth gain invaluable educational experience from a variety of individuals but community cohesiveness would be promoted. Here is where President Clinton's notion of government as a coordinating agent can be put to democratic use. In this coordinated context that brings together a plethora of educational, governmental, civic, social, and commercial agencies, apprenticeships could prosper. Special forms of learning could take place, and as part of its coordinating activity, government could help create and encourage various agencies to generate high-skill, high-paid jobs for graduating apprentices. Such apprenticeships would not merely be occupied by students tracked into vocational education but by all students regardless of their backgrounds. The great power of such vocational and civic experiences, when properly questioned and analyzed in more traditional school classrooms, could help reform the entire enterprise of American education (Hamilton and Hamilton, 1992; Raizen, 1989; Nichols, 1996).

The Future Role of Government: Accomplishing Socially Beneficial Tasks While Reducing Bureaucracy

A vocational education that fails to connect students with academic knowledge and the ability to produce knowledge while preparing them for jobs that have migrated to Singapore is of little worth. The well-being of working Americans is dependent on a rigorous, untracked, and vocationally and academically integrated education combined with good jobs that contribute to rebuilding communities and forging new social connections between people from diverse backgrounds. As maintained in previous chapters, we must find new ways to accomplish this necessary task. The quality of life we will experience in the twenty-first century is dependent on the success of our efforts. As more and more workers find themselves either unemployed or in the low-wage, no-benefit contingent (part-time) labor pool, millions of talented individuals will find themselves with time on their hands. Is it possible to devise creative strategies to make personally rewarding, socially beneficial use of the abilities of these individuals—even if it is outside of the boundaries of what we call the public and private sectors?

When asked, most people value the concept of community service. The success of programs such as Habitat for Humanity is testimony to the prevalence of this social value. Critical vocational educators believe that this common value of community service can be used to help mobilize a social and educational movement to redesign the money-saturated political system described in this book. Politically speaking, Americans at the end of the century are in a bad mood. Angry at the failure of bureaucratic government to respond efficiently to their needs, they are suspicious of any governmental program. Convinced by the corporate media that big government exercises its evil exclusively in the areas of placing senseless bureaucratic regulations on good corporate citizens and throwing away tax dollars on the poor, these angry working citizens sometimes end up exacerbating the problems they face. They are often not aware of the fact that the social agencies benefiting the most from big government, as it is now constituted, are the megacorporations. It will take tremendous effort on the part of a variety of cultural workers to counter the corporate information blitz that has planted these perspectives in the minds of so many.

One way to begin the important work of talking back to the corporations and their well-financed political puppets is to find common areas of agreement with conservative critics of government. On one level, their critique of bureaucracy is on target—but the problem is that they condemn only governmental bureaucracy, leaving corporate bureaucracy intact. The nonpublic and nonprivate third sector (civil sector) discussed here would be grounded on an understanding of the failure of centralized bureaucracies and dedicated to a decentralization of some of the socially beneficent tasks assumed over the last six or seven decades by centralized government. Great caution must be taken in any discussion of this civil sector: The advocacy of support for such a sector cannot dismiss the necessity of public government as a countervailing force to corporate power. We are not talking about George Bush's "thousand points of light," which he and other politicians have cynically used to refute and dismantle government's role as a protector of individuals from the ravages of the free market. Republican and some Democratic politicians have used third-sector rhetoric as a device to covertly promote a free market economy in which industry is deregulated, corporate taxes are lowered, and social services and entitlements for the poor are eliminated.

Thus, the use of this third civil sector is important and can accomplish much, but it can never take the place of government. It is just one of a variety of strategies we can use to promote a critical vocational education connected to a socially and economically just social vision. Finances for the civil sector would not just magically appear. Governments of local, state, and national varieties would have to help finance social and educational agencies devising locally conceived and administered programs. Many third-sector programs, therefore, would provide humane and personal ways of implementing the social dreams of those who take democracy seriously. Such third-sector activity would not be entirely altruistic, however, as individuals reeling from the economic (and thus psychological) effects of the deindustrialization of globalism would connect with nongovernmental organizations out of self-interest, out of concern for their futures. Only with grassroots local organizations connected to national and international coordinating agencies can economically displaced individuals survive globalized capital migration and the automation that accompanies it.

Critical vocational educators must connect with these NGOs, which have sprung up over the last few decades at the local, national, and international levels and have formed around opposition to macrodynamics such as the harmful effects of modernity or to microdynamics such as the destruction of a particular forest. A civil international order is developing; critical vocational educators and other cultural workers must develop the insight to devise ways of working in cooperation with it that contribute to the social good and promote good work for vocational students as they graduate from high school. As the civil sector works to rebuild local communities, vocational students could participate in third-sector apprenticeships that could not only teach them practical work skills but could involve them in civic activities and political action. Workers displaced by globalization could earn a living both through working on beneficial community projects and by teaching vocational students the skills they have acquired in their previous work experiences. Vocational educators could help build networks of people who have particular academic and vocational skills who could be called upon to use these abilities in a wide variety of civic and educational projects. Third-sector work would require a wide range of abilities, including construction skills, engineering skills, administrative skills, and research skills, just to name a few.

As an alternative to traditional forms of welfare, local, state, and federal governments could provide grants to secondary school vocational programs to educate former welfare recipients in integrated academic and vocational educational programs and move them into work roles in the civil sector. Such alternative programs could be financed by funds once relegated to traditional welfare systems. The establishment of these alternative programs is merely one of many steps that must be taken to lessen the disparity of income that, if left unaddressed, will ignite violent social explosions around the world in the twenty-first century. Faced with this frightening possibility and the reluctance of corporate-dominated governments to address it, NGOs that reject both the free market ideology that has allowed the creation of multinational corporate tyrants as well as the dead-end politics of nationalism are seeking a better way. Despite the despair felt by many progressives at the end of the century, the existence of critical pedagogies of vocational and academic education, progressive third-sector NGOs, and a new vision for organized labor remind us that change is possible (Rifkin, 1995; Chesneaux, 1992; Ferguson, 1984).

The Corporate Construction of Good Times in an Era of Downsizing

By the late 1990s, the cheap-labor policies of American corporations were producing record profits and unprecedented salary increases for upper management. Numerous corporations incorporated superlative celebrations of their good times into their advertisements, attempting to convince workers that this was the best of times. "Is this a great time or what?" companies reminded workers, ignoring issues of worker unemployment, underemployment, and stress derived from living with a precarious job and an uncertain future. The Clinton administration, of course, went along with the corporate celebration, taking credit for the success. Together, President Clinton, Vice President Gore, and Speaker of the House Gingrich—disagreeing on only a few particulars—admonished Americans to prepare for the sci-fi postmodern era with its glass and silicon, instant global communications, the often-invoked information superhighway, virtual reality, and automated factories. Making use of vocational education as panacea, political leaders from both parties assured Americans that all they needed to prosper in this future techtopia was a little retraining for high-tech jobs—jobs, unfortunately, that simply do not exist.

But the stock market continued to rise, "proving" the superiority of unbridled free enterprise, or at least indicating how beneficial cheap labor is to short-term corporate profits. "But employment has increased in this economic upswing," corporate apologists respond to our cynicism. Only because, we answer, of stagnant wages and increased part-time, no-benefit jobs. The power of corporate information control reveals itself yet again, as some workers cheered the rising stock market as a sign of their increased chance for prosperity. Some workers bought into the neoclassical economic wisdom that any increase in their wages was bad for the stock market and thus bad for future prosperity. So powerful was the stock market–induced optimism of some of the workers that they overspent their earnings, pushing consumer debt to unprecedented heights. The rising stock market, they reasoned, would enable them to earn the money to pay off these debts. Many workers believed this even at a time when corporations were gutting employee pension plans. Riding on the Teflon magic carpet of illusory prosperity, the Clinton administration did little to protect workers from the global forces lurking in the shadows of the future.

Analysis of these ominous shadows indicates that without the types of governmental, educational, and civil sector policies advocated here, corporate and political leaders will find it more and more difficult to maintain the illusion of prosperity. Even in the "best of times"—defined by rising corporate profits and record-setting stock prices—few high-paid, high-skill jobs have been created. Indeed, the 1990s have been a watershed in American economic history—increased profits and business prosperity accompanied by minimal job creation, especially good job creation. This watershed is characterized by a basic change in the relationship between capital and labor; any semblance of the old Fordist compromise that crumbled in the early 1970s has been erased. Corporate leaders in the late 1990s do not even feel compelled to speak a language of concern for their workers' well-being. Another aspect of the watershed involves the institutionalization of labor competition among Japan, Western Europe, and the United States. Such competition will induce corporations to operate at an accelerating intensity, with a need for greater speed and flexibility and lower overheads—all of which exerts negative pressures on workers' interests.

When growing numbers of elite workers willing to work for less from developing countries such as India, China, and Malaysia are added to the competition from Europe and Japan, the problems faced by twenty-first-century American workers will intensify. Many economists portray this competitive future as a good thing, as a creative process of capitalism shedding its worn-out skin and emerging triumphant from the metamorphosis. Critical vocational educators, however, are too aware of the fact that the benefits of the change go to the managers, while the workers, left in the wake, struggle to rebound from declining wages and life disruptions. They are also aware that many of the government-sponsored innovations in school-to-work programs of the 1990s still channel students into the bad work of the globalized economy's contingent labor force. The American public's consciousness of these looming realities has been forestalled by millions of women entering the service workforce to provide families with two incomes. Still, a pessimism about the future is creeping up on American workers, expressed in their worry about their children's economic future. Deep in the recesses of the American worker's subconscious, a knowledge of these dire future possibilities resides. For the time being, such men and women would like to forget about it; their political representatives are all too happy to oblige their continuing repression of this harsh reality (Rifkin, 1995; Wolman and Colamosca, 1997; Carlson, 1997).

The Possible Moral Backlash Against Inhumane Global Economics

Among specific groups in American culture, evidence is emerging that the virtue of unbridled global capitalism is being questioned. John Sweeney,

Dennis Rivera, and many of the workers they represent do not accept the globalized "inevitability" that commerce is everything and only the financial accounting of short-term profits matters. Some argue that to some degree Bill Clinton's reelection in 1996 indicated discomfort with the unbridled expansion of the globalized free market; if this is so, then Clinton's labor policy in his second term has disappointed many of his supporters. The Teamsters' strike against UPS in August 1997 illustrated the moral backlash of working Americans toward inhumane economic policies of globalized corporations. Ron Carey and the Teamsters saw their strike as a direct attack on the corporate politics of lowering labor costs. Over 128,000 Teamsters work part-time for UPS, receiving low wages and no benefits. Most part-timers hold down two or more jobs, and 10,000 Teamsters work more than thirty-five hours per week for UPS under part-time contracts.

Reflecting the actions of hundreds of other U.S. corporations, UPS hired primarily contingent workers; since 1993, over four out of five new hires are part-time. Such dramatic cutbacks in labor costs might have been more understandable if the company was losing money and near bankruptcy, but UPS was setting new records for one-year profit margins. In 1996, for example, the company made a *$1,115,000,000 profit*. To maintain such record profit levels, many U.S. corporations are banding together to develop trade strategies for controlling labor and public opinion. The Employer Group is an organization dedicated to keeping worker wages under $8 per hour by recruiting workers living in poverty from East Asia and Mexico, by soliciting charitable and other nonprofit agencies to run low-cost day care centers for working mothers, and by building cheap dormitories for low-wage workers (in the nineteenth century, firms built so-called "company housing" for miners and other workers). At the end of the twentieth century, the exploitative practices of management many thought were the product of a bygone era are back with a vengeance (Slaughter, 1997; Seymour, 1997; Wolman and Colamosca, 1997). Critical vocational educators and labor were heartened by the speed of UPS's concession to several of the Teamsters' demands. Despite corporate media coverage that for the most part denied the validity of labor's concerns with downsizing and part-time job growth, many Americans understood the Teamsters arguments. The strike stands as an important moment in contemporary labor history, as it articulated for a wide audience the underside of the dynamically flexible post-Fordist economy.

Smart governmental intervention, progressive unions, third-sector civil programs, and an integrated critical vocational and academic education offer us hope for the future. I am encouraged by the development of new programs that address the realities delineated in this book. For example, the Labor in the Schools Committee of the California Federation of Teachers (CFT) has developed a program about work entitled "The Yummy Pizza

Company." As the project puts students to work in the pizza business, it introduces them to everyday forms of worker exploitation. Confronted with workplace problems, students explore ways that unions might help them address their problems. Given the procorporate information environment in which student consciousness is formed, young people are often shocked to discover the restrictions employees encounter in the workplace. The Yummy Pizza Company helps students understand that the U.S. Constitution protects individuals from government but not from employers. For most students, this is a profound and shocking revelation (Hiber, 1997).

Programs of this sort, of course, are a rarity in the corporate-influenced schools at the end of the twentieth century. Critical vocational educators understand that simulation games like this could be used as a fun way to engage students in a profound analysis of work in the late twentieth century. The teaching of the social, economic, historical, and philosophical foundations of work are appropriate at any grade level. Ordinary citizens will be thwarted in their efforts to build communities of solidarity and to shape their own lives until we figure out a way to tell present workers and future workers how work is related to philosophical views of the role of humans in the world, to historical tendencies in the pursuit of commerce, to economic theories that underlie the organization of the economy and the workplace, to social questions of justice around issues of racism, sexism, and class bias, to political issues concerning the role of government in a democratic society, and to cultural questions concerning the ways consciousness is constructed and identity is formed in a world characterized by unprecedented technopower. It is my profound hope that the vocational educational issues delineated in this book will play a positive role in the struggle for an informed view of the context in which work takes place—good work, and a renewed vision of democracy in American life. The ways the society chooses to tell the workers of tomorrow about these dynamics will profoundly shape America's future.

References

Adams, F., and G. Hansen. (1994). "Business and democracy: Implications for education." In R. Lakes (ed.), *Critical education for work: Multi-disciplinary approaches.* Norwood, NJ: Ablex.

Allison, C. (1995). *Present and past: Essays for teachers in the history of education.* New York: Peter Lang.

Alvesson, M., and H. Willmott. (1992). "On the idea of emancipation in management and organizational studies." *Academy of Management Review* 17, 3, pp. 432–464.

Amott, T. (1993). *Caught in the crisis: Women and the US economy today.* New York: Monthly Review Press.

Anderson, James D. (1988). *The education of blacks in the South, 1860–1933.* Chapel Hill: University of North Carolina Press.

Anthias, F., and N. Yuval-Davis. (1992). *Racialized boundaries: Race, nation, gender, color, and class and the anti-racist struggle.* New York: Routledge.

Apple, M. (1985). "Teaching and women's work: A comparative historical and ideological analysis." *Teachers College Record* 86, 3, pp. 455–473.

———. (1992). "Constructing the captive audience: Channel One and the political economy of the text." Unpublished manuscript. University of Wisconsin.

———. (1993). "Constructing the 'other': Rightist reconstructions of common sense." In C. McCarthy and W. Crichlow (eds.), *Race, identity, and representation in education.* New York: Routledge.

Arnot, M. (1992). "Schools and families: A feminist perspective." In K. Weiler and C. Mitchell (eds.), *What schools can do: Critical pedagogy and practice.* Albany, NY: SUNY Press.

Arnott, T., and J. Matthaei. (1991). *Race, gender, and work: A multicultural economic history of women in the U.S.* Boston: South End Press.

Aronowitz, S. (1973). *False promises.* New York: McGraw-Hill.

———. (1983). "The relativity of theory." *Village Voice,* December 27, p. 60.

———. (1989). "Working-class culture in the electronic age." In I. Angus and S. Jhally (eds.), *Cultural politics in contemporary America.* New York: Routledge.

———. (1992). *The politics of identity: Class, culture, and social movements.* New York: Routledge.

Aronowitz, S., and H. Giroux. (1991). *Postmodern education: Politics, culture, and social criticism.* Minneapolis: University of Minnesota Press.

Aronowitz, S., and W. DiFazio. (1994). *The jobless future: Sci-tech and the dogma of work.* Minneapolis: University of Minnesota Press.

Atkins, M. (1986). "The pre-vocational curriculum: A review of the issues involved." *Journal of Curriculum Studies* 19, 1, pp. 45–53.

Babich, B. (1981). "Toward a liberating interpretation of philosophy for vocational education." *Viewpoints in Teaching and Learning* 57, 4, pp. 1–6.

Bacon, D. (April 1, 1996). "For a labor economy." *Nation* 262, 13, p. 14.

_____. (July 8, 1996). "Will the Labor Party work? *Nation* 263, 2, pp. 22–24.

Balsamo, A. (1985). "Beyond female as variable: Constructing a feminist perspective on organizational analysis." Paper presented to Critical Perspectives in Organizational Analysis Conference, New York.

Banducci, R. (1985). "From school to work: International perspectives." *Educational Digest* 50, pp. 48–51.

Banfield, B. (1991). "Honoring cultural diversity and building on its strengths: A case for national action." In L. Wolfe (ed.), *Women, Work, and the Role of Education*. Boulder, CO: Westview Press.

Barnet, R., and J. Cavanagh. (1994). *Global dreams: Imperial corporations and the new world order.* New York: Simon and Schuster.

Barrow, R. (1984). *Giving teaching back to teachers.* Totowa, NJ: Barnes and Noble Books.

Beane, D. (1985). Mathematics and science: Critical filters for the future of minority students. Washington, DC: American University, Mid-Atlantic Center for Race Equity.

Beck, R. (1991). *General education: Vocational and academic collaboration.* Berkeley: NCRVE.

Beed, C. (1991). "Philosophy of science and contemporary economics: An overview." *Journal of Post-Keynesian Economics* 13, 4, pp. 459–494.

Bellah, R. et al. (1991). *The good society.* New York: Vintage Books.

Berger, B. (1995). "Methodological fetishism." In R. Jacoby and N. Glauberman (eds.), *The bell curve debate: History, documents, and opinion.* New York: Random House.

Bhatnagar, D. (1988). "Professional women in organizations: New paradigms for research and action." *Sex roles* 18, 5–6, pp. 343–355.

Biklen, S. (1978). "The progressive education movement and the question of women." *Teachers College Record* 80, 1, pp. 316–335.

Block, A. (1995). *Occupied reading: Critical foundations for an ecological theory.* New York: Garland.

Block, F. (1990). *Postindustrial possibilities: A critique of economic discourse.* Berkeley: University of California Press.

Bluestone, B. (1988). "Deindustrialization and unemployment in America." *Review of Black Political Economy* 17, 2, pp. 29–44.

Bluestone, B., and B. Harrison. (1982). *The deindustrialization of America: Plant closings, community abandonment, and the dismantling of basic industry.* New York: Basic Books.

Bluestone, B., and I. Bluestone. (1992). *Negotiating the future: A labor perspective on American business.* New York: Basic Books.

Bluestone, I., and A. Brown. (1983). "Foreword." In A. Wirth, *Productive work—In industry and schools: Becoming persons again.* Lanham, MD: University Press of America.

Bohm, D., and F. Peat. (1987). *Science, order, and creativity.* New York: Bantam Books.

Bohm, D., and M. Edwards. (1991). *Changing consciousness.* San Francisco: Harper.

Borgmann, A. (1992). *Crossing the postmodern divide.* Chicago: University of Chicago Press.

Bovard, J. (1987). "The failure of federal job training programs." *USA Today* 116, pp. 12–17.

Bowers, C. (1982). "The reproduction of technological consciousness: Locating the ideological foundations of a radical pedagogy." *Teachers College Record* 83, 4, pp. 529–557.

Bowles, S., D. Gordon, and T. Weisskopf. (1990). *After the wasteland: A democratic economics for the year 2000.* Armonk, NY: M. E. Sharp.

Bozik, M. (1987). "Critical thinking through creative thinking." Paper presented to the Speech Communication Association, Boston.

Brecher, J. (1972). *Strike.* Boston: South End Press.

Brosio, R. (1985). "A bibliographic essay on the world of work." Paper presented to the American Educational Studies Association, Chicago, Illinois.

_____. (1994). *The radical democratic critique of capitalist education.* New York: Peter Lang.

_____. (n.d.). "The worker-citizen concept as it evolved in American social thought: Accent John Dewey." Unpublished manuscript. Ball State University.

Bullock, H. (1967). *A history of Negro education in the South: From 1619 to the present.* New York: Praeger.

Candaele, K., and P. Dreirer. (December 16, 1996). "Canadian Beacon." *Nation* 263, 20, p. 20.

Carby, H. (1992). "The multicultural wars." In G. Dent (ed.), *Black popular culture.* Seattle: Bay Press.

Carlson, D. (1992). *Teachers and crisis: Urban school reform and teachers' work culture.* New York: Routledge.

_____. (1997). *Making progress: Education and culture in new times.* New York: Teachers College Press.

Carnevale, A. (May 1992). "Skills for the New World Order." *American School Board Journal* 179, 5, pp. 28–30.

Case, R. (1985). *Intellectual development: Birth to Adulthood.* New York: Academic Press.

Chesneaux, J. (1992). *Brave modern world: The prospects for survival.* New York: Thames and Hudson.

Cockburn, A. (May 17, 1993). "Clinton and labor: Reform equals rollback." *Nation* 256, pp. 654–655.

Collins, J. (1989). *Uncommon cultures: Popular culture and postmodernism.* New York: Routledge.

Cook, J., and M. Fonow. (1990). "Knowledge and women's interest: Issues of epistemology and methodology in feminist sociological research." In J. Nielsen (ed.), *Feminist research methods: Exemplary reading in the social sciences.* Boulder: Westview Press.

Coontz, S. (1992). *The way we never were: American families and the nostalgia trap.* New York: Basic Books.

Cooper, M. (April 8, 1996). "Harley riding, picket walking socialism haunts Decatur." *Nation* 262, 14, pp. 21–25.

_____. (May 27, 1996). "Class war @ Silicon Valley: Disposable workers in the new
economy." *Nation* 262, 21, pp. 11–16.

_____. (March 24, 1997). "Labor deals a new hand." *Nation* 264, 11, pp. 11–16.

Copa, G., and E. Tebbenhoff. (1990). *Subject matter of vocational education: In
pursuit of foundations.* Berkeley: NCRVE.

Cotton, J. (1992). "Towards a theory and strategy for black economic development." In J. Jennings (ed.), *Race, politics, and economic development: Community
perspectives.* New York: Verso.

DeVore, P. (1983). "Research and industrial education searching for direction." Paper presented at the American Vocational Association Convention, Anaheim, California.

Dewey, J. (1908). *Ethics.* New York: Holt and Company.

_____. (1916). *Democracy and education.* New York: Free Press.

DeYoung, A. (1989). *Economics and American education.* New York: Longman.

Dornsife, C. (1992). *Beyond articulation: The development of tech prep programs.*
Berkeley: NCRVE.

DuBois, W. (1973a). *The education of black people: Ten Critiques, 1906–1960,* ed. H.
Aptheker. New York: Monthly Review Press.

_____. (1973b). *The future and function of the private Negro college (1946).* In
W.E.B. DuBois, *The education of black people,* ed. H. Aptheker, Amherst: University of Massachusetts Press.

Du Gay, P. et al. (1997). *Doing cultural studies: The story of the Sony Walkman.* London: Sage Publications.

Early, S. (January 6, 1997). "The Teamsters' new contract." *Nation* 264, 1, pp.
20–23.

Edson, C. H. (1979). "Sociocultural perspectives on work and schooling in urban
America." *Urban Review* 11, 3, pp. 127–148.

Eiger, N. (1982). "The workplace as classroom for democracy: The Swedish experience." *NYU Educational Quarterly* 7, 2, pp. 19–24.

Eisner, E. (1984). "Can educational research inform educational practice?" *Phi
Delta Kappan* 65, 7, pp. 447–452.

Ellwood, D. (1988). *Poor support: Poverty in the American family.* New York: Basic
Books.

Ellwood, D., and D. Wise. (1983). "Youth unemployment in the 1970s." In R. Nelson and F. Skidmore (eds.), *American families and the economy: The high cost of
living.* Washington, DC: National Academy Press.

Emery, F., and E. Thorsrud. (1976). *Democracy at work.* Leiden: Martinus Nijhoff.

Falk, W., and T. Lyson. (1988). *High tech, low tech, no tech: Recent industrial and occupational change in the South.* Albany, NY: SUNY Press.

Fee, E. (1982). "Is feminism a threat to scientific objectivity?" *International Journal
of Women's Studies* 4, 4, pp. 378–392.

Feffer, A. (1993). *The Chicago pragmatists and American progressivism.* Ithaca: Cornell University Press.

Feinberg, W., and B. Horowitz. (1990). "Vocational education and the equality of
opportunity." *Journal of Curriculum Studies* 22, 2, pp. 188–192.

Ferguson, K. (1984). *The feminist case against bureaucracy.* Philadelphia: Temple University Press.

Ferguson, M. (1980). *The Aquarian conspiracy: Personal and social transformation in our time.* Los Angeles: J. P. Tarcher.

Fine, M. (1993). "Sexuality, schooling, and adolescent females: The missing discourse of desire." In *Silenced Voices: Class, Race, and Gender in the United States Schools.* Albany, NY: SUNY Press.

Fiske, D., and R. Shweder. (1986). *Metatheory in social science: Pluralisms and subjectivities.* Chicago: University of Chicago Press.

Frankenberg, R. (1993). *The social construction of whiteness: White women, race matters.* Minneapolis: University of Minnesota Press.

Frantz, N. (1992). "Voices of change." *Vocational Education Journal* 67, 7, p. 26.

Fraser, N. (1994). "Rethinking the public sphere: A contribution to the critique of actually existing democracy." In H. Giroux and P. McLaren (eds.), *Between borders: Pedagogy and the politics of cultural studies.* New York: Routledge.

Fraser, N., and L. Nicholson. (1990). "Social criticism without philosophy: An encounter between feminism and postmodernism." In L. Nicholson (ed.), *Feminism/Postmodernism.* New York: Routledge.

Freeman, R., and D. Gilbert. (1992). "Business, ethics and society: A critical agenda." *Business and Society* 31, 1, pp. 9–17.

Freire, P., and D. Macedo (1987). *Literacy: Reading the word and the world.* South Hadley, MA: Bergin and Garvey.

Fusco, C. (1992). "Pan-American postnationalism: Another world order." In G. Dent (ed.), *Black Popular Culture.* Seattle: Bay Press.

Gabbard, D. (1995). "NAFTA, GATT, and Goals 2000: Reading the political culture of post-industrial America." *Taboo: The Journal of Culture and Education* 2, pp. 184–199.

Gaines, D. (1990). *Teenage wasteland: Suburbia's dead-end kids.* New York: Harper-Perennial.

Gans, H. (June 9, 1993). "Scholars' role in planning a post-work society." *Chronicle of Higher Education,* p. 83.

Gardner, H. (1991). *The unschooled mind: How children think and how schools should teach.* New York: Basic Books.

Garrison, J. (Summer 1989). "The role of postpositivistic philosophy of science in the renewal of vocational education research." *Journal of Vocational Education Research* 14, 3, pp. 39–51.

Gaskell, J. (1987). "Gender and skill." In D. Livingstone (ed.), *Critical pedagogy and cultural power.* South Hadley, MA: Bergin and Garvey.

Gee, J., G. Hull, and C. Lankshear. (1996). *The new work order: Behind the language of the new capitalism.* Boulder, CO: Westview Press.

Gergen, K. (1991). *The saturated self: Dilemmas of identity in contemporary life.* New York: Basic Books.

Gibson, R. (1986). *Critical theory and education.* London: Hodder and Stroughton.

Gilligan, C. (1981). *In a different voice: Psychological theory and women's development.* Cambridge: Harvard University Press.

Giroux, H. (1988). *Schooling and the struggle for public life.* Minneapolis: University of Minnesota Press.

_____. (1992). *Border crossings: Cultural workers and the politics of education*. New York: Routledge.

_____. (1993). *Living dangerously: Multiculturalism and the politics of difference*. New York: Peter Lang.

_____. (1997). *Pedagogy and the politics of hope: Theory, culture, and schooling*. Boulder, CO: Westview Press.

Giroux, H., and R. Simon. (1989). "Popular culture as a pedagogy of pleasure and meaning." In H. Giroux and R. Simon (eds.), *Popular culture: Schooling and everyday life*. Granby, MA: Bergin and Garvey.

Goodlad, J. (February 19, 1992). "Beyond half an education." *Education Week* 11, 22, pp. 34, 44.

Gordon, D. (June 17, 1996). "Values that work." *Nation* 262, 24, pp. 16–22.

Gowen, S. (1994). "The 'literacy myth' at work: The role of print literacy in school-to-work transitions." In R. Lakes (ed.), *Critical Education for Work: Multidisciplinary Approaches*. Norwood, NJ: Ablex.

Greider, W. (1992). *Who will tell the people? The betrayal of American democracy*. New York: Touchstone.

Gresson, A. (1995). *The recovery of race in America*. Minneapolis: University of Minnesota Press.

Grossberg, L. (1992). *We gotta get out of this place*. New York: Routledge.

Grubb, N. (Spring 1978). "The phoenix of vocationalism: Hope deferred is hope denied." *New Directions for Education and Work* 1, pp. 71–89.

Grubb, N., G. Davis, J. Lum, J. Phihal, and C. Morgaine. (1991). *The cunning hand, the cultured mind: Models for integrating vocational and academic education*. Berkeley: NCRVE.

Gruber, H., and J. Voneche (eds.). (1977). *The essential Piaget*. New York: Basic Books.

Hacker, A. (1992). *Two nations: Black and white, separate, hostile, unequal*. New York: Ballantine Books.

Hacker, S. (1989). *Pleasure, power, and technology: Some tales of gender, engineering, and the cooperative workplace*. New York: Routledge.

Hamilton, S. (1986). "Excellence and the transition from school to work." *Phi Delta Kappan* 68, pp. 239–242.

_____. (September 30, 1992). "School-work nexus: If any road can take you there, you don't know where you're going." *Education Week* 12, 2, p. 36.

Hamilton, S., and M. Hamilton. (1992). "A progress report on apprenticeships." *Educational Leadership* 49, 6, pp. 44–47.

Hamper, B. (1992). *Rivethead*. New York: Warner.

Hannam, M. (1990). "The dream of democracy." *Arena* 90, pp. 109–116.

Harp, L. (September 23, 1992). "Scuttled program's work, skill themes enjoying resurgence." *Education Week* 12, 3, pp. 1, 13.

Harris, M. (1981). *America now*. New York: Simon and Schuster.

Hartsock, N. (1989). "Foucault on power: A theory for women?" In L. Nicholson (ed.), *Feminism/postmodernism*. New York: Routledge.

Harvey, D. (1989). *The condition of postmodernity*. Cambridge: Basil Blackwell.

Hatcher, R. (1992). "Conclusion." In J. Jennings (ed.), *Race, politics, and economic development: Community perspectives*. New York: Verso.

Haymes, S. (1995). *Race, culture, and the city: A pedagogy for black urban struggle.* Albany, NY: SUNY Press.

Heilbroner, R. (1977). *The economic transformation of America.* New York: Harcourt Brace Jovanovich.

Held, D. (1980). *Introduction to critical theory: Horkheimer to Habermas.* London: Hutchison.

Herrnstein, R., and C. Murray. (1994). *The Bell Curve: Intelligence and class structure in American life.* New York: Free Press.

Hershbach, D. (1994). "The right to organize: Implications for preparing students for work." In R. Lakes (ed.), *Critical education for work: Multidisciplinary approaches.* Norwood, NJ: Ablex.

Hiber, A. (August 11, 1997). "See Dick strike. Strike, Dick, strike." *Nation* 21, 19, p. 10.

Hillison, J., and W. Camp. (1985). "History and future of the dual school system for vocational education." *Journal for Vocational and Technical Education* 2, 1, pp. 48–56.

Hinchey, P. (October 27, 1993). "Lost in translation: Perils on the uncertain route from reform theory to practice." *Education Week* 13, 8, pp. 22, 24.

Hirsch, E. D. (1987). *Cultural literacy.* Boston: Houghton Mifflin.

Holtz, H. et al. (1989). "Introduction: Education, politics, and ideology." In H. Holtz et al., *Education and the American dream: Conservatives, liberals, and radicals debate the future of education.* Granby, MA: Bergin and Garvey.

hooks, b. (1993). *Sisters of the yam: Black women and self-recovery.* Boston: South End Press.

Hossfeld, K. (1994). "Hiring immigrant women: Silicon Valley's simple formula." In M. Zinn and B. Dill (eds.), *Women of color in U.S. Society.* Philadelphia: Temple University Press.

House, E. (1978). "Evaluation as scientific management in US school reform." *Comparative Education Review* 22, 3, pp. 388–401.

Hudelson, D. (1992). "Roots of reform: Tracing the path of 'workforce education.'" *Vocational Education Journal* 67, 7, pp. 28–29, 69.

Jackson, J. (October 5, 1997). "Business-as-usual labor coverage." *In These Times* 21, 20–22, p. 8.

Jacobs, F., and D. Phillips. (1979). "Beyond the little red schoolhouse." *Change* 11, 5, pp. 5–10.

Jacoby, R. (1975). *Social amnesia.* Boston: Beacon Press.

Jacques, R. (1992). "Critique and theory building: Producing knowledge 'from the kitchen.'" *Academy of Management Review* 17, 3, pp. 582–606.

Jankowski, M. (1991). *Islands in the street: Gangs and American urban society.* Berkeley: University of California Press.

Jennings, J. (1991). "Minorities and vocational education: The challenges." *Vocational Educational Journal* 66, 4, pp. 20–21, 45.

_____. (1992). "Blacks, politics, and the human service crisis." In J. Jennings (ed.), *Race, politics, and economic development: Community perspectives.* New York: Verso.

Jhally, S., and J. Lewis. (1992). *Enlightened racism: The Cosby show, audiences, and the myth of the American dream.* Boulder, CO: Westview Press.

Johnson, W. (1991). "Model programs prepare women for skilled trades." In L. Wolfe (ed.), *Women, work and school: Occupational segregation and the role of education*. Boulder, CO: Westview Press.

Jonathan, R. (March/April 1990). "The curriculum and the new vocationalism." *Journal of Curriculum Studies* 22, 2, pp. 184–188.

Jones, M. (1992). "The black underclass as systematic phenomenon." In J. Jennings (ed.), *Race, politics, and economic development: Community perspectives*. New York: Verso.

Kallick, D. (November 11, 1996). "Left turn ahead." *Nation* 263, 15, pp. 22–24.

Kantor, H. (1994). "Managing the transition from school to work: The false promise of youth apprenticeship." *Teachers College Record* 95, 4, pp. 442–461.

Kellner, D. (1989). *Critical theory, Marxism, and modernity*. Baltimore: Johns Hopkins University Press.

Kincheloe, J. (1991). *Teachers as researchers: Qualitative paths to empowerment*. New York: Falmer.

———. (1993). *Toward a critical politics of teacher thinking: Mapping the postmodern*. Westport, CT: Bergin and Garvey.

———. (1995). *Toil and trouble: Good work, smart workers, and the integration of academic and vocational education*. New York: Peter Lang.

Kincheloe, J., and S. Steinberg. (1993). "A tentative description of post-formal thinking: The critical confrontation with cognitive theory." *Harvard Educational Review* 63, 3, pp. 296–320.

Kincheloe, J., S. Steinberg, and A. Gresson (eds.). (1996). *Measured lies: The bell curve examined*. New York: St. Martin's Press.

Kincheloe, J., S. Steinberg, and P. Slattery. (1999). *Contextualizing Teaching*. New York: Longman.

King, J., and C. Mitchell. (1996). *Black mothers to sons*. New York: Peter Lang.

Klahr, D., and J. Wallace. (1976). *Cognitive development: An information processing view*. Hillsdale, NJ: Erlbaum.

Kliebard, H. (1987). *The struggle for the American curriculum, 1893–1958*. New York: Routledge.

———. (Spring 1990). "Vocational education as symbolic action: Connecting schooling with the workplace." *American Educational Research Journal* 27, 1, pp. 9–26.

Kneller, G. (1984). *Movements of thought in modern education*. New York: John Wiley and Sons.

Kolberg, W., and F. Smith. (1992). *Rebuilding America's workforce: Business strategies to close the competitive gap*. Homewood, IL: Business One Irwin.

Koller, A. (1981). *An unknown woman: A journey to self-discovery*. New York: Bantam Books.

Kozol, J. (1991). *Savage inequalities: Children in America's schools*. New York: Crown Publishers.

Kroc, R. (1977). *Grinding it out: The making of McDonald's*. New York: St. Martin's Press.

LaBrecque, R. (Winter 1974). "What is to be done? Pragmatism at the crossroads." *Studies in Philosophy and Education* 8, 3, pp. 183–204.

Lakes, R. (Fall 1985). "John Dewey's theory of occupations: Vocational education envisioned." *Journal of Vocational and Technical Education* 2, 1, pp. 41–47.

_____. (1990). "The importance of social skills on the shop floor." *Journal of Industrial Teacher Education* 28, 1, pp. 71–74.

_____. (1991). "Critical pedagogy for vocational-technical educators: Some considerations." *Journal of Studies in Technical Careers* 13, 4, pp. 299–305.

_____. (1994a). "Critical education for work." In R. Lakes (ed.), *Critical education for work: Multidisciplinary approaches.* Norwood, NJ: Ablex.

_____. (1994b). "Is this workplace democracy?: Education and labor in postindustrial America." In R. Lakes (ed.), *Critical education for work: Multidisciplinary approaches.* Norwood, NJ: Ablex.

Lamphere, L. (Fall 1985). "Bringing the family to work: Women's culture on the shop floor." *Feminist Studies* 11, 3, pp. 519–539.

Lankshear, C. (1995). "And where do we go from here? Lifeless factories, dry streams and 'the new competition.'" *Taboo: The Journal of Culture and Education* 2, pp. 154–183.

Lasch, C. (1979). *The Culture of Narcissism.* New York: W. W. Norton and Company.

Lather, P. (1991). *Getting smart: Feminist research and pedagogy with/in the postmodern.* New York: Routledge.

Lave, J. (1988). *Cognition in practice.* Cambridge: Cambridge University Press.

Lavine, T. (1984). *From Socrates to Sartre: The philosophic quest.* New York: Bantam Books.

Lawler, J. (1975). "Dialectical philosophy and developmental psychology: Hegel and Piaget on contradiction." *Human Development* 18, pp. 1–17.

Leshan, L., and H. Margeneu. (1982). *Einstein's space and Van Gogh's sky: Physical reality and beyond.* New York: Macmillan Publishing Company.

Letiche, H. (1992). "Having taught postmodernists." *International Studies of Management and Organization* 22, 3, pp. 46–70.

Levi, L. (June 17, 1996). "We left it at the movies." *Nation* 262, 24, pp. 28–30.

Levin, H. (1984). "Jobs: A changing workforce." *Change* 16, pp. 32–37.

Levine, D. (1994). "The school-to-work opportunities act of 1994: A flawed prescription for education reform." *Educational Foundations* 8, 3, pp. 33–51.

Litz, C., and B. Bloomquist. (April 1980). "Adult education: Resolution of the liberal-vocational debate." *Lifelong Learning in the Adult Years*, pp. 12–15.

Livingstone, D. (1987). "Upgrading and opportunities." In *Critical pedagogy and cultural power.* South Hadley, MA: Bergin and Garvey.

Livingstone, D., and M. Luxton. (1988). "Gender consciousness at work: Modification of the male breadwinner norm among steelworkers and their spouses." Unpublished manuscript.

Lowe, D. (1982). *History of Bourgeois Perception.* Chicago: University of Chicago Press.

Lucas, C. (1985). "Toward a pedagogy of the useful past for teacher preparation." *Journal of Thought* 20, pp. 19–33.

Luethemeyer, J. (1974). "Some fundamental differences: Between industrial arts and vocational education." *Man/Society/Technology* 33, 8 pp. 236–238.

Luttrell, W. (1993). "Working-class women's ways of knowing: Effects of gender, race, and class." In Louis Castnell and William Pinar (eds.), *Understanding curriculum as a racial text: Representations of identity and difference in education.* Albany, NY: SUNY Press.

Lyons, R. (Fall/Winter 1988). "Scarcity, conflict, and work: An essay on schooling." *Journal of Thought* 23, 2/3, pp. 6–27.

Macedo, D. (1994). *Literacies of power: What Americans are not allowed to know.* Boulder, CO: Westview Press.

MacLeod, J. (1987). *Ain't no making it.* Boulder, CO: Westview Press.

Maher, F., and C. Rathbone. (1986). "Teacher education and feminist theory: Some implications for practice." *American Journal of Education* 94, 2, pp. 214–235.

Mahoney, M., and W. Lyddon. (1988). "Recent developments in cognitive approaches to counseling and psychotherapy." *Counseling Psychologist* 16, 2, pp. 190–234.

Malveaux, J. (1992a). "Popular culture and the economics of alienation." In G. Dent (ed.), *Black popular culture.* Seattle: Bay Press.

_____. (1992b). "Popular economy of black women." In J. Jennings (ed.), *Race, politics, and economic development: Community perspectives.* New York: Verso.

Marable, M. (1992). "Race, identity, and political culture." In G. Dent (ed.), *Black popular culture.* Seattle: Bay Press.

Marcuse, H. (1955). *Eros and Civilization.* Boston: Beacon Press.

Margo, R. (1990). *Race and schooling in the South, 1880–1950: An economic history.* Chicago: University of Chicago.

Margonis, F. (1989). "What is the meaning of contemporary educational nationalism?" In J. Giarelli (ed.), *Proceedings of the Forty-fourth Annual Meeting of the Philosophy of Education Society.* Normal, IL: Philosophy of Education Society.

Marshak, D. (June 2, 1993). "What employers know that educators may not." *Education Week* 12, 36, pp. 25, 28.

Marsick, V. (1989). "Examining new paradigms for workplace learning." In C. Coggins (ed.), *Proceedings of the Annual Adult Education Research Conference.* Madison, WI: Madison Department of Continuing and Vocational Education.

McCarthy, C., and M. Apple. (1988). "Race, class and gender in American educational research: Toward a nonsynchronous parallelist position." In L. Weis, *Class, race, and gender in American education.* Albany, NY: SUNY Press.

McClure, L. (1992). "Democracy for unions, too?" *Progressive* 56, 6, pp. 21–23.

McDermott, J. (1980). *The crisis in the working class and some arguments for a new labor movement.* Boston: South End Press.

McIntosh, P. (1995). "White privilege and male privilege: A personal account of work in women's studies." In M. Anderson and P. Collins (eds.), *Race, class, and gender: An anthology.* Belmont, CA: Wadsworth.

McLaren, P. (1986). *Schooling as ritual performance: Toward a political economy of educational symbols and gestures.* London: Routledge and Kegan Paul.

_____. (1992). "Literacy research and the postmodern turn: Cautions from the margins." In R. Beach et al., *Multidisciplinary perspectives on research.* Urbana, IL: National Council of Teachers of English.

_____. (1994). *Life in schools: An introduction to critical pedagogy in the foundations of education.* White Plains, NY: Longman.

McLaren, P., R. Hammer, S. Reilly, and D. Sholle. (1995). *Rethinking media literacy: A critical pedagogy of representation.* New York: Peter Lang.

Meissner, M. (1998). "The reproduction of women's domination in organizational communication." In L. Thayer (ed.), *Organization, Communication.* Norwood, NJ: Ablex Publishing.

Melman, S., and L. Dumas. (April 16, 1990). "Planning for economic conversion." *Nation* 250, 15, pp. 509, 522–528.

Mingers, J. (1992). "Recent developments in critical management science." *Journal of the Operational Research Society* 43, 1, pp. 1–10.

Moberg, D. (April 1, 1996). "The new union label." *Nation* 262, 13, pp. 11–15.

_____. (December 16, 1996). "Labor as neighbor." *Nation* 263, 20, pp. 18–21.

Mostern, K. (1994). "Decolonization as learning: Practice and pedagogy in Frantz Fanon's revolutionary narrative." In H. Giroux and P. McLaren (eds.), *Between borders: Pedagogy and the politics of cultural studies*. New York: Routledge.

Mullings, L. (1994). "Images, ideology, and women of color." In M. Zinn and B. Dill (eds.), *Women of color in U.S. society*. Philadelphia: Temple University Press.

Murray, J., and J. Ozanne. (1991). "The critical imagination: Emancipatory interests in consumer research." *Journal of Consumer Research* 18, 2, pp. 129–144.

Murray, R. (1992). "Fordism and post-Fordism." In C. Jencks (ed.), *The post-modern reader*. New York: St. Martin's Press.

Nation. (April 8, 1996). "Class act," 262, 14, p. 3.

Nation. (October 14, 1996). "Labor and academe," 262, 22, pp. 5–6.

Nation. (October 28, 1996). "Labor goes to college," 262, 13, pp. 4–5.

NCRVE (National Center for Research in Vocational Education). (1992). "Vocational education: A special tip sheet for educational writers." Berkeley: NCRVE.

Nelson, R., and J. Watras. (Spring 1981). "The scientific movement: American education and the emergence of the technological society." *Journal of Thought* 16, 1, pp. 49–71.

Nichols, M. (1996). "Initiatives in worker training and continuous learning." *Community College Journal* 7, 3, pp. 24–27.

Nightingale, C. (1993). *On the edge: A history of poor black children and their American dreams*. New York: Basic Books.

Nooteboom, B. (1991). "A postmodern philosophy of markets." *International Studies of Management and Organization* 22, 2, pp. 53–76.

Oakes, J. (1985). *Keeping Track: How Schools Structure Inequality*. New Haven: Yale University Press.

_____. (1988). "Tracking in mathematics and science education: A structural contribution to unequal schooling." In L. Weis (ed.), *Class, race, and gender in American education*. Albany, NY: SUNY Press.

Oakes, J., and M. Lipton. (1990). *Making the best of schools: A handbook for parents, teachers, and policymakers*. New Haven: Yale University Press.

Olson, L. (May 5, 1993). "School-to-work initiative goes beyond apprenticeships." *Education Week* 12, 32, pp. 22–23.

_____. (May 12, 1993). "Skepticism, concern greet fast-track plan for skills standards." *Education Week* 12, 33, pp. 1, 20.

_____. (May 26, 1993). "Rising to the task." *Education Week* 12, 25, pp. 1–3.

_____. (June 2, 1993). "Senate committee approves skills-standards board." *Education Week* 12, 36, p. 22.

_____. (June 23, 1993). "Clinton to urge state systems for school-job link." *Education Week* 12, 39, pp. 1, 36.

_____. (January 19, 1994). "Enrollments in vocational education down from 1982 to 1990." *Education Week* 13, 17, pp. 1, 19.

_____. (January 26, 1994). "Bridging the gap: The nation's haphazard school-to-work link is getting an overhaul." *Education Week* 13, 18, pp. 20–25.

_____. (February 23, 1994). "On the career track." *Education Week* 13, 22, pp. 28–31.

_____. (March 2, 1994). "Skills standards for high-tech workers unveiled." *Education Week* 13, 23, p. 12.

Palmer, P., and R. Spalter-Roth (1991). "Gender practices and employment: The Sears case and the issue of choice." In L. Wolfe (ed.), *Women, work, and school: Occupational segregation and the role of education.* Boulder, CO: Westview Press.

Parnell, D. (Fall 1990). "Why applied academics?" *Balance Sheet*, pp. 12–14.

Pascall, G. (1994). "Women in professional careers: Social policy developments." In J. Evetts (ed.), *Women and career: Themes and issues in advanced industrial societies.* New York: Longman.

Perez, L. (1993). "Opposition and the education of Chicana/os." In C. McCartthy and W. Crichlow (eds.), *Race, identity, and representation in education.* New York: Routledge.

Phillips, K. (1970). *The emerging Republican majority.* New York: Anchor Books.

Piaget, J. (1970). "Piaget's theory." In P. Mussen (ed.), *Manual of child psychology,* vol. 1. New York: Wiley.

Piaget, J., and B. Inhelder (1968). *The psychology of the child.* New York: Basic Books.

Pincus, F. (August, 1980). "The false promises of community colleges: Class conflict and vocational education." *Harvard Educational Review* 50, 3, pp. 332–361.

Pitsch, M. (April 6, 1994). "With students' aid, Clinton signs Goals 2000." *Education Week* 13, 28, pp. 1, 21.

Pollin, R. (September 30, 1996). "Economics with a human face." *Nation* 263, 9, pp. 21–23.

Pollin, R., and A. Cockburn. (February 25, 1991). "The world, the free market, and the left." *Nation* 252, 7, pp. 224–236.

Poster, M. (1989). *Critical theory and poststructuralism: In search of a context.* Ithaca: Cornell University Press.

Powderly, T. (1889). *Thirty years of labor, 1859–1889.* Columbus, OH: Excelsior Publishing House.

Press, E. (April 8, 1996). "Union do's: Smart solidarity." *Nation* 262, 14, pp. 29–32.

Pullin, D. (1994). "Learning to work: The impact of curriculum and assessment standards on educational opportunity." *Harvard Educational Review* 64, 1, pp. 31–54.

Raizen, S. (1989). *Reforming education for work: A cognitive science perspective.* Berkeley: NCRVE.

Raizen, S., and R. Colvin. (1991). "Apprenticeships: A cognitive-science view." *Educational Week* 7, 11, p. 26.

Rehm, M. (1989). "Emancipatory vocational education: Pedagogy for the work of individuals and society." *Journal of Education* 171, 3, pp. 109–123.

Reich, C. (1995). *Opposing the system.* New York: Crown Publishers.

Reinharz, S. (1992). *Feminist methods in social research.* New York: Oxford University Press.

Rendon, L., and A. Nora. (1991). "Hispanic women in college and careers: Preparing for success." In L. Wolfe (ed.), *Women, work, and school: Occupational segregation and the role of education.* Boulder, CO: Westview Press.

Richmond, S. (December 1986). "The white paper, education, and the crafts: An assessment of values." *Journal of Educational Thought* 20, 3, pp. 143–155.

Riegel, K. (1973). "Dialectic operations: The final period of cognitive development." *Human Development* 16, pp. 346–370.

Rifkin, J. (1995). *The end of work: The decline of the global labor force and the dawn of the post-market era.* New York: Tarchner/Putnam.

Ritzer, G. (1993). *The McDonaldization of society.* Thousand Oaks, CA: Pine Forge Press.

Rizvi, F. (1993). "Children and the grammar of popular racism." In C. McCarthy and W. Crichlow (eds.), *Race, identity, and representation in education.* New York: Routledge.

Robbins, D. (1991). *The work of Pierre Bourdieu.* Boulder, CO: Westview Press.

Roberts, M., and R. Wozniak. (1994). *Labor's key role in workplace training.* Washington, DC: AFL-CIO.

Roditi, H. (March 16, 1992). "High schools for docile workers." *Nation* 254, 10, pp. 340–343.

Rodriguez, L. (July/August 1994). "Rekindling the warrior." *Utne Reader* 64, pp. 58–59.

Roediger, D. (1991). *The wages of whiteness: Race and the making of the American working class.* New York: Verso.

Rosser, P. (1989). *The SAT gender gap: Identifying the causes.* Washington, DC: Center for Women Policy Studies.

Rubin, L. (1994). *Families on the faultline: America's working class speaks about the family, the economy, race, and ethnicity.* New York: HarperCollins.

Rumberger, R. (January, 1984). "The growing imbalance between education and work." *Phi Delta Kappan* 65, 5, pp. 342–346.

Rury, J. (1991). *Education and women's work: Female schooling and the division of labor in urban America, 1870–1930.* Albany, NY: SUNY Press.

Samper, M., and R. Lakes. (1994). "Work education for the next century: Beyond skills training." In R. Lakes (ed.), *Critical education for work: Multidisciplinary approaches.* Norwood, NJ: Ablex.

Schied, F. (1993). *Learning in social context: Workers and adult education in nineteenth-century Chicago.* DeKalb, IL: LEPS Press.

Schon, D. (1987). *Educating the reflective practitioner.* San Francisco: Jossey-Bass Publishers.

Schwartz, B. (1994). *The costs of living: How market freedom erodes the best things in life.* New York: W. W. Norton.

Senge, P. (1990). *The fifth discipline: The art and practice of the learning organization.* New York: Doubleday.

Serrin, W. (January 28, 1991). "The wages of work." *Nation* 252, 3, pp. 80–82.

Seymour, C. (August 11, 1997). "Low-wage innovations." *In These Times* 21, 19, pp. 18–20.

Shapiro, S. (1995). "Reply to Gabbard: Capitalism, the state, and political power." *Taboo: The Journal of Culture and Education* 2, pp. 200–205.

Shelton, B. (1984). "The development of vocational education in Buffalo." *Urban Education* 18, 4, pp. 466–476.

Sherman, R. (Winter 1974). "Vocational education and democracy." *Studies in Philosophy and Education* 8, 3, pp. 205–223.

Sherman, S. (March 10, 1997). "An appeal to reason." *Nation* 264, 9, pp. 15–19.

Shor, I. (1986). *Culture wars: School and society in the conservative restoration.* Chicago: University of Chicago Press.

_____. (1988). "Working hands and critical minds: A Paulo Freire model for job training." *Journal of Education* 170, 2, pp. 102–121.

Shor, I., and P. Freire. (1987). *A pedagogy for liberation: Dialogues on transforming education.* South Hadley, MA: Bergin and Garvey.

Sidel, R. (1992). *Women and children last: The plight of poor women in affluent America.* New York: Penguin Books.

Simon, R., and D. Dippo. (1987). "What schools can do: Designing programs for work education that challenge the wisdom of experience." *Journal of Education* 169, 3, pp. 101–116.

Simon, R., D. Dippo, and A. Schenke. (1991). *Learning work: A critical pedagogy of work education.* Westport, CT: Bergin and Garvey.

Slattery, P. (1995). *Curriculum development in the postmodern era.* New York: Garland.

Slaughter, J. (August 11, 1997). "Face-off at UPS." *In These Times* 21, 19, pp. 6–7.

Sleeter, C. (1993). "How white teachers construct race." In C. McCarthy and W. Crichlow (eds.), *Race, identity, and representation in education.* New York: Routledge.

Smart, B. (1992). *Modern conditions, postmodern controversies.* New York: Routledge.

Smith, J. (1983). "Quantitative versus qualitative research: An attempt to clarify the issue." *Educational Researcher* 12, pp. 6–13.

Spencer, B. (1995). "Old and new social movements as learning sites: Greening labor unions and unionizing the greens." *Adult Education Quarterly* 46, 1, pp. 31–42.

Spring, J. (1972). *Education and the rise of the corporate state.* Boston: Beacon.

_____. (April 1984). "Education and the Sony war." *Phi Delta Kappan* 65, 8, pp. 534–537.

_____. (1989). *The sorting machine revisited: National educational policy since 1945.* New York: Longman.

Spring, J. (1994). *The American school: 1642–1993.* New York: McGraw-Hill.

Stack, C. (1994). "Different voices, different visions: Gender, culture, and moral reasoning." In M. Zinn and B. Dill (eds.), *Women of color in U.S. society.* Philadelphia: Temple University Press.

Stafford, W. (1992). "Whither the great neo-conservative experiment in New York City." In J. Jennings (ed.), *Race, politics, and economic development: Community perspectives.* New York: Verso.

Steinberg, S., and J. Kincheloe. (1997). *Kinderculture: The corporate construction of childhood.* Boulder, CO: Westview Press.

Thompson, I. (1989). "Cultural literacy and the auto mechanic: Teaching reading and writing to technical students." *Teaching English in the Two-year College* 16, 1, pp. 43–48.

Tomaskovic-Devey, D. (1993). *Gender and racial inequality at work: The sources and consequences of job segregation.* Ithaca, NY: ILR Press.

Tozer, S., P. Violas, and G. Senese. (1993). School and society: Educational practice as social explanation. New York: McGraw-Hill.

Trend, D. (1994). "Nationalities, pedagogies, and media." In H. Giroux and P. McLaren (eds.), *Between borders: Pedagogy and the politics of cultural studies.* New York: Routledge.

Ulmer, G. (1989). "Mystory: The law of idiom in applied grammatology." In R. Cohen (ed.), *Future literary theory.* New York: Routledge.

Valli, L. (1988). "Gender identity and the technology of office education." In L. Weis (ed.), *Class, race, and gender in American education.* Albany, NY: SUNY Press.

Vattimo, G. (1991). *The end of modernity.* Baltimore: Johns Hopkins University Press.

Violas, P. (1978). *The training of the urban working class.* Chicago: Rand McNally.

Walkerdine, V. (1984). "Developmental psychology and the child-centered pedagogy: The insertion of Piaget into early education." In J. Henriques, W. Holloway, C. Urwin, C. Venn, and V. Walkerdine (eds.), *Changing the subject.* New York: Methuen.

_____. (1988). *The mastery of reason: Cognitive development and the production of rationality.* London: Routledge.

Wallace, M. (1993). "Multiculturalism and oppositionality." In C. McCarthy and W. Crichlow (eds.), *Race, identity, and representation in education.* New York: Routledge.

Webster, F. (1985/1986). "The politics of new technology." *Socialist Register*, pp. 385–411.

Weis, L. (1988). "High school girls in a de-industrializing economy." In L. Weis (ed.), *Class, race, and gender in American education.* Albany, NY: SUNY Press.

Weisman, J. (1991). "Some economists challenging view that schools hurt competitiveness." *Education Week* 9, 11, pp. 1, 14–15.

Welch, S. (1991). "An ethic of solidarity and difference." In H. Giroux (ed.), *Postmodernism, feminism, and cultural politics: Redrawing educational boundaries.* Albany, NY: SUNY Press.

West, C. (1992). "Nihilism in black America." In G. Dent (ed.), *Black popular culture.* Seattle: Bay Press.

_____. (1993). *Race matters.* Boston: Beacon Press.

Williams, S. (1992). "Two words on music: Black community." In G. Dent (ed.), *Black popular culture.* Seattle: Bay Press.

Willis, P. (1977). *Learning to labour: How working-class kids get working-class jobs.* Farnsborough, England: Saxon House.

Wilms, W. (Fall 1979). "New meanings for vocational education." *UCLA Educator* 21, 1, pp. 5–11.

Wirth, A. (1983). *Productive work—in industry and schools.* Lanham, MD: University Press of America.

Wolfe, L. (1991). "Introduction." In L. Wolfe (ed.), *Women, work, and school: Occupational segregation and the role of education.* Boulder, CO: Westview Press.

Wolff, J. (1977). "Women in organizations." In S. Clegg and D. Dunkerly (eds.), *Critical issues in organizations*. London: Routledge Direct Editions.

Wolman, W., and A. Colamosca. (1997). *The Judas economy: The triumph of capital and the betrayal of work*. New York: Addison-Wesley.

Woods, P. (1983). *Sociology and the school: An interactionist viewpoint*. London: Routledge and Kegan Paul.

Zachariah, M. (1987). "The school in planned social change: Problem or solution?" *Education with Production* 5, 2, pp. 6–26.

Zieger, R. (1994). *American workers, American unions*. Baltimore: Johns Hopkins University Press.

Zinn, M. (1994). "Feminist rethinking from racial-ethnic families." In M. Zinn and B. Dill (eds.), *Women of color in U.S. Society*. Philadelphia: Temple University Press.

Zinn, M., and B. Dill. (1994). "Difference and domination." In M. Zinn and B. Dill (eds.), *Women of color in U.S. society*. Philadelphia: Temple University Press.

Zunker, V. (1986). *Career counseling: Applied concepts of life planning*. Monterey, CA: Brooks/Cole Publishing.

Zweigenhaft, R., and G. Domhoff. (1991). *Blacks in white establishment*. New Haven: Yale University Press.

Index